WE WILL REMEMBER THEM

Biographies of the Great War dead
whose names are recorded
on the memorials
in St Matthew's Church, Weeke
and St Paul's Church, Fulflood

Derek Whitfield
Geraldine Buchanan
Josephine Coleman
Cheryl Davis
Steve Jarvis
Jenny Watson

Editor: Derek Whitfield
Desktop publishing: Richard Buchanan
Printed 2021 by Sarsen Press, Winchester

They shall grow not old, as we that are left grow old:
Age shall not weary them, nor the years condemn.
At the going down of the sun and in the morning
We will remember them.

For The Fallen by Robert Laurence Binyon, 1914

Cover photograph: Edward Joseph Austin (Jack) Tunks of Sussex Street, Winchester, 1898-1918.
Taken by Rider's Studios, Winchester. Signed: 'Jack, May 1917'.
Photograph now held in Royal Hampshire Regiment Museum.
Jack Tunks's biography is on pp. 323-326.

Contents

Acknowledgements 1

Abbreviations 2

Background Information

Introduction 3

The Fulflood and Weeke Memorials 11

A history of Weeke – From Kingelis to the Great War 15
By Barrie Brinkman

How the other half lived - Weeke Within on the eve of the Great War 19

The Biographies

Index to biographies 30

Biographies of the Great War Dead 32

Appendices

    i.   The 4th Hampshires in Mesopotamia 375
          The role of the 4th Battalion, The Hampshire Regiment in
          Mesopotamia and at the Siege of Kut-al-Amara, 1915-16

    ii.   The Battles of 1916-1918 387
          The major British offensives on the
          Western Front during the Great War

    iii. The "Missing" Men 393
          Men listed in the Winchester War Service Register
          but not included on either church memorial

    iv. A guide to the British Army 1914-18 394
          A simplified structure of the Army, and the role
          of the battalion, the 'home' of the British soldier

Index to street addresses, and a note on re-numbering 396

Bibliography 401

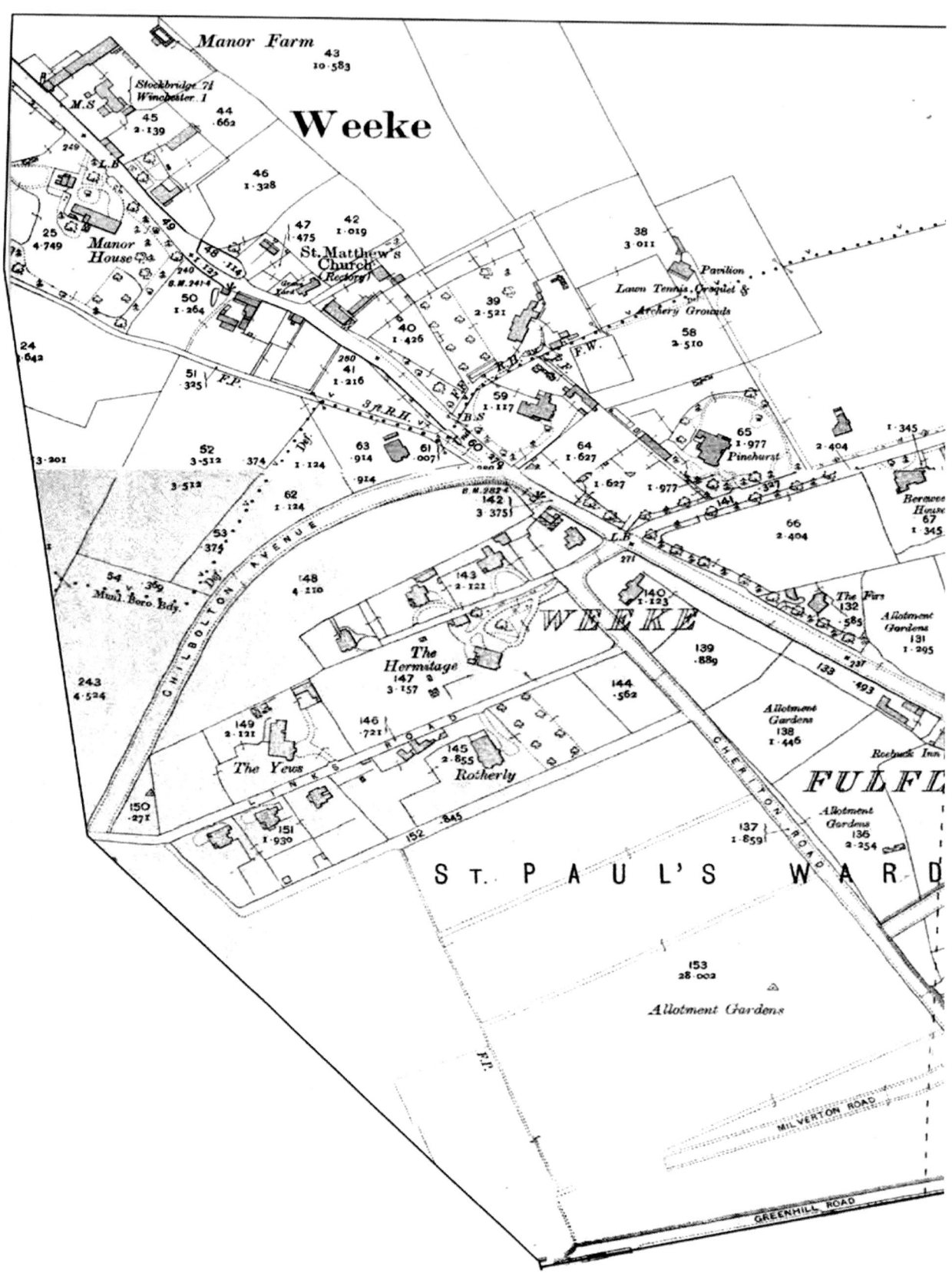

Map of Weeke and Fulflood

from Ordnance Survey, 1909 (Hampshire Record Office) Scale approx. 1:4,000 .   100m

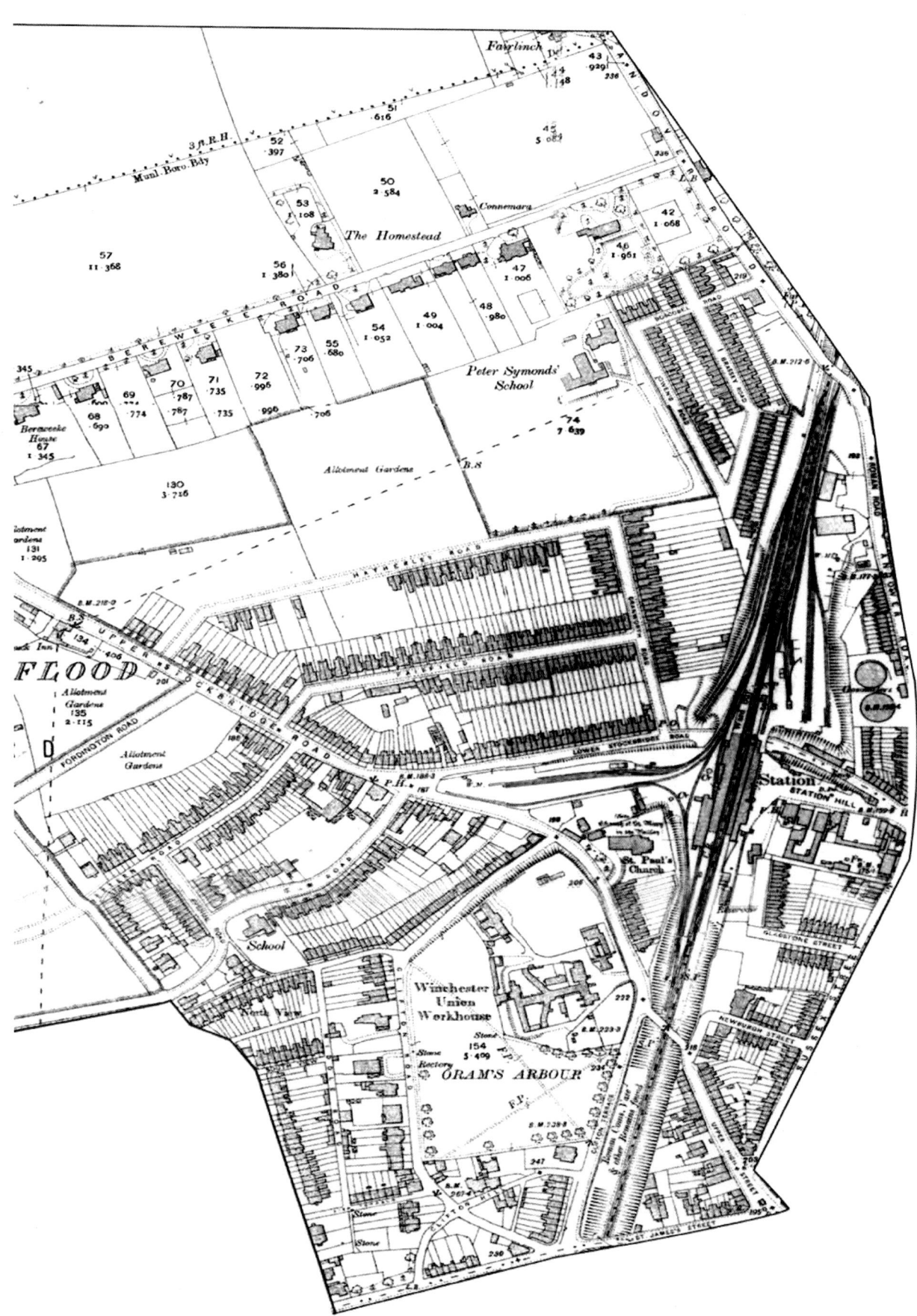

This book is dedicated
to all the men of the parish of Fulflood and Weeke
who lost their lives in the Great War,
and to their families.

Acknowledgements

As we started our work, Steve and Jenny Jarvis's website on the Hampshire War Memorials and Jen Best and Tom Beaumont James's work on the Winchester Debt of Honour project were crucial in providing basic information about most of the men who are the subject of this book. Tom's excellent introduction to Debt of Honour also helped to explain why Winchester, unlike most British towns and cities, has no single stone memorial listing the names of its Great War dead and why the people of Fulflood and Weeke, like other parishes, erected their own parish memorials.

There are others who we would like to thank for their help with this book. Barrie Brinkman kindly contributed a history of Weeke which describes the many changes that took place in that half of the parish in the years leading up to the Great War. Colin Bulleid, curator of the Royal Hampshire Regiment Museum and Archive, Winchester, cheerfully answered queries about the regiment's role in the war and provided access to the rich seam of records relating to the 4th Battalion, The Hampshire Regiment. The staff at the Hampshire Record Office, Winchester, also patiently dealt with our many research enquiries. We are grateful to the Hyde 900 and King Alfred College (Diocesan Training College) Great War memorial projects for their mutual support.

The changes to house numbering and street names that have taken place in the parish – particularly in Fulflood – have made tracing some of the men difficult in the extreme. However, thanks to the original work of Chris Piles who made us aware of the problem, and the help of Polly Cook we believe we may have succeeded in unravelling this particular 'Gordian Knot'. Thanks, too, to Andrew Hoggart, lately of The Roebuck Inn, Stockbridge Road, who pointed us in the direction of its role in the community.

Richard Buchanan spent many hours collating the material and preparing it for publication. He also produced the Street Index which shows where in Fulflood, Weeke and elsewhere in Winchester the parish's Great War dead lived.

Geoff Cuell, Janice Merritt and Christine Vear kindly shared family memories of Reginald Clark, Herbert Tong and Leslie Jacob respectively and provided photographs. Thanks, too, to Rob and Penny Matthews, of 14, Avenue Road, for allowing us to copy the photograph of Harold Forster. Incredibly, it was still in the house when they moved in – 90 years after Harold lived there!

Simon Newman took the photographs of the St Paul's Memorial Board and the Memorial Book at St Matthew's featured in the section on the origins of the parish memorials as well as the photograph of the St Thomas School Memorial, now held at Kings School. The photographs of the houses in which the parish fallen lived were taken by the authors.

The people listed below made generous donations to assist in the publication of the book and the overall project. We would particularly like to thank the parish of St Matthew's with St Paul's for their help and financial assistance, and the Winchester Cathedral Guides for their large donation following a tour of the Western Front conducted by Derek Whitfield in September 2018.

John Brewer.	Jonathan Frere.	Philip Morgan.
Bevis Clarke-Smith.	Marian Frere.	Christopher Pankhurst.
Colin Cook.	John Jenkyn.	Rosalind Pollock.
Deborah Dalton.	Stephen Jones.	Natalie Shaw.
Clare Dixon.	Janice Merritt (in memory of Herbert Lewis Tong).	Hugh Woodd.
Andrew Ferguson.		Winchester Cathedral Guides

Abbreviations

ACEF	Armoured Car Expeditionary Force
AIF	Australian Infantry Force
AOC	Army Ordnance Corps
APC	Army Pay Corps
ASC	Army Service Corps
BEF	British Expeditionary Force
CO	Commanding Officer
CSM	Company Sergeant Major
CWGC	Commonwealth War Graves Commission
DCLI	Duke of Cornwall's Light Infantry
DD	Discharged Dead
DSO	Distinguished Service Order
EAMR	East African Mounted Rifles
GR	Grave Reference
GWDFW	Great War Dead of Fulflood and Weeke
HRO	Hampshire Record Office
HQ	Headquarters
IWM	Imperial War Museum
KRRC	King's Royal Rifle Corps
MC	Military Cross
MCC	Marylebone Cricket Club
MGC	Machine Gun Corps
MM	Military Medal
MMR	Mercantile Marine Reserve
NCO	Non-Commissioned Officer
NLS	No Longer Standing
NSW	New South Wales
OBLI	Oxfordshire and Buckinghamshire Light Infantry
OLI	Oxford Light Infantry
OTC	Officer's Training Corps
PoW	Prisoner of War
PPCLI	Princess Patricia's Canadian Light Infantry
PR	Pier Reference
RCR	Royal Canadian Regiment
RFA	Royal Field Artillery
RFC	Royal Flying Corps
RGA	Royal Garrison Artillery
RHA	Royal Horse Artillery
RNACD	Royal Naval Armoured Car Division
RNAS	Royal Naval Air Service
SDGW	Soldiers Died in the Great War 1914-1919
WVS	Womens Voluntary Services
WWMHS	Winchester Working Men's Housing Society
WWSR	Winchester War Service Register
YMCA	Young Men's Christian Association

Introduction

The aftermath of the Great War saw tens of thousands of monuments built to honour the dead in what remains Britain's biggest-ever wave of public commemoration. Most cities, towns and villages chose to build permanent stone memorials inscribed with the names of the fallen. Winchester is unusual in that no such monument was ever erected. This is not to say that the city authorities never considered commissioning one. Various plans – including a Temple of Honour on St Giles Hill and a memorial roadway to be called the Scared Way, running from the cathedral to Southgate Street – were discussed but rejected on cost grounds. The memorial that was eventually erected at the west end of the cathedral on 31 October 1921 remembered the fallen from the county, from the Hampshire Regiment and from Winchester but, crucially, the individual names of the fallen were not commemorated.

By contrast, the memorials at St Paul's Church, Fulflood, and St Matthew's Church, Weeke, are inscribed with the names of many, although not all, of the men associated with the parish who died in the war. The oak Memorial Board at St Paul's commemorates 91 men who gave their lives – 78 from Fulflood and 13 from Weeke. The red, leather-bound Memorial Book held in St Matthew's lists 90 men.

Both memorials are representative of a complex national response to the trauma of the Great War. The sheer scale of the public's involvement inevitably fed into this response when the war ended. For the first time in a major conflict, volunteers and conscripts had vastly outnumbered professional soldiers and so memorials needed to cater for the wishes of the civilian population as well as the military.

The parish memorials therefore served an important purpose in the years after the Great War. Many of those who died once worshipped at the churches and the memorials would have provided a tangible focus for their loved ones' grief. However, as the years passed, and those surviving relatives also slipped into memory then so the names on the memorials became less familiar. Today, other than on Remembrance Sunday, it is unlikely they receive a second glance from visitors or congregation.

That is why in 2015 two people, Geraldine Buchanan and Josephine Coleman, began working on the Great War Dead of Fulflood and Weeke (GWDFW). By 2016, two people had become six. As Britain marked the centenary of the conflict, the painstaking task of researching the 91 names on the two memorials carried on. The aim was to uncover the 'lost' stories behind those names and bring them together in a book and on the group's website (www.greatwardeadwinchesterfulfloodweeke.com) compiled by Steve Jarvis. The stories are, of course, deeply poignant but they also provide a fascinating snapshot of life in the early days of the modern parish.

The men listed on the memorials came from different socio-economic backgrounds which largely reflected the class division between the two halves of the parish. The population in 1914 stood at around 4,800, the great majority of whom lived in Fulflood. However, Weeke was more well-heeled. As Barrie Brinkman shows on pp. 15 - 17, the late 19th Century exodus of middle-class residents from Winchester's increasingly crowded city centre led to the establishment of a prosperous new community in Weeke, centred on Bereweeke Road, Chilbolton Avenue and upper Cheriton Road. The Weeke men remembered on the memorials are therefore overwhelmingly officers, many of whom – like 2nd Lieutenant Henry Gould, son of parish rector Charles Gould - had been educated at public school.

In Fulflood, the late Victorian and Edwardian period had seen development on both sides of the Stockbridge Road. In terms of the scale of building and the type of housing, this half of the parish was the Badger Farm of its day and home to teachers, clerks, railway workers, soldiers and sailors, builders, gardeners and many more. An address in Fulflood may not have carried the same cachet as one in Bereweeke Road, but with its solid middle class and aspirational working-class residents who believed in self-help, the family and individual responsibility, the area was overwhelmingly God-fearing and respectable.

Of the 13 men listed on the memorials who had addresses in Weeke, nine were commissioned officers, reflecting the area's higher social status. Of course, several of the Fulflood fallen did serve as officers but the majority did so as rank and file or NCOs. This did not make them lesser fighting men. Henry Churcher, a gardener from Avenue Road who enlisted in 1914 at the age of 23, proved to be a natural soldier and leader of men, winning promotion to Company Sergeant Major and the Military Medal for gallantry.

Breaking the men down by individual services, 82 served in the British Army, of whom 15 were officers and 68 'rank and file' (Privates and NCOs). Five men served in the Royal Navy and Mercantile Marine and four in the Royal Flying Corps and Royal Naval Air Service. Together, they fought in most of the principal theatres of war – the Western Front, Gallipoli, Mesopotamia (modern Iraq), Egypt, Palestine, Persia, East Africa and even Russia.

Men from Canada, Australia, New Zealand and East Africa with family connections to the parish, volunteered to fight for the 'Mother Country' and they, too, are remembered on the memorials. One of these, James Dennistoun, had been on Captain Scott's expedition to Antarctica in 1912. He survived that only to die in a German prisoner-of-war camp.

Researching the project

The men's stories were compiled using a range of sources. The websites www.ancestry.co.uk and www.findmypast.co.uk give access to the decennial census records of 1841 to 1911 which provide details such as family relationships, ages, addresses and occupations. Other records available through the websites include registers of births, marriages and deaths, electoral rolls, school rolls, details of wills and probate, trade union membership and emigration and immigration, to name but a few. The websites also provide information on the men's military service – enlistment and military pension records, medal entitlement, casualty and prisoner-of-war lists and the official War Office publication Soldiers Died in the Great War 1914-1919. However, the destruction of many soldiers' records during the Blitz in 1940 remains a major stumbling block to researchers.

One important local source was the Winchester War Service Register (WWSR) of 1921. Published by the city authorities to commemorate those men from the city who served in the armed forces 'from the Declaration of War to the Signing of the Armistice', it contains 3,454 names, including some 770 men from Fulflood and Weeke. It also identifies 459 city men who were killed or died, of whom about 20 per cent came from the parish. Although one of the criteria for inclusion in the WWSR was that the man had to have lived in Winchester in 1914, this was not followed to the letter. The aforementioned James Dennistoun, for example, was living in New Zealand running his parents' sheep station when the Great War began. James's family clearly pulled strings with the compilers of the Register to get his name included.

The WWSR gives each man's name and address (although these are sometimes misleading) together with his rank, date of enlistment, the branch of the forces and unit(s) in which he served and details of where he served. It also lists any medals awarded for gallantry and whether he was wounded. If the man was killed, then details of where and when he died are also given.

The WWSR undoubtedly contains the names of the great majority of Winchester men who served in the Great War, but it is not a complete list. Several of those listed on the memorials at St Matthew's and St Paul's do not appear in the Register – Charles Goodwin, Leopold Sothcott and Charles Hawker to name but three. In fact, it is the belief of Steve Jarvis, who has spent many years compiling a database of

Hampshire war memorials, that there are 108 additional men listed on surviving Great War memorials across Winchester who do not appear in the WWSR.

Debt of Honour, by Jen Best and Tom Beaumont James, fleshes out the basic facts given in the WWSR by providing more information on the 459 city dead, including most of those researched for this book. However, while extremely useful, the amount of detailed information given on each man is still limited.

The aim of the GWDFW project has been to provide a fuller, more rounded biography of each of the 91 men and in the process bring to life a defining period in the history of Fulflood and Weeke. To that end, we made use of other primary sources such as local newspapers, street directories and regimental archives and war diaries. We also spoke to several of the men's descendants whose recollections and photographs enriched those biographies immeasurably.

Editorial method

In preparing each biography we have endeavoured to give the address that the man was living at when he went to war or his last address before he was killed. However, correctly identifying where the men lived has not always proved straightforward. Fulflood and Weeke were both expanding in this period and there were frequent changes to house numbering and road names. For example, both the WWSR and Debt of Honour (which uses the same addresses as the WWSR) record Andrew Bogie living at 2, St Paul's Terrace, an address which is 20, St Paul's Hill today.

Moreover, the addresses in the WWSR are sometimes different from those given in earlier census records. Often, this was because by 1921, when the WWSR was published, families had moved from the homes they had occupied when their menfolk went to war. For example, the WWSR gives Francis Forder's address as 75, Parchment Street (his mother's address from 1918) whereas in 1914, when he enlisted with the 4th Battalion, The Hampshire Regiment, he was living with his mother and grandmother at 30, North View in Fulflood.

To help readers, this book gives the man's original wartime address and the modern address if it has changed. We have indicated this in the title piece introducing each biography by listing the modern address in brackets after the original address. Likewise, if a property is no longer standing then that is also indicated in brackets.

Each man's rank (the highest shown in the various records) is also given together with his service number - or numbers – and the military unit in which he served. In the case of soldiers this is his battalion and regiment and for sailors the ship on which he was serving when he was killed. Details of the men's medal entitlement are listed together with their place of burial or commemoration plus any wording that appears on their grave or memorial.

The biographies differ in length and detail according to the amount of information uncovered. Some men proved extraordinarily difficult to research – Charles Goodwin and William Mitchell, for example. Indeed, Goodwin is the only name of the 91 listed on the memorials for whom a Fulflood or Weeke connection has yet to be discovered.

In several cases the chronology of a man's military service has been difficult to unravel. Often this was because he had transferred between battalions or regiments on unspecified dates. Signaller Jack Fifield, for example, served with three battalions of the Hampshire Regiment (the 1st, 14th and 15th) between 1916 and 1918 but no record has been found showing when he moved from one to the other. Without these details it has occasionally been necessary to employ a degree of educated guesswork to try to reconstruct what happened to individual men during the war.

In general, the military backgrounds of those men who served as officers proved easier to research as they figure more frequently in battalion war diary reports, regimental journals and newspaper reports. The wealth of material relating to Brigadier-General Ronald Maclachlan and Major Harold Forster enabled us to produce detailed biographies of both men. By contrast, far less could be gleaned about Lance-Corporal Frederick White who consequently remains a more shadowy figure.

There are, of course, exceptions to the above rule. Those men of the 4th Battalion, The Hampshire Regiment who died in Turkish captivity after the siege of Kut-al-Amara are well documented in the Comforts Fund ledgers of Mrs Esme Bowker, widow of the battalion's CO. These fascinating records, and many others, are now held at the Royal Hampshire Regiment Museum.

The parish response to war

Fulflood and Weeke's response to the outbreak of war in August 1914 was determined by many factors but, initially at least, by Winchester's status as a garrison city. While most Britons did not discover that the country was at war until the morning of 5 August 1914 (and much later in remote areas), the situation in Winchester was different. Reservists for the Hampshire Regiment and the two Rifles regiments began to arrive at the city's Army depots on 4 August, even before Britain's ultimatum to Germany had expired. By the following day, the depots were packed. The Hampshire Chronicle reported that:

> ... [t]he Royal Proclamation to mobilise the Army has had an extraordinary effect upon the military forces. On Wednesday [5 August] there were scenes of such enthusiasm as have rarely accompanied military preparations in this country. Battalions gave way from time to time to their feelings by vociferous cheering, and as one passed barrack-rooms the vocal evidence of satisfaction were volleyed out of the windows in unmistakeable fashion. The spirit of the Army has shown itself to be magnificent, and the contrast from the quiet, strained demeanour... during the days of suspense was most remarkable. Probably never before has the Army mobilised with such evidence of rejoicing.

Over the following weeks, the 'militarisation' of Winchester continued as troops mobilised on the downs surrounding the city and there were soon 20,000 men – equivalent almost to Winchester's entire population – living in makeshift camps. A number of men from Fulflood and Weeke, almost certainly caught up in the excitement of the moment, enlisted at this time, helping to make August 1914 the parish's peak recruitment month of the entire war rather than September which had the highest rate nationally.

Different factors influenced the men who joined up in September. The initial surge of enthusiasm had by then given way to a more sober mood, described by the Hampshire Chronicle as one 'of grim determination, of the calm that comes to men with minds made up to see a thing through'. The pages of the Chronicle clearly show that most people, shocked by the invasion of Belgium and reports of German atrocities there, regarded Britain's cause as just.

Overlaid on this was a strong sense of duty, particularly evident among men who enlisted immediately after the publication of the Amiens Dispatch in The Times on 29 August. This laid bare the scale of the British Army's defeat at the Battle of Mons a few days earlier and its subsequent retreat. In the six days between 30 August and 5 September 1914 nearly 175,000 across Britain volunteered for military service. This compared to 100,000 who had done so in the three weeks between 4 and 22 August. These slightly later volunteers therefore enlisted not at the moment of greatest jingoistic enthusiasm but when it appeared that Britain might be about to lose the war.

Men were also motivated by other factors, especially a belief in the justness of Britain's cause, a growing hatred of Germany, a desire to be seen to be behaving appropriately and a sense of duty. There was also an intense social pressure to enlist, particularly among friends. This helps to explain why no fewer than

17 of the 91 names (nearly 1 in 5) on the parish memorials are men who served in the 4th Battalion, The Hampshire Regiment.

The 4th Hampshires were Winchester's equivalent of a Pals' Battalion. Several men had joined as Territorials in the pre-war years – among them Andrew Bogie, Frank Coles and Eric Rule - and in August and September 1914 the 4th Hampshires became the 'go to' battalion for even more. William Hooker, of 71, Western Road (a house later renumbered and now in Cheriton Road), wrote later about how he came to enlist with the 4th Hampshires on 5 September 1914:

> *The daily papers were calling out for recruits to join the forces. I was just 18 and considered it was my duty to go. I talked it over with my father who said he would put nothing in my way. Some of my friends had joined the local Territorial [battalion] in Winchester so I went along and became a soldier.*

A sense of duty, establishment pressure via the newspapers and social pressure from his friends – William Hooker was a very typical volunteer in 1914.

Although money was a motivating factor in more deprived areas of Britain, there is little evidence it played an important role in Fulflood and Weeke where unemployment was low, and most families were either solid working class or lower middle class. The list of occupations among the fallen from the 4th Hampshires shows that the recruits were overwhelmingly 'respectable' – Andrew Bogie, for example, was a schoolteacher, Eric Rule an auctioneer's clerk, Leslie Jacob an apprentice dentist, Cecil Shefferd a council clerk, Frank Coles a printer's compositor and Frank Chapman a legal clerk. These men did not volunteer for the money, but rather because it was the 'right thing to do'.

The human cost of war

Calculating the percentage of serving men from Fulflood and Weeke's who died is tricky. The 91 men listed on the memorials do not represent the total parish death toll as the WWSR includes at least another seven men who died and had lived in the parish and there may well be more. (See Appendix iii.) Nor, as we have seen, does the WWSR include everyone with a strong Winchester connection who served. However, it is estimated that around 12 per cent of those parish men listed on the memorials were killed or died from wounds or illnesses whilst still in the Army (91 deaths out of about approximately 770 parish names in the WWSR). This is higher than the national average of 11.5 per cent but lower than the overall Winchester figure of 13.2 per cent. However, if one adds the parish men who died but who are not included on the memorials – at least seven - then the figure is approaching the same as the Winchester average.

Of course, this figure only represents the dead; the great majority of men who served in the forces came home at the end of the war. Looking through the WWSR, one is struck by the number of men from the parish who enlisted. In some streets virtually every household had a family member serving at home or overseas. One might expect this to be the case after the introduction of conscription in early 1916, but what is significant about Fulflood and Weeke (and Winchester in general) is just how many men *volunteered* in 1914 and 1915. In fact, between August and December 1914 alone, voluntary recruitment in Winchester exceeded that in all of 1916, the most successful recruiting year under conscription.

Many households in the parish sent two, three or more men to serve. For example, five Soffe brothers fought in theatres as far afield as France, Salonika and Mesopotamia. Four lived – or had lived – with their parents at 17, St Paul's Hill (8, Upper Stockbridge Road before the road was renamed and renumbered) while the other brother lived at 22, North View. Two of the brothers, George and Henry, were killed and both are mentioned on the parish memorials. The Stroud family of 7, Western Road also lost two sons, Bertram and George, as did James Wedge, of 8, Andover Road, whose sons Charles and

James were killed. Other families were more fortunate: all six Snow brothers, of 41, Fairfield Road, served and survived.

Several schools attended by the fallen still exist. Many went as infants to Western School, then in Elm Road, and from there to St Thomas Church of England Elementary School in Mews Lane, which was eventually amalgamated into Kings' School. There, they are remembered on the St Thomas School Memorial Board. Some attended Peter Symonds Grammar School, now the Sixth Form College, and they too have a memorial board. Others went to prep schools and public schools such as Winchester College, whose dead are remembered on a magnificent War Cloister. A handful trained to be teachers at the Winchester Diocesan Training College, whose buildings now form part of Winchester University.

Although parish men joined Army regiments from across Britain – and, indeed, the Empire – many enlisted with those based in Winchester, namely The Rifle Brigade, The King's Royal Rifle Corps and The Hampshire Regiment. No fewer than 30 of the 91 men commemorated on the memorials served with the Hampshires and the first of the book's four appendices examines the role of the regiment's 4th Battalion in Mesopotamia in 1915 and 1916, particularly at the siege of Kut and during its tragic aftermath.

The second appendix provides a chronology of the major British offensives on the Western Front between 1916 and 1918. By this stage of the war the British Expeditionary Force numbered more than two million men, up from just 75,000 in 1914, and was mounting increasingly complex, multi-phase campaigns lasting several months. The Somme Offensive, fought between 1 July and 18 November 1916, is usually described as a single battle whereas it comprised 12 battles and three distinct phases. Rather than simply state that a man 'was killed at the Battle of the Somme' we have tried, wherever possible, to identify the specific military action he was fighting in at the time of his death. Readers can then use the appendix to place that action within the context of the whole campaign.

The battles of 1914 and 1915 do not feature in the appendix. This is not to belittle their importance but simply a recognition that these were smaller operations, usually comprising a single phase. They are covered – as are the Battle of Jutland and the Gallipoli campaign - in the biographies of the men who died fighting in them.

A third appendix lists the men from the parish who died in the war but who are not mentioned on either of the church memorials. The final appendix provides a guide to the structure of the British Army during the war, including the composition of the various units and who commanded them. There is also a short section on the role of the battalion which, along with the regiment, was regarded by soldiers as their military 'home'.

We hope that the book will be read by local historians as well as by those in the parish, and wider Winchester, who want to learn more about a defining period of our recent history. We particularly hope that it will prove a valuable resource for local schools where the Great War continues to be an important component of the history curriculum.

Inevitably, the book will contain errors and the authors have worked hard to keep them to the minimum, checking and re-checking sources. There can be errors in the original documents and even on memorials. As more and more records are put online and more cross-referencing can be done, it will be possible gradually to reduce the amount of error. More information about these men will become available and for those particularly interested in an individual there could already be more material to be found online. We welcome any corrections and amendments or new information that adds to their story. Let us know via our email address: *greatwardeadwinchesterfulfloodweeke@outlook.com*

The project's website *www.greatwardeadwinchesterfulfloodweeke.com* ,which is a work in progress, will eventually contain all the men's biographies. Additions and amendments will be included in the website.

The project has opened a window on a different world. We would probably recognise the streets and buildings of the parish 100 years ago, but so much else would be unfamiliar – the importance of Christian faith and patriotism, the way in which several generations of a family lived together in often cramped conditions and above all, perhaps, the proximity of death. Antibiotics and mass immunisation programmes did not exist and diseases such as tuberculosis, pneumonia, diphtheria and enteritis wreaked havoc, particularly among young children. Many of the families researched for this book lost one or more children to disease only to be visited by tragedy once more in the Great War.

The book does not seek to glorify war. However, it does recognise that the men of Fulflood and Weeke, like millions more across Britain, answered the call to arms in the full knowledge of what it might ultimately cost. It is for that selflessness that we remember them.

Derek Whitfield
Geraldine Buchanan
Josephine Coleman
Cheryl Davis
Steve Jarvis
Jenny Watson

Spring 2021

The Fulflood and Weeke Memorials

St Matthew's Church, Weeke, and St Paul's Church, Fulflood, where the two memorials to the Great War dead can be seen today

St Paul's Church Memorial Board

The large two-panelled wooden Memorial Board in St Paul's Church, Fulflood, is made of oak and was designed in 1920 by the architect B.D. Cancellor, who lived in Weeke and practised from offices at Queen Anne Chambers on Winchester High Street. Cancellor's other works in Winchester include Peter Symonds Grammar School (c.1899) and the front of Godbegot House in the High Street (1900). From 1894 to 1910 he was in partnership with Henry L.G. Hill, who is believed to have designed the memorial window to his son, Captain Nicholas Hill, at St Matthew's Church.

Across the top of the Memorial Board is the text:

TO THE GLORY OF GOD AND IN THE MEMORY OF THE MEN WHO GAVE THEIR LIVES
1914-1918 THEIR NAME LIVETH FOR EVERMORE

Each of the Memorial Board's two panels is 63in (160cm) wide by 47in (119cm) high and contains four columns of inscribed men's names. Seven columns feature the names of 11 men, while the eighth has 14, making a total of 91. There is no hierarchy to either the St Paul's or Matthew's memorials - the men are simply listed alphabetically without their rank.

The Memorial Board was originally located in the church's Lady Chapel but was moved to its current position on the south wall in the 1980s. It is situated below the memorial window to Kathleen Gould, daughter of Charles Gould, Rector of Weeke with St Paul's from 1900-1915, and sister of 2nd Lieutenant Henry Gould, who was killed in the Great War and whose name appears on the Memorial Board.

Fundraising for the Memorial Board began in early 1919 and six donations, amounting to £7 18s 0d had been received by the end of the financial year on 31 March 1919. The bulk of the fundraising came in 1919-20 when a further 96 donations were made. By 31 March 1921, the fund had amassed £128 4s 2d and the final figure on 31 March 1922 was £177 6s 5d (about £5,000 in today's money). The fund was spent at some point between April and December 1922. The families of men listed on the memorial board, as well as local organisations, all gave money to the fund. They included the following:

The Fulflood and Weeke Memorials

The carved oak Memorial Board in St Paul's Church with the inscribed names of the 91 men who died in the Great War. Below: the panels in close-up *(Photos: Simon Newman)*

- Mrs E. Drake [mother of Private Thomas Drake] who gave 2 guineas on 2 June 1920.
- Reverend Gould [father of 2nd Lieutenant Henry Gould] who gave 2 guineas on 23 July 1920.
- Western Girls School which gave £3 14s 2d on 2 September 1920.
- Muldowney family [of Private John Muldowney] who gave 5s on 2 September 1920.
- Miss Cole who gave £2 on 2 guineas on 12 January September 1920.
- Warrens the Stationers which gave £4 1s 5d on 12 December 1920.
- Mr E.W. Fifield [father of Signaller Jack Fifield] who gave £5 5s on 15 December 1920.
- Mrs Gould [mother of 2nd Lieutenant Henry Gould] who gave 2 guineas on 12th January 1921.

12

The Fulflood and Weeke Memorials

The church vestry minutes of a meeting held on 31 March 1921 record that 'on association with proposed war memorial the following resolution was proposed by W.E Madams and F.T. Brown and carried unanimously. That the Weeke Parochial War Memorial be carried out in accordance with plan of B.D. Cancellor and that the rector and churchwardens be empowered to apply for necessary faculty'.

This faculty was applied for by C.S Woolridge on 22 October 1922 for £1 10s. It is believed that the Memorial Board was installed in St Paul's in November 1922.

St Matthew's Church Memorial Book

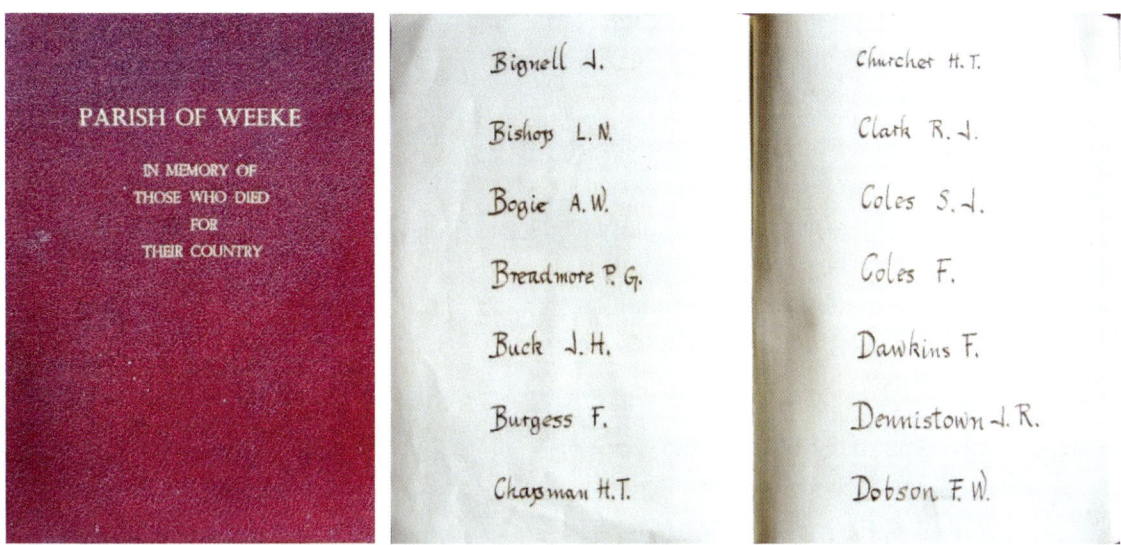

Above left: The cover of the Memorial Book at St Matthew's Church and, right, the opening pages
(Photos: Simon Newman)

St Matthew's Church, Weeke, contains a red leather-bound Memorial Book that lists the names of 90 men who died in the Great War. The book may not have been compiled until after the Second World War as the names of the men lost in both wars are listed in the same handwriting. The front of the book reads:

PARISH OF WEEKE.
IN MEMORY OF THOSE WHO DIED FOR THEIR COUNTRY

The men's names are handwritten on 13 pages, with seven names listed on 12 pages and six names on the other.

While all 91 names on the St Paul's memorial have been traced, no record has yet been found for H.T. Chapman listed only in the Memorial Book at St Matthew's. Indeed, no record may ever be found, for it is the group's belief that the entry is an error and should read F.J. Chapman whose name precedes H.T. Churcher on the St Paul's memorial. It is thought that the person responsible for inscribing the St Matthew's book may have made a simple mistake and used the initials H.T. for both Churcher and Chapman (see photographs above).

The only name on the St Paul's Memorial Board that does not appear in the Weeke Memorial Book is Harold Forster. The reason for the omission is unclear.

St Matthew's also houses a memorial window to Captain Nicholas Weatherby Hill. Nicholas lived with his parents in nearby Butt's Close in a house designed by his architect father Henry L.G. Hill, who probably also designed the window. Nicholas won the Military Cross shortly before his death on 16 January 1917.

Other memorials

Sixteen of the 91 men commemorated at St Paul's and St Matthew's are also listed on the wooden memorial board erected at St Thomas Senior Church of England Boys' School. The school used to be in Mews Lane, Winchester, but the building is now a private residence and the memorial is today held at Kings' School, Romsey Road, Winchester.

Many boys in Fulflood and Weeke moved on to St Thomas School from Western School in Elm Road, Fulflood – there was an infants and girls' school on the site. However, not all boys who attended St Thomas's and later died in the war are included on the memorial – for example, neither Leslie Jacob nor Jack Fifield are listed.

There is also a memorial to the fallen in the chapel of the former Winchester Diocesan Training College, later King Alfred Teacher Training College and now part of Winchester University. The wooden 'War Rail' commemorates the 60 men associated with the College who died in the Great War. Two of them, Andrew Bogie and Basil Vokes, also feature on the memorials at St Matthew's and St Paul's.

The St Thomas School Memorial now held at Kings School, Winchester *(Photo: Simon Newman)*

The Diocesan Training College memorial was erected by past and present students and dedicated by the Bishop of Winchester at a service on 25 September 1920. It consists of oak panelling around the lower part of the chapel walls, as well as extra stalls at the west end and two inscribed panels. The names of the fallen are inscribed upon the frieze of the panelling. On the north wall there is a panel inscribed:

To the Glory of God and in Memory of those Members of this College who gave their Lives in the Great War 1914-1918. This panel work is placed by Masters and Students Past and Present

On the south wall is a quote from 2 Maccabees vi 31:

These men died leaving their deaths for an example of a noble courage and a memorial of virtue, not only unto young men but unto all their nation

Changes to the chapel since the original dedication have resulted in sections of the rail, and part of the inscription, being moved to different parts of the chapel.

DEREK WHITFIELD and JENNY WATSON

A History of Weeke – from Kingelis to the Great War

Weeke in 1914 was a parish on the cusp of change. Although its outer reaches were still very rural – and would remain so until after World War Two – those closer to Winchester had seen a significant middle-class influx during the three decades leading up to the Great War. Crucially, too, Weeke's agricultural community was facing an uncertain future following the death of one the parish's two biggest landowners.

Weeke was unusual for a village in that it had no shops or pubs. The small population simply could not justify the usual village services so getting hold of food and other supplies meant a trip down Stockbridge Road into 'town'. The nearest pubs were the Roebuck Inn, on Stockbridge Road, and the Jolly Farmer, on the Andover Road.

This lack of services meant that St Matthew's Church became the hub of the community. Although small in size, St Matthew's was perfectly adequate for Weeke in the years before the Great War. The church, whose history dates to the 11th Century, was originally a chapel of ease for the local population. Its 'mother' church was St Mary in the Valley, situated near the junction of Andover Road and Swan Lane. In medieval times, substantial settlements were clustered around Winchester's city walls, including in Weeke parish. However, the Black Death of 1348 decimated the population of the city and led to many churches being abandoned, including St Mary in the Valley.

In the 1490s, St Matthew's was created by rebuilding the chapel of ease, but the St Mary's name lived on for hundreds of years. As late as 1911, the Census still referred to Weeke as the parish of St Mary's of Wyke – a recognition of the ancient association with St Mary in the Valley as well as one of the name variations for Weeke. The modern spelling of Weeke was established in the Ordinance Survey maps of the late 19th Century and has remained the same ever since.

The growth of Winchester from beyond its old city walls was already well underway in 1914. The first boundary extension had been in 1802 and the Roebuck Inn was subsequently built on the new 'city limit'. In 1902 the boundary was extended to a line close to Chilbolton Avenue and it would be pushed out further still to the outer limits of Weeke at Salters Lane in 1932. Meanwhile, with the building of the railway in 1840 and the subsequent sale of land by the Church Commissioners, the areas outside the city walls slowly grew in population to form Fulflood.

If St Matthew's Church was Weeke's communal hub in 1914 then 18th Century Weeke Manor was its major employer. For nearly 100 years, the Burnett Hitchcock family had lived in the Manor (opposite Bere Close on Stockbridge Road) from where they had managed the cluster of farms that formed the basis of the Weeke community. The first of these, Weeke Manor Farm, was a mixed farm and the farmhouse still stands on Stockbridge Road behind the Weeke fish and chip shop. Part of Teg Down Farm, which had sheep on the downs, was also in Weeke and the farmhouse is on Sarum Road. The third, Pipers Farm, was a poultry farm, but is now gone. It used to stand opposite Weeke pond on Stockbridge Road.

For hundreds of years the lands of Weeke were owned by the Church, having been given to the Bishop of Winchester in 636AD by Kingelis, the King of Wessex. The land was leased to many families over the centuries, including the Burnett Hitchcocks from the early 19th Century. Then from the 1860s, the family started purchasing much of the land when the Church decided to sell off some of its holdings.

A History of Weeke

The view up the Stockbridge Road from Weeke pond with the tower of St Matthew's Church visible in the top left. Weeke Manor stood further up the hill on the right. Judging by the ladies' attire, the photograph was probably taken in the early 1900s

Colonel Thomas Burnett Hitchcock took over the ownership and management of Weeke Manor and the associated properties and farms when his father died in 1887.

A much-respected pillar of the community, Colonel Burnett Hitchcock became a JP and was involved in the early days of Hampshire County Council. However, when he died in 1909 his family decided to leave Weeke Manor.

In 1911 the Colonel's assets were taken over by a trust for the benefit of his family, and by 1914 there was no family living in Weeke Manor. The house was rented out until 1920 when the family sold it to John Norton, 5th Baron Grantley, who held the property until 1942 when it was requisitioned to house schoolboys evacuated from war-ravaged Portsmouth. In 1945 the Red Cross purchased the house as their headquarters before it was finally converted into housing in 2006.

As Winchester's population grew in the 1880s, a number of middle-class residents began to build large houses beyond the city boundary close to the village of Weeke. The first houses, such as The Vicarage, Arnwood, The Hermitage and Springhill, were at the Weeke end of Cheriton Road. The Firs, meanwhile, was built on the eastern side of Stockbridge Road, just north of the Roebuck Inn. Large properties also began to appear along Bereweeke Road and this development continued until around 1910.

Inevitably, this type of housing boom changed the social complexion of Weeke. The newcomers were often clergymen or Army officers, both retired and serving. With two Army barracks in Winchester, there was a clear need for accommodation suitable for senior military personnel and these new residents were no doubt welcomed by the Burnett Hitchcocks. Many would have attended St Matthew's Church which almost certainly ranked over St Paul's in Fulflood in terms of social status. Indeed, the number of middle-class 'locals' worshipping at St Matthew's probably exceeded the farm workers.

In the 1880s a group of gentlemen set up the Winchester Golf Club on land near Morn Hill. The club thrived, but the three landlords could not agree on a long lease for the land. Consequently, in 1901, the club moved to an area of Teg Down owned by the Church Commissioners, who were prepared to offer a long lease. Golf was the perfect leisure activity for Weeke's new middle classes - Colonel Burnett Hitchcock even provided a silver salver for a club competition. The club's location, not far from the station and close to stabling at The Old Red Deer and Roebuck Inns on Stockbridge Road, was ideal and membership grew steadily up to 1914.

The Hermitage, at the Weeke end of Cheriton Road, was typical of the large houses built in the area from the 1880s as middle-class residents moved out of increasingly crowded Winchester. The house still stands today

Golf was not the only middle-class leisure activity to take root in Weeke in this period. In 1906 a group of Winchester residents met to discuss the idea of forming a tennis club. Colonel Burnett Hitchcock agreed to lease more than five acres of land along Bereweeke Road and by February 1907 the greens and courts had been laid out. After the Colonel's death in 1909 his son, Captain Burnett Hitchcock, continued the family's support and in 1913 agreed to sell the land in Bereweeke Road to the club. During the Great War numerous Army and Navy officers were allowed temporary membership of the club.

The opening of the Golf Club and the Tennis Club increased the urbanisation of Weeke and further marginalised the local farming community. This process continued in the 1920s and 1930s with the construction of houses in Bereweeke Avenue and Stoney Lane. However, the major developments took place after World War Two. In 1957 Weeke Manor Farm closed, paving the way for the Weeke Manor council estate. Pipers Farm was sold as four building plots in 1961, although it is unclear how long the farm had been closed before the sale. Finally, the Teg Down housing estate was built on the down lands during the 1960s. Although Harestock Farm was part of Littleton parish it was bounded on the city side by Weeke Manor Farm. It closed in the early 1970s allowing the Harestock estate to be built.

The urbanisation of Weeke was complete.

BARRIE BRINKMAN

How the Other Half Lived
– Weeke Within on the Eve of the Great War

As the arrival of a wealthy social elite transformed the appearance of the 'upper', or northern, part of Weeke in the late 19th Century, a different type of development was taking place 'down the hill' in that area of the parish closest to Winchester city centre. Here, rather than the large, elegant houses set in spacious grounds which typified the new properties in Bereweeke Road and the top of Cheriton Road, streets of mainly terraced properties sprang up to cater for a predominantly working and lower middle class population.

This distinction was officially recognised in 1894 when Weeke parish was split into two – Weeke Within (the southern half) and Weeke Without. While the latter lies outside the city boundary of 1802, Weeke Within is inside. Its northern limit is marked by The Roebuck public house on the Stockbridge Road and it stretches on the east side as far as Andover Road, the western end of City Road and both sides of Sussex Street as far south as Newburgh Street, which, along with the northern half of Oram's Arbour, Greenhill Road, and approximately along the line of Sarum Road, forms the southern boundary of the parish. The western boundary is mainly along the line of Lanham Lane off Sarum Road.

Before the second half of the 19th Century, much of what was to become Weeke Within was covered in orchards, market gardens, allotments and grazing areas. The arrival of the railway in Winchester in 1840 began the process of change, not only by dividing the southern part of Weeke parish in two but by encouraging the development of light industry and trade and commerce. The other major significant factor in the area's development was the decision by the Ecclesiastical Commissioners, who owned much of the land on the western side of Winchester, to free it up for sale from the late 1850s.

From the 1870s, Weeke Within became part of the rapid development of Winchester's western suburbs. Its growth mirrored that of Winchester as a whole. The city's population more than doubled in the 19th Century – from 9,000 in 1837 to 23,500 by 1911. The population of Weeke parish in 1911 was 4,600, the largest in the city. Of those, 4,492 lived in Weeke Within despite it comprising just 90 of the parish's 1,094 acres.

This chapter charts the development of the three distinct parts of Weeke Within: Oram's Arbour, the area around the station and the suburb of Fulflood, where the pre-1914 boom was most apparent.

Oram's Arbour

Although the urbanisation of Weeke Within did not truly take off until the 1870s some limited development had started to reshape Oram's Arbour even before the railway was built. Owned by the city, the Arbour was the surviving remnant of an Iron Age enclosure which once probably stretched down to the pre-Roman course of the River Itchen in the valley bottom. In 1837 the New Winchester Union Workhouse was built within the Arbour boundary and by the 1881 Census it housed 10 members of staff and 129 inmates, mostly aged over 50. There were also some mothers with young children as the workhouse had become a place where unmarried mothers were sent to give birth. By the early 1900s attitudes and systems had improved. Old age pensions and national health insurance were introduced and gradually the Winchester workhouse moved towards its 20th Century role as a hospital. It was used as such by the military authorities during the Great War, for soldiers convalescing and undergoing minor operations. Its role as a hospital ended in 1998 and shortly afterwards it was converted into residential accommodation in a development called Oram's Mount, which has retained much of the original style externally.

From the 1840s, Oram's Arbour also became the first part of Weeke Within to be developed for housing. The parish boundary crosses Clifton Terrace in an approximate continuation of the line from Newburgh

Street and passes through the Arbour just to the south of the Union Workhouse. This means that the northern half of Clifton Road is in Weeke parish, as is North View. Most of the mainly piecemeal developments along the top of Clifton Road were aimed at Army officers at the nearby Winchester Barracks and the increasing number of professional people in Winchester. North View, meanwhile, provided more modest accommodation.

Winchester Union Workhouse – built in 1837, it was one of the earliest developments in Weeke Within

(Photo: photosfromwinchester.blogspot.com)

The Station Area

The division of the southern part of the parish by the railway line influenced the way in which the two areas subsequently developed. Building in Fulflood in the second half of the 19th Century would be confined to land to the north-west of the railway, while the area around the station developed from 1840 in a slightly different and more commercial way.

City Road, formerly Northgate Street, was built to make access to the routes to Andover, Stockbridge and Salisbury and the station easier from the city. For centuries before that, travellers had gone down Hyde Street and along Swan Lane, but from the mid 1800s the latter could not cope with the increase in traffic. The route to Weeke and Stockbridge had probably continued in a straight line from Swan Lane up what is now Station Hill and across to join the bottom of the modern St Paul's Hill. The station was built across this route and as the railway also needed an embankment to cross the Fulflood valley, one was built with a 'tunnel' through it to create the new line of the route to Weeke. It was eventually named Lower Stockbridge Road, although occasional references to Weeke or Wyke Road still occurred after its official renaming. The route to Weeke from the Westgate was renamed Upper Stockbridge Road (now St Paul's Hill), once it passed over the railway bridge.

As well as the changes in road patterns, the development around the station particularly reflected the needs of travellers. Other than trains and the very occasional car, travel for the better off and trade was still horse-drawn and there was still a farrier at 19, Lower Stockbridge Road (38, Stockbridge Road today and currently home to Hayward's Guitars). The blacksmiths in 1914, Thomas Barnett and his son Charles, were the in-laws of Percy Norgate whose name is on the Great War memorials at St Paul's and St Matthew's churches. Nearby, shops, pubs and hotels – including temperance hotels – were built along from the corners of each of the six roads that still meet close to the station. The Carfax Hotel, which opened in 1918 on the corner of Station Hill and Sussex Street, had been converted from Saunders cycle shop. The Eagle Hotel stood on the corner of Swan Lane and Andover Road from 1848. (It was converted into flats in 2001 and is now known as Eagle Court.) The Albion pub, still on the corner of Stockbridge and Andover Roads, was there from the mid-1850s.

Businesses lined the left side of Station Hill all the way up to the station. Nearly all these buildings were demolished from the 1970s to allow eventually for the construction and landscaping of the Hampshire Record Office, which opened in 1993. These included The Carfax Hotel (closed in 1967), Whites' Removal Offices, the Railway Tavern and Wykeham Motors. The one building to survive – although its business closed in 1992 - was the South Western Inn at the top of Station Hill which had been originally been known as the Licensed Refreshment Rooms when it opened sometime before 1873. Around the corner in Sussex Street, stood the Cowdray Hotel, and two pubs, The Criterion and The Gladstone Arms. The Gladstone had distinctive exterior tiling similar to that surviving at The Fulflood Arms.

Station Hill in the early 20th Century. Note the shops and businesses lining the left side of the road leading up to the station - nearly all have now gone. Below: Carfax Hotel stood on the corner of Station Hill and Sussex Street. It was ideally placed to cater for travellers *(Photos: City of Winchester Trust)*

Terraced housing in this part of the parish began early. At right angles to the Barnett's smithy, in the then Lower Stockbridge Road, a terrace of houses was built by the time of the 1870-71 Ordnance Survey (OS) Map (the site is now a car park). Gladstone Street is marked on the same map; the south side survives but the first two houses in that terrace and the adjoining Gladstone Arms were demolished for the widening of Sussex Street in the 1970s. By 1880, Ashley Terrace had been built and lay at right-angles between Gladstone Street and the station, with its front gardens facing the railway. (Until the 1960s there was no Station Road linking Upper High Street to the station, just a pathway.) The northern side of Gladstone Street was demolished for the widening of that street and Sussex Street while Ashley Terrace was knocked down to make way for Station Road.

The terraced housing in Newburgh Street, just inside the southern edge of the parish, was built by 1889 and both sides have survived, although some properties were lost for the widening of Sussex Street. At the west end of Newburgh Street stood Newburgh House. Built before the terraced houses, it was probably the largest property in Weeke Within (according to the 1911 Census it had 27 rooms). From the mid 1880s to the turn of the century, the house, then known as Betchworth, was home to the large family of the Reverend Richards, Rector of St Laurence-in-the-Square. By 1911 it had been renamed Purbeck House and was home to the private Southend School for girls. By 1916 the school had moved to Clifton Road and the property is thought to have then reverted to a private residence. In the late 1920s it was briefly offices for the agricultural section of Hampshire County Council. By 1930 the site was in military hands and has remained so, but the original Newburgh House was demolished in the 1960s, no doubt to make room for the new Station Road and more modern premises for the military.

Sussex Street developed in a more varied way than the 'purpose built' streets of terrace houses described above. Between Gladstone Street and Station Hill were almost entirely commercial premises - pubs, hotels and shops. Between Gladstone and Newburgh Streets stood a row of terrace houses. These were subsequently demolished to make way for a modern terrace built further back to allow for a wider Sussex

Street. On the city side of Sussex Street, to the north of Tower Street, stood large semi-detached and detached houses, most of which survive. Between Tower Street and Westgate Lane, the junction of which marked the southern end of the parish, were smaller, terraced houses. (This part of the original Sussex Street, and Westgate Lane, now lie under the Hampshire County Council offices.)

On Andover Road, the southern end of which was in Weeke Within, commercial premises with accommodation above sprang up on both sides. On the east side terraced housing continued as far as Worthy Lane, but this was demolished in the 1960s. Likewise, the two gasholders set back from the road between the shops and the houses on the west side of Andover Road, there by 1889 and a familiar sight on the pre-war parish landscape, have also been knocked down. However, the shops and much of the terraced housing survives on this side. Before 1914 there was no further development on the western side of Andover Road before the railway bridge, at which point Weeke Within becomes Weeke Without.

Fulflood

In the 40 years before the Great War, the area of Fulflood, which had been covered in orchards, market gardens, grazing areas and allotments, gradually became a bustling, mainly lower middle and working class suburb of western Winchester, with a village feel about it. However, it remained in a state of flux, with piecemeal development and road names and numbers being changed as more houses were built.

Fulflood is named after an intermittent spring which rises between the top end of Greenhill Road and Byron Avenue. Whether its original name was Foul-flood or the more salubrious Full-flood is a matter for discussion. It is now culverted as it makes its way downhill (crossing Cheriton Road, Stockbridge Road, Cranworth Road and Andover Road) to join the web of streams in Hyde which flow into the River Itchen. Fulflood Farm, which seems to have been the only farm in Weeke Within by the 19th Century, was comparatively small - the occupant of the farmhouse in the 1861 Census was directly responsible for only 11 acres. The farmhouse, which dated back in parts to the 1600s, ended up being hidden behind the parade of shops along the Stockbridge Road. The building eventually became derelict and was demolished in the 1950s.

By the time of the 1870-71 OS Map, Fulflood had begun to grow. Moderately sized houses had been built in what was then known as Green Lane, and sometimes as Green Hill (now the southern end of Cheriton Road). These houses included The Rosery, now on the corner of Western Road and Avenue Road, and Laurel Cottage (later The Laurels and today Fig Lodge), now in Cheriton Road. By 1889, Green Lane and Green Hill had become Western Road which reflected what had been their route by extending around the corner by The Fulflood Arms as far as West End Terrace. The name Cheriton Road did not appear until about 1909, but Western Road still 'encroached' into modern Cheriton Road until 1914.

Avenue Terrace, on the west side of the newly created Avenue Road, had also been built by 1870-71 and was the first terraced housing in the area. It had been built in a more sophisticated style than much of the similar housing that had been erected in the inner city and the Soke. (This was to be true of most of Fulflood's terraced housing.) Avenue Cottages, on the steps between Avenue Road and North View, had also been built. These houses now form part of Avenue Road.

Elm Road began to be developed in the 1870s. It was initially named Elmville and was planned for the upper end of the market, as Oram's Arbour had been. Why else was it made wider than the average side road in the neighbourhood? The two substantial pairs of semi-detached houses, Nos 1-2 and 3-4, on the left just off the Stockbridge Road, which were the first to be built in the road in the 1870s, give an indication of what the Elmville Estate Company had planned for the whole road. However, it seems that Elmville was too close to the railway station, especially in the days of steam trains. With a goods and shunting yard just across the main road (now one of the station car parks) and cows, pigs and sheep passing by on the untarmaced main road to be sold in the Winchester market or to be carried by trains to other markets, it must have been a very dirty and smelly environment to live close to. (The regular use of dustcarts in the summer to spray the roads with water was a common site in pre-Great War Fulflood.) Consequently, development in Elm Road became more modest in scale as it did in other parts of Fulflood. A few large houses with mews had been built on St Paul's Hill between Clifton Road and Elm Road and were therefore even closer to the station with all its disadvantages. These have long since been demolished.

By 1878, a pair of semi-detached houses, Highgrove Villas (by 1891 Glenwood Villas, now 2 and 4, Cheriton Road), had been built between Avenue Road and North View. Around the same time two pairs of semi-detached houses, Greenhill Villas, were built, just below Avenue Road. All these were probably the last moderately sized houses to be built in this part of Fulflood. There then followed a period of mainly terraced, but also some semi-detached, development on both sides of Western Road. These properties, which still stand linked up with The Rosery and The Laurels (now Fig Lodge) which had previously been isolated. Terraced housing was also built from The Fulflood Arms up to Greenhill Villas. These are also now part of Cheriton Road.

From the late 1880s sets of terraced houses were built below Winchester Prison. One of these, Hillgrove Terrace, was on what was then Western Road (now Nos 1-19 Cheriton Road) and the others in the new Greenhill Road. Greenhill Avenue was built at right angles to Greenhill Road and led to what was then the back entrance of the prison. Greenhill Terrace, much further up, was also built earlier, also at right angles to Greenhill Road. These were probably cottages for workers at the then adjacent Hilliers Nurseries. Probably the last development to the west of the Stockbridge Road in Fulflood before the Great War was built by the Winchester Working Mens' Houses Society, formed by 1912. Its cottage-style houses built in the triangle between Greenhill Road, Milverton Road and Cheriton Road, were a forerunner of the post-war change in architectural fashions.

As late as 1889, the Fulflood stretch of the Stockbridge Road, between the bridge under the railway and The Roebuck pub, remained largely undeveloped. Other than The Roebuck itself and The Old Red Deer (a pub which stood on the corner of Stockbridge Road and Elm Road), the only other development was a small number of houses across the road from Elm Road. These included a moderately large detached property known as Bradford House (modern No. 106). The occupant in the 1911 Census was Charles Henry Ellis, the manager of the Maypole Dairy in Winchester High Street. During the Great War soldiers from the Hampshire Carabiniers Yeomanry broke the shop's windows as it was thought that Mr Ellis, who sported a Kaiser-like bristly moustache, was a German!

By 1894, terraced housing was being built on the west side of the railway bridge on what was then called Lower Stockbridge Road. The houses between The Old Red Deer and Western Road, which are now all commercial properties, had also been built. Gradually, housing began to creep up Stockbridge Road, especially on the north-east side, and by 1909 development extended up to just beyond Hatherley Road. The houses beyond Fairfield Road were mainly moderately large semi-detached properties. Slightly later, in the 1890s and early 1900s, Fairfield Road, Cranworth Road, Brassey Road, Boscobel Road and Owens Road were developed, again mainly with terraced housing. Houses on Hatherley Road, however, were built to the standard of those on Stockbridge Road above Fairfield Road, but its north side was not completed until after the Great War. With so much development going on during the 30 years or so prior to the war, the new suburb of Fulflood must have resembled a permanent building site.

All this building took place within the ancient parish of Weeke and as early as the 1860s it was apparent that the small medieval church of St Matthew's could no longer cope with the increasing population. Besides, the new Fulflood looked more towards Winchester than the still rural village of Weeke. Work on St Paul's Church began in 1870 on what was then Union Hill, later Upper Stockbridge Road and now St Paul's Hill. The architect, John Colson, chose a Victorian Gothic design but, with money apparently in short supply, building work took almost 40 years. The chancel was consecrated in 1872 and work finally completed in 1910. The north wall was decorated with graffito work by George Heywood Sumner, one of the leading Art Nouveau artists of his time and son of Mary Sumner, founder of the Mothers' Union. Fashions change, however, and Sumner's work was painted over with limewash in 1963, although a small patch has since been uncovered, and the cartoons for the original work are now in the Hampshire Record Office.

Weeke Within – Fulflood, Oram's Arbour and the Station Area

As the suburb developed, a Mission Hall in Brassey Road, now a private residence numbered 41A, was built for the parish and by 1914 held a weekly service every Thursday. There was another Mission Hall to the west of the railway arch on Stockbridge Road by 1923 but it has not yet been researched. It was demolished recently for housing.

According to the 1914 Warren's Directory, Weeke Within had several church social groups, including a number that catered for children. The main parish Sunday school for older boys was held at 3pm and its superintendent was a Mr Fifield. This could be the father of Basil 'Jack' Fifield who is listed on the parish war memorials. The girls and infants had their Sunday School at 3pm at Western School in Elm Road. The Brassey Road Mission Hall's Sunday school was at 10am for boys, girls and infants. On a more obviously sociable level, the Boys Club met on Monday evenings and the Girls Club on Thursday evenings in St Paul's Church Rooms which had been built alongside the church in 1912. There was also a parish social club for the men, presumably to provide an alternative to the pubs, which ran from 6-11pm Monday to Friday and on Saturday from 2pm. Billiards and whist were two of its activities.

The parish had another hall, built by 1909, at the bottom of what is now St Paul's Hill. During the Great War when Winchester was surrounded by military camps, it would have been conveniently placed to provide refreshments to soldiers arriving or departing from the station as well as a recreational space for reading newspapers and writing letters. A further communal building, Western Hall, was adjacent to the later Vokes & Becks Monumental Masons' site (now Becks Mews). The premises, probably run by the Evangelical Free Church, were there by 1895 and were used as a public hall and a Sunday School.

Every 'village' had to have a school. In 1878, Western Church of England School was built at the upper end of Elm Road. It had a dual purpose, as a mixed infants catering for ages 5-7 and as a girls' elementary school, educating pupils from 7-13. As a primary school, it moved to its present site in Browning Drive, at the top end of Fulflood, in 1975. The old Western School building survives and from 1997 it was converted into apartments and renamed Bankside House.

For many of the men of the parish who died in the Great War, Western School would have been their first. However, Weeke had no boys' elementary school. The bright ones went to St Thomas Elementary School in Mews Lane (off Romsey Road) or other elementary schools in the city. Those even brighter, and who could get their fees paid for by an award, moved from St Thomas's at the age of 13 to the Peter Symonds Grammar School which opened in its new building in 1899. Four of the six names on the Peter Symonds Great War Memorial Board and which also appear on the parish memorials lived in Fulflood and had their fees paid.

Those girls bright and fortunate enough could get grants to go to the fee-paying Winchester County Girls School, now The Westgate School. Founded in 1909, it moved to the then new building in Cheriton Road in 1911. The school aimed to educate girls up to the age of 16-17 to prepare them to run a home or to become teachers. In January 1915, as the Great War entered its sixth month, the Army requisitioned the school building, along with many others in Winchester, as troop accommodation. The winter of 1914-15 was appallingly wet and cold and the military authorities feared for the wellbeing of the thousands of troops mobilising in camps on the downs around the city, many just in bell tents. The school moved to a pair of semi-detached houses, later the site of Nethercliffe School, in Hatherley Road. Here the girls grew vegetables throughout the war. After they were able to return, probably later in 1915, the school used the huts built by the Army as much needed extra classrooms.

Weeke Within briefly had a private girl's school when the aforementioned Southend School moved to Newburgh House by 1911. The school had been started by a Miss Lunn as a kindergarten in St Thomas Street, expanded to Southgate Street as a day and boarding school before relocating to Newburgh House. By 1916, however, it had moved again, to 3-4 Clifton Road, and was outside the parish. Doris Burniston, born in 1899, attended Southend School when it was at Newburgh House and she described it as a school for trades people's daughters: her father was a solicitor's clerk.

The new 'village' of Fulflood had houses, a church and a school. Another essential component, shops, often just sprang up. It was easy to turn a front room into a general store - for example, 52, Western

Road (the address then and now) was Brading's off-licence. Some roads seem to have been developed with a shop at the corner as part of the design. Examples of these were on the western corner of Stockbridge Road and Cranworth Road which has only recently been converted into purely residential use, and Smith's at 7, later 13, Brassey Road on the western corner with Boscobel Road. There were two sub-post offices in Fulflood in 1914. The Warren's Directory of that year does not specify where, but Smith's may have been one of them as it was a post office by 1921.

With no domestic refrigeration, fresh milk had to be purchased from one of Fulflood's several dairies. According to the 1914 Warren's Directory, Mrs J. Lay's Dairy stood at the corner of Western Road and Stockbridge Road (currently Solutions Dental Clinic). The 1908 Directory shows a dairy at 22, Western Road (part of The Rosery site) run by a Mrs Montague, but it was no longer listed as such by 1914. The 1881 Census showed that Fulflood Farm had also become a dairy, with its address given as 20, Week (sic) Road. Again, however, it was not listed as a dairy in 1914.

By 1914, the biggest concentration of commercial premises in Fulflood had been established on the Stockbridge Road between Elm Road and Western Road, with the proprietors usually living above the shops. Two have been mentioned already - The Old Red Deer at one corner and Lays' Dairy at the other. In between were several general stores, a butcher and a fishmonger. There was also a newsagent run by the Tong family whose son, Herbert, is listed on the parish memorials. This property, now No. 11, is the derelict site alongside the still surviving archway to what had been J. H. White's coal stores.

On the opposite side of Western Road from Lays' Dairy was The Omega off licence. Already there in the late 1800s, the property remained an off licence until the early 21st Century. There was a further off licence across the Stockbridge Road (now Pi restaurant) which only closed in the 1990s.

Two shops stood in Western Road by 1914, the aforementioned Bradings at No. 52, and H. Sealey at No. 24 (the address then and now), on the corner with Avenue Road opposite The Rosery. Sealey was listed as a grocer, baker and pastry cook and his shop known as Western Supply Stores. It later became a Co-op. Avenue Road had a grocer, George Winkworth, at No. 22, up the steps at the other end. Doris Burniston, mentioned earlier, recalled sweets being sold from the shop through the railings to Western School children, a tradition carried on well into the 20th Century.

Amidst all the housing, workshops sprang up to provide further employment. This was a typical arrangement throughout areas of terraced housing in Winchester. Vokes and Beck, the monumental masons, took over from John Marsh in 1901 at what is now 108, Stockbridge Road, by the modern roundabout with St Paul's Hill. The firm left Fulflood in 2005 and was the last prominent workshop style business to leave the area. Today the only clue to the firm's long association with Fulflood is in

A poor quality photo from the early 1900s looking up what was then Lower Stockbridge Road. The shop on the right stands on the corner of Cranworth Road and judging by the line of children probably sold sweets!

the name of Becks Mews, the recent housing development on the former Vokes and Beck site. Basil Vokes, son of one of the founders of the business, is listed on the parish memorials.

J.H. Whites Coal Stores was situated at the then 87, Stockbridge Road, through the still surviving archway in the row of shops, between the modern Nos 9 and 11. Whites was one of the coal businesses responsible for organising rationing in Winchester during the Great War when there was a shortage of domestic coal due to priority being given to the needs of the armed services and industry. In 1914 Southern Counties Agricultural Trading Society (SCATS) had their registered office and stores on Cranworth Road near the railway bridge, next to the Mission Hall. The SCATS store is still in Winchester, in Winnall, and is known today as Moles Country Store.

What of non-church related leisure facilities? By 1914, men (mainly) had several pubs to choose from as well as the parish social club. The Roebuck, probably one of the earliest and a pub that still survives, was built on Stockbridge Road and opened as The Three Horse Shoes in the 1830s. The 1841 Census showed that it had become The New Bridge Inn and by 1851 it had been renamed The Roebuck, with the publican being also described in that year's Census as a farmer. When first built, The Roebuck stood in the middle of agricultural land which increasingly became used for horticulture and later for housing.

As well as being the point at which Weeke Within became Weeke Without, The Roebuck also marked the city and Parliamentary boundary for many years and a small boundary marker is still embedded in the front wall. The pub also owned some of the land on the opposite side of the Stockbridge Road (now Langton Close), which from at least 1869 to about 1902 was the site of an annual sheep and lamb fair. The 1870-71 OS Map marks a cricket pitch on the site and from 1902 until 1914 it was also home to Winchester Football Club, with the pub being used as the changing rooms. In 1917, when wartime food shortages were becoming a problem, The Roebuck's football pitch was divided up into allotments. After the war, the club relocated to Bar End. A number of Winchester FC players were killed or wounded in the Great War, including Edwin 'Teddy' Smith who lived in Fairfield Road, close to the club ground. He is listed on the parish memorials.

Mark Wakeford, the publican of The Roebuck in the 1881 Census, also built The Old Red Deer, as a family hotel and pub at the corner of Elm Road and Stockbridge Road. It had opened in 1881 and was extended in 1889 to include stabling. (That building still survives.) By 1899, the pub was being run by Thomas Shefferd whose son Cecil also worked there and who is listed on the parish memorials. Just down the road, Cecil's uncle, William Shefferd, was the publican at The Albion. In a large yard behind The Old Red Deer (now Red Deer Court) a barn provided space for carriages and wagons. Being so close to the station, it must have been well placed for guests and a delivery business to the surrounding villages. Behind The Roebuck was a field (now Pilgrim's Gate) that was used for grazing the Old Red Deer horses and for holding circuses. There was also at some stage a Red Deer cricket team. Despite its good location, The Old Red Deer had become solely a pub in 1916. It closed in 1983 but the building survives with Winchester Travel Health on the corner and Fulflood Gallery & Framing next door.

The Railway on St Paul's Hill opened in 1883, presumably also to serve the needs of travellers as well as locals. The now famous music venue at the back may have been used as a livestock store for animals being transported by train. The Railway and The Old Red Deer should have done well in the war. The huge influx of soldiers meant Winchester's population more than doubled between 1914-18 with no fewer than one million soldiers estimated to have passed through the city during the period. Most arrived and departed by train and it is inconceivable that they did not visit pubs like The Railway and Old Red Deer, just a stone's throw from the station.

The Fulflood Arms, still on the corner of Western Road and Cheriton Road, was opened in 1871 and still has the original green glazed tiles on the outside that marked it out as a Winchester Brewery

Company pub. The Volunteer, on the corner of North View and Middle Road, was there before 1880 and was formerly The Woolpack. It closed in the 1970s and is now a private residential house.

By the outbreak of the Great War, Weeke Within on both sides of the railway was a thriving and virtually self-sufficient part of Winchester. The many occupations listed in the censuses showed that much of the male population was skilled, with men working as joiners, carpenters, decorators, plasterers, builders, boot and shoe makers, plumbers, bricklayers, printers, glaziers, tailors, bakers, domestic gardeners and coopers.

The Volunteer pub on the corner of North View and Middle Road is now a private residential house *(Photo: Lloyd Phillips)*

Others worked in what today we would describe as service industries – as shopkeepers, clerks, hotel waiters and cooks. Still more worked in the slowly expanding public sector as prison wardens, postmen, policemen and, of course, as soldiers and sailors. There were also men still working in jobs related to horse-drawn transport, such as farriers, harness makers, grooms, carters and carmen. However, while some described themselves as railway porters and jobbing gardeners, there were very few listed as just labourers. In the larger middle class properties on the Stockbridge Road and on Fairfield Road and Hatherley Road lived businessmen and men and women teachers (including singing and music teachers). Winchester's Chief Post Office Clerk and a Times correspondent also lived here.

Dressmaking and domestic service were the most common occupations for single women, but they could also be milliners or work in or even run – as in the case of Mrs Lay – a dairy or a shop. Some had jobs as clerks. Very few married women were listed as having an occupation: most still faced the onerous daily task of running homes without the labour-saving domestic appliances we take for granted. In the larger houses in Weeke Within there was often one living-in servant. Most families in Weeke Within had enough money to afford to rent their new houses from their the husband's and maybe their offsprings' wages. Some took in the occasional boarder to supplement the finances. Several widows were recorded running boarding houses as an occupation, and a few worked as laundresses.

The impact of the Great War on Fulflood and Weeke, like the rest of Winchester, was immediate and profound. The arrival of thousands of troops at the nearby barracks in early August 1914 galvanised the local population in a way that areas more 'remote' from the war never were. People responded by supporting the war effort in myriad ways – billeting troops, giving to, or working for one of the many war charities, enrolling as nurses, working as ambulance drivers or helping out at the 'clubs' – at Weeke Parish Hall, for example – that provided soldiers with refreshments and entertainment. Some families may have housed Belgian refugees. All this represented a voluntary, rather than a state-led, response. Moreover, although patriotism and enthusiasm did initially play a part in driving this response, most people were motivated more by a sense of duty and a strong belief in the righteousness of Britain's cause. The same factors drove military recruitment and explain why more of the Weeke parish men who fought in the Great War were volunteers rather than conscripts.

The war affected people in other ways, too. The coal shortages mentioned earlier not only caused hardship during the winter months but led to travel restrictions, particularly on the trains. At a more basic level, the sights and sounds of everyday life changed: contemporary accounts describe how Winchester became a 'sea of khaki', its roads choked with military vehicles and the paraphernalia of war. The building of the Army mobilisation camps around the city altered the physical landscape even more dramatically, to the regret of some. Unfamiliar accents – Scots, Welsh, Canadian and, later American – became commonplace on the streets and in shops and pubs. Black American servicemen, who arrived with the US Army in 1917-18, would undoubtedly have been the subject of lively conversation among curious locals.

However, the biggest challenge families faced was the strain of living with the knowledge that their menfolk might be killed in battle. From early in the war, it became apparent that losses would be on a previously unimaginable scale, and mourning, not just for immediate family but for friends and neighbours, became the norm. For many, the trauma cast a shadow for years to come. Some never fully came to terms with their loss.

The end of the war in November 1918 and the return of servicemen over the following months would be bittersweet in Weeke parish, as elsewhere. The parish memorials list 91 men who died but our research has shown the true figure to be over 100 and many more returned home disabled physically and/or mentally scarred. The Spanish Flu pandemic of 1918-19 then heaped further misery on an exhausted population. The communal effort in the publication of the Winchester War Service Register in 1921 and the creation of the memorial boards for the men of Fulflood and Weeke at St Paul's Church in 1922 would have hopefully provided some solace.

GERALDINE BUCHANAN

Index to the biographies

The biographies are in alphabetical order, with the subject name appearing in the page heading.

B

Bignell, Jesse	32
Bishop, Leonard Newman	35
Bogie, Andrew William	37
Breadmore, Percy George	42
Buck, James Henry	44
Burgess, Frank Ernest	48

C

Chapman, Frank James	53
Churcher, Henry Thomas	55
Clark, Reginald James	59
Coles, Frank	65
Coles, Sidney James	68

D

Dawkins, Frank	71
Dennistoun, James Robert	73
Dobson, Frances William	76
Douglas, Charles Edwin Gardiner	78
Douse, Clifford Tom	81
Drake, Thomas Harold	85

E

Edwards, Frederick	88

F

Fifield, Basil Jack	90
Forbes, John	93
Forder, Francis James	95
Forster, Harold Thomas	98
Francis, Albert Edward	103
Fraser, Frank	106

G

Gambling, Albert Victor	109
Goodridge, George	112
Goodwin, Charles Francis	116
Goodyear, George Frederick	119
Gould, Henry Charles Hamerton	121
Gye, Denison Allen	124

H

Halls, Harold Charles	126
Hammond, Charles Walter	129
Hawker, Charles William Seymour	132
Hawkins, Sidney Michael	136
Head, Frank Joseph	138
Hill, Arthur Samuel	141
Hill, Nicholas Weatherby	146
Hounslow, George Horace	150

I

Illingworth, Thomas William	152
Inge, Sidney George	154

J

Jacob, Leslie John	156
Johnson, Archibald Leonard	160

K

Ketley, Charles Walter	168

L

Lawrance, Ernest Albert	170
Lever, George Thomas	175
Lovelock, George Allan	178

M

Maclachlan, Ronald Campbell	182
Maidment, Hubert George	193
Male, Reginald Harry	196
Middleton, Bertram Charles	202
Mitchell, William James	207
Morrah, John Henry	217
Morrison, David Thomson	226
Muldowney, John Henry	230

N

Newby, William Ernest Herbert	235
Newton, Alan Herbert	242
Norgate, Percy Douglas	245

Index to Biographies

P

Payne, Henry John 249
Powell, Cyril Edward 251
Powney, William Benjamin 253
Prior, George 255

R

Richards, Frederick Charles 258
Rule, Eric Granville Sutherland 262

S

Scadden, Alfred 266
Seward, John William 269
Shears, Samuel 276
Shefford, Cecil 279
Simmons, John 283
Smith, Archibald Charles 288
Smith, Edwin Alfred 291
Smith, Horace 294
Soffe, George 299
Soffe, Henry James 302
Sothcott, Leopold George 305
Stevens, Ernest 308
Stroud, Bertram Edward 310

Stroud, George 313

T

Thompson, Richard James 315
Tong, Herbert Lewis 318
Tunks, Edward Joseph Austin 323

V

Vandeleur, John Beauclerk 327
Vokes, Basil 334

W

Wake, Frederick William 339
Wand-Tetley, Clarence Ernest 341
Ward, Donald Henry Charles 347
Wedge, Charles Edward 353
Wedge, James Charles Thomas 359
Whitcher, Edwin Walter 363
White, Frederick Alexander 367
White, William Edward 369
Winter, Charles John 371

BIGNELL, Jessie

Acting Corporal JESSE BIGNELL
34, Stockbridge Road, Winchester (no longer stands)
Service Number 16309. 2nd Battalion, The Essex Regiment
Killed in action, Belgium, 8 October 1917

Jesse Bignell's birth in Longstock, near Stockbridge, was registered in the first quarter of 1883, so he could also have been born in late 1882. He was the eldest child of Thomas and Louisa Bignell. His father had been born in March 1859 in Easton, near Winchester, where Jesse's paternal grandfather Henry was working as an agricultural labourer. Henry and his wife Sarah already had four daughters, all born when they lived in Kings Worthy, near Winchester. Sarah was about 44 when she gave birth to Thomas.

Jesse's father appears to have worked with horses all his life. He had moved to Winchester by 1881, working as a groom and living in lodgings at 83, Cheesehill Street (now 36 Chesil Street). The householder of No.83 was Charles Whitcher who later moved to Avenue Road, Fulflood, with his wife Ann. Edwin Whitcher, the couple's son, later died in the Great War and he is commemorated on the Fulflood and Weeke memorials. Edwin Whitcher's biography is on pp 363.

Living at 4, Cheesehill Street (now 2, Cheshil Street) in 1881 was Louisa Brock who worked as a cook to the Shenton family, a name well-known in Winchester. Louisa was the daughter of David Brock and Sarah (née Webb) and had been born in Longstock in around 1859. Romance flourished in Cheesehill Street and she and Thomas Bignell married in Winchester in 1883.

By 1884, the couple must have been living in Winchester as all their subsequent three surviving children were born there. In 1891 Thomas and Louisa were living at 5, Lower Stockbridge Road (now 10, Stockbridge Road) with their four children – Jesse, by then aged eight, Ethel, aged seven, four-year-old Leonard, and William, aged 19 months. William had had a twin Harry who died in early 1890. The elder three children were listed as scholars. Thomas, their father, was working as a stableman to a butcher. The Bignell's home was a large property and it must have been part of their financial plan to take in lodgers when they started to rent it as, in 1891, there were four lodgers living with the family.

By 1901, Thomas and Louisa and their four children were living at 17, Lower Stockbridge Road, a much smaller property. It was part of a terrace of houses, which has subsequently been demolished, and which stood at right angles to the rest of Lower Stockbridge Road. It would have been overlooked by the Victorian gasometer off Andover Road. This terrace when first built was numbered 9-18, Lower Stockbridge Road. When the road was renumbered and renamed it became 18-36, Stockbridge Road. The access, which now leads to a private car park, was between what is now Haywards Guitars, 38, Stockbridge Road (which was 19, Lower Stockbridge Road) and 16, Stockbridge Road (previously 8, Lower Stockbridge Road.) After the terrace was demolished, Stockbridge Road was not renumbered so the gap in the numbers remains to this day.

The 1901 Census shows that three of the four Bignell children were working. Jesse, by then 18, was a grocer's porter, Ethel's occupation was described as 'nursemaid domestic' and Leonard, aged 14 was a milk boy. Presumably the youngest, William, aged 11, was still at school. By the time of the 1911 Census, most of the Bignell family were still at 17, Lower Stockbridge Road with Thomas working as a butcher's stableman, Leonard as a milkman and William as a boot repairer. Jesse, however, was recorded working as a grocer's assistant in Abridge, near Romford, Essex, in the household of Alfred Bayle, a grocer, and presumably his employer.

BIGNELL, Jessie

Some confusion surrounds which battalion of the Essex Regiment Jesse served with during the Great War. The records of the Commonwealth War Graves Commission state that he was with the 10th Battalion but his Medal Index Card and Army casualty records both list him with the 2nd Battalion. In this case, it has been decided to follow the Army records and assume that Jesse enlisted with the 2nd Battalion in Warley, the main regimental depot in Essex, in December 1914.

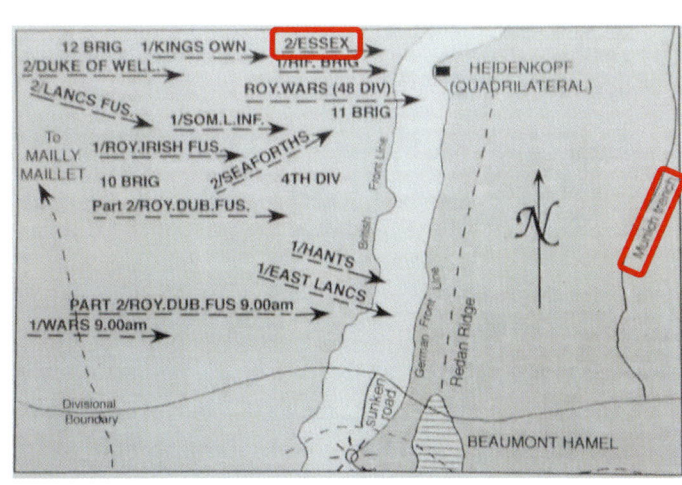

The attack by 4th Division on 1 July 1916, the first day of the Battle of the Somme. Jesse Bignell's battalion, the 2nd Essex, are on the extreme left of the British line

The 2nd Essex was a Regular Army battalion under the command of 12th Brigade, part of the 4th Division. The Division had moved to France at the end of August 1914 and fought at the battles of Le Cateau, the Marne, the Aisne and Armentieres that year. In 1915 it suffered heavy casualties at the Second Battle of Ypres (22 April-25 May) which saw the first use of poison gas and flamethrowers in the war. Jesse is recorded joining the 2nd Essex in France on 25 May 1915, the last day of the battle, probably as a much-needed reinforcement.

Jesse was with D Company of the 2nd Essex for the start of the Somme Offensive (1 July-18 November 1916 – see page 387). The attack by 4th Division on German positions north of the village of Serre on 1 July proved a disaster. Losses for the day amounted to 5,752, more than half its fighting strength. Jesse's battalion somehow managed to reach Munich Trench (see map above) despite heavy German machine-gun fire. However, enemy counter-attacks meant these gains had to be abandoned and by the following day the men of 4th Division were back in their own trenches.

The shattered 4th Division did not return to the front line on the Somme until the autumn when it fought at the Battle of Le Transloy (1-18 October). The 12th Brigade went into action at 2.05pm on 12 October when troops attacked Spectrum Trench just to the north of the village of Lesboeufs. The assault, which followed a heavy Stokes mortar bombardment of German positions, was badly hampered by appalling battlefield conditions and made little progress.

At some stage Jesse Bignell was made Acting Corporal which meant he would have overseen 10-15 men. On 13 December 1916 he was taken to Casualty Clearing Station No.34, possibly after contracting trench foot. He was transferred to a sick convoy two days later and may have been sent back to England to recover.

Jesse was almost certainly back on the Western Front in time for the Arras Offensive (9 April-16 May 1917, see page 388). The offensive opened with the Battle of Vimy Ridge (9-14 April) and the parallel First Battle of the Scarpe – in which 4th Division fought – and saw the biggest Allied successes of the war up to that date. However, the campaign bogged down. The 4th Division also took part in the unsuccessful Third Battle of the Scarpe (3-4 May).

The 4th Division played no part in the opening phase of the Third Battle of Ypres, better known as Passchendaele (31 July-15 November 1917, see page 389). However, it did feature in the subsidiary attacks at Polygon Wood and Broodseinde in late September and early October. Using 'bite and hold' tactics, with objectives limited to what could be held against enemy counter-attacks, the assaults proved highly successful and dented German morale so severely that they began to make plans to withdraw from the Belgian coast. In the event, the Germans did not need to withdraw: the rain, which had blighted British efforts during the early weeks of the battle, returned after Broodseinde to effectively blunt subsequent attacks.

Jesse Bignell, who had been wounded on 3 September, was killed in action on 8 October 1917, aged 34. He probably died that night as the 2nd Essex moved up the line in torrential rain before going over the top at 5.20am the following day at the start of the Battle of Poelcapelle.

Jesse's youngest brother William also fought in the Great War after enlisting with the 2/4th Battalion, The Hampshire Regiment in August 1914 (see page 375). He served in India for more than two years before transferring to Egypt and then Palestine where he took part in the advance on Jerusalem. In June 1918, the 2/4th Hampshires moved to the Western Front where they swiftly gained a reputation as a formidable fighting unit. William served alongside Henry Churcher, who lived at 3, Avenue Road, Winchester. Henry was killed during this final phase of the war.

After the war, Thomas and Louisa Bignell continued to live at 34, Stockbridge Road. Louisa died in 1934, aged about 75, and Thomas in September 1937. All of Jesse's siblings married. Ethel married Cornelius 'Frank' Hillyer in 1912 in Winchester. Frank went on to serve on the home front in the Great War. Ethel and Frank, who had no children, were living at 11, North Walls, Winchester, in 1939. Ethel died in Winchester in 1952, aged 68.

In the 1939 Register, Jesse's brother Leonard was a works contractor labourer. He and his wife Sarah were living at 31, Fairdown, Winchester. Leonard died in Winchester in 1955. His youngest brother, William was a clerk at the Records Office and he and his wife Elsie were at 63, Stanmore Lane, Winchester. Both couples appear to have had children.

Medals and memorials for Jesse Bignell

Acting Corporal Jesse Bignell was buried in Nine Elms British Cemetery (above), Poperinge, West Flanders, Belgium (GR. IV. B. 6.). He was entitled to the 1914-15 Star, the Victory Medal and the British War Medal. His name is the first on the memorials at St Paul's and St Matthew's churches, Winchester.

Researchers – GERALDINE BUCHANAN and JOSEPHINE COLEMAN

Additional sources
- The Essex Regiment: http://www.essexregiment.co.uk.

BISHOP, Leonard Newman

Private LEONARD NEWMAN BISHOP
1, Cromwell Terrace, Romsey Road, Winchester (house no longer stands)
Service number 9416. 1st Battalion, The South Wales Borderers
Killed in action, France, 26 September 1914

Leonard Newman Bishop, the son of Edward and Sarah Bishop, was born in the first quarter of 1885. His father worked as a warder at Winchester Prison for many years and the family lived in prison service accommodation nearby. Leonard served in the Army for a decade before the Great War and was sent to France shortly after hostilities began in August 1914. He was killed in action the following month.

Leonard's father, Edward (1841-1911), was born in Winchester, the son of Benjamin and Elizabeth. Bishop. Benjamin worked as a shoemaker and then as a messenger (possibly for Winchester College) and the family lived at 7, Canon Street. In the 1861 Census Edward, then 19, was recorded working as a servant at Winchester College and living at the Commoners' Hall. He married twice. His first wife was born Elizabeth Wisbey in 1827, making her some 14 years his senior. Edward and Elizabeth married in 1867 and in 1871 they were living at 5, County Cottages, Winchester, close to the prison where Edward was working as a warder, a job he continued in until about 1891.

It is believed that Elizabeth gave birth to a son in 1871 but he died the same year. Elizabeth herself died on 5 January 1877, aged 50, and is buried at West Hill Cemetery, Winchester.

In May 1878 Edward remarried. His second wife, Sarah Rebecca Newman, was the daughter of carpenter Charles Newman and his wife, also called Sarah. Sarah Jnr had been born in Cambridgeshire (probably in the village of Isleham, near Newmarket) in 1840. In 1871 she was living and working as a servant in Oxford and seven years later she and Edward married in Henley on Thames. The 1881 Census showed them living at 8, Prison Quarters, Winchester. The couple had four children, all born in Winchester: Edward Charles (1879), Edith Annie (1880), Lilian 'Lily' Lucy (1883) and Leonard (1885). Tragically, Sarah died in Winchester in 1887, aged 47, leaving Edward widowed for a second time.

It appears that Edward enlisted the services of an elderly aunt, Mary Carney, to help him look after his young children. In 1891 Mary was living with the family at their new home at 1, Cromwell Terrace, Winchester. (The house was part of a short row of properties on the Romsey Road close to the Royal Hampshire County Hospital which have since been demolished.) Mary was still with the family ten years later by which time Edward had retired from the prison service. Two children remained at home – Leonard who was working as a postman and Edward Jnr as an organ builder.

Shortly afterwards, Leonard moved to London where he found work as a postman in Isleworth. Then in 1904 he joined the Army, enlisting in Winchester with the 1st Battalion, The Dorsetshire Regiment (service number 7325). He served in India with the Dorsets and then in South Africa with the 2nd Battalion, The South Wales Borderers before transferring to the 1st South Wales Borderers (service number 9416).

When the Great War began in August 1914, Leonard was serving with D Company of the 1st South Wales Borderers. The battalion came under the orders of 3rd Brigade, part of the British 1st Division which arrived in France on 13 August. The Borderers first saw action at the Battle of Mons (23 August) when the British Expeditionary Force (BEF) attempted to hold up the advancing German First Army. The heavily outnumbered British inflicted heavy casualties on the Germans but were eventually forced to retreat. The retreat lasted for two weeks and took the BEF to the outskirts of Paris before it counter-attacked with the French at the Battle of the Marne (6-12 September). This forced the German armies to retire northwards until they in turn halted the pursuing British at the Battle of the Aisne (12-15 September). Both sides then began to dig in, marking the start of trench warfare on the Western Front.

Fighting north the Aisne, however, continued. On 26 September 1914, 1st Division took part in an action near the village of Chivy on the Chemin des Dames ridge. In his diary, Captain C.J. Paterson of the 1st South Wales Borderers described the day's events:

BISHOP, Leonard Newman

The most ghastly day of my life and yet too one of the proudest because my Regiment did its job and held on against heavy odds. At 4.15am Germans attacked. Main attack apparently against my Regiment, which is the left of our line. D and A Companies in the trenches. B and C hustled up to support, and soon the whole place alive with bullets. News comes that they are trying to work round our left. The CO asked the Welsh Regiment to deal with this, which it did. Poor D Company had to face the music more than anyone else.

Presently the news comes that the Germans are in a quarry in the middle of our line ... [but] C Company drove them clean out. About 3pm things began to quieten down. D and A Companies had done their share of the work on the right and left. We were able to reorganise more or less, except for D Company's far advanced trenches, and those we searched at night and found James wounded, Sills and Welby killed. Total casualties. Killed - Welby, Simonds, Coker, Sills and 86 men; wounded – Pritchard, James and Gwynn slightly, and 95 men; and missing 12.

Leonard Bishop was 28 years old when he was killed during the fighting described above. His body was never found.

Leonard's father, Edward, is believed to have continued living in Winchester after the war although there is no trace of him there in the 1911 Census or subsequent electoral records. He died in the city in 1935, aged 93.

Leonard's brother Edward Charles, the organ builder, married twice. His first wife, Emily, whom he wed in 1903, gave birth to a son, Wilfred, in Winchester in 1904 but she died the following year. In 1908 Edward remarried. His second wife, Margaret Frances Carpenter, had been born in Bangalore, India, in 1887. The couple initially lived in Bournemouth where a son, Kenneth Leonard, was born in October 1910. Edward Charles served in France and Belgium during the Great War with the Royal Berkshire and Gloucestershire Regiments. He did not enlist until 1917 which means he was probably conscripted. After the war he, Margaret and Kenneth moved back to live in Winchester at 50, Fairfield Road. Edward died in Bournemouth in 1946 at the age of 66.

Leonard's sister Edith had a daughter, Ethel, in 1896 when she was just 16. In 1902 she married John Whitear (it is unclear whether he was Ethel's father) in Winchester and they had a son, Francis, and a daughter, Marjorie, together. The family lived for a time in Fulflood, first in Greenhill Road and then Avenue Road before also moving to Bournemouth where Edith died in 1961, aged 81. Leonard's younger sister, Lily, was working as a domestic servant in Winchester in 1901. Ten years later she was helping to run a hotel in Bournemouth, but no record of her can be found after that date.

Leonard Newman does not figure in the Winchester War Service Register, although his brother Edward does, with his address given as 50, Fairfield Road. However, Edward may have been responsible for Leonard's name appearing on the memorials at St Paul's and St Matthew's. Leonard was killed several years before Edward moved to Fairfield Road and so never lived in or visited the property. For that reason, this biography gives Leonard's address as 1, Cromwell Terrace. It may have been situated just outside the Fulflood and Weeke parish boundary, but it is the house most closely associated with him.

Medals and memorials for Leonard Newman Bishop

Private Leonard Newman Bishop was entitled to the 1914 (Mons) Star, the British War Medal and the Victory Medal. He is commemorated on the La Ferte-Sous-Jouarre Memorial, Seine-et-Marne, France. He is also listed on the memorials at St Matthew's and St Paul's churches, Winchester.

Researcher – JENNY WATSON

BOGIE, Andrew William

Company Quarter Master Sergeant ANDREW WILLIAM BOGIE
2, St Paul's Terrace, Winchester (20, St Paul's Hill today)
Service numbers 4/149 and 200023. 1/4th Battalion, The Hampshire Regiment.
Died in captivity, Turkey, 22 September 1916

Andrew William Bogie, the son of Peter and Catherine Bogie, was born in 1882 in St Peter Port, Guernsey. Andrew moved to Winchester in the early 1900s to train to be a teacher and after qualifying he taught at St Thomas Church of England Boys' School. Married with one son, he joined the Hampshire Regiment's 1st Volunteer Battalion which later became the 4th Battalion, The Hampshire Regiment. During the Great War, he served in India and Mesopotamia and died of disease while in Turkish captivity after being taken prisoner following the siege of Kut-al-Amara in 1916.

Andrew's father was born in Marwick, Fifeshire, in 1852, and worked for most of his life as a gardener – both domestic and as a market garden trader - in Scotland and England. Andrew's mother was born Catherine Webb in Malta in 1857 and was known as Kate. Her father, William Webb, was a soldier with the 1/21st (Royal North British Fusiliers) Regiment of Foot, later the Royal Scots Fusiliers. The regiment had arrived in Malta from the Crimean War in June 1856, shortly before Kate's birth, and remained on the island until March 1860. It was stationed at Fort Ricasoli and formed part of the British garrison.

The 1871 Census listed Kate, then 14, as a scholar at the Royal Victoria Patriotic Asylum for Girls in south-west London. Paid for through public donations and opened in 1859, the Asylum educated and trained 300 orphan daughters of soldiers and sailors who had died in the Crimean War. Clearly William Webb was not killed in Crimea because he was with his regiment on Malta when his daughter was born in 1857. When he did die is unclear.

On 27 December 1880, Peter Bogie and Kate Webb married in Croydon, Surrey, where she was living at the time. The marriage certificate gives Peter's place of residence as St Andrew, Guernsey, and the couple were recorded as living on the island in the 1881 Census just a few months later.

Following Andrew Bogie's birth in 1882 Peter and Kate went on to have another son, Alfred, born in Guernsey in July 1884, and a daughter, Catherine, born in Bracebridge, Lincolnshire, in April 1886. Census records show that they also had two other children who died.

The family moved around the country a great deal as Peter Bogie sought work. In 1891 they were living at 58, Lansdowne Road, Croydon, with Peter employed as a gardener/domestic servant. By 1901 they had moved back to Guernsey, with Peter working from home as a self-employed fruit grower. Andrew,

BOGIE, Andrew William

by then 19, was a schoolteacher although he had received little or no training. Meanwhile Alfred, following in his father's footsteps, was working as a gardener.

In 1902 Andrew enrolled at the Diocesan Training College, now the University of Winchester, where he underwent two years of formal teacher training. The college magazine states that Andrew was a regular speaker at debates, including one that asked, 'Would conscription be beneficial to the country?' He played for the college reserves football team and was part of the Volunteer Company of the Hampshire Regiment that all students were obliged to join, quickly winning promotion to corporal. Andrew qualified in 1904 and became a master at St Thomas Elementary Boys' School, the college's Practising School in Winchester. He was a member of the National Union of Teachers.

In 1910 Andrew married 23-year-old Florence Hannah Moss in her hometown of Great Yarmouth, Norfolk. The 1911 Census showed the couple living at 11, Highfield Villas, St Cross Road, Winchester, but by 1913 they had moved to 2, St Paul's Terrace. The house was renumbered 20, St Paul's Hill (the address then and now) during the Great War and is the address given for Andrew in the Winchester War Service Register (WWSR). On 23 February 1913 Florence gave birth to a son, Kenneth, probably at the family home in St Paul's Terrace.

20, St Paul's Hill, Winchester – this house was 2, St Paul's Terrace in October 1914 when Andrew Bogie went to war

Living next door to the Bogies at 3, St Paul's Terrace in 1914 were Ernest and Charlotte Fifield and their son, Jack, who was to be killed while serving with the Hampshire Regiment in the Great War. A few houses further up the hill at No. 10 lived Eric Rule who served in the same battalion as Andrew Bogie. He would die in 1916 during an attempt to rescue Andrew and other Hampshire soldiers trapped in the besieged British garrison at Kut-al-Amara.

Andrew Bogie continued serving as a part-time soldier with the 1st Volunteer Battalion of the Hampshire Regiment until 1908 when the Territorial Force came into being and the unit was redesignated the 4th Battalion, The Hampshire Regiment. His original Army service number (4/149) shows that he transferred to the 4th Hampshires in May 1908. By 1914 he had reached the rank of Sergeant serving in his battalion's B Company. When the 4th Battalion split into two in September that year Andrew was assigned to the 1/4th Hampshires. He volunteered for service overseas and in October sailed for India.

According to a report in the Hampshire Chronicle of 12 December 1914, Andrew was made Acting Company Quarter Master Sergeant (his responsibilities included ensuring his men were supplied with food, clothing and ammunition) and Orderly Room Sergeant shortly after arriving in India. The 1/4th Hampshires spent just four months there before being sent to Mesopotamia in mid-March 1915. Here they fought several encounters with the Ottoman Turks just north of their base at Basra, including the capture of the town of Nasiriyah on the River Euphrates.

BOGIE, Andrew William

Sergeant Andrew Bogie (circled) with other men of B Company, 4th Battalion, The Hampshire Regiment. The photograph was taken in July 1914, just days before the outbreak of war, while the battalion was on its annual camp on Salisbury Plain. *(Photo: Royal Hampshire Regiment Museum)*

In December 1915, Andrew Bogie found himself among the Hampshire men besieged in the British garrison at Kut-al-Amara (for details of the siege see pp.378). During the five-month siege, Andrew displayed gallantry that earned him the Military Medal – gazetted in 1919 - to go alongside his Meritorious Service Medal. He was also mentioned in dispatches.

After the surrender of the Kut garrison on 29 April 1916, Andrew and the surviving British and Indian soldiers were marched off to prisoner-of-war camps hundreds of miles away in Turkey. The conditions on the march were appalling and many men succumbed to disease. Interestingly, although he had only been in Mesopotamia for a year, Andrew had managed to learn the Turkish language. Evidence of this comes in a letter written by another 1/4th Battalion POW, Regimental Sergeant Major William Leach, who had also been at Winchester Diocesan Training College. In the letter, William describes how a soldier had been flogged and kicked by the Turkish guards during the march into captivity:

> *[Private Wood's] belt had been stolen by the escort and his shirt was very much torn. His body was one mass of scars and bruises which he accounted for by the brutal treatment he had suffered. He was flogged and kicked and hit with rifles and was absolutely unable to pick out or recognise the man who had treated him this way owing to his weak condition. I took him with Coy. QM Sgt Bogie (acting as interpreter) to Kashmi Effendi, and showed him how the man had been treated, but owing to the man not being able to pick his assailants no visible sign of notice seemed to be taken.*

Andrew eventually reached the POW camp at Yarbaschi in the Amanus Mountains, where those men fit enough worked on the construction of the Baghdad railway. Little is known of Andrew's short time in captivity at Yarbaschi. Most of the information we do have is contained in the Prisoner of War Comforts Fund records compiled on the Hampshire Regiment POWs by Mrs Esme Bowker, widow of the 1/4th Battalion's CO. These state that Andrew Bogie was 5ft 10in tall, wore size 9 boots and a six and three-quarters cap. His adopter in England was a Mr Stillwell of The Pines, Windlesham, Surrey,

BOGIE, Andrew William

who sent him aid parcels containing a jacket, overcoat, trousers, cardigan and socks as well as a Christmas parcel with plum pudding, sweets, a pipe, cigarettes, soap and other items.

Unfortunately, Andrew probably never received any of these parcels because on 22 September 1916 he died of dysentery, aged 34. New of his death did not reach England for more than a year. The Hampshire Regimental Journal of October 1917 states:

> *QMS Bogie - Official information has this week been received that QMS Andrew William Bogie, Hampshire Regiment, died of dysentery while a prisoner of war at Yarbaschi, Turkey. This news corning after a long period of suspense is very painful, and much sympathy will he expressed with his wife, who resides at No. 1, St Paul's Terrace. Winchester.*
>
> *The late QMS Bogie joined the Hampshire Territorials in May 1908 and went out with the Battalion to India early in the war, subsequently proceeding to Mesopotamia. He was in Kut at the time of General Townshend's surrender. For ... something approaching twelve months his wife had not heard from him, nor could tidings he gleaned from any other source. QMS Bogie was one of the best-known NCOs of the Battalion, and always enjoyed the highest confidence of his officers, and the warmest esteem of his fellow non-commissioned officers and men, by all of whom he has, no doubt, been greatly missed. In civil life he was an assistant master at St. Thomas Boys' School, Winchester, the Headmaster of which on Thursday afternoon communicated the sad intelligence to the pupils.*

The Army Registers of Soldiers' Effects 1901-29 shows that the War Office paid £32 4s 3d to Florence Bogie on 27 March 1918, in respect of Andrew's effects and back pay. She also received payments of £12 in October 1919 and £4 in April 1920 which were possibly war gratuities. Probate records reveal that she received £137 19s 11d from her late husband's estate in February 1918.

The Warren's Winchester Directory of 1918 records Florence living at 22, St Paul's Hill. The houses in St Paul's Terrace were renumbered during the war, with No. 22 corresponding to the old 1, St Paul's Terrace (next to the church). It therefore appears that Florence had moved to the house next door – this tallies with the address given for her in the Hampshire Regimental Journal report above. The Electoral Register of 1920 shows a William Coates also living in the house – perhaps he was a lodger – but Florence was on her own again by the following year.

At some point after 1911, Andrew's parents moved to Winchester. They were living at 100, Cromwell Road, on the new estate at Stanmore, from 1923 until Peter Bogie's death in 1925, aged 73. Andrew's mother subsequently moved to Aldershot and she passed away in Winchfield Hospital on 20 February 1938 at the age of 81.

Florence Bogie was still living at 22, St Paul's Hill when she died on 16 May 1932. She was buried at West Hill Cemetery, Winchester. The inscription on her gravestone, which has since been removed, read: 'In ever loving memory of Andrew William Bogie who entered the higher life at 34 when in his country's service and of Florence his wife who re-joined him May 16 1932 age 44 years'.

Florence left her estate, valued at £597 14s 5d, to her son Kenneth who went on to marry Hazel Gladys Clark in the New Forest in 1935. Kenneth worked as a branch manager for an insurance broker and he and Hazel had two daughters and a son. Kenneth died in Salisbury in 1999 and Gladys in 2004. Andrew's sister Catherine, who in 1911 had been working as a schoolteacher on Guernsey, married widower William Tanner, a 55-year-old builder, on 24 May 1922 in Grayshott, Hampshire. She is believed to have died in Surrey in 1955, aged 69.

Alfred Bogie, Andrew's brother, joined the 2nd Battalion, Seaforth Highlanders as a professional soldier sometime after 1901. During the Great War he fought as a Private on the Western Front from August 1914 before being transferred to the 1st Garrison Battalion, Seaforth Highlanders. He is believed to have served with them in Salonika from 1916-1918. Alfred was entitled to the 1914 (Mons Star), the British

BOGIE, Andrew William

War Medal and the Victory Medal. He later emigrated to Canada and lived in Toronto where he married Mabel Polley on 12 December 1930. However, the marriage was short-lived, Mabel dying in 1932. It is believed Alfred continued to live in Toronto up to his death on 1 December 1972, aged 88.

Medals and memorials for Andrew William Bogie

Company Quarter Master Sergeant Andrew William Bogie was entitled to the 1914-15 Star, the British War Medal and the Victory Medal. After the war, his body was disinterred and reburied at Baghdad (North Gate) War Cemetery, Iraq (GR. XXI. R. 21.). Andrew's name appears on the memorials at St Paul's and St Matthew's churches as well as those in the Winton Memorial Room at the University of Winchester's King Alfred College Campus Old Chapel (the former Diocesan Training College) and the St Thomas Church of England Boys' School Memorial, now at Kings School, Winchester. His name also appears on the memorial in St Peter Port, Guernsey, the town of his birth.

Researcher - DEREK WHITFIELD

BREADMORE, Percy George

Private PERCY GEORGE BREADMORE
188, Stockbridge Road, Winchester
Service numbers 3388 and 37641. 2/4th Battalion, The Royal Berks Regiment
Killed in action, France, 28 April 1917

Percy George Breadmore was born in Stockbridge on 3 June 1894, the only son of Albert and Ada Breadmore. Percy's connection with Winchester came through his uncle, a prosperous corn merchant who lived on Stockbridge Road. It was this address that Percy used when he joined the Army in November 1914. Percy died in April 1917 on the Western Front. His uncle and nephews all served in the Great War and survived.

The Breadmores were a well-known family in the Stockbridge area. Percy's grandfather, George (1828-1893), worked as a maltster in the nearby village of Wherwell before moving to Stockbridge where he established a corn merchant business. Percy's father, Albert, was born in Wherwell and went to school in Andover. He later set up a coal merchant business in Stockbridge.

Percy's mother was born Ada Bryant in Islington, north London, in 1868. She and Albert married in Lambeth, south London, in 1890 by which time Albert had started his Stockbridge coal business. Ada gave birth to Percy in 1894 but she died in Lambeth the following year, aged 27. Albert died in 1898.

With his grandparents also dead, it is not clear who looked after Percy in his early years. The next record of him comes in 1901 when he was seven years old and living with bricklayer John Froud and his wife Sarah at their home at Greenhill View, Owslebury, near Winchester. It is not known whether Percy was related to the Frouds. By 1911 he was living at 9/10 North Street, Chichester, West Sussex, and working as a draper's assistant.

Percy's uncle Charles Breadmore ran a successful corn merchant business at 120, High Street, Winchester. Charles had been born in Stockbridge in 1869 and by 1901 he was married with five children. One of them, Reginald, was the same age as Percy. Charles was also an award-winning sweet pea grower and he named several new varieties.

By 1914 Charles Breadmore, along with his wife Beatrice and their younger children, had moved to Sunnyside, 188, Stockbridge Road (the address, then and now). This is the address that Percy used when he enlisted in Reading with the 2nd Battalion, The Royal Berkshire Regiment in November that year. His service number was 37641.

Army records show that Percy later transferred to the 2/4th Royal Berkshires with the service number 3388. Although we do not know when he switched, the fact that Percy did not serve overseas until 1916 indicates that it was quite soon after he joined up.

The 2/4th Royal Berkshires were a Territorial battalion raised at Reading on 6 November 1914, around the time that Percy enlisted. The battalion came under the orders of 2nd South Midland Brigade, later part of the 61st Division. After training at Maidenhead,

188, Stockbridge Road, Winchester – the home of Percy Breadmore's uncle, Charles. Percy gave this address when he enlisted in 1914

BREADMORE, Percy George

Northampton and Chelmsford, the Division moved to Salisbury Plain in March 1916 before departing for the Western Front two months later.

The 61st Division first saw action on 19-20 July 1916 in a joint assault with the 5th Australian Division against German positions at Fromelles. Planned as a diversionary attack to draw German troops away from the Battle of the Somme, which was raging some 40 miles to the south, it proved a disaster. The British and Australians suffered 7,080 casualties in just one day. Such was the damage to the 61st Division and its reputation that it was not used again other than for holding trench lines until 1917.

According to the Winchester War Service Register (WWSR), Percy Breadmore was wounded in August 1916. However, the battalion was not in action that month, so it is possible that he had been wounded at Fromelles.

The 61st Division returned to action during operations on the River Ancre between 11 and 13 March 1917. During this period, the Germans withdrew from the positions they had defended so ferociously during the Somme Offensive to new, even more formidable, defences known as the Hindenburg Line. The 61st was one of the Divisions that cautiously pursued the retreating Germans, capturing the towns of Chaulnes and Bapaume in the process.

Percy Breadmore was killed in action on 28 April 1917 during the Arras Offensive. The WWSR states that he fell while fighting at Gouzeaucourt, near St Quentin, close to the Hindenburg Line. He was 23 years old.

Charles Breadmore, Percy's uncle, served with distinction during the war. Commissioned as a Lieutenant in the Royal Army Service Corps (RASC) in November 1915 at the age of 46, he served in France, Belgium and Italy and reached the rank of Staff Major. He was mentioned in dispatches three times.

Charles's three sons, Percy's cousins, also served. Cyril Breadmore was commissioned in October 1914 as a 2nd Lieutenant in the RASC (Mechanical Transport) and reached the rank of Captain. He served in France and Belgium and was twice mentioned in dispatches. Reginald Breadmore also won a commission with the RASC in October 1914. He served in Egypt and Salonica, possibly with the Indian Army, reaching the rank of Major. Douglas Breadmore appears to have moved to Australia before the war because he joined the Australian Imperial Force in Belmont, Western Australia, in November 1914. He fought in France and Belgium and was wounded three times. He was a Sergeant when the war ended.

After the war, it appears that Charles and Beatrice Breadmore divorced. The 1925 Warren's Winchester Directory shows Beatrice living at 2, Step Terrace, Winchester. She died in 1943. In 1939, Charles was the proprietor of a private hotel in Uckfield, Sussex, with his second wife, Lilian, the manageress. After a remarkably varied and full life, Charles died in Crowborough, Sussex, in June 1960, aged 91.

Reginald Breadmore continued his military career after the war and was appointed the Indian Army's Chief Inspector of Mechanical Transport in the 1920s. Awarded the OBE, he was promoted to Lieutenant-Colonel in the Indian Army Ordnance Corps (AOC). Reginald died at sea, aged 57, while on active service on 29 March 1941. He is buried at New Sandwick Cemetery, Sandwick, Shetland.

Medals and memorials for Percy George Breadmore

Private Percy George Breadmore was entitled to the British War Medal and the Victory Medal. He is buried at Villers-Guislain Communal Cemetery, Pas De Calais, France (GR. B. 10), and is mentioned on the memorials at St Matthew's and St Paul's churches, Winchester.

Researchers - JENNY WATSON and DEREK WHITFIELD

BUCK, James Henry

Private JAMES HENRY BUCK
17, Andover Road, Winchester
Service number 3854. 2/4th Battalion, The Hampshire Regiment
Died of disease, Quetta, India, 13 July 1916

James Henry Buck was born in 1892 in Gibraltar, the fourth child of Tom and Harriet Buck. James, known to family and friends as Harry, came from a military background, but his life was marred by personal difficulties and tragedy. His father died when he was 10 years old and by the time he was 18 he had been admitted to the workhouse in Winchester. James may therefore have viewed the outbreak of war in 1914 as an opportunity to improve his lot and see the world. Instead, he suffered an unpleasant death from disease contracted while fighting with the Hampshire Regiment in Mesopotamia.

James's father, Tom Buck, was the youngest of three brothers and was born in 1863 or 1864 in the village of Rolleston-on-Dove, Staffordshire. Tom's father, Henry, worked as a gardener. His mother, Emma (née Cryer) had been born in 1835 but she died when Tom was in his early teens. By 1881, when the family was living in the hamlet of Castle Bromwich, near Birmingham, Henry had taken a second wife, Bridget, by whom he had a son and two daughters.

Tom Buck worked briefly as a gardener before enlisting with the King's Royal Rifle Corps (KRRC) on 2 January 1883.

James Buck's mother, Harriett (née Dicks), was born on 24 October 1866 at the Curragh Army Camp in County Kildare, Ireland. Her father, Isaac Dicks (1833-), was a Nottingham-born brickmaker who had married 17-year-old Emma Skidmore in 1852. Given Harriet's birthplace, it is likely that Isaac later joined the Army, although no records can be found to confirm this. After Isaac's death, Emma married James Edward and in 1891 the couple were living at 10, Upper Brook Street, Winchester. Emma, then aged 55, was working as lace maker and 41-year-old James as a labourer.

Little is known of Harriett Dicks's early life. In 1884 she and Tom Buck married at Stoke Damerel, Plymouth, Devon. Tom, by then serving with the KRRC, had almost certainly been posted to the area as Devonport, besides being an important Royal Navy base was also one of England's foremost garrison towns.

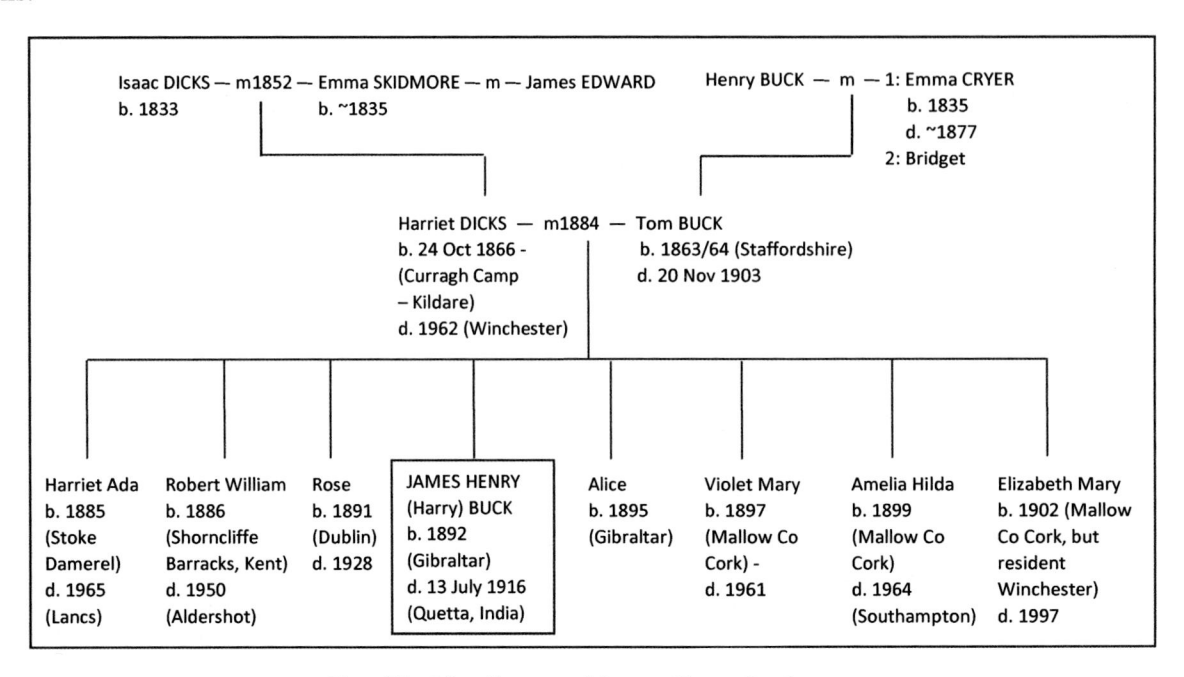

Simplified family tree of James Henry Buck

BUCK, James Henry

In 1885 Harriett gave birth to a daughter, Harriett Ada (known as Ada) in Stoke Damerel. A son, Robert William, was born the following year at Shorncliffe Barracks, Kent, followed by another daughter, Rose, in Dublin in 1891. Tom Buck was clearly moving around the country a great deal with the KRRC, but by the time of James's birth in 1892 the family had moved abroad and were living in Gibraltar. Another daughter, Alice, was born in Gibraltar in 1895, but by the time Violet Mary and Amelia Hilda arrived, in 1897 and 1899 respectively, the Bucks were living in Mallow, County Cork, where the British Army had an infantry barracks.

By 1901 the Bucks had moved to Winchester, home to the King's Royal Rifles Corp depot, and were living at 45, Wharf Hill (no longer standing), probably James' first Winchester home. Tom's name does not appear on that year's census record, but his wife indicated on it that he was serving with the Army in South Africa. Harriett gave birth to her last child, Elizabeth Mary, in 1902. Oddly, despite the family living in Winchester, Harriet had the baby in Mallow. Perhaps she had relatives or friends there and, with Tom overseas, wanted to be close to familiar faces?

The year 1903 was a traumatic one for the Buck family. Five-year-old Violet died in Mallow just a few months after her sister Elizabeth's birth. Then, on 20 November, Colour Sergeant Tom Buck, who had returned from fighting in the Second Boer War, passed away in Winchester at the age of 39. The cause of his death is not known.

The Army Registers of Soldiers' Effects, 1901-1929 shows that on 2 February 1904 the Army paid £12 15s to Harriett and £3 12s 11d to both daughter Ada and son Robert. A week later Harriett received a further £18 4s 2d for her five remaining dependent children.

Harriet remarried in 1908. Her new husband, handyman Arthur Allassandro Mundy, had been born in Winchester in 1883 and was therefore some 16 years younger than Harriett. The 1911 Census records Arthur, Harriett and Elizabeth living with Arthur's mother at 5, Princes Buildings, Middle Brook Street, Winchester. This was one of the most deprived areas of the city with much dilapidated and unsanitary housing. Two of the Buck daughters, Ada and Alice, are recorded on the Census as being in service in London while Rose was working as a servant in Winchester.

For two of the Buck children, however, life was clearly difficult. Amelia, then aged 10, was an inmate of the Royal Victoria Mental Asylum in Wandsworth, London. As for 18-year-old James, he had been admitted to the Winchester Workhouse in Upper Stockbridge Road, adjacent to Oram's Arbour. On the official workhouse return he is recorded as being born in 1883, not 1892, which would have made him 28. It is not known whether this was an error on the return or whether James, who is listed as a general labourer, needed to increase his age. Quite why he had been admitted to the workhouse is unclear as there is no record of any disability. Perhaps he had fallen out with his stepfather who, after all, was only a few years older, or maybe there was simply no room for him in the family home.

While James had fallen on hard times, his brother Robert was making a career in the Army. He had enlisted in the King's Royal Rifle Corps as a musician and then, in 1910, married 22-year-old Winchester girl Kate Temple. The following year the couple were living at 3, Alma Road, in Cheriton, Kent. This was the home of the Shorncliffe Barracks where Robert had been born some 25 years earlier.

James Buck's brother Robert, who served in the King's Royal Rifle Corps, and wife Kate

BUCK, James Henry

Soldiers of the 2/4th Hampshires, James Buck's original battalion, take a break from training in the mountains near Quetta, India, in 1915 *(Photo: Royal Hampshire Regiment Museum)*

In 1914 Harriett and Arthur Mundy were living at 17, Andover Road, Winchester (the address then and now) – James Buck's address in the Winchester War Service Register (WWSR). Among their neighbours in the years leading up to the Great War were young men who would serve with the Hampshire Regiment in the conflict. Albert Francis (see page 103) and his parents lived at 15, Andover Road, while Francis Forder (see page 95) and his mother were at No. 11 until around 1911-12. James Buck and Francis Forder served in the same battalion, though not at the same time. All three men died in the war and are listed on the parish memorials.

According to the WWSR, James Buck enlisted for military service with the Hampshire Regiment in 1915, although no month is given. There is some confusion about which battalion he joined: according to the Regimental Medal Roll it was the 2/4th Hampshires, but the website Soldiers Died in the Great War (SDGW) lists him as serving with the 1/4th Battalion. What happened is that James was initially assigned to the 2/4th Battalion before later being posted to the 1/4th Hampshires as a draft (or reinforcement).

James is not thought to have been with the 2/4th Hampshires when they deployed to India in January 1915. He probably joined up with the unit in India later that year after enlisting in England and then spent the remainder of 1915 training and preparing for active service.

James entered a theatre of war in 1916. Although no records can be found to directly confirm this, his entitlement to the British War Medal and the Victory Medal - which were awarded only to men who had served in a theatre of war - indicate that he must have done. Moreover, the fact that he was not entitled to the 1914-15 Star shows that James did not enter a war theatre in either of those years. We also know that he must have fought in Mesopotamia as this was the only combat zone in which the 4th Hampshires were operating in 1916. Although neither mention James by name, the Hampshire Regiment's official history and the 2/4th Battalion's war diary lend weight to this theory. Both contain reports from early 1916 of large numbers of 2/4th drafts being sent to Mesopotamia to reinforce the 1/4th Battalion which had suffered heavy casualties fighting the Turks while trying to relieve the besieged British garrison at Kut-al-Amara.

However, it is not known precisely when James arrived in Mesopotamia. Possibly it was in time to join the 1/4th Hampshires as they attempted, unsuccessfully, to break through to their comrades trapped inside

Kut in January 1916. A more likely scenario is that James arrived for the later attempts to relieve Kut in March and April. These proved equally fruitless and the garrison finally surrendered to the Turks on 29 April.

What happened to James Buck once he arrived in Mesopotamia is also a mystery. Presumably, he was either wounded in battle or fell sick. Either way he would have been transported back to India on a hospital ship. One of the few established facts is that James died at Quetta (in modern Pakistan) of enteric fever - or typhoid - on 13 July 1916. He was 24 years old.

After the war James's mother and his stepfather Arthur Mundy continued to live in Winchester. They went on to celebrate 40 years of marriage before Arthur's death in 1948. Harriett lived on to the age of 96 before her death in Winchester in 1962.

Robert Buck, James's brother, probably served during the Great War, but no records have been found to confirm this. His wife, Kate, had given birth to a son, Leslie, in Farnham, Surrey, in 1913. By 1939 they were living in Aldershot, Hampshire, where Robert died in December 1950, aged 64. Kate also died in Aldershot, on 18 October 1974. She was 85.

17, Andover Road, Winchester - James Buck's mother and stepfather lived here in 1914. It is James's address in the Winchester War Service Register

James's sister Harriet married Herbert Everett, a sailor, in Camberwell, south London, in October 1915. She died in Lancashire in 1965, aged 80. Sister Elizabeth married Sidney Vardy in Southampton in 1923. She, too, lived a long life before dying in 1997 at the age of 95. The three other sisters never married. Rose died in 1928, aged 37, and Violet in 1961 at the age of 64. Despite her afflictions in early life, Amelia lived to be 93 before her death in Southampton in 1964.

Medals and memorials for James Henry Buck

Private James Henry Buck was entitled to the British War Medal and the Victory Medal. He was buried at Karachi Cemetery, but according to the Commonwealth War Graves Commission has no known grave. This suggests that he may have been buried in haste due to the virulent nature of enteric fever. James is commemorated on the Delhi Memorial (India Gate), India (PR. Face 23) – pictured right -and on the memorials at St Matthew's and St Paul's churches, Winchester.

Researcher – DEREK WHITFIELD

BURGESS, Frank Ernest

Sergeant FRANK ERNEST BURGESS
26, Clifton Road, Winchester
Service number 6505. 1st Battalion, The King's Royal Rifle Corps
Died of wounds, Flanders, 28 October 1914

Frank Ernest Burgess was born in Winchester on 5 March 1888. His place of birth, according to his Army enlistment papers, was in St Paul's parish (more correctly St Matthew's with St Paul's parish), which was part of the growing Winchester suburbs of Fulflood and Weeke. He was probably born at 2, Greenhill Terrace, off Greenhill Road, as his parents were living there from at least 1886.

Frank's father, William, was born in Beauworth, near Cheriton, Hampshire, in about 1857 and worked variously as a drayman and a bricklayer's labourer. Frank's mother was born Emmeline (also known as Emily) Kennison in Northington, near Winchester, in 1862. The couple must have met or at least consolidated their friendship in Kingston-upon-Thames, Surrey, as they were both living there in 1881. They married in 1882 in Alresford.

By the time Frank was born in 1888, William and Emmeline already had a daughter, Alice Maud, who had been born on 7 July 1883. They also had a two-year-old son, William, who died when Emmeline was pregnant with Frank. However, Emmeline went on to give birth to three more children: Eva Florence in 1890, Reginald on 22 May 1895 and Edward on 14 December 1902. All were born in Winchester. The 1891 Census records the Burgess family living at 26, Clifton Road, Winchester (the address then and now). In 1901 Frank and his family were still at 26, Clifton Road.

Frank attended Western Infants School, then in Elm Road, before moving on to St Thomas National Church of England Boys' School in September 1895. He would have remained there until he was 13 or 14 years old.

In May 1905 Frank, aged 18, enlisted for 12 years – nine in active service and three in the Reserve - with The King's Royal Rifle Corps (KRRC). On his enlistment papers he put his prior occupation as 'porter' and was recorded as being 5ft 8in tall, weighing 9st 6lbs, and of 'good physical development'. Frank was posted to the 1st Battalion, The King's Royal Rifle Corps on 7 September of that year.

The 1st KRRC had served in South Africa during the Boer War. When that ended, they moved to Malta in 1902 and stayed there until 1905 when the battalion was divided into three. Two contingents went to Crete and Cyprus to help the Turkish authorities put down risings. (Until the early 20th Century, it was a key principle of British foreign policy to prop up the Turkish Empire against Russian advances towards the Mediterranean, which, together with the Suez Canal, formed part of the vital British sea route to India.) The third KRRC contingent, which included the Battalion HQ staff, was sent to Cairo. (Egypt was in theory independent but still technically part of the Turkish Empire and was under strong British influence to protect the Suez Canal.) Frank, attached to the third contingent, left the UK for Cairo on 26 September 1905.

**26, Clifton Road, Winchester –
Frank Burgess' childhood home.**

BURGESS, Frank Ernest

In March 1906, the two detachments on Crete and Cyprus re-joined the rest of the 1st KRRC in Egypt. They were on the move from October 1906 onwards, south to Khartoum in the Sudan, where they remained until towards the end of 1907. (That 'troublesome' area was then under British and, nominally, Egyptian control.) In 1907 Frank was appointed lance-corporal on 16th January, and was later hospitalised in Khartoum for a time. The 1st KRRC remained in Egypt until January 1909 when they embarked for England, to be stationed at Gosport. Meanwhile his mother Emmeline had died in 1907, aged 45. Frank was promoted to Lance-Sergeant on 18 January 1910, but ended the year by being severely reprimanded for being still in his bed at the Gosport Barracks at 6:45 am.

Frank Burgess's name on the St Thomas School admissions register of 1895

By 1911 William Burgess, Frank's father, had become a night-watchman. He had his two younger children at home with him – Reginald, aged 15, was working as a golf caddie, while nine-year-old Edward was at school. William's sister, Martha Burgess, aged 51, was also living with the family and possibly acting as the housekeeper, since Frank's younger sister Eva had married in 1910. Eva had probably stepped up to run the household , aged 17, after her mother died in 1907.

Apart from training periods at Wool, Dorset, and Parkhouse Camp in Salisbury, Frank was stationed in Gosport from 1909 until September 1911, when the 1st KRRC moved to Aldershot. They remained there until the outbreak of war in August 1914. From Gosport or Aldershot Frank could easily have visited his family in Winchester.

While at Gosport, Frank met Ethel Hooker and the couple married on 6 April 1912 in St Thomas's Church, Portsmouth, now the city Cathedral. Ethel had been born to a military family in Dover, Kent, in 1889. She and her five siblings were put into care after their mother's death in 1891, but they seem not to have been scattered as they were all living in Chelmsford, Essex, as adults. By 1911 – around the time she met Frank - Ethel was in Portsmouth and working as a housemaid at 3, The Parade, HM Dockyard. On 5 November 1912 Ethel gave birth to a son, Frank Richard, always known as Guy, in Farnham, near Aldershot.

In May 1913 Frank extended his military service to 12 years. That August he gained promotion to Sergeant and the following year he further extended his Army service to 21 years. He was described in a 1913 report as 'a thoroughly capable, hard-working NCO. Has been through a course of mounted infantry. Thoroughly trustworthy and sober'. Ten days after that report, he was absent from 8pm to 10.55pm and subsequently reprimanded.

When war broke out in August 1914, the 1st KRRC were at Aldershot, under the orders of 6th Brigade, part of 2nd Division. The 2nd Division was ordered to France as part of I Corps, led by General Sir Douglas Haig. The 1st KRRC left Salamanca Barracks, Aldershot, at 3.30am on 12 August, entrained at Farnborough and arrived at Southampton at 9am. They sailed at noon in a converted cattle ship and disembarked at Rouen the following day.

Before going into action, the 1st KRRC encamped near Hannappes with the rest of the 6th Brigade. On 21 August 'in the hottest of weather', the battalion advanced towards the Germans with the rest of the Brigade and two days later took part in the Battle of Mons, the first British military action of the war.

At Mons, the British Expeditionary Force (BEF) joined the French army in attempting to halt the German advance on Paris. However, the stand soon turned into a retreat when the French unexpectedly

BURGESS, Frank Ernest

began to withdraw, leaving the British no choice but to pull back as well to avoid being outflanked. The retreat was a disciplined one with 1st KRRC in the rearguard. The withdrawal lasted from 24 August until 5 September, but the objective was achieved: the Germans were stopped within 20 miles of Paris.

The KRRC Chronicle of 1914 contains a detailed account of the 1st Battalion's engagement with the Germans at the Battle of the Marne. The battle, which would save Paris, opened on 6 September with a British and French counter-attack which forced the Germans to retreat. The 1st KRRC, part of an advance guard, pursued the Germans northwards, crossing the River Marne on 9 September. The following day the battalion arrived at the southern end of the village of Hautesvesnes, where they caught up and then attacked a 1,200-strong German rearguard battalion. After some tough fighting, the Germans surrendered. They explained later that the 1st KRRC's skirmishing and marksmanship were so good that they could neither move nor return fire. In those early weeks of the war, before the advent of trench warfare, the riflemen's traditional skills of 'fire and movement' stood them in good stead. The encounter cost the 1st KRRC 14 men killed and 60 wounded with some men missing.

From the Marne, the German army retreated northwards pursued by the Allies until they reached the heights on the east side of the River Aisne. It was here that Frank next saw action between 13 and 27 September at the Battle of the Aisne. Late in the evening on 13 September, the BEF crossed the river under cover of a thick mist. Fierce fighting ensued over the following days with heavy losses on both sides. The Germans could not push the British back over the Aisne and the British could not push the Germans off the heights. The stalemate led to both sides digging in – trench warfare had begun. The 1st KRRC suffered 149 casualties in the battle, including 27 men killed and eight missing. Three more men were killed and 11 wounded on 28 September when a shell exploded in a trench north of Verneill.

The BEF's final major encounter of 1914 was the First Battle of Ypres, which opened on 19 October. Frank Burgess was wounded in action near Zonnebeke on 26 October and admitted to the 6th Field Ambulance the following day. He died of the bullet wounds to his left leg and foot on 28 October, aged 26. (The previous day, Prince Maurice of Battenburg, Queen Victoria's youngest grandson and a Lieutenant in Frank's battalion, was killed in action while fighting at Zonnebeke. A memorial tablet to Prince Maurice - and his brother Leopold who died in 1923 - stands in the south presbytery aisle of Winchester Cathedral.)

Shortly after Frank's death his widow Ethel and son Frank Jnr (Guy) moved to Chelmsford. Her address on the Imperial War Graves Commission form organising the inscriptions to be put on graves is given as Chale, 34, Henry Road, Chelmsford, which was her father's home. Another of Ethel's sisters was also living in the house, with a third at No. 35. Besides her husband, Ethel lost two brothers in the war.

The Winchester War Service Register gives rather confusing details about Frank's military service. It states, for example, that he was 'believed killed in action at Mons' when we know from Commonwealth War Graves Commission records that he died of wounds nearly two months later. The details were almost certainly supplied by Frank's father in Winchester and, depending on how much contact he had with Ethel Burgess, Frank's widow and legal next-of-kin, he may have been uncertain as to where and when his son died. The Register gives Frank's address as 10, Ashley Terrace, Winchester, and although there are no Burgesses listed in Warren's Directories as living at that address before, during or after the war it is possible that his father William was lodging there. However, in the absence of any clear indication of when William may have moved to 10, Ashley Terrace, this study has chosen to give Frank's address as 26, Clifton Road, a house he knew well.

Frank's father, William, left 26, Clifton Road shortly after the 1911 Census. However, with so many Burgesses living in Winchester and more than one with the initial W it has not yet been possible to pin down where he moved to. Nor is it known when he died.

BURGESS, Frank Ernest

There is also a mystery as to whether Frank's younger brother, Reginald, served in the Great War or not. He was born in 1895 and therefore of military age during the war and single. No certain military record for him has yet been found. According to the WWSR 1921, the only Reginald Burgess who served in the war, (and who lived at the then 54 Sussex Street, Winchester), enlisted in 1910 in the KRRC. Frank's Reginald would have only been 15 then and besides he was listed at being at home at 26, Clifton Road in the 1911 Census and working as a golf caddie. Reginald married in 1923. In the 1939 National Register he was listed working as a domestic gardener and living in Farleigh Wallop, near Basingstoke, with his wife Ellen and son Gerald who had been born in 1925. Reginald died in Basingstoke in September 1973, aged 78.

Frank's older sister, Alice Maud, had married Lewis Jones, a house carpenter, in 1905 in Winchester, By 1911 they were living at 6, Boscobel Road where they remained until 1922. Lewis Jones is in the WWSR 1922, having been a sapper in the Royal Engineers. His service dated from 10 May 1915 and he was invalided out from Chatham, Kent, on 22 June 1918. He was given a Silver War Badge to denote his honourable discharge. By 1923, Alice Maud and Lewis were living on the new council housing estate at 101, Stanmore Lane. For the first two years, Alice Maud's brother, Edward Silas was living with them. They were there until at least 1927. In the 1939 Register, they were at 3, Fairfield Road and by the 1950s, they were at 5, Cranworth Road. They appeared to have never had children. Lewis died in 1963 at St Paul's Hospital, changed from its original purpose as the Union Workhouse. Alice Maud was to die in the same place in June 1967. She left her estate of £1,609 to her brother Reginald Burgess.

In 1910 Frank's younger sister Eva married George Alborough in Winchester. George was a career soldier who had been born in Carlow, Ireland, in 1884. His home address was given in his military records as 3, Greyfriars Terrace, Winchester. He rose to be a Sergeant in the 3rd KRRC and in 1911 he and Eva were living at the overseas military unit at Dagshai, India. George was killed in action at Ypres on 3 February 1915. In 1917 Eva joined the Women's Army Auxiliary Corps (formed that year to make better use of women labour within the armed forces and free up men for the frontline) and she was stationed at Colchester, Essex, where there was a large military hospital. It may be that having lost two close family members she wanted to 'do her bit' for the war effort. It is unlikely that she and George had had children. In 1919 Eva re-married in Winchester, this time to George J. Hunter. She died in Greenwich, south-east London, on 30 November 1964, aged 74.

Little is known about Frank's youngest brother, Edward Silas, born in 1903. He was living at 101 Stanmore Lane with his sister, Alice Maud, and her husband, Lewis in 1923 and 1924. He and his wife Mabel were listed in the 1939 Register, when they were living at 30, St. Catherine's Road, Winchester, and he was working as a builder's lorry driver. Edward died in the city in 1959, aged 56.

Grave of Frank Burgess at Ypres Town Cemetery *(Photo: Andrew J. Begent)*

BURGESS, Frank Ernest

Medals and memorials for Frank Ernest Burgess

Sergeant Frank Ernest Burgess was entitled to the 1914 (Mons) Star, the British War Medal and the Victory Medal. He is buried at Ypres Town Cemetery, Ypres, West Flanders, Belgium (GR. C. 1.) and his headstone is inscribed with the words:
GONE BUT NOT FORGOTTEN.
He is mentioned on the memorials at St Matthew's and St Paul's churches, Winchester, and also on Chelmsford's parish memorial in the Cathedral and on a bronze plaque in the Chelmsford Civic Centre.

Researchers – GERALDINE BUCHANAN and JOSEPHINE COLEMAN

Additional sources

ANDREW J. BEGENT
see http://www.chelmsfordwarmemorial.co.uk/first-world-war/chelmsford/burgess-frank-ernest.html

War Memorial in Chelmsford Cathedral
IWM © Christopher R Weekes (WMR-45576)

CHAPMAN, Frank James

Private FRANK JAMES CHAPMAN
4, Andover Road, Winchester
Service numbers 4/3238 and 201058. 1/4th Battalion, The Hampshire Regiment
Died of disease in captivity, Mesopotamia, 15 October 1916

Frank James Chapman was born in 1894 in the village of Rustington, near Littlehampton, Sussex. He did not come to Winchester until 1906 when his father took over the running of a public house in St Cross. Frank worked as a legal clerk and volunteered for the 4th Battalion, The Hampshire Regiment shortly after the outbreak of war in 1914. He died in Turkish captivity after being taken prisoner following the siege of Kut-al-Amara in 1916.

James Chapman, Frank's father, was born in Hurstpierpoint, West Sussex, on 26 February 1866. James, one of nine siblings, was the son of Robert Chapman (1833-1902) and his wife Jane (née Brooker) who had married in Petworth, Sussex, in 1860. Robert hailed from Cuckfield, West Sussex, and spent his life working as a gardener and a domestic servant. Jane was born in Farnham, Surrey, in 1835.

Frank's mother was born Catherine Ruce in Ipswich, Suffolk, in 1866. Catherine, known to family and friends as Kate, was the daughter of John and Mary Ruce. John (1830-1911) had been born in Brightwell, Suffolk, and worked as an ostler - a groom or stableman who took care of horses at an inn. Mary, who was born in Stowmarket, Suffolk, had one other daughter, Ellen.

In 1881, 15-year-old James Chapman was working as assistant gardener and living at the family home in Cuckfield. Kate Ruce, meanwhile, had moved away from Suffolk and had found employment as a nursemaid at the home of draper David Manning and his wife Bertha in Clerkenwell, London.

James and Kate married in 1890 and the following year were living at Mews Brook Cottage, Rustington, along with their five-month-old daughter, Elsie. James was working as a domestic gardener. Little had changed in the family's circumstances by the 1901 Census, other than the birth of Frank in 1894. They lived in the same house and James was still employed as a gardener.

In 1906 the Chapmans moved to Winchester where James took over the running of the White Horse public house at 3, Front Street, St Cross. (The property remained a pub until 1998 when it was converted into a private residence. The address today is 55, St Cross Road.) Quite why James opted for such a radical 'career change' is not known, but he may have been influenced by Kate's father who worked in pubs and inns. Frank, meanwhile, had left school and was working as a law clerk.

By 1914 James and Kate had moved again, this time to 4, Andover Road, Winchester. Presumably, James was no longer running the White Horse, but no record can be found of his occupation at the time. Little else is known about Frank Chapman other than a few brief physical details contained in later Regimental documents. These show that he was 6ft tall, wore size 9 shoes and a size 7 cap.

Frank's first service number, 4/3238, indicates that he enlisted with the 4th Battalion, The Hampshire Regiment in September 1914, just weeks after the Great War began. At the time, the battalion was in the process of being split into two because of the surge of recruits and Frank, after volunteering for service overseas, was assigned to the 1/4th Hampshires. Having said farewell to his family, he sailed with the battalion for India in October, arriving the following month.

The 1/4th Hampshires remained in India until March 1915 when they were ordered to Mesopotamia. Frank arrived at Basra by troopship on 18 March. Almost immediately the battalion began operations in the region against the Ottoman Turks, firstly to defend British oil supplies and later along the Euphrates river, culminating in the capture of the towns of Nasiriyah and Amara.

CHAPMAN, Frank James

*Above left: 4, Andover Road, Winchester – home to Frank Chapman and his family in 1914.
Right: Until 1998 this building at 55, St Cross Road, Winchester, was the White Horse pub where James Chapman, Frank's father, was landlord for several years from 1906. It is now a residential property but the post-box (inset) is a reminder of its previous use*

Frank was part of the garrison at Kut-al-Amara besieged by the Turks from early December 1915. When the garrison surrendered on 29 April 1916, he and some 13,000 British and Indian soldiers were taken prisoner. (For details of the Siege of Kut see pp.378.) Those fit enough were marched off to prisoner-of-war camps, but they had to endure soaring temperatures and brutal treatment on the way and many men fell sick. According to Regimental Sergeant Major William Leach, a fellow 1/4th Hampshire prisoner, Frank was among these casualties and had to be treated in hospital in Tikrit, north of Baghdad. However, he apparently recovered sufficiently to reach the Turkish PoW camp at Airan in Turkey.

According to the Comforts Fund set up by Mrs Esme Bowker for the Hampshire Regiment soldiers captured at Kut, Frank was 'adopted' by Mrs Webb of Westfield, Hatch End, north London. She sent him parcels of food and clothing, but he was probably dead before they arrived. According to Mrs Bowker, Frank died at Airan, aged 22. All the sources except the Hampshire Regimental Journal give his date of death as 18 October 1916. The Winchester War Service Register states that he was suffering from enteric (typhoid) fever.

After the war Frank's parents continued to live at 4, Andover Road until 1927. In 1939 James Chapman, by then 73 and an invalid, was living at Glendale, Kings Worthy, near Winchester, with his daughter Elsie caring for him. James died in Winchester in 1941. No record can be found of Kate Chapman's death.

Medals and memorials for Frank James Chapman

Private Frank James Chapman was entitled to the 1914-15 Star, the British War Medal and the Victory Medal. He has no known grave and is commemorated on the Basra Memorial, Iraq (PR. 21 and 63) as well as the memorials at St Matthew's and St Paul's churches, Winchester.

Researcher – DEREK WHITFIELD

CHURCHER, Henry Thomas

Company Sergeant Major HENRY THOMAS CHURCHER M.M.
3, Avenue Road, Winchester.
Service numbers 3303 and 201109. 2/4th Battalion, The Hampshire Regiment.
Died of wounds, France, 19 September 1918

Henry Thomas Churcher was born on 11 March 1891 in Bemerton, Wiltshire, the eldest son of Lot and Elizabeth Churcher. In the early 1890s the family moved to Winchester where Henry, known as Harry to family and friends, went to school. He became a gardener before enlisting with the Hampshire Regiment when Britain went to war in 1914. He quickly won promotion and reached the rank of Company Sergeant Major in just a year. He won the Military Medal shortly before being killed in action in France, just two months before the war ended.

Henry's father Lot was born in 1865. His birthplace is listed both as Romsey (1871 Census) and Fareham (1911 Census) although the England and Wales Birth Register gives it as Fareham. In 1871 Lot was living with his parents, Henry, a gardener, and Charlotte, at 4, Church Lane, Bemerton, then a village on the western fringes of Salisbury but today a suburb of the city. He was still living in Church Lane in 1881, but as a lodger with Robert and Harriet Vining. From the census records it appears that Lot, like his father, spent his working life as a gardener.

Henry's mother was born Elizabeth Joiner in Bere Regis, Dorset, in 1862. Her father, Thomas Joiner, an agricultural labourer, died before she married. Her mother, also a native of Bere Regis, was born Jane Phillips in 1837.

Lot and Elizabeth married at Bere Regis on 26 May 1890. The following April they were living with one-month-old Henry in Bemerton. The address on the census entry is difficult to read but it appears to be 12, Sidney Cottages. Henry was christened at Bemerton on 26 April 1891.

The Churchers went on to have six children, five of whom were surviving in 1911. The other surviving children, all boys, were Harold, Ernest, William and Alfred (1903-1971). Harold was born in Bemerton in July 1892, but by the time that the next brother, Ernest, arrived in June 1894 the family had moved to Winchester. Two other boys, William and Alfred, were also born in Winchester, in 1900 and 1903 respectively.

Henry attended Western Infants School in Elm Road before moving on to St Thomas Senior Church of England Boys' School in February 1898. At the time the family were living at 6, Queen's Terrace in the parish of St Faith Within and they were still there in 1901. By 1911, however, the Churchers had moved to 3, Avenue Terrace, Avenue Road, Fulflood. Henry Churcher, by then 20, was working as a domestic gardener and his brothers Harold and Ernest as bakers. William and Alfred were at school.

CHURCHER, Henry Thomas

Henry enlisted with the 4th Battalion, The Hampshire Regiment on 16 September 1914. His brother Harold also joined up with the 4th Hampshires, probably on the same day judging by the proximity of their service numbers – Henry was 3303 and Harold 3311. Both brothers were assigned to the newly-formed 2/4th Battalion on 1 October 1914.

Two months later the 2/4th embarked for India, arriving on 11 January 1915. Home for the next two years was the British Army base at Quetta (in modern Pakistan) where the battalion trained in mountain warfare. Henry Churcher clearly displayed leadership qualities from an early stage because by October 1915 he had been appointed Company Sergeant Major of A Company. This made him the senior non-commissioned officer (NCO) in his unit. It was an important role with responsibilities that included administration and discipline. In combat, Henry's main responsibility was the supply of ammunition to his company. Harold Churcher, meanwhile, had been promoted to Corporal.

On 29 April 1917, the 2/4th Hampshires left India for Egypt, reaching Suez on 15 May. Henry Churcher's first experience of combat came in Palestine in November when the battalion was involved in follow-up operations after the Third Battle of Gaza. Henry then fought with the battalion as it formed the part of the spearhead of the advance through the Judean Hills towards Jerusalem, a period of fighting in which his brother Harold was wounded.

3, Avenue Road, Winchester – Henry Churcher's home in 1914

In May 1918, the 2/4th Hampshires transferred to the Western Front. Harold Churcher is thought to have recovered from his wounds by then and he and Henry were with the battalion in late July then they took part in a French counter-offensive against the Germans in the Ardre valley, north of the River Marne. In fierce fighting the battalion lost a total of 174 men killed and as many again wounded, but the Churcher brothers came through unscathed. In his history of the 2/4th Hampshires 1914-1919, the Commanding Officer, Lieutenant-Colonel F. Brook, wrote of the Ardre battle:

> *In these nine days the Battalion had borne itself in a manner which could not have been excelled by the oldest of veterans. It had learned that in war there need not be dismay when the task seems impossible, and it had shown to the rest of the Division that, as a Battalion and individually, in comparative method it was a force to be reckoned with. It was the Battalion's first fight on the Western Front; a battle which, taken as a whole, was destined to be the turning point of the war and bring the end in sight. A considerable number of honours fell to the Battalion ... and there is not enough room to mention those who were worthy of mention. One might refer to Sergt. Major Churcher, who was a tower of strength to his Company ...*

After just a fortnight's rest Henry and Harold were back in action again around Behagnies and Beugnatre, north of the River Somme. By this stage, the Germans were retreating on much of the Western Front, but they continued to resist and their machine-gunners inflicted heavy losses on the advancing British. The 2/4th Hampshires suffered another 150 casualties.

On 8 September, less than a fortnight before he died, Henry Churcher was presented with the Military Medal for his outstanding service on the Ardre. The award was given to soldiers below commissioned rank who had displayed 'acts of gallantry and devotion to duty under fire'.

CHURCHER, Henry Thomas

Officers and NCOs of the 2/4th Hampshires in India in October 1915. CSM Henry Churcher is on the second row from the front, third from left *(Photo: Royal Hampshire Regiment Museum)*

Henry's final battle was the 2/4th Hampshires' capture and defence of the village of Havrincourt between 12 and 14 September 1918. The initial attack cost the battalion 200 casualties and although it spent the following two days in reserve heavy German shelling killed or wounded nearly a further 100 men.

In his book The Royal Hampshire Regiment 1914-1918, C.T. Atkinson writes:

> *These two days [13 and 14 September] bought the total casualties up to nearly 300, including 2/Lt Bryant and 75 men killed and missing, among them CSM Churcher of A Company, an admirable Warrant Officer.*

It is unclear precisely when Henry was wounded but he died at the 14th General Hospital on 19 September, aged 27. The Hampshire Regimental Journal of October 1918 states:

> *CHURCHER - On September 19th, at the 14th General Hospital, France, Company Sergt. Major H.T. Churcher, died of wounds, the dearly-loved eldest son of Mr and Mrs L. Churcher, 3, Avenue Terrace, Fulflood, Winchester. 'God's Will be done'.*

> *Company Sergt. Major H.T. Churcher, Hampshire Regiment, who died in a General Hospital in France on September 19th of wounds, received a day or two previously, was the eldest son of Mr and Mrs Lot Churcher, of 3, Avenue-Road, Fulflood, Winchester. C.S.M. Churcher, whose age was 27 last March, had been in the Army just four years, having joined a battalion of the Hampshires on September 16th 1914, and had been on service in India before going to France. He has two brothers serving in the Army.*

Harold Churcher survived the Great War and ended up with the rank of Acting Lance-Sergeant. Ernest Churcher also served in France as a Lance-Corporal in the Army Service Corps. He was wounded on 5 October 1918 but survived.

The Churcher family remained in Winchester after the war and maintained close ties with Fulflood. Henry's parents both lived into old age. His mother, Elizabeth, died in Winchester in May 1944, aged 80, while his father Lot passed away on Christmas Eve 1954 at the age of 89.

CHURCHER, Henry Thomas

Harold Churcher married Gertrude Goater in Winchester in 1922. Their son John had three children all of whom were born in the city. Two of these subsequently married in Winchester. Harold died in Winchester in August 1983, aged 91.

Ernest Churcher married Muriel Taylor in Winchester in July 1920. Muriel died in 1942 after which Ernest married Annie Fayne the following year. He was living at 54, Western Road when he died on 22 August 1959, aged 65.

William Churcher does not appear to have married. He lived in Fulflood for the remainder of his life and was at 19, Avenue Road when he died, aged 75, in 1975.

Alfred Churcher married Dorothy Barratt in September 1929 and they had two sons. In 1939 the family was living at 85, Greenhill Road, with Alfred working as a plumber and fitter. He died in Winchester in June 1971, aged 67.

Medals and memorials for Henry Thomas Churcher

Company Sergeant Major Henry Thomas Churcher M.M. was entitled to the Victory Medal and the British War Medal. He is buried in Terlincthun British Cemetery (above), Wimille, Pas de Calais, France (GR. IV. B. 4.) and is mentioned on the memorials at St Matthew's and St Paul's churches in Winchester.

Researcher – DEREK WHITFIELD

CLARK, Reginald James

Rifleman REGINALD JAMES CLARK
40, Fairfield Rd, Winchester
Service Number S/33649, 12th (Service) Battalion, The Rifle Brigade
and 0195193 Army Ordnance Corps
Killed in action, France, 30 November 1917

Reginald James Clark was born in Salisbury, Wiltshire, on 12 July 1884, the youngest child of Henry and Elizabeth Clark. Reginald's father had been born in Wilton, near Salisbury, and worked as a carpenter. His mother was from Laverstock, near Salisbury. William Clark, Reginald's eldest brother was born in 1875 in Wilton, followed by Thomas, Amy, Ethel, Beatrice and Reginald, all born in Salisbury.

By 1890, the family must have been living in Milford, then on the edge of Salisbury, as on 1 December of that year, six-year-old Reginald entered St Martin's Church of England School. According to the 1891 Census, the family were living in Wellington Cottage, Southampton Road, Milford, although the school record gives Waterloo Gardens as the address. His three eldest siblings were already out at work - even 13-year-old Amy was recorded working as a dressmaker. Reginald progressed through Standard I-V and left in his Standard VI year, in October 1897, aged 13.

By the 1901 Census, the Clarks had moved to Portswood, Southampton, and were living at Primrose Cottage, Ash Tree Road. Only Amy, still a dressmaker, and Reginald, by then aged 16 and a builder's clerk, were living at home with their parents.

However, by the time of the 1911 Census, Reginald also had flown the nest and was living at a boarding house at 17, Eastgate Street, Winchester (the property has the same number today). Besides the landlady, the household consisted of four young men and one single woman, a teacher at the Girls' High School. Reginald was working as an ironmonger's clerk and it was presumably here that he met his future wife, Millicent Cuell, known as Milly to her family and friends, who worked as a cashier for an ironmonger.

In the 1911 Census, Milly, then aged 22, was living with her parents, Henry and Rose Cuell at Rosebank, Worthy Lane (now Church Lane), in Easton, near Winchester. Intriguingly, her father had been an inmate in Winchester Prison in the 1901 Census, but it has not yet been possible to find out what crime he had committed. Milly's elder sister, Ethel, had died aged 18 in 1905, just 13 days after marrying. Reginald's eldest brother, Frederick (known as Jack), had left home in 1910 to join the Royal Navy. His four other siblings were still at home in 1911: Henry Jnr and Ernest were self-employed market gardeners while 11-year-old Albion (known as Alb) was at school. Gwen, aged two, was the baby of the family.

CLARK, Reginald James

The Clark brothers (from left to right) – Thomas, William and Reginald. The photograph is believed to have been taken shortly before the Great War *(Photo: Cuell family)*

17, Eastgate Street, Winchester, where Reginald Clark was lodging in 1911

Reginald Clark's future wife Milly Cuell (far right, second row down in dark jacket), pictured at Easton School in 1898. Her brothers Frederick (known as Jack) and Ernest are in the centre and on the far right of the front row respectively *(Photo: Cuell family)*

40, Fairfield Road, Winchester, where Reginald moved with his wife Milly after they married in 1911. Following Reginald's death, Milly remained in the house until 1921 when she moved back to Easton

CLARK, Reginald James

Reginald Clark and Milly Cuell married towards the end of 1911, presumably at St Mary's Church in Easton. By 1913 they were living at 40 (then and now), Fairfield Road, Winchester, within the parish of St Matthew's and St Paul's. Presumably, Reginald was still working in the ironmongery business.

Reginald was 26 when the Great War broke out in August 1914. For reasons that we will probably never know, he chose not to enlist as a volunteer even though others in his extended family did so. It may have led to a degree of social ostracism as there was pressure on all able-bodied men to answer the call to arms. Reginald was finally called up under conscription in June 1916, just a month after the Military Service Act of January that year was extended to include married as well as single men.

Milly Clark was some four months pregnant when Reginald went off to war. On 28 November 1916 she gave birth to a son, Cyril Clive, in Marylebone, London. It is not known whether she had gone to London to see Reginald while he was on leave or whether they had set up a temporary home there. However, the Warren's Winchester Directories show that their house at 40, Fairfield Road was held in the name of R.J. Clark from 1913 until about 1921. According to Milly's descendants in the Cuell family, Reginald definitely met baby Cyril before he was killed in late 1917.

Reginald served initially as a Private in the Army Ordnance Corps (the Royal prefix was added in 1918) which dealt with the supply and maintenance of weapons, munitions and other military equipment. He received the service number 0195193. At some stage, however, he transferred to the 12th Battalion, The Rifle Brigade with the new service number S/33649.

The 12th (Service) Battalion, The Rifle Brigade had been raised in Winchester in September 1914 as part of Lord Kitchener's Second New Army and was assigned to 60th Brigade in 20th (Light) Division. Sent to the Western Front in July 1915, it saw action at the Battle of Loos and then the following year at the Battle of Mount Sorrel and in several operations during the Battle of the Somme.

Given that Reginald served initially with the AOC after being conscripted, he would not have figured in the Somme fighting which ended in November 1916. Although the date of his transfer to the 12th Rifle

Milly Clark (front row, far left) with her father Henry and mother Rose (both front row) at the wedding of her brother Henry Jnr and Ada Quick in 1912

CLARK, Reginald James

Brigade has not been established, it is possible that he was with the battalion at the Third Battle of Ypres (Passchendaele) during the late summer and autumn of 1917. The 12th Rifle Brigade took part in some of the costliest fighting of the campaign at the Battle of Langemarck as well as the more successful Battles of the Menin Road and Polygon Wood.

The battalion – with Reginald Clark definitely among its ranks - next saw action at the Battle of Cambrai (20 November - 7 December 1917). The offensive towards Cambrai, a strategically important enemy supply point, some 30 miles east of Arras, was followed by the biggest German counter-attack against the British since 1914.

Today the Battle of Cambrai is remembered chiefly for seeing the first mass use of tanks in warfare although other developments which had been maturing since 1915, such as predicted artillery fire,

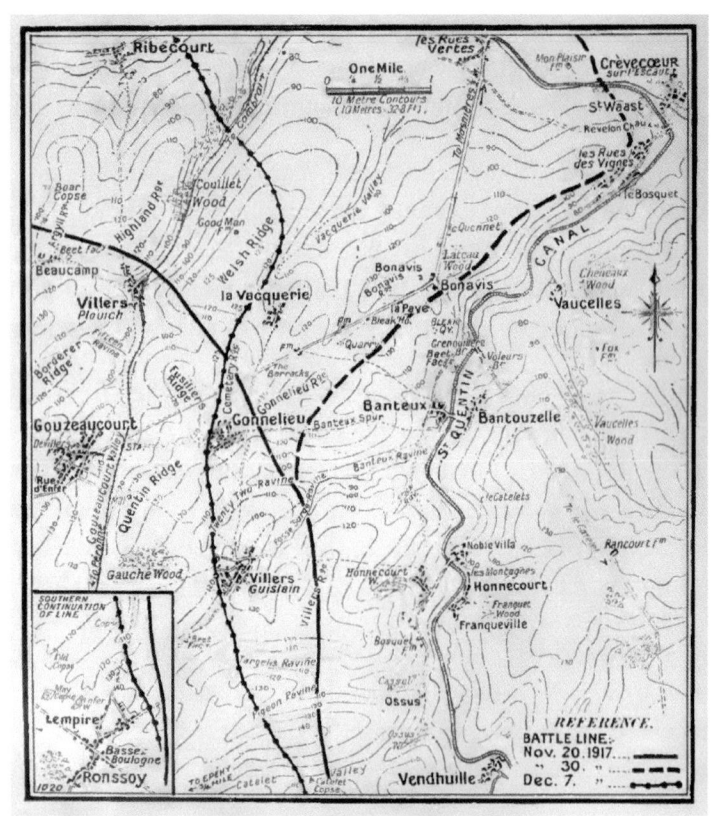

The Cambrai battlefield showing the furthest extent of the British advance and the German counter-attack. Reginald Clark was involved in fighting at La Vacquerie on 20 November 1917 and was killed near Gonnelieu ten days later

sound ranging, infantry infiltration tactics and close air support, were actually more important to British success in the early stages of the fighting.

The battle began at dawn on 20 November, with a bombardment by 1,000 guns on German defences, followed by smoke and a creeping barrage to cover the first advances. The attacking force comprised six infantry divisions of the III Corps on the right and IV Corps on the left, supported by 437 tanks. Initially, there was considerable success: even the Hindenburg Line, previously believed to be virtually impregnable, was breached by tanks as the British advanced up to five miles. The 12th Rifle Brigade formed part of 20th Division's attack, forcing a way through the village of La Vacquerie before digging in after achieving all its objectives. One company alone took more than 130 prisoners and captured a trench mortar and six machine-guns. The battalion's losses for the day totalled one officer killed and 40 men killed or wounded – remarkably low by Great War standards.

The British made similar early gains elsewhere along the line, but a combination of German resistance and the unreliability and vulnerability of the tanks – 180 were out of action at the end of the first day – meant the advance gradually stalled. Between 21 and 27 November the 12th Rifle Brigade consolidated its defensive positions before going into reserve the following day in a captured stretch of the Hindenburg Line.

On 30 November, the Germans launched a massive and unexpected counter-attack, firing a short but intense artillery barrage and using infantry tactics that would be employed to devastating effect again in their 1918 Spring Offensive. The previous night the 12th Rifle Brigade had camped in Fifteen Ravine, near the village of Gonnelieu. They were woken by the German artillery barrage and as the men attempted to move into a nearby trench, they were strafed by machine-gun fire from more than 30 enemy aircraft flying low overhead.

CLARK, Reginald James

All that morning panic reigned in the British lines as commanders tried to come to terms with the scale of the German assault. The 12th Rifle Brigade was first ordered to occupy the high ground between La Vacquerie and Quentin Mill and then, a short while later, to advance towards Gonnelieu. Here the battalion spent the remainder of the day attempting to repulse furious enemy attacks and it was possibly during this fighting that Reginald Clark was killed. Although his body was never found, and he was officially listed as 'Missing', it is likely that he was killed in action.

The Cambrai fighting continued for another week at which point the British withdrew, giving up most of the gains they had made in the battle. The British suffered some 40,000 casualties, of which the 12th Rifle Brigade lost 13 other ranks killed and four officers and 84 other ranks wounded. The number of men missing, presumed killed, totalled 32, including Reginald Clark.

Reginald's mother, Elizabeth Clark, died in March 1918, only a few months after her son's death. His father Henry died in 1929. Of Reginald's siblings, his two brothers, William, a currier, and Thomas, a bootmaker, seemed to have stayed in Salisbury when their parents and younger siblings moved to Southampton. Both married and had families. Thomas died in Southampton in 1957. Amy and Ethel both married and had families and remained living in Southampton. Amy died there in 1967 and Ethel in 1972. Beatrice, the sibling nearest in age to Reginald, married and had family and by 1911 she was living back in Salisbury. She died in Surrey 1972.

Three of Milly Clark's brothers also served during the war and all survived. 'Jack', who had joined the Royal Navy in 1910, fought at the Battle of Jutland in 1916 aboard HMS King George V. Ernest, meanwhile, appears to have volunteered in 1914 and served in the 9th Lancers and the Royal Field Artillery. Albion, who was not called up until May 1918, was assigned to the Royal Navy but never went to sea. Milly's older brother, Henry Jnr, was a market gardener, which became a reserved occupation. He supplied produce to the army camps on Morn Hill, Winchester.

As for Milly herself, she returned to Easton in about 1921 with her son Cyril and went to live with her mother Rose at Rosebank. (Her father had died in 1916.) Cyril attended school at Easton, as his mother had done, along with his cousin Eddy, son of Henry George Jnr and his wife Ada. The two boys were the same age and lived next door to each other, Cyril in Rosebank and Eddy in Jasmine Cottage, both properties being owned by Rose Cuell. According to the family, Cyril and Eddy were like brothers and their friendship carried on into adulthood.

In 1925 Rose Cuell remarried and moved to West End, Southampton. That probably left Milly and Cyril with her younger brother Ernest at Rosebank. Ernest never married and, again from information supplied by the family, he acted as a father figure to Cyril. Ernest ran a garage in Easton which provided a coach, lorry and taxi service. The 'family' of three were still at Rosebank in 1939 according to the Register of that year which also stated that Cyril was working as a civilian engine fitter at HMS Kestrel at Worthy Down, near Winchester.

Milly Clark never remarried. She remained at Rosebank until she became seriously ill and went to a nursing home in Crawley, near Winchester, where she died in 1962, aged 72. She was buried in St Mary's churchyard in Easton, but has no gravestone so she, like her husband, has no known grave. Ernest, her younger brother and surrogate father to Cyril, died in 1989, aged about 95. He would have been the last of Reginald's generation to have known him. Cyril seems to have worked all his life as an air mechanic. He did marry but had no children and died in 2000 in Southampton, aged 83.

CLARK, Reginald James

Above: Elizabeth and Henry Clark's grave in Salisbury and, below, the inscription bearing their son Reginald's name on the edging (Photos: Geoff Cuell)

Medals and Memorials for Reginald James Clark

Rifleman Reginald James Clark was 33 years old when he died. He was entitled to the British War Medal and the Victory Medal. He has no known grave, but is listed on the Cambrai Memorial at Louverval, Nord Calais, (PR. Panel 10 and 11). Reginald is remembered in the Memorial Book at St Matthew's Church, Weeke, and on the Memorial Boards at St Paul's Church, Fulflood. His name also appears on the edging of the grave of his parents, Elizabeth and Henry Clark, (Plot K573) in London Road Cemetery, Salisbury, Wiltshire. The inscription reads:

[TO THE MEMORY ....]

AND OF THEIR SON REGINALD JAMES MISSING IN FRANCE NOV 30 1917

Researchers – GERALDINE BUCHANAN and DEREK WHITFIELD

Additional sources

- Seymour, William: *The Rifle Brigade 1914-1918, Vol II 1917-1918* (The Rifle Brigade Club Ltd, London, 1936).
- Interview with Geoff Cuell, great nephew of Millicent Clark (née Cuell).

COLES, Frank

Company Sergeant Major FRANK COLES
2, Andover Road, Winchester
Service numbers 4/42 and 200011. 1/4th Battalion, The Hampshire Regiment
Died in Turkish captivity, Mesopotamia, between 16 and 18 September 1916

Frank Coles, the son of Charles William and Elizabeth Coles, was born in Alresford in the first quarter of 1885. Frank was a pre-war Territorial soldier with the 4th Battalion, The Hampshire Regiment and he worked as a printer's compositor before joining his father's tailoring business shortly before 1914. A respected figure in Winchester, Frank died a prisoner of the Turks after the fall of Kut-al-Amara in 1916.

Frank's father Charles was born in Chelsea, west London, in around 1861. No record can be found of Charles's parents. Frank's mother was born Elizabeth Camis in Hinton Ampner, near Winchester, in September 1860. Her father, Thomas, was born in Avington, near Winchester, around 1814 and worked as an agricultural labourer. Elizabeth's mother, Mary, was born in nearby Kilmeston in around 1821.

Charles and Elizabeth married in Alresford in July 1882. On 7 June 1883 Elizabeth gave birth to a daughter, Daisy, in Alresford. Frank was born two years later and christened on 26 July 1885. The couple had two other children, but neither survived into adulthood. In 1891 the Coles family were living in a cottage in Cheriton with Charles working as a tailor. Frank and Daisy were both at school, presumably in the village, but no record can be found to confirm this. By 1901 the family had moved to Winchester and were living at 2, Andover Road. By this stage Charles was a self-employed tailor working from home. Frank, aged 16, was working as a printer's compositor's apprentice and Daisy as a parlour maid.

In 1906 Daisy married George Mariner in Twyford, Hampshire, and she gave birth to a son, William, in 1909. By 1911 Frank was still living with his parents at 2, Andover Road and had qualified as a compositor. However, it appears that shortly afterwards he joined his father in the family tailoring business.

There are several inconsistencies in Frank's military record. According to the Winchester War Service Register (WWSR) he did not join the Army until August 1914. However, his original service number 4/42 indicates that he was a pre-war Territorial soldier with the 4th Hampshires. Indeed, Frank comes so close to the start of the battalion numbering sequence that he must have been among the first to enlist with the unit when the Territorial Force was created in 1908.

Another clue that Frank had been a part-time soldier for some time before the war broke out is that he played in the Soldiers' Home Band. Had he enlisted in August 1914 there would have been little chance to display any musical prowess since military training was the urgent priority for new recruits.

The other major discrepancy concerns Frank's rank when he died. Most sources give it as Company Sergeant Major but some, notably the Commonwealth War Graves Commission, state that he had only reached Lance-Sergeant. This was an appointment given to a Corporal so that they could fill a post usually held by a Sergeant. The Hampshire Regimental Journal of July 1916 lists Frank as a Lance-Sergeant in its roll call of men taken prisoner at Kut, but then in a February 1917 obituary states that he was a Company Sergeant Major. This biography has opted for the more senior rank.

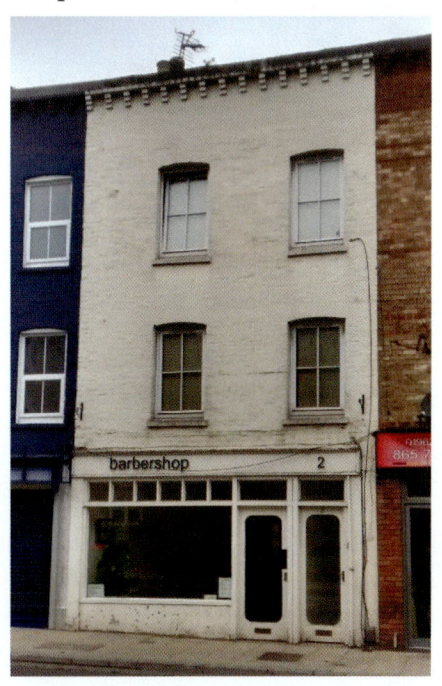

2, Andover Road, Winchester – Frank Coles's home from around 1900

COLES, Frank

Right: Major Foster Footner's letter in the Hampshire Regimental Journal of April 1918 confirming the death of Frank Coles. Note the inclusion on the list of Andrew Bogie, Frank Richards, Cecil Shefferd and Francis Forder whose names also appear on the memorials at St Matthew's and St Paul's and whose biographies can be found in this book

> Afian Kara Hissar,
> January 13th, 1918.
>
> Dear ———, Thank you very much for your letter of August 25th. I am afraid that I cannot give you much help as to the fate of the men, as we are allowed no communication with the men.
>
> I know of thirty-six men who were alive and well lately, of thirty-three whose death is practically certain, and of eleven exchanged, making a total of eighty. Of the rest of the men I know nothing except rumours. The thirty-three dead are the following:—Batts, Sergt. Bogie, Sergt. Coles, Sergt. Raynbird, Corpl. Harman, Loveland, Coombes, Elkins, Goodchild, Hall, King, Miles, Warner, Richards, Shefferd, Vokes, Lansley, Bartraham, Churcher, Forder, Gardiner, Howell, Kille, Lce.-Corpl. Lucas, Marriner, Morgate, Stevens, Whitehead, Sergt. Odell, Bell, Wakeford, Woods, and Bartlett. I saw Elton and Lacey a few weeks ago. They were going from Kastamouni to Geddes, having given a promise not to escape, with about seventy others. They were fit and well. Smith, Roberts and Harrison were orderlies with the party, and were well. Forbes is at Stamboul; Harris and Patmore, being "Die Hards," remained at Changiri. Jones is at Belamadih.
>
> All well. I hope you and yours are quite well also. Please remember me to Mrs. Barton.
>
> Yours sincerely,
> F. L. FOOTNER.

In October 1914 Frank sailed to India with the 1/4th Hampshires and from there to Mesopotamia, arriving in a theatre of war on 18 March 1915. He served with A Company and was almost certainly already an NCO – Corporal or even Sergeant – so would have had been responsible for leading men during the battalion's early encounters with the Ottoman Turks in the spring and summer of 1915 (see pp. 377 for details).

In December 1915 Frank found himself among the 13,000-strong force trapped in the British-Indian Army garrison at Kut-al-Amara. This included nearly 197 officers and men of the 1/4th Hampshires. When the garrison fell to the Turks on 29 April 1916 after a five-month siege, Frank, together with the other 187 surviving Hampshire soldiers, was marched off to the notorious prisoner of war camp at Afrum Karra Hissa (modern day Afyonkarahisar) in Turkey. Frank's name appeared in a list of men from the 1/4th Hampshires taken at Kut published by the Hampshire Chronicle on 10 June 1916.

The letters and records of Sergeant William Leach, a fellow 1/4th Battalion prisoner, reveal that Frank was sick when the convoy of prisoners reached the city of Mosul, north of Baghdad. Frank then had the misfortune to end up at a PoW camp that was presided over by a bullwhip-wielding commandant and widely regarded as the worst for Allied prisoners at the time.

Frank Coles died from dysentery at the camp in September 1916. He was 31 years old. The precise date of his death is unclear, with the CWGC giving 18 September and regimental and newspaper sources 16 September. An entry in the 1917 Hampshire Regimental Journal states:

> *COLES - Died from dysentery on September 16th, 1916, as a prisoner of war at Afrum Karra Hissa, Co Sergt. Major Frank Coles, Hampshire Regiment, only son of Mr C. W. Coles 2, Andover Road, Winchester.*

On 3 February 1917, under the headline 'Death of Sergeant Major Frank Coles', the Hampshire Observer newspaper reported:

> *Many in Winchester will read with great regret the news of the death ... on September 16 last, at Hissa, where he was a prisoner of war, of Sergeant Major Frank Coles, of the Hampshire Regiment. The deceased who succumbed to dysentery at the age of 31, was the only son of Mr C.W. Coles of Andover Road, Winchester. He assisted his father in his tailor's business, was a member of the Soldiers' Home Band and was much esteemed by all who knew him.*

In April 1918 the Hampshire Regimental Journal published a letter from Major Foster Footner, the senior 1/4th Hampshire officer in Kut and a fellow prisoner at the Afrum Karra Hissa camp, in which he confirmed Frank's death along with several more men whose names appear on the memorials at St Matthew's and St Paul's. In February 1918, the Army paid Charles Coles £35 2s 9d in respect of his late son's effects and back pay. He also received a £10 war gratuity in October 1919.

COLES, Frank

Frank's parents continued to live in Winchester after the war. Elizabeth died there in December 1925, aged 65, and was buried at Magdalen Down Cemetery. Charles died at St Catherine's Lodge, Garnier Road, Winchester, in January 1940. He was 79 years old and was laid to rest with his wife at Magdalen Down (Ground 6, Section 3rd. Grave L3 77). Frank's sister Daisy died in Bishopstoke on 10 September 1957, aged 74.

Medals and memorials for Frank Coles

Company Sergeant Major Frank Coles was entitled to the 1914-15 Star, the British War Medal and the Victory Medal. After the war, his body was disinterred and reburied at Baghdad (North Gate) War Cemetery, Iraq (GR. XXI. K. 16.). He is mentioned on the memorials at St Matthew's and St Paul's churches, Winchester.

Researcher – DEREK WHITFIELD

COLES, Sidney James

Private SIDNEY JAMES COLES
68, Western Road, Winchester (No. 44 today)
Service numbers 4/3237 and 201057. 1/4th Battalion, The Hampshire Regiment
Killed in action, Mesopotamia, 21 January 1916

Sidney James Coles was born in Portaferry, County Down, Northern Ireland, in late 1894, the son of Thomas Henry and Rose Coles. His name is spelt Sydney in the Winchester War Service Register and on the memorials at St Matthew's and St Paul's, but his birth was registered as Sidney and that is how it appears on most official records. Part of a well-respected family with close connections to St Paul's Church in Fulflood, Sidney enlisted with the Hampshire Regiment shortly after the outbreak of war. He was killed in Mesopotamia (modern Iraq) in 1916 during an attempt to relieve the besieged British garrison at Kut-al-Amara.

Little is known of Sidney's father except that he was born around 1870. Given Sidney's birthplace, it is possible that Thomas Coles was a serving soldier - it would certainly help to explain his absence in the official census records. Sidney's mother was born Rose White in Winchester in 1871 and was one of 11 children. Her father, George (1842-1905), was born in Micheldever, near Winchester, and worked as a carpenter. Her mother Mary, born around 1841, was from Fareham. In 1871 the family were living at 15, Upper High Street, Winchester. Ten years later they had moved to Western Road in Fulflood.

The 1891 Census shows Rose White working as a domestic servant for a family in Portsmouth. She married Thomas Coles in Winchester later that year. Sidney's birth was registered in Downpatrick in the final quarter of 1894, but at some stage between then and 1901 his father died.

In the 1901 Census Rose and Sidney were living at her parents' home at 68, Western Road. It is thought that they continued to live there until 1914, by which time the householder, according to Warren's Winchester Directory, was Rose's brother, Alfred White. The house became No. 44 when the street was renumbered after the war, and this is the address that appears in the Winchester War Service Register of 1921. However, this biography uses No. 68, the address when Sidney went to war in 1914.

By 1911 Mary White, Sidney's grandmother, was also widowed. In that year's Census his mother Rose was recorded working as an assistant wardress at HM Prison – presumably Winchester – while 16-year-old Sidney had left St Thomas Church of England Boys' School and was working as a coach trimmer with Messrs Easther Ltd in Jewry Street. This was skilled work and involved making and fitting the leather upholstery to the interior of horse-drawn coaches.

The Census also reveals how the family was continuing to prosper despite the deaths of Sidney's father and grandfather. His mother's younger sister, Marian White, was working as an assistant schoolmistress while her younger brother, Alfred, had moved on from his job as a machinist in 1901 to become verger at St Paul's Church. The Coles-White family had other links with St Paul's – young Sidney was a chorister there and a member of the St Paul's Amateur Dramatic Society. Clearly a young man of some promise, Sidney moved to a new job in Reading, Berkshire, sometime before 1914 to further his career.

Right: 44, Western Road – this was No. 68 when Sidney Coles lived here from the early 1900s

COLES, Sidney James

Soldiers of the 1/4th Hampshires at their first camp near Basra after arriving in Mesopotamia in March 1915. Sidney Coles was with the battalion at this time, but was killed ten months later at the Battle of El Hanna *(Photo: Royal Hampshire Regiment Museum)*

Sidney enlisted with the 4th Battalion, The Hampshire Regiment in September 1914, a few weeks after the outbreak of war. From military records we know that he was 5ft 11½in tall, wore a size 9 shoe and a size 7 hat. He was given the service number 4/3237 and assigned to the 1/4th Battalion. Having volunteered for service overseas, Sidney sailed for India with his battalion in October 1914, arriving the following month. He had only been in India a matter of weeks when his mother remarried in Winchester. Her second husband was Robert Flitton and the couple set up home at 9, Gladstone Street, Winchester.

After four months of training in India Sidney was sent to Mesopotamia with his battalion. After arriving there on 18 March 1915, the Hampshires took part in operations against the Ottoman Turks around Basra, but at some stage Sidney contracted fever and was sent back to India to recuperate.

On returning to Mesopotamia, Sidney joined the relief force under General Fenton Aylmer as it attempted to break the Turkish siege of the British garrison at Kut-al-Amara where nearly 200 officers and men of the 1/4th Hampshires were among the 13,000 British and Indian troops trapped. (For details of the siege and of operations by the 1/4th Hampshires in 1915 see pp. 377.) On 21 January 1916, the remainder of the 1/4th Battalion joined an attack by 9th Brigade on Turkish positions at El Hanna on the north bank of the River Tigris which blocked the way to Kut. In his book, The Royal Hampshire Regiment 1914-1918, the historian C.T. Atkinson describes the early stages of the battle:

> *The Hampshires had been under fairly heavy long-range rifle fire even before 'Zero' and had had a few men hit ... but directly the advance had begun rifles, machine-guns and field guns had opened a heavy fire, and with the ground flat and affording no cover casualties quickly mounted up... Before reaching [the battalion's old front trench] Colonel Bowker [the battalion commander] had been hit, but pushed on nevertheless, to be hit again and killed.*

The attack failed and when it was called off that night the Hampshires had lost 13 officers and 230 men killed, missing and wounded out of 16 and 339 in action. Among the missing was 21-year-old Sidney Coles whose body was never found. Also killed were the 1/4th Battalion's Commanding Officer, Lieutenant-Colonel Francis Bowker, and 37-year-old Company Sergeant Major Eric Rule who lived in St Paul's Terrace, Winchester (now St Paul's Hill), a short distance from Sidney's home.

COLES, Sidney James

Sidney's mother waited nearly two years for news for her son before finally being informed that he was 'presumed dead'. The Hampshire Regimental Journal of December 1917 states:

After an elapse of almost two years of anxious suspense, official news has been received of Pte Sidney James Coles, Hampshire Regiment (3237). He was reported as missing after an engagement somewhere in Mesopotamia on January 21st 1916, and no further tidings being received relative to him, the Army Council conclude his death must have taken place on that date. He was the son of Mrs. R. Mitten [sic], 9, Gladstone Street, formerly Mrs Coles, 68, Western Road, Winchester, and was apprenticed as a trimmer with Messrs. Easther, Ltd., Jewry Street (now Mr. F. J. Matthews), and afterwards secured a good position at Reading.

He went out to India in 1914 with the Regiment, under the command of the late Colonel Bowker and went with the first force to the Persian Gulf where he contracted fever and was sent back to India. After recuperating on the hills of Sabathe, he went to Quetta, and from there back to the Gulf, and was serving with the Kut relief force, under General Aylmer, up to the date he was reported missing. He was well known in the parish of Weeke, and as a boy was a chorister of St Paul's Church choir. He was also a member of St Paul's Amateur Dramatic Society.

After the war, Sidney's mother Rose continued to live with her husband Robert Flitton at 9, Gladstone Street. The couple were still there in 1927. Rose Flitton is believed to have died in Gosport in 1963, aged 93.

Medals and memorials for Sidney James Coles

Private Sidney James Coles was entitled to the 1914-15 Star, the British War Medal and the Victory Medal. He is commemorated on the Basra Memorial, Iraq (PR. Panel 21 and 63) and on the memorials at St Matthew's and St Paul's churches, Winchester. He is also listed on the St Thomas Church of England Boys' School Memorial, now held by Kings' School, Winchester.

Researcher – DEREK WHITFIELD

DAWKINS, Frank

Private FRANK DAWKINS
8, Greenhill Terrace, Winchester
Service numbers 72137 and 3972. 9th (Service) Battalion, The Cheshire Regiment (Transferred from Devon Yeomanry)
Killed in action, Belgium, 29 April 1918

Frank Dawkins was born in Winchester on 6 February 1899, the son of George and Emma Dawkins. One of five children, Frank left school just a year before the Great War broke out. He enlisted in 1917 and was killed the following year during the German Spring Offensive.

Frank's father George was born in Winchester in 1861 and grew up in a tenement in Middle Brook Street. He followed his father into the plumbing trade and was listed as a plumber's assistant in the 1881 Census when he was living with his parents and siblings at 63, Middle Brook Street.

Frank's mother was born Emma Mullins in Winchester in 1865. She was daughter of gardener Charles Mullins who was born in Winchester in 1832, and his wife Heneritte, born in Winchester in 1841. In 1881 Emma was living at St Peter's Villa, St Peter's Street, Winchester, where she was working as a domestic servant to nurseryman William Blackmore and his wife Elizabeth.

George and Emma married in Winchester in 1890 and their five children were all born in the city - George (1891), Bessie (1893), Agnes May (1896), Frank (1899) and Florence (1902).

The 1901 Census found the family living at 8, Greenhill Terrace, Fulflood, with George Snr working as a painter's labourer. On 1 February 1906 Frank, then aged six, enrolled at St Thomas Elementary School, Winchester. The family were at the same address in 1911. Father George was a painter and George Jnr a gardener while daughters Bessie and Agnes May were working as housemaids. Frank left school on 21 March 1913, aged 13, and presumably went to work.

Frank joined the Army in Winchester on 9 March 1917, shortly after his 18th birthday. He may have volunteered but was probably conscripted. What remains of his enrolment form (it was severely damaged in the Blitz in 1940) shows that he joined the Devon Yeomanry with the service number 3972. He then appears to have transferred to an infantry battalion of the Devonshire Regiment as a Private (service number 69344) before moving a final time to the 9th Battalion, The Cheshire Regiment (service number 71237).

Interestingly, the Cheshire Regiment's Victory Medal and British War Medal Roll shows Frank's name amid dozens of other former Devonshires. This suggests that Frank's battalion was one of the many disbanded in early 1918 and amalgamated with other units.

Frank would almost certainly have been with the 9th Cheshires at the start of the German Spring Offensive on 21 March 1918. This massive assault on British positions in Picardy, northern France, was intended to drive a wedge between the British and French armies, capture the strategically important city of Amiens and bring Germany victory in the war.

8, Greenhill Terrace, Winchester – the house where Frank Dawkins grew up

71

DAWKINS, Frank

The 9th Cheshires, who came under the orders of 56th Brigade in 19th Division, entered the fray on 22 March, taking up a defensive line at Delsaux farm, south of Beugny (a village to the north west of the town of Bapaume). A German attack on 24 March forced them back but the battalion then counter-attacked and regained some lost ground. They were then ordered back to a new line west of Bapaume, but before they could complete the move a further withdrawal to Grevillers was ordered. The Germans attacked again on 25 March forcing the Cheshires to pull back again at which point they were withdrawn into reserve.

All the available records and sources state that Frank Dawkins was killed in action on 29 April 1918 and buried in a military cemetery at Kemmel in Flanders. This was the region attacked by the Germans in their second spring offensive, the Battle of the Lys (9 April-29 April 1918).

However, there is no record of the 9th Cheshires, nor the 19th Division, fighting in the Lys area in April 1918. Of the Cheshire battalions, only the 10th and 11th were in action there at the time.

So, what happened? One clue is the place that Frank is buried. On the day that he died (29 April), British and French troops were fighting off a German assault against the Scherpenburg, a high point close to Kemmel. It is possible that Frank had been rushed to the area as a reinforcement to help stem the attack on the Scherpenburg, was killed and then buried at Kemmel.

Another possibility is that he was killed a few days earlier and, in the chaos of the time, the date of his death wrongly reported. This second theory does have some credibility. On 16 April, following a severe mauling at the hands of the Germans, the 10th Cheshires had been formed into a composite unit with *other* troops. Then, on 26 April, they took part in an attack on Kemmel which had been in German hands since the previous month. The attack failed and the 10th Cheshires lost 27 men killed. Could Frank Dawkins have been one of them? We will probably never know for certain.

Frank was 19 years old when he died. His brother George served in the war as a Royal Navy stoker aboard HMS Constance and survived. Frank's parents continued to live at 8, Greenhill Terrace after the war. George Snr died in Winchester in 1925 and Emma in 1950.

Medals and memorials for Frank Dawkins

Private Frank Dawkins was entitled to the British War Medal and the Victory Medal. He is buried at Klein-Vierstraat British Cemetery (above), Kemmel, West Flanders, Belgium, (GR. V. D. 6.) and the inscription on his headstone reads:

**SLEEP ON DEAR SON AND TAKE YOUR REST
WE MISS YOU MOST WHO LOVED YOU BEST**

Frank's name appears on the memorials at St Matthew's and St Paul's churches, Winchester, and on the St. Thomas School Memorial now held at Kings School, Winchester.

Researchers – JENNY WATSON and DEREK WHITFIELD

DENNISTOUN, James Robert

Lieutenant JAMES ROBERT DENNISTOUN
The Lodge, Bereweeke Road, Winchester (no longer stands)
2nd North Irish Horse (attached to 23rd Squadron, Royal Flying Corps)
Died of wounds while a prisoner of war, Germany, 9 August 1916

The derring-do exploits of James Robert Dennistoun make him one of the most colourful of the men listed on the memorials at St Matthew's and St Paul's churches. His parents married in Winchester and then emigrated to run a sheep station in New Zealand where James was born in 1883. He loved the outdoor life and became a keen adventurer and mountaineer. Between 1911 and 1912 he took part in Captain Scott's ill-fated Terra Nova Expedition to Antarctica. On the outbreak of war in 1914, James returned to England and joined the Army before transferring to the Royal Flying Corps in 1916. He was shot down on his first mission and died of his wounds in a hospital in Germany a few weeks later.

James Dennistoun was born in Peel Forest, South Island, New Zealand on 7 March 1883, the son of George (1848-1921) and Emily (1852-1937) Dennistoun. George, who came from an old Scottish family, was born in Glasgow. His own father died when he was very young and by 1851 he was living at Admanton, a large country property owned by his aunt in Monkton, Ayrshire. (Today the house is a country hotel on the edge of Glasgow). George's mother, Barbara (1822-1910), was living off an annuity so the family was clearly wealthy. By 1861 George was a naval cadet aboard HMS Britannia.

James's mother was born Emily Russell, the daughter of Lieutenant-Colonel Andrew Hamilton Russell (1812-1900) and his wife Eliza (1815-1891). Colonel Russell had a glittering Army career and he and Eliza had three children together. Two were born in Ireland where, presumably, their father was posted.

In 1879 George Dennistoun married Emily Russell at St Bartholomew's Church, Hyde, Winchester. The Reverend Stephen Bridge, a member of the Russell family, officiated at the wedding. At the time, Emily's parents were living at Hyde Lodge, Worthy Lane, Winchester, where they remained until moving to Newton Abbot, Devon, sometime after 1881.

George and Emily Dennistoun moved to New Zealand shortly after marrying to take over a sheep station at Peel Forest, north of the town of Geraldine on South Island. It was here that James was born in 1883 and his brother, George Jnr, the following year. In 1896 James and George Jnr were admitted to Wanganui Collegiate, a boys' boarding school on North Island. Two years later, James travelled to England to become a pupil at Malvern College, Worcestershire. He remained at the school until 1901 when he returned to New Zealand to help run Peel Forest. His brother, meanwhile, had enlisted as a cadet with the Royal Navy in 1899 and he remained with the service for more than 20 years.

Once home, James took up mountaineering and in 1910 he became the first non-Maori to climb Mitre Peak, which rises 5,550ft above Milford Sound, today one of New Zealand's most famous tourist

DENNISTOUN, James Robert

destinations. His notebooks and diaries from this period were published in 1999 as The Peaks and Passes of JRD.

In 1911, James accompanied Captain Robert Scott on his Terra Nova Expedition to the South Pole and was put in charge of the mules. The same year he received the King's Antarctica Medal and the Royal Geographical Society Medal. In 1912 he was made a member of the Alpine Club.

James did not immediately volunteer for military service after the outbreak of war in August 1914. Instead, he waited some seven months before sailing to England to enlist. He arrived on 14 April 1915 and went to stay with relatives in Winchester. James initially considered the Argyll and Sutherland Highlanders, but eventually he travelled to County Antrim where, on 14 May, he obtained a commission as a 2nd Lieutenant with the North Irish Horse, part of the elite Household Cavalry regiment.

James Denniston aboard Terra Nova on Captain Scott's South Pole expedition of 1911-12

James was assigned to the 2nd North Irish Horse and sent for training at the cavalry school at Netheravon, Wiltshire, where he also visited the nearby flying school. James returned to his regiment and sailed for France with his squadron on 18 November 1915, the same day that he was promoted to Lieutenant.

After spending some months as an Intelligence Officer in the 33rd Division – of which the North Irish Horse were part – James was attached to 23rd Squadron the Royal Flying Corps on 8 June 1916. His cousin, Lieutenant Herbert ('Herbie') Russell, was already serving as a pilot with the squadron which operated two-seater FE2b biplanes from an airfield at Izel-le-Hameau, west of Arras. On 26 June, James took off on a bombing raid, his first - and last – RFC operation. Herbert was piloting the FE2b and James was in the observer's seat when they were shot down. Herbert wrote later:

> *When the machine was wheeled out, I noticed it had no bomb-racks or bomb sights fitted ... I pointed this out to the CO. He replied, 'Never mind, let Dennistoun take them up in his arms and throw them over when you think you are about right; you've had enough experience by now!'*

James and Herbert were heading for home when three German aircraft attacked their plane over the town of Biache St Vaast. James took three machine-gun bullets to the stomach and Herbert was shot in the lungs. Their aircraft caught fire, and both were burned as it crashed landed behind German lines. Although seriously wounded, James survived the landing and he and Herbert were taken prisoner. James was admitted to hospital in Hamblain the same day and operated on. He remained there until 28 July when he was moved to another hospital at Douai before being sent to a prisoner-of-war camp at Ohrdruf in Thuringia, Central Germany, on 3 August.

On the 29 June, nurse Lili Eidam, who was caring for James, wrote to his mother saying they expected him to pull through. However, she had not reckoned on the terrible 36-hour train journey to Ohrdruf. For the first 19 hours, James had to lie on a rough wooden stretcher, with no blankets or food. Crucially, his wounds were never dressed during the entire journey. James arrived at Ohrdruf on 6 August and three days later had another operation. He did regain consciousness but died the same day, aged 33.

DENNISTOUN, James Robert

An FE2b biplane of the Royal Flying Corps like that in which James Dennistoun and his cousin Lieutenant Herbert Russell (right) were shot down over German lines

Herbert Russell recovered from his wounds. He was transferred to Switzerland on 9 December 1917 and repatriated to England on 24 March 1918. During the Second World War he was made Acting Air Vice-Marshal and became Air Vice-Marshal on 8 May 1949. Herbert died on 9 May 1963, aged 68.

James's parents returned to England in 1918 and went to live at The Lodge in Bereweeke Road, Winchester. They would have ensured that James's name appeared on the memorial at St Paul's church and in the Winchester War Service Register. In 1920 the Dennistouns moved to Torquay, Devon where George died on 7 May 1921, aged 73.

James's brother George served in the Royal Navy during the war and took part in its first naval engagement on Lake Nyasa (Lake Malawi) in Central Africa in August 1914. He was awarded the Distinguished Service Order in 1916 and made a Commander in December 1918. He retired from the Navy in 1922 and returned to Peel Forest. During the Second World War, George served as commanding officer of a naval training establishment at Lyttleton, near Christchurch, and was awarded the OBE. He died in New Zealand in 1977, aged 93.

Medals and memorials for James Robert Dennistoun

Lieutenant James Robert Dennistoun was entitled to the 1914-15 Star, the British War Medal and the Victory Medal. He is buried in the Niederzwehren Cemetery (grave right), Kassel, Germany, Hesse (GR. IV. H. 2.) and the inscription on his headstone reads:
THOU WILT SHEW ME THE PATH OF LIFE IN THY PRESENCE IS FULNESS OF JOY.
His name (spelt Dennistown) appears on the memorials at St Matthew's and St Paul's churches. There is also a memorial window to James Robert Denniston [sic], Terra Nova Expedition, at St Stephen's Church, Peel Forest, South Canterbury, New Zealand.

Researcher – JENNY WATSON

Additional sources
- http://www.antarctic-circle.org/llag.church.htm
- http://navymuseum.co.nz/worldwar1/people/captain-george-hamilton-dennistoun-dso-obe/
- http://www.rafweb.org/Biographies/Russell_HB.htm

DOBSON, Francis William

Private FRANCIS WILLIAM DOBSON
County High School for Girls, Cheriton Road, Winchester
(now Westgate School)
Service number 11114. 1st Battalion, The Coldstream Guards
Killed in action, France, 22 December 1914

Francis William Dobson, the eldest child of Jesse and Ellen Dobson, was born in Winterbourne Bassett, near Marlborough, Wiltshire, on 24 September 1893. The family lived in Wiltshire and the New Forest area until shortly before the Great War when Francis's father became caretaker/groundsman at the County High School for Girls (now Westgate School) in Cheriton Road, Winchester. In August 1914, Francis enlisted with one of the British Army's elite regiments, but he was killed in action in December, less than a month after arriving on the Western Front.

Jesse Dobson, Francis's father, was born on 16 October 1867 in Winterbourne Bassett where his own father, Jeremiah, worked as a farm labourer. Jesse was listed as a plough boy on the 1881 Census. Francis's mother, Ellen, born in April 1874, was the daughter of farm labourer William Decox and his wife Bertha. She and Jesse Dobson married in Hilmarton, near Calne, Wiltshire, on 15 July 1893, just two months before Francis's birth.

In 1896, Francis, Ellen and Jesse were living in Woodborough, near Pewsey, Wiltshire. It was there that Ellen gave birth to three more children: Tom, on 23 March 1896; Violet, on 8 November 1899; and Stanley on 17 February 1902. The children all went to Woodborough School, with Francis enrolling there on 23 October 1898.

Francis left Woodborough School on 1 May 1906 at the age of 13 having reached Grade V. The school logbook reveals that he was wanted at home, presumably to start work. The other children also departed the school in 1909 when the family left the village.

In 1911 the Dobsons, minus Francis and Tom, were living in Lymington, Hampshire, where Jesse was working as a groom and gardener. It is thought that Francis was working as one of a team of ten servants at Berry Court, a house in St Peter's Road, Bournemouth.

Sometime before 1914, Francis's parents moved to Winchester where his father had found work as the groundsman/caretaker at the County High School for Girls in Cheriton Road, Fulflood. It is not known whether Jesse ever lived there, but it was the address he gave when he joined the 1st Battalion, The Coldstream Guards in August 1914, shortly after the Great War broke out.

In 1914, new Army recruits would spend at least three months undergoing basic training before being sent into combat. The fact that Francis was immediately sent to the Western Front strongly suggests that he had previous military experience. This may have been as a Special Reservist – a part-time soldier similar to a Territorial – although no military record has yet been found to confirm this.

The Coldstream Guards were one of the seven regiments in the Household Division, the personal troops of King George V. The 1st Coldstream Guards, a Regular Army battalion, landed in France on 14 August, just nine days after Britain declared war. The battalion came under the orders of the 1st (Guards) Brigade, 1st Division and fought at the Battle of Mons (23-24 August) and the subsequent retreat, the Battle of the Marne (6-12 September) and the Battle of the Aisne (13-28 September). It was then virtually annihilated during the First Battle of Ypres (19 October-22 November 1914), losing all its officers. By 1 November, the battalion had been reduced to just 150 men and the Quartermaster. Francis joined the battalion on 26 November, shortly after its mauling at Ypres.

DOBSON, Francis William

On 20 December the 1ˢᵗ (Guards) Brigade was ordered to the northern French village of Givenchy which, together with an important length of British front-line trenches, had been captured by the Germans. The Brigade, with the 1ˢᵗ Coldstream Guards and Cameron Highlanders leading, attacked the following afternoon in a heavy hailstorm and succeeded in retaking a line of old French trenches. A report of the 1ˢᵗ Coldstream Guards' part in the fighting that followed stated:

> *Lieutenant Colonel John Ponsonby established his HQ in the end house of Givenchy village with a Company in trenches nearby. A patrol under 2nd Lieutenant Mills went forward to the end of Givenchy village and reported it clear of the enemy so far as the church. Attempts were made overnight to straighten up the line and get in touch with the Gloucesters on the left and the Cameron Highlanders on the right, but proper touch could not be obtained.*
>
> *Lieutenant Colonel Ponsonby, assisted by Captain Daniels (15th Sikhs), made a reconnaissance and found a Company of the London Scottish on the left rear of No .2 Company of the Coldstream Guards which were almost immediately withdrawn. At 5.45am on the 22ⁿᵈ December the three Companies in the forward trenches attacked the German trench along the road leading from Givenchy to Chapelle St. Roche. [They] took it, but being without any support on their flanks, they were bombed out of it about 8am and retired to the north of the ruins of the church in Givenchy having lost over 50 per cent of their strength.*
>
> *With the Scots Guards and the London Scottish holding the remaining parts of Givenchy, so began the daily routine of siege warfare in this area of Givenchy. At 9pm on the 22nd December the battalion was relieved by the Black Watch and marched back to billets in a village south of the canal at Pont Fixe.*

Francis Dobson, aged 21, was almost certainly killed in this fighting, less than one month after he had arrived in France. He was listed as missing, believed killed, although his Medal Index Card states that he was killed in action. His mother Ellen was awarded a dependent's pension of 5s a week after the war.

It is thought that Francis's brother Tom fought with the West Yorkshire Regiment in the Great War. He survived and is believed to have gone on to become a police inspector in Portsmouth.

The County High School in Cheriton Road is thought to have been requisitioned by the Army during the war. In 1939, Francis's mother, father and sister Violet were living at 1, Cheriton Road with Violet working as a short-hand typist. His father Jesse died in March 1942, aged 74, and was buried at Morn Hill Cemetery, Winchester. His mother Ellen passed away in Winchester in 1952 at the age of 78 and Violet in 1982, aged 82.

Medals and memorials for Francis William Dobson

Private Francis William Dobson was entitled to the 1914 (Mons) Star, the British War Medal and the Victory Medal. He is commemorated on the memorial to the missing at Le Touret Military Cemetery (above), Pas de Calais, (front panel 2 and 3) and on the memorials at St Matthew's and St Paul's churches, Winchester.

Researchers – JENNY WATSON and DEREK WHITFIELD

DOUGLAS, Charles Edwin Gardiner

Private CHARLES EDWIN GARDINER DOUGLAS
22, Cheriton Road, Winchester.
Service number 2147. 1/4th Battalion, The Hampshire Regiment
Died of disease, Mesopotamia, 12 June 1915

Charles Edwin Gardiner Douglas, the elder son of Charles Henry and Elizabeth Douglas, was born in Winchester on 23 May 1895. Charles appears to have come from a comfortable background. His father was a cabinet maker and, although not wealthy, provided a stability which enabled his family to thrive. Charles won a place at Peter Symonds School before becoming a clerk with Hampshire Council. He died from disease in 1915 while serving with the Hampshire Regiment in Mesopotamia.

Charles's father was born in January 1866 in South Stoneham, near Eastleigh, the son of James Douglas (1824-1896) and his wife Ann (1829-1898). James, who worked for much of his life for the Ordnance Survey in Southampton, had been born in Ireland. Ann (née Clay) was born in Portsmouth.

Charles's mother was born Elizabeth Gregory in Toxteth Park, Liverpool, in November 1866. Her parents were photographer Charles Gregory and his wife Agnes. In the 1881 Census Elizabeth was listed as a visitor at 148, High Street, Southampton, the home of John and Lydia Sewell, a family of outfitters and tailors. Presumably, she and Charles's father met in Southampton and they married in the city in 1889.

By 1891 Charles and Elizabeth Douglas had moved to Winchester and were living at 36, Western Road, Fulflood, where they remained for more than 50 years. The house stood in what is now Cheriton Road, a few doors up from the Fulflood Arms. It was renumbered 22, Cheriton Road in 1914.

In 1892 Elizabeth Douglas gave birth to a daughter, Ada, who died sometime before 1911. After Charles Jnr's birth in 1895, his parents had to wait another nine years for their third child, Frank, who was born in Southampton in 1904.

Charles attended Western Infants School in Elm Road, Fulflood, before enrolling at St Thomas Church of England Senior Boys' School in February 1903. He was clearly an above average scholar because five years later he moved to Peter Symonds Boys' Grammar School which had opened in 1897.

The Peter Symonds Admissions Register shows that Charles entered the school on 21 September 1908, aged 13. He received a grant covering his fees from St John's Hospital, Winchester, so his family did not have to pay for his education. The grant was initially for two years, but later extended to cover the three years that Charles spent at the school. He left on 27 July 1911, aged 16, to become a clerk with Hampshire County Council.

As a Symonds pupil, Charles would have had experienced the eccentric ways of Telford Varley, the school's first headmaster. Ordained as a priest in 1908, Varley was held in awe by the boys. He was prone to fearsome outbursts of temper and for designing strange punishments for those who misbehaved. He memorably caught one boy climbing through a classroom window and invited him to climb in and out of it 50 times after school while he himself sat in the room marking.

22, Cheriton Road, Winchester - Charles Douglas's home from 1895

DOUGLAS, Charles Edwin Gardiner

Right: Soldiers of the 1/4th Hampshires at the battalion's annual camp on Salisbury Plain in the summer of 1914. Charles Douglas would almost certainly have been at the camp which coincided with Britain declaring war on Germany on 4 August
(Photo: Royal Hampshire Regiment Museum)

All Symonds boys were required to join the school's Officer Training Corps which provided basic military training and was a natural conduit into the Army. In 1913 Charles, then aged 18, enlisted as a Territorial soldier with the 4th Battalion, The Hampshire Regiment with the service number 2147.

In the summer of 1914 Charles would have travelled to Salisbury Plain with the 4th Hampshires for the battalion's annual camp. The men were still at camp on 4 August when Britain declared war on Germany and mobilisation began. Charles was assigned to the 1/4th Hampshires which was created after the huge influx of recruits led to the battalion splitting into two. He volunteered to serve overseas and sailed for India with his battalion in October 1914, arriving the following month. (For details of the 1/4th Hampshires' time in India see pp. 375)

In early March 1915, the battalion was sent to Mesopotamia, arriving at Basra in the middle of the month. Charles's Army records show him entering a theatre of war on 18 March 1915. Charles, who served with ''A Company, was in Mesopotamia for just three months before he died. He would have taken part in operations against the Ottoman Turks aimed at securing British oil supplies in the region. These engagements took place in April on the lower Euphrates river and in Arabistan the following month.

The battalion was in action again in late May and early June, manning a flotilla of steamers and bellums – large, flat-bottomed boats – which were used to capture the town of Amara. However, these were exhausting operations, involving long marches in intense heat and fighting in mosquito-infested marshes. In his book The Royal Hampshire Regiment 1914-1918, the historian C.T. Atkinson describes how the fighting and the climate took its toll on the battalion:

> *By this time the climate and particularly the moist heat was making itself felt, sick in hospital were up to 180 by June 16th, half a dozen men had died [Charles Douglas was almost certainly one of them], mainly from heatstroke, and on June 17th 84 men were invalided to India.*

Charles Douglas died of disease - or possibly heatstroke - in Basra on 12 June 1915, less than one month after his 20th birthday.

Charles's parents continued to live at 22, Cheriton Road after the war. Elizabeth Douglas died in the city in 1944, aged 77, and Charles Snr in 1952 at the age of 86. Charles Douglas Jnr's brother, Frank, married Violet Palfrey in Winchester in December 1934. The couple, who do not appear to have had any children, were living at 14, Cheriton Road, when Frank died on 1 February 1955, aged 53.

DOUGLAS, Charles Edwin Gardiner

An Army hospital boat on the River Tigris in Mesopotamia during the Great War – Charles Douglas may have been evacuated to Basra on a vessel like this after being taken sick *(Photo: Royal Hampshire Regiment Museum)*

Medals and memorials for Charles Edwin Douglas

Private Charles Edwin Gardiner Douglas was entitled to the 1914-15 Star, the British War Medal and the Victory Medal. He was buried in Basra War Cemetery, Iraq (GR. VI. B. 3.). Charles is mentioned on the church memorials at St Matthew's and St Paul's churches, Winchester, as well as those at Peter Symonds School and St Thomas School Church of England Boys' School. The latter is now held at Kings School, Winchester. His name also appears on the Hampshire County Council memorial in Winchester.

Researcher – DEREK WHITFIELD

DOUSE, Clifford Tom

**Private CLIFFORD TOM DOUSE (DOWSE on memorials),
5, Andover Road, Winchester.
Service numbers 2180 and 204744. 3/1st Hampshire Carabiniers Yeomanry
and 15th (Service) Battalion, The Hampshire Regiment.
Killed in action, Belgium, 4 September 1918**

Clifford Tom Douse was born in Winchester on 5 September 1889, the son of William and Sarah Dowse, who were then living at 55, Winnall (Wales Street). Although the family surname is spelt Dowse on the memorials at St Paul's and St Matthew's, it is Douse on most official documents, such as census records and the Register of Births.

Clifford, known to family and friends as Tom, was one of seven siblings to survive into adulthood. The eldest, William Jnr, was born in 1870 followed by Mary (1871-1951), Frederick (1875-1945), Caroline Rose 1876-1942) and Eva Jane (1879-1962). After Tom's birth another sister, Maria, arrived in 1894. Tom was the first of the Douse children to be born in Winchester, all his older siblings being born in the nearby village of Easton.

Tom's father, William Douse, was also born in Easton, in 1842. He spent his life working as an agricultural labourer on farms in Easton and on Winchester's eastern fringes, including the no doubt appropriately named Mud Farm on the Alresford Turnpike Road in Easton.

In 1870 William married Sarah Allen who had been born in 1851 in Kings Worthy. In 1871 the couple were living at the Bat and Ball Inn in Easton. The 1881 Census showed the family living at another pub in the village, the Chestnut Inn (today the Chestnut Horse), which stood next to the Bat and Ball.

By 1891 the Douses, including young Tom, had moved to 55, Winnall in Winchester. The family were at the same address in 1901 when Tom's mother Sarah was supplementing the household income by working as a laundress with daughter Eva. The census also shows that William and Sarah's two-year-old grandson, Ernest, was living with them. This was possibly the son of Mary Douse who had married in 1899.

On 27 February 1894, Tom Douse entered St John's National Church School, Winchester, aged four. It is not known when he left.

By 1911 the Douse family had moved a short distance to 26, Colson Road, just off Wales Street, and close to the First In Last Out pub. Tom, 21, was working as a butcher's assistant. A tribute published in the Hampshire Regimental Journal in October 1918, shortly after his death, states that he worked for Mr H. Elkington, almost certainly Howard Elkington, who was Mayor of Winchester in 1912-13.

It is not immediately clear what connection Tom Douse had to Fulflood or Weeke. The Winchester War Service Register (WWSR) gives his address as 5, Andover Road (today a Chinese fast food business) but his name does not appear in any Warren's Winchester Directory of the period.

5, Andover Road, Winchester – Tom Douse's address in the WWSR

DOUSE, Clifford Tom

His parents are listed but they continued to live in Colson Road during and after the war. However, one clue can be found in the Warren's Directory of 1915 which records a 'Butcher, Z.Z' living at 5, Andover Road. In the directories of 1916 and 1917 the address is marked 'void'. Given that Tom was a butcher's assistant, it is possible that he was running a branch of Mr Elkington's business from there and living over the shop. Or he may have been renting the property from Elkington. Certainly, the initials Z.Z are highly unusual while it seems more than coincidental that the address became void the year that Tom went off to war. By 1918, when he was dead, the house was occupied once more.

Although old enough to volunteer for military service on the outbreak of war in August 1914, Tom Douse was not swept up in the 'rush to the colours' This was probably due to the nature of his work; as a butcher he would have been kept busy supplying the Army camps which sprang up around Winchester in 1914 and 1915. With labour in short supply, Mr Elkington would have been reluctant to lose him.

Late 1915 was a momentous time for Tom. Not only is he believed to have volunteered for military service, but he became a husband and a father. Tom married Lillian Russell (known as Lily to family and friends) on 29 December 1915 at All Saints Church, Banstead, Surrey. The wedding certificate shows that the couple were living at 6, Canon Lane, Burgh Heath, Surrey. Tom's profession is listed as butcher. The couple already had a son, Ernest, who had been born in Epsom on 7 September 1915. It is unclear why Tom and Lily had moved to Surrey in mid to late 1915, but it is possible that it was to escape the opprobrium that may have surrounded Lily's pregnancy.

One of seven surviving siblings, Lily had been born in Willesden, north London, on 3 February 1885. Her father, John Thomas Russell, was born in 1862 in Brightling, Sussex, and her mother, Elizabeth, in Kilburn, north London, in about 1864. In 1891 the family was recorded living at 6, Deanery Villas, Godalming, Surrey, with John's occupation given as former professional cricketer.

By 1901 the Russells had moved to Winchester and were living at 6, Ilex Terrace. Lily, then 16, was working as a laundry maid and her father as the cricket professional at West Downs School, Winchester. In 1911 the family were living at 1, Highland Terrace, West Hill, Romsey Road, Winchester, with Lily and her sister Jessie both working as laundresses.

It is believed that Tom attested for military service in late 1915 and was then called up the following April. He joined the 3/1st Hampshire Carabiniers Yeomanry with the service number 2180. This cavalry unit had remained in Britain during the first two years of the war, but in 1916 several squadrons were transferred to France with the remainder following in 1917.

Troopers of the Hampshire Carabiniers Yeomanry at their summer camp in 1915. Tom Douse grew up on farms and would have been comfortable working with horses (*Photo: Royal Hampshire Regiment Museum*)

DOUSE, Clifford Tom

The Carabiniers served as Corps Cavalry for IX Corps until late July 1917, doing useful work during the attack on Messines in Flanders – patrolling, locating the enemy and carrying information. By this stage of the war, however, the Army was having difficulty finding fresh drafts of men to replace those killed and wounded. One solution was to convert Yeomanry units into infantry, and so in October 1917 Tom Douse, by then service number 204744, found himself absorbed into the 15th Battalion, The Hampshire Regiment.

The 15th Hampshires were a Service Battalion assigned to 41st Division. The battalion had a close association with Portsmouth and had been raised during the of peak of voluntary recruitment in the first year of the war. By the time Tom Douse joined it had already seen action during the Somme Offensive and at the Third Battle of Ypres, better known as Passchendaele.

Tom was fortunate to miss the fighting at Ypres. Instead, in November 1917, he found himself dispatched to Italy with the 15th Hampshires to help stem an Austro-German breakthrough at Caporetto in the Italian Alps. The five British divisions sent to Italy travelled by train from Paris, via Lyons and Marseilles to Cannes. From there they continued along the Riviera to Genoa and on to Modena and finally Mantra where they disembarked on 17 November. In his book The Royal Hampshire Regiment, 1914-1918, the historian C.T. Atkinson states:

> *The six-day journey had been an interesting experience, the entirely new scenes and the enthusiastic welcome received in Italy compensating for its length and cramped conditions, while everyone was glad the battalion was not returning, as had been expected, to the Ypres Salient.*

The British then marched 100 miles to reach the River Piave where they hoped to stop the Italian retreat. In the event they saw little action as the enemy offensive had already run out of steam. The Italian front, however, was a world away from the mud and desolation of France and Flanders as Atkinson records:

> *... on the evening of November 20th the Division began the relief of the Italians in the Montello sector, NE of Montebelluno, where the Piave bends southward round a steep ridge, from which splendid observation could be enjoyed over the plains to the SE. The 15th had their first turn in the line here from December 8th to 15th. The ridge was largely covered with woods and elsewhere with vineyards and fields of maize, and with the country virtually as yet undamaged by war no greater contrast with Flanders could have been imagined.*

Seeing Italy must have been a tremendous adventure to Tom Douse, but it proved short-lived. On 1 March 1918, the 15th Hampshires left Italy for the Western Front where they arrived four days later, just in time to meet the full fury of the German Spring Offensive.

The onslaught began on 21 March. The Hampshires went into action the following day between Bapaume and Sapignies, north of the River Somme. In bitter fighting, the battalion held their line against repeated assaults by the Germans whose corpses 'were piled in heaps in front of the wire'. The following days brought little respite - on 24 March the Hampshires, with some Argyll and Sutherland Highlanders, took part in a bayonet charge to halt a German attack and the following night fought a fine rearguard action as the British pulled back.

In April, the battalion was moved out of the line and transferred north to the British Second Army to the east of Ypres. Here it took part in the British withdrawal almost to the gates of Ypres itself, in the process giving up most of the ground won during the bloody Passchendaele campaign just a few months earlier.

On 9 August, as the tide of the war turned in the Allies' favour, the 15th Hampshires were in action once more near Clytte in Flanders. The attack cost 42 men killed or missing, including three officers from the Carabiniers. Tom Douse, however, came through unscathed.

DOUSE, Clifford Tom

Tom was killed in action on 4 September 1918 (the WWSR incorrectly has it as the 14th), the day before his 29th birthday. His battalion was ordered at short notice to attack a strong German position near Vierstraat, south of Ypres. An artillery barrage aimed at silencing German machine-gun posts fell short of its target which meant the Hampshires came under withering fire when they advanced. Tom Douse was among those to fall, along with two company commanders and 95 other officers and men. More than 220 other men were wounded or gassed, including the battalion Commanding Officer.

An entry in the Hampshire Regimental Journal of October 1918 states:

> *Douse - Killed in action on September 4th, Pte T. Douse, Hampshire Regiment, son of Mr. and Mrs W. Douse, 26, Colson Road, Winnall, Winchester.*
>
> *Pte. T. Douse, Hampshire Regiment, killed in action on September 4th, was the son of Mr and Mrs W. T. Douse, of 26, Colson Road, Winnall, Winchester. Before the war he was in the employment of Mr. H. Elkington as a butcher, and married the eldest daughter of Mr. J. Russell, cricket professional at West Downs, Winchester. Deceased leaves one child, a son, aged three years.*

Tom's widow Lily received £4 12s 9d from the Army authorities on 14 December 1918 in respect of his personal effects. She received an additional £3 8s 9d on 29 January 1919 and a war gratuity of £10 10s on 11 December 1919.

Less than a year after Tom's death, Lily remarried. Her second husband was Nicholas Hankin. Lily died in Winchester in September 1973, aged 88. Ernest Douse, her son by Tom, married in Winchester in 1949. No details of his wife have yet been found, but the couple are believed to have had one child. Ernest died in the New Forest in November 2002 at the age of 87. Tom's parents, William and Sarah Douse, died within months of each other in 1931, aged 90 and 80 respectively.

Most of Tom's siblings had married and moved away from Winchester before the war, ending their close connections to the city. The exception was his younger sister Maria who married Charles Haines in Winchester on 29 August 1914. Charles served with the 2nd Battalion, The King's Royal Rifle Corps and was killed on 1 July 1916, the first day of the Battle of the Somme. Maria is not believed to have remarried and she died in Winchester in April 1984, aged 89.

Tom's elder brother, William Jnr, did have a son, Charles, who was born in Easton in 1900. Charles later married and went on to live in Surrey where he died in 1933.

Medals and memorials for Clifford Tom Douse

Private Clifford Tom Douse was entitled to the British War Medal and the Victory Medal. (These appear to have been returned to the military authorities by his family in June 1923.) He was buried at Messines Ridge British Cemetery (above), West-Flanders, Belgium (GR. III. C. 7.). His name appears on the memorials at St Matthew's and St Paul's churches, Winchester.

Researcher – DEREK WHITFIELD

DRAKE, Thomas Harold

Private THOMAS HAROLD DRAKE
Wyke Hill House, Weeke, Winchester
Service number 125. The East African Mounted Rifles
Killed in action, East Africa, 3 November 1914

Thomas Harold Drake was born in Stratford, east London, on 2 December 1883. He came from a prosperous family background: his father was a doctor and his grandfather a gentleman farmer and brewer. Thomas attended Marlborough College before emigrating to East Africa in the early 1900s. He joined the East African Mounted Rifles when Britain went to war in August 1914 and was killed in action near Mount Kilimanjaro two months later.

The Drake family came from Kingsclere, near Newbury, on the Hampshire-Berkshire border. Thomas's father Arthur (1849-1895) and grandfather William (1803-1881) were both born there as were his uncles and aunts. William Drake was a master brewer and farmer who, in the 1851 and 1861 Censuses, lived with his wife Sarah at The Brewery in Duke Street, Kingsclere. Sarah had been born in Barton Stacey, near Winchester, in 1809.

In 1861 William's farm amounted to 250 acres and he employed seven labourers and three boys. Two of his sons, William Jnr and Edward, were also in the brewery trade while a third, Thomas, had qualified as a doctor in 1861 but was not practising. Arthur was at school.

Thomas's mother was born Emily Courtney in Woodmancote, near Basingstoke, in 1858. Little is known of her early life or of her parents, William and Mary-Ann Courtney.

In 1871, most of the Drake family were still living in Duke Street, Kingsclere. William Snr's farm had expanded to 280 acres and he employed nine men. Arthur Drake, although just 22, had qualified as a surgeon while his brother William Jnr was running 490-acre Dummer Down Farm, near Basingstoke.

Arthur married Emily Courtney in Winchester in 1879, around the time that his parents moved to 12, Southgate Street, Winchester, where William Snr died in 1881, aged 78. That year's census shows, rather oddly, that Arthur was living with his widowed mother in Southgate Street while Emily was with her parents a short distance away at 10, St James's Villas.

However, this appears to have been a temporary arrangement because a few months later, on 7 September 1881, Emily gave birth to a son, Arthur Edward, in West Ham, East London. The couple had presumably moved to the area because of Arthur's work as a doctor. In 1883, Emily and Thomas – probably twins - were born in Stratford.

The 1891 Census shows the family living in Romford Road, West Ham, with Arthur working as a medical practitioner. However, while his siblings were at home, eight-year-old Thomas was boarding at a small school run by his aunt, Charlotte Drake, in Swan Street, Kingsclere. The school also had an

DRAKE, Thomas Harold

assistant teacher and the students were predominantly siblings from various families, aged between seven and 11.

The same census reveals that William Drake Jnr, Thomas's uncle, was running the 1100-acre New Down Farm at Micheldever, near Winchester. Two of Thomas's other uncles and aunts were Winchester residents: Elizabeth Drake was at Fernlea, St Thomas Street, and living off her own means (her mother Sarah had died in 1886), while Thomas was a doctor and living at 44, Hyde Street.

Thomas's father Arthur died in Nursling, Southampton, in 1895. The same year, Thomas enrolled at Temple Grove School, East Sheen, Surrey, where fellow pupils included the composer Sir Sydney Nicholson, who founded the Royal School of Church Music, and Sir Ronald Storrs, the first British governor of Jerusalem.

Wyke Hill House, Weeke – Thomas Drake's mother moved here in around 1900 shortly before he emigrated to East Africa

In 1897 Thomas was admitted to Marlborough College where he remained until leaving at Easter 1901, aged 17. It is thought that his brother, Arthur Jnr, also went to Marlborough before going on to Cambridge to study medicine. In 1911 Arthur Jnr was working as a physician and surgeon and living in Rochester, Kent, with his wife Ethel and their young son.

Sometime before 1901, Thomas's mother moved back to Winchester to live at Wyke Hill House, Weeke.

Around 1902, Thomas Drake emigrated to British East Africa (later Kenya) where he settled and farmed in Molo, a fertile area in the south-west of the country. The British government offered leases of up to 999 years as well as exemption from land tax to encourage settlers to move to East Africa. The incentives worked. In 1903 there were fewer than 400 European settlers in British East Africa; by 1912 the figure had risen to 1,000.

Shortly after the Great War began in August 1914, British East Africa found itself threatened by German East Africa (now Tanzania), the neighbouring colony to the south. German raiding parties ambushed British detachments and attacked the Uganda Railway. In response, many young settlers and coffee planters joined the East African Mounted Rifles (EAMR), a corps raised in Nairobi on 5 August 1914.

By the end of the month, the EAMR ranks had swelled to more than 400 volunteers. Most were expert riders and crack shots with the advantage of knowing the country and Swahili. They knew little and cared less about formal soldiering and they were somewhat taken aback when they found themselves being issued with regulation uniforms and expected to undergo formal training. However, as they prepared for war in August, the EAMR developed into a more uniform and disciplined unit - the only concession to individuality being to allow the members of 'Bowker's Horse' – a detachment which included Thomas Drake - to retain the letters BH on their helmets.

DRAKE, Thomas Harold

At the end of October, the 4,000-strong British Indian Expeditionary Force 'C', commanded by Brigadier General J. M. Stewart, gathered near the border with German East Africa ahead of a two-pronged invasion of the colony. The first thrust involved attacks on the port of Tanga and the German settlement at Longido on the slopes of Mount Kilimanjaro. On 3 November 1914, some 1,500 Punjabis of the British force advanced at night up the slopes near Longido. However, when daylight came, they were caught in the crossfire of a strong German defensive position and suffered heavy casualties.

Thomas Drake was killed in action at Longido on 3 November. His friends buried him where he fell, together with seven other men who lost their lives. Following the battle, British troops became widely scattered and commanders, deciding that their position was hopeless, pulled out and marched back to British East Africa, having accomplished nothing.

Thomas's brother Arthur served as a doctor and surgeon in the Great War. He enlisted in 1914 and became a Captain with 28th Hospital Unit, 25th Casualty Clearing Station, Royal Army Medical Corps, attached to 86th Brigade, Royal Garrison Artillery. At some point after the war he and his wife Ethel move to Chesterton, Cambridgeshire, where he worked as a physician and surgeon.

Thomas's mother Emily continued to live at Wyke Hill House in Weeke after the war and would have been responsible for her son's name appearing on the memorial at St Paul's. She died in Winchester in 1926, aged 68.

Medals and memorials for Thomas Harold Drake

Thomas Drake's entry in the Marlborough College Roll of Honour

Private Thomas Harold Drake was entitled to the 1914 Star, the British War Medal and the Victory Medal. His remains were later removed from Longido to Dar es Salaam War Cemetery, Tanzania (GR. Coll. Grave 8. E. 6-13.). The inscription on his headstone reads:
KILLED TRYING TO RESCUE.
Thomas is commemorated on the Marlborough College War Memorial and in its Roll of Honour. His name also appears on the memorials at St Matthew's and St Paul's churches, Winchester.

Researcher – JENNY WATSON

EDWARDS, Frederick

Private FREDERICK EDWARDS
1, Greenhill Road, Winchester
Service numbers 2418 and 241286. Hampshire Royal Garrison Artillery
and 2/5th Battalion, The Hampshire Regiment
Died of wounds, Palestine, 25 May 1918

Frederick Edwards was born on 7 June 1885 in Sixpenny Handley, a Dorset village on Cranborne Chase, ten miles east of Blandford Forum. Known as Fred to his family, friends and on official documents, he was born Henry Fred J. Ingram, the illegitimate son of Amelia Clara Ingram. Amelia, also illegitimate, was the daughter of Charlotte Ingram and had been born in Handley in 1861. Charlotte had married a Samuel Joy in 1864.

In 1881 Amelia was working as a servant at West Tytherley Rectory, near Stockbridge. By 1891 she was employed as a cook at a house in Culvers Close, Winchester. Five-year-old Fred, meanwhile, was living in Handley with his grandmother Charlotte who by this time was widowed. In late 1891 Amelia married John Edwards in Winchester.

John Edwards had been born in 1855 in Shoreditch, London. In 1873, he married his first wife, Sarah Emily Burgess, who had been born in Selborne, Hampshire, in 1855. By 1881 the couple were living at 36, North Walls, Winchester, with their three children - John Jnr, born in London in 1877, and Caroline and Charles, both born in Winchester in 1879 and 1880 respectively.

John Edwards was then struck by a succession of tragedies, beginning in 1881 with the death of his son, Charles. In 1886 his wife Sarah also died, followed by another daughter, Annie, who was barely a year old. By 1891 John was working as a muffin baker and living with his surviving children in Little Minster Street, Winchester.

Later that year, John Edwards married Amelia Ingram, who thereafter was known as Clara. Fred joined his mother and stepfather in Winchester and the new family expanded with the births of Fred's half-brother and half-sister, Hector and Mabel, in 1893 and 1894. Fred attended Western Infants School in Elm Road – but probably only for a short time given that he had been living in Dorset in 1891 - before entering St Thomas Church of England Senior Boys' School, in 1893, aged eight. It is not known when he left school.

In 1894 the Edwards family moved to 1, Greenhill Road, Fulflood, which would remain their home up to the Great War and beyond. In 1901 John Edwards was operating a muffin and breadmaking business from the property, assisted by his elder son. Meanwhile, Fred was working part-time as an errand boy for a pork butcher.

By the time of the 1911 Census John Edwards was no longer a baker, but was working instead as a house painter, employing John Jnr and Hector as labourers. Fred, too, had found steady work as a bricklayer. The Trade Union Membership Register 1914-16 reveals that during that period he was a member of the Operative Bricklayers' Society and that he received sickness payments from the union.

1, Greenhill Road, Winchester - Fred Edwards was brought up in the house

EDWARDS, Frederick

The inauguration of Ramleh Cemetery, near Tel Aviv, Israel, in 1927. Fred Edwards is buried here

Fred Edwards did not join the rush to the colours in the early months of the Great War. Two possible explanations suggest themselves. First, John Edwards Snr died early in 1914 and Fred may have felt he should stay at home and support his widowed mother. The second explanation is less altruistic. In late 1914 and 1915, with military camps going up all round Winchester, the construction industry was booming. For builders like Fred the opportunity to make good money may have proved irresistible.

The Winchester War Service Register states that Fred Edwards enlisted with the 2/5th Battalion, The Hampshire Regiment in March 1916. However, research has revealed that he attested under the Derby Scheme at the end of 1915 and was called up on 14 February 1916 at Hilsea, Portsmouth, where he joined the Hampshire Royal Garrison Artillery (RGA) with the service number 2148

It is unclear how long Fred served with the RGA before transferring to the 2/5th Hampshires. Nor do his Army records state when he entered a theatre of war. The 2/5th Hampshires were sent to India at the start of the war and remained there until March 1917 when they deployed to Palestine. It is possible that Fred became bored with a home posting (the Hampshire RGA did not serve overseas) and transferred soon after enlisting. In this case he may have served in India before being sent to Palestine to fight at the Third Battle of Gaza in November 1917 and then in the advance on Jerusalem and the capture of the port of Jaffa the following month.

What is known is that Fred Edwards was wounded and taken prisoner by the Turks on 10 May 1918 when the 2/5th Hampshires attacked the village of Berukin (present day Bruqin, situated within the Palestinian-controlled West Bank), north of Jerusalem. The battle, which began the previous day, saw fighting against both Turkish and German forces. The 2/5th Hampshires lost four officers and some 50 men killed and missing and a further 90 men wounded in its last major engagement before being disbanded three months later. Fred died of his wounds in captivity at Jabez on 25 May 1918, aged 32.

Fred's family continued to reside at 1, Greenhill Road after war. In 1939 his mother Clara was living there with her stepson John Jnr and daughter Mabel who, by this time, was married to Frederick Newman. John Jnr was selling cakes assisted by Mabel and Frederick. It is not known when Clara Edwards died.

Medals and memorials for Frederick Edwards

Private Frederick Edwards was entitled to the British War Medal and the Victory Medal. He is buried at Ramleh War Cemetery, near Tel Aviv, Israel (PR. V. 28. Special Memorial) and is mentioned on the memorials at St Matthew's and St Paul's churches, Winchester. His name also appears on the St Thomas Boys' School Memorial, now held at Kings School, Winchester.

Researcher – DEREK WHITFIELD

FIFIELD, Basil Jack

Signaller BASIL JACK FIFIELD
Winford, 1, Elm Road, Winchester.
Service number 24686. 1st Battalion, The Hampshire Regiment
and 14th and 15th (Service) Battalions, The Hampshire Regiment
Killed in action, Belgium, 17 August 1918

Basil Jack Fifield was born in Winchester on 31 August 1897, the second of Ernest and Charlotte Fifield's three children. Known as Jack to family and friends, he worked as a railway clerk and enlisted as a Signaller in the Army during the Great War. Jack served with three battalions of the Hampshire Regiment before being killed in August 1918.

Jack Fifield's parents married in Bromley, Kent, in 1895. His father Ernest, the son of a gamekeeper, had been born in Micheldever, Hampshire, in 1869. Ernest worked as a clerk for the London and South Western Railway at the company's offices in Eastleigh and by 1918 was head accountant in the Carriage and Wagon Department. Jack's mother was born Charlotte Wren in Clifton, Bristol, in 1869. She was a National Schoolteacher in Bristol before marrying Ernest Fifield. The couple's other children were Queenie, born in 1896, and Nina, born in October 1902.

In 1901 the Fifields lived at 3, St Paul's Terrace, Upper Stockbridge Road, Winchester (St Paul's Hill today), and they were still there in 1911 when they employed a live-in female domestic servant. In 1914 their neighbours at 2, St Paul's Terrace were Andrew and Florence Bogie. Andrew also served with the Hampshire Regiment in the Great War and died in Turkish captivity after the siege of Kut-al-Amara in Mesopotamia. Further up the hill at No.10 lived Eric Rule who served alongside Andrew Bogie in the war. He was killed in action in 1916.

Jack enrolled at St Thomas Senior Church of England Boys' School in Winchester in August 1906. (He is not, however, mentioned on the school's war memorial.) In 1914 his sister Nina entered the County High School for Girls in Cheriton Road (known as The Westgate School today).

Jack followed his father into the service of the London and South Western Railway. In March 1914 he was working as a junior clerk in the Locomotive Accounts Office in Eastleigh, earning £26 a year. Two years later - when the family moved to their new home, Winford, 1, Elm Road, Fulflood - his annual salary had risen to £60.

Jack Fifield was too young to volunteer for military service when the Great War broke out. In late 1915, after turning 18, he may put his name forward under the Derby Scheme, which allowed a man to 'attest' his willingness to fight, enabling him to be called up later. Alternatively, he may have been among the first wave of young men conscripted into the armed forces in early 1916.

Jack entered military service with the Hampshire Regiment on 25 May 1916. After a period of training he joined the 1st Battalion on the Western Front in March 1917 as a signaller.

Right: 1, Elm Road, Winchester - Jack Fifield moved here with his family in 1916

FIFIELD, Basil Jack

Jack's work involved providing signals communications back to his unit. Wired telephones were used where possible, but this meant laying landlines which was dangerous work due to enemy shelling.

Jack probably took part in the 1st Battalion's attack near the French village of Fampoux on 9 April 1917, the opening day of the Arras Offensive. At some point later that year he was transferred to the 14th (Service) Battalion, one of Lord Kitchener's New Army units raised in 1914 and 1915. Jack's obituary in the Hampshire Regimental Journal states that he saw action at Ypres, but whether that was with the 1st Battalion or the 14th is not known. Both battalions took part in the Third Battle of Ypres (better known as Passchendaele), but it was the 14th Battalion which saw more of the fighting, distinguishing itself on 31 July 1917, the opening day of the offensive.

The Roll of Honour at Waterloo Station commemorating the London and South West Railway workers – including Jack Fifield – who gave their lives in the Great War

The 14th Battalion was disbanded in February 1918 and Jack Fifield was transferred once more, this time to the Hampshire Regiment's 15th Battalion, another New Army unit. The 15th Hampshires were heavily involved trying to stem the German Spring Offensive in March 1918 during fighting to the north of the town of Bapaume, in the Somme valley.

The following month the 15th Hampshires moved to Flanders where, on 9 August, they fought a fierce engagement at La Clytte, near Ypres, losing 42 officers and men killed or missing along with 104 wounded. Jack Fifield survived this but was killed a week later, on 16 August, when a German shell exploded in his trench, apparently while the battalion was out of the front line. He was just a few days short of his 21st birthday.

His obituary in the Hampshire Regimental Journal of September 1918 states:

> *Signaller Basil (Jack) Fifield, Hampshire Regiment, killed in action on August 16th, was the only son of Mr and Mrs E. W. Fifield, of Winford, Elm Road, Winchester, who received the official notification of his death in action on Thursday. Private information had reached them a few days previously that Signaller Fifield was killed in the trenches by shell fire, a chum of his (Pte. Hughes, son of Mr and Mrs Hughes of Avenue Road, Winchester) having observed his dead body being brought in on a stretcher. Signaller Fifield, who was only 20 years of age (he would have been 21 on August 31st), joined up in May 1916, and went overseas in March of last year. During that seventeen months on active service he was in the thick of the heavy fighting, first at Ypres, and subsequently at Peronne. He was killed on Mount Hamel. Before enlisting, he was in the office of his father, who is the head accountant in the Carriage and Wagon Department of the London and South-Western Railway, Eastleigh, and enjoyed the esteem of many friends, both at Eastleigh and Winchester.*

The obituary is mistaken when it gives Jack Fifield's place of death as Mount Hamel. The Winchester War Service Register (WWSR) states that he died at Kemmel, the sector near Ypres in Belgium where the 15th Battalion was fighting at the time he was killed and that is almost certainly correct. The WWSR

FIFIELD, Basil Jack

also gives Jack's date of death as 17 August, rather than the 16th and given the previous error in the obituary this biography uses the later date.

Jack's mother Charlotte served as a volunteer British Red Cross nurse throughout the war, clocking up 3,258 hours of service in hospitals and sanatoriums in Winchester and Shawford.

After the war, the Fifields gradually moved away from Winchester. Jack's elder sister Queenie married Herbert Davidge in the city in 1919, but by 1927 they were living in Swaythling, Southampton. His younger sister Nina married Donald Laverty in 1928 in Southampton where she eventually died, aged 76, in 1978.

In 1939 Jack's parents, then both aged 70, were living at 29, Wellbeck Avenue, Southampton, together with 18-year-old Brian Davidge, the son of Queenie and Herbert. Ernest Fifield died in Southampton in 1965, aged 96.

Medals and memorials for Basil Jack Fifield

Signaller Basil Jack Fifield was entitled to the British War Medal and the Victory Medal. He is buried at Lijssenthoek Military Cemetery (grave pictured right), Poperinge, West Flanders, Belgium (GR. XXV. E. 27A.). Jack is commemorated on the memorials at St Paul's and St Matthew's churches, Winchester. His name is also inscribed on the Roll of Honour at Waterloo Station commemorating the workers of the London and South Western Railway Company who gave their lives in the Great War. He was among the company's men remembered at a commemorative service held at St Paul's Cathedral in 1919.

Researcher – DEREK WHITFIELD

FORBES, John

Private JOHN FORBES
25, Sussex Street, Winchester (no longer stands)
Service number S/9037. 8th (Service) Battalion, The Seaforth Highlanders
Killed in action, France, 19 August 1916.

John Forbes was born in Dalry, Edinburgh, in 1879, one of 12 children. A stone cutter by profession, he is believed to have moved to Winchester for work in the 1890s but returned to Scotland to enlist in a Highland Regiment when the Great War broke out. He was killed in 1916 during the Battle of the Somme.

John's father, Alexander Forbes (1844-1907), was born in Cullen, Banffshire, in around 1844 and was one of nine children. He worked as a stonemason and, like his son, appears to have travelled around the country for work because when he died in 1907, he was living in Wandsworth, south London. Alexander's father, William, was also a stonemason and he lived and worked in Cullen. William Forbes and his wife Helen married in around 1830.

John Forbes's mother was born Eliza Constant or Cousant in 1848. The census entries for her place of birth are very vague – 'from England'. Although mostly a housewife, she did leave home to work as a nurse in Aberfoyle, Perthshire, in the early 1900s.

Alexander and Eliza married on 15 October 1866 in Cullen and their first son, William, was born there in 1867. Three more children, twins Alexander and Ellen (1868) and Eliza (1870), were born in Aberdeen. The remaining children were all born in Edinburgh – Mary (1875), Catherine (1877), John (1879), Thomas (1881), Margaret (1882), James (1884), Peter (1886) and Robina (1891)

By 1901 John had moved to Winchester and was living at 4, Tower Street. His occupation on that year's census was stone cutter. John married Ethel Bubb in Winchester in 1906. Ethel had been born in the city on 4 April 1882 and she lived with her parents at 25, Sussex Street (the house no longer stands). Her father, Charles, born in Porton, Worcestershire, in 1849, worked as a coachman and fly driver. (A fly was a one-horse, two-wheeled light carriage.) Ethel's mother, Esther, had been born in Sparsholt, near Winchester in 1857. Her brother Walter worked as a hairdresser in Winchester.

John and Ethel had one daughter, Marjorie, who was born in Winchester in 1907. They continued to live at 25, Sussex Street with Ethel's parents for many years so money may have been tight. Either that or John had to travel a lot to find work.

In 1915, the second year of the Great War, John returned to Edinburgh where he enlisted with The Seaforth Highlanders (Ross-shire Buffs, Duke of Albany's). He was assigned to the 8th (Service) Battalion, formed mainly of volunteers, with the service number S/9037.

The 8th Seaforth Highlanders had been raised at Fort George, Inverness, in September 1914 as part of Lord Kitchener's Second New Army. The battalion came under the command of 44th Brigade in the 15th (Scottish) Division. The 8th Seaforths moved to Aldershot for training and from there to Petersfield in November 1914. On 22 January 1915, the 15th Division was inspected by Lord Kitchener himself. The following month they were at Chisledon Camp on Salisbury Plain and then moved to Tidworth in May for final training. In July, the battalion sailed for France with the rest of 15th Division.

Private John Forbes arrived in France on 12 October 1915, towards the end of the Battle of Loos (25 September-15 October 1915). The 8th Seaforths had been in the first wave of troops to attack on 25 September and captured the town of Loos itself early on before being pushed back. The battalion suffered 502 casualties in the battle, around half its total strength, so John was probably sent out as a draft, or reinforcement.

FORBES, John

John would have been with the 8th Seaforths when the Germans launched two gas attacks on 15th and 16th Divisions at Hulluch, near Loos, on 27 and 29 April 1916. The first gas cloud – a mixture of phosgene and chlorine - and accompanying artillery bombardment were followed by raiding parties which led to the temporary capture of sections of the British line. In the second attack, two days later, the wind turned and blew the gas back over the German lines, causing heavy casualties. The PH gas helmets worn by many British troops performed badly during the attacks. As a result, production of the more effective Small Box Respirator was accelerated.

On 11 May 1916, the Germans launched a massive artillery bombardment on 15th Division positions near Loos known as the Kink Salient. Specially trained assault teams rushed the survivors and captured the British front and second lines. Among those taken prisoner were British tunnellers trapped underground. The Germans repulsed a series of hasty counter-attacks by the British who eventually withdrew and consolidated a new, less exposed, line further back.

John Forbes was killed in action on 19 August 1916 at the Battle of Pozieres (23 July-3 September) during the Somme Offensive. The fighting for Pozieres and nearby Mouquet Farm was among the bloodiest of the entire Somme campaign, particularly for the Australians who suffered 23,000 casualties.

John Forbes was 37 years old when he died. His body was never found. After his death, his widow Ethel continued to live at 25, Sussex Street until 1918 when she moved the short distance to No. 47. She died in Winchester in 1940, aged 58.

Medals and memorials for John Forbes

Private John Forbes was entitled to the 1914-15 Star, the British War Medal and the Victory Medal. He has no known grave, but his name is listed on the Thiepval Memorial (above), Somme, France (Pier & Face 15C) and on the memorials at St Matthew's and St Paul's churches, Winchester.

Researcher – JENNY WATSON

Private FRANCIS JAMES FORDER
30, North View, Winchester
Service number 4/1417. 2/4th Battalion, The Hampshire Regiment
(attached 1/4th Battalion)
Died in Turkish captivity, Mesopotamia, 7 July 1916.

Francis James Forder, the illegitimate son of Blanche Forder, was born in South Stoneham, Eastleigh, on 23 September 1892. Before the Great War he worked as a plumber and served as a Territorial soldier with the Hampshire Regiment. He served in India and Mesopotamia (modern Iraq) and was taken prisoner by the Turks following the siege of Kut-al-Amara in 1916. He is believed to have died from disease during the forced march to a prisoner-of-war camp in Turkey.

Francis's mother Blanche was the daughter of James and Jane Forder and was born in West Meon in 1873. James and Jane – Francis's grandparents - had married in Lyndhurst on 10 December 1872. James had been born in Southampton in about 1838. The 1841 Census showed his family living in Nursling, on the outskirts of Southampton. Blanche's mother was born Jane Read in the New Forest village of Stoney Cross in around 1832.

Francis Forder's grandfather James died on 22 April 1888. Three years later his widow and daughter were living in Lyndhurst High Street with Jane working as a confectioner. In 1900 Blanche and eight-year-old Francis moved to 4, Andover Road, Winchester, where she took up work as a dressmaker. Meanwhile, Francis's grandmother Jane, by then 66, was a live-in servant for Lieutenant-Colonel William Tilden, a retired Army officer living at 1, St James's Lane, Winchester.

In 1903 Francis and his mother moved a few houses up the street to 11, Andover Road. At the time Francis was a pupil at Hyde Infants School, but on 21 March 1904 he enrolled at St Thomas Senior Church of England Boys' School in Mews Lane. By the time of the 1911 Census Francis had left school and was working as a plumber's mate. He, his mother and grandmother were all living at 11, Andover Road.

By 1912, however, Blanche Forder had moved from Andover Road. The Warren's Winchester Directories of 1912-1917 have no entries in her name and she does not reappear until 1918 when she is listed living at 75, Parchment Street, Winchester. This is the address given for Francis Forder in the Winchester War Service Register.

But where were Blanche and Francis living between 1912 and 1918? The answer can be found in the Hampshire Regiment's list of men taken prisoner at Kut-al-Amara in Mesopotamia 1916. This gives his address as 30, Arbour Terrace, Winchester, and names his mother as next of kin. The Warren's Directories for the period show Francis's grandmother Jane as the head of the house, although it is listed as 30,

Right: 30, North View, Winchester – Francis Forder was living here with his mother and grandmother in 1914

FORDER, Francis James

Right: Part of the 250-strong detachment of drafts from the 2/4th Hampshires – which included Private Francis Forder - leaves Quetta for Mesopotamia in October 1915 *(Photo: Royal Hampshire Regiment Museum)*

North View. Clearly the family had chosen to live together once more – probably as an economy measure – and it was from 30, North View, Fulflood, that Francis went off to war in 1914.

Francis Forder's service number, 4/1417, indicates that he joined the 4th Battalion, The Hampshire Regiment as a Territorial in 1910, the year of his 18th birthday. The reasons behind his decision to join are not known, but possibly he had been influenced by his grandmother's former employer, Lieutenant-Colonel Tilden.

As an experienced Territorial soldier, one would expect Francis to have been assigned to the 1/4th Battalion, The Hampshire Regiment when it was formed shortly after the outbreak of war in 1914. He would then have sailed for India with the battalion in October 1914 before being sent to Mesopotamia in mid-March 1915. However, his Medal Index Card reveals that he did not enter the Asiatic theatre of war until 25 October 1915, eight months after the 1/4th Battalion first arrived there.

What happened is that Francis Forder served with the 2/4th Battalion, The Hampshire Regiment in India until October 1915 when he was sent out to Mesopotamia as a reinforcement for the 1/4th Battalion. This is confirmed by the death notice for Francis in the Hampshire Regimental Journal in October 1916 which states:

> *FORDER - On July 17th, at Baghdad, prisoner of Kut, Pte. F. J. Forder, 1417, 2/4th Hampshire Regt, aged 23.*

Francis's name also appears in a report published by the Hampshire Chronicle on 10 June 1916 listing Hampshire Regiment prisoners captured at Kut. The report clearly shows him to be from the 2/4th Battalion but attached to the 1/4th.

Clearly, Francis had been assigned to the newly-formed 2/4th Hampshires in October 1914. Perhaps the battalion commander decided that he would provide the 2/4th – which was largely composed of raw recruits – with much-needed experience. The 2/4th Hampshires followed the 1/4th Battalion to India in early 1915 and remained there until 1917. However, regimental records show that in late October 1915 the 2/4th Hampshires sent a draft of 250 men to Mesopotamia. Francis Forder was almost certainly among them.

Once attached to the 1/4th Battalion, Francis was then assigned to the company of Hampshire troops that formed part of the British-Indian garrison at Kut-al-Amara which was besieged by Turkish forces for

FORDER, Francis James

Francis Forder's name on the Hampshire Regiment's list of men taken prisoner at Kut in 1916. It confirms both his address and his battalion - 2/4th attached 1/4th *(Photo: Royal Hampshire Regiment Museum)*

five months from December 1915. (For details of the siege see pp. 378.) When the garrison surrendered on 29 April 1916 Francis and his surviving comrades were marched off into captivity. Conditions on the march were appalling and according to another Hampshire prisoner, Regimental Sergeant Major William Leach, Francis became sick and was left behind at Baghdad. He died there on 17 July 1916, aged 23.

After the war, Francis's mother and grandmother continued to live in Winchester. It is not known when or where Blanche died. His grandmother Jane passed away in Winchester in 1928, aged 95.

Medals and memorials for Francis James Forder

Private Francis James Forder was entitled to the 1914-15 Star, the British War Medal and the Victory Medal. He was buried in Baghdad (North Gate) War Cemetery, Iraq (GR. VI. H. 8.) and is mentioned on the memorials at St Matthew's and St Paul's churches, Winchester. His name also appears on the St Thomas Church of England Boys' School memorial, which is held today at Kings School, Winchester.

Researcher – DEREK WHITFIELD

FORSTER, Harold Thomas

Major HAROLD THOMAS FORSTER (or FOSTER) DSO and Bar, MC and Bar
14, Avenue Road, Winchester
Service number 5670. 1st Battalion, The Royal Berkshire Regiment
(Attached to 2nd Battalion, The Northamptonshire Regiment)
Died of wounds, France, 29 May 1918

Harold Thomas Foster was born in the Winchester parish of St Faith on 14 November 1878, the son of William Earle and Lydia Foster. Intriguingly, the family changed their surname to Forster around 1890 and inverted their Christian and middle names. Hence Harold's name appears as Forster in many of the census and Army records. A remarkably brave soldier, he was awarded the Distinguished Service Order and Bar and the Military Cross and Bar during the Great War. He was also a talented sportsman and played first-class cricket for Hampshire.

Harold's father, William, was born in 1848 in Pimlico, London, the son of a builder also called William. Harold's mother was born Lydia Lloyd on 19 March 1848 in Westminster, London. Her father, James Lloyd, worked as a coachman. Lydia's mother was born Mary-Ann Williams in Winchester in June 1816. William and Lydia married in Twickenham, Middlesex, on 22 August 1869. William was a joiner at the time. The following year, when the couple were living at 61, Swinbroke Road, Kensington, west London, Lydia gave birth to a daughter called Lydia Annie. Their first son, Percy, was born in Paddington, west London, on 17 October 1874.

Sometime between 1871 and 1878 the Fosters moved to Winchester where Harold and twins Edith and Ernest (1881) were born. The 1881 Census shows Lydia and the children living at 20, North View. William Foster, however, was recorded living as a boarder at 92, Broad Street, Portsmouth, and working as a furniture packer. It is believed he moved there for work while the family remained in Winchester. Shortly afterwards Lydia moved to Portsmouth to join her husband, but it is possible that the three older children, Lydia Annie, Percy and Harold, remained behind to continue their schooling.

Tragedy struck the family in 1883 when two-year-old Ernest Foster, Harold's younger brother, died of burns after his nightshirt caught fire. At the inquest William's employment was listed as builder's foreman. The same year Lydia gave birth to another son, Sidney, in Portsmouth.

According to family memory, William Foster spent time in Winchester Prison during 1886 and Lydia moved back to the city, presumably so that she could visit him more easily. It is not known why William was jailed. Lydia's parents had moved to Winchester from London by this time and were living at 14, Queen's Road, so it is possible that she lived with them.

On his release from prison, William was apparently set to be immediately rearrested on a theft charge, but the prison authorities did not want him back in jail, so they handed him over into the care of his wife. However, the spell in prison appears to have affected William's health because in 1887 he died of tuberculosis, aged 39. To compound the tragedy, Harold's youngest brother Sidney died in the same year.

Above left: 32, Clifton Road, Winchester – Harold Forster's home at the start of the Great War. Right: 14, Avenue Road, where he and his wife Ethel moved in 1917 or 1918

By 1888, Lydia's parents, James and Mary-Ann Lloyd, had moved to 10, Arbor View, Fulflood. Mary-Ann died the following year. In the 1891 Census, Lydia was living with her father and children at 32, Clifton Road. The census also reveals how members of the family had changed their names – Harold, for example, had become Thomas H. Forster while his sister Edith became Mary E. Forster. Why they did this is unclear, but perhaps it had something to do with the shame of William Foster being sent to prison.

By 1895 Harold's mother Lydia was living at 15, Romsey Road. Two years later she remarried. Her new husband, Edwin Jeffery, had been born in Winchester in 1841. In the 1901 Census the couple were recorded as living at 9, Avenue Road, Fulflood, with Edwin working as a grocer's warehouseman. Lydia and Edwin remained at the address until 1909 when they disappear from the Warren's Directory.

Harold Forster attended St Thomas Church of England Senior Boys' School before enlisting with the Royal Marines Light Infantry in 1897 when he was 19. Two years later, however, he bought himself out and joined the 1st Battalion (Princess Charlotte of Wales), The Royal Berkshire Regiment as a Private, initially serving in Ireland.

In 1905 Harold married Ethel May Smith in Dublin. They had three sons together. William and Victor are both believed to have been born in Ireland. The third son, Owen, was born in Winchester in 1918, but sadly Harold was killed in action the same year and never met him. In 1908 Harold's mother died of cancer in Winchester, her death being recorded by Harold who must have come over from Ireland.

By 1911 Harold and his family had moved back to England and were living at military quarters at Fort Burgoyne in Dover. The census of that year also showed that his brother Percy had married and was living with his wife Beatrice and two daughters in Willesden, London. Percy was employed as a railway coachmaker.

Harold's prowess as a cricketer shone through when he made his first-class debut for Hampshire against MCC in May 1911. A left-arm slow-medium bowler, he took 5 for 38 in the MCC's first innings and finished with match figures of 9 for 92. In all, he played five first-class matches for Hampshire that season. Later in the year he also played hockey for his battalion.

At the start of the Great War in August 1914, Harold was a Company Sergeant Major (CSM) with the 1st Royal Berkshires. The battalion quickly mobilised and on 13 August arrived in France where, as part of 2nd Division, it took part in the Battle of Mons (23-24 August) and the subsequent retreat (24 August-5 September). Harold is also believed to have seen action at the First Battle of the Aisne (12-15 September) before being wounded on 30 October.

Harold was sent to England to convalesce before returning to the front. Commissioned on 15 June 1915, he was posted to the 2nd Battalion, The Royal Berkshire Regiment, part of 8th Division, and promoted to Lieutenant on 28 December. In June 1916 he was Mentioned in Dispatches and on 19 August he was awarded the Military Cross for bravery. The award was backdated and referred to his time as a Company Sergeant Major. His citation read:

> *Coy S./M. (now 2nd Lt.) Harold Thomas Forster, R. Berks. R.*
>
> *For gallantry and devotion to duty. A very gallant warrant officer, he has maintained the same standard in the performance of his duties.*

Harold Forster while he was a Sergeant Major in The Royal Berkshire Regiment

Harold fought at the Battle of Albert (1-13 July 1916), the opening phase of the Somme Offensive, and on 22 October he became the battalion's Adjutant - a staff officer who advised the Commanding Officer. He was Mentioned in Dispatches for a second time on 25 May 1917.

During the Third Ypres (Passchendaele) campaign between July and November 1917, Harold saw action at the Battle of Pilckem Ridge (31 July-2 August) and the Battle of Langemarck. On 26 September he was awarded a Bar to his Military Cross and the Distinguished Service Order (DSO). He was Mentioned in Dispatches again on 21 December. The citations for the DSO and the Bar to the MC followed on 9 January 1918. The citation for his Bar to the MC read:

> *Lt. Harold Thomas Foster, M.C. R. Berks. R.*
>
> *For conspicuous gallantry and devotion to duty. He took over command of his battalion when his colonel had become a casualty, and led them with great skill to their objective, twice changing direction in order to avoid hostile barrage. He then made a personal reconnaissance and ascertained the position of the enemy, after which he formed a defensive flank, and was able to re-establish his line when it had been driven back by determined hostile counter-attacks. He remained perfectly cheerful throughout, showing a fine example of fearlessness and contempt for danger.*

FORSTER, Harold Thomas

The citation for his DSO read:

> *Lt. Harold Thomas Forster, DSO, MC, R. Berks. R.*
>
> *For conspicuous gallantry and devotion to duty during an attack. He performed invaluable work as Adjutant throughout the day, rallying and controlling the men and showing great grasp of the situation. He set a fine example of courage and resource to all.*

In April 1918 Harold was attached to the 2nd Battalion, The Northamptonshire Regiment (also in 8th Division) as an Acting Major and Second-in-Command. He wrote several letters home to his wife Ethel during this period, including this one:

> *My Own Darling Girl,*
>
> *Just received your letter and very pleased to get it. The weather appears to have changed there as it has here. Yes Kiddie, you must tell Gash that he cannot have the ground after Xmas as we want it ourselves, then next year we can plant nearly all of it with potatoes which should keep you going as the back garden does not appear to be any good. As you say he had a cheek, but I know him. He would soon collar the lot if he had a chance.*
>
> *I do hope you won't have any bad weather when Percy is there, perhaps you would get him to put some winter cabbages in which will come in very handy to you.*
>
> *I wish I could get home for a time to square up things a bit but if I do, I don't want anyone else staying there. I want you and the boys all to myself. If I am lucky enough to get leave soon I expect you will be on your own, all the visitors will have gone. As we shan't be out of here till the 1st I wonder if Joe will manage to come down or not.*
>
> *We have the parson to tea in the trenches too, but he is a jolly fine chap.*
>
> *Now my darling girl I will close, kiss the boys. With all my love to my darling girl.*
>
> *I remain your loving husband*
> *Harold Forster*

Another letter gives an idea of conditions in the trenches:

> *My Darling Kid,*
>
> *I was looking forward to a letter today but there is no mail, so we are all disappointed. Never mind, perhaps we shall do better tomorrow. It's been raining nearly all the time since I wrote yesterday and the place is awful. We had a dugout fall in on three men this morning owing to the rain, but we dug them out in time. The trenches are rotten today.*
>
> *We have had some good news today so altogether we are doing grand. Our new armoured cars are doing well evidently.*
>
> *Well I have no news Kiddie dear.*
>
> *Kiss Vic for me.*
>
> *With all my love to you.*
> *Your loving husband*
> *Harry*

Harold took over command of the 2nd Northamptonshires when the CO was killed on 24 April at the Second Battle of Villers-Brettoneux during the German Spring Offensive. Today the battle is notable for being the first occasion that tanks fought against each other. In May 1918, 8th Division was sent south to the River Aisne area to rest and recuperate having suffered heavy casualties during the early spring fighting. There, however, the Division inadvertently found itself in the path of another major German attack (Operation Blucher, 26 May-3 June) against French forces on the Aisne.

Harold died on 29 May 1918 after a shell exploded beneath his horse at Bouleuse Ridge, near Ventelay. He suffered chest and face injuries and was taken to a field dressing station after which there was confusion about what had happened to him. Harold's wife Ethel still believed him alive months later, but in March 1919 the Army concluded that he had died on 29 May. His grave was not located until sometime later.

On 16 September 1918, more than three months after his death, Harold was awarded a Bar to his DSO for the first few days of his command of the 2nd Northamptonshires. The citation read:

Lt. (A./Maj.) Harold Thomas Forster, DSO MC, R. Berkshire Regiment attd North'n R.

For conspicuous gallantry and devotion to duty. He assumed command of his battalion when his colonel was killed, and by his coolness and skill extricated it from a critical situation and formed a defensive flank of the utmost importance. For three days and nights, by his pluck and energy, he set an example to his men of inestimable value under adverse conditions of heavy and continuous shellfire.

At some point in 1917 or 1918 Harold and Ethel had moved to 14, Avenue Road, Fulflood. As it has not been possible to pinpoint where Harold's family were living in 1914, this biography uses the house in Avenue Road as his address. Ethel remained at the property until 1923 (she is listed as Foster in Warren's) when she moved to 3, Stuart Crescent, Stanmore, Winchester, which was a new estate at the time. She was still living there in 1931. Harold's brother Percy remained in the east London area after the war.

Medals and memorials for Harold Thomas Forster

Beside his DSO and Bar and MC and Bar, Major Harold Thomas Foster was also entitled to the 1914 (Mons) Star, the British War Medal and the Victory medal. He is buried at Terlincthun British Cemetery (above), Wimille, Pas de Calais, France (GR. VII. A. C. 12.) and is mentioned on the memorials at St Matthew's and St Paul's churches, Winchester. His name also appears on the St Thomas Church of England Boys' School memorial, now held at Kings School, Winchester, and the memorial at the Aegis Cricket Bowl, Southampton.

Researchers – JENNY WATSON and DEREK WHITFIELD

Additional sources
- N. McCrery: *Final Wicket: Test and First-Class Cricketers Killed in the Great War* (Barnsley: 2015).
- Renshaw (ed.): *Wisden's Lives Cricket's Fallen, 1914-1918.* (London: 2014).

FRANCIS, Albert Edward

Private ALBERT EDWARD FRANCIS
15, Andover Road, Winchester
Service numbers 2275 and 205506. Hampshire Carabiniers Yeomanry and 15th (Service) Battalion, The Hampshire Regiment
Killed in action, France, 25 March 1918

Albert Edward Francis was born in Putney, south-west London, in 1880 or 1881. One of eight children, he served as a professional soldier in the early 1900s before marrying in Winchester where he became a policeman. In 1916 he joined the Hampshire Carabiniers Yeomanry, a cavalry unit which amalgamated with the 15th Battalion, The Hampshire Regiment in 1917. He was killed in action during the German Spring Offensive the following year.

Albert's father, John Francis (1837-1902), was born in Westhampnett, Chichester, Sussex, the son of Charles (1786-1871) and Martha (1786-1864) Francis. One of ten children, John suffered great hardship in his early years. The 1851 Census recorded him living as a pauper in the Westhampnett workhouse despite being just 13 years old. Why Albert's father should have been abandoned by his family to such a miserable existence is unclear but, interestingly, both his parents later died in the same workhouse.

Sometime in the late 1850s or early 1860s, John Francis enlisted in the Grenadier Guards. Joining the Army was a common means of escaping poverty in the Victorian period and it would have provided John with a regular wage and a roof over his head. On Christmas Eve 1862 he married Emma Gerrish at St Mary's Church, Lambeth, south London. Emma had been born in North Bradley, near Westbury, Wiltshire, in 1838. Her father John, also from North Bradley, worked as an agricultural labourer. Her mother Hannah had been born in Beckington, Somerset, in 1821.

John and Emma Francis soon started a family. Their first son, Alfred, was born in Lambeth in 1864 followed four years later by a daughter, Edith, born in Putney. By 1871 John had left the Army to work as a railway porter and he and Emma were living with their two children in Harris Yard, Putney. The couple had a second son, Henry, in 1874 and a third, William, in 1878.

Albert Francis was just a few months old by the time of the 1881 Census when the Francis family were still in Putney and John was working as a carman. By 1891 they had moved to 34, College Street, Winchester. Albert's father was still working as a carman and his eldest brother Alfred was a gardener.

We know nothing of Albert Francis's education, but he would probably have left school aged 12 or 13 having received basic schooling. On 9 April 1898, aged 18, he joined the Army as a gunner with the Royal Horse Artillery (RHA). By April 1901 he was based at barracks in Aldershot. Albert served with Y Battery in the RHA and spent a total of seven years in the Army (plus five in the Reserve) before leaving in 1905. On 7 September the same year, he joined the City of Winchester Police Force as a Constable 3rd Class on a starting wage of 23 shillings a week. According to the Force Staff Register he was 25 years old when he joined which confirms Albert's year of birth as 1880 or 1881, not 1876 as stated in some sources.

On 29 January 1906 Albert married Mary Gilbert in Winchester. One of seven children, Mary was the daughter of agricultural labourer George Gilbert (1851-1935) and had been born in the hamlet of Newton Stacey, near Winchester in 1879. Her mother was born Elizabeth Waters (1852-1934) in nearby Barton Stacey. In 1901, 21-year-old Mary was working as a cook and domestic servant for playwright David Jones and his wife Caroline, a music teacher, at their house in Putney.

On 30 March 1907 Mary gave birth to a son, also called Albert, followed by a daughter, Winifred, on 1 August 1908. Meanwhile, Albert Snr, continued to work as a policeman, enjoying regular pay rises until by September 1909 he was earning 27 shillings per week.

FRANCIS, Albert Edward

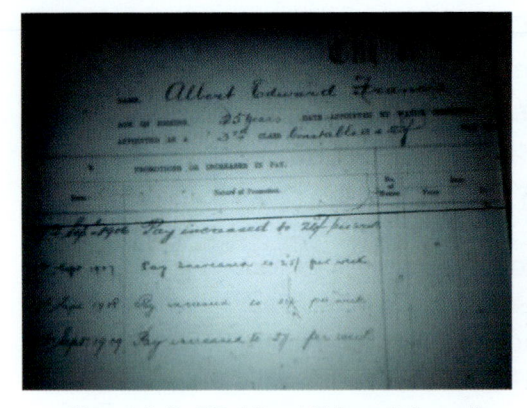

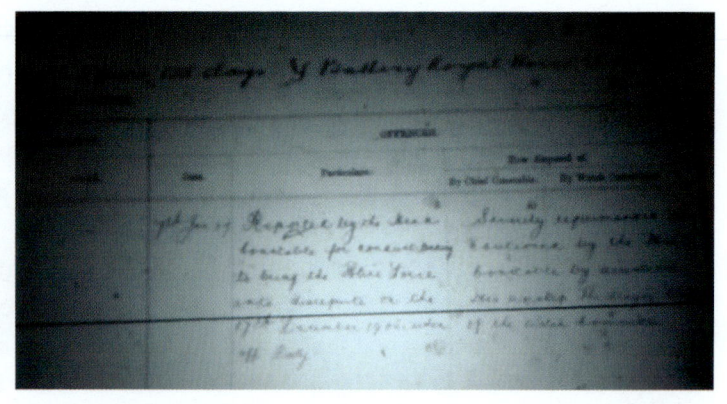

Above left: PC Albert Edwards's police record in 1909 and, right, showing his official reprimand for 'conduct tending to bring the Police Force into disrepute'

However, an incident in 1908 reveals that perhaps not all was well in Albert Francis's life. In December that year he was caught fighting with PC William Pike when off duty. Both men were reported by the Chief Constable for 'conduct tending to bring the Police Force into disrepute'. The Winchester City Police Staff Register records that they received a severe reprimand and caution.

Albert remained with the police until 26 April 1911 when he was discharged from the force on medical grounds. The Force Conduct Book states that he was suffering from neurasthenia, a condition similar to chronic fatigue syndrome with symptoms such as headaches and irritability. This must have made Albert a difficult man to live with and perhaps goes some way to explaining the incident in 1908. It is not known if Albert managed to find work after leaving the police force.

Albert and Mary appear to have lived at several addresses in Winchester. An A. Francis was first listed in Warren's Winchester Directory in 1906, living at 22, St John's Road. In 1911 he was at 35, Hyde Street, but by the following year, after leaving the police force, he had moved to 15, Andover Road. His address remained the same until 1917 when, oddly, there was no A. Francis listed living in Winchester. By 1918, however, Albert Francis was back and living at 11, Andover Road so the family had clearly moved. The Winchester War Service Register and most other sources give Albert's address as 11, Andover Road, but this study uses No. 15 which is where he was living when he left to go to war in 1916.

When the Great War began in August 1914 Albert was no longer on the Army Reserve List so was not liable to be called up. Nor did he join the early rush to volunteer for military service. Indeed, it was not until May 1916, at the age of 35, that he joined the Hampshire Carabiniers Yeomanry, possibly as a conscript. (Conscription was extended to married men on 25 May 1916.)

Albert joined the 3/1st Hampshire Carabiniers with the service number 2275. The Carabiniers were mounted soldiers who carried a carbine (a shorter version of a rifle) and among those who had joined the unit the previous month was Tom Douse who lived a few houses away from Albert at 5, Andover Road. The Carabiniers had remained in Britain during the first two years of the war, but in 1916 several squadrons were transferred to France with the remainder following in 1917.

The Carabiniers served as Corps Cavalry for IX Corps at the Battle of Messines in June 1917 before being absorbed into the 15th (Service) Battalion, The Hampshire Regiment in October. The amalgamation took place because by this stage of the war the British Army was finding it difficult to replace those men who had been killed and wounded. One of many solutions was to convert Yeomanry units into infantry.

FRANCIS, Albert Edward

Troopers of the Hampshire Carabiniers Yeomanry in 1914 before the outbreak of war. Albert Francis joined them from the Royal Horse Artillery in 1916 *(Photo: Royal Hampshire Regiment Museum)*

In November, with the new service number of 205506, Albert was sent to Italy with the 15th Battalion – a unit with close ties to Portsmouth - to help stem an Austro-German breakthrough at Caporetto in the Italian Alps. (Details of the battalion's time in Italy can be found in Tom Douse's biography on pp. 81.)

The 15th Hampshires returned to the Western Front in early March 1918, just as the Germans were preparing to launch their Spring Offensive. The onslaught began on 21 March and the 15th Battalion went into action the following day between Bapaume and Sapignies, north of the River Somme. In bitter fighting, the battalion courageously held their line against repeated German assaults. In his book The Royal Hampshire Regiment 1914-1918, C.T. Atkinson describes the fighting:

> *The [Hampshires'] line was sited on a reverse slope, and though in places the Germans got within 50 yards their corpses were piled in heaps in front of the wire and none got through.*

The following days brought little respite. On 24 March, the battalion took part in a bayonet charge to halt another German attack and on the night of 25-26 March they fought a fine rearguard action as the British pulled back. Despite the intensity of the fighting, the Hampshires casualties were comparatively light but among those killed was Albert Francis. He was 37 or 38 years old.

In July 1918 Albert's widow Mary received a payment of £7 19s 11d in respect of his effects and back pay and then, in November 1919, an £8 war gratuity. Mary continued to live in Winchester after the war and was still at 11, Andover Road in 1961. She died in 1966, aged 86. Albert and Mary's daughter Winifred married William Hopwood in Winchester in April 1935. She died in the city in August 1908 at the age of 63. Albert Edwards Jnr died in South-East Hampshire in 1974, aged 67.

Medals and memorials for Albert Edward Francis

Private Albert Edward Francis was entitled to the British War Medal and the Victory Medal. He is buried in Achiet-le-Grand Communal Cemetery Extension (right), Somme, France (GR. II. I. 1.) and is mentioned on the memorials at St Matthew's and St Paul's churches, Winchester.

Researchers – DEREK WHITFIELD and CHERYL DAVIS

FRASER, Frank Arthur

Signaller FRANK ARTHUR FRASER
Culduthel, Links Road, Winchester
Service number 5795. 18th Battalion, Australian Infantry Force
Killed in action, Belgium, 9 October 1917

Frank Arthur Fraser was born in Notting Hill, west London in 1882, the third of the four sons of Charles and Margaret Fraser. Frank served in the Royal Navy before emigrating to Australia and is not thought to have ever lived in Winchester. However, his parents moved to the city in around 1910 and they are thought to have been responsible for his name appearing on the memorials at St Matthew's and St Paul's. Frank was killed at the Third Battle of Ypres (Passchendaele) in 1917.

Frank's father was born in Wimborne, Dorset in 1855. In August 1874, aged 18, he joined the Scots Guards in Wimborne but left in September 1878. The same year, he married Margaret Griffiths in Surrey. Margaret, the daughter of a bootmaker, had been born in Beaumaris, on the island of Anglesey, North Wales, in 1854. She worked as a domestic servant before marrying.

The Frasers moved to London where, for the next 20 years, Charles worked as a coachman, living at various mews houses in Kensington, Paddington and Chelsea. The couple's three other sons, William, Charles and Richard, were born in London in 1878, 1880 and 1886 respectively.

In 1900 Frank Fraser joined the Royal Navy, enlisting for 12 years. He would have spent much of that period overseas – in the 1911 Census he was recorded serving as a Leading Signalman aboard the cruiser Grosephine (Josephine). The ship was stationed in the East Indies, but in port at Aden at the time of the Census.

The same Census showed that Frank's parents had moved to Winchester. Charles was no longer a coachman but working instead as the publican of The Queen inn in Kingsgate Street. The couple's nine-year-old grandson, William, was living with them on the premises. He was possibly the son of Frank's older brother, William, who had married Florence Tebbut in Northamptonshire in 1900.

Frank Fraser left the Navy in 1912 and emigrated to Australia where he worked as a clerk, living in Darlinghurst, a suburb of Sydney, New South Wales. Frank enlisted as an infantryman with the Australian Imperial Force at Victoria Barracks on 8 May 1916. After completing his basic training, he left Australia by troopship on 7 October 1916, arriving at Plymouth on 21 November. For his military training, he was assigned to the 5th Training Battalion based in Rollestone, Wiltshire. He then embarked at Folkestone for the Western Front on 14 June 1917, arriving at Le Havre the next day.

On 3 July 1917 Frank joined the 18th (New South Wales) Battalion, the Australian Infantry Force (AIF) in France. His brief entry in the Winchester War Service Register states that he served as a Signaller. The 18th NSW Battalion, which came under the orders of 5th Brigade, part of the Australian 2nd Division, had suffered heavy casualties at Gallipoli in 1915 and then again during the Somme Offensive in 1916, particularly at the Battle of Pozières which raged from late July to early September. (Charles Bean, the Australian official historian of the Great War, wrote that the Pozières ridge 'is more densely sown with Australian sacrifice than any other place on earth'.) In early 1917 the battalion was in action at Warlencourt during the German army's retreat to the Hindenburg Line and then, in late spring, at the Second Battle of Bullecourt, part of the Arras campaign.

Frank Fraser's first experience of combat is thought to have been at the Battle of the Menin Road Ridge (20-25 September 1917), part of the Third Ypres campaign in Flanders. The attack aimed to capture sections of the curving ridge, east of the town of Ypres. It saw the first involvement of Australian units in the Third Ypres campaign and was successful on its entire front. Advancing under an intense supporting artillery barrage, the troops overcame formidable German defensive positions which included concrete pill-box strongpoints. The two AIF divisions suffered 5,013 casualties.

After a fortnight's rest - during which time Australian troops spearheaded further successes at Polygon Wood and Broodseinde - Frank was back in action on 9 October at the Battle of Poelcapelle (also called the First Battle of Passchendaele). The objective was to capture the ridge on which the village of Passchendaele stood.

The plan was similar to that used at the Menin Road battle: British and Australian troops would secure a series of intermediate objectives under the protection of a heavy artillery barrage before seizing the ridge. However, rain had turned an already poorly drained battlefield into a quagmire which meant that not enough heavy guns could be brought within range. The infantry attack bogged down in the mud and although the Australians managed to secure some of their objectives for a short time, they were eventually forced to withdraw.

Culduthel in Links Road is Frank Fraser's address in the WWSR. It was owned by Ada Fraser, possibly a relative who allowed Frank's parents to lodge there

The 2nd Australian Division sustained 1,250 casualties at the Battle of Poelcapelle. Frank Fraser was among those killed on the opening day. He was 35 years old.

Frank's military records list his mother Margaret as his next of kin. She applied to the Australian government for her son's medals on 12 December 1921. Her address in Frank's records is given first as Culduthel, Links Road, Winchester, and then as 35, Monks Road, Winchester. The Winchester War Service Register gives Frank's address simply as Links Road.

Culduthel, which still stands, is a large house and one that would have been beyond the means of Frank's parents. In fact, the householder during the war was Ada Albinia Fraser, widow of Colonel Alexander Fraser, formerly of the Hampshire Regiment who had died in 1901. (In the 1911 Census Ada was listed as the householder for Winnall Manor.) Although a Scot by birth, it seems likely, given the surnames, that the Colonel was related to Frank Fraser. If so, then it is possible that his widow may have allowed Frank's parents to lodge at Culduthel. The arrangement would have ended when Charles and Margaret Fraser moved to 35, Monks Road – this is Charles's address in the Electoral Registers of 1920 and 1921.

Frank's brother, Charles Jnr, also served in the Great War. Commissioned into the Royal Army Service Corps in 1915, he later transferred to the City of London Yeomanry, a cavalry unit known as the Rough Riders which had taken its name from the volunteer horsemen who had fought under Colonel (later President) Theodore Roosevelt in the Spanish-American War of 1898. Charles, who ended the war as a Lieutenant, saw action in France and Belgium. His address in the WWSR is also given as Links Road.

Two of Ada Fraser's sons fought in the war and survived. Major Alexander Fraser served with the Royal Berkshire Regiment and was wounded twice. He won the Military Cross and was twice Mentioned in Dispatches. Francis Fraser was a Staff Officer. Wounded once, he won also won the Military Cross as well as the Distinguished Service Order and was Mentioned in Dispatches.

FRASER, Frank Arthur

Charles Fraser, Frank's father, died at 35, Monks Road in 1922. His mother died there in 1931. Of Frank's brothers, William worked as a coachman in London all his life. He married and raised a family before his death in 1951, aged 81.

Charles Jnr never married and died in Winchester in 1933 at the age of 53. He was living at 37, Monks Road at the time of his death. The youngest brother, Richard, also worked as a coachman before joining the Dragoon Guards in 1909. He, too, is believed to have fought in the Great War. It is not known whether he married.

Medals and memorials for Frank Arthur Fraser

Signaller Frank Arthur Fraser was entitled to the British War Medal and the Victory Medal. He was buried at Dochy Farm New British Cemetery (above), West Flanders, Belgium (GR. VIII. D. 17) and his name appears on the memorials at St Matthew's and St Paul's churches, Winchester. He is also commemorated on the Australian Roll of Honour.

Researchers – CHERYL DAVIS, STEVE JARVIS and DEREK WHITFIELD

GAMBLING, Albert Victor

Air Mechanic (2nd Class) ALBERT VICTOR GAMBLING
Hope Villas, 16, Western Road, Winchester
Service number 24215. Royal Flying Corps
Honourably discharged because of illness, 19 April 1917
Died, Winchester, October 1919

Albert Victor Gambling, known as Bertie to family and friends, was born in Winchester on 16 November 1888, the son of John and Sarah Gambling. John had been born in Preston Plucknet, Somerset, and baptised there on 11 August 1857. John's father, George Gambling, born around 1831, also in Preston Plucknet, was a leather dresser. His mother, Emily, whom George married in 1857, worked as a leather glover. Emily died in 1862, aged 25.

On Christmas Day 1863 George Gambling remarried. His second wife, 19-year-old Jane Raison also lived in Preston Plucknet and she went on to give birth to five sons: Thomas, George, Mark, William and Walter. Jane died in 1876 while giving birth to Walter, who survived. Just a few months after Jane's death, George married for a third time. His new wife, Eliza Eglen (Eglon), was John Gambling's second stepmother but by this time he was 19 years old. Eliza died in 1896 and George in 1899.

On 11 September 1882, John married Angelina Ann Young in Preston Plucknet. A trained tailor, John had already moved to Winchester to work and he brought his new bride to live in the city. Winchester offered good prospects to tailors as there was a strong sartorial tradition among the Army officers, Winchester College boys, cathedral clergymen, lawyers and doctors who made up the city's elite. Also, the population increased sharply in the late 19th Century, further raising demand for tailoring among Winchester's burgeoning middle classes. However, it is unlikely that John Gambling ever ran his own business: the 1911 Census recorded him working at home, but for an employer.

In 1883, at the age of 27, Angelina Gambling tragically died in childbirth. The following year John remarried in Winchester. His second wife, Sarah Hallett, had been born in Thorncombe, Dorset, in 1857 and was the daughter of a glover in Chard, Somerset.

In 1885, John Gambling was recorded in Warren's Winchester Directory for the first time, living at 20 (now No. 3) North View, Fulflood. On 17 April that year, Sarah gave birth to a son, Ernest John, followed by Percy George on 2 October 1886 and Albert, known as Bertie to family and friends, in 1888. All three boys went to Western Infants School, then in Elm Road. At the age of six or seven, the boys moved on to St Thomas Higher Grade National/Senior Church of England School, an elementary school in Mews Lane - Ernest in 1893, Percy in 1894 and Bertie in 1895. Their address on admission was 18, (now No. 5) North View. By 1896 the family had moved again, to Hope Villas, 16, Western Road (the house has the same name and number today) where Bertie's only sister, Ivy Louise, is believed to have been born in 1898.

Ernest left school in 1899 to start work as an apprentice to a cabinet maker while Percy later became a tailor's apprentice. Bertie was still at school in 1901 but would have left shortly afterwards. His sister Ivy would probably have started at Western Infants in about 1903 and then gone on to Western Elementary School for Girls on the same site at the age of seven. The 1911 Census shows Ivy still at school (she would have left soon afterwards) and living with her parents at 16, Western Road, along with her eldest brother Ernest, by then a qualified cabinet maker.

Meanwhile, Percy and Bertie Gambling, had both moved to London. Percy, aged 24, was in lodgings and working as a military tailor while 22-year-old Bertie was boarding at 36, Fitzroy Street, off Tottenham Court Road. The 1911 Census recorded him working as an accountant in the automobile trade. It is possible that he met his future wife, Eva Goodchild, in London in this period.

GAMBLING, Albert Victor

On 27 November 1915 Bertie attested (registered his willingness) to serve in the armed forces, probably under the Derby Scheme. His enlistment papers give his address as 394, Uxbridge Road, Shepherds Bush, London, and his occupation as an insurance broker. He was placed on the Army Reserve list the following day and mobilised on 29 February 1916. Bertie joined the Royal Flying Corps (RFC) at South Farnborough, Surrey, on 1 March as an Air Mechanic, 2nd Class, with the service number 24215. His enlistment papers reveal that he was 5ft 10ins tall, with blue eyes and brown hair.

Bertie embarked for France on 9 November 1916, but just a month later he began to fall ill with a cough. His medical reports and discharge papers record that in January 1917 he was diagnosed with tuberculosis in the left lung after coughing up blood. On 28 February, it was decided to send him back to England. After being discharged from 10 Stationary Hospital on 1 March, he embarked on the hospital ship Princess Elizabeth on 13 March. Bertie probably disembarked at Liverpool as he was sent to Windsor Street Military Hospital there. The Army doctor who signed his medical report on 22 March confirmed the tuberculosis diagnosis. Bertie's illness had been brought on by his war service – the winter of 1916-17 was exceptionally bitter – and being on guard duty had further worsened his condition. The doctor concluded that Bertie should be discharged from the services and that he was permanently disabled and entitled to a military disablement pension of 40s (£2) per week.

Bertie was officially discharged on 19 April 1917. His address on discharge was Hope Villas, 16 Western Road, Winchester - his parents' address - and his trade listed as storeman. On 7 May 1917 he was issued with a Silver War Badge, signifying that he had been honourably discharged because of a wound or illness. The badge, worn on civilian clothing, was intended to deter 'white feather wavers'.

Bertie married Eva Goodchild in Camden, London, in early 1918. Eva had been born in St Albans, Hertfordshire, in 1896. Her father was a gardener, but the rest of the family worked in the clothing industry with Eva herself listed as a silk worker in the 1911 Census. After the marriage, she and Bertie made their home with his parents in Winchester. Bertie appears in the 1918 Winchester electoral records at 16, Western Road and as the householder for the same address in the 1919 Warren's Directory even though it was his parents' home as well.

Bertie Gambling died in Winchester on 27 October 1919, aged 30. The cause of his death is not known but may well have been linked to his tuberculosis. He was buried on 1 November 1919 in West Hill Cemetery, Winchester. There is an intriguing reference to Bertie being mentioned in the London Gazette which would only happen if he had carried out an action that was above and beyond the normal line of duty. His name does not appear in the Winchester War Service Register (WWSR), presumably because he did not live in the city at the beginning of the war.

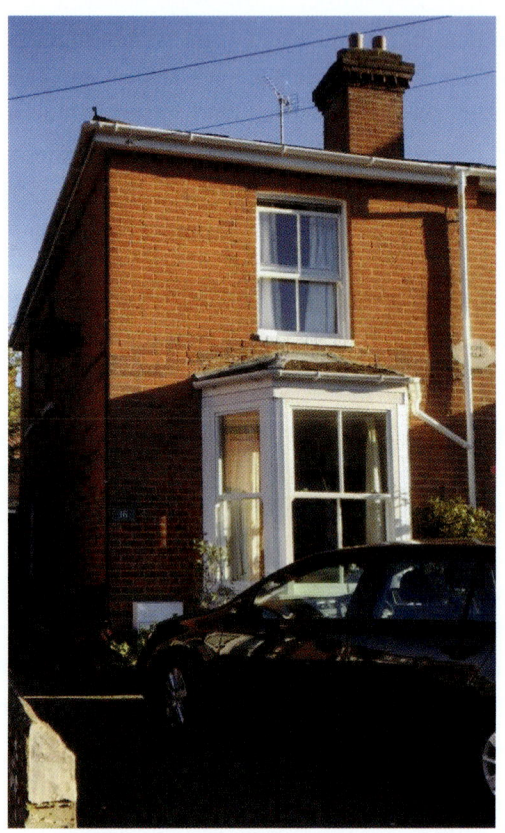

16 Western Road, home to Bertie and Eve Gambling and to Bertie's parents.

After Bertie's death, his parents remained at 16, Western Road for the rest of their lives. Sarah Gambling died in 1930 and John in 1935. Bertie's widow Eva remarried in St Albans in 1929. Her husband was Charles Almond and by 1939 they were living in Bletchley, Buckinghamshire. The couple had at least three children. Eva died in 1968 in Leighton Buzzard, aged 71.

GAMBLING, Albert Victor

Bertie's eldest brother Ernest served in the war as an Air Mechanic, 1st Class (service number 211240) with the Royal Naval Air Service (RNAS). He enlisted in February 1916 and served on the home front. He would have been transferred to the RAF in April 1918 when the RNAS and the RFC merged. His address in the WWSR is given as 9, St. Catherine's Road. According to the electoral records he must have been married by at least 1923 as his wife Agnes joined him on the electoral list that year. Ernest's name and trade (carpenter), appeared in a National Union of Railwayman membership list for 1926, the year of the General Strike. He joined on 10 May 1926, the day before the Trades Union Congress called off the strike. It is possible that he worked at the Eastleigh railway carriage works. Ernest and Agnes remained at 9, St. Catherine's Road until their deaths within a short time of each other in 1963.

Bertie's other brother Percy also served with the RFC as an Air Mechanic, 1st Class and he, too, survived the war. Percy appears to have been based at the No.1 Aircraft Unit at St Omer, near Calais, which was the RFC's main repair and maintenance base. After the war, Percy seems to have returned to work in London. In 1939 he married Mary Smith in Kensington. At 53, Percy was considerably older than his 31-year-old wife. The couple are not believed to have had children and both died in London, Percy in 1957 and Mary in 1987.

In 1924, Bertie's sister Ivy married William A. White in Winchester. In the WWSR there is a William A. White who enlisted as a Private in September 1914 and went on to become a Staff Sergeant in the Royal Army Service Corps. He served in Gallipoli, Egypt, France and Salonika. His Winchester address was 9, Cathedral View.

Ivy and William appear in the 1939 National Register, with William listed as an architect's chief clerk. The couple lived at Hill Crest (unnumbered then, but now No. 137), Greenhill Road, one of the inter-war semi-detached houses. There were six in the household so Ivy and William possibly had four children, but the records that would confirm this are still closed. They were still living there by 1973. Ivy is believed to have died in Basingstoke the following year. She was the last person to die who would have known Bertie.

Medals and memorials for Albert Victor Gambling

Air Mechanic (2nd Class) Albert Victor Gambling was entitled to the Victory Medal and the British War Medal. His grave in West Hill, Cemetery, St. James' Lane, Winchester (GR. 2183), is not maintained or listed by the Commonwealth War Graves Commission as he died after discharge. Nor, for reasons not known, is Bertie on the St Thomas School War Memorial, now held at Kings' School, Winchester. However, he is remembered on the memorials at St Paul's and St Matthew's churches, Winchester.

Researcher – GERALDINE BUCHANAN

GOODRIDGE, George

Private GEORGE GOODRIDGE
69, Greenhill Road, Winchester
Service number 6609. 1st Battalion, The Hampshire Regiment
Killed in action, Belgium, 14 May 1915

George Goodridge was born in Gomeldon, near Salisbury, in 1880. From an agricultural background, he worked initially as a shepherd on farms across Wiltshire and Hampshire before becoming a professional soldier with the Hampshire Regiment in the early 1900s. Two of his four children were born in Winchester and following his death in 1915 his widow returned to the city. She would have been responsible for George's name appearing on the memorials at St Matthew's and St Paul's churches, even though it does not feature in the Winchester War Service Register (WWSR).

George's father, Eli Goodridge, was born in around 1850 in the village of Martin, near Fordingbridge, on the northern fringes of the New Forest. Eli's father, Henry, a shepherd, had also been born in Martin in 1817. Henry's wife, Emma, was born in 1830 and she and her husband had many children together.

In 1873 Eli Goodridge married Sarah Foster who had been born around 1853 in Dorset. Three sons, Edwin, James and Francis were born around 1875, 1877 and 1879 respectively. By the time of the 1881 Census, when George Goodridge was just a few months old, the family were living in Idmiston, near Amesbury, Wiltshire. Eli was working as a shepherd.

By 1891 the family had moved to Gothic Cottages, East Grimstead, Alderbury, Wiltshire. The three elder Goodridge sons were working as agricultural labourers while ten-year-old George was at school. Tragically, the Census also reveals that Sarah Goodridge had been admitted as a patient to the lunatic asylum in Devizes, Wiltshire. She remained there until her death in 1919, aged 64. In Sarah's absence George employed a housekeeper, 71-year-old Jane Lanham.

By the time of the 1901 Census, George Goodridge's brothers had left home and he and his father were living at Charity Down in Longstock, near Stockbridge, together with a new housekeeper, Sarah Jenkins, aged 57. George was working as a shepherd, probably with his father.

In 1905 George married Annie Jenkins, the daughter of the family's housekeeper, in Alresford. Annie had been born on 1 July 1880 in Fordington, near Dorchester, Dorset. Her father, Thomas, was a Welshman born in 1831. Her mother, Sarah, had been born in 1841 in Beaminster, Dorset.

Three years before he married, George Goodridge had joined the Army. No attestation papers can be found, but his service number (6609) indicates that he enlisted with the 1st Battalion, The Hampshire Regiment in late 1902. He probably signed up for seven years plus five in the Reserve. This means he would have left the Army in late 1909 but was still liable for call up when Britain went to war in August 1914.

Mary, the first of George and Annie Goodridge's three daughters, was born in Winchester in late 1906. The second, Evelyn, was born in two years later, also in Winchester. **By the 1911 Census the family had moved again.** On the census document George has written his address as Dean Hill, Salisbury, Wiltshire. This has been transcribed on the Findmypast website as Dean Hill, East Dean, Romsey, Hampshire, and is almost certainly correct. The house or cottage was tiny with just three rooms, one of them probably a kitchen. Despite this, the family had managed to squeeze a visitor into the house – Annie's 32-year-old sister Mary Jenkins who was employed (although probably not by the Goodridges) as a domestic servant. George, who had left the Army by this stage, was working as a shepherd.

The year 1911 saw the birth in East Dean of George and Annie's third daughter, Gladys. The couple's only son, Henry, was born in 1913 in Stratford sub Castle, a small village north of Salisbury, and the

GOODRIDGE, George

Goodridge family were almost certainly living there when George was called up when war broke out the following year.

George Goodridge's Medal Index Card shows that he entered a theatre of war on 6 September 1914. In his book, The Royal Hampshire Regiment 1914-1919, the historian C.T. Atkinson states that the 1st Battalion, The Hampshire Regiment, which had just been involved in the gruelling Retreat from Mons, received its first reinforcements on 6 September. These numbered some 52 men under Captain R.D. Johnston. George was almost certainly one of them.

George linked up with the 1st Hampshires just in time to take part in the First Battle of the Marne (6-12 September 1914). Having been pursued southwards by German forces for more than a week, the French and British took advantage of a gap that had opened between the two advancing enemy armies. A counter-attack along the River Marne by six French armies and the British Expeditionary Force (BEF) forced the Germans to retreat.

The Hampshires, part of 11th Brigade in 4th Division, joined the pursuit northwards, but it was not until 13 September that they engaged the Germans again. At 3am that morning, the Hampshires crossed the River Aisne and swept up the steep slopes that led down to the river valley. At the top they came across several German outposts, but the troops

69, Greenhill Road, Winchester - George Goodridge's wife Annie moved here in 1916 following his death the previous year

manning them were taken completely by surprise and immediately withdrew. Unfortunately, the British were unable to take advantage of this advantageous position, due to the difficulty in bringing up artillery. Instead, stalemate set in and the Aisne became the Hampshires' introduction to trench warfare.

On 4 October the 1st Hampshires headed north to Flanders to take part in the advance towards the River Lys. The battalion saw action around the town of Armentieres before being ordered up to Ploegsteert. By the end of October, the First Battle of Ypres was raging just to the north but fighting spilled into the Hampshires' sector as the Germans attempted to overrun their positions in Ploegsteert Wood.

Between 28 October and 7 November, the 1st Hampshires were subjected to almost continuous German artillery bombardments and infantry attacks in the wood. However, they proved a match for their opponents. Describing an attack on 30 October, one officer wrote: 'They came on so thick you couldn't miss them. It was just like shooting rabbits on Shillingstone Hill.' Nevertheless, the Hampshires lost 134 men killed and missing in the defence of Ploegsteert Wood along with 143 wounded.

On 21 November, Charles Goodwin, another soldier whose name appears on the memorials at St Matthew's and St Paul's, joined the 1st Hampshires as a reinforcement. It is not known whether he and George Goodridge knew each other, but over the next five months they endured the same hardships and fought in the same battles before both were killed in action within a day of each.

By the end of November, the worst of the fighting in Ploegsteert Wood had subsided, but it also marked the start of months of bad weather. Heavy rain flooded the battalion's trenches which, even when free of water, were knee-deep in slush. C.T. Atkinson describes how the Hampshires learned to adapt to the unfamiliar conditions:

GOODRIDGE, George

> *Some [trenches] had to be abandoned and sandbag breastworks built up instead, while many experiments were made with bricks and wooden floors to keep men above the water level when in trenches. However, arrangements had to be made to give the men baths and clean clothes when they came out of trenches absolutely plastered with mud. Brewers' vats made excellent baths and ample supplies of clothing and 'comforts' arrived regularly, supplementing the ample but rather monotonous rations. The clothing included 'some extraordinary garments with fur outside'. 'One has only got to go on one's knees and growl to be like a bear in the pantomime,' one officer wrote.*

George Goodridge may have witnessed or even taken part in the 1914 Christmas Day 'Truce', now part of Great War legend. The Hampshire Regimental Journal of January 1915 contains a remarkable eye-witness account by an anonymous 1st Battalion officer of the moment that British and German soldiers in Ploegsteert Wood left their trenches to fraternise together, even swapping rifles and equipment.

The weather in much of northern Europe in early 1915 was appalling. In Flanders, a wet January ended with frost and snow which continued into February. Sickness – mainly bronchitis, frostbite and trench foot – took a heavy toll and hundreds of 1st Hampshire men were admitted to hospital. No major offensives were launched over the winter, but 'harassing' of the enemy continued and George Goodridge and Charles Goodwin are likely to have been involved in raids on German trenches and in trying to capture prisoners for interrogation.

On 15 April 1915 the 1st Hampshires came out of the line at Ploegsteert Wood and spent a week billeted in farms near Bailleul. On 22 April news arrived of a major German attack around Ypres, involving the first use of poison gas in the war. The attack, the start of what became known as the Second Battle of Ypres (22 April-25 May 1915), completely surprised the French troops holding the line north of Ypres and they gave way, leaving a large gap in the Allied line.

The 1st Hampshires were rushed north by train to Poperinge, near Ypres, where they found the rumours about the gas attack confirmed by the smell of chlorine and the sight of French soldiers suffering from the effects of gas. Over the following month, George Goodridge and his comrades took part in what some have described as the most difficult fighting the battalion experienced in the whole war. Often referred to as a 'soldiers' battle' because it featured the elite of Britain's pre-war professional army, the Second Battle of Ypres not only saw the introduction of poison gas to the battlefield, but the deployment for the first time of massed heavy artillery. Both weapons were to become symbolic of the horrors of trench warfare.

Between 25 April and 3 May, the 1st Hampshires held the line near Berlin Wood, north of Ypres, against repeated German attacks. On 26 April, the battalion was subjected to an intense artillery barrage that lasted all day. C.T. Atkinson describes the soldiers' ordeal:

> *Directly the mist lifted, a most tremendous bombardment started, salvo after salvo of heavy shell descending upon the line in rapid succession; shells at times were coming down at the rate of 50 a minute and that anyone survived was a marvel. The German tactics were to drench the ground with shells and then push infantry forward, thinking to take easy possession of a destroyed line; but heavily as they shelled the Hampshires they did not shift them and any effort to advance was promptly checked. In places the Germans could get up close by using old trenches and saps, but they could not oust the Hampshires.*

The battalion's casualties on 26 April came to 150, including 59 men killed and missing. Over the following days the Germans continued to press and on 29 April hammered the Hampshires with another bombardment. When it ceased, German infantry advanced towards the battalion's trenches, but were repulsed by rifle and machine-gun fire. By 3 May, when the 1st Hampshires were taken out of the front line, they had lost six officers and 116 other ranks killed and missing, among them some irreplaceable NCOs. A further five officers and 116 other ranks had been wounded.

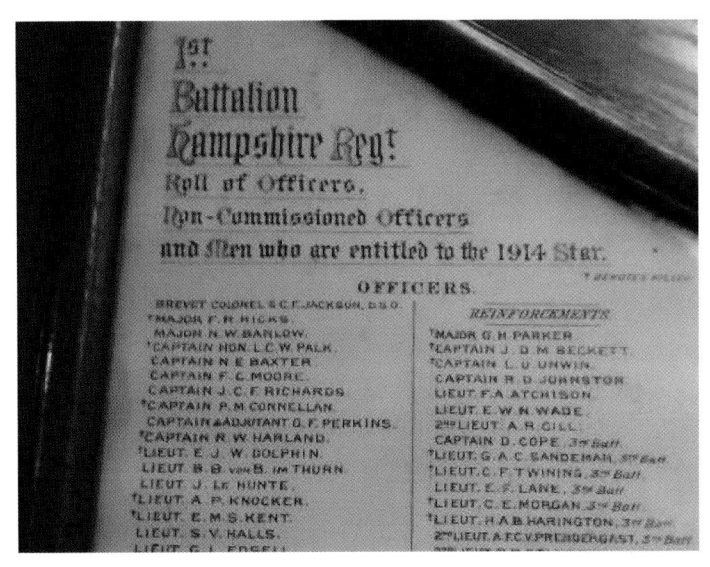

GOODRIDGE, George

Above: George Goodridge's name on the Roll of Officers, NCOs and Men of the 1st Battalion, The Hampshire Regiment who were entitled to the 1914 Star. The Roll (left) is held by the Royal Hampshire Regiment Museum in Winchester

After a brief period resting, during which time the British withdrew to new positions, the 1st Hampshires found themselves back in the thick of the fighting on 8 May, this time just south of Canadian Farm, near the village of Wieltje. Once again, German artillery pounded the Hampshires, fatally wounding the Commanding Officer, Lieutenant Colonel F.R. Hicks.

The biggest attack came on 13 May with the bombardment opening at daylight. One officer wrote that 'at one time the whole line of trench disappeared in a yellow cloud of smoke and the earth was absolutely rocking'. This hurricane of shells was followed by renewed German infantry attacks, yet somehow the Hampshires clung on, inflicting heavy casualties on the enemy.

The 1st Hampshires were relieved once more on 14 May, the same day that George Goodridge was killed at the age of 34. Charles Goodwin is recorded as being killed on 15 May, but by that time the Hampshires were out of the front line. Neither man's body was ever found so it is possible that both died in the bombardment of 13 May. However, with no concrete evidence to support this, the dates of death given here are those recorded by the Commonwealth War Graves Commission.

For Annie Goodridge, George's widow, 1915 proved an awful year. Shortly before her husband's death, her mother Sarah had died in Amesbury. With her husband gone, Annie may have had to vacate a tied agricultural property in Wiltshire and by 1916 she and her young family had moved to 69, Greenhill Road, Winchester, where she continued to live for more than 20 years. In 1939 she was recorded living at the house with daughter Gladys, by then working as a Co-op clerk, and son Henry, a water inspector.

George's sister Constance married gardener George Quartermain in Winchester in 1933. By 1939 the couple were living at Kilmeston, together with Mary Jenkins, Annie Goodridge's sister. Constance is believed to have died in Winchester in 1942.

Following the death of his wife Sarah in a lunatic asylum, George's father Eli remarried in Amesbury in 1926 at the age of 76. His new wife, Sarah Frampton, was 21 years younger. Eli lived to be 93 before he died in 1946 in Trowbridge.

Medals and memorials for George Goodridge

Private George Goodridge was entitled to the 1914 (Mons), the British War Medal and the Victory Medal. He is commemorated on the Menin Gate Memorial, (Panel 35), Ypres, West Flanders, Belgium, and on the memorials at St Matthew's and St Paul's, Winchester. His name also appears on the Roll of Officers, NCOs and Men of the 1st Hampshires who were entitled to the 1914 Star. This is held in the Royal Hampshire Regiment Museum, Winchester.

Researcher – DEREK WHITFIELD

GOODWIN, Charles Francis

Private CHARLES FRANCIS GOODWIN
Address unknown
Service number 3/3129. 1st Battalion, The Hampshire Regiment
Killed in action, Belgium, 15 May 1915

The biography of Charles Francis Goodwin proved difficult to research. Although his name appears on the memorials at the parish churches of St Matthew's and St Paul's, it does not feature in the Winchester War Service Register. In fact, Charles does not appear to have had any Winchester connection, except for one possible, albeit speculative, link that is discussed below. Records for his parents and siblings are scarce and with so many 'dead ends' his life remains shrouded in mystery.

The Soldiers Died in the Great War (SDGW) records give Charles Goodwin's place of birth as St Andrew's, Plymouth. The UK Registration of Births Index shows that a Francis Charles Goodwin was born in Plymouth on 18 July 1893. He was christened at Christ Church, Plymouth, on 24 August the same year and the baptism certificate states that his parents, George and Frances, lived at 10, York Place, Plymouth. George's occupation was given as tailor.

Eight years earlier, the 1881 Census had recorded a George and Frances Goodwin living at 7, St Peter Street in the London parish of St James. Both were aged 27. Significantly, George was working as a tailor which suggests that he and Frances are the same couple recorded living in Plymouth in 1893 following Charles Goodwin's birth. In 1881 the couple had two daughters - Emma, aged five, and three-year-old Sophie. Also living in the house were Frances's father, 64-year-old Francis Cunneford, and her sister Sophie, aged 17.

The 1881 Census shows George and Frances as already being married. However, just over two years later, on 17 December 1883, George and Frances Goodwin are recorded marrying at St Philip's Church, Lambeth, south London. Both were 30 years old and were living together at 7, St Peter Street, London. Frances's father is given as Francis Cunneford, a salesman. George's father is listed as engineer William Robert Goodwin, deceased. George Goodwin gave his birthplace as St George, Middlesex, and his occupation as tailor. Frances's birthplace is recorded as St Pancras, Middlesex, while the daughters were born in St James (probably in the family home).

Clearly, the George and Frances Goodwin on the census are the same people as the couple recorded marrying two years later. They may have lied about their marital status on the census to conceal the fact that their daughters were illegitimate.

After 1893, the year that Charles Goodwin was born, the trail of records for the family goes cold. There is one showing that a Charles Goodwin, aged six, was admitted to the Fulham Road Workhouse in Westminster, London, on 24 May 1899, but it is not known whether this was George and Frances's son. If it was, then the family had moved back to London from Plymouth. It also suggests that the Goodwins had fallen on hard times and would help to explain why they disappear from the official records. (An interesting aside is that Francis Cunneford, Frances Goodwin's father, was also briefly admitted to Fulham Road Workhouse in 1886. The record lists his occupation as 'hawker', rather than the grander sounding 'salesman' on his daughter's marriage certificate!)

To date, the only other reliable information about Charles Goodwin has been gleaned from his Army records. It shows that he enlisted in Winchester and the prefix 3 on his service number (3/3129) indicates that he was a Special Reservist with the 3rd Battalion, The Hampshire Regiment. A Special Reservist was a part-time soldier, like a Territorial. A man would enlist in the Special Reserve for six years and was liable for call-up in the event of war. His service period started with six months' full-time training on the same pay as a Regular soldier. He then returned to civilian life, but still had to complete three to four weeks' military training each year.

GOODWIN, Charles Francis

Soldiers of the 1st Battalion, The Hampshire Regiment in Ploegsteert Wood during the winter of 1914-15. Charles Goodwin was among those who had to endure flooded trenches which led to dozens of cases of trench foot *(Photo: Royal Hampshire Regiment Museum)*

Although his name appears on the St Matthew's and St Paul's memorials, there is no record of Charles Goodwin living in Weeke or Fulflood. However, Warren's Winchester Directory for 1914 does show a W. Goodwin living at 38, Greenhill Road. He cannot be found in any other year at that address, or anywhere else in Winchester. Nor is there a W. Goodwin on the burgess roll or voting lists. One possibility, albeit a remote one, is that this W. Goodwin was related to Charles. If so, then he may have lived briefly in Winchester and allowed Charles to lodge with him.

As a Special Reservist, Charles Goodwin was called up for military service when Britain declared war on Germany on 4 August 1914. He would probably have made his way to the Hampshire Regimental Depot in Winchester where he would have joined hundreds of other Reservists from the Hampshires and the two Rifles regiments also based in the city. After several weeks in Winchester, Charles was sent to join the 1st Battalion, The Hampshire Regiment on the Western Front.

Charles's Medal Index Card records that he entered a theatre of war on 12 November 1914. The War Diary of the 1st Hampshires states that 260 men from the 3rd Battalion arrived as reinforcements on 21 November – Charles Goodwin was almost certainly among them. The 1st Hampshires, one of the regiment's two Regular battalions, had already seen three months of fierce fighting as the initial war of movement on the Western Front gave way to stalemate in the trenches.

Also serving with the 1st Hampshires when Charles joined the battalion was George Goodridge, another soldier whose name features on the memorials at St Matthew's and St Paul's. George and Charles fought together for five months before both were killed within a day of each other at the Second Battle of Ypres. George's biography contains an account of the 1st Battalion's actions between November 1914 and mid-May 1915 and can be read on pp. 114.

Charles Goodwin is recorded as being killed in action on 15 May, the day after George Goodridge. Given that neither man's body was ever found, and that the 1st Hampshires had been pulled out of the line on 14 May, it is possible that both men died in the German artillery bombardment of the battalion's position on 13 May. However, there is no firm evidence to support this, so the dates of death used here are those recorded by the Commonwealth War Graves Commission.

GOODWIN, Charles Francis

Above: Charles Goodwin's Army pension record showing his mother Frances as the claimant. **Right:** An extract from the Hampshire Regimental Journal of July 1915 showing some of the 1st Battalion casualties at the Second Battle of Ypres. Charles Goodwin and George Goodridge are among those listed as killed in action

Charles was 21 years old when he died. Army records show that on 8 October 1915, the sum of £5 9s 11d was paid to his father George, probably in respect of his personal effects.

After the war, Charles's mother Frances claimed an Army war pension in respect of her son. Records held by the Western Front Association show that she received regular pension payments up to her death at the end of 1931. Her address on the pension records is 23, Wybert Street, NW1, a short distance from Regent's Park, and in the same area that the Goodwins were recorded living in 1881. It is not known when Charles's father died or what became of his sisters Emma and Rose.

Medals and memorials for Charles Francis Goodwin

Private Charles Francis Goodwin was entitled to the 1914 (Mons) Star, the British War Medal and the Victory Medal. He is commemorated on the Menin Gate Memorial (Panel 35), Ypres, West Flanders, Belgium. His name also appears on the memorials at St Matthew's and St Paul's churches, Winchester.

Researchers - DEREK WHITFIELD and CHERYL DAVIS

GOODYEAR, George Frederick

Able Seaman GEORGE FREDERICK GOODYEAR
17, Milverton Road, Winchester
Service number – unknown. Mercantile Marine Reserve
Drowned while serving on HM Yacht Zaza, 12 March 1917

George Frederick Goodyear was born in Bethnal Green, east London, on 10 September 1888, the eldest of the four children of George and Alice Goodyear. George Goodyear Snr was born in Dunstable, Bedfordshire, in 1861. In late 1887 he married Alice Simmons in Bethnal Green, east London. Alice had been born in nearby Shoreditch in 1867.

The 1891 Census recorded George and Alice living in Deptford, south-east London, together with George Jnr, who was nearly three years old. That same year, Alice gave birth to a second son, Albert, who was followed by Frank in 1896 and Lilian in 1898. All the children were born in London.

By 1901 the Goodyears were living in West Ham in the east London borough of Walthamstow where George's father was employed as a 'foreman of carriers'. By 1911 the family had moved to another address in Walthamstow. George, his father and brother Albert were all working as clerks while brother Frank was a jeweller's assistant.

In late 1912 George Goodyear married Clara Hyder in West Ham. Clara, a dressmaker, was the daughter of master plasterer Harry Hyder (1851-1913) and his wife Elizabeth (née Bewick, 1849-1923). Harry and Elizabeth had married in Edmonton, north London, in 1874 and had gone on to have six children, including Clara who had been born in 1881. The Hyders were recorded living at different London addresses in the census returns of the late 19th Century, but all within the Leyton area.

George and Clara Goodyear are believed to have moved to Winchester shortly after marrying - the 1914 Warren's Winchester Directory lists 'G.F. Goodyear' living at 17, Milverton Road. George had found work in the city with Hampshire County Council, possibly as a clerk. The house at Milverton Road was one of a number owned by the Winchester Working Men's Housing Society, which had been founded in 1911 to provide affordable homes to rent in the city. Among George and Clara's neighbours was George Lever, who was living with his mother-in-law at 11, Milverton Road. He served with the Hampshire Regiment in the Great War and was killed in action in Flanders in October 1914. George Lever's biography is on pp.175.

We know few details of George Goodyear's wartime military career, largely because he served with the Mercantile Marine Reserve (MMR) and was not issued with a service number. Thus, we do not know for certain his date or place of enlistment or medal entitlement. Also, the history of the MMR before and during the Great War is a neglected subject which further shrouds George's military career in mystery.

The years before the outbreak of war had seen the British Admiralty significantly expand its reserve forces. By 1914 these numbered some 18,000 officers and men of the Royal Naval Reserve, all of whom were trained in war duties, plus

17, Milverton Road, Winchester – George and Clara Goodyear's home in 1914

GOODYEAR, George Frederick

the 170,000 men of the MMR and 100,000 fishermen. At the beginning of August 1914, 147,667 men served with the Royal Navy; in November 1918, when the Armistice was signed, it had been increased by some 200,000 officers and men, in addition to making good a wastage of about 80,000. These recruits came largely from the MMR and fishermen.

A builder's model of the yacht Zaza on which George Goodyear served

At the time he that died, George Goodyear was serving as an Able Seaman aboard HM Yacht Zaza which had been requisitioned by the Admiralty as an Auxiliary Patrol Vessel on 29 September 1914. Zaza had been built on the Clyde and was launched in 1905. During the war it is believed the vessel may have served as an Auxiliary Patrol Group Leader or been a part of special yacht squadrons, at home or in the Mediterranean. Zaza weighed 423 tonnes and was armed with one 12-pounder gun and two 6-pounder anti-aircraft guns. She left Royal Navy service on 30 March 1919 but was requisitioned again in the Second World War before being scrapped in Southampton in 1952.

George Goodyear drowned on 12 March 1917 while serving on HMS Zaza. He was 28 years old. We do not know exactly where he died but, given that he is buried in a British cemetery, it was almost certainly in British waters.

George's name does not appear in the Winchester War Service Register of 1921, probably because his wife Clara had returned to London when the Register was being compiled and she was therefore not in Winchester to supply the necessary details. Clara was recorded living at 32, Colchester Road, Leyton, at the time of her husband's death. She died in Surrey in 1948, aged 68.

Medals and memorials for George Frederick Goodyear

Able Seaman George Frederick Goodyear's medal entitlement is unclear since it is not known whether he ever entered a theatre of war. He was buried at Queen's Road Cemetery (right), Walthamstow, London E17 (GR. C06. P. 120A), which contains graves from the Great War. One assumes that he was buried there at the request of his family, who lived locally. George is mentioned on the memorials at St Matthew's and Paul's churches, Winchester, and his name also appears on the Hampshire County Council Memorial in Winchester, although it incorrectly states that he served with the Royal Navy.

Researchers – CHERYL DAVIS and DEREK WHITFIELD

GOULD, Henry Charles Hamerton

2nd Lieutenant HENRY CHARLES HAMERTON GOULD
14 Bereweeke Road, (Bereweeke House) Winchester
32nd Brigade, Royal Field Artillery
Died of wounds, France, 15 April 1917

Henry Charles Hamerton Gould was the only son of Charles Gould, Rector of St. Matthew's, Weeke with St Paul's, Fulflood, between 1900 and 1915. Henry attended Twyford School and Winchester College where he requested he be put into the Army Class after the Great War began. He joined the Royal Artillery in 1916 and died after being gassed at the Battle of Arras in April 1917.

Henry was born in Holmwood, near Dorking, Surrey, on 26 April 1897 while his father, Charles Hamerton Gould, was vicar there. Charles had been born on 1 March 1865 in Ecclesall Bierlow, Sheffield, Yorkshire. He attended Harrow School and then New College Oxford where in 1887 he obtained a Third-class degree in history. His clerical preparation included a year at Wells Theological College, Somerset, in 1888 followed by a Masters degree. Between 1889 and 1893 Charles served as Curate at Portsea, Hampshire, before moving to be in charge of St. Mary's, Holmwood, Surrey, in 1894, the year he married Mary Sumner. Mary (Henry's mother) was born in 1873 in Buriton, Hampshire, and was the daughter of the Reverend Henry Le Couteur Sumner and his wife Rhoda Anna. Charles. Mary's marriage was registered in Hartley Wintney and so, presumably, they were married at St. Peter's, Yately, where Mary's father was the vicar.

Charles and Mary had four children while living in Holmwood, Surrey – Kathleen Mildred, born 27 February 1896, Henry (1897), Marion Edith (14 May 1899) and Monica Margaret (26 February 1900).

In 1900 the family moved to Bereweeke House, Bereweeke Road, Winchester, following Charles' appointment as Rector of Weeke/Wyke with St Paul's. The Goulds lived comfortably: Bereweeke House had 16 rooms and by 1911 the Goulds employed four live-in servants, including a cook. Today, Bereweeke House has been converted into several residential flats and is numbered 14, Bereweeke Road.

Bereweeke House - the Gould family home from 1900

In about 1904 Henry was sent to Twyford School, a prep school near Winchester. He was to lose his elder sister, Kathleen Gould, Charles and Mary's eldest child, who died, aged 10, in 1906. A memorial

GOULD, Henry Charles Hamerton

window dedicated to her was installed at St Paul's Church – it is on the south side with a brass plaque to the right. In 1910 Henry entered Winchester College where he was in D House. In the 1911 Census he was listed living at Culver House, Culver Close, Winchester as a boarder/school boy.

Henry showed some promise as a scholar but when war broke out in 1914 he asked to be transferred from Senior Division, Sixth Book, to the Army Class. In June 1915 he entered Woolwich, the Royal Artillery's officer training school. The same year his family moved to the New Forest after Charles Gould was appointed Vicar of Fawley with Langley.

> Much regret is felt here at the death of Second-Lieutenant Henry Charles Hamerton Gould, Royal Field Artillery, only son of the Rector of Fawley, and Mrs. Gould, who was killed in action on Sunday last, at the early age of 19 years, and deep sympathy is felt with the Rector, Mrs. Gould, and the two daughters in their bereavement. It is a rather singular coincidence that the late Rector (Rev. Thirlwell Gore Brown) and the present Rector should have each had a son and two daughters, and that both have lost their only son in this terrible war, the son of the late Rector having been killed last year.

2nd Lieutenant Henry Gould's death is announced in the Hampshire Advertiser on 21 April 1917

In February 1916 Henry enlisted with Royal Field Artillery (RFA) and was posted to the 27th Battery as 2nd Lieutenant. The RFA was the largest of the Royal Artillery's three arms, with responsibility for the Army's medium calibre guns and howitzers. Henry's battery formed part of 32nd Brigade, RFA which came under the command of 4th Division. A field artillery brigade had a total strength of just under 800 men, so was broadly comparable to an infantry battalion (just over 1,000).

It is not known precisely when Henry entered a theatre of war, but it is thought to have been in 1916, probably in time for the Somme Offensive (1 July-18 November). During the Somme campaign, 4th Division fought at the Battles of Albert (1-13 July) and Le Transloy (1-18 October). Henry was in action again during the Arras Offensive (9 April-16 May). The campaign began well, with the Canadians capturing Vimy Ridge and the British advancing three miles in places. A key factor in this success was the huge artillery barrages, using high explosive and gas shells, that preceded the attacks.

Henry died of wounds on 15 April 1917 after a gas shell hit his dug-out, near the village of Aubigny. It took rescuers four hours to extricate him from the wrecked shelter and he survived for 'a day and a half of suffering, very bravely borne.' Henry was a week short of his 20th birthday when he died.

After the war, Charles Gould moved with his family from Fawley to become Vicar of Highcliffe, Christchurch, Dorset, from 1925. It has been difficult to find information on Henry's younger sisters as adults: Marion Edith, born 1898, and Monica Margaret, born 1900. Neither married. The youngest daughter, Monica Margaret, probably stayed living with her parents as The Vicarage at Highcliffe is the address given as her abode in her probate records. She died on 18 February 1939, aged only 38, at Millbrook Nursing Home on Jersey. (Her mother was a Sumner with close family connections in the Channel Islands.) Charles and Mary had had the grief of losing three of their four children. They were still at Highcliffe in the 1939 Register, and Mary was volunteering as a WVS Canteen Manager. Presumably on Charles retirement, perhaps hastened by Monica's death, he and Mary moved to Winchester, to Wellisford House on Links Road. Charles died on 4 June 1944, aged 79, leaving over £26,000 to his wife.

Their surviving offspring, Marion Edith, is also to be found in the 1939 Register, surprisingly, as a Hospital Sister at Park Pruett Hospital, near Basingstoke. It was a mental hospital before and after World War II and a military hospital during the war. Marion did not need to work. She must have had a vocation to care for people and possibly a wish to be independent. At some point, she too moved to Winchester. It is possible that her widowed mother, Mary, came to live with her as Mary does not feature as an independent householder at some stage after her husband's death in 1944. Miss M. E. Gould is the householder for Downside on St. Giles Hill in Warren's Directory of 1953/4. Her mother, Mary, died in 1962 at the age of 89. She was buried with her husband in Winchester, probably in Magdelen Hill

Cemetery. By 1964, Marion Edith was living at 26, Quarry Road, according to Kelly's Directory. She was to make at least one more move to 6, Great Minster Street. She died on 4 July 1984 aged 86.

Medals and memorials for Henry Charles Hamerton Gould

HENRY CHARLES HAMERTON GOULD
2ND LIEUT. ROYAL ARTILLERY †AUBIGNY

2nd Lieutenant Henry Charles Hamerton Gould was entitled to the British War Medal and the Victory Medal. He was buried at Aubigny Communal Cemetery Extension, Pas de Calais, France (GR. VI. B. 6.) and the inscription on his headstone reads:
FAITHFUL UNTO DEATH BLESSED ARE THE PURE IN HEART
Henry is commemorated on the memorials at St Matthew's and St Paul's churches, Winchester, and on a memorial plaque on the wall of All Saints Church, Fawley. He is also listed on the memorials at Winchester College (above) and Twyford Preparatory School. The east window of St Paul's Church was dedicated to the Reverend Gould and his family.

Researcher – JENNY WATSON

Additional sources

- https://www.winchestercollegeatwar.com/archive/henry-charles-hamerton-gould/

GYE, Denison Allen

Acting Captain DENISON ALLEN GYE
Piper's Field, Chilbolton Avenue, Winchester (house no longer stands)
15th Brigade, Royal Horse Artillery
Killed in action, France, 28 February 1917

Denison Allen Gye was born in Kensington, west London, in 1882, the first son of Percy and Sarah Gye. Percy Gye, a barrister and later County Court judge, had been born in London in 1845. His wife was born Sarah Sant in London on 9 June 1856. Both of Percy's parents were from wealthy backgrounds. His father, Frederick, was the proprietor of the Royal Station Opera in London while his mother, Elizabeth (née Allen), was the daughter of an artist.

Percy and Sarah Gye married in 1880. On the 1881 Census they were recorded living in Kensington and employing three servants. Following the birth of Denison, the couple had two more children. A second son, James Addison, was born on 18 July 1886 and a daughter, Sylvia, on 2 August 1890. Both were born in London.

The family cannot be found on the 1891 Census, possibly because they were abroad. By 1901, however, they were living at Abbey Hill, Worthy Road, Winchester, where they employed five servants. Denison, who had been educated at Charterhouse School, near Guildford, Surrey, was 19 years old and single. He had no occupation at the time. By the 1911 Census, the Gyes were living at Piper's Field, Chilbolton Avenue, Winchester. Denison, however, was not recorded as being there. Percy Gye died in the house in 1916, aged 70. The property no longer stands.

Denison appears to have enlisted in August 1914, shortly after the start of the Great War. He was commissioned as a 2nd Lieutenant in the Zion Mule Corps, part of the Army Service Corps. At some stage, however, he transferred to the 15th Brigade, the Royal Horse Artillery (RHA) which had been formed in Leamington, Warwickshire, in January 1915. Denison's uncle, Lionel Gye, served in the same unit during the war.

The 15th Brigade, RHA came under the orders of 29th Division and first saw action at Gallipoli in 1915. After landing at Cape Helles on 25 April, the Brigade took part in the capture of Sedd-el-Bahr (26 April), the First, Second and Third Battles of Krithia (28 April, 6-8 May and 4 June respectively), the Battle of Gully Ravine (28 June-2 July) and the Battle of Krithia Vineyard (6-13 August). The Brigade remained on the Gallipoli peninsula until it was evacuated on the night of 7-8 January 1916.

It is not known whether Denison was with 15th Brigade during its time in Gallipoli – the Army record which gives details of his 1914-15 Star shows him with the Zion Mule Corps, so it is likely that he switched units later.

After Gallipoli, 15th Brigade, RHA moved to Suez and then, in March 1916, to France. As part of VIII Corps in the British Fourth Army, it fought at the Battle of Albert on 1 July 1916, the opening day of the Somme Offensive. Denison Gye was almost certainly with 15th Brigade by this stage and he appears to have come through the Somme campaign unscathed.

However, Denison was killed in action at Combles, some eight miles south of the town of Bapaume, in the Somme valley, on 28 February 1917. His death, at the age of 34 or 35, is somewhat puzzling: Combles had been captured by British and French forces the previous September and should have been a comparatively quiet area in February 1917.

At the time of his death, Denison had reached the rank of Acting Captain. Probate records show that he left £1798 15s 3d.

Denison's brother James served with the Royal Flying Corps (the Royal Air Force from April 1918) during the Great War and survived. He went on to marry in Switzerland in the early 1920s and in the 1939 National Register he and his wife Olive were living in Kenilworth, Warwickshire, with James working as a translator.

In the same year, Denison's mother Sarah and sister Sylvia were living in Newport Pagnell, Buckinghamshire. It is not known when they died.

Medals and memorials for Denison Allen Gye

Acting Captain Denison Allen Gye was entitled to the 1914-15 Star, the British War Medal and the Victory Medal. He was buried at Guards Cemetery (above), Combles, Somme, France (GR. I. D. 2) with Christian symbolism on his headstone. Denison is mentioned on the memorials at St Matthew's and St Paul's churches, Winchester.

Researchers – STEVE JARVIS and CHERYL DAVIS

HALLS, Harold Charles

Private HAROLD CHARLES HALLS
95, Greenhill Road, Winchester
Service number 203628 6th (Service) Battalion, The Dorsetshire Regiment
(also 2021 Hampshire Carabiniers Yeomanry
and 100737 East Yorkshire Regiment)
Died in France, 25 October 1918

Harold Charles Halls was born in Southbourne, near Bournemouth, in 1897, the eldest child of Henry and Minnie Halls. Harold's ties to Winchester were not close. His parents moved to the city in around 1910 after his father retired from the Coastguard Service, but Harold himself was away at school in London until about 1912. He enlisted in 1915 and served on the Western Front for nearly three years before dying shortly before the Great War ended.

Henry Halls, Harold's father, was born in Middlesex on 27 March 1868. His parents, James (born 1844) and Jane (1838), were Londoners and Henry spent his early life in the East End. In 1871 James Halls was working as an ale cellar man in Mile End. Twenty years later he and Jane had moved to 16, George's Street, West Ham, with James employed as a painter and decorator. Henry's two brothers, Thomas and James Jnr, were also living in the house. James, however, was not and it is possible that he had joined the Royal Navy.

Harold's mother was born Minnie Carver on 9 September 1874 in Shenfield, Essex. Her father, Thomas, had been born in 1845 in Finchingfield, Essex, and her mother Emma in Bocking, Essex, in 1841. In 1881 the family were living at Rose Valley, Shenfield, with Thomas working as a market gardener. By 1891, Minnie had left home to work as a maid for the Rector of Little Oakley, Clacton, Essex.

Henry and Minnie married in 1895 in Billericay, Essex, but they moved shortly afterwards to Southbourne when Henry joined the Coastguard Service. Harold was born there in 1897. In the 1901 Census his father is recorded living at Coastguard Station 1, Southbourne. The cottages, on Hengistbury Head, still stand today.

Coastguards were normally recruited from the Royal Navy and the service was viewed as an auxiliary to the Navy. All personnel were required to practise gunnery and signalling while life-saving was regarded as a secondary role. Coastguards were not encouraged to become too friendly with the local people (a legacy from the smuggling days) and consequently they were transferred frequently. Henry was soon moved to the Isle of Wight where Minnie gave birth to two sons, Victor in Newport in 1902, and Cecil three years later in East Cowes.

Sometime between 1905 and 1910, Harold obtained a place at the Royal Hospital School in Greenwich – presumably as a result of his father's work for the Coastguard Service. Seafaring traditions were an important element of the school's life and Royal Navy uniforms (sailor suits) were issued to all pupils and used for ceremonial and formal events. Harold was listed living at the school in the 1911 Census. His parents, meanwhile, had moved to 48, Greenhill Road, Winchester, following Henry's retirement from the Coastguard Service. By then Henry was working as a chauffeur while sons Victor and Cecil were both at school locally. The house at 48, Greenhill Road became No. 95 when the street was renumbered in around 1913.

Harold probably left the Royal Hospital School in about 1912, when he was 14. He must have returned to live with his parents in Winchester because at some point before the Great War – and despite being under-age - he joined the Hampshire Carabiniers Yeomanry (service number 2021). This unit formed part of the Territorial Force and had detachments in Winchester, Portsmouth, Bournemouth and Southampton.

HALLS, Harold Charles

The entrance to the Royal Hospital School in Greenwich in 1905. Harold Halls, the son of a coastguard, was a pupil there at around this time

Harold did not become old enough for military service until 1915, at which point he enlisted with the East Yorkshire Regiment (service number 100737). He then transferred to the 6th (Service) Battalion, The Dorsetshire Regiment (service no. 203628), but it is not known precisely when. The identity of the East Yorkshire Regiment battalion he served in is also not known for certain, but it may have been the 7th as this was in 50th Brigade, part of 17th Division, the same as the 6th Dorsets.

Given this, Harold probably served with 50th Brigade during the war which makes it possible to establish a chronology of events. Harold did not serve overseas in 1915 because he was not entitled to the 1914-15 Star. However, if he was in France in time for the start of the Somme Offensive (1 July-15 November 1916) then he would have taken part in the capture of the village of Fricourt on 1 July and then in the bloody fighting around Mametz Wood and in Delville Wood.

In 1917, 50th Brigade moved north and saw action in the First and Second Battles of the Scarpe and in the capture of Rouex during the Arras Offensive (9 April-16 May 1917). In the autumn, the Brigade fought in the First and Second Battles of Passchendaele at the end of the Third Ypres campaign (31 July-10 November 1917).

The Brigade spent the early part of 1918 resting after the battles of the previous year. However, its battalions were heavily engaged during the German Spring Offensive, followed in the autumn by the Battle of Epehy and the Battle of Cambrai, both part of the British Army's attempt to break through the German Hindenburg Line.

Once through these formidable defences, the Allied armies found themselves fighting in open country on the Western Front for the first time since 1914. The retreating Germans attempted to make stands along a series of rivers in northern France and Belgium and it was at one of these, the Battle of the Selle (17-25 October 1918), that Harold Halls was killed.

The battle opened on 17 October with the British Fourth Army forcing crossings over the River Selle. By nightfall, German defences on most of the ten-mile front had been shattered and the town of Le Cateau captured. Fighting continued on 18-19 October as Fourth Army advanced more than five miles, pushing the Germans back towards the Sambre-Oise Canal. A surprise night attack on 20 October by the British Third Army secured the high ground east of the river and the momentum was maintained on 23 October with a combined assault by the Fourth, Third and First Armies.

HALLS, Harold Charles

Nothing is known of Harold's death, at the age of 21, on the last day of the battle. His Medal Index Card does not even state whether he was killed in action or died because of sickness.

Harold's father Henry served at sea as a Petty Officer in the Great War and survived. He and Harold's mother remained at 95, Greenhill Road until 1927 when they left Winchester to return to Essex. In 1939 they were living in Ilford where Henry died in 1946, aged 78, and Minnie in 1958 at the age of 84. Harold's younger brother Victor also went to live in Ilford.

Medals and memorials for Harold Charles Halls

Private Harold Charles Halls was entitled to the British War Medal and the Victory Medal. He was buried at Abbeville Communal Cemetery Extension (above), Somme (GR. IV. J. 20.) with the following inscription on his headstone:
SLEEP DEAR ONE TAKE YOUR REST WE MISS YOU MOST WHO LOVED YOU BEST.
His name also appears on the memorials at St Paul's and St Matthew's churches, Winchester.
(His initials are A. C.)

Researchers – JENNY WATSON and DEREK WHITFIELD

HAMMOND, Charles Walter

Private CHARLES WALTER HAMMOND
Kingscote, 36A Clifton Road, Winchester (37, Clifton Road today)
Service numbers 2157 and 200333. 1/4th Battalion, The Hampshire Regiment
Died in Turkish captivity, Mesopotamia, August 1916

Charles Walter Hammond was born in Orpington, Kent, in January 1897, the son of John Lovick Hammond and his wife, Elizabeth. Charles's father was a career soldier and his grandfather may possibly have had military links in India. Charles joined the Hampshire Regiment as a Territorial in 1913 and served in India and Mesopotamia in the Great War. He died in Turkish captivity in 1916 after being taken prisoner at the siege of Kut-al-Amara.

Charles's father John was born in Romford, Essex, in 1853, the son of Cornelius Hammond, an agricultural labourer and Louisa, a dressmaker. John worked briefly as a groom before enlisting in the Army on 24 January 1871. When his 12 years' service expired, he signed up again and rose to become a Company Quarter Master Sergeant in the Durham Light Infantry. He served in India where he met Elizabeth Neville. Elizabeth had been born in 1862 in Bengal which suggests that her father may have had military connections.

John and Elizabeth married in Bombay on 4 September 1876. Elizabeth gave birth to two daughters, Alice and Ellen, in India, in 1879 and 1885 respectively. By the time that their first son, Thomas, was born in 1889 the family were back in England living in Army barracks in Newcastle upon Tyne. In 1892 a third daughter, Ada, was also born in Newcastle, followed three years later by Charles in Kent.

John Hammond left the Army in April 1894 and took his Army pension. However, he retained strong military ties and became a messenger for the War Office. In June 1900 he successfully applied for a one-year Short Service Attestation, becoming a Quarter Master Sergeant in the Royal East Reserve Regiment.

By the following year, when Charles was four years old, the Hammonds had moved again and were living in Gresham Road, Shenfield, Essex. John was approaching the end of his short commission while 15-year-old Ellen was a pupil-teacher at a local school. On 26 June 1903, Elizabeth gave birth to another son, Eric, in Brentwood, Essex.

By the time of the 1911 Census, the Hammonds had moved to the Winchester area and were living at Armagh, a five-room property in the village of Littleton. John was an Army pensioner, but also working as a clerk. The Census does not state whether 14-year-old Charles was working or still at school – in fact, nothing is known about his education. Intriguingly, however, it shows that his mother had given birth to a total of eight children, of whom six had survived. No record can be found of John and Elizabeth's other two children.

The Warren's Winchester Directory of 1914 reveals that the Hammonds were living at Kingscote, 36A, Clifton Road, Winchester. The house was later renumbered 37, Clifton Road and still stands today.

Right: 37, Clifton Road, Winchester – this was No. 36A when Charles Hammond and his family lived here in 1914

HAMMOND, Charles Walter

Right: Charles Hammond's name appeared in the Hampshire Chronicle on 10 June 1916 when the newspaper published the list of Hampshire Regiment men who had been taken prisoner at Kut. Note the other Fulflood and Weeke names – Andrew Bogie, Frank Chapman, Frank Coles, Fred Richards, Cecil Shefferd, George Soffe and William White. All died in captivity and are mentioned on the parish memorials

Charles Hammond's service number 4/2157 indicates that he enlisted with the 4th Battalion, The Hampshire Regiment at some point in 1913. He was 17, old enough to join the Territorials but too young to serve overseas (the lower age limit for foreign service was 19).

Charles is believed to have been with the 4th Hampshires for their annual summer training camp on Salisbury Plain in late July and early August 1914. The camp took place against the backdrop of the European crisis which followed the assassination of the Austrian Archduke Franz Ferdinand in Sarajevo on 28 June. The 4th Hampshires were still at camp when Britain declared war on Germany on 4 August and mobilisation began.

When the surge of recruits led to the 4th Battalion splitting in two, Charles was assigned to 'A' Company in the 1/4th Battalion. He volunteered for service overseas and in October sailed to India, arriving the following month. The 1/4th Hampshires spent just four months in India before being ordered to Mesopotamia. They arrived at Basra on 18 March 1915.

Charles took part in the Hampshires' early forays against the Ottoman Turks – first in Arabistan, then along the Tigris and Euphrates rivers before helping to capture Nasiriyah in July 1915. The latter operations were carried out in the inhospitable creeks and marshes of the Euphrates delta and many men fell victim to the intense heat and disease.

In December 1916, Charles Hammond was part of the contingent of 1/4th Hampshires that became cut off in the British garrison of Kut-al-Amara. Besieged by the Turks for five months, the garrison finally surrendered on 29 April 1916 and Charles and his comrades were marched off into captivity along with thousands of other British and Indian troops. (For details of the Kut siege and its aftermath, see pp. 378.)

It is unlikely that Charles ever made it to a Turkish prisoner-of-war camp. His name appears on a list of Hampshire Regiment prisoners taken at Kut published in the Hampshire Chronicle on 10 June 1916, but it seems he may already have been seriously sick or wounded when captured. According to Mrs Esme Bowker, who established a Comforts Fund for the Hampshire Regiment prisoners, Charles was sick and in a field ambulance when the prisoner column reached Shumran, a short distance from Kut. Regimental Sergeant Major William Leach, a fellow prisoner, wrote that Charles died in hospital at Shumran.

The precise date of Charles's death is not known. The Commonwealth War Graves Commission and Soldiers Died in the Great War both state that it was on 20 September 1916, but this seems too late given the observations of RSM Leach and Mrs Bowker. The Winchester War Service Register simply says August 1916 and that is probably about as accurate as it is possible to be. Charles was 19 years old.

HAMMOND, Charles Walter

The wedding of Charles Hammond's sister Ada and Captain Montague Atkinson in India in 1925. Charles's father, Sergeant Major John Hammond (front row), cuts an imposing figure with his sword and medals

John and Elizabeth Hammond moved to 54, St Catherine's Road, Bar End, Winchester, but at some stage they moved away from Winchester. In 1939 the couple were living together in Wandsworth, south London. John died in Surrey in September 1949, aged 96. It is not known when Elizabeth died.

Charles's sister Ada married Captain Montague Parker Atkinson – who had spent his early years in St Mary Bourne, near Andover – on 21 September 1925 in Shillong, Bengal, India. In December 1934, Ada and Montague travelled to Canada and the United States, with her husband described on the shipping line's records as 'Officer Commanding British Forces, Peshawar, India'. Ada died in April 1979 in Poole, Dorset, aged 86, and Montague in Alton, Hampshire, in 1990, aged 95.

Eric Hammond, Charles's brother, went on to become a professional soldier like his father. He married in 1929 and died in Broadstairs, Kent, in September 1978, aged 75. It is not known what became of Charles's other siblings.

Medals and memorials for Charles Walter Hammond

Private Charles Walter Hammond was entitled to the 1914-15 Star, the British War Medal and the Victory Medal. He is commemorated on the Basra Memorial, Iraq (Panel 21 and 63), and on the memorials at St Matthew's and St Paul's churches, Winchester.

Researcher – DEREK WHITFIELD

HAWKER, Charles William Seymour

Lieutenant CHARLES WILLIAM SEYMOUR HAWKER
Arnwood, Weeke, Winchester (house no longer stands)
13th (Service) Battalion, The Hampshire Regiment
Died of illness contracted during war, Switzerland, 13 March 1918

Charles William Seymour Hawker was born in Newtown, near Wickham, Hampshire, on 26 February 1889. Although English by birth, Charles's immediate roots lay thousands of miles away in South Australia where, in 1840, his grandfather and great uncles had arrived as settlers from England. Tough, resourceful men, the Hawkers adapted well to pioneer life, becoming wealthy outback sheep farmers and then influential politicians. Charles's father later returned to England, bringing with him a share of the family fortune. This enabled his son to enjoy a gilded Edwardian upbringing – fine houses, servants and governesses and a Winchester and Oxford education. Charles enlisted with the Public Schools Battalion on the outbreak of war in 1914 but transferred to the Hampshire Regiment after obtaining a commission. He does not appear to have served overseas and was discharged from the Army in 1916 before dying two years later. His name does not appear in the Winchester War Service Register.

Charles's father, Frederick Hawker, was born on 6 December 1851 in Adelaide, South Australia, the son of Charles Hawker (1823-1861) and his wife Emma. Charles Hawker Snr and his brother George (1818-1895) were the sons of Admiral Edward Hawker (1782-1860) who lived in Petersfield and who was godfather to one of Jane Austen's nieces. In 1840, armed with a small amount of capital, they and another brother emigrated to the Colony of South Australia, eventually establishing a sheep station north of Adelaide which came to be known as Bungaree.

George Hawker eventually bought out his brothers and extended his land until he had some 80,000 acres. He paid much attention to the breeding of his sheep, and his wool gained a high reputation. In 1858 George entered the South Australian House of Assembly and two years later was elected Speaker. He retired from Parliament in 1865 but returned in 1874 and was a member until his death. He also added the posts of Chief Secretary of South Australia and Treasurer to those he held during his long political career. A follower of cricket and horse racing (the town of Hawker still holds an annual Hawker Cup), George was due to be knighted, but died before he could receive his award. However, his wife – by whom he had 12 children - was known as Lady Hawker until her death.

After being bought out by his brother, Charles Hawker returned to England in 1850 and married Emma Digby. He later returned to South Australia where he founded the Anama sheep stud. He died in Adelaide in 1861 as he and his family, including 10-year-old Frederick, were preparing to return to England.

HAWKER, Charles William Seymour

Above: Charles Hawker's great uncle George who set up the Bungaree sheep station in South Australia which was the basis of the family wealth. He later served in the state parliament. Left: Lincolnville, the house in Cheriton Road where Charles's mother lived from around 1920

On 10 November 1874 Frederick Hawker married Blanche Bridger at St John's Church in Paddington, London. Blanche, the daughter of William Bridger, had been born in London in 1849. No record can be found of her mother. In 1876 Blanche gave birth to twins, Arthur and Blanche, in Winchester.

By 1881 the family were living at Wood End House, Newtown, near Wickham, Hampshire. Built in the late 18th Century, the property was enlarged in the mid-1800s, probably before the Hawkers moved there. It still stands today. In the 1881 Census Frederick Hawker is described as a landowner. The family employed five servants, including a nurse, a nursemaid, a domestic maid, a footman and a cook.

Arthur Hawker died in 1886, aged 10. However, in 1888 Blanche and Frederick had a second daughter, Irene, born in Winchester. Charles was born the following year, probably in Wood End House. The Hawkers were still living in the house in 1891 and were employing even more servants, including two nursemaids and a school governess who would have tutored the younger children.

Frederick Hawker, Charles's father, died at Bembridge, on the Isle of Wight, on 1 June 1893, aged just 41. Probate records show that he left £2651 11s 11d to his widow. He is buried in St Nicholas churchyard, Wickham. Blanche did not remarry following her husband's early death, but she did move to Winchester with her children. In 1901 she was living at Kingsmead, a house in Kingsgate Street. She continued to employ servants although their number had been reduced to four, including a governess.

In the late 1890s Charles Hawker attended Eagle House School in Sandhurst, Berkshire, one of the country's oldest preparatory schools. In 1901, aged 13, he entered Winchester College where he was in E House. He remained at the College until 1905 when he went up to Oxford.

By 1911, Charles, then aged 21, had left home and was boarding in the home of retired farmer Henry Westbrook, in the hamlet of Standon, near Winchester. The house may have been Standon Farmhouse, which still stands on the junction of Sparsholt Road and the A3030, just north of Hursley. Charles is recorded as living on his own means, so he may not have been working. Sharing the house with him was 21-year-old Geoffrey Corbett. He, too, was of independent means so it is possible that he and Charles were friends. Charles's mother, meanwhile, had moved to Arnwood, a 13-room house at the top of

HAWKER, Charles William Seymour

Cheriton Road in Weeke where she was living with her younger daughter Irene and three servants. The house no longer stands.

In 1914 Charles was learning estate management, but when war broke out that August he enlisted with one of the Public Schools Battalions. These 'Pals' battalions were raised as part of Kitchener's New Armies and were originally made up exclusively of former public schoolboys. After being taken over by the British Army they formed battalions of the Middlesex Regiment and the Royal Fusiliers.

Charles spent just one month with his Public Schools Battalion. In September 1914 he gained a commission with the Royal Hampshire Regiment and joined the 13th (Service) Battalion which officially came into being the following month. The 13th Hampshires were formed on the Isle of Wight as a battalion in Fourth Army, but in April 1915, they became a Reserve battalion and were posted to Wareham, Dorset. In September they moved to Bovington and from there to Wool in September 1916. The battalion then converted into the 34th Training Reserve Battalion of 8th Reserve Brigade.

For much of this period Lieutenant Charles Seymour acted as battalion transport officer; he was later appointed transport officer at Brigade Headquarters at Wool. However, in January 1916 he was invalided out of the Army, suffering from illness contracted on service. It is unclear what illness Charles was suffering from, but just over two years later, on 13 March 1919, he died in Switzerland where he may have been sent to recuperate.

Charles's sister Irene served as a Red Cross Volunteer in Winchester Hospital during the war. She died in 1919, possibly from Spanish flu, aged 31. After Irene's death, Charles's mother Blanche moved into a smaller house, Lincolnville, which was situated further down Cheriton Road between Western Road and Fordington Road, and which still survives. She was still there in 1939, dying early in 1940 at the age of 91.

Charles cousin, Charles Allan Seymour Hawker, also served in the Great War. A grandson of George Hawker and the son of the manager of the family sheep stations in South Australia, he was studying at Cambridge when war broke out. He enlisted on 11 August 1914 and was commissioned as a temporary **Lieutenant in the** 6th (Service) Battalion, The Somerset Light Infantry on 1 August 1915. He saw action in Flanders and was injured on 11 August 1915 and again on 24 September at the Battle of Loos when he lost an eye. Despite his injuries, Charles Allan returned to the front in May 1917 with the rank of Captain. He was wounded again on 4 October 1917 during the Passchendaele campaign and paralysed from the waist down. However, after a series of operations and rehabilitation, he was able to walk with two sticks, although his legs remained in surgical irons for the rest of his life.

Charles Allan returned to South Australia in 1920, resumed his studies and became involved in family agricultural holdings. He also enjoyed a distinguished political career before he was killed in air crash in 1938. The Canberra suburb of Hawker is named in his honour.

HAWKER, Charles William Seymour

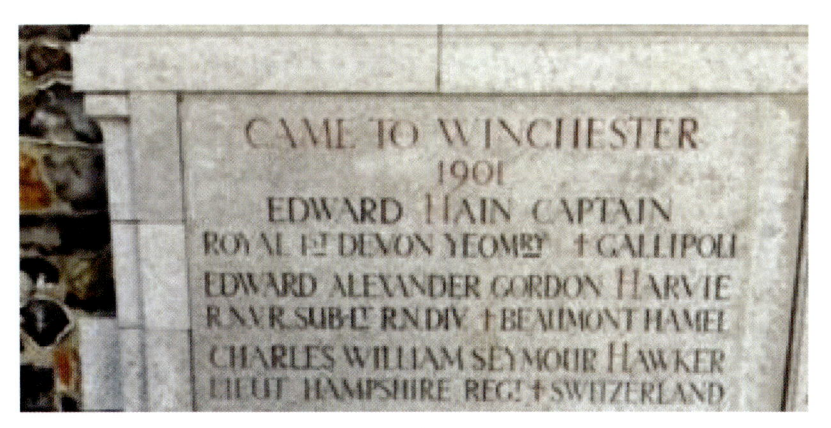

Charles Hawker's name on the
Winchester College War Cloister

Medals and memorials for Charles William Seymour Hawker

It is thought that Lieutenant Charles William Seymour Hawker was not entitled to any medals because he never served in a theatre of war. He was buried at Vevey (St Martin's) Cemetery, Switzerland (GR. 1A.) and is mentioned on the memorials at St Matthew's and St Paul's churches, Winchester. Charles's name also appears on the Winchester College War Cloister (Outer C1). At St Nicholas Church, Wickham, there is a brass memorial which reads:

'In ever loving memory of Frederick Arthur Hawker of Wickham, died June 1st 1893 aged 42 [sic], also of his elder son Arthur F.B. Hawker died September 29th 1886 aged 10 and of his younger son C.W. Seymour, Lieutenant, Hampshire Regiment, died of illness contracted during the War, March 13th 1918 aged 29, also of his younger daughter Irene Laura Maud Hawker died April 9th 1919'

Researchers - DEREK WHITFIELD, GERALDINE BUCHANAN and CHERYL DAVIS

HAWKINS, Sidney Michael

Air Mechanic 2nd Class SIDNEY MICHAEL HAWKINS
Piper's Farm, Weeke, Winchester (no longer stands)
Service number 63786. Royal Flying Corps
Died in England, 6 April 1917

Sidney Michael Hawkins was born in Sparsholt, near Winchester, in 1898. His parents, Jesse and Caroline, were from long-established farm worker families in villages near Winchester. Before the Great War, Sidney worked as a taxi driver and it was probably an interest in engines that lay behind his decision to enlist as a mechanic with the Royal Flying Corps (RFC) in March 1917. He died in the north of England just a few weeks later.

Sidney's father Jesse was born in Sparsholt in 1868, the son of farm worker Charles Hawkins (born 1839) and his wife Jane. The Hawkins family were all baptised at St Stephen's Church, Sparsholt, and at the time of Sidney's birth could trace their roots in the village back to 1798. Jesse's mother was born Jane Wareham in 1839. She came from a farming family in the nearby village of Crawley.

Jesse Hawkins was one of five siblings. In 1871 the family were living at Lower Dean, a hamlet between Sparsholt and Winchester, and were still there ten years later by which time Jesse, his elder brother and father were all working as agricultural labourers. Charles Hawkins died sometime before the 1891 Census, leaving his widow Jane and their children living at 40, Home Lane, Sparsholt.

Sidney's mother was born Caroline Carter in Meonstoke in 1864. Her father, also called Jesse and born in 1841, worked as a carter. Caroline's mother, Sarah, had been born in Somerset in 1835. In 1871 Caroline was living at Lower Farm, Droxford, with her parents and two brothers. She enrolled at Exton village school the following year. By 1881 the family had moved to a cottage next to the vicarage in nearby Corhampton and Caroline was working as a dressmaker. The family were at the same address in 1891. Jesse Hawkins and Caroline Carter married in Droxford in 1892 and went to live in Sparsholt where Sidney was born in the early winter of 1898. The 1901 Census recorded the family living at Upper Dean with Jesse working as a domestic gardener. Shortly after the census Caroline gave birth to a daughter, May, who was baptised at St Stephen's on 4 August.

By 1911 the Hawkins family were living in the Crabwood area of Sparsholt in a three-roomed dwelling. Sidney, then aged 12, and nine-year-old May were at school – probably in the village. Sidney's grandmother Jane and aunt Ellen were still living in Home Lane, Sparsholt, with Jane working as a laundress.

After leaving school in around 1913 it is likely that Sidney worked on local farms. However, he also worked as a taxi driver because that is the occupation that he gave on his enlistment papers in March 1917. All drivers at the time needed a basic knowledge of how cars worked and how to repair them. Sidney may have learned this from working on farm tractors which were starting to make an appearance in the English countryside.

Cars were also an increasingly common sight on roads despite being expensive. Drivers did not need to take a test and the roads in large towns and cities could be busy. There were no traffic lights or pedestrian crossings although the speed limit was 20mph. However, despite the growth in the number of private cars most people's first car journey was in a taxi

In March 1917 Sidney, aged 18, enlisted with the RFC as an Air Mechanic, 2nd Class. It is not known whether he volunteered or was conscripted. By this stage in the war the Allies had more than 20,000 aircraft and each required a team of up to 40 mechanics.

HAWKINS, Sidney Michael

Right: A Royal Flying Corps advertisement for recruits, including air mechanics

The government launched a major drive to recruit air mechanics and in 1917 alone 14,000 men and women were trained at the RFC base in Halton, Buckinghamshire. Recruits were paid two shillings a day.

The skills needed by an Air Mechanic, 2nd Class were varied but the RFC was particularly keen to recruit those who had worked as armourers, welders, blacksmiths, coppersmiths, tinsmiths, engine fitters, mechanics, electricians, machinists or fitters. It is believed that Sidney was sent to Leeds for training - the Blackburn Aeroplane and Motor Company had opened its Olympia Works in the Roundhay area of the city in 1914 and a new factory was also established at Brough, in the East Riding of Yorkshire, in 1916.

However, Sidney's time in the RFC proved short-lived. He died in Leeds on 9 April 1917, aged 18, just a few weeks after enlisting. How he died is a mystery. It may have been the result of illness or he may have been involved in an accident while training – it was common in the early days of flying for mechanics to walk into a propeller.

Sidney's parents – and probably his sister May - moved to live on Piper's Farm, Weeke, in 1917. The farm was one of three in the village that had been owned by the Burnett Hitchcock family of Weeke Manor before 1911. The name of the farm has been perpetuated in the recent developments of Pipers Field and Pipers Gardens in Chilbolton Avenue. Sidney's father, Jesse, died in Winchester in 1919, aged 50, and his sister, May. in 1921 at the age of 20. His mother, Caroline, continued to live on Piper's Farm and she would have been responsible for ensuring Sidney's name appeared on the parish war memorial. In the space of four years she had lost her husband and both her children. She remained at the farm until 1936 when she is believed to have died, aged 72.

Medals and memorials for Sidney Michael Hawkins

Air Mechanic 2nd Class Sidney Michael Hawkins never entered a theatre of war so was not entitled to any military medals. After his death, his body was brought back to Sparsholt and laid to rest in St Stephen's churchyard (left)). His name appears on the Sparsholt War Memorial (right) and on the memorials at St Matthew's and St Paul's churches, Winchester.

Researcher – JENNY WATSON

HEAD, Frank Joseph

Petty Officer FRANK JOSEPH HEAD
14, Romsey Road, Winchester
Service number 214768. HM Submarine C34, Royal Navy
Killed in action, North Sea, 21 July 1917

Frank Joseph Head was the second of six children born to William James and Eliza Ellen Head. A Winchester boy, he joined the Royal Navy in 1902 at the age of 14 and served on battleships, cruisers and destroyers before transferring to submarines. He was killed in 1917 in the North Sea after his submarine was torpedoed and sunk by a German U-Boat.

Frank was born on 2 March 1888 although he gave his year of birth as 1886 when he enlisted in the Royal Navy, presumably so he could sign up earlier. His father William was a farmer who was born on 6 April 1860 in Chenole, near Sherborne, Dorset. William's father, Joseph (born 1808), had also been a farmer. Joseph was married to Mary Head, who had been born in 1821.

Frank's mother was born Eliza Elston in New Cross, Deptford, south London, in 1862. She and William married in the mid-1880s and moved to Winchester where Eliza gave birth to six children - Ethel (born 1886), Frank (1888), Ada (1889), Harry (1892), Mabel (1895) and Arthur (1896). The 1891 Census showed the Heads living at 37, Parchment Street with William working as a tailor. The family were still there in 1901.

On 31 January 1902, Frank joined the Royal Navy as a Bugler and Boy 2nd Second Class even though he was at least a year under-age. He did his training at the Royal Naval Boys Training Establishment HMS St Vincent in Gosport, near Portsmouth, where he remained until 23 March 1904. The main qualifications for acceptance as a boy sailor were the parents' signed permission, the ability to read and write, a character reference from a professional person and a clean record. The boy also had to pass an academic assessment, be of a certain height and pass a thorough medical examination. Only around one in four applicants was successful.

On 2 April 1904 Frank (service number 214768) was rated-up to Ordinary Seaman and his Navy career began in earnest. His early training would have involved a study of basic seamanship skills such as ropes, knots and splices, sailing small boats, gaining familiarity with dropping and recovering an anchor and parade ground marching. He served on a range of ships as shown in the table overleaf.:

Frank's career as a submariner began in 1910 when he entered the Royal Navy's Torpedo School at HMS Vernon, a shore establishment in Portsmouth. Founded in 1876, HMS Vernon pioneered the development of underwater weapons such as the torpedo and the depth charge and it is likely that it was also a centre for submarine training.

Right: A C-class submarine like that on which Frank Head was serving when it was sunk by a German U-boat in 1917. Life on board for the crew was hot, cramped and dangerous

HEAD, Frank Joseph

Petty Officer Frank Head's Navy record 1904-1917

Name of Ship	Date FH Joined	Date FH Left	Class of Ship
Formidable	15/11/1904		Battleship
Formidable	26/06/1905	01/10/1906	
Venomous	02/10/1906	04/05/1907	Destroyer
Victory 1	05/05/1907	01/06/1907	
	02/06/1907	21/09/1907	
Victory	22/09/1907	22/11/1907	
Crescent	23/11/1907	11/01/1908	
King Alfred	12/01/1908	24/05/1910	Cruiser
Victory	25/05/1910		
Vernon	04/09/1910	13/05/1911	Torpedo school Portsmouth
Mercury	14/05/1911	30/06/1911	Training ship Chatham
Arrogant	01/07/1911	13/07/1911	Depot ship
Bonaventure	14/07/1911	14/10/1912	Depot ship
Maidstone	15/10/1912	26/02/1913	Depot ship
	27/02/1913	19/03/1913	
Rosario	20/03/1913	12/03/1915	Depot ship
Dolphin	15/03/1915	13/08/1915	Depot ship
Maidstone	14/08/1915	07/11/1915	Depot ship
Arrogant	08/11/1915	27/11/1916	Depot ship
Dolphin	28/11/1916	31/03/1917	Depot ship
Maidstone	01/04/1917	30/06/1917	Depot ship
Lucia	01/07/1917	21/07/1917	Depot ship

Frank then served a short spell at HMS Mercury which could have been to bring him up to date with signalling practices. In July 1911 he transferred to HMS Arrogant, one of four submarine depot ships he served on between 1911 and 1917, and on 4 March 1913 he passed his Petty Officer exams. Frank was passed professionally competent for Petty Officer rank on 5 February 1914.

As Frank's naval career blossomed, his family continued with life in Winchester. They had moved to 29, Staple Gardens by 1907, the same year that Arthur, the youngest son, entered St Thomas Senior Church of England Boys' School. By 1911 the Heads had moved again and were living at 14, Romsey Road, on the very edge of the parish. William Head was still working as a tailor while Ada was a dressmaker, Harry a house painter, Mable a draper's assistant and Arthur a builder's apprentice. Ethel and Frank had left home.

At just 5ft 4ins tall, Frank was the ideal stature for the Navy's cramped and claustrophobic submarines. It is not known when he joined the crew on submarine C34, but the vessel was attached at various times to the depot boats that Frank served on – HMS Dolphin in November 1916, HMS Maidstone in 1917 and HMS Lucia in July 1917.

Life aboard a submarine of the Great War period was extremely hard. There were no showers or air conditioning and the smell of diesel was all-pervasive. The vessel constantly sprang leaks and there was rarely any realistic means of escape if it was sunk. Privacy, too, was non-existent. Comfort on the C Class submarine was sacrificed to its most essential equipment – the engines, hydraulic systems, torpedo tubes and depth and directional control gear.

HEAD, Frank Joseph

So, what tempted sailors to volunteer? There was the novelty factor, plus extra pay for being a member of the submarine service and extra pay for each night spent on board (which earned it the nickname 'hard lying allowance'). Promotion within the service was also a little faster than in the general service Royal Navy. At sea, the men passed the time playing cards, sleeping, knitting and on watch duty.

In 1915, C34 moved to Harwich from where it was sent out on 'U-boat Trap' patrols to try to disrupt the German submarines then causing mayhem in the North Sea. The trap involved a 'bait' vessel, usually an armed trawler, towing a submerged submarine. When challenged by a U-boat, the trawler alerted the submarine which then slipped its tow and attempted to torpedo the U-boat.

14, Romsey Road, Winchester - Frank Head's family home in 1914 at the start of the Great War

On 21 July 1917, a torpedo fired from the German submarine U52 near Shetland struck C34, sinking it with the loss of all but one of the 18-man crew. The sole survivor was picked up by the U-boat and taken to Germany as a prisoner of war. Among those killed was 29-year-old Frank Head who was third in command of C34.

After the war Frank's parents William and Eliza moved to 59, Milverton Road, Winchester, which is his address in the Winchester War Service Register. This biography, however, uses 14, Romsey Road, the family's home in 1914 and one that Frank would have known well.

Ada Head, Frank's sister, went on to marry Theodore Matthews, a master coach builder, and in 1939 they were living with her parents at 15, Eastgate Street, Winchester. William died in 1940 at the age of 80. It is not known when Eliza or Ada died.

Medals and memorials for Frank Joseph Head

Petty Officer Frank Joseph Head was entitled to the 1914-15 Star, the British War Medal and the Victory Medal. He is commemorated on the Portsmouth Naval Memorial (PR. 24) and on the memorials at St Matthew's, St Paul's and St Thomas's churches, Winchester. His name also appears on the Great War memorial (right) at the United Church, Jewry Street, Winchester.

Researcher – JENNY WATSON

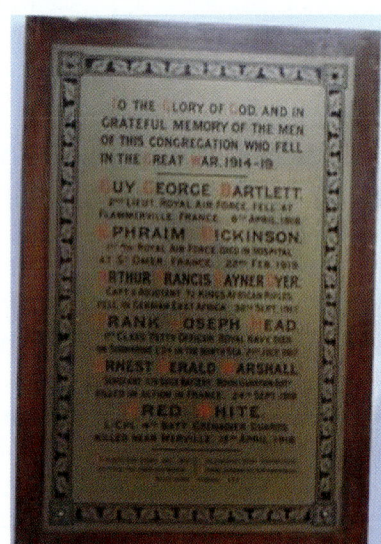

HILL, Arthur Samuel

Rifleman ARTHUR SAMUEL HILL
Service number R/31897. 17th (Service) Battalion, The King's Royal Rifle Corps
9, Union Street (NLS) (and 69, Fairfield Road), Winchester
Missing, believed killed, Belgium, 3 August 1917

The entry in the Winchester War Service Register (WWSR) for Arthur Samuel Hill reads

> ✠ HILL, ARTHUR S. (69, Fairfield Road) K.R.R.C., July 1916, Rfn. Flanders. *Missing (believed killed), Aug. 3, 1917.* :

It is the address '69, Fairfield Road' that links Arthur to the parish of St Matthew's with St Paul's. However, as will become clear below, it has not been possible to confirm that he lived at the address or, indeed, anywhere else in the parish before, during or after the Great War. For that reason, the presence of his name on the two church memorials remains a mystery requiring further research.

Arthur was born in Winchester in about 1888, the sixth child of Edwin and Elizabeth Hill. His father was a bootmaker who was born in Portsmouth in about 1852 and his mother, whose maiden name was Youren, was born in Southampton in about 1857. Her family were originally from Cornwall. The couple married in 1877 and their first three children, Stephen, (his mother was only 16 when he was born), Blanche and Violet were born in Southampton.

By 1881, the family had moved to Winchester and were living at 42, Upper Wolvesey Terrace in the parish of St Peter's, Cheesehill. By 1886, they had moved to Union Street, at the eastern end of North Walls, living initially at No. 26. In 1888 and 1889 they were at No. 35, but by 1890 Edwin and Blanche (that seemed to be her preferred Christian name) had settled at 9, Union Street where they lived for the next 33 years. (All Hill family addresses in Union Street were demolished, mainly in the Friarsgate redevelopment of Winchester in the 1960s and by the creation of the one-way road system.) By 1891, they had four further children. Lily was born about 1883, whilst they were still at Upper Wolvesey Terrace, Edwin Jnr in 1886, by which time they had moved to Union Street, Arthur in 1888 and Ada who was less than one year old in the 1891 Census.

Lily, Edwin Jnr, Arthur and Ada would have gone to the local infants' school, Holy Trinity - Lily and Ada to the girls' section in the building which still stands in Upper Brook Street behind Holy Trinity Church, and Edwin and Arthur to the boys' school in Cossack Lane. This had formerly been St Maurice's School and it, too, was subsequently demolished during the Friarsgate development. (Cossack Lane survives today as the street forming the entrance and exit to the Middle Brook Street car park and the school was on the north-east corner of it.)

In 1901, Edwin Hill was working as a self-employed bootmaker at home with his son, Edwin Jnr, aged 15, helping him. Arthur, then aged 12, and ten-year-old Ada would have been at elementary school. Their four eldest siblings, Stephen, 26, Blanche, 23, Violet, 21, and Lily, 18, appear to have left home. In 1906 Blanche married Albert Chapman in Winchester and five years later the couple were living at 36, Union Street, with Albert working as a baker. After the war they moved to 8, Union Street, which may have been even closer to her parents' address. In 1909 Violet married Charles Hart and they went to live in Ipswich, where a daughter was born the following year.

According to an advertisement in the 1910 Warren's Winchester Directory, the Hill shoe and boot making business was established in 1895. However, the first reference to it is in the 1903 edition of Warren's when the business was based at 19, Union Street. In 1905, the entry in Warren's trade section proudly reads 'Hill & Son' in enlarged and bold lettering and it is still at No. 19.

The move to combine home and residence at 9, Union Street occurred by 1909. With fewer children

HILL, Arthur Samuel

at home - possibly only Edwin Jnr as Arthur and Ada may have left by then - there would have been more space at 9, Union Street and it must have made economic sense.

Arthur's eldest brother Stephen may have already left home by 1891 as he was not at 9, Union Street on the census night of that year. By 1901 Stephen was married, working as an agricultural labourer and living in a cottage in Stockbridge Road, King's Somborne, near Winchester, with his wife Jane and the first three of their children.

The advertisement for Hill & Son bootmakers in the 1910 Warren's Directory. Edwin and Blanche Hill are pictured outside 9, Union Street
(Photo: Hampshire Record Office)

A return to the countryside may suggest that this is not the right Stephen Hill, but their children have so many Hill-Youren Christian names that it does seem likely. In the 1911 Census, Stephen, by then aged 36, was back in an urban environment, working as a general labourer and living at 20, Mortimer Road, Itchen, Southampton, together with Jane and their six surviving children.

Edwin Jnr, Arthur's elder brother, married 21-year-old Margaret Roberts in 1910 in South Stoneham, near Eastleigh, and in the 1911 Census they were living at 37, Brassey Road, Winchester. Margaret's occupation was dressmaker, working on her own account. By 1912, the couple had moved a short distance to 1, Cranworth Road where they remained for many decades. Meanwhile, Arthur's youngest sister Ada was recorded in 1911 working as an assistant in a Bournemouth draper's business.

Arthur himself had also left home by 1911 and cannot be found in Winchester. However, there was an Arthur S. Hill, born in Winchester and of the right age (23), boarding at 56, Great College Street, Camden, London. He was single and his occupation was given as a printer. He appears to have remained single as no marriage record can be found for him.

Arthur Hill enlisted (he was probably conscripted) in the district of St Pancras, London, in July 1916 when he was still living in Camden. He was assigned to the 17th (Service) Battalion, The Kings Royal Rifle Corps (KRRC) as a Rifleman, with the service number R/31897. The 17th KRRC had been formed by the British Empire League in 1915 as part of Lord Kitchener's New Armies. It came under the orders of 117th Brigade, itself part of 39th Division. The battalion arrived in France in March 1916 and were in support during the Battle of the Ancre (13-16 November), the final major British assault of the Somme campaign. Arthur probably just missed the battle as he would have had to complete his 13 weeks' basic training before joining his battalion late in 1916.

Although 1917 was a year of bitter fighting on the Western Front with major British offensives at Arras and Messines in the spring and early summer, for 17th KRRC the first six months were relatively quiet. The Regimental Chronicle of 1917 reported that the period prior to the launch of the Third Battle of Ypres (or Passchendaele) on 31 July saw few casualties among the battalion which was based in the Ypres area of Flanders:

HILL, Arthur Samuel

The routine work was fairly dull, but undoubtedly good training for a comparatively young Battalion, and by the end of June we knew all there was to know about trench warfare... [In July] For the first time for many months we left the neighbourhood of Ypres for a few days and carried out special training over a model course at St. Omer. We returned to E Camp (by bus) on July 21st, and on the 28th moved up to our battle front, in the left portion of the Hill Top sector, having two companies in the front line and two in support.

Led by Lieutenant-Colonel A.P.H. Le Prevost, 17th KRRC took part in the Battle of Pilckem Ridge (31 July-2 August 1917), the opening engagement of the Third Ypres campaign. The battalion formed up for the attack in trenches on the extreme left of the 39th Division, by then part of XVIII Corps of the Fifth Army. The Rifles had five objectives with the overall aim of breaking through the German front-line system in their sector. The Regimental Chronicle described the beginning of the assault:

At zero minus 5 minutes, the attack was opened at 3.50am by a deluge of oil drums which made matters remarkably unpleasant in the German's front trenches. This was followed by a terrific barrage of all-calibre guns and the assaulting waves moved forward as the barrage lifted.

The German front-line trench, the first objective, was captured by 4.20am. All the other objectives were also achieved, in the process of which the battalion captured two German officers, 64 other ranks and one machine gun. The 17th KRRC lost one officer and eight men killed, one officer and 60 men wounded and eight missing.

However, it was not until 5 August when the battalion was withdrawn from the front line that the final casualty list was established. At that stage four men were still missing, among them Arthur Hill, who was aged about 29. There are conflicting reports as to how he died with some sources saying he died of wounds. Perhaps his comrades saw him go down wounded but could not stop to give him aid. It did not help that on 2 August the weather turned very wet and it rained continuously for the next three days. According to the Regimental Chronicle '[t]he men had for the most part been knee deep in water and mud' before they were relieved on 5 August. Arthur's body was probably lost in the churned-up battlefield. He was formally reported missing, believed killed in action.

The WWSR of 1921 creates a conundrum with references to two Hills who served in the war. In the Register, Arthur Hill's address is given as 69, Fairfield Road while Stephen R. Hill, who could be Arthur's brother, is listed at No. 67. However, according to the Warren's Directories, there was no Arthur Hill or Stephen Hill based in Fairfield Road before, during or after the war. One possibility is that Arthur had returned from London shortly before the outbreak of war and lodged with Edward Williamson, who lived at 69, Fairfield Road from 1914 until 1920. Perhaps he had then returned to Camden and enlisted from there in 1916? Without an August 1914 Winchester address, Arthur Hill should not have been in the WWSR. It is only the Fairfield Road address that links 'A. S. Hill' on the St Matthew's and St Paul's memorials to the parish and his entitlement to be in the Register.

The Warren's Directory does show an Edward Hill living at 69, Fairfield Road from 1921 until 1923. If he were a relative of Arthur's this would give the WWSR address some credibility as Edward Hill may have wanted his relative commemorated in his local church. However, there is an obvious problem with these two theories: why did the WWSR give Arthur's address as Fairfield Road and not his parent's address in Union Street? As yet, there is no satisfactory answer to this question.

HILL, Arthur Samuel

What of Stephen R. Hill whose name also appears in the WWSR? Was he Arthur's brother? That, too, remains unclear. The Register states that Stephen had already been in the Royal Army Service Corps and re-joined the Army in September 1914 as a Private in the Royal Engineers. He served in France and Italy, rose to be a Corporal and survived the war. Unfortunately, it has not been possible to find a service number or any details of Stephen's military service other than those given in the WWSR. Neither the 1901 nor 1911 Censuses indicate that Stephen Hill served in the forces.

The next mention of the Stephen Hill who definitely was Arthur's brother is in the 1939 Register, when he was living with his wife Jane at 17, Pound Road, now in King's Worthy but then in the Rural District of Winchester. Aged 65, he was working as a plumber's mate. Stephen died in Winchester in June 1949, aged 74.

6, Cranworth Road, Winchester, the home of Arthur Hill's parents, Edwin and Blanche, from 1925 to 1940

Edwin Hill Jnr, Arthur's brother who had gone into the family bootmaking business, seems to have had no interest in remaining in it once his father had retired. The business is believed to have been sold to an R. Jackson in the early 1920s and there are no further E. Hills listed as bootmakers in Warren's Directories after 1923. Edwin Jnr and his wife Margaret had been living at 1, Cranworth Road since 1912 and by 1925 his parents had moved just a few doors away to No. 6. This terraced house still survives with an archway alongside, which in those days led to a workshop area.

In the 1927 Warren's Directory, Edwin Jnr is described as a motor haulage contractor and he used the yard behind his parents' house nearby as a garage until 1938. This is the last mention of Edwin Jnr being a motor haulage contractor and in the 1939 Register he was a taxi driver/owner. By then he was 53 years old and whether the change of career was for health or financial reasons is not known. He retained the garage behind 6, Cranworth Road even after the deaths of his parents in Winchester in 1940, his father at the age of about 88 and his mother at 82. Edwin Jnr himself died in Winchester in 1966, aged 80.

Of Arthur's older sisters, Blanche appears to have remained in Winchester with her husband Albert and she died in the city in 1970. It is not known whether Lily married or not, nor when she died, while Violet died in Ipswich in 1972. Arthur's younger sister Ada was living in Bournemouth when the 1939 Register was drawn up. There is no mention of a husband, but her status is 'married'. Her occupation is given as a demonstrator of a Welgard Cleaner. Perhaps her stay

Arthur Hill's name on the Commonwealth War Graves Commission's original typed list of names for inclusion on the Menin Gate
(Photo: CWGC)

144

HILL, Arthur Samuel

there was only temporary. Her husband died on 11 September in 1966 in Croydon, Surrey. That was in the same quarter of the year that her brother Edwin's death was registered in Winchester. Ada's death was registered in Croydon in 1977. She would have been the last member of her generation to have known Arthur alive.

Medals and memorials for Arthur Samuel Hill

Rifleman Arthur Samuel Hill was entitled to the British War Medal and the Victory Medal. He has no known grave and is commemorated on the Ypres (Menin Gate) Memorial, Belgium (PR. Panel 51 and 53) and in the churchyard of Holy Trinity, on North Walls, Winchester (photos left and above). It is believed that he is the 'A.S. Hill' on the memorials on the memorials at St Matthew's and St Paul's churches, Winchester.

Researchers – GERALDINE BUCHANAN and JOSEPHINE COLEMAN

Additional sources

- The Kings Royal Rifle Chronicle 1917.
- Hare, Major-General Sir Steuart. *The Kings Royal Rifles Annals (Vol. IV).*

HILL, Nicholas Weatherby

Captain NICHOLAS WEATHERBY HILL, M.C.
Butts Close Cottage, Weeke
2nd Battalion, The Oxford and Buckinghamshire Light Infantry
Killed in action, France, 16 January 1917

Nicholas Weatherby Hill was the only son of Henry L.G. Hill, an architect based in Winchester from 1894 to 1917, and his wife, Mary. Nicholas was born in Weeke - then just outside Winchester - on 7 August 1896. The first mention of his father in Winchester is in the Warren's Winchester Directory for 1894 when a Hill is listed living at the Manor Farm House in Weeke, and the Winchester architect B.D. Cancellor was recorded taking on a Mr Hill as a partner. Their offices were in Jewry Street and the partnership lasted until 1910. The Farm House remained Henry Hill's home address until 1898.

Henry had married Mary in about 1895. She had been born in Bayswater, London, in around 1858. Six of her brothers had gone to Winchester College which strongly suggests that she was from a wealthy background. Nicholas, the couple's only child, was born while they were living at the Farm House. By 1899, according to the Warren's Winchester Directory, they were living at 'the Cottage Weeke', later described as Butts Close Cottage. The house was designed by Henry Hill in the Arts and Craft style and it features in the Hampshire volume of Nicholas Pevsner's Buildings of England series. Henry Hill is also mentioned in Pevsner as the architect of the Science School at Winchester College.

Butts Close Cottage was subsequently divided into two with the right wing, formerly the servants' quarters, known as Butts Cottage, while the Hill family's part of the house was called Butts House. In the 1901 and 1911 Censuses, the Hills employed three servants.

In about 1903, at the age of seven, Nicholas went to Horris Hill Preparatory School in Newtown, Hampshire, just south of Newbury. The school had strong connections with Winchester College which it retains today. Nicholas was obviously a very able child as he was placed high up on the roll to attend Winchester College in two successive years, but he elected to take an Exhibition rather than the Scholarship entrance exam. This entitled him to live in a Commoner's House which in his case was Culverlea Boarding House or House G (now Serjeant's and familiarly known as Phil), accessed today from Romans Road.

Nicholas arrived at the College in 1909 and was at his boarding house at the time of the 1911 Census. He displayed a great variety of talents whilst at Winchester. He possessed a strong feeling for art and played the piano with great ability. He displayed his leadership by becoming Senior Commoner and therefore Joint Head of School alongside a Scholar. Had he remained at the College rather than leave early to join the Army then he would almost certainly have been made captain of the cricket team, as he had already played for the First XI in the two summers prior to leaving.

Nicholas won a Classical Scholarship to New College, Oxford, which he was scheduled to take up

HILL, Nicholas Weatherby

in the autumn of 1916. However, in 1915, with the Great War almost a year old, he opted instead to leave Winchester to go to Sandhurst Military College. After completing his officer training there, he was gazetted on 19 October 1915 as 2nd Lieutenant in the 2nd Battalion, The Oxfordshire and Buckinghamshire Light Infantry (OBLI). This had been the old 52nd Regiment, which, on the initiative of John Colborne, a Wykehamist, had attacked the flank of Napoleon's Old Guard at Waterloo in 1815, a turning point of that battle. Was Nicholas inspired by this famous Wykehamist to join his former regiment? (A statue of Sir John Colborne, later Lord Seaton, has stood outside the Rifles Museum in Peninsula Square, Winchester, since the 1990s.)

By October 1915, 2nd Lieutenant Hill was on active service in France. Early in 1916, the 2nd OBLI were moved to the area of Notre Dame de Lorette, north of Arras, to relieve French troops who were required for the defence of Verdun. They then moved south to take part in the Battle of Albert (1-13 July 1916), the opening phase of the Somme Offensive. The battalion was in action again on 30 July, during the second phase of the campaign, attacking from Delville Wood towards Guillemont and Ginchy.

Despite appalling weather and a battlefield turned into a sea of mud, the Somme campaign continued through the autumn of 1916. On 13 November, the 2nd OBLI went over the top once more at the start of the Battle of the Ancre, the final British assault of the campaign. The battalion attacked German trenches north of the village of Beaumont Hamel and suffered heavy losses among officers and men. It is believed that this was the occasion mentioned in the Winchester War Service Register when Nicholas was injured, as well as the action in which he won the Military Cross. The citation for the M.C. in the London Gazette in February 1917 reads:

> *2nd Lt. (Actg. Capt.) Nicholas Weatherby Hill, Oxf. and Buck. L.I. For conspicuous gallantry in action. He assumed command of his company in the attack with marked courage and ability. Later, although wounded, he continued to encourage his men.*

The OBLI won battle honours for their actions at the Battles of Albert, Delville Wood and the Ancre. It is not known whether Nicholas had sufficiently recovered from his wounds to spend Christmas 1916 with his battalion, which had a period of rest and training near the forest of Crecy under something approaching peacetime conditions, or even whether he got home on leave.

Nicholas probably won promotion to Acting Captain because of his bravery at the Battle of the Ancre. In January 1917, the 2nd OBLI, presumably with Nicholas among their number, returned to the scene of the July 1916 Somme fighting, and for many weeks, and under appalling conditions, held a line of posts along the Albert-Bapaume road.

The memorial window to Nicholas Hill in St Matthew's Church, Weeke. It was designed by his father Henry *(Photo: Simon Newman)*

HILL, Nicholas Weatherby

Above left: The brass memorial plaques to Captain Nicholas Hill, left, and the original wooden cross placed on his grave in France. All are now in St Andrew's Church, Donhead, near Salisbury, Wiltshire.
The larger plaque inscription reads:
'To the Glory of God and in Proud and Loving Memory of Nicholas Weatherby Hill MC Cap^{tn} 2nd Batt^{n} Oxford & Bucks Light Inf^{ty} Born at Weeke near Winchester Aug 7 1896 Who fell in Action in the Somme on the night of January 16 1917 and lies in the Military Cemetery at Courcelette France'
Below: A Military Cross which Nicholas was awarded posthumously in February 1917

In his history of the regiment, the 2nd OBLI's Commanding Officer at the time, Lieutenant-Colonel Richard Crosse, said the battalion suffered:

... very severe winter weather with little protection from shell fire and none from the wet and cold, and with only such cooking in the forward posts as was possible with a short allowance of solidified alcohol.

On the night of 16 January 1917 Nicholas Hill was killed by shellfire near the village of Courcelette while making his way to the frontline trenches. Hopefully, his Commanding Officer had told him before his death that he was being put forward for a Military Cross and that Nicholas was then able to let his parents know.

Nicholas's father, Henry, also served in the war. He worked for the War Office in the Directorates of Recruiting and Mobilisation, reaching the rank of Major. He was awarded the O.B.E. for his services.

On Saturday 17 February 1917, a memorial service was held for Nicholas at Winchester Cathedral,

HILL, Nicholas Weatherby

attended by many of the 'Gentlemen of the College'. Given the ethos of the time, he would have been an inspirational figure to them.

By early 1917, Henry and Mary Hill had left Butts Close Cottage in Weeke and moved to Donhead, near Salisbury, where they arranged for a large brass memorial to Nicholas to be erected in the local church. However, they did not forget Nicholas's birthplace and his father designed a memorial window which can still be seen in St Matthew's Church today.

Medals and memorials for Nicholas Weatherby Hill

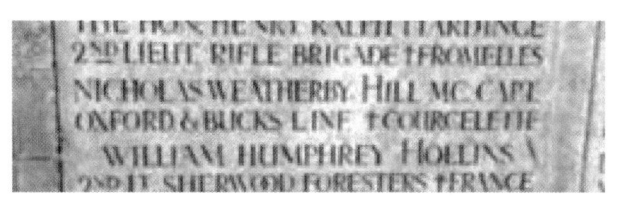

Captain Nicholas Weatherby Hill was entitled to the British War Medal and the Victory Medal. He is buried in Courcelette British Cemetery, Somme, France (GR. I. D. 13). Nicholas is remembered in St Matthew's, Weeke, with a window on the south side dedicated to him and his name is among those in the church's Memorial Book. Nicholas is also listed on the Memorial Boards at St Paul's Church, Fulflood, and Horris Hill School. He is listed on the walls (Outer F1) of Winchester College War Cloister (above) and there is a brass plaque dedicated to him, together with the wooden cross from his initial grave in France, in St Andrew's Church, Donhead, near Salisbury, Wiltshire.

Researchers – GERALDINE BUCHANAN and JOSEPHINE COLEMAN

Additional sources

- Winchester College website: www.winchestercollegeatwar.com/archive/nicholas-weatherby-hill/
- Crosse, R.B. *A Short History of the Oxfordshire and Buckinghamshire Light Infantry, 1741-1922 for the Young Soldiers of the Regiment* (Gale & Polden, 1925).
- The Oxfordshire & Buckinghamshire Light Infantry, The Great War 1914 – 1919, 2nd Battalion (52nd Light Infantry). Website created by Mr. Tobin. https://oxandbuckslightinfantry.weebly.com/1st--2nd-battalions-in-the-great-war.html
- Information from Mr and Mrs Somerville, the current owners of Butts Close.
- Hampshire Observer, 17 February 1917.

HOUNSLOW, George Horace

Gunner GEORGE HORACE HOUNSLOW M.M.
30, Brassey Road, Winchester (was 57 North Hill Terrace)
Service number 24461. 3rd Siege Battery, Royal Garrison Artillery
Died of wounds, France, 5 August 1917

George Horace Hounslow was born in Wareham, Dorset, in 1887, the eldest of the three children of William and Florence Ann Hounslow. The family moved to Winchester in around 1900 and a few years later George joined the Army as a gunner with the Royal Garrison Artillery. During the Great War he fought in France and Flanders and died of his wounds at the start of the Third Battle of Ypres (better known as the Battle of Passchendaele) in August 1917.

George's father William was born in Ashfield, near Romsey, in 1867 to George Hounslow, a painter's labourer, and his wife Jane (née Archer). Jane gave birth to two more children – Harry, in 1871, and Horace George in 1874. (Predictably, there is much confusion between George Horace and his uncle Horace George). In the 1881 Census, the Hounslows were recorded still living in Ashfield. Jane Hounslow died in 1889.

George's mother was born Florence Judd in Starcross, near Exeter, Devon, on 3 November 1859. Her father, Charles, had been born in the village of Winterslow, near Salisbury, and he worked as an agricultural labourer. Her mother Mary was also born in Starcross.

George's parents are thought to have married in Wareham, Dorset, in October 1886. George was born the following year and shortly afterwards the family moved to Wellow, near Romsey, where a second son, Frank, was born on 24 October 1890. (Interestingly, the parents of the pioneering nurse Florence Nightingale lived in Wellow and she was buried in the churchyard there in 1910. It is possible that young George Hounslow knew Florence from her visits to the village.) A daughter, Winifred Florence, was born in Winchester on 4 November 1894.

School records suggest that the Hounslow family spent a short time living in Basingstoke before moving to Winchester. The family were living at 8, St Cross Road in 1900, the same year that George's nine-year-old brother Frank was admitted to St Thomas Church of England Boys' School.

By the 1901 Census, the Hounslows had moved again – to 6, Westgate Lane, Winchester. William, aged 38, was working as a domestic coachman while 13-year-old George, who had left school, was a milk boy, sorting out the bottles for the milkman. Frank and Winifred were both at school.

The 1911 Census records the Hounslows living at 57, North Hill Terrace, Brassey Road, Winchester. William was still working as a coachman with Frank, 20, employed as a house carpenter and 16-year-old Winifred as a milliner's apprentice. George was not with the family; he had enlisted with the Royal Garrison Artillery and was stationed in Portsmouth. His Uncle Horace had served in the same unit. By 1913 57, North Hill Terrace had been renumbered 30, Brassey Road which remains the address today.

George was 27 years old when the Great War broke out in August 1914. At the time, the Royal Garrison Artillery (RGA) largely comprised fortress-based heavy guns located on the British coast. Among these were Fort Nelson and Fort Southwick on Portsdown Hill overlooking the naval base of Portsmouth and this is probably where George was stationed early in his Army career.

The British Army possessed little heavy artillery in 1914, but the demands of trench warfare on the Western Front meant that it quickly grew in importance. The Army eventually acquired huge numbers of heavy guns and howitzers of immense destructive power. These were positioned some way behind

HOUNSLOW, George Horace

the front line. Siege batteries of the RGA were equipped with heavy howitzers, which fired large calibre high explosive shells in a high trajectory. The usual armaments were 6-inch, 8-inch and 9.2-inch howitzers, although some batteries had huge railway or road-mounted 12-inch howitzers. All were capable of firing shells many miles. As British artillery tactics developed, the siege batteries were most often used to destroy or neutralise enemy artillery, as well as putting down destructive fire on strongpoints, supply dumps, stores, roads and railways behind enemy lines.

A heavy artillery battery would typically be made up of five officers and 180 other ranks, more than 100 horses (mainly heavy draught), three two-horse carts and ten four-horse wagons. The battery would normally be teamed with three others under the command of a Siege Brigade.

The 3rd Siege Battery went out to the Western Front on 17 September 1914. However, George's Medal Index Card shows that he did not enter a theatre of war until 20 May 1915, so it is possible that he was not originally part of 3rd Siege Battery.

30, Brassey Road, Winchester – George Hounslow's family home at the outbreak of war in 1914

Sometime during 1916 George was wounded – probably during the Somme Offensive - and awarded the Military Medal. He was wounded again at the Battle of Pilckem Ridge, the opening phase of the Third Ypres campaign (31 July-10 November 1917) and died on 5 August 1917 at 22nd General Hospital in Etaples, northern France. He was 30 years old.

On 8 December 1917, the Army sent George's father William a payment of £24 15s 6d, probably in respect of his son's effects and back pay. William also received a war gratuity of £17 10s on 10 November 1919.

George's family remained in Winchester after the war. In 1920, his brother Frank was registered on the Electoral Roll living with his parents at 30, Brassey Road. George's father William died in Winchester in 1934, aged 77, and his mother Florence in 1943 at the age of 83.

George's sister Winifred married Maurice Brewer in Winchester in 1922. She died in Devizes, Wiltshire, in 1985, aged 90. Brother Frank married Mable Newman in Winchester in 1943, the same year that his mother died. Frank died in Winchester Hospital in 1962, aged 71. He was living at 1, Trussell Crescent, Weeke, at the time of his death.

Medals and memorials for George Horace Hounslow

Gunner George Horace Hounslow was entitled to the 1914-15 Star, the British War Medal and the Victory Medal. He is buried at Etaples Military Cemetery (right), Pas de Calais, France (GR. XXV. L. 4A) with the following inscription on his headstone:
GONE BUT NOT FORGOTTEN.
He is also mentioned on the memorials at St Matthew's and St Paul's churches, Winchester.

Researcher – JENNY WATSON

ILLINGWORTH, Thomas William

Private THOMAS WILLIAM ILLINGWORTH
86, Brassey Road, Winchester
Service number 36708. 10th (Service) Battalion, The Gloucestershire Regiment
Died of wounds, France, 18 November 1916

Thomas Illingworth was born in Hornchurch, Essex, in 1892, the youngest of Henry and Jane Illingworth's seven children. Thomas moved to Winchester shortly before the Great War to work as a dental assistant. He enlisted with the Gloucestershire Regiment in 1915 and died the following year from wounds received while fighting at the Battle of the Somme.

Thomas's father was born in Hoxton, Middlesex, in 1850. His mother was born Jane Bolas in Bethnal Green in London's East End. Besides Thomas, Jane gave birth to three other sons and three daughters. They were: Elizabeth (born 1873); Herbert George, born in south London in 1878; Gwenfrewi (1881); Olivia (1884); Oswald Walter, in Beckenham, Kent, in around 1885; Charles (1887).

Henry Illingworth's earliest listed occupation is bootmaker. In 1881 he and his family were living at the Boot Shop, 183, Old Kent Road, south London. Ten years later they had moved to Tindall Villas, Brentwood Road, Hornchurch, with Henry working as a travelling draper. Thomas was born the following year. The 1901 Census records the Illingworths living 19, Tilia Road, Lower Clapton, Hackney, London. By then Henry was employed as an insurance agent. The elder children were also working - Herbert as a waiter, Gwenfrewi as a dressmaker and Oswald was an errand boy. Thomas and Charles were both at school.

Thomas's father died sometime before 1911. That year's Census showed his widow Jane was still at Tilia Road with Herbert working as a hotel waiter, Oswald as boot and shoe salesman and Thomas as a dental assistant. All the Illingworth daughters had left home, along with son Charles who was a furniture salesman in Walthamstow, east London, where he lived with his wife Nellie and baby son.

The dental profession that Thomas Illingworth worked in was quite unlike that of today. The biggest difference was that most dentists were unqualified. Indeed, it was not until 1921 that dentists were legally required to undergo a period of formal training. In the years before the Great War they increasingly used foot-operated drills which made the process of filling much quicker than previously. For those needing false teeth, the development of vulcanite dentures ensured a far better fit.

Thomas married in Clapton on 3 August 1913. His bride, Constance, was the daughter of pawnbroker Joseph Long and his wife Susan. Constance, known as Connie to family and friends, had been born in Islington, London, in early 1891. On their wedding certificate she and Thomas were recorded living together in Clapton, but within a year the couple had moved to Winchester where Thomas had found work.

The Warren's Winchester Directories of 1914 and 1915 show him as the householder for 86, Brassey Road (the address then and now).

An early 20th Century dentists' chair – this would have been a familiar sight to Thomas Illingworth

ILLINGWORTH, Thomas William

Thomas is thought to have joined the Army as a volunteer in 1915. He enlisted in Winchester with the 10th Battalion, The Gloucestershire Regiment – commonly referred to as The Glosters - and was assigned the service number 36708. The battalion had been raised in Bristol in September 1914 as part of Lord Kitchener's massive expansion of the British Army following the outbreak of war. It was initially attached to 26th Division.

After two periods of training on Salisbury Plain the battalion moved to France in August 1915 where it joined 1st Brigade in 1st Division. Thomas was not with the 10th Glosters at this stage as his Medal Index Card shows that he did not arrive on the Western Front until 1916. The 1st Division was at the forefront of fighting at the Battle of Loos in September and October 1915 and it remained in the Loos sector until early 1916 when Thomas Illingworth joined up with the 10th Glosters.

The 10th Glosters fought several actions during the Somme Offensive. On 23 July, during the Battle of Pozieres, the battalion attacked the German line east of the village and it was involved in two further attacks in the same area in August. Its final action of the Somme campaign came on 9 September in a failed assault on High Wood in which it lost 122 men killed, missing and wounded. Thomas died of wounds near Becourt, close to High Wood, on 18 November 1916. He was 24 years old. He probably received the wounds in the attack of 9 September. The 10th Glosters saw no fighting in 1917 and were disbanded in February 1918.

86, Brassey Road, Winchester – Thomas and Connie Illingworth lived in the house after moving from London in 1913 or 1914

After her husband's death, Connie Illingworth continued to live at 86, Brassey Road until 1921 when her name disappears from the Winchester electoral records. No trace can be found of her after that date. It is not known whether she and Thomas had any children. Connie was probably responsible for her late husband's name appearing on the Fulflood and Weeke church memorials. However, Thomas's name does not figure in the Winchester War Service Register, which is somewhat surprising given that Connie was still living in the city when it was being compiled in the early 1920s.

Oswald Illingworth, Thomas's brother, joined the Royal Army Medical Corps in 1917 at the age of 31. He is believed to have survived the war.

Medals and memorials for Thomas William Illingworth

Private Thomas William Illingworth was entitled to the British War Medal and the Victory Medal and is buried at Becourt Military Cemetery (right), Becordel-Becourt, Somme, France (GR. I.F.14.). His name appears on the memorials at St Matthew's and St Paul's churches, Winchester.

Researcher – JENNY WATSON

INGE, Sidney George

Private SIDNEY GEORGE INGE
Venclyst, 90, Fairfield Road, Winchester
Service number 3818. 2nd Battalion, Lancashire Fusiliers
(Previously 37549, The Royal West Kent Regiment)
Killed in action, France, 3 September 1918

Sidney George Inge was born in late 1885 in Canterbury, Kent, the seventh of the nine children of May and Amelia Inge. Sidney's parents had both been born in Kent in 1845.

According to census records from 1881 and 1891, Sidney's father worked as a grocer in Canterbury, employing two men and a servant. By the 1901 Census, he was still in Canterbury but working as a brick merchant. Meanwhile, Sidney had left school and was employed as an ironmonger's assistant.

May Inge's change of occupation appears to have led him and the family to move to Winchester during the early 1900s because in the 1911 Census they were recorded living at Holbury, 8, Hatherley Road with May listed as a brick maker. Two children had died by this time and three daughters had married. This left Bessie (born 1878), Percy (1884) and Harry (1887) living at home. By 1912 Sidney's brother Percy had moved a few doors along the road and was living at 20, Hatherley Road.

In 1915 May and Amelia moved to Venclyst, 90, Fairfield Road, Winchester, which is the address given for Sidney in the Winchester War Service Register (WWSR).

However, Sidney was not living in Winchester when the Great War broke out; in fact, he was not even in the country. At some point before 1911 (he is not listed in that year's census) he is believed to have emigrated to South Rhodesia. We know this because Commonwealth War Graves Commission (CWGC) records state that he travelled from there to join the Army in England in 1916.

Sidney enlisted at Herne Bay, Kent, on 31 October 1916 but it is not clear which Regiment he joined. According to the WWSR it was the Royal West Surreys, while Soldiers Died in the Great War states that he joined the Queen's Own (Royal West Kent) Regiment. Given Sidney's affiliation with Kent and the fact that he enlisted there, it is more likely to have been the latter.

In early 1918 Sidney transferred to the 2nd Battalion, Lancashire Fusiliers. The British Army disbanded many under-strength battalions at this time, redeploying the troops with other units and this is probably what happened to Sidney's battalion. The 2nd Lancashire Fusiliers, who came under the command of 12th Brigade, part of the Army's 4th Division, fought at the Battle of the Lys (7-29 April 1918) during the German Spring Offensive. They helped to ensure that the Germans did not break through to the strategically important Allied railhead at Hazebrouk in Flanders.

Later that summer, Sidney would have taken part in the Second Battle of the Somme (21 August-2 September 1918), part of the Hundred Days Campaign, in which Allied forces retook most of the territory captured by the Germans in their spring offensives.

90, Fairfield Road, Winchester - Sidney Inge's parents moved here from Hatherley Road in 1915

INGE, Sidney George

On 2 September 1918, the 2nd Lancashire Fusiliers formed part of an assault by the British 4th Division and Canadian 4th Division on the Drocourt-Queant Line, an 11-mile-long German trench system which made up part of the Hindenburg Line. The system incorporated numerous fortifications including concrete bunkers, machine-gun posts and deep belts of barbed wire. It is believed that Sidney was killed on 3 September, the second day of the attack. He was 33 years old.

On 17 November 1919, the Army sent May Inge, Sidney's father, a payment of £19 16s 3d in respect of his son's effects and back pay. A war gratuity of £8 10s was also sent on 19 December 1919. May applied for Sidney's medals in April 1921.

Percy and Harry Inge, Sidney's brothers, both fought in the Great War and survived. Percy went on to marry and his children, Robert James (Jimmy), Eric and Kathleen all became dental surgeons working in City Road, Winchester. Harry Inge married and later became an optician, also working in City Road.

Sidney's father May died in 1925, aged 80, and his mother Amelia the following year, aged 81. Percy Inge passed away in 1957 at the age of 73 and Harry in 1967, aged 80.

Medals and memorials for Sidney George Inge

Private Sidney George Inge was entitled to the British War Medal and the Victory Medal. He was buried (grave pictured right) in Eterpigny British Cemetery, Pas de Calais, France (GR. A. 5). He is mentioned on the memorials at St Matthew's and St Paul's churches, Winchester, and also on the memorial at St Peter Street Methodist Church, Winchester.

Researchers – CHERYL DAVIS, DEREK WHITFIELD and STEVE JARVIS

JACOB, Leslie John

Private LESLIE JOHN JACOB
79, Western Road , Winchester (No. 57 today)
Service numbers 4/3326 and 201125
2/4th Battalion, The Hampshire Regiment (attached 1/4th Battalion)
Died in captivity, Turkey, between October 1916 and 12 February 1918

Leslie John Jacob was born at 9, Elm Road, Fulflood, Winchester, on 3 February 1895, the son of John Henry and Winifred Annie Jacob. In the years before the Great War the Jacobs were a well-known family in Fulflood, with Leslie's parents, grandparents, uncle and cousins all living in the parish. In the summer of 2020, a family link still existed in the person of Leslie Jacob's niece, Christine Vear, who was living at 39, Stockbridge Road. This is the same house in which Leslie's parents lived after the Great War.

John Henry Jacob, Leslie's father, was born in Winchester around 1870 and spent most of his working life as a carpenter. John Henry came from a thriving working-class background. His father, John Wise Jacob, born in Tichborne, near Alresford, in 1849, owned his own building company and in 1871 he had seven men and one boy working for him. The census of the same year showed John Wise and his family living at 20, Clifton Road, Winchester, where they employed one servant.

John Wise Jacob's wife, Sarah, was born in Wimborne, Dorset, around 1849. The couple had three other children besides John Henry - Eva, born in 1873, William (1877) and Arthur (1883). By 1881 the family had moved to 40, Weeke Terrace, Winchester, with John Wise working as a carpenter employing one man and two boys. By 1891 the Jacobs were living at 27, Lower Stockbridge Road, Winchester. On that year's Census John Wise was listed as a builder while his son John Henry was working as a carpenter and William as an apprentice. Eva was a dressmaker.

John Leslie Jacob's mother was born Winifred Annie Andrews in Winchester on 18 January 1871. Her father, Jacob Andrews, had been born in Leckford, near Stockbridge, on 10 February 1842. He spent most of his life working as a tenant farmer across the county. On 5 April 1862 Jacob married Emily Eades, who had been born on 13 March 1842 in Hazeley Heath, near Hook, Hampshire. Winifred was one of 11 children, all of whom survived into early adulthood and beyond.

JACOB, Leslie John

Left: 9, Elm Road, Fulflood - Leslie Jacob was born here on 3 February 1895

Right: 57, Western Road, Fulflood, where Leslie Jacob lived in 1914 (when it was No. 79)

John Henry Jacob and Winifred Andrews married in Botley, near Southampton, on 7 August 1893. By 1895 the couple had moved to Fulflood, living first at 5, Fairfield Terrace (which became 25, Fairfield Road when the street was renumbered around this time) and then 9, Elm Road, the house where Leslie was born. By 1901, the Jacobs had moved a short distance to 79, Western Road. The house became No. 57 when the street was renumbered after the war, which explains the discrepancy in addresses between the Warren's Directory of 1914 and the Winchester War Service Register (WWSR) published in 1921.

On 11 December 1902 Winifred gave birth to a daughter, Winifred Marjorie, who was usually known by her middle name, presumably to distinguish her from her mother. According to Marjorie's daughter, Christine Vear, her mother attended Western Primary School in Elm Road. It is likely that Leslie was also a pupil there. He is then believed to have moved on to St Thomas Higher National Church of England Boys' School – the school records list an L. Jacob as being a pupil there.

The extended Jacob family would have been familiar faces in Fulflood. In 1911, Leslie, by then working as a dentist's assistant, and his parents and sister were still at 79, Western Road. Meanwhile, his grandparents lived at 57, Lower Stockbridge Road with their daughter Eva, then aged 38 and married with a 12-year-old daughter, Audrey Eva. William Jacob, Leslie's uncle, was living with his wife Ada and their two children at 41, Lower Stockbridge Road.

Leslie's mother Winifred played an active role in the local community. At the turn of the 20th Century she helped to start the Salvation Army movement in Winchester and was for many years in charge of its Sunday School. During the Great War, when large numbers of troops were billeted in the city and great concern was being expressed in some circles about the moral welfare of women, Winifred joined the voluntary force of women who patrolled Winchester offering help and advice. Leading on from this, she became an important figure in the establishment of the Winchester Women Citizens' Association.

Leslie Jacob enlisted as a volunteer with the 4th Battalion, The Hampshire Regiment in September 1914, one month after the start of the Great War. Although several records place him with the 1/4th Battalion it appears that he was originally assigned to the 2/4th Battalion before later joining the 1/4th. The 2/4th Hampshires sailed for India in December 1914, arriving in Bombay the following month. From here

JACOB, Leslie John

they moved to the British Army base at Quetta (in modern Pakistan) where the men spent the following months training and acclimatising.

In October 1915 Leslie Jacob was one of 250 men of the 2/4th Battalion sent as drafts to the 1/4th Battalion in Mesopotamia. Leslie's move to the 1/4th Battalion is confirmed both by his Medal Index Card, which shows him entering the Asiatic theatre of war (Mesopotamia) on 25 October 1915, and by the Prisoner of War Comforts Fund records of Mrs Esme Bowker which state that Leslie was '2/4th attached to the 1/4th'.

Leslie Jacob with his father John, mother Winifred and sister Marjorie. The photograph is believed to have been taken in around 1910 in the garden of the family's home at 79, Western Road, Winchester (No.57 today)
(Photo: Christine Vear)

Once in Mesopotamia, Leslie Jacob is believed to have been assigned to 'A' Company of the 1/4th Battalion which, just over a month later, found itself trapped inside the British garrison at Kut-al-Amara by a besieging Turkish force. When the British surrendered the garrison on 29 April 1916 Leslie was not initially among the thousands of British and Indian troops marched off into captivity in Turkey. According to Regimental Sergeant Major William Leach, a fellow prisoner, Leslie stayed behind at Kut as a guard at the hospital which housed those men too sick to travel. However, he must have subsequently re-joined his comrades because, according to Mrs Bowker, by 4 October 1916 he was incarcerated at Baghdadbau II PoW Camp, Entilli, Turkey.

Under the headline 'Casualties Among Local Men', the Hampshire Regimental Journal of September 1917 states:

> Pte L.J Jacob - Mrs J. Jacob, 79, Western Road, Winchester, has received official information that Pte L. J. Jacob, 3326 Hampshire Regiment, is a prisoner of war at Entilli, Turkey.

Prisoners of war at Entilli, in the Amanus Mountains, were used as forced labour in the building of the Baghdad Railway. The camp was under the control of a German construction company, but conditions were nevertheless extremely harsh with only those prisoners fit enough to work provided with food. Mrs Bowker's records of July 1916 provide some interesting details about Leslie Jacob. He was a tall man for the time, 6ft 1ins, with size nine boots and a 7⅛ cap. As a PoW, he was adopted by Mr Lionel Dugdale of Crathorne Hall Farm, Yarm, Yorkshire, who sent him parcels of clothing and blankets in October and November 1916.

Whether or not Leslie was still alive to receive the parcels is not known because the precise date of his death is unknown. According to the WWSR it was in September 1916 but given that Mrs Bowker placed him at Entilli in October this seems unlikely. Both the CWGC and SDGW state that he died on 12

JACOB, Leslie John

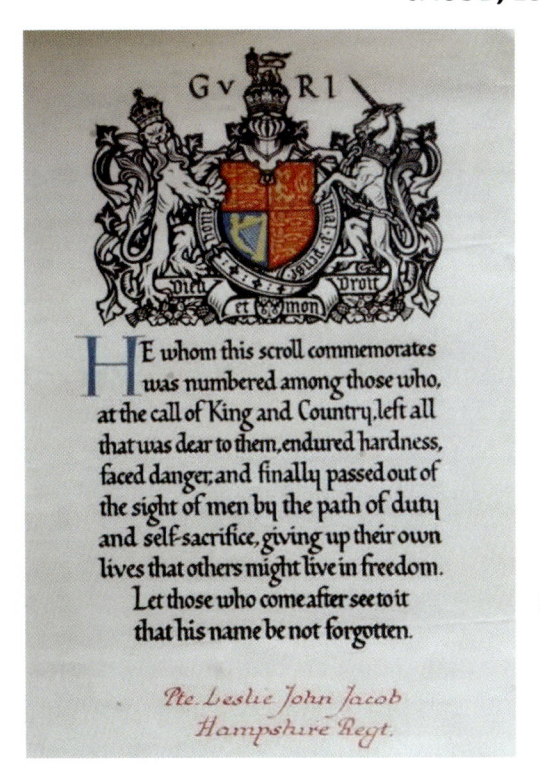

Above: The Great War Memorial Plaque inscribed with Leslie Jacob's name which belonged to his parents. **Left:** The Great War Memorial Scroll, which also bears his name and regiment.
(Photographs by kind permission of Christine Vear)

February 1918, but the fact is we do not know for certain. The most we can say is that Leslie died in captivity sometime between October 1916 and 12 February 1918.

After the war Leslie's parents moved to 39, Stockbridge Road and later to the house next door, No. 41. His father John died at Park House Nursing Home, Winchester, in October 1937, aged 67. Winifred, his mother, died in March 1955, aged 84. The couple are buried together at West Hill Cemetery, Winchester.

Leslie Jacob's sister Marjorie married Arthur Vear in Winchester on 23 August 1924. Arthur had served overseas with the Rifle Brigade during the Great War. In 1959 he was awarded the MBE for his services with the Royal Observer Corps in Winchester during the Second World War. Arthur and Marjorie had two daughters: Mavis, born in September 1929, and Christine, on 28 November 1935. The family were living at 39, Stockbridge Road – Marjorie's parents' old house – in 1939. Arthur, who worked as a local government accountant, died in 1973, aged 74.

Leslie's uncle William lived at 43, Stockbridge Road in the 1930s meaning that, for a time, members of the Jacob family occupied three successive properties. William died in Winchester in June 1954, aged 77, and Leslie's aunt Eva in March 1956 at the age of 83. Eva's daughter Audrey died in Winchester in July 1986, aged 87.

Medals and memorials for Leslie John Jacob

Private Leslie John Jacob was entitled to the 1914-15 Star (right), the British War Medal and the Victory Medal. In 1927 his body was among hundreds exhumed from PoW graves across Turkey and reburied in the CWGC Baghdad (North Gate) War Cemetery, Iraq (GR. XXI. P. 7). He is mentioned on the memorials at St Matthew's and St Paul's churches, Winchester.

Researcher – DEREK WHITFIELD

Additional sources
- Interview with Christine Vear, niece of Leslie Jacob.

JOHNSON, Archibald Leonard

Petty Officer Motor Mechanic ARCHIBALD LEONARD JOHNSON
11, Newburgh Street, Winchester
Service number F/1996. 18 Squadron, Armoured Car Division (Russia),
Royal Naval Air Service
Died of disease, Russia, 17 or 18 July 1916

Archibald Leonard Johnson was born in Petersfield, Hampshire, on 15 May 1889. Details of his early life, and those of his parents, are at times confusing and contradictory, but he appears to have moved to Winchester in the early 1900s. Known as Archie to family and friends, he worked as a cycle agent before the Great War. In November 1914 he enlisted as a mechanic with the Royal Naval Air Service (RNAS) and served in an armoured car squadron. He spent a short time on the Western Front before joining the Armoured Car Expeditionary Force (ACEF) which was sent to Russia at the end of 1915. He died of food poisoning in southern Russia in July 1916 before the ACEF fired a shot in anger.

Archie was the son of Nathaniel Luther and Alice Sarah Johnson. Nathaniel's parents, William (1828-1885) and Fanny Johnson, had married in 1852. William, who had been born in London, worked as a tailor. Fanny died in 1855, two years after giving birth to Nathaniel in Portsmouth. In 1856 William Johnson remarried, his second wife being Sarah (nee Moss), and the couple went on to have four children together.

The 1861 Census recorded William and Sarah Johnson living in Portsmouth with their first two children. Nathaniel, however, was not with them. Instead, he was listed living at a different Portsmouth address with shipwright Hiram Mildred and his family. Hiram is thought to have been Nathaniel's uncle.

By 1871, Nathaniel, then aged 17, was still living with Hiram and working as a carpenter. Nathaniel clearly had an aptitude for business because by 1881, when still only 28, he had his own building firm which employed 60 workers. He was also able to join the Freemasons. In the summer of 1881, he married 24-year-old Alice Sarah Drew, the daughter of a dockyard worker, in her hometown of Portsmouth. The couple's first child, Ernest, Archie's older brother, was born in Portsmouth on 11 November 1883.

However, in the years before Archie was born, something happened in Nathaniel's life which led to him being excluded from the Freemasons. Whether he had been made bankrupt or involved in a scandal is not known, but the apparent result was that he left the building trade and by 1891 was working as an assistant superintendent for an assurance company.

That year's census recorded a 'Nath. L. Johnson' living in Station Road, Petersfield, with his wife Alice T. (not Alice S). To further muddy the waters, this 'Nath' gave his birthplace as Stepney, London, not Portsmouth as on the previous census listings for Nathaniel Johnson. However, the evidence suggests that 'Nath' and Nathaniel are the same person. All the family's names, initials, ages and birthplaces are correct, apart from Alice's middle initial and Nathaniel's place of birth. Another clue is Archie Johnson's birth in 1889. This was registered in Petersfield which, of course, is where the Johnsons were recorded living in the 1891 Census.

At some point over the next four years Archie Johnson's family moved to Twyford, near Winchester, and it was there that Alice gave birth to a daughter, Florence Dorothy, on 9 March 1895.

The 1901 Census failed to restore complete consistency to the information about the Johnsons. The entry for the family showed that Nathaniel, aged 47, was living with his wife and three children in Park Lane, Twyford, and had returned to his original trade of carpenter and joiner. However, he no

JOHNSON, Archibald Leonard

longer had his own business but was working as an employee. His wife was correctly listed as having been born in Portsmouth, but her name had changed from Alice to Annie and her age had increased by two years. Meanwhile, although Archie, Ernest and Florence had the correct names and ages, Archie's birthplace was put down as Portsmouth, not Petersfield. Census inconsistencies were certainly not uncommon in this period, but the number in the case of Nathaniel Johnson and his family are unusual. The reason, however, remains unclear.

Nathaniel died in 1905, aged 52, with his death registered in Winchester. By the time of the 1911 Census his widow Alice - not Annie as in 1901 - had moved to Winchester where she and her grown-up children were living at 11, Newburgh Street. (The property, next to Newburgh House, still stands.) Ernest, the elder son, was 27 years old and working as a carpenter like his father. No occupation was given for Florence, 16, but 21-year-old Archie was a self-employed cycle agent – in effect a bike mechanic.

Archie Johnson was 25 and still unmarried when war broke out in August 1914. Three months later, on 12 November, he volunteered for military service as a Petty Officer Air Mechanic with the RNAS and was assigned the service number F/1996. Archie's Navy record card provides some interesting personal details – he was just under 5ft 10ins tall with a 33ins chest, brown hair, grey eyes and a fresh complexion. In the 'Character and Ability' section he was twice rated V.G. (Very Good) for character and Sat. (Satisfactory) once for ability. He enlisted for the duration of the war.

The RNAS was the air arm of the Royal Navy and came into being because of the inter-service rivalry between the Navy and the Army. When the Royal Flying Corps (RFC) had been established under Army control in 1912 it was intended to encompass all military flying. However, the Navy was not willing to cede control over all forms of naval aviation and soon formed its own, unauthorised, flying branch. In July 1914, the RNAS was officially recognised by First Lord of the Admiralty, Winston Churchill. It was separate from the Royal Flying Corps and became in effect a rival air force. Ultimately, it would merge with the RFC in 1918 to form the Royal Air Force (RAF).

When war broke out in 1914, the RNAS sent a squadron under Commander Charles Samson to the Continent to support Allied ground forces. However, with too few aircraft at his disposal, Samson sent his men to patrol the French and Belgian countryside in the privately owned cars that some of them had taken to war. Samson had two RNAS vehicles, a Rolls-Royce and a Mercedes, fitted with armour plate and a single machine-gun. Within a month most of the cars had been armed and armoured and these were soon joined by others which had been armoured at Navy workshops.

The success of Samson's forces in reconnaissance missions and rescuing downed pilots so impressed Churchill that in September 1914 he established the Royal Naval Armoured Car Division (RNACD). However, with the loss of Antwerp the following month the armoured cars were withdrawn to England and reorganised. During the winter of 1914-15 they were deployed to East Anglia as part of the anti-invasion force before returning to France in March. Shortly afterwards one squadron was sent to South West Africa and two squadrons to Gallipoli.

The RNACD eventually boasted 20 squadrons. Its vehicles, mainly Lanchesters and Rolls Royces, were commandeered from across the country and then strengthened to carry armour plate and a revolving machine-gun turret. Heavier cars carried a three-pounder gun to deal with enemy strongpoints. Each squadron consisted of three sections of four armoured cars plus a heavy section. There was also a support section of lorries, a motor ambulance; a wireless vehicle and a mobile workshop which is where Archie Johnson would presumably work.

JOHNSON, Archibald Leonard

Above: An early RNAS Lanchester armoured car, complete with revolving machine-gun turret. As a mechanic, Archie Johnson would have been responsible for servicing and maintaining vehicles such as this

Left: 11, Newburgh Street, Winchester, where Archie was living with his family when he enlisted with the Royal Naval Air Service in November 1914

The cost of forming armoured car squadrons was relatively high so the Admiralty accepted officers from wealthy individuals who offered to pay for them. Two such men were the Duke of Westminster and Oliver Locker-Lampson, the latter being commissioned as a Lieutenant Commander and his unit designated No.15 Squadron.

Obtaining sufficient personnel for the RNACD posed problems as motoring was still relatively new. Only the well-off could afford cars, few men could drive and even fewer could maintain them.

Officers and men of the ACEF in Vladikavkas, southern Russia, in August 1916. Archie had died there the previous month. Oliver Locker-Lampson, Commander of the ACEF, is seated second left and Ted Lockie is standing on the far right *(Photo: Rushden Research)*

For the relatively small numbers of men in these categories the Navy was in competition with the Army, which needed men with the same skills for its Service Corps. While drivers could be trained easily, skilled mechanics could not, and so suitably qualified men were recruited with the rank of Petty Officer Mechanic and the appropriate level of pay - £3 a week. This is the rank that Archie was given when he enlisted.

JOHNSON, Archibald Leonard

Like all military recruits, Archie underwent a period of training after joining up. His service records (right) show that he was posted to two ships – HMS Pembroke III, from 12 November 1914 to 31 March 1915, and HMS President II, from 1 April 1915 until his death the following year.

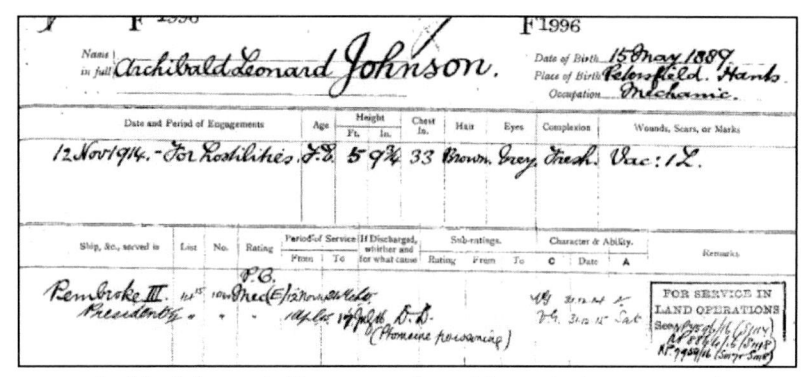

Archie Johnson's Navy record card *(www.findmypast.co.uk)*

These 'ships' were not actual vessels but shore establishments which the Navy used for training and administrative purposes. However, while HMS Pembroke II was a well-known RNAS training base on the Isle of Sheppey, Kent, during the Great War, no record can be found of an HMS Pembroke III in this period. HMS President II, which has been traced, was a Navy accounting base, located variously at Chatham, Crystal Palace, Chingford and Shrewsbury. During his training Archie would have learned how to service, maintain and repair armoured cars. Although he had been a bicycle mechanic in civilian life, working on engines was far more complex, but the character reports on his military records suggest that he rose to the challenge.

After completing his training, Archie was assigned to 18 Squadron RNACD and posted to the Western Front in 1915 – his entry in the Winchester War Service Register (WWSR) states that he served in Belgium as well as Russia. By this time, however, the increasingly static nature of trench warfare greatly inhibited the use of armoured cars on the Continent. The Admiralty also began to question why it was involved in what was clearly not a naval function and so in mid-1915 most of the squadrons were transferred to the Army.

However, in the autumn of 1915, with Britain keen to bolster the faltering Russian war effort on the Eastern Front against Germany and the Austro-Hungarian Empire, the Admiralty agreed to send a Division (three squadrons) of its remaining armoured cars to Russia where operational conditions for the vehicles were more favourable.

The new Division was placed under the command of Oliver Locker-Lampson who had lobbied strongly for an armoured car force to be sent to the Eastern Front. It was created around the nucleus of his 15 Squadron and the detachment of 17 Squadron heavies which was then serving with it. The unit's active service strength was 32 officers and 372 men plus 21 officers and 83 men at base in England. Additional personnel to complete the complement came from volunteers from the disbanded squadrons. It is likely that these volunteers included Archie Johnson.

Six weeks were needed to equip the force with Lanchester cars and winter clothing, followed by a short spell of leave, during which time Archie Johnson no doubt visited his family in Winchester. Then, on 3 December 1915 and buoyed by messages of goodwill from King George V and Rudyard Kipling, the Division, now called the Armoured Car Expeditionary Force, sailed from Liverpool aboard SS Umona for the Russian port of Archangel. (The expedition had to use the northern route via the Arctic Ocean because the southern access to Russia through the Black Sea had been blockaded by the Turks.) In the hold were 45 cars, 15 lorries and 50 motorcycles. Conditions for the men were cramped: in peacetime the liner had accommodation for only 75 crew and 58 passengers. On 5 December, Umona ran into a storm that nearly sank her. Petty Officer Ted Lockie, who was serving with the ACEF, described the conditions on board:

> *We lost a couple of lifeboats and several temporary buildings on the well decks [were] smashed to splinters by the tremendous seas that broke over us ... The situation became critical; over 500 men, including experienced sailors, were sick as horses. The Captain never*

JOHNSON, Archibald Leonard

left the bridge for over 24 hours, and at one time the ship listed to port so far that it was feared she would capsize ... The sanitary conditions were bad, the water froze, and the ship was covered in snow and ice...

Umona was blown 150 miles off course in the storm. The hold in which the men were sleeping filled with 18ins of water so that clothes and mess utensils floated about. Three days later the storm blew itself out, but life aboard the battered ship remained grim. Below deck, in stinking conditions, the men were allowed no heat or cigarettes for fear of igniting the ammunition stored beneath them.

Ten days out from Liverpool, having rounded the Northern Cape of Norway, Umona anchored in Ukansky Bay to make urgent repairs. The expedition very nearly ended here. By then the White Sea was frozen, closing the route to Archangel and the expedition received orders to return home. However, Locker-Lampson connived with the senior medical officer to persuade the Admiralty that a pneumonia epidemic was likely unless they could get the men ashore. The ploy succeeded and Umona was allowed to proceed to the ice-free port of Alexandrovsk (later Murmansk), which it reached on Christmas Day.

The men went ashore to be billeted among the Laplanders. Rations were augmented with black bread and reindeer meat, which Ted Lockie found 'bitter and unpalatable'. The men kept fit with training sessions and helping to develop their base. However, the storm at sea had damaged many armoured cars, so these, together with the repair staff – including, presumably, Archie Johnson - and the sick, were brought home.

Umona reached Newport in South Wales, the Division's home base and workshop, on 26 February 1916. A week was needed to unload the ship and discharge patients before the men were allowed home on leave. If Archie was indeed among the men sent home, then this would be the last time that his family would ever see him.

In May 1916, Umona, with the repaired armoured cars and Archie Johnson and the other mechanics on board, sailed for Alexandrovsk once more. The spring thaw allowed them to reach Archangel uninterrupted, and on 30 May they came ashore to a rousing welcome from their colleagues who had remained in Russia. (These men had earlier made their way to Archangel independently on another ship.) Two days later the day the ACEF entrained for Moscow.

The journey south, aboard primitive rolling stock, took almost five days. The Russian authorities used the journey as a public relations exercise and no opportunity was missed en route to fête the unit, deliver speeches, and present them with gifts. One officer recalled this as 'more of a nuisance than a pleasure' as it meant sleeping fully clothed and being frequently woken in the middle of the night. In Moscow, the British were received by the Grand Duchess Elizabeth, sister of the Tsarina.

Another member of the expedition, Tom Garner, who knew Archie Johnson, kept a diary of his time in Russia. The entries for the period spent in Moscow state:

6 June 1916 *Go into city. Everybody looking at us. Cannot stand still as a huge crowd gathers round us and [people] feel our clothes. Terribly hot. Meet two people who speak English and go home with them.*

7 June 1916 *See our friends again and go shopping. Visit a music shop where the 'Old Boy' plays all the English tunes he has on the pianola and gramophone and we have to sing Tipperary. Go to a nice cafe for dinner and in the afternoon see the Kremlin, Big Bell Czar's Chapel, Ball Room, Throne, etc.*

8 June 1916 *March through the city to the English Church with the band leading us and Cossacks each side. Flags out and people cheering as we pass along. Terribly hot, fellows dropping out as we go. Have a service in the church and then march back to the station.*

JOHNSON, Archibald Leonard

Tom Garner's map showing the route taken by the Armoured Car Expeditionary Force to Russia on SS Umona in December 1915. The port of Alexandrovsk (later Murmansk) is marked with a cross
(Olney & District Historical Society)

On 10 June, the ACEF, now under the command of the Russian Army, left Moscow by train for Vladikavkaz (then spelt Vladikavkas), some 1,100 miles south in the foothills of the Caucasus Mountains. (Today, Vladikavkas is the capital of the Russian Republic of North Ossetia-Alania.) Tom Garner's diary tells the story of the journey, of the sickness that struck the party, and of Archie Johnson's death:

12 June 1916 *Very nice country. Heaps of flies and mosquitos. Have a swim in the [River] Don. One of our fellows drowned. Arrive at Rostov [670 miles south of Moscow]. Grand reception. Lovely town and people. March through the streets strewn with roses to open air gardens. Have a swell feed which was provided by the people of the town. Sit in open air theatre and hear ladies sing and see a lot of Cossack dances. Given cigarettes and march back to train loaded with flowers.*

14 June 1916 *Arrive at Vladikavkas in the Caucasus [430 miles south of Rostov] where a Cossack band leads the procession to the Kardetski Korpus, a fine boarding college for officers, 5 miles away. [The Division was comfortably quartered in the Patriotic Warrior of 1812 Officer Training College.] Have a good wash and then get on the trams which were decorated for the occasion and are taken to the Banqueting Hall. After leaving that and feeling happy and contented go into the park and on the lake in boats.*

15 June 1916 *Sleep in sheets for the first time since leaving England.*

16 June 1916 *Review by a Russian General. Very hot. Can see Mount Kazbek in the distance with snow on its peaks.*

18 June 1916 *Terribly hot, nearly everyone sick. Hospital full up with dysentery cases.*

23 June 1916 *Bendixen dies of dysentery. [Petty Officer Mechanic C.C. Bendixen, who, like Archie Johnson, was buried in Vladikavkaz Hospital Cemetery.]*

25 June 1916 *Funeral, I am one of the firing party.*

JOHNSON, Archibald Leonard

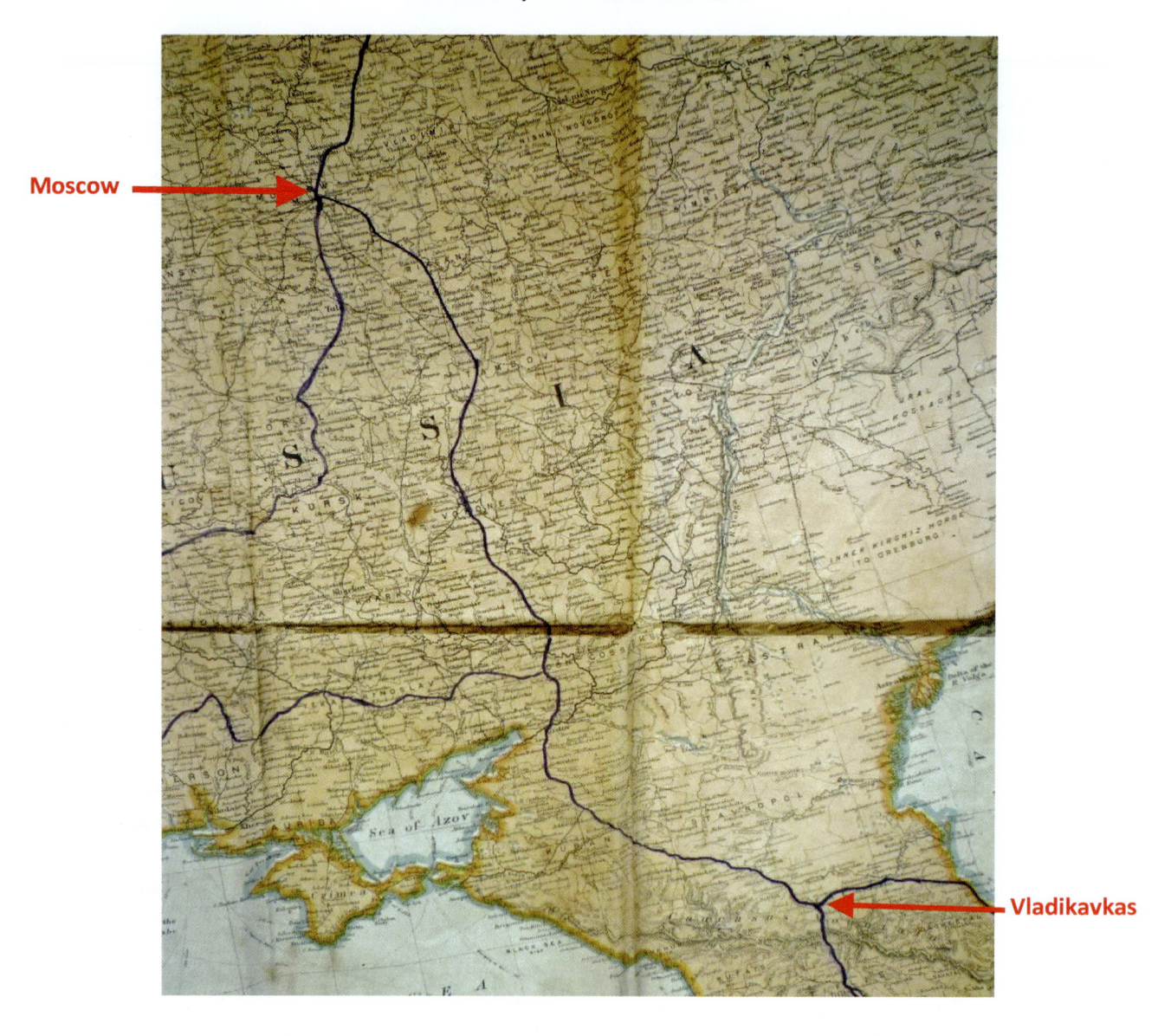

Tom Garner's map showing the route taken by the ACEF from Moscow to Vladikavkas where Archie Johnson died in July 1916. The other routes trace the subsequent progress of the ACEF until it left Russia following the Bolshevik Revolution of October 1917
(Olney & District Historical Society)

27 June 1916 *Go for a route march in our shirts and shorts.*

8 July 1916 *Go for another route march and sleep out the night.*

9 July 1916 *Our fellows give a concert in the theatre for Red Cross.*

10 July 1916 *In hospital. On low diet. Breakfast, two cups of che [tea]. Dinner, one plate of soup. Tea, egg and milk.*

14 July 1916 *Mail arrives, great excitement.*

17 July 1916 *Out of hospital. Sea Base Arrive. Firing practice with 3 PR [pounder]. Johnson dies.*

According to Tom Garner, Archie died on 17 July 1916. His Navy records give the same date but other sources state 18 July. His death in Vladikavkaz Hospital aged 27 was due to ptomaine poisoning caused by bacteria in tinned food. Although he had been with the ACEF for seven months, Archie never saw action. (Following Archie's death, the ACEF operated in Asia Minor, Romania, Austria and Russia itself, fighting against Turks, Kurds, Bulgarians, Germans and Austrians. The men served with Cossacks and Siberian Army Regiments. Once back in England, many of the men transferred to the Motor Machine Gun Corps and were sent out to Baku on the Caspian Sea under General Lionel Dunsterville to defend the oilfields there.)

JOHNSON, Archibald Leonard

Archie's mother Alice continued to live at 11, Newburgh Street after the Great War. Her daughter Florence was also living in the house in 1939 together with her husband Joseph Hayter, who she had married in Winchester ten years earlier. Alice died in 1947, aged 90, and was buried in Magdalen Hill Cemetery. Joseph, who ran a dry stores business, died in 1951. Florence, who is not believed to have had any children, was still at 11, Newburgh Street when she died in 1982, aged 87. She was buried in the same plot as her mother (and presumably her father and husband).

It is not known whether Archie Johnson's brother Ernest served in the Great War. Ernest had married Maud De La Saux Simmonds in London in 1914. Maud had been born on Jersey in 1883 and worked as a dressmaker before marrying. She and Ernest had a daughter, Muriel, who was born in Camberwell, London, in 1915. The family remained in Camberwell and in 1939 Ernest was working there as a builder and decorator. Maud Johnson died in 1951 and Ernest four years later. Muriel, who married in Camberwell in 1954, died in 1990.

Medals and memorials for Archibald Leonard Johnson

Petty Officer Motor Mechanic Archibald Leonard Johnson was entitled to the 1914-15 Star, the British War Medal and the Victory Medal. He was buried at Vladikavkaz Hospital Cemetery, Vladikavkaz, Beslan, South Ossetia-Alania, Russian Federation. After the war, the CWGC planned to erect a headstone stating that Archibald Johnson was 'buried near this spot', but as relations with the Soviet Union deteriorated the Commission felt that any grave was unlikely to be maintained. For this reason, Archie is commemorated on the Haidar Pasha Memorial (Panel 12) in Istanbul, Turkey, along with other servicemen whose graves could no longer be maintained in the southern parts of the former Russian empire (see below). His name also appears on the church memorials at St Paul's and St Matthew's churches, Winchester.

CWGC document showing the addition of names to the Haidar Pasha Memorial.
Archie Johnson's name is in column four

Researchers – GERALDINE BUCHANAN, DEREK WHITFIELD
and JOSEPHINE COLEMAN

Additional sources

- Rushden Research. *Wm 'Ted' Lockie's War Service*. Researched by Derek Savory, 1997-8.
  https://www.rushdenheritage.co.uk/war/lockieWm-serviceWWI.html
- Olney & District Historical Society. *Tom Garner's First World War Diary*.
  http://www.mkheritage.org.uk/odhs/tom-garners-first-world-war-diary-preface/
- Alston, Charlotte. *Encounters on the Eastern Front: The Royal Naval Armoured Car Division in Russia 1915-1920*. (War in History, 25 (4). pp. 485-510.)
  Accessed via http://nrl.northumbria.ac.uk/32425/1/Armoured%20Cars%20WIH.pdf

KETLEY, Charles Walter

Corporal CHARLES WALTER KETLEY M.M.
72, Brassey Road, Winchester.
Service number 42855. 15th Signal Company, Royal Engineers
Killed in action, France, 11 April 1917

Charles Walter Ketley was born in 1896 in Beckenham, Kent, the only child of Frederick and Annie Ketley. Charles did not have close links with Winchester: his parents moved to the city in 1914, shortly after war was declared, and moved away again when hostilities ended in 1918. However, his parents ensured that his name appeared on the memorials at St Matthew's and St Paul's and in the Winchester War Service Register.

Frederick Ketley, Charles's father, had been born in Langford, Essex, in 1858, the son of Charles Snr, an agricultural labourer and later pork butcher, and his wife Mary Ann. In 1871 the family were living in Maldon, Essex, where Frederick worked as a gardener.

In 1880 Frederick married Annie Springett in Maldon. Annie had been born in Great Totham, Essex, in 1862. The newly-weds were living in Maldon in 1881 with Frederick working as a carman.

By the 1891 Census, Frederick and Annie had moved to Beckenham, the birthplace of Frederick's mother, Mary Ann. Frederick had become a colporteur (a peddler, especially of religious tracts and books). After apparently being childless for some time, Annie gave birth to Charles Walter in 1896. The family had one servant and Annie's sister living with them.

In 1901 the family were living at 10, Blakeney Avenue, Beckenham, together with Annie's brother. By 1911 Frederick Ketley had become a Congregational Church minister and the family were living at the Manse, Tolleshunt D`Arcy, Essex. Charles Walter, by then aged 15, was employed as a butcher's assistant.

In late 1914 Frederick and Annie moved to 72, Brassey Road, Winchester. The reason for their move is unclear, but it could possibly have been connected to Frederick's religious duties during the Great War.

Charles enlisted in the Royal Engineers in London in September 1914 and arrived in France on 8 July 1915. He served as a signaller. At battalion level this meant passing communications between the battalion commander and his various company and platoon officers. With the limited technology available at the time this would have involved being a runner and carrying messages by hand. It was dangerous work and the life expectancy of a runner was short.

In September 1915, Charles was gassed but he recovered. He rose to become a Corporal, possibly for the action where he won his Military Medal. The award is listed in the London Gazette (supplement 29794, page 10219) of 21 October 1916.

On 9 April 1917, Charles took part in the First Battle of the Scarpe. The battle, together with the action at Vimy Ridge, opened the Arras Offensive which saw the British and Canadians make impressive early gains. The village of Feuchy was captured in the first phase of the battle by troops of the British Third Army who advanced more than three miles in places, the furthest by the Allies on the Western Front up to that date.

Charles was killed in action at Feuchy on 11 April 1917, two days after the start of the Arras Offensive. He was around 20 years old.

KETLEY, Charles Walter

After the war Frederick Ketley received an Army pension in respect of his son. His address on the military pension records in 1918 was the Sailors Rest Home, Meadow Street, Avonmouth, near Bristol. At some point Frederick returned to Essex, together with Charles's mother Annie. A later pension record gives his address as Park View, Tiptree Road, Great Totham, Essex, which is the village where Annie Ketley had been born. Frederick Ketley died in Maldon in 1938, aged about 80, and Annie in 1944 at the age of 82.

Medals and memorials for Charles Walter Ketley

Corporal Charles Walter Ketley was entitled to the 1914-15 Star, the British War Medal and the Victory Medal. He is buried in Feuchy Chapel British Cemetery (above), Wancourt, Pas de Calais, France, and is mentioned on the memorials at St Matthew's and St Paul's churches.

Researchers – STEVE JARVIS and CHERYL DAVIS

LAWRANCE, Ernest Albert

Private ERNEST ALBERT LAWRANCE
56/86 Lower Stockbridge Road, Winchester (now 15, Stockbridge Road) and 25, Greenhill Road
Service numbers 5091 and 33643. 2/5th Battalion, The Gloucestershire Regiment and 1st Battalion, The Devonshire Regiment
Killed in action, France, 22 April 1918

Ernest Albert Lawrance was born on 10 August 1884 in Winchester. He was the fifth child of gardener Charles Lanham Lawrance, who was born in Romsey in 1851 and his wife Betsy (née Grass) She had been born in 1851 or 1852 in Tollard Royal, Wiltshire. As an adult Ernest was probably known as Albert as his military service records show his two birth names switched round – he is listed as Albert E. Lawrance in the Winchester War Service Register (WWSR), for example. To avoid confusion, this biography uses the Christian name Ernest throughout but does state when he chose to use Albert. The family's surname was also spelt variously Lawrance and Lawrence, but the former is used here.

Ernest's parents married in Romsey in 1873 and by the 1881 Census they were living at 24, North Walls, Winchester, with three children. The eldest, Frances Mildred, aged six and at school, had been born in Romsey, while four-year-old Frederick Charles and William, aged one, were both born in Bighton, near Alresford. Their ages suggest that the Lawrances had moved to Winchester in about 1879 or 1880. The family home has long been demolished but used to be one of several houses and two pubs that once stood in the gap that is now the pedestrian entrance to St Peter's car park. The 1881 Census records that there were 16 occupants in No. 24 made up of four families.

Charles and Betsy were to have three more children, all born in Winchester. Edith Rose was born on 9 July 1881 and Ernest followed three years later. The last child, Alfred Henry, is believed to have been born on 4 August 1887.

The Warren's Directory of 1884 shows the family living at 22, Wyke Road, Fulflood, which is probably where Ernest was born. The Lawrances stayed at the house until at least 1897. Fulflood was an expanding suburb at that time and there were frequent re-numberings and changes of road names. Thus, the address of the Lawrances' home was recorded variously as 22, Wyke Road, 56, Lower Stockbridge Road and 86, Lower Stockbridge Road. The modern address is 15, Stockbridge Road, the right-hand half of Ripples bathroom store. In the late 1890s it was part of a row of residences with The Red Deer public house on the corner of Elm Road as the only commercial premises.

The 1891 Census showed that Ernest's eldest sister, Frances, had left home to train as a housemaid at 'the House for Training Servants' in Whippingham, within the royal estate of Osborne on the Isle of Wight. In the same census, Frederick Lawrance was recorded working as an errand boy while William, Edith and six-year-old Ernest were all at school. All three may have gone to Western Infants School in Elm Road with Edith probably moving up into Western Girls Elementary School on the same site.

Which elementary school Ernest and William attended is not known but it may have been St Thomas Church of England Boys' School in Mews Lane, Winchester. The youngest Lawrance child, Alfred, almost certainly went there - according to the school's records an Alfred Henry Lawrence, born on 4 August 1887, and who lived in Lower Stockbridge Road, entered St Thomas's on 4 March 1895, from Western Infants School. It is believed that this is the correct Alfred Lawrance, although the father's name was given as Thomas, not Charles. According to the school records, Alfred was readmitted on 20 January 1897 and again on 5 April with no reason given for the need for re-admission. However, the final entry records that he left on 8 July 1897, aged nine, because of illness.

LAWRANCE, Ernest Albert

Above left: 15, Stockbridge Road, Winchester. Ernest Lawrance is believed to have been born in 1884 in the right-hand side of what today is Ripples bathroom store and spent his childhood living there. Originally, the house was 22, Wyke Road and later became 56 and then 86, Stockbridge Road before finally being renumbered No. 15. Right: 25, Greenhill Road, where Ernest's sister Edith moved with her husband and family in 1914 – it is Ernest's address in the Winchester War Service Register

Ernest's father died in Winchester in 1897, aged 46. His widow, Betsy, was listed in the Warren's Directory the following year (confusingly, at 87, Lower Stockbridge Road, not 86), but this is the last time she was recorded living in Winchester under the name of Lawrance. It is believed she may have married a John Coster sometime before 1901 because the census of that year showed a John and Betsy Coster living as boarders at 54, Lower Brook Street, Winchester, together with Alfred Lawrance, then aged 14.

No records have been found for John and Betsy Coster's marriage nor can either be found in the 1911 Census as a couple or John Coster on his own. However, the census does have an entry for a Betsy Lawra/ence (the spelling is not clear), a widow, who was an inmate at the Hursley Workhouse in Hursley Road, Chandlers Ford. Her previous occupation was a 'domestic'. If this is Ernest Lawrance's mother, the wrong age, 49, was given for her. She was in fact 59 but workhouse records were often inaccurate and significantly the workhouse entry does give Betsy's correct birthplace. The fate of John Coster is unclear although the death of a man of that name, aged 64, was recorded in 1915 at Andover, not far from his birthplace at Amport.

In 1900, 16-year-old Ernest Lawrance joined the Royal Navy at Portsmouth, using the Christian name Albert. He is believed to have signed up for 12 years and gave his previous occupation as a bugler with the 3rd Hampshire Militia. In his service record he is described as 5ft 4½ins tall, with dark brown hair, grey eyes and a dark complexion. He was already well tattooed on both arms with horseshoes, whips, butterflies, a heart with an arrow through it and an anchor on each arm. He also had a scar on one of his wrists.

LAWRANCE, Ernest Albert

The battleship HMS Exmouth on which Able Seaman Albert Lawrance served between 1904 and 1905

On 17 December 1900 Ernest, with the rating of Boy 2nd Class, was sent to HMS Boscowen, a boys' naval shore training establishment at Portland, Dorset. In the 1901 Census, he was among a long list of '2nd Class Boys' on HMS Boscawen. From 14 June 1901 his sub-rating was that of Bugler. Ernest appears to have served mainly on older ships that were accommodation vessels for HMS Boscawen, and therefore permanently moored off Portland.

As a bugler, Ernest's duties would have included signalling wake up and lights out as well as taking part in the ceremonial aspects of ship's life. He would also have been fully trained as a naval rating. On 5 June 1902 Ernest was sent to the accommodation ship HMS Agincourt and made Boy 1st Class. Just a few weeks later, he transferred to HMS Camperdown and on 10 August was promoted to Ordinary Seaman.

HMS Camperdown had been recommissioned in 1900 as a Royal Navy coastguard ship, patrolling near the coastguard station on the shores of Lough Swilly, County Donegal. The loch provided sheltered anchorage for the Royal Navy on the Western Approaches to the British Isles and a Royal Artillery fort at the entrance testified to its importance. The son of the coastguard from 1896-1901 remembered as a child what a dramatic picture the Channel Fleet made steaming out of the lough and how on one occasion the coastguard families were invited aboard HMS Camperdown. Ernest served on Camperdown from 6 August 1902 until 5 May 1903, around the time that she was paid off and put into the reserve fleet.

On 18 May 1904 Ernest Lawrance was promoted to Able Seaman and assigned to the battleship HMS Exmouth, flagship of the Vice Admiral of the Home Fleet, Sir Arthur Wilson. Ernest spent a year on HMS Exmouth before being sent to HMS Excellent, the Navy gunnery school, on Whale Island, Portsmouth, in May 1905. The following month his sub-rating became Seaman-Gunner, but within days he was transferred again, this time to Nelson's flagship HMS Victory, which was then being used as an accommodation vessel. On 4 January 1906, Ernest was invalided out of the Navy at the age of just 21.

By the 1911 Census, the former seaman was calling himself Ernest Lawrance once more and working as a gardener in Chandlers Ford. He was living with his sister Frances, her husband George Goodall and their three children in a house in Southampton Road, which they shared with another family.

Frances and George had married in Winchester in 1895 and by 1901 they were living at 2, Mill Yard, Laverstoke, near Basingstoke, where George worked as a stoker in the local paper mills (started by the Huguenot Portal family in 1719 and now the Bombay Sapphire Distillery). The couple had two young sons, Frederick and Bertram, and a daughter, Ethel, was born in 1902. By 1911 the family had moved

LAWRANCE, Ernest Albert

to Chandler's Ford with George, then aged 40, employed as a carter to a coal merchant. However, early the following year, Frances Goodall died aged just 37.

Ernest's eldest brother, Frederick, can also be traced up to 1911. Frederick married in 1900 – his wife Alice had been born in Vernham, Berkshire – and in the following year's census the couple were recorded living at 12, Winchester Road, Eastleigh, a property they shared with another couple and their young child. Frederick worked as a coal merchant's carman. By 1911, the Lawrances, still childless, were living at 23, Winchester Road (possibly the renumbered No.12). That year's census also provides reasonably convincing evidence of the correct spelling of the family surname – Frederick, by then a railway contractor's porter, has clearly signed the census form as 'Lawrance'. After the 1911 Census, records for Frederick and Alice Lawrance become less certain.

What of Ernest's other sister, Edith? In 1901, aged 20, she was one of three laundry maids at the Andover Road Laundry which served Winton House school. Two years later Edith married Walter Herridge in Winchester and the newly-weds went to live with Walter's father, jobbing gardener Edward Herridge, at 9, Greenhill Road (now No.17). Edward, Walter and Edith were still at the house in 1911 when Walter was working as a labourer. The couple had three children – Elizabeth, Albert and Edward and a fourth, Edith (named after her mother), was born in 1914. The extended Herridge family may have lived at 11, Brassey Road for a while but the records in Warren's do not paint a clear picture. By 1914 Edward Herridge was back in Greenhill Road but at No. 25 (the house number then and now), and the address given in the WWSR in 1921 for Ernest Lawrance.

Ernest's younger brother Alfred has been more difficult to trace. As mentioned earlier he may have been living with at 54, Lower Brook Street in 1901 with his mother Betsy and her new husband John Coster. In 1903 an Alfred Lawre/ance (the signature on his attestation papers is difficult to read) enlisted with the Hampshire Regiment as a militiaman, the forerunners of the Territorials. He signed up for six years with the service number 617. On his attestation papers, dated 26 August 1903, he gave his occupation as labourer. Nothing is known about Alfred's military career nor has he been found in the 1911 Census. However, there is a record for an Alfred Lawrance's death in Winchester in the late summer of 1913 at the age of 25 which would be the correct age if he died before 4 August.

In March 1916, 31-year-old Ernest Lawrance joined the British Army as Albert E. Lawrance. His service records show that he was living in Eastleigh at the time, possibly still with his brother Frederick and sister-in-law Alice. The date of March 1916 suggests that he may have been among the first waves of single men aged 18-40 to be conscripted – the introduction of compulsion had begun two months earlier.

Ernest enlisted as a private with the 2/5th Battalion, The Gloucestershire Regiment in Winchester. The 2/5th Glosters were a Territorial battalion formed in Gloucester in September 1914 and were assigned to 184th Brigade in 61st Division. The battalion spent the early years of the war serving on the home front before moving to the Western Front in May 1916. It is unlikely that Ernest would have been with them at this stage because he would have been completing his training. However, he may well have joined up with the Glosters by the time the battalion first saw active service in July 1916 when 61st Division joined the 5th Australian Division in an attack on Fromelles, about ten miles west of Lille. The assault cost the Australians 5,500 casualties and the 61st 1,550. The 2/5th Glosters were in reserve for the attack and had the depressing task of bringing in and burying the dead, which took four days.

At some stage, Ernest transferred from the 2/5th Glosters to the 9th Battalion, The Devonshire Regiment, acquiring a new service number (33643) in the process. He later moved to the 8th Devons and eventually to the 1st Devons. It has not been possible to determine when these transfers took place, but as all the

LAWRANCE, Ernest Albert

battalions with which he was associated fought at the Third Battle of Ypres in the summer and autumn of 1917, we can assume that he took part in that campaign. He may also have taken part in the Battle of Arras in April and May of the same year.

Ernest was definitely with one of the three Devonshire battalions sent to northern Italy as part of 7th Division in November 1917 following the Austro-German breakthrough at Caporetto. The Devons held the line near Vicenza and served on the River Piave front. Ernest was probably serving with the 1st Devons when they transferred to Italy because he was certainly with that battalion when it was recalled to France in early April 1918, shortly after the start of the German Spring Offensive.

During the Battle of the Lys (7-29 April 1918), the second of the German spring attacks, the 1st Devons were assigned to hold the British line in the Nieppe Forest, near Armentieres in northern France. As part of 95th Brigade, they threw back numerous German attacks - on 13 April alone, the battalion repulsed no fewer than four assaults in 'last ditch' engagements. Ernest Lawrance was killed in action on 22 April in the vicinity of Nieppe Wood. He was 33 years old. Following his death his personal effects, amounting to £14 15s 11d, were sent to his sister Edith at 25, Greenhill Road.

It is not known for certain whether any of Ernest's brothers served in the Great War. As stated above, Alfred Lawrance is believed to have joined the Army in 1903 but then died in 1913. The last definite mention of William Lawrance, meanwhile, is in the 1891 Census and records for Frederick are similarly scarce. Given that Ernest's family went to the trouble of ensuring that he was listed in the WWSR in 1921, it seems unlikely that they would have failed to mention any other brothers who served.

Albert's brother-in-law, Walter Herridge, Edith's husband, did. He joined up in July 1917, aged 38, and was probably conscripted. As happened to many older married men with children, he served on the home front as a private in the Labour Corps.

Ernest Lawrence's mother Betsy is believed to have died in Winchester in 1936, aged 85. She was buried at Magdalen Hill Cemetery on 31 March that year. Edith Herridge, Ernest's sister, remained at 25, Greenhill Road until around 1925 when she and her husband Walter moved a short distance to 16, North View. In the 1939 Register, Walter's occupation was given as bricklayer. After her husband's death, Edith continued to live at 16, North View at least until 1964. The couple's fourth child, also called Edith, married William White in Winchester in the spring of 1941. She died in Winchester in 1999, aged 85.

Frederick Lawrance and his wife Alice continued to live in Eastleigh after the war, but no definite records for have yet been found for them or Ernest's other brother, William, after the 1920s.

Medals and memorials for Ernest Albert Lawrance

Private Ernest Albert Lawrance was entitled to the British War Medal and the Victory Medal. He is buried at Morbecque British Cemetery, Nord, France (GR. Plot I. Row C. Grave 6). The name on his headstone reads Private A. Lawrence. He is commemorated as Lawrance A.E. on the Memorial Board at St Paul's Church, Fulflood, and in the Memorial Book at St Matthew's, Weeke, where his name is written with the initials A.F.

Additional sources

- Memories of being brought up on a coastguard station on Lough Swilly, Donegal, Ireland. https://www.coastguardsofyesteryear.org/articles.php?article_id=34
- Conversation with Mike Brentnall, builder, about 15, Stockbridge Road.

Researchers – GERALDINE BUCHANAN and JOSEPHINE COLEMAN

LEVER, George Thomas

Private GEORGE THOMAS LEVER
11, Milverton Road, Winchester
Service number 7009. 1st Battalion, The Hampshire Regiment.
Killed in Action, Belgium, 19 October 1914

George Thomas Lever was born on 6 September 1885 in Kingston-upon-Thames, Surrey. He moved to Winchester after enlisting with the Hampshire Regiment in the early 1900s. George married a Winchester girl but his family life was blighted by the early deaths of two daughters and also of his wife due to complications in childbirth. George was recalled to military service as a Reservist in August 1914 and killed in action two months later.

George's father, Robert, was born in 1859 in Fisherton Anger, Salisbury, the son of James and Caroline Lever. James, a boot and shoemaker, had been born in Ansty, Wiltshire, around 1821 and Caroline in Tisbury, Wiltshire, some eight years later. George's mother was born Eliza Allen in Reigate, Surrey, in 1857. Her father, Robert, was born in Kennington, south London, around 1829 and worked as a labourer. Eliza's mother, Sarah, was also born in Surrey in about 1826.

Robert and Eliza married on 20 October 1878 at the Parish Church in Reigate. In the 1881 Census the couple were living in Caterham, Surrey, where Robert worked as an attendant at the town's asylum. Their first son, Robert Arthur, was born in Caterham in 1881. The following year Robert secured a job as a carriage cleaner with London and South Western Railway earning 15 shillings a week.

Robert's new job involved him working in Kingston-upon-Thames, Surrey, where the Lever's second son, William, was born in 1882. George arrived three years later and was baptised on 10 February 1886. In 1891 the family were living at 18, Hudson Road, Kingston, with Robert working as a railway porter.

In March 1892 Eliza Lever gave birth to a daughter, Elizabeth, but the child died at just a few weeks old on 17 May. Eliza herself passed away early in 1893 when George was seven. It appears that over the next few years he and his brothers were cared for by their father who eventually remarried in 1898.

Robert's new wife, Selina Eidmann, had been born in Dalston, Middlesex, in 1860. In 1881 Selina was living with her widowed mother in Leyton, Essex, and working as an English and music teacher. In 1901 Robert and Selina were living in St Paul's Road, Bournemouth, with her mother and two boarders. However, neither George, then aged 15, nor his two brothers were recorded as living at the house.

George Lever joined the Army in November 1903, soon after his 18th birthday. He enlisted with the Hampshire Regiment with the service number 7009, probably for a period of seven years with another five as a Reservist. According to the Hampshire Regimental Journal of January 1906 he received a first Good Conduct Badge while serving with the 2nd Battalion. In December, the same year he was awarded the same badge by the 1st Battalion.

11, Milverton Road, Winchester – the home of George Lever's mother-in-law Maria Holt from 1915-17 and his address in the WWSR

LEVER, George Thomas

The 1st Battalion, The Hampshire Regiment on 23 August 1914, the day before they embarked for France. Private George Lever is somewhere among their ranks *(Photo: Royal Hampshire Regiment Museum)*

On 17 June 1906 George married Mary Agnes Holt at St Peter's Roman Catholic Church, Jewry Street, Winchester. It is possible the couple had met while George was stationed at the regimental barracks in the city. Mary was born in Winchester in 1886, the daughter of Samuel and Maria Holt. Samuel, listed as an Army pensioner in the 1901 Census, had also been born in Winchester in around 1847. Maria was from Galway, Ireland. The couple, who also had two sons, lived at 25, Middle Brook Street, Winchester.

Just a few months after her wedding, Mary Lever gave birth to a daughter, but the child died shortly afterwards. A son, George Jnr, was born safely in Winchester on 16 March 1908, but a second daughter, Lily, born on 12 March 1909, died of convulsions at just five days old. To complete the tragedy, Mary Lever also died on 21 March from puerperal fever contracted during childbirth. Her husband was at her bedside when she passed away. George Lever left the Army in 1910 and the following year was working as a builder's labourer and living with his in-laws and young son at 20, Water Lane, Winchester. However, further misfortune hit the family when Mary's father, Samuel Holt, died, aged 54, that year.

George's address in the Winchester War Service Register (WWSR) is 11, Milverton Road, Fulflood. There is no Lever at that address in the 1914 Warren's Directory, but the 1915, 1916 and 1917 volumes show a Mrs Holt living there. This is almost certainly George's mother-in-law Maria who would have ensured that his name appeared on the memorial at St Paul's church after the war.

Maria Holt's home at 11, Milverton Road was built and owned by the Winchester Working Men's Housing Society which had been founded in 1911 to provide affordable homes for rent in the city. One of 82 houses in Milverton Road, Greenhill Road and Cheriton Road, it was first rented out in 1912. Initially rents were charged from six shillings to 8/6d per week. The homes, which still stand today, were luxurious compared to the slums in the Brooks area of the city centre at the time and all had their own gas supply. In March 1912, the Hampshire Chronicle reported the housing was for 'the working classes, on a breezy hillside'.

Although no longer a full-time soldier in August 1914, George was still a Reservist and was immediately called up for military service when Britain went to war. According to the WWSR he enlisted on 1 October 1914, but this is contradicted by his Medal Index Card which states that he entered a theatre of war with the 1st Battalion, The Hampshire Regiment on 24 August 1914. This is confirmed by the inclusion of George's name on the board in the Royal Hampshire Regiment Museum commemorating the officers and men of the 1st Battalion entitled to the 1914 Star. George therefore was an 'Old Contemptible', one of that elite band of British Regular Army soldiers who were the first to see action in the Great War.

George fought with the 1st Hampshires at the Battle of Le Cateau on 26 August 1914 after the British and French retreat from Mons three days earlier. Despite the 7,812 British casualties at Le Cateau, George came through unscathed and took part in the subsequent Allied retreat to the River Marne. In

LEVER, George Thomas

early September, as the tide of the war turned, the Hampshires, part of 11th Brigade in 4th Division, re-crossed the Marne and joined in the Allied pursuit of the German army to the River Aisne.

On 12 September the 1st Hampshires led 11th Brigade's crossing of the Aisne and only narrowly failed to gain a decisive victory over the German army. This effectively marked the end of the war of movement on the Western Front and the beginning of four years of trench warfare. On 12 October the 1st Hampshires transferred to Flanders where they were ordered to occupy Nieppe on the River Lys.

Quite how and when George Lever met his death is unclear. The WWSR has him 'Missing (believed killed), Belgium, Oct. 3, 1914'. However, on that date the battalion was still working on improving defences on the Aisne and, according to the unit's war diary, was 'unmolested by the enemy'. George's listing in Soldiers Died in the Great War, 1914-1919 states that he was killed in action on 19 October and the Commonwealth War Graves Commission website lists him as dying on the same day. The Hampshire Regimental Journal states that he went missing on 19 October while his Medal Index Card lists him as 'Presumed Dead'

The 1st Battalion War Diary entry for 19 October is brief and states merely that the unit retired from the town of Armentieres due to heavy German shelling. The entry for the following day describes how a Company commander, Major P. Connellan, and one other unnamed soldier were killed. Given the virtual unanimity among the various sources on the date of George's death, the most likely explanation is that he was killed by shellfire on the retreat from Armentieres and his body never found. George Lever was 29 years old when he died. The Registers of Soldiers Effects 1901-1929 indicates that £2 17s 1d was paid to his mother-in-law in May 1916 for the benefit of his son, George Jnr. A war gratuity of £5 was also paid out in 1919.

On 25 April 1931 George Lever Jnr married Olive Young at St Peter's Church, Jewry Street, Winchester, the church where his parents had married 25 years earlier. Olive gave birth to three sons in Winchester: Robert (1934-1979), William (1935-2015) and John (1940-1986). George Jnr died in Winchester in 1973, aged 65, and Olive in March 1990 at the age of 81.

George Lever's father died in Bournemouth in 1933, aged 74. His brother Robert worked as a carter and married Kate Joynes in Christchurch, Dorset, in 1901. In 1911 the couple were living in Bournemouth, with their four daughters. A Robert Arthur Lever served as a transport corporal in the Royal Army Medical Corps during the Great War, but it has not been possible to establish whether this was George's brother. Robert is believed to have died in Epsom, Surrey, in 1956 at the age of 75. George's other brother, William, married Fanny Emily Groves on the Isle of Wight in 1908. The couple lived on the island for many years and had four daughters and a son. It is not known whether William served in the Great War. He died in Bournemouth in 1957, aged 75.

Medals and memorials for George Thomas Lever

Private George Thomas Lever was entitled to the 1914 (Mons) Star, the British War Medal and the Victory Medal. He is commemorated on the Ploegsteert Memorial, Comines-Warneton, Hainaut, Belgium (PR. Panel 6) and on the memorials at St Matthew's and St Paul's churches, Winchester. His name also appears on the 1st Battalion, The Hampshire Regiment's Roll of Officers, NCOs and men who were entitled to the 1914 Star. This is held in the Royal Hampshire Regiment Museum, Winchester.

Researcher - DEREK WHITFIELD

LOVELOCK, George Allan

Private GEORGE ALLAN LOVELOCK
10, Greenhill Road, Winchester
Service number 3/4553. 10th (Service) Battalion, The Hampshire Regiment
Killed in Action, Gallipoli, between 9 and 21 August 1915

George Allan Lovelock was born on 23 March 1882, one of the 11 children of Thomas and Sarah Lovelock. George joined the Army in 1901 but was discharged the same year. However, he joined the Special Reserve and was called up for military service with the Hampshire Regiment when Britain went to war in August 1914. He was killed in action at Gallipoli the following year.

George's father Thomas was born in about 1847 in St Cross, Winchester. In the 1851 Census Thomas was recorded living at 28, Back Street, St Cross, with his parents, William and Sarah Lovelock and elder sister Daisy. William Lovelock, a farm labourer, had been born in the village of Compton, near Winchester, in about 1793, and Sarah in neighbouring Otterbourne in about 1803.

In 1861 the family still lived in Back Street and young Thomas was working as a shop boy. Ten years later, with William Lovelock dead, Sarah and Thomas were boarding at 1, Back Street, the widow working as a laundry charwoman and her son as a domestic gardener.

George's mother was born Sarah Hopkins in Winchester in about 1852, the daughter of George and Elizabeth Hopkins. George Hopkins had been born in Christchurch, near Bournemouth, in around 1818. In 1851 he was living with his wife and two elder daughters at 8, Sussex Street, Winchester, and working as a journeyman tailor. Ten years later he was a pork butcher and the family, including nine-year-old Sarah, were living at 17, High Street, Winchester. By 1881 George was working as a tailor once more and living with his wife at 35, Jewry Street, Winchester. Elizabeth Hopkins (née Bishop) had been born around 1815. Her place of birth is given variously as London and Colerne, Wiltshire, on the censuses.

Thomas Lovelock and Sarah Hopkins married in Weeke, Winchester, on 28 October 1874. Two years later the first of their children, Sarah Jnr, was born in Winchester. She was followed by Louisa (1878), William (1879), Ellen (1880), George himself in 1882, Thomas (1883), Alice (1885), Amelia (1886), Eva (1888, but died the same year), Daisy (1889) and Horace (1891, but died the same year). Sarah gave birth to all the children in Winchester apart from Amelia and Daisy who were born in Longparish, near Andover.

In 1881 Thomas, Sarah and their four elder children were living at 4, Abbey Passage, Winchester. Thomas was working as a gardener. By 1891 the family had moved to 15, Elm Road, Fulflood, and in that year's census no fewer than 12 people were recorded living in the house. George, by then nine, was a pupil at Central Infants School in Winchester. He moved up to St Thomas Senior Church of England Boys' School on 21 February 1893 and left on 12 March 1896, as he approached his 14th birthday. A few months earlier, on 9 December 1895, his mother had died, aged just 43. One wonders just how much the strain of giving birth to, and caring for, 11 children in 17 years contributed to her early death.

George Lovelock joined the Army on 26 March 1901 with the service number 8378. He signed up with the Rifle Brigade for seven years plus five years in the Reserve. His attestation papers reveal that he was working as a labourer when he enlisted and that he had been serving in the Militia. The Militia was Britain's military reserve force which was transformed into the Special Reserve in 1908 when the

LOVELOCK, George Allan

Territorial Force also came into being. George's Army records also reveal that he had previously been rejected for military service because he was underweight.

Within a few days of joining up, George was stationed in barracks in Gosport. However, his time in the Army proved short-lived as he was discharged the same year, possibly on physical fitness grounds. This setback failed to put George off the Army because at some point in the following years he joined the Special Reserve.

In July 1910 George married Lillian Jeffery In Winchester. Lillian had been born in Otterbourne in August 1883, one of the seven children of William and Ann Jeffery. By the following year's census, the newly-weds were living at 14, Staple Gardens, Winchester, with George working as a house painter. By 1912 they had moved to 85, Upper Stockbridge Road, and in 1914 were living at 10, Greenhill Road which is George's address in the Winchester War Service Register (WWSR).

In 1914, 10, Greenhill Road was just two years old. It was built and owned by the Winchester Working Men's Housing Society (WWMHS) which provided affordable homes for rent in the city. One of 82 houses in Milverton Road, Greenhill Road and Cheriton Road, it was first rented out in 1912. Among those living in a WWMHS property was George Lever who was lodging with his mother-in-law Maria Holt at 11, Milverton Road. George Lever was killed in action in France in October 1914 and his name appears with George Lovelock's on the memorials at St Matthew's and St Paul's churches. His biography appears on pp. 175.

10, Greenhill Road, Winchester - George Lovelock was living here in August 1914

As a Special Reservist (his service number 3/4553 confirms this), George Lovelock would have been called up when Britain declared war in August 1914. He was assigned to the 10th (Service) Battalion, The Hampshire Regiment, which was initially composed of Reservists and volunteers. The 10th Battalion was originally formed in Winchester, but after being attached to 10th Division, which was made up largely of Irish units, it was sent to Dublin to complete its formation. The battalion later moved to Mullingar where the men underwent rigorous training.

In May 1915, the 10th Hampshires returned to England with 10th Division for final training in the Basingstoke area. It was assumed that 10th Division would be sent to the Western Front, but in June it received orders to prepare for service at Gallipoli. The change of destination meant much re-equipping and re-fitting but on 6 July 1915 the battalion embarked at Liverpool for the Mediterranean.

George Lovelock entered a theatre of war on 22 July when the battalion landed at Lemnos, an island in the eastern Mediterranean close to the Turkish coast and the 'jumping off point' for troops engaged in the attack on Gallipoli. Today Lemnos is a pleasant Greek tourist destination, but it was utterly different in 1915. According to C.T. Atkinson, the Hampshire Regiment's official biographer of the war, the 10th Battalion quickly became acquainted with 'the flies, the dust, the thirst … and the diarrhoea which were the chief features of residence on Lemnos'.

LOVELOCK, George Allan

British troops on Lemnos in training for Gallipoli in the summer of 1915. Many older Reservists such as George Lovelock were found to be in poor physical condition when they reached the island. George was killed within a month of arriving here

Atkinson states that many of the battalion's experienced soldiers – Reservists such as George Lovelock – were in a poor physical state when they were sent into battle at Gallipoli. This was because they were generally older and because the ship that had transported the battalion to the Mediterranean had been so crowded that physical exercise had been impossible.

George Lovelock died at Gallipoli in August 1915 although the exact date and place of his death are unclear. According to the WWSR it was on 9 August, during the Battle of Sari Bair (6-21 August 1915), the final attempt by the British to seize control of the Gallipoli Peninsula from the Turks. The battle proved costly for the 10th Hampshires who lost 10 officers and 155 other ranks killed or missing and 276 wounded between 6 and 10 August. However, both the Commonwealth War Graves Commission and Soldiers Died in the Great War state that George was killed on 21 August in the attack on a Turkish position known as Hill 60. Here the 10th Battalion lost another 43 men killed and missing and 110 wounded. George's body was never found. He was 33 years old when he died.

George's brother Thomas also served in the Great War. After marrying Louisa Budd in Winchester in 1911, he signed up with the Rifle Brigade in Basingstoke in January 1915, aged 33. His attestation papers show that he was living and working as a butler in Preston Candover, near Basingstoke, and that he had previously served with the Rifle Brigade for eight years. Thomas survived the war, but no record can be found of his life afterwards or when he died.

Lillian Lovelock, George's widow, never remarried. In 1941 she was living at 47, North Walls, Winchester, and she died in the city in June 1965 at the age of 81. George's father remained a widower until his death in Winchester in 1929, aged 82.

Apart from sister Sarah, all of George's siblings moved away from Winchester. Sarah married John Page in 1896 and the couple's first daughter, Henrietta, was born the following year. A second girl, Violet, arrived in 1900 and by 1901 the family were living at 23 Union Street, Winchester, together with George and Sarah's younger sister Amelia, then aged 14. One assumes this arrangement was to help ease the burden on their widowed father. In 1911 the Pages were living at 85, Upper Stockbridge Road, together with Henrietta and Violet as well as Louise Lovelock, 33, another sister of George and Sarah. No record can be found of Sarah, Amelia or Louise's death.

LOVELOCK, George Allan

Medals and memorials for George Allan Lovelock

Private George Allan Lovelock was entitled to the 1914-15 Star, the British War Medal and the Victory Medal. He is commemorated on the Helles Memorial (above), Turkey (PR. Panel 125-134 or 223-226, 228-229 & 328.) and on the memorials at St Matthew's and St Paul's churches, Winchester. His name also appears on the St Thomas Church of England Boys' School Memorial, which is now held at Kings' School, Winchester.

Researcher – DEREK WHITFIELD

MACLACHLAN, Ronald Campbell

Brigadier-General RONALD CAMPBELL MACLACHLAN
Langhouse, Chilbolton Avenue, Weeke (no longer stands)
General Staff. Commander, 112th Infantry Brigade
Previously Commanding Officer, 8th Battalion, The Rifle Brigade
Killed in action, Belgium, 11 August 1917

Brigadier-General Ronald Campbell Maclachlan is the highest-ranking name on the Fulflood and Weeke memorials. From a wealthy, high-achieving Scots background, he moved to Weeke with his wife and family a few months before the outbreak of war in 1914 and consequently his Winchester connections did not run deep. Ronald was one of four brothers who served in the Army. He fought in the Boer War and served in other theatres in the British Empire. Later he earned a reputation as an inspirational leader and trainer of men. In the Great War he commanded a new battalion of the Rifle Brigade on the Western Front before winning promotion to Brigadier-General. He appeared destined for even higher command before a German sniper's bullet cut short his life in 1917 at the Third Battle of Ypres.

Ronald Maclachlan was born on 24 July 1872 in Newton Valence, a small village south of Alton. He was the seventh of nine children born to the Reverend Archibald Neil Campbell Maclachlan, patron and vicar of the parish, and his wife Mary. The family boasted a strong military tradition: Ronald's paternal grandfather, also called Archibald, had been a career soldier with the 69th Regiment of Foot (later the Welch Regiment) and reached the rank of Lieutenant-General. Like his wife Jane (née Campbell), Archibald had been born in Argyllshire, the heartland of the Maclachlan clan which had links to the Campbells. Jane's brother, Neil Campbell, was also a soldier and saw action in the Napoleonic Wars. He was appointed to accompany Napoleon into exile on Elba in 1814 and then fought at Waterloo the following year.

Archibald and Jane Maclachlan married in 1811. By the 1841 Census they were living in Southampton, then a fashionable spa town and retirement location for the wealthy. Their house, a handsome, newly-built terraced property in Rockstone Place, off The Avenue, was later numbered 8 and remained in the family for the next 60 years. The census showed that several relatives were living in the house with them.

The Maclachlans had three children. Their elder son, James, served in the Army but died of yellow fever in Jamaica in the early 1840s while their daughter, also called Jane, died in India in 1838, possibly in childbirth. The couple's surviving son, Archibald Neil (Ronald's father), went on to study at Exeter College, Oxford. After graduating, he was ordained into the Church of England and

MACLACHLAN, Ronald Campbell

in 1846 became curate at New Alresford, near Winchester, and shortly afterwards at Old Alresford. In 1850, aged 30, he became chaplain of St Cross Hospital in Winchester.

By the 1851 Census Archibald and Jane Maclachlan had moved from Southampton to 19, Albion Street, Paddington, west London. However, the couple must have returned to Southampton because Lieutenant-General Maclachlan's death in 1854 was recorded there. Jane then continued to live at 8, Rockstone Place until her own death in 1878.

In 1855 the Rev. Archibald Neil Maclachlan married Mary Elizabeth Sidebotham in Whittington, near Worcester. Mary, then aged about 22, had been born in Worcester and was the daughter of Charles Sidebotham, a barrister and police magistrate, and his wife, also called Mary. Five years passed before the couple's first child, Mary Abigail, was born in Worcester on 22 September 1860. Following her birth, the family moved to Newton Valence where Archibald had bought the patronage of the living from the incumbent vicar of St Mary's Church which meant he was able to nominate himself as the new vicar.

The Maclachlan family went to live in The Vicarage, a large 19-room house, where they employed three live-in servants and a groom-gardener. More children quickly followed: Eveleen on 12 February 1862, Archibald in about 1864, Neil (1865), Lachlan (1868) and Elsie Jean, who was born on 12 November 1869. Interestingly, the 1871 Census recorded the Maclachlans living not in Newton Valence, but with the Rev. Maclachlan's mother at 8, Rockstone Place in Southampton. This was probably because Newton Valence had been struck by an outbreak of diphtheria at the time – one family alone lost no fewer than six children.

The diphtheria danger had clearly passed by 1872 because on 24 July that year Ronald Maclachlan was born in the village. Mary gave birth to two more sons in Newton Valence - Alexander Fraser, on 23 July 1875 and Ivor Patrick in 1878. Tragically, Ivor was born mentally handicapped and he spent much of his life being cared for by private nurses. (A later census described him as an 'imbecile from birth', although the term 'imbecile' in the 19th Century did not have the same negative connotations that it does today and meant a person with development issues.)

By the 1881 Census, three of the Maclachlan boys were at boarding school – Archibald and Neil at Eton and 12-year-old Lachlan at Cheam Preparatory School, situated between Basingstoke and Newbury. Shortly afterwards, Ronald also started at Cheam where he remained until 1886 when he joined his brother Lachlan at Eton. A fine sportsman, Lachlan played for the Eton Cricket XI and excelled at the college's traditional games of Wall and Fives. From Eton he went straight to Sandhurst before joining the King's Royal Rifle Corps (KRRC) in 1888, the same year that Neil Maclachlan was commissioned into the 1st Battalion, The Seaforth Highlanders.

On 25 March 1891, the Rev Archibald Maclachlan died, aged 61. The subsequent disposal of his financial assets gives a glimpse of the family's wealth. In June 1891 Great Western Railway shares owned by the Rev. Maclachlan and valued at £48,329 0s 9d were transferred to his widow. Today these would be worth nearly £6 million, and this probably represented just a fraction of the vicar's total estate. An interesting footnote is that following her husband's death Mary Maclachlan was passed the right to nominate the new vicar of Newton Valence. She chose her eldest son, Archibald, who took up the post in early January 1895. Archibald had studied theology at Oxford and after completing his training for the priesthood had been ordained by the Bishop of Winchester in Winchester Cathedral in December 1893.

MACLACHLAN, Ronald Campbell

Meanwhile, Ronald Maclachlan was following in the military footsteps of his other older brothers. After leaving Eton in 1892 he went to Sandhurst before being commissioned into the Rifle Brigade on 8 July 1893 as a 2nd Lieutenant. He was promoted to Lieutenant on 27 November 1895 and then posted to Rawalpindi in northern India (modern Pakistan) with the 3rd Battalion. While an excellent career move, for Ronald the posting would have been tinged with sadness because on 10 March 1895 his brother Lachlan, serving with 1st KRRC, had been killed in a polo accident in Rawalpindi. Lachlan was aged just 27 and had been stationed on India's North West Frontier for the previous four years. There is a lancet window in Newton Valence church in his memory.

In another part of the British Empire, Captain Neil Maclachlan was distinguishing himself with the 1st Seaforth Highlanders. In 1897 he served in the international military occupation of Crete, aimed at helping the Greek occupants who had rebelled against Ottoman Turk rule. The following year he joined up with British forces in the Sudan under General Horatio Kitchener who were fighting to recover the region from the Mahdists/Dervishes and to avenge the death of General Charles Gordon at Khartoum. Neil was seriously wounded at the Battle of Atbara in April 1898 but recovered to take part in the decisive British victory at Omdurman in September for which he was mentioned in dispatches. He also received the British Medal and the Khedive's Medal with two clasps. After a spell in Cairo, Neil was promoted to Major in 1903 and posted to India with his battalion.

In September 1899 Ronald Maclachlan was sent to South Africa with 2nd Rifle Brigade to fight in the Second Boer War (1899-1902). He was joined there by his young brother Alexander who had been commissioned into 3rd KRRC earlier that year, making him the fourth Maclachlan brother to pursue a military career. Alexander had previously been to Eton and Magdalen College, Oxford, before enrolling at Sandhurst for his officer training.

While in South Africa, Ronald and Alexander were fighting quite close to each other at times, although it is not known whether they met up. Ronald arrived at Durban on 26 October 1899 to assist in the defence of the British garrison at Ladysmith in Natal. The subsequent siege by a large Boer force lasted from 2 November to 28 February 1900 when the garrison was finally relieved, after several failed attempts, by General Redvers Henry Buller (with one Lieutenant Winston Churchill among the first group of soldiers to arrive).

The intervening three months saw several fierce engagements, including the Battle of Wagon Hill on 6 January 1900 in which Ronald Maclachlan was severely wounded in the chest. He had recovered enough to take part in the action at Laing's Nek in June and subsequent operations in the Transvaal. In August he was promoted to Captain and saw action at the Battle of Bergendal where, according to The Rifle Brigade Chronicle he 'did good service with the machine-guns'. The battle, the last set-piece encounter of the war, saw the men of 2nd Rifle Brigade storm formidable Boer positions on top of Bergendal kopje (hill), winning praise from General Buller for their bravery under withering enemy fire. For his services during the South Africa Campaign, Ronald was mentioned in dispatches (Gazette, 24 April 1900) and received the Queen's Medal with three clasps.

Meanwhile, Alexander Maclachlan, who had arrived in South Africa on 24 November 1899 with the 3rd KRRC, took part in General Buller's attempts to relieve Ladysmith, including the fierce fighting at Spion Kop in January 1900. He also saw action in the big push of 12-27 February and was gravely wounded in the fight to capture the final Boer position on Pieter's Hill. At the end of the war in 1902, Alexander, still only a 2nd Lieutenant, was made a Companion of the Distinguished Service Order (DSO) for gallantry. He also received the Queen's Medal with four clasps, the King's Medal with two and was mentioned in dispatches.

MACLACHLAN, Ronald Campbell

The 2nd Rifle Brigade storm Boer positions at the Battle of Bergendal in August 1900 when Captain Ronald Maclachlan was said to have done 'good service with the machine guns'

Meanwhile, Alexander Maclachlan, who had arrived in South Africa on 24 November 1899 with 3rd KRRC, took part in General Buller's attempts to relieve Ladysmith, including the fierce fighting at Spion Kop in January 1900. He also saw action in the big push of 12-27 February and was wounded in the fight to capture the final Boer position on Pieter's Hill. At the end of the war in 1902, Alexander, still only a 2nd Lieutenant, was made a Companion of the Distinguished Service Order (DSO) for gallantry. He also received the Queen's Medal with four clasps, the King's Medal with two and was mentioned in dispatches.

In 1901 or 1902 Captain Ronald Maclachlan returned to 3rd Rifle Brigade in India as Adjutant. In 1904 he served as a transport officer in the Tibet Campaign under Colonel Francis Younghusband. Effectively a military invasion, the Younghusband 'expedition' aimed to stem what was perceived as growing Russian influence in the semi-autonomous state which was nominally under Chinese protection. The Tibetan army resisted fiercely but its troops, overwhelmingly peasants, were no match for the British. The harsh terms of the resulting treaty outraged many influential Britons and in 1906 Anglo-Tibetan relations were renegotiated, with China agreeing not to let any other foreign state interfere in Tibet. Britain for its part promised to keep out and not interfere in Tibetan matters. Ronald Maclachlan received the Tibet Campaign Medal with clasp.

Back in England, Ronald's mother was by 1901 living at 8, Rockstone Place, his grandparents' old home. Two of Ronald's sisters, Eveleen and Elsie, were living with her, together, presumably, with his mentally handicapped brother, Ivor. The Rev. Archibald Maclachlan was still at The Vicarage in Newton Valence, together with his eldest sister Mary Abigail. This was not an uncommon situation at that time: an unmarried sister who did not need to work would keep house for her unmarried brother. By 1903 Mary Maclachlan had returned to Newton Valence, her address in Kelly's Hants & IOW Directory being given simply as 'the Village'. Elsie Maclachlan died on 15 May the same year, aged 33. Like her brother Lachlan, Elsie has a lancet window dedicated to her by her family in Newton Valence church while the altar cross was paid for by friends in her memory.

MACLACHLAN, Ronald Campbell

Ronald Maclachlan and Elinor Trench's marriage certificate from 7 January 1908

On 7 January 1908 Captain Ronald Maclachlan, then aged 35, married Elinor Mary Trench, a 37-year-old widow at St Mark's Church, North Audley Street, London. His brother Archibald conducted the service. On the marriage certificate, Ronald's address was given as 13, North Audley Street and Elinor's as Tidmington, Worcestershire. The daughter of James Charles Cox, a well-known doctor and scientist, and his first wife, Margaret, Elinor had been born in Australia in about 1871. She married William Le Poer Trench in London in 1891 and they had one daughter, Beth, born in Sydney, Australia, in about 1902. William died in Eton, Berkshire in 1904, aged 37.

A few weeks after the wedding, on February 1, Ronald was appointed Adjutant of Volunteers and six months later was made Adjutant of the Officers' Training Corps (OTC) at Oxford University. In between the two appointments, however, came the news that his brother Neil had been accidentally killed while on active service in India with the 1st Seaforth Highlanders. We know nothing about the circumstances of the accident except that it happened while Neil, aged 43, was taking part in the Mohmund Campaign against 'rebels' on the North West Frontier.

Ronald held the post of OTC Adjutant at Oxford until 30 September 1911 and was responsible for its evolution from the old University Rifle Corps. In his history of The Rifle Brigade 1914-18, William Seymour states: 'So successful was he [Ronald] that, though his own personality, the somewhat unpopular "dog shooters" gave place to a body of enthusiasts with a waiting list containing the best men in the University…' He was promoted to Major in January 1910 and at the end of his appointment the university awarded Ronald an Honorary MA Degree in recognition of his work.

The 1911 Census showed that he and Elinor, together with her daughter Beth, were living at Elmthorpe, a 17-room property on Oxford Road, Cowley, then a prosperous, leafy suburb. The census also revealed that Ronald's mother Mary, aged 76, had moved to The Cottage in East Tisted, close to Newton Valence. Although she employed several servants, the only family member living with her was her youngest son Ivor, 33. Her daughter Eveleen, who had been with her in 1901, was by then living with her brother Archibald and sister Mary at The Vicarage in Newton Valence.

At the end of his posting in Oxford Ronald returned to his regiment and gained promotion to Colonel. The next phase of his career is somewhat unclear. According to his obituary in The Times in August 1917 (and re-published in The Hampshire Chronicle a few days later), he moved to Winchester with Elinor in around May 1914, apparently to take up command of the Rifle Brigade Depot. The obituary stated that the couple took up residence in their new home, Langhouse, in Chilbolton Avenue, Weeke (the house no longer stands).

MACLACHLAN, Ronald Campbell

Churn Army Camp on the Berkshire Downs in 1914 or 1915 where Ronald Maclachlan trained men of the Oxford University OTC

However, Ronald never became Depot commander. Instead, in June 1914, he was appointed Colonel of the Oxford University OTC and over the following three months he trained 500 officers, mainly at the Churn Camp on the Berkshire Downs. According to William Seymour: 'When war came in 1914 it was thanks to Maclachlan at Oxford ... that the Regiment obtained such a magnificent band of young officers.'

Shortly after the outbreak of war, Ronald took command of the newly-formed 8th (Service) Battalion, The Rifle Brigade. Formed at Winchester on 21 August 1914 as part of Lord Kitchener's First New Army, the battalion joined 41st Brigade in 14th (Light) Division. Under Ronald's guidance, these volunteers trained initially at Aldershot before moving to Grayshott, near Haslemere, Hampshire, and then returning to Aldershot in March 1915 for final training. They then proceeded to France, landing at Boulogne on 19 May.

The 8th Rifle Brigade first saw action on 5 July but its real baptism of fire – literally - came at the end of the month. On 19 July, the British exploded a large mine under German trenches at Hooge, a small village about two miles east of Ypres in Flanders. The blast left a crater some 120ft wide and 20ft deep with a lip 15ft high which British troops immediately occupied. German retaliation came on 30 July. The British 41st Brigade had taken over the line just a week earlier with 8th Rifle Brigade holding the lip of the crater. At around 3.15am a devastating enemy artillery and machine gun barrage opened up and hissing jets of flame shot across from the German trenches. It marked the first use of flamethrowers in warfare against the British and the weapon spread terror and consternation among the troops of 8th Rifle Brigade. An officer of a battalion occupying neighbouring trenches described the scene:

> [T]he Bosch attacked our right flank held by R. Maclachlan's battalion (8th) and drove them out with liquid fire. It was just at dawn when suddenly flares and star shells arose all together and then the horrible fire jets which look just like a fire hose, except they are fire instead of water. After a couple of minutes of this up went the Bosch red rockets, the signal for their artillery, and from that moment till Monday night, about four days, we lived through continuous bombardments day and night.

One company of around 200 men was virtually obliterated early in the attack. Other men fled their trenches and were either picked off by machine guns or pulverised by artillery as they sought the sanctuary of the support trenches. Many of those who remained in the front trenches died in hand-to-hand fighting with German troops and virtually all the forward positions held by 41st Brigade had to be abandoned. Ordered to counterattack the same afternoon, 8th Rifle Brigade suffered more casualties in a futile assault on the Germans now dug in at the crater. The day's fighting cost the battalion 19 officers and 469 other ranks killed, wounded and missing. Shortly afterwards, Ronald wrote to the parents of an officer killed in what quickly became known as the Hooge Liquid Fire Attack:

> *It is a cruel story: it was a sudden attack under cover of liquid gases that set the trench aflame. In spite of all the horror and confusion, your boy, apparently with two other officers ... rallied the men at once and firing hard through the flames, held their ground. It was simply heroic and just what we all knew could and would be done by your boy in a tight corner.*

Contrary to what Ronald Maclachlan's obituary in The Times stated, he is not believed to have been wounded at Hooge. Rather, he survived unscathed only to be severely wounded on 29 December 1915 while serving with his battalion near Ypres. Nothing is known about how he received the wounds which were serious enough to put him out action for nine months. Ronald would have been evacuated to England for treatment, so he almost certainly spent time with his family in Winchester. On 3 June 1916, while still recuperating, Ronald received the DSO for distinguished service in the field.

Ronald resumed command of 8th Rifle Brigade on 23 September 1916 during the Somme Offensive. The battalion had just taken part in the Battle of Flers-Courcelette (12-17 September), one of the most successful British attacks of the campaign. However, it also proved to be its last action there and in mid-December the battalion, together with the rest of 14th Division, moved north to trenches near Arras.

On 30 December 1916 Ronald Maclachlan was mentioned in dispatches. Then, just a week later, his 23-year association with the Rifle Brigade came to an end when he was promoted to Brigadier-General, commanding 112th Infantry Brigade in 34th Division. The appointment was clearly sudden because Ronald did not even have time to say farewell in person to his battalion. Instead, he wrote a short note in pencil on a sheet torn from his field message book which was then read out to his assembled men at a special parade. In it, Ronald spoke of his pride at having commanded the battalion for so long and of its 'splendid spirit' despite 'constant fighting and incessant losses'.

The battalion's response, also read out, demonstrated the respect and deep affection that the men felt for their Commanding Officer:

> *The Battalion wish to express what a lasting debt they owe to you for the skill, energy and devotion with which you have trained and nursed them in their early days and led them and inspired them in active service. We feel that any success that has fallen to the Battalion has been founded on your example and leadership. Those who have served under you will never forget what you have done for them and will strive to pass on the high tradition of the Regiment which you have established in the 8th Battalion. All ranks unite in wishing you happiness and highest success in your new command and in any higher post to which you may be called.*

Ronald's promotion put him on the Army's General Staff with responsibility for some 4,000 men in four battalions, plus support troops. In April 1917 he commanded 112th Brigade during first three phases of the Arras Offensive (9 April-16 May) and his inspirational leadership was a key factor in the capture of the village of Monchy-le-Preux during the First Battle of the Scarpe (9-14 April). Major-General Hugh Bruce-Williams, commander of 37th Division, wrote later:

MACLACHLAN, Ronald Campbell

Brigadier-General Ronald Maclachlan's grave, fourth from right, at Locre Hospice Cemetery, Belgium

> *We wondered how it was possible for the Germans to have let his [Ronald's] men get to the summit of the ridge where there was not a blade of cover. It was his personal example and personal influence only that did it. He was right up at the front, almost in the front line.*

With the end of the fighting at Arras, 37th Division moved north to Flanders. The 112th Brigade did not figure in the start of the Third Battle of Ypres (Passchendaele) which began on 31 July 1917, but it did subsequently take over a stretch of line between Bee Farm and Forret Farm, near Hollebeke, south-east of Ypres.

In reality this 'line' consisted of a stretch of shell holes with little cover and the Brigade War Diary noted ominously on 7 August that enemy snipers were harassing troops trying to make their way to the front. It proved a tragically prescient observation. Four days later, as Ronald Maclachlan made an early morning visit to the line, he was shot and killed by a German sniper. He was 45 years old. His obituary in The Times stated that he had attended a senior officers' course in England just three weeks before his death and one wonders whether he took the opportunity to visit his family in Winchester for what would have been the last time.

Ronald, who was posthumously mentioned in dispatches in December 1917, was one of more than 200 British generals killed in action in the Great War. The fact that he was prepared to put himself in harm's way endeared Ronald to his men. According to The Rifle Brigade Chronicle 1917, 'the large number who attended his funeral [on 13 August] was eloquent testimony of the esteem in which he was held by all'. William Seymour wrote:

> *In the Regiment he was universally beloved: an exceedingly smart adjutant, a good sportsman, a charming companion and a master of his profession, there was no height to which he could not have risen had he been spared. But what distinguished Ronnie Mac above all else was that amazing personality which enabled him to get the best out of all with whom he came into contact. It is unlikely the Regiment will ever again see his equal in character: his superior – never.*

MACLACHLAN, Ronald Campbell

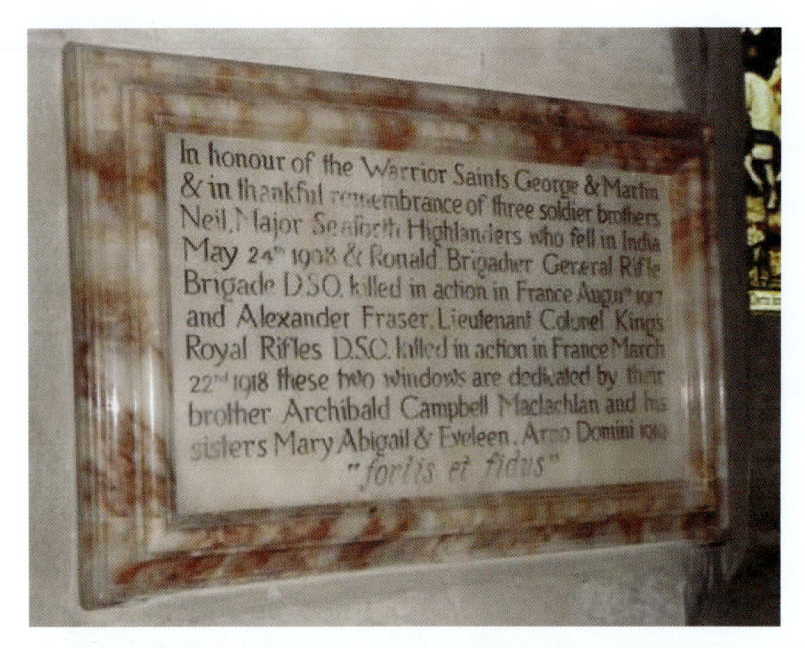

Above and right: the stone tablet and stained-glass window in memory of Ronald, Neil and Alexander Maclachlan. They were placed in St Mary's Church, Newton Valence, near Alton, by the brothers' surviving siblings

Left: the stone tablet to Ronald in Winchester Cathedral, placed there by his widow, Elinor

Below: Rookley House, King's Somborne. Elinor Maclachlan moved here in about 1920 from the Winchester home she shared with Ronald

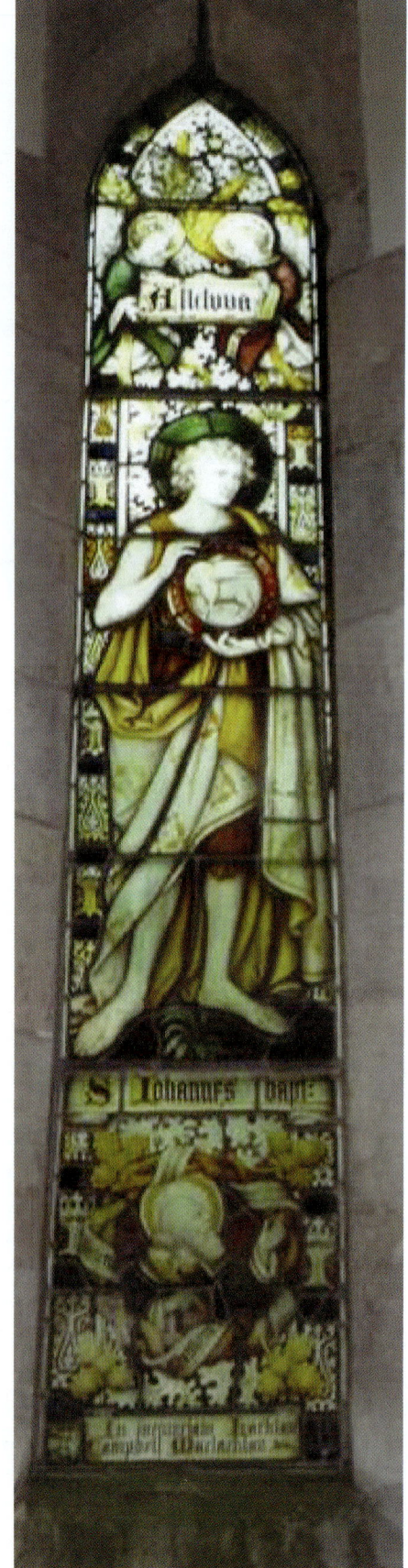

MACLACHLAN, Ronald Campbell

The following obituary appeared in The Times on 14 August 1917 and then, four days later, in the Hampshire Chronicle (Page 5):

Brig-Gen R.C. Maclachlan DSO, who fell in France on August 11th, was a son of the late Rev A. Maclachlan, of Newton Valence, Alton, Hants. He was educated at Eton and Sandhurst and joined the Rifle Brigade in 1896. During the South African War, he was mentioned twice in dispatches, was severely wounded and went through the Siege of Ladysmith. He afterwards took part in the Tibet Campaign. In 1908 he became Adjutant of the Oxford University O.T.C., an appointment he held for four years, on giving it up, the honorary degree of M.A., for service rendered to the University. He was very much identified with the Public Schools Camp as Brigade Major.

During the present war he was severely wounded at Hooge on July 30th, 1915, received the D.S.O., and had been twice mentioned in dispatches. He married in 1906 Elinor Mary, daughter of Dr J.C. Cox, of Sydney, NSW. Brig-Gen and Mrs Maclachlan took up their residence in Winchester at Langhouses, Chilbolton Ave about three months before the war started. The gallant officer, who was then a Colonel in the Rifle Brigade, was coming, we believe, in command of the Rifle Depot. On the outbreak of the war he was appointed Colonel of the Oxford University O.T.C. He trained 500 officers at the Chum Camp. After that he trained and commanded one of the new Battalions of the Rifle Brigade and took them to the Front in July 1915.

A brave and conscientious officer, he would never give an order to his men and hesitate to share in the danger of it himself. The men under his command not only respected but invariably beloved him. Death came to him when engaged in a typical action, for he was sniped on the way to the front line trenches. Brig-Gen Maclachlan was in England three weeks ago for a senior officers' course in the Midlands.

He was one of four soldier brothers. The eldest was an officer in the Seaforth Highlanders, and he met a soldier's death on the Indian frontier; another brother was accidentally killed while playing in a polo match at Rawal Pindi several years ago; and another brother is an officer in the King's Royal Rifle Corps on active service (not in France). A brother, the Rev. A.C. Maclachlan, is Vicar of Newton Valence, and is patron of the living. In Winchester, the deepest sympathy will go out to Mrs Maclachlan, who has been such a kindly and devoted worker for the good of soldiers in general and of the Rifle Regiments in particular.

For Ronald's mother, his death must have come as a shattering blow. Further bad news followed on 22 March 1918 when Lieutenant-Colonel Alexander Maclachlan, the fourth and last surviving Army brother, was killed in action on the Western Front during the German Spring Offensive. He had been Commanding Officer of 12th Rifle Brigade for just three weeks when, like Ronald, he was shot dead while reconnoitring front-line trenches.

Alexander had enjoyed an illustrious military career. After serving in South Africa, he had been made Captain in 1906 and Adjutant the following year. During King George V's visit to India in 1911-12 he was appointed an Aide-de-Camp to His Majesty. At home on leave when the Great War began, Alexander was posted to 1st KRRC and took part in the Mons Retreat and the Battle of the Aisne where he was seriously wounded. He rejoined 3rd KRRC in the autumn of 1915 and after being promoted to Major was sent with the battalion to Salonika. In late 1916 he took command of 13th Battalion, The Middlesex Regiment on the Lake Doiran front where, according to the KRRC Chronicle of 1918, 'he earned further distinction by his example and leadership'. However, the climate affected his health and he was invalided home in the summer of 1917. After being promoted to Lieutenant-Colonel a few months later, he took temporary command of 11th and 12th KRRC before his final posting to 12th Rifle

MACLACHLAN, Ronald Campbell

Brigade. During the war he received a Bar to his DSO, the Serbian Order of Kara George with Swords and four mentions in dispatches.

Nor was that the end of the Maclachlans' misfortune. In late 1918, Ivor, the youngest brother, died at the age of about 40, becoming the sixth of Mary Maclachlan's nine children to predecease her. Mary appears to have had no grandchildren – her three daughters, together with Ivor and Archibald, never married and there is no evidence that any of the four Army brothers had children. By 1923 Mary had moved back to The Vicarage in Newton Valence where she lived with her three surviving children. She died on 12 June 1925, aged about 92. Her daughter Mary Abigail died in 1941 at the age of 81 and Archibald in 1944, aged 79. Eveleen remained in the Newton Valence area, passing away in 1953, aged 91.

Ronald's widow, Elinor, devoted herself to the welfare of Rifle Brigade soldiers during the war – her name crops up in several letters in which men remark on parcels - of books, for example – they had received from her. She continued to live at Langhouse immediately following Ronald's death but by 1920 had moved to Rookley House, Kings Somborne. However, in the Winchester War Service Register of 1921, she gave Ronald's address as Langhouse, presumably because it was the last one associated with him. By 1925 Elinor had moved again to St Vincents on the Salisbury Road in Upper Clatford, near Andover. She lived there until at least 1937 and died in the Andover area in 1949, aged 79. Nothing is known of what became of her daughter Beth, although she may have returned to Australia.

Medals and Memorials for Ronald Campbell Maclachlan

Brigadier-General Ronald Campbell Maclachlan was buried at Locre Hospice Cemetery, Heuvelland, West Flanders, Belgium (GR. II. C. 9). In addition to the decorations mentioned above, he was entitled to the 1914-15 Star, the British War Medal and the Victory Medal. Ronald is remembered on the memorials at St Paul's and St Matthew's churches, Winchester. He is commemorated on a stone tablet in Winchester Cathedral, placed there by his wife Elinor, and also on the Rifle Brigade Roll of Honour in the same building. His surviving siblings, Archibald, Mary Abigail and Eveleen dedicated a window and a tablet at St Mary's Church, Newton Valence, to Ronald and his brothers Alexander and Neil who were also killed on military service. Ronald and Alexander are also listed in the Eton College Memorial Book of those who fought in the Great War.

Researchers – GERALDINE BUCHANAN and DEREK WHITFIELD

Additional sources

- William Seymour: *The Rifle Brigade 1914-1918*, 2 Vols. (London, The Rifle Brigade Club Ltd, 1936).
- The Rifle Brigade Chronicles, 1914, 1915, 1916, 1917 and 1918.
- The King's Royal Rifle Corps Chronicle 1918.
- Cheam School Archives.
- 112th Brigade War Diary, 1917.

MAIDMENT, Hubert George

Sergeant HUBERT GEORGE MAIDMENT
2, Gladstone Street, Winchester (no longer standing)
Service number 2760. 2nd (City of London) Battalion, The London Regiment (Royal Fusiliers)
Killed in action, France, 17 September 1916

Hubert George Maidment was born in Winchester in 1892, the second child of William and Alice Maidment. He trained to be a teacher before volunteering for military service with the City of London Battalion. Hubert fought at Gallipoli in 1915 and at the Battle of the Somme the following year where he was killed in action.

Hubert's father William was born in Wilton, near Salisbury, on 24 April 1865, the son of agricultural labourer John Maidment. William worked first as a florist and fruiterer and later as a gardener and nurseryman. Hubert's mother was born Alice Bell in Sunderland, County Durham, on 6 March 1861. William and Alice also had a daughter, Alice Lizzie, who was born in Winchester on 21 November 1888.

The 1891 Census showed the Maidments living at 10, Boundary Street, Winchester, with William employed as a gardener. (Boundary Street was Hubert's probable birthplace, but the address no longer exists. The street was at right angles to and on the western side of Eastgate Street.) After Hubert's birth the following year, the family moved at some stage to 153, High Street, Winchester, to the west of Cross Keys Passage, which is where they were listed in the 1901 Census. William was a florist and fruiterer so presumably had a shop there.

By 1908 the Maidments had moved to 2, Gladstone Street, Winchester, where they remained for many years. In the 1911 Census, William Maidment was to put its former address, 2 Gladstone Terrace. In that census he was working as a gardener and nurseryman and daughter Alice, 22, as a dental secretary. Hubert, meanwhile, was studying to be a teacher. (The evidence suggests that this was not at the Diocesan Training College in Winchester.) Nothing is known of his earlier education, but he was clearly an able student.

The Maidments remained at 2, Gladstone Street until 1913 when they moved next door to 1, Gladstone Street. So that would have been the family address from which Hubert went to war and that explains why it is 1, Gladstone Street that appears in the Winchester War Service Register of 1921. The Maidment family are believed to have worshipped at the Primitive Methodist chapel in Parchment Street as Hubert's name appears on the memorial board there. It is possible that the chapel supported Hubert financially through his teacher training. After qualifying as a teacher Hubert moved to London, where he started work as a teacher employed by London County Council

Hubert enlisted with the 2nd (City of London) Battalion, The London Regiment (Royal Fusiliers) with the service number 2760 on 21 September 1914, about six weeks after the start of the Great War. As volunteers flocked into its ranks the 2nd Royal Fusiliers were divided into first, second, third and, eventually, fourth line battalions – namely the 1/2nd, 2/2nd, 3/2nd and 4/2nd.

The Winchester War Service Register (WWSR), in which his name appears as Herbert, states that Hubert served in Malta and Gallipoli with the Royal Fusiliers. The 1/2nd and 2/2nd Battalions were both stationed on Malta and both saw action at Gallipoli in 1915. However, whereas the 1/2nd Battalion fought for the whole of the Gallipoli campaign, landing there on 25 April 1915, the 2/2nd did not arrive until much later in the year. Hubert almost certainly served with the 2/2nd Battalion as his Medal Index Card shows him entering the Egyptian theatre of war on 30 August 1915, the same day that the 2/2nd arrived

MAIDMENT, Hubert George

there from Malta. The 2/2nd remained in Egypt for about six weeks before embarking for Gallipoli, landing at Cape Helles on 13 October when they joined 2nd Brigade in the Royal Naval Division.

The Allies had started to run down the Gallipoli campaign by the time Hubert arrived and the battalion's time in the trenches was quiet compared to what had gone before. He did, however, endure a great storm and blizzard at the end of November. In December, the battalion was evacuated from Gallipoli and sailed via the Greek island of Lemnos to Egypt, arriving there on 24 January. In April, the 2/2nd Royal Fusiliers transferred to France where they were disbanded the following month with most men sent to other units. Among these were three officers and 126 other ranks who were sent to the 1/2nd Battalion and it is thought they included Hubert Maidment.

The 1/2nd Royal Fusiliers had been assigned to 169th Brigade in the 56th (London) Division when it arrived in France from Gallipoli in February 1916. After joining his new battalion, Hubert began training for the British summer offensive on the Somme. He had probably already been promoted to Lance-Corporal and would go on to reach the rank of Sergeant.

The Parchment Street Methodist Church memorial to Hubert Maidment, now held at the United Church in Jewry Street

On 1 July 1916, the first day of the Somme Offensive, 56th Division took part in a diversionary assault on the village of Gommecourt, at the northern end of the British Army's 13-mile long attack sector. It proved a disaster, with the Division losing more than 4,000 men killed, missing and wounded. The Division was then pulled out of the line until 9 September when it returned to take part in the Battle of Ginchy. A week later, 52nd Division went over the top again at the Battle of Flers-Courcelette (15-22 September) which featured the first use of tanks in military history. Hubert Maidment was killed in action on the opening day of the battle, aged 24. His body was never found.

Hubert's parents, William and Alice, remained at 1, Gladstone Street until about 1930, when they moved to 53, Brassey Road. William Maidment continued to work as a market gardener after the war. In 1939 he and Alice were still living at 53, Brassey Road together with their 23-year-old granddaughter Ruth Hunter. Ruth was the daughter of Hubert's sister Alice and her husband Cecil Hunter, a dentist, who had married in 1914. William Maidment died in Winchester in 1946.

MAIDMENT, Hubert George

Medals and memorials for Hubert George Maidment

Sergeant Hubert George Maidment was entitled to the 1914-15 Star, the British War Medal and the Victory Medal. He is commemorated on the Thiepval Memorial (above), Somme, France (Pier & Face 9D & 16B). His name also appears on the memorials at St Matthew's and St Paul's churches, Winchester (although as H.S. Maidment), and on a special memorial erected at Parchment Street Methodist Church, Winchester, and now held at the United Church, Jewry Street.

Researchers – JENNY WATSON and DEREK WHITFIELD

MALE, Reginald Harry

Lance-Corporal REGINALD HARRY MALE
Trevenna, Stockbridge Road, Winchester (No. 176 today)
Service Number 46366. 6th Battalion, Machine Gun Corps
(Previously Trooper 1249, Hampshire Carabiniers Yeomanry)
Killed in action, France, 18 September 1918

Reginald Harry Male, the son of George Henry and Caroline Fanny Male, was born in Southampton (not Wyke Hill, Winchester, as stated in several sources) on 24 February 1897. He came from a comfortable background: his father was Superintendent of Winchester Post Office while Reginald himself attended Peter Symonds School before becoming a bank clerk in 1913. When war broke out, he enlisted with the Hampshire Carabiniers Yeomanry and later transferred to the Machine Gun Corps. Reginald served for two years on the Western Front and saw action in some of the bloodiest fighting there. He was killed in action in September 1918 during the British Army's final advance to victory.

Reginald's father George was the son of Henry Male and his wife Caroline Kate (née Leverton and known by her middle name). Henry, a master mariner, had been born in Weymouth, Dorset, in around 1841 and Kate in Whiteparish, near Romsey, in March 1846. In the 1851 Census, Kate was at her maternal grandfather's inn, The Three Tuns in Romsey, with her mother Louisa Leverton, a farmer's wife. By the 1861 Census, Kate, then aged 16, was living with her brother William Leverton, by then the publican of The Three Tuns, and his wife Emma and their family.

Henry Male and Kate Leverton married in Mottisfont, near Romsey, on 16 April 1867. The following year, on 28 October, Kate gave birth to George – Reginald Male's father - in Romsey. The 1871 Census recorded Henry, Kate and young George living at 10, Aberdeen Road, St Denys, Southampton. However, on 21 December 1875 Kate died at the age of just 29.

On 15 August 1877 Henry Male remarried. His second wife, Fanny Oake (1840-1922), had been born on the Isle of Wight in around 1840 and in 1861 she was employed as a maid in the Ryde home of Augustus Clifford, a retired Royal Navy Admiral. Fanny and Henry married in Lewisham, Kent, and in 1878 the couple had a son, Charles, a step-brother for George. The 1881 Census listed Fanny living at 3, Brighton Terrace, Southampton, with her occupation given as 'lodging housekeeper'. Although young Charles was living with her on Census night Henry Male was not, although this was probably because he was at sea.

Meanwhile, George Male, Henry's son by his first marriage, was being looked after by his uncle

MALE, Reginald Harry

and aunt, William and Emma Leverton, at their home, Trout Cottage, Chilbolton, near Stockbridge, Hampshire. William was no longer a publican but employed as a schoolmaster. The 1881 Census also recorded another nephew living with the Levertons – nine-year-old Harry Male, probably George's brother. No further record can be found of Harry Male, but it is worth noting that Reginald Male's middle name was Harry.

There is no trace of George Male in the 1891 Census, but in 1893 his marriage to Caroline Lock was registered in Andover. Caroline had been born in Ringwood, Hampshire, on 23 January 1870. On 20 June 1894 she gave birth to a son, William, and a daughter, Winifred, on 15 August 1895. Both children were born in Southampton, as was Reginald, who arrived in 1897 and Gladys, born in 1900. It is possible that all the children were born at 84, Gordon Avenue, Portswood, Southampton, as this was the address given for the family in the 1901 Census. George, then aged 32, was working as a Post Office clerk and he and Caroline were prosperous enough to employ a live-in servant.

Reginald and William Male both attended Southampton Boys' College, a private secondary school. However, in 1908 their father was appointed Chief Clerk at Winchester Post Office, then situated in Parchment Street, with the result that on 7 May 1909 Reginald and William were admitted to Peter Symonds School. (Reginald's date of admission on the Peter Symonds records is given as 7 May 1907 but this is almost certainly an error.) The grammar school records do not show either boy receiving any sort of grant so one must assume their parents could afford the fees.

The Commonwealth War Graves Commission wrongly gives Reginald's birthplace as Wyke Hill, Winchester. In fact, the Males moved from Southampton to live at Trevenna, Upper Stockbridge Road, which had previously been known as Wyke/Weeke Road or Hill. This may partly explain the error. Today, the house is No. 176, Stockbridge Road, although the name Ecclesfield – the name given to the property by the occupiers after the Males - also appears above the doorway.

William Male left Peter Symonds School in February 1911 to become an apprentice locomotive engineer, probably at the Eastleigh railway works. Reginald left just over two years later, on 7 June 1913. He joined the Alton branch of the Union of London and Smith's Bank as a clerk and was working there when Britain went to war in August 1914.

The following month, aged 17, Reginald Male volunteered for military service, joining the Hampshire Carabiniers Yeomanry as a trooper with the service number 1249. The Hampshire Yeomanry, part of the Territorial Force, were trained and equipped as mounted infantry. The Drill Hall in Hyde Close, Winchester (a carpet showroom today and originally, in the mid-1800s, the city's first museum), served as the unit's headquarters and there were four Squadrons (A, B, C and D) based at Portsmouth, Winchester, Southampton, and Bournemouth. Which squadron Reginald joined is not known for certain, but it is likely that it was B, given that it was based in Winchester where he lived and had a detachment in Alton where he worked.

Reginald did not fight overseas with the Hampshire Yeomanry. Instead he completed his basic training with them and then served on the home front, first in Portsmouth and then in Sussex. In April 1916 he was compulsorily transferred to the Machine Gun Corps (Infantry), which had been formed in September the previous year, and allocated the new service number 46366. Reginald was sent to the MGC HQ and Training Centre at Belton Park, near Grantham, Lincolnshire, for an intensive gunnery course before embarking for France in September as part of 16th Machine Gun Company in 6th Division.

MALE, Reginald Harry

176, Stockbridge Road, Winchester, was the Male family home from 1908 to 1916 when it was known as Trevenna

The old Winchester Post Office in Parchment Street in the 1970s. Reginald Male's father was Chief Clerk and then Superintendent here from 1908 to 1916

The Drill Hall in Hyde Close, Winchester, was the Hampshire Carabiniers Yeomanry HQ at the outbreak of the Great War when Reginald Male joined. Today it is a carpet showroom

A contemporary artist's impression of a Machine Gun Corps transport limber going into action

In 1916, when Reginald Male arrived on the Western Front, all MGC teams were formed into Companies - one to each Brigade – comprising about 150 men and fielding 16 heavy Vickers MK1 machine guns. These were each operated in by a team of six men – No. 1 who fired the gun, No. 2 who assisted, feeding ammunition belts, No. 3 a range taker using an optical instrument, No. 4 the signaller, and Nos. 5 and 6

MALE, Reginald Harry

who carried boxes of ammunition and doubled up as runners or scouts. This accounted for 96 men. The majority of those remaining served in the transport section which operated six four-wheeled limbers (wagons) drawn by horses or mules. Their purpose was to keep the guns supplied with ammunition, spares and other materials from dumps several miles behind the front line. It was an arduous and dangerous job since the Germans kept all the roads and tracks leading to the front under constant bombardment.

It appears that Reginald initially served with the gun section and that he also doubled as servant to one of the Company officers. He later transferred to the transport section, no doubt because of his expertise with horses gained while serving with the Hampshire Carabiniers. He would have enjoyed periods of home leave, but from 1917 these would have been spent in Pembroke, South Wales, where his father had been appointed Postmaster at the docks Post Office.

The heavy machine gun was one of the most effective weapons of the Great War and there are numerous instances of a single well-placed weapon cutting great swathes in attacking infantry – most notably on 1 July 1916, the first day of the British Army's Somme offensive. It followed that multiple machine guns, with interlocking fields of fire, were an incredibly destructive defensive weapons system and the Germans employed them in huge numbers after withdrawing to the Hindenburg Line in spring 1917. The British copied this but also used machine guns during attacks – in particular, creeping barrages, where fire fell ahead of the artillery barrage to catch enemy troops moving to the rear. Machine gunners like Reginald would also concentrate fire on specific targets or sweep the ground behind the enemy's front and support positions. For these tasks, machine guns were generally placed about 1000 yards behind the advancing infantry and then moved up as soon as the enemy positions were captured.

The Somme Offensive was still raging when Reginald arrived in France in September 1916. The precise date that he joined his unit is unknown, but it may have been in time for him to see action at the Battle of Flers-Courcelette (15-22 September), the capture of Lesboeufs (25 September) and the Battle of Morval (25-28 September). He almost certainly took part in the Battle of the Transloy Ridges (9-18 October). The following year 16th Machine Gun Company was involved in the fighting on Hill 70 near Lens (13-22 April 1917) and then in the tank attack at Cambrai (20-21 November), the capture of Bourlon Wood (23-28 November) and helping to stem the German counter-attacks (30 November-3 December).

By the start of 1918 Reginald Male was a hardened veteran of the Western Front and had been promoted to Lance-Corporal. That spring the four Machine Gun Companies in each Division were amalgamated to form Machine Gun Corps Battalions, the old 16th Company becoming A Company of the 6th Battalion MGC. The unit was heavily involved during the German Spring Offensive – at the Battle of St Quentin (21-22 March), the Battle of Bailleul (13-15 April), the Second Battle of Kemmel Ridge (25-26 April) and the Battle of the Scherpenberg (29 April).

Reginald survived this bitter fighting after which 6th MG Battalion enjoyed a period out of the front line to rest and re-equip. During the summer, the tide of the war began to change in favour of the Allies and by September the British Army had recaptured much of the ground lost in the spring. On 18 September, Reginald – by this stage serving in the battalion's transport section – took part in a major assault on the French village of Epehy, which guarded the approach to the Hindenburg Line. He was killed in action the same day, aged 21.

On 28 September 1918, under the headline Roll of Honour (page 5), the Hampshire Chronicle reported:

MALE, Reginald Harry

Lance-Corpl. R.H. Male MGC – the many friends in Winchester of Mr G.H. Male, Postmaster of Pembroke Docks (formerly Superintendent at Winchester Post Office), will regret to hear that he has this week received the news that his youngest son, Reginald Harry, was killed in action in France on September 18th.

Lance-Corpl. Male – whose age was 21 – previous to joining the Army was a clerk in the Union of London and Smiths Bank at Alton. In September 1914, at the age of 17, he joined the Hampshire Carabiniers Yeomanry. In April 1916 he was transferred to the Machine Gun Corps Depot at Grantham and proceeded overseas to France in September 1916.

Trefcon British Cemetery at Caulaincourt, northern France, where Reginald Male is buried

The Commanding Officer of the section, in a letter to Mr Male informing him of his son's death, writes: 'Personally, I viewed Lance-Corpl. Male's career with the greatest interest. He was my personal messenger a good while ago, when we were both in the gun sections, and as such I had many opportunities of observing his unswerving devotion to duty and the high personal regard with which he imbued all those with whom he came into contact. The Battalion has lost a good soldier, but we of the Transport have lost more than that – we have lost a loveable and faithful comrade.'

Reginald's parents had, of course, moved from Winchester by this time but they clearly still had friends in the city, including, presumably, in Fulflood and Weeke. This explains why they decided to have their son's name included on the parish war memorial. The Commonwealth War Graves Commission gives George and Caroline Male's address as **Holland House, Church Street, Malvern, Worcestershire**, which is possibly the address to which they moved after George was transferred by the Post Office from Pembroke in the early to mid-1920s.

By 1939 George Male had retired and he and Caroline were living at 10, Brightlands Avenue, Bournemouth, along with their daughter Winifred who was unmarried. George died in Bournemouth on 26 February 1941, aged 72. In his will he left £443 5s to Caroline who died in early 1963 at the age of 92 or 93. Winifred Male was recorded working as an ARP warden in the 1939 Register. No further record of her has been found to date.

It is not known whether William Male, Reginald's elder brother, served during the Great War; it is possible that his job as a railway engineer was a reserved occupation. In 1929 he married Mildred Morgan in Ashby-de-la-Zouch, Leicestershire. Ten years later, the couple were living in Birmingham with William employed as an inspector of engineering parts at the Austin works where he was also an ARP warden. It is not believed that he and Mildred had any children. William died in Birmingham on 3 April 1974, aged 79, leaving £9,289 in his will.

Reginald's younger sister, Gladys, is thought to have married Alfred Walker in Southampton in 1932 and died in Winchester in September 1998, aged 98.

MALE, Reginald Harry

Medals and memorials for Reginald Harry Male

Lance-Corporal Reginald Harry Male was entitled to the British War Medal and the Victory Medal. He is buried at Trefcon British Cemetery, Caulaincourt, Aisne, France (GR. B. 10). His headstone is inscribed with the following:

THY WILL BE DONE

Reginald is mentioned on the memorials at St Paul's and St Matthew's churches, Winchester, as well as on the Peter Symonds School War Memorial. His name also appears on the National Provincial and Union Bank of England War Memorial in the City of London, the Pembroke and Monkton War Memorial in Pembroke, Dyfed, and the memorial at St Mary the Virgin Church, Pembroke.

Researchers – GERALDINE BUCHANAN, DEREK WHITFIELD and JOSEPHINE COLEMAN

Additional sources

- We are grateful to Graham Sacker of the Machine Gun Corps Database for his assistance in tracing Reginald Male's service with 16th Company MGC and 6th Battalion MGC and for explaining the role of the MGC transport section.
- Trefcon British Cemetery - WW1 Cemeteries.com
  https://www.ww1cemeteries.com/trefcon-british-cemetery.html
- See also https://astreetnearyou.org/person/273271/Lance-Corporal-Reginald-Harry-Male

MIDDLETON, Bertram Charles

Lance-Corporal BERTRAM CHARLES MIDDLETON
50, Western Road, Winchester (7, Cheriton Road today)
Service number S/16457. 1/8th Battalion, Argyll and Sutherland Highlanders
Died of wounds, England, 21 May 1918

Bertram Charles Middleton, the eldest child of John and Charlotte Middleton, was born in Winchester on 24 October 1892. His father worked as a tailor and his mother was a trained dressmaker. One of four siblings, Bertram – or Bertie as he was known to family and friends - enlisted shortly after the outbreak of war in 1914 and served initially with the Army Pay Corps. He later transferred to the Argyll and Sutherland Highlanders and is believed to have fought with no fewer than four of the famous Scottish regiment's battalions. He died of his wounds in England in 1918 after being wounded in Flanders during the German Spring Offensive and is buried in Winchester.

John Middleton, Bertram's father, was born in Hythe, near Southampton on 21 March 1865 and was one of six children. John's father, William, worked as a gardener and had been born in Netherhampton, near Salisbury, in around 1828. John's mother was born Caroline Palmer in the Berkshire village of Eastbury, between Newbury and Hungerford, in 1836. John had an older sister, Elizabeth (born 1863) as well as two younger sisters, Caroline (1866) and Alice (1869) and two brothers, William (1870) and Ernest (1874).

By 1871 William and Caroline Middleton had moved to Winchester and were living at 2, Queen's Terrace, off the Romsey Road. Five years later, Caroline died at the age of just 40, leaving her widower husband to bring up their young family. The Middletons were still living in Queen's Terrace in 1881 with 16-year-old John working as a tailor's apprentice.

William Middleton died in Winchester in 1887, aged 60. His daughter Caroline had married the previous year and emigrated to Australia where, between 1888 and 1906, she had a large family of seven children (two more died in infancy). She died in Western Australia in 1908, aged 41. Ernest, the youngest sibling, also moved to Western Australia where he died in 1910 at the age of 37. By the time of the 1891 Census only John and Elizabeth Middleton were left living in the family home in Queen's Terrace.

In 1891 or 1892, John Middleton married Charlotte Wood in Winchester. Charlotte had been born in Hursley, near Winchester, on 11 April 1865 and was the daughter of greengrocer Charles Wood and his wife Maria. In the 1891 Census, Charlotte was recorded living with her parents at 7, St James's Street, Winchester, and working as a dressmaker. (The house is now 10, Romsey Road and in early 2020 was the unoccupied last shop up from The Westgate public house). Charlotte had a younger brother, William, who was a book binder.

John and Charlotte quickly started a family, with Bertram being born in October 1892. Charlotte then gave birth to a daughter, Freda, in early 1895, followed by Harold on 6 December 1896 and Lena on 11 November 1900. All the children were born in Winchester. By 1896 the family were living at 50, Western Road, Winchester, a six-room property in Fulflood. The house was later renumbered 7, Cheriton Road. John and Charlotte may have moved there earlier as the Warren's Winchester Directories list an S. Middleton living at the house in 1891 and again from 1893-5 (the 1892 directory in the Hampshire Record Office is missing), but it is not known whether this is a typographical error.

MIDDLETON, Bertram Charles

On 1 February 1900, seven-year-old Bertram entered St Thomas National Church of England Boys' School, Winchester, having previously been a pupil at Western Infants School in Elm Road, Fulflood. His younger brother Harold also attended Western School between February 1904 and October 1910.

The Middletons were still at 50, Western Road in the 1911 Census which listed John as a tailor, Bertram, then 18, as a law clerk and 16-year-old Freda as a millinery apprentice. Harold and Lena, meanwhile, were both described as being at school, although Harold had probably already left by this time. Also living in the house was 81-year-old Maria Wood, Charlotte Middleton's mother.

Bertram Middleton volunteered for military service in November 1914. This was at least three months after Britain declared war on Germany, suggesting that his decision to enlist was not taken in haste. He initially joined the Army Pay Corps (APC), which perhaps suited him given his civilian job as a clerk, but at some point he transferred into one of the British Army's most famous fighting regiments, the Argyll and Sutherland Highlanders.

According to the World War One Service Medal and Award Rolls, 1914-20, Bertram served with four battalions of the Argylls – the 10th, the 11th, the 2nd and the 1/8th. Although it was common for men to join more than one battalion, to serve with four was rare. One possible explanation is that because these four battalions all fought on the Western Front, and the Argylls were often in the thickest of the fighting, casualties would have been high. Consequently, reinforcements from other units within the regiment (and elsewhere) would have been constantly required.

7, Cheriton Road, Winchester (it had been 50, Western Road before being renumbered after the Great War). Bertram and his family lived here from at least 1896. His parents were recorded still living there as late as 1942

Unfortunately, no record has been found to indicate the dates when Bertram joined these battalions and nor does his Medal Index Card show when he first entered a theatre of war. Without these details it is extremely difficult to accurately piece together his military background. However, by using a degree of informed guesswork we can establish a rough outline.

What is known is that Bertram was not entitled to the 1914-15 Star which means that the earliest he could have seen action was 1916. Given that he served with four battalions, he must have been on the Western Front for a considerable time - it was unheard of for a man to serve with four battalions in six months or even a year. Therefore, it is not unreasonable to conclude that Bertram was posted to France sometime in 1916 after leaving the APC. If one accepts this premise, then it is possible to unlock some of the details of his military service.

MIDDLETON, Bertram Charles

The four battalions with which Bertram Middleton has been linked all fought in the major campaigns on the Western Front from 1916 until the spring of 1918 – namely the offensives on the Somme, at Arras and at Passchendaele plus the defensive battles during the German Spring Offensive. Although we cannot identify the individual actions in which he took part, Bertram probably fought in most, or all, of these campaigns. It also means that by the time of his death he was a tough, battle-hardened soldier.

While accepting that the precise details of where and when Bertram fought will never be known, it is believed that that he may have first seen action at the Battle of the Somme on 14 July 1916. Why? The four battalions as listed on Bertram's Service Medal and Award Rolls begin with the 10th Argylls and end with the 1/8th. If the list is chronological, then Bertram was serving with the 1/8th Argylls when he suffered his fatal wounds in 1918. This is supported by the Soldiers Died in the Great War (SDGW) records but contradicted by Commonwealth War Graves Commission records which give his unit as the 2nd Argylls. For this biography it has been assumed that the last battalion Bertram served in was the 1/8th Argylls and that he began his fighting career in France with the 10th Argylls in 1916.

The 10th (Service) Battalion, The Argyll and Sutherland Highlanders had been formed at Stirling in August 1914 and came under orders of 27th Brigade in 9th (Scottish) Division. The battalion moved to billets in New Alresford, near Winchester, in November the same year and then to Bramshott in east Hampshire in February 1915. In May 1915, the Argylls were sent to France and transferred to 26th Brigade, also in 9th Division.

The 10th Argylls had been on the Western Front for about a year when Private Bertram Middleton is thought to have joined them. The battalion was in reserve on 1 July 1916, the opening day of the Somme Offensive, when the British Army suffered more than 57,000 casualties. However, it did take part in the dawn attack of 14 July on objectives that included the village of Longueval and Delville Wood. The assault involved new tactics, with some 22,000 men secretly assembling in the dark and then creeping forward into no-man's land just before zero hour to reduce the distance to the German trenches.

In places, the British forced their way into the German line within seconds. The Argylls, who were attacking Longueval, had to cut their way through the barbed wire, but eventually broke through into the village. German troops in orchards on the northern edge of Longueval poured machine-gun fire on to the attackers, but the Argylls pushed on and even established a foothold in Delville Wood. The Argylls, with the rest of 26th Brigade, fought on for most of the day until exhausted and although unable to capture all of Longueval they did manage to consolidate and construct strongpoints before the Germans counter-attacked.

It is possible that Bertram Middleton took part in the action at Longueval, but for the reasons outlined above the details of the remainder of his military service on the Western Front remain obscure, with one exception – his final battle.

On 21 March 1918, the Germans launched their Spring Offensive in a bid to win the war before the arrival in Europe of hundreds of thousands of American troops. Having failed to achieve a decisive breakthrough in March, they turned their attention the following month to Flanders at the Battle of the Lys (7-29 April).

As stated previously, Bertram is believed to have been serving in Flanders with the 1/8th Argylls when the Lys offensive began. (Incidentally, the 2nd Argylls, listed by the CWGC as Bertram's unit

MIDDLETON, Bertram Charles

at the time, was posted in the same area.) The 1/8th Argylls, who came under orders of 183rd Brigade in 61st (South Midland) Division, found themselves blocking a German advance towards the strategically important railway town of Hazebrouck. So serious was the situation that on 11 April the British Commander-in-Chief, Field Marshal Sir Douglas Haig, issued a Special Order of the Day:

> *There is no other course open to us but to fight it out. Every position must be held to the last man: there must be no retirement. With our backs to the wall and believing in the justice of our cause each one of us must fight on to the end. The safety of our homes and the freedom of mankind alike depend upon the conduct of each one of us at this critical moment.*

Between 12-15 April desperate fighting raged in the villages, fields and forests around Hazebrouck. On 12 April, Bertram Middleton

Bertram Middleton's Commonwealth War Graves Commission headstone in Winchester (West Hill) Cemetery.

was seriously wounded and after being taken from the battlefield to a Casualty Clearing Station he was evacuated to England. Despite being treated in hospital for more than a month he died of his wounds on 21 May 1918, aged 25. According to the Winchester War Service Register, he was a Lance-Corporal at the time he was wounded, but the date of this appointment is unknown.

After the war, John and Charlotte Middleton continued to live at 7, Cheriton Road and were still there in 1942. Army records show two war gratuity payments in respect of Bertram's effects being made to Charlotte in 1918 and 1919. Although it has not been possible to establish when John died, records show that Charlotte passed away in Bournemouth in early 1957, aged 90.

Harold Middleton, Bertram's brother, also fought in the Great War. He enlisted in 1916 and served as a sapper with the Royal Engineers on the home front, reaching the rank of Sergeant. He was not entitled to any medals because he did not enter a theatre of war. In 1923 Harold married 25-year-old Irene White in Winchester and the couple had a son who they named Bertram after Harold's brother. Harold and Irene later moved to Reading where he worked as a clerk at a Ford car distributor. It is not known when Harold died.

Bertram's eldest sister Freda married Edgar Bolwell in 1923. Edgar had served in the Great War with the Royal West Kent Regiment, rising from the ranks to become a 2nd Lieutenant before being discharged – presumably because of wounds – in June 1916. The couple, who are believed to have had one child, moved to Horsham, West Sussex, where Edgar worked as a teacher. He died in Bournemouth in 1963, but the date of Freda's death is unknown.

Lena Middleton, Bertram's youngest sibling, married Ernest Yaldren in Winchester on 17 December 1921. Ernest, who served in France with the Royal Berkshire Regiment in the war, came from a Winchester family and he and Lena appear to have remained in the city after marrying – in 1928 they were living at 28, Greenhill Road, Fulflood, and later moved to 76, Stuart Crescent, Stanmore.

MIDDLETON, Bertram Charles

The couple had three children – Myra (1924-2012), Kenneth (1929-2013) and Cyril (1925-2008) – all of whom were born in Winchester. After Ernest's death at St Paul's Hospital, Winchester, in 1957, Lena remained in Stanmore until 1972 when she moved to 25, Godson House, Lawn Street, Winchester. She died on 14 February 1978, aged 77.

Medals and memorials for Bertram Charles Middleton

Private Bertram Charles Middleton was entitled to the British War Medal and the Victory Medal. He is mentioned on the memorials at St Paul's and St Matthew's churches, Winchester, and on the St Thomas School War Memorial, now held at Kings School, Winchester. Bertram is buried in Winchester (West Hill) Cemetery (GR. 16516). In 1977 his gravestone was replaced by the Commonwealth War Graves Commission and now bears the following additional inscription:

IN LOVING MEMORY
HAROLD, FREDA AND LENA
BROTHERS AND SISTERS

Researchers – GERALDINE BUCHANAN, JOSEPHINE COLEMAN and DEREK WHITFIELD

MITCHELL, William James

Officers Steward 1st Class WILLIAM JAMES MITCHELL
Associated Winchester address – 80, Stockbridge Road (No. 27 today)
Service number 353613. Royal Navy, HMS Invincible
Killed in action, North Sea (Battle of Jutland), 31 May 1916

William James Mitchell was one of the most difficult of the names on the parish memorials to link with Winchester, let alone with Fulflood and Weeke. Many Mitchells with different initials and Winchester connections were researched. However, through work found in the Hampshire Record Office carried out by anonymous researchers in the 1990s, the link was made. William Mitchell's stepsister, Laura Page, lived at 80, Stockbridge Road (No. 27 today), and was presumably responsible for having his name placed on the parish memorials. So far, this is his only known link with the area, that of a much-loved brother and uncle and therefore presumably a visitor when he got leave from the Navy. From subsequent research an interesting, complex and poignant, family history emerged.

Laura Page was born in Winchester on 16 May 1872, but her maiden name was not Mitchell as one would have expected but Gale. Her mother was Lucy Sophia Gale, the daughter of Charles and Eliza Gale. The name of Laura's father is unknown, although one does appear on her marriage certificate.

Laura's grandfather Charles was born in Garrowby, Yorkshire, in about 1816. By the 1871 Census he, his wife Eliza and their family had been living in Winchester at 19, (now No. 4), North View for about three years. Before that, they had lived in Kings Worthy and Hursley. Charles must have had some formal education beyond elementary age because in 1851 he was a schoolmaster in Kings Worthy with ten residential pupils. In the succeeding censuses his occupation and a small change to his birthplace make interesting reading. By 1861, he was a relieving officer in Hursley, i.e. he collected money for the parish union workhouse. In 1871, he stated he was an accountant and had added Hall to his birthplace of Garrowby. Garrowby Hall is the ancestral home of the Earls of Halifax!

Charles Gale's wife Eliza, whom he married in the 1840s, was born in Droxford, Hampshire, in about 1819. She had no occupation listed in the 1851 Census but was presumably busy looking after her young family and ten residential pupils. There were no pupils mentioned in the 1861 Census, but Eliza does not appear to have needed to work.

By 1871, however, the Gales seem to have fallen on more difficult times. Eliza was by then an upholsterer and their two adult children, including Laura's mother Lucy, then 18, also had to earn a living. Living with Charles, Eliza and Lucy were the eldest Gale daughter, Julia, aged 30, a son Frederick, 16, a further daughter Caroline, aged 10, and two grandchildren aged three and one, all with the Gale surname. Lucy was recorded working as a machinist and Julia as a dressmaker.

Laura was born to Lucy Gale in Winchester in 1872 and by the 1881 Census she was living at 8, Avenue Terrace (now Road) with her grandmother Eliza, who was by then a widow. Laura's unmarried aunt, Caroline, a dressmaker, was also living at the house. Laura would probably have been one of the earliest pupils to attend Western School, which opened in 1878, and was just across the road from her home.

Laura's mother Lucy, meanwhile, had married William Thomas Mitchell towards the end of 1880 in Winchester. William, aged about 35, had been a sailor in the Royal Navy before becoming a beer retailer. He was also a widower (his first wife, Jane Long, had died in 1879) with a young son, William James Mitchell, who had been born on 29 December 1874 in Gosport, Hampshire.

MITCHELL, William James

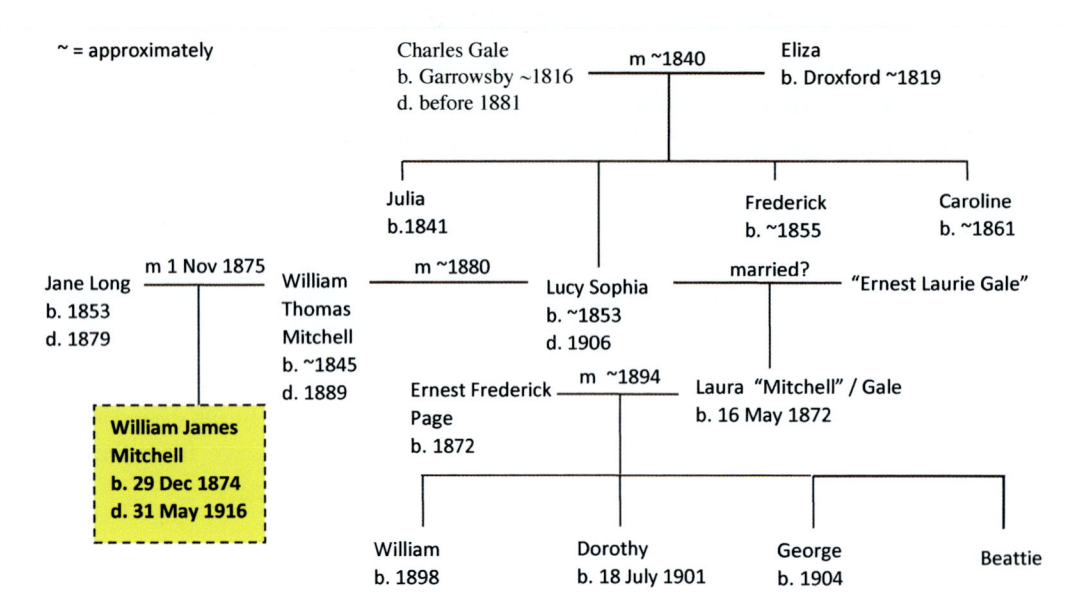

```
                                    Charles Gale      m ~1840    Eliza
                                    b. Garrowsby ~1816 ─────────  b. Droxford ~1819
~ = approximately                   d. before 1881
                                    ┌──────────────────┬──────────────────┐
                                    Julia              Frederick          Caroline
                                    b. 1841            b. ~1855           b. ~1861

                m 1 Nov 1875                m ~1880                married?
Jane Long ─────────────── William ───────────────── Lucy Sophia ─────────── "Ernest Laurie Gale"
b. 1853                   Thomas                    b. ~1853
d. 1879                   Mitchell                  d. 1906
                          b. ~1845       Ernest Frederick   m ~1894   Laura "Mitchell" / Gale
                          d. 1889        Page ──────────────────────  b. 16 May 1872
       ┌──────────────┐                  b. 1872
       │ William James│
       │ Mitchell     │
       │ b. 29 Dec 1874│
       │ d. 31 May 1916│
       └──────────────┘
                          ┌──────────────┬──────────────┬──────────────┐
                          William        Dorothy        George         Beattie
                          b. 1898        b. 18 July 1901 b. 1904
```

William James Mitchell – family tree

Through the marriage William James became Laura Gale's younger stepbrother, although there was no blood relationship. In the 1881 Census, the newly married Lucy and William Mitchell were living in Alverstoke, near Gosport, with William Jnr.

It is not known when Laura joined her mother, stepfather and stepbrother in the Portsmouth area, but it was certainly early enough for her and William James to develop a close sibling relationship. Perhaps Laura left Winchester to join them in 1881, shortly after her mother's marriage and after the census in April 1881 was compiled. Or maybe it was after she had finished her time at Western School in about 1885, when she was 13 and William nearly 11.

William Thomas Mitchell died in 1889. By the 1891 Census his widow Lucy was living in Portsea (Portsmouth) with her daughter Laura. Lucy was working as a laundress and Laura, whose surname was given as Mitchell, as a domestic servant. There were also two lodgers at the address. Back in Winchester, Laura's grandmother, the redoubtable Eliza, by then 72, was sharing a household with another widow and her family at 21, Lower Stockbridge Road (now 52, Stockbridge Road). She was still working as an upholsterer and had three grandchildren, aged from one to 14. living with her,

By 1891 William James Mitchell, then aged 16, appears to have left home; indeed, no trace of him has so far been found in that year's census. Nor is it known whether he was present when his stepsister Laura married Ernest Page in Alverstoke in the spring of 1894. On the marriage certificate she gave her name as Laura Laurie Gale and her father's as Ernest Laurie Gale, an agent. It has not been possible to trace this name and it has been suggested that it was a fabrication to cover the fact that Laura was illegitimate. Laura gave birth to a son, Ernest, later in 1894 but he died two years later.

The year 1894 was a landmark, too, for 19-year-old William Mitchell who joined the Royal Navy at Portsmouth as a Domestic (3rd Class), service number 353613. His service record has survived and it gives a physical description of William: he was 5ft 3ins tall, with hazel eyes, a fresh complexion and fair hair. The record also lists all the ships that he served on from 1894 to 1916.

William served on his first ship, HMS Seahorse, from 1894 until 28 February 1900. Seahorse had been built in 1880 as a sea-going tug, but she was also used for salvage, as a tender, a survey ship and occasionally as a gunship. She was based at Portsmouth so William would have had plenty of opportunity to visit family there and in Winchester.

MITCHELL, William James

William James Mitchell's Navy career

DATE	SHIP	RANK / EVENT
1894	Joined RN	Domestic 3rd class
11 October 1894	Seahorse	
28 February 1900	Duke of Wellington	
07 March 1900	Warspite	
01 July 1902	Duke of Wellington	
26 July 1902		Domestic 2nd class
09 November 1902	Good Hope	
01 April 1905		Domestic 1st class
15 July 1907	Victory I	
01 October 1907		Officers Steward 2nd class
02 October 1907	Illustrious	
02 June 1908	London	
04 October 1908	Surprise	
08 October 1908		Officers Steward 1st class 'Captain's Steward'
26 March 1909	Victory I	
14 April 1909	Ariadne	
26 August 1910	Victory I	
25 November 1910	*Gap in service records*	
10 December 1910	Hermes	
01 January 1913	Hyacinth	
23 January 1913	Victory I	
20 April 1913	Achilles	
01 March 1915	Invincible	
31 May 1916	Invincible	'Discharged Dead Killed in Action' Battle of Jutland

The first mention in Warren's Directory of Ernest Page (the husband of William's stepsister Laura) being a householder in Winchester was in 1896, when he was listed at 14, Elm Road - the address then and now – which was probably the couple's first home together. Ernest, one of six children, had been born in Winchester in 1872. His mother died when he was young and he was looked after by his father who worked as a carpenter as well as publican of the Mildmay Arms in Eastgate Street where the family lived for a time.

By 1897, the year after the death of their young son, Laura and Ernest had moved to 24, Elm Road (the number then and now). In 1898 Laura gave birth to a son, William, and a daughter, Dorothy, on 18 July

MITCHELL, William James

1899. Dorothy was christened at St Matthew's Church, Weeke, on 13 August the same year. She was to grow up and play an important part in the life of Bertram Stroud, another man whose name is on the parish memorials.

In the 1901 Census Laura and Ernest Page were still at 24, Elm Road, Fulflood, with their two young children. However, not all appears to have been well in the life of Lucy Mitchell, Laura's mother and William Mitchell's stepmother, who was recorded living at the Winchester Union Workhouse, then in Upper Stockbridge Road, now St Paul's Hill. Her age was given as 49 and her occupation as a barmaid. Perhaps Lucy was ill in the infirmary or the isolation ward and not in the workhouse proper. If she were ill that would explain why she was not living with her daughter.

It should be noted that by 1901 workhouses were not the grim institutions depicted by Charles Dickens in Oliver Twist. If Lucy were actually in the main workhouse then there may have been all sorts of reasons why she could not live with Laura and Ernest. Space, for example, may well have been a problem. Although the Elm Road property had three bedrooms, the Gale family was expanding and there were also two lodgers living there.

Meanwhile, William Mitchell's naval career was progressing well. He left HMS Seahorse on 28 February 1900 and after a brief posting on HMS Duke of Wellington he moved to HMS Warspite on 7 March 1900 and was recorded among the ship's crew in the 1901 Census. William remained with HMS Warspite until 1 July 1902. There followed another period based on HMS Duke of Wellington at Portsmouth and on 26 July 1902 he was promoted to Domestic (2nd Class). No date is given in his service record for leaving HMS Duke of Wellington and he was not appointed to his next ship HMS Good Hope until 9 November 1902. The Good Hope was a new armoured cruiser brought into service under the command of Captain Charles Madden. William was promoted to Domestic (1st Class) on 1 April 1905.

William's time on HMS Good Hope coincided with his stepsister Laura and family moving to 80, Stockbridge Road (No. 27 today) where a second son, George, was born in 1904. In 1906, William's stepmother Lucy died at the Winchester Workhouse, aged 54. She was almost certainly buried in West Hill Cemetery, probably by the southern wall where workhouse inmates were put in unmarked graves.

In 1906 HMS Good Hope became the flagship of the Admiral of the First Cruiser Squadron in the Atlantic Fleet. This was based at Gibraltar and for the first time William would have had a chance to 'see the world' rather than simply the waters around the British Isles. William served on HMS Good Hope until 15 July 1907. There then immediately followed time on HMS Victory I, Nelson's former flagship and another accommodation and stores ship at Portsmouth.

William became Officers' Steward (2nd Class) on 1 October 1907 and the next day was posted to HMS Illustrious where he remained until 1 June 1908. These dates coincide with those of the captaincy of Hugh H.D. Tothill who was to be captain of HMS Conqueror in the Second Battle-Cruiser Squadron at the Battle of Jutland in 1916.

After HMS Illustrious, William Mitchell went to serve on HMS London, another pre-Dreadnought battleship, from 2/3 June to 4 October 1908 when it was part of the Channel Fleet. He was then immediately assigned to HMS Surprise and promoted to Officers' Steward (1st Class) on 8 October. It is probably from this point in his career that William's family would have referred to his role as the 'Captain's Steward'. HMS Surprise, a small despatch boat, was different to any vessel William had previously served on. Its role was to carry military dispatches as quickly and as safely as possible. Surprise was not as high profile as some of his previous ships, but perhaps new Officers Stewards (1st Class) had to work their way up to the more prestigious warships?

MITCHELL, William James

Left: 14, Elm Road, Winchester, and right 24, Elm Road. William Mitchell's stepsister Laura lived at these properties with her family from 1896 to 1897 and 1897 to 1904 respectively. William probably knew both houses well

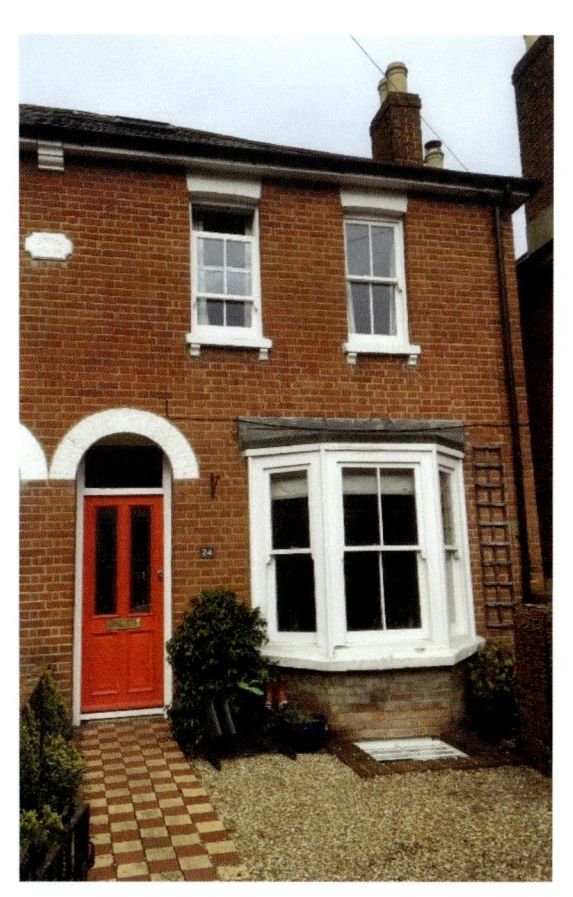

From the time that William Mitchell joined the Navy in 1894, he had always got 'Very Good' in his annual assessments. His role, along with his fellow 1st Class Officers' Stewards, would have been to keep the officers' uniforms in good repair, to lay and serve at their tables and look after the silver tableware. When the ship was at 'Battle Stations' he might have had an active role as a first-aider. HMS Invincible, the last ship William served on, had 12 such Officers Stewards (1st Class) working the three-watch system, so possibly three or four of them would be on duty at any one time.

After leaving HMS Surprise on 26 March 1909, William had just over a fortnight based at HMS Victory 1 at Portsmouth. He was then assigned to the cruiser HMS Ariadne from 14 April 1909 until 26 August 1910. After this posting, he was based again at HMS Victory 1 for more than two months until 25 November 1910. Intriguingly, there is then a gap of just over two weeks in his service record, until 10 December 1910 when he was assigned to HMS Hermes.

The 1911 Census shows William's stepsister Laura and her family still living at 80, Stockbridge Road. The names of three children are given: William, aged 13, who was at school but also earning money as a newsboy; Dorothy, 11, and also at school; and seven-year-old George. Another daughter, Beattie, who had been born after the 1901 Census, was listed staying with her father Ernest's younger sister, Henrietta, and her husband George Powell.

William Mitchell has not yet been found on the 1911 Census but from his service record we know that he was on the cruiser HMS Hermes in April that year. Hermes was the flagship of Sir Paul Warner, Commander-in-Chief of the Cape of Good Hope and West Africa Stations, based at Cape Town, South Africa. This must have been a prestigious posting for William as there would have been much official entertaining. While on Hermes he had his annual assessment on 31 December 1911, and from then on, the word 'Supr.' (Superior) was added to his usual 'Very Good'.

MITCHELL, William James

The battle-cruiser HMS Invincible, William Mitchell's last ship

William was signed off from HMS Hermes on 31 December 1912 when the ship returned to England for a refit. He was reassigned on 1 January 1913 to another cruiser, HMS Hyacinth, but only for three weeks before being posted home to Portsmouth where he served on HMS Victory 1 from 23 January to 19 April 1913.

The following day, William joined HMS Achilles, part of the Second Cruiser Squadron. The squadron was itself part of the First Fleet, within the Home Fleet. The First Fleet and part of the Second Fleet became the Grand Fleet in August 1914. HMS Achilles was one a group of ships sent on 2 August 1914 to defend the Shetland Islands, while the newly-formed Grand Fleet went to its battle stations at Scapa Flow in the Orkney Islands. The Second Cruiser Squadron, including HMS Achilles, was assigned to the Grand Fleet after the Great War broke out on 4 August. It was based at Rosyth, in the Firth of Forth, under Rear-Admiral Sir David Beatty's Battle-Cruiser Squadron. William Mitchell remained on board HMS Achilles until 28 February 1915.

On 1 March 1915 William Mitchell joined his last ship, the battle-cruiser HMS Invincible, under Captain Arthur Cay. Built in 1907, Invincible was comparatively lightly armoured but fast and bristling with heavy guns. She had already seen action in the North Sea in August 1914 at the Battle of Heligoland Bight.

On 8 December 1914, Invincible, together with another battle-cruiser, HMS Inflexible, had sunk the German armoured cruisers Gneisenau and Scharnhorst in the South Atlantic. Invincible had then joined Beatty's Battle-Cruiser Squadron based at Rosyth. In March 1915 she was joined there by the battle-cruiser HMS Indomitable and then HMS Inflexible in June. Together, the three ships formed the Third Battle-Cruiser Squadron with Invincible designated the flagship of Rear-Admiral Sir Horace Hood from 27 May 1915.

There were no major actions for HMS Invincible in 1915. However, William managed to get some shore leave because in the second quarter of that year he married Blanche E. Volker. Blanche was from Portsmouth so she and William may have met when he was on shore leave in the city. Their wedding, however, took place in Winchester and one wonders if Laura Page and her family helped to host the celebrations for her stepbrother and his bride.

The year 1916 was much more active for HMS Invincible and William Mitchell. On 24-25 April, a squadron of German warships bombarded Yarmouth and Lowestoft and Beatty was sent to intercept

MITCHELL, William James

them with the First and Third Battle-Cruiser Squadrons. In the bad weather, they missed the German force, but on the way back to base Invincible had the indignity of being rammed by a smaller British boat and had to limp home to Rosyth for repairs which lasted until 22 May. Almost immediately the Third Battle-Cruiser Squadron was sent to Scapa Flow for gunnery practice. Scapa Flow was the main base for the British Grand Fleet and here Invincible came under the control of Admiral Sir John Jellicoe. For this reason, William Mitchell's squadron fought at Jutland under Jellicoe's leadership and not with the other battle-cruiser squadrons under Beatty.

The Battle of Jutland was conceived as one of several German plans to lure Beatty's force into the North Sea and to defeat it before the Grand Fleet could join them from Scapa Flow. This would give the German Navy parity with the British in the North Sea and make it possible for them to get out into the Atlantic and break Britain's vital trade routes, especially with North America. (Previous German attempts in 1914 are described in the biography of Bert Newby on p. 239.)

Jutland was fought over 36 hours from 31 May-1 June 1916 between the British Grand Fleet and the German High Seas Fleet off Denmark's Jutland Peninsula. It involved much manoeuvring and had three phases. The first involved contact between Vice-Admiral Franz Von Hipper's fast scouting group of five modern battle-cruisers and Beatty's two battle-cruiser squadrons from Rosyth. Hipper's force was used as 'bait' to lure Beatty into the path of the main German fleet.

Because the German naval codebooks had been captured by the Russians in 1914 and shared with her allies, the British knew the German High Seas Fleet was planning to come out of harbour, but owing to a failure of communication between the Admiralty and Jellicoe they did not know when. On 30 May the Grand Fleet under Jellicoe left Scapa Flow. The force included the Third Battle-Cruiser Squadron under Rear-Admiral Hood on board HMS Invincible, which was under orders to rendezvous with Beatty's Battle-Cruiser Fleet coming out from Rosyth. Beatty's role was to try to cut off Hipper's advance force from its base. However, the British did not know that the High Seas Fleet under Admiral Reinhard Scheer had left harbour and was close behind Hipper's force.

Once Beatty's and Hipper's ships came within gunnery range on 31 May, Hipper was the first to fire at 3.48pm and HMS Indefatigable, in Beatty's Second Battle-Cruiser Squadron, was sunk at 4.05pm. HMS Queen Mary, in the First Battle Cruiser Squadron with Bert Newby and Charles Winter on board, was sunk by 4.26pm. (This first phase of the battle is described in more detail on page 239.)

Towards 5pm Beatty was told that the German High Seas Fleet had been sighted. This was the first news that Beatty - and, shortly afterwards, Jellicoe - had that Scheer's battle fleet was at sea. HMS Invincible had not been involved in the first phase of the battle, but at 5.30pm Jellicoe ordered Hood and the rest of the Third Battleship Squadron to go to assist Beatty. Hood was on the bridge of Invincible with his Flag Captain Cay when he sighted Beatty's force at 6.10pm.

The second phase of the battle, when the two nations' fleets engaged each other for the first and last time in the Great War, opened with HMS Invincible firing on and disabling the German ships Wiesbaden and Pillau. She then inflicted two serious hits on the battle cruiser Lutzow. At 6.30pm, however, Invincible suddenly appeared as a clear target for Lutzow and Derfflinger. (Changing visibility created by the smoke, mist, and the light of the setting sun played a vital role in the battle.)

The two German ships each fired three salvoes at Invincible. A shell from the third salvo blew the roof off her Q-turret, detonating the ammunition below and causing the ship to blow up and sink in just 90 seconds. Eyewitness accounts reported that flames shot up from Invincible and then a huge fiery burst with huge columns of dark smoke, mottled with blackened debris, swelled up hundreds of feet into the air.

MITCHELL, William James

Above: HMS Invincible, with William Mitchell on board, explodes after being hit by a salvo of German shells at the Battle of Jutland on 31 May 1916. The photo was taken from a nearby British destroyer. Below: Invincible's bow and stern protruding from the sea after the explosion

The explosion caused HMS Invincible to split into two with its bow and stern sticking in the air before both halves sank. All but six of her crew of 1,032 were killed. Among the dead were Rear-Admiral Hood, Captain Cay and William Mitchell.

The third and final phase of the battle occurred during the night of 31 May/1 June with sporadic fighting by both sides in the dark. By early morning, the German High Seas Fleet was heading for its home base and safety. The Germans quickly claimed victory – after all, they had lost fewer ships and men – but historians today generally agree that the battle resulted in a British strategic victory because the German fleet did not venture out of port for the rest of the war. At the time, however, the outcome caused consternation in the British Admiralty and among a public who had always assumed the overwhelming supremacy of the Royal Navy. This was reflected in the sombre reports that appeared in all newspapers, including the Hampshire Chronicle, immediately after the battle.

A total of 8,645 men were killed and 1,178 wounded at Jutland. Of these, the British lost 6,094 with 674 wounded and the Germans 2,551 and 504 wounded. British shipping losses amounted to 113,000 tons compared to 62,300 tons for the German fleet. Alarmingly for the British, three modern battle-cruisers – Invincible, Indefatigable and Queen Mary – all sank very rapidly after suffering internal explosions. An investigation revealed that ammunition handling practices caused flash fires after a ship was hit. These then spread rapidly to the ammunition stores resulting in the subsequent devastating explosions. The findings led to changes in ammunition handling aboard British ships.

After the war, Invincible was located by a Royal Navy minesweeper lying on a sandy bottom at a depth of 180ft. The ship's stern was right-side up and the bow upside-down. Today, the wreck of HMS Invincible is subject to the Protection of Military Remains Act 1986.

MITCHELL, William James

A modern scan of the wreck of HMS Invincible 180ft down on the bed of the North Sea

In June 1917 three In Memoriam notices were published together in the Hampshire Chronicle to commemorate the first anniversary of William Mitchell's death. The first, which contains a poem adapted from 'Maud' by Alfred Tennyson, was from his wife, Blanche, although she did not give her name, only her address. (In the transcription by Ancestry of the Navy Grave Roll 1914-1919, the name of William's wife is given as Blanche Elizabeth Mitchell with the same address in Portsmouth as on the notice.) The notice reads:

In ever loving memory of my dearly beloved husband, William James Mitchell (Captain's Steward), killed in action on May 31st 1916 on HMS Invincible.

Ah! Christ if it were possible
For one short hour to see
The face I love, that he might tell me
How and where he be
I miss him and mourn him in silence, unseen
And I think of the days that might have been.

FROM HIS SORROWING WIFE
19, St. George's Road East Southsea.

As no child is mentioned, it can be presumed that William and Blanche had no children. They had only been married for about a year, most of which William had spent at sea.

The second notice, from William's stepsister Laura Page, reads:

In ever loving memory of my dearly beloved brother, James Mitchell
(Captain's Steward), who lost his life 31st May 1916 on HMS Invincible.
Gone but not forgotten
From his loving sister Laura.

The final notice was from Laura and Ernest Page's surviving children, William, Dorothy, Beattie and George:

In loving memory of our dear Uncle William James Mitchell who lost his life 31st May 1916 on
HMS Invincible.
From his loving nieces and nephews
Dorsie, Beattie, Willie & George

MITCHELL, William James

Dorothy (Dorsie) Page, William Mitchell's niece, suffered a further bereavement in October 1916 when her fiancée Bertram Stroud was killed at the Battle of the Somme (see his biography on pp. 310). Dorothy later married Harry Pheby and they went to live at 20, Cranworth Road, Winchester. The couple are not thought to have had any children. After Harry's death, Dorothy was recorded living with her mother Laura at 27, Stockbridge Road. Dorothy died in Portsmouth in 1983.

Ernest Page may have died in Winchester in 1928, aged 58, but this age does not tally with other records for him. The last mention of him in Warren's as the householder for 27, Stockbridge Road was in 1929 after which his wife Laura, William Mitchell's stepsister, took over as the householder. In the 1939 Register Laura was still at the same address together with her daughter Dorothy and Kenneth H. Page. Kenneth, who was single, had been born on 29 September 1913 and was a Winchester City Police Constable. His relationship to Laura is unclear. Laura remained at 27, Stockbridge Road until her death on 29 October 1954, aged 82. She had lived at the house since 1904.

Beattie Page, William's youngest niece, married Thomas Pratt in Winchester in 1928. In 1939 they were living in Chichester where Thomas worked as a cinema projectionist. The Pratts do not appear to have had any children. Beattie died in Southampton in 1996, aged about 95.

Medals and memorials for William James Mitchell

William James Mitchell, Officers' Steward (1st Class) was entitled to the British War Medal and the Victory Medal. His final resting place, HMS Invincible, off the coast of Denmark, is a protected war grave. William's name appears on the Naval Memorial (above and right) on Southsea Common in Portsmouth (GN 21) and in Winchester on the memorials at St Paul's and St Matthew's churches.

Researchers – GERALDINE BUCHANAN, JOSEPHINE COLEMAN and CHERYL DAVIS

Additional sources

- http://www.northeastmedals.co.uk/britishguide/jutland/hms_invincible_casualty_list_1916.htm
- http://www.naval-history.net/OWShips-WW1-02-HMS_Invincible.htm
- Corbett, Sir Julian. *Official History Naval Operations Great War*, Vol. III. (Longmans 1923).
- Hampshire Record Office – Ref TOP343//3/679. Six A4 typed and printed pages. No date. No author. Colonel Darroch, Royal Hampshire Regiment Museum, was named as assisting the research.
- www.memorialsinportsmouth.co.uk/pnm-panels.htm

MORRAH, John Henry

**Major JOHN HENRY MORRAH
25, Cranworth Road, Winchester
1st Battalion, The King's Own Royal Lancaster Regiment
Killed in action, France, 18 October 1914**

John Henry Morrah was a career soldier who served throughout the British Empire for nearly 20 years before the Great War. He came from a distinguished upper middle-class family. His father, also an Army officer, later served as Mayor of Winchester while his elder brother was a President of the Oxford Union and later found success as a poet and novelist. John, known as Micky to his Army colleagues, was decorated for gallantry during the Boer War. In the Great War he was one of the 'Old Contemptibles' who fought on the Western Front in the summer and autumn of 1914. He was killed by a German sniper in Flanders in October 1914.

John Morrah was born in Derby on 20 July 1875. His parents were living at 93, Friar Gate at the time and it is likely that his mother, Mary, gave birth to John in the house. James Morrah, John's father, was a Captain in the 60th Rifles (later the King's Royal Rifle Corps) based in Derby. James had been born in 1832 in Chelsea, west London, where his father, also called James, was a surgeon. James Morrah Snr's brother (John's great uncle) also practised medicine and had been assistant surgeon in the 1st Battalion, the 4th Regiment of Foot at the Battle of Waterloo. The 4th Regiment of Foot later became the King's Own Royal Lancaster Regiment in which John Morrah served. James Morrah Snr's wife, Elizabeth (née Pasmore), had lived in Clifton, Bristol, where the couple married before moving to London.

James Morrah Jnr went to Westminster School, where he was a Queen's Scholar, before going on to Oxford. He joined the Army in 1854 and between September and December served briefly with the 3rd West India Regiment and the Cape Mounted Rifles. In 1855 he was commissioned into the 60th Rifles as a Lieutenant and served at that rank for five years. In 1860 he became Adjutant of the 2nd Battalion which took part in the capture of the Taku Forts and the surrender of Peking that year. He was awarded the China War Medal with two clasps in recognition of his service during the campaign.

James was Adjutant of the 7th Battalion at Winchester from 1863 to 1870 when he was appointed Staff Officer of Pensioners, serving in King's Lynn, Canterbury and Woolwich. He retired with the honorary rank of Colonel on 20 March 1887. James Morrah married twice. He had four daughters by his first wife, Emma (née Boulton), although only two, Frances and Emily, survived into adulthood. Emma died in Winchester on 13 May 1867, aged 37, possibly from complications while giving birth to Emily.

James married for a second time on 24 August 1869 in Kingston-upon-Thames, Surrey. His new wife, Mary Lister, had been born in Norton, Derbyshire on 24 June 1844 and was the daughter of civil engineer

MORRAH, John Henry

John Lister and his wife Elizabeth. Mary was living in Kingston and James in Winchester at the time of their marriage.

The couple quickly started a family. A son, Herbert, was born in Winchester in 1870 followed by William in King's Lynn the following year. In late 1872 Mary Morrah gave birth to a daughter, Gertrude, in King's Lynn and then a third son, Edward, also in King's Lynn, in 1874. After John's birth in Derby in 1875 the Morrahs had a sixth child, Mary, who was born in Derby in 1876.

93, Friar Gate, Derby - the house where John Morrah is thought to have been born on 20 July 1875

In 1888, following James's retirement from the Army, the Morrahs moved to Westgate House, 81, High Street, Winchester. The 1891 Census showed four daughters and four servants residing at the property in addition to James and Mary. The daughters included Frances, then 27, and Emily, 23, James's children by his first wife Emma. The census also revealed that the Morrahs' sons, John and Edward, were boarders at Eastbourne College, Sussex.

John's father eschewed a quiet retirement and threw himself into local politics. In 1889 he was elected to Winchester Town Council as a Conservative member for St Thomas ward. Two years later he became Mayor of Winchester, a significant achievement for a man with little political experience. James Morrah served on no fewer than nine council committees in addition to his official duties as mayor.

James continued as a councillor until his death on 14 May 1893, aged 61. Among his many other roles he was chairman of the Executive Committee of the Conservative Association, a member of the Primrose League (an organisation founded in 1883 to spread Conservative principles throughout Britain), treasurer of the Elementary Schools Council and president of the Winchester Volunteer Fire Brigade. Clearly hugely respected, the Hampshire Chronicle's report of his death (Death and Funeral of Col. J.A. Morrah, 20 May 1893, p.5) noted of his time as Mayor: 'How worthily he fulfilled the duties of the office during the year 1890-91 is still fresh in the memories of the citizens.' James's funeral was held at St Thomas's Church with his coffin carried by sergeants of the Rifles. In his will he left £11,871 9s 3d (equivalent to more than £1.5 million in 2019) to his wife Mary and son Herbert.

Mary Morrah continued to live at Westgate House until 1895 when she moved to Glasnevin, a large property in Barnes Close, St Cross, Winchester. The house, No. 3 on the north side of the road, was later renamed Trevean. Mary remained there until 1905 when she moved a short distance to The Willows, another imposing house, on the western side of St Cross road. The property no longer stands and today the site is occupied by modern homes. In 1911 Mary moved once more, this time to West Dene at 25, Cranworth Road, thus beginning the Morrah family's association with Fulflood and Weeke.

In 1893, the year that his father died, John Morrah won a Queen's Cadetship to Sandhurst. He was helped in this by the interest of several influential military figures, including the Duke of Connaught, son of Queen Victoria and Prince Albert, who later became a Field Marshal in the British Army. Such prominent connections show that John and his family moved within the very highest echelons of British society.

MORRAH, John Henry

John Morrah (pictured seating second from the right, second row up) with his fellow battalion officers in around 1910

John left Sandhurst in 1895, was commissioned into the 1st Battalion, The King's Own Royal Lancaster Regiment in March the following year and appointed Lieutenant in November 1897. In the 1901 Census he was living at Tournay Barracks, part of the Aldershot Garrison.

Although the 1st King's Own never fought in South Africa during the Second Boer War John Morrah did. In October 1901 he was sent out to command the regiment's 27th Company of Mounted Infantry and took part in operations in the Transvaal, Orange Free State and Cape Colony before being severely wounded in an engagement with Boer forces at Vredefort in the Orange River Colony on 17 December. Invalided home in February 1902, he spent several months recuperating before rejoining his regiment. John was awarded the Queen's Medal with four clasps for his services during the campaign.

On 19 November 1903 John, by then based in Malta, married Maud Macgregor at St George's Church, Hanover Square, London. Four years older than her husband, Maud had been born in October 1871 in Bombay (modern Mumbai), India. Her father, Cortlandt Macgregor (previously Macgregor-Skinner), was born in Bombay in 1841 and later became a Major in the Royal Engineers. After retiring from the Army, he held the post of Registrar at the Royal College of Science, which was later absorbed into Imperial College. He died in 1893 in Germany. Maud's mother, Sophie (née De Koehler and known as Zosha), was born in Warsaw, Poland, in February 1848. In the 1901 Census, Maud was living with her mother at 15, Carlisle Place, Hanover Square,

Maud's elder sister, Alice, had married John's brother Herbert in 1895 so it is likely that John and Maud had known each other for some time. The newlyweds initially lived in London where a daughter, Marjorie, was born in 1904. Maud gave birth to a son, Michael, in 1907 in Lancaster where, presumably, her husband was stationed at the time.

It has been difficult to precisely track the progress of John Morrah's military career, but it is believed that he also served overseas in Hong Kong, Singapore and Burma (modern Myanmar). Between 1908 and 1910 he held a special staff appointment as Adjutant of the Madras (modern Chennai) Volunteer Guards. The United Grand Lodge of Freemason Membership Registers (Colonial and Foreign section) reveal that John was initiated into the Freemasons in October 1908 when he was living in Lebong, near Darjeeling in northern India. It is not known whether John's family accompanied him to India. However, the 1911 Census, compiled after John had returned to England, showed Maud and the two children living at 29, Cardigan Road, Richmond, west London. John, meanwhile, was recorded as residing in Winchester at The Willows, together with his mother and sister Mary Grace. It is likely that John was merely visiting at the time of the census because by 1912, the year he was promoted to Major, his wife gave birth to a second daughter, Joyce, in Dover where his battalion was stationed at the time.

MORRAH, John Henry

The British Army base at Lebong, near Darjeeling, northern India, where John Morrah was stationed in 1908. It was while here that he was initiated into the Freemasons

What, meanwhile, of John's siblings? The eldest brother, Herbert Morrah, is perhaps the most interesting. Educated privately at Highgate School, London, he later attended St John's College, Oxford, where he was President of the Union. Herbert made several influential friends at Oxford, including F.E. Smith, later a leading Conservative politician, who would rescue Herbert's reputation from potential scandal in the 1920s.

On 13 June 1895 Herbert married Alice Elise Macgregor in Kensington, West London, and the couple's first child, Dermot, was born in Ryde, Isle of Wight, on 26 April 1896. By this time Herbert had already embarked on a literary career. This had begun in 1894 with a volume of verse, 'In College Fields', followed by three novels, 'A Serious Comedy' (1896), 'The Faithful City' (1897) and 'The Optimist' (1898). In February 1898 Alice gave birth to a daughter, Stella Margaret, in Ryde followed by a second girl, Kathleen Cecilia, in London in November 1901. The census in April of that year showed the family living at 51, Ravenscourt, Notting Hill, west London, with Herbert working as an author and editor.

By 1911, Herbert, Alice and their children had moved to 14, Addison Gardens, Kensington, west London. That year saw the publication of Herbert's book Highways and Hedges in which he describes the charm of English country life. His words are accompanied by romantic colour landscape plates by the artist Berenger Benger. By contrast, the life of Edward Morrah was blighted by tragedy. After leaving Eastbourne College he served an apprenticeship as an electrical engineer and was inducted into the Institute of Electrical Engineers in 1899. However, on 15 January 1900 Edward was admitted as a patient to Menston Lunatic Asylum, near Leeds, Yorkshire, where he died three months later, on 25 April at the age of 26.

John Morrah's other brother, William, was musically gifted and he worked for a time as a 'vocalist'. In April 1903, William married French-born Marguerite Longhurst, the daughter of a journalist. By 1911 the couple were living in Friern Barnet, Middlesex, with their daughter, Marie. The census of that year recorded William's profession as a 'traveller in motorists'.

Gertrude Morrah, John's elder sister, qualified as a midwife in 1902 and by 1904 she was working at Guy's Hospital, London. On 26 January 1909 Gertrude married Leonard Latham Wickham, the son of

MORRAH, John Henry

Winchester clergyman Henry Wickham, in Vepery, Madras, India. Leonard worked as an executive engineer for the Madras Public Works Department before retiring in 1914. At this point the couple returned to England and Gertrude went back to work at Guy's Hospital.

The 1st King's Own (Royal Lancaster) Regiment were still based in Dover serving with 12th Brigade, part of 4th Division, when the Great War broke out in August 1914. Fears of a German invasion meant the Division was held back from the original British Expeditionary Force (BEF) sent to the Continent, but when it became clear that the Germans did not intend to cross the Channel this decision was reversed and the 4th Division embarked for France aboard the SS Saturnia, landing at Boulogne on 23 August. The same day the BEF fought its first major engagement of the war at the Battle of Mons.

25, Cranworth Road, Winchester – home to John Morrah's mother and, following her death in 1920, his sister Mary Grace

Within days, John Morrah's battalion was involved in fierce fighting at the Battle of Le Cateau. Early on 26 August, after an all-night march to cover the retreat of the main body of the BEF from Mons, the King's Own were resting at Haucourt, near Le Cateau, when they suddenly came under murderous German artillery and machine-gun fire. The battalion suffered more than 430 casualties in a single two-minute burst of machine-gun fire which nearly destroyed it as a fighting unit. Among the 64 men killed was the Commanding Officer, Lieutenant-Colonel Alfred Dykes.

Captain (later Colonel) Lionel Cowper was among those who fought with the King's Own at Le Cateau and he later described his devastating first experience of modern industrial warfare. The men, he wrote, were waiting to have their breakfasts when 'a tremendous burst of machine-gun fire opened on them, killing Colonel Dykes almost immediately [his dying words were 'Goodbye, boys']. Then the German artillery began to shell the battalion's positions:

> *At first their fire was short, but they soon found the range and the shells started to burst about thirty to fifty yards in front of the leading company. The first burst of fire did not touch the transport and some of the drivers tried to turn their horses round and get them to cover, but the machine guns then appeared to lengthen the range and bullets began to drop amongst them. Then came the shells, and chaos ensued. The first shell hit the cooker; the mess cart was immobilised with the horses dead between the shafts; the remaining horses bolted and some of the vehicles got locked together; others, both horse and vehicles, galloped off in all directions; the jackets of the machine guns were reported to have been holed and therefore useless. The small dog, for which the men had made a coat out of a Union Jack, was killed as he stood next to the driver of a wagon. One by one company commanders tried to get their men to cover, but 'C' Company was almost entirely wiped out.*

MORRAH, John Henry

Fighting raged for most of the day with the King's Own continuing to take casualties. Following the death of Colonel Dykes and with the second in command temporarily missing, John Morrah took over as CO. Captain Cowper's account continues:

> [W]hen it was later possible to discover the losses in the battalion they were found to be five officers killed, six wounded, of whom two were taken prisoner, and one missing; no less than 431 other ranks were killed, wounded and missing, a total which, even in the bloody battles of Ypres and the Somme, was never reached again in a single day by the 1st Battalion. This introduction to war was a rude shock to the majority who had never previously a shot fired in anger. Even those who had served in South Africa were unprepared for anything of the sort, and Grover declared that Spion Kop was 'child's play' in comparison.

Over the following days the King's Own, together with the rest of the BEF, were pushed back towards Paris by the advancing German armies. Although no longer CO, John Morrah is believed to have been second in command and his military experience would have proved invaluable in maintaining his men's morale during this period of exhausting forced marches. The King's Own then featured in the Allied counterattack at the Battle of the Marne (5-9 September) which first halted and then pushed back the Germans. John was appointed temporary CO on 9 September and he led his battalion during the Battle of the Aisne (12-15 September). At the Aisne, the Germans began to dig in along the high ground of the Chemin des Dames ridge, signalling the start of trench warfare on the Western Front.

After nearly a month on the Aisne, the King's Own were sent north to Flanders with the rest of the 4th Division, arriving at Hazebrouck on 12 October. Nine days earlier, John Morrah's spell in charge of the battalion had come to an end with the appointment of Lieutenant-Colonel Herbert Creagh-Osborne as CO. This was probably more to do with John's relative inexperience rather than a reflection of his performance as acting CO – after all, he had been a Major for less than two years.

On 13 October, the King's Own joined an attack by the British III Corps on the town of Meteren during the opening phase of the Battle of Armentieres (13 October-2 November). The battalion advanced across flat country through a thick early morning fog which unfortunately lifted as the troops approached Meteren where the Germans occupied houses with an excellent field of fire. Captain Cowper was again in the thick of the action:

> As soon as the battalion emerged from the lane it came under machine-gun and rifle fire, but there was no hesitation and the men continued to advance in perfect order by the orthodox method of the time, in short rushes. The plan was for the machine guns to cover the advance by engaging with fire the enemy on the southern outskirts of the village, but no sooner did [Lieutenant Anthony] Morris emerge from the farm enclosures than he was seen from the church tower. He took up a position behind a scanty hedge, where he and his team were later found in a tidy row of eight, all dead and their gun out of action.

> Visibility was so poor that the artillery was never able to support the advance, and with the battalion machine guns out of commission there was nothing to hinder the enemy fire. So heavy did it become that all four companies were driven to find cover as best they could in the wet ditches and hedgerows on their right and in their rear ... Sergeant E. Howard crawled out into the open to find out why twelve men who were lying there did not fire, though he shouted at them to do so. He found them all dead. The Lancashire Fusiliers were ordered to fill the gap on the right of the King's Own, but by nightfall they had not arrived and the Regiment had to continue to protect its own flanks.

> After dark, the wounded were collected up in the farmhouse, and the Lancashire Fusiliers not only came up on the right of the King's Own but pushed on into Meteren, which they found deserted. Most of the next day was spent in clearing the battlefield ... The men were horrified to see how little of Meteren was still standing. Whole families were homeless, and the small children who begged for bully beef did not ask in vain.

MORRAH, John Henry

Right: A newspaper report of Major John Morrah's death in 1914 and, far right, his Queen's Medal with four clasps which he received for his bravery during the Second Boer War in 1901

The attack on Meteren cost the King's Own another 36 men killed, 34 wounded and 15 missing. Seven more died of wounds over the next two days.

On 18 October, Major John Morrah was shot dead by a German sniper near Armentieres as he attempted to signal to officers of a neighbouring regiment. Colleagues reported that he died instantly. John fought on the Western Front for less than two months, but in that time he impressed with his bravery, coolness under fire and inspirational leadership. He was posthumously mentioned in BEF Commander-in-Chief Sir John French's Despatch of 14 January 1915. News of his death soon reached Winchester and on 7 November 1914 the Hampshire Chronicle published the following obituary (The Casualty List, p. 10):

Major John Henry Morrah, the King's Own Royal Lancaster Regiment, who was killed in action on October 18th, aged 39, was the youngest son of the late Col. James Arthur Morrah, formerly of the King's Royal Rifle Corps, and was educated at Eastbourne College and Sandhurst. He received his commission in March 1896 and was appointed Lieutenant in November 1897, Captain in May 1901 and Major in December 1912. He served in the South African campaign, in which he was severely wounded, receiving the Queen's medal with four clasps, and was afterwards continuously employed on active service in India and other parts of the Empire viz, at Malta, Hong Kong, Singapore, Calcutta, Burma, Darjeeling, Madras (as Adjutant of the Madras Volunteer Guards), South Africa etc. The late Major Morrah was dangerously wounded near Vredefort on December 17th 1901. He married, in 1903, Maud Florence, younger daughter of the late Major Cortlandt Macgregor RE, and leaves a widow and three children, for whom, together with his mother and two sisters, who reside at Winchester, much sympathy will be felt.

A brother officer wrote of him: 'He really was a gallant officer, how gallant only we who saw him from day to day can tell, going about among the men with conspicuous coolness when danger was greatest and bullets were thickest – an example of sterling bravery. Today the Regiment that has done so much, and is still going to do more, is the poorer by a gallant officer, an English gentleman, and a sincere and keen soldier.'

Another correspondent writes: Major John Henry Morrah was the youngest son of the late Colonel James Arthur Morrah, whose connection with the city of Winchester dated from the year 1854, when he received his first commission in the 60th Rifles, and was continued in various ways until his death in 1893, including the Mayoralty, which he held in the year 1891.

The late Major Morrah, who received the honour of a Queen's Cadetship at Sandhurst, through the kindly interest of the late General Montgomery and other Riflemen, including H.R.H. the Duke of Connaught, received his earlier education at Eastbourne College, of which he remained always a loyal and attached member. His choice of the King's Own Royal

MORRAH, John Henry

Lancaster Regiment was due to the association therewith of his great uncle, William Morrah, whose record was one of considerable distinction and included the Battle of Waterloo.

The late Major Morrah was gazetted to his Regiment in 1896. His promotion was rapid – in 1901 he secured his company and in 1912 his majority. He served in a number of different stations, such as Hong Kong, Singapore, Burma, as well as in England, and on the staff he held a special appointment from 1908 to 1910 as Adjutant of Indian Volunteers at Madras. In the South African War he took part in the operations in the Transvaal, the Orange River Colony, and Cape Colony and during the campaign he was very severely wounded. He held the Queen's medal with four clasps.

In the present campaign the deceased officer had taken part in many important engagements and during the whole of the time up to the middle of October his letters had been full of interesting details, written with the spirit for which he was famous in his Regiment and amongst a large circle of friends. He fell the victim of a German sniping bullet, and his death was mercifully instantaneous. It is understood that at the moment of the fatal shot he was standing up to signal to the Seaforth Highlanders across the river, and that the operations, which were shared by Major Lysons and Captain Lendon of the same Regiment, took place in the neighbourhood of Le Touquet. These two officers subsequently fell and the three were buried side by side.

Of his brilliantly sunny temperament, as well as of his fine soldierly gifts and qualities, 'Micky' Morrah, as he was often familiarly known, leaves an ineffaceable impression, and many accounts received from the front since his lamented death speak in the most glowing terms of his admirable courage, cheerfulness and unselfishness, whatever the circumstances.

Maud Morrah and her three children were living at 129, Hamlet Gardens, Ravenscroft Park, west London, when John died. However, when probate was granted, on 29 April 1915, her address was given as 77, The Esplanade, Dover. John left his wife an estate valued at £1,373 15s 3d. Army records show that Maud also received £29 13s in respect of lost kit in May 1915, a further payment of £21 in July 1915 and a £60 war gratuity in September 1919. Maud never remarried. She later emigrated to Southern Rhodesia (modern Zimbabwe) to be with her daughter Marjorie who had moved there in 1946 with her husband Linzee Otho Wooldridge. Maud died in Salisbury (now Harare) on 12 April 1959, aged 87. Marjorie died in 1982, aged 78.

Michael Morrah, John's son, trained as an accountant. He married Catherine Day in Bromley, south London, in 1935 and spent much of his working life overseas, particularly in the Caribbean and the United States. The couple had at least one child, a daughter called Anne, born in 1937. Michael returned to England and died in Ploughley, Oxfordshire, in December 1977, aged 71.

John's youngest child, Joyce, was recorded working as a shorthand typist in 1939 and living with her elderly mother at 156, Sussex Gardens, Paddington, London. In 1946, the same year that her sister Marjorie moved to Rhodesia, Joyce married Charles Stumbles, the Civil Commissioner for Southern Rhodesia in Durban, South Africa. Her place and date of death are not known.

Mary Morrah, John's mother, continued to live at 25, Cranworth Road, Winchester, until her death in 1920, aged 76. Her daughter, Mary Grace, had presumably been living with her for some years because her name then appears as the householder of the property in Warren's Directories until 1929. In 1931 Mary was recorded as living with her sister Gertrude and husband Leonard Wickham at 10, Compton Road, St Cross, Winchester. Gertrude is believed to have died in Winchester in 1932 and the same year Mary Grace moved to 2, St James's Villas, Winchester, where she remained until her death, aged 76, on 11 December 1942. Interestingly, Mary Grace's stepsister, Emily, who it is believed served as a nurse at Guy's Hospital while Gertrude Morrah worked there as a midwife, was living with her when she died.

MORRAH, John Henry

William Morrah, John's brother, does not appear to have fought in the Great War. Instead, he continued to live in London with his family; by 1936 he and wife Margueritte were in Harrow and in 1939 in Wembley with William recorded working as a 'superintendent at Selfridges'. He is thought to have died in St Albans, Hertfordshire, in March 1953, aged 81.

Herbert Morrah, John's artistic eldest brother, enlisted in the Royal Navy Voluntary Reserve in 1914 and worked for the Admiralty in Room 40, a top-secret intelligence department. The predecessor of the code-breaking centre at Bletchley Park in the Second World War, Room 40 provided vital intelligence to the British military and their allies between 1914-18. Its main task was to intercept and decrypt German wireless and telegraph messages, particularly those relating to German shipping and U-boats.

After the war Herbert returned to civilian life, but in 1927 found himself at the centre of a scandal when he was prosecuted for what the newspapers of the day somewhat coyly described as 'an offence in a West End theatre'. Fortunately, he was able to call upon his old university friend F.E. Smith - by this time Lord Birkenhead and Lord Chancellor of England – as a character witness and his evidence led to Herbert's acquittal. Herbert's wife Alice died in Bristol in September 1930, aged 61. Herbert himself died in hospital in Sutton, Surrey, on 20 March 1939, aged 68. His son Dermot, by this time a successful journalist with the Daily Mail, had also served in the Great War as a Lieutenant in the Royal Engineers. Dermot's grandson is the journalist Tom Utley, a long-time columnist on the Daily Mail.

Medals and memorials for John Henry Morrah

Major John Henry Morrah was entitled to the 1914 (Mons) Star, the British War Medal and the Victory Medal. He is buried at Le Touquet Railway Crossing Cemetery (grave right), Comines-Warneton, Hainaut, Belgium, (GR. A. 6). His name appears on the memorials at St Paul's, St Matthew's and St Thomas's churches, Winchester, and the Eastbourne College and Royal Lancaster Regiment memorials. There is also a pew plaque (above) commemorating John Morrah in St Mary's Priory Church, Lancaster.

Researchers – DEREK WHITFIELD, JENNY WATSON and GERALDINE BUCHANAN

Additional sources

- Colonel Lionel Cowper: *The King's Own, The Story of a Royal Regiment, Volume III, 1914-1950.* (Oxford, 1939)
- https://www.eastbourne-college.co.uk/wp-content/uploads/2018/08/esorg-roll-of-honour-2018-08-15.pdf
- https://weaponsandwarfare.com/2017/10/05/room-40-at-the-admiralty
- https://www.greatwarforum.org/topic/137935-kings-own-royal-lancaster-regiment-war-diaries/
- http://www.kingsownmuseum.com/fww-centenary1914augactions.htm

MORRISON, David Thomson

Armourer Sergeant-Major DAVID THOMSON MORRISON
(Believed to be A. Morrison listed on memorials)
19, Brassey Road, Winchester
Service numbers 655 and A/1663. 12th Section, Army Ordnance Corps
Died in Winchester, 24 February 1919

There is uncertainty over the identity of the soldier listed as A. Morrison on the memorials at St Paul's and St Matthew's churches. No one of that name appears in the Winchester War Service Register, the official censuses or Warren's Winchester Directory. However, the records of the Commonwealth War Graves Commission do include a David Thomson Morrison, a pre-war Regular soldier who lived in Brassey Road. He served with the Army Ordnance Corps (which became the Royal Army Ordnance Corps in 1918) during the Great War and died in Winchester in early 1919. Errors on war memorials are not unknown and so, in the absence of an alternative explanation, the authors of this book believe it is likely that David Morrison is the man listed on the two memorials.

David Morrison was born in Edinburgh on 8 February 1866, the youngest of six children. His father, Alexander, was born in Salton, East Lothian, in 1824 and worked as a blacksmith. On 1 June 1846 Alexander married Isabella Harrison in Edinburgh. Isabella, who had been born around 1826, was the daughter of Edinburgh shoemaker William Harrison and his wife, also called Isabella. Alexander and Isabella went on to have five children in addition to David: Anna, born in 1850, Jane (1855), William (1858), John (1861) and Jessie (1863). All were born in Edinburgh.

David spent his childhood in Edinburgh. The 1871 Census showed the Morrisons living at 83, Rose Street, which is possibly where David had been born. Nothing is known of his education, but by 1881 when the family were at 108B, Rose Street, he was working as an apprentice to Edinburgh gunsmith John Dickson & Son, based in nearby Princes Street. Established in 1820, Dickson & Son had gained fame for their unique gun trigger plate mechanism

An advertisement for Edinburgh gunsmith John Dickson & Son with whom David Morrison was apprenticed in the 1880s

that was admired for its strength, elegance and balance. David's brothers were also working by this time - William as a printer's machine-man and John as a blacksmith.

On 29 October 1888 David Morrison joined the Army in Birmingham, enlisting as a Private with the Corps of Armourers, a branch of the Army Ordnance Corps (AOC), for seven years plus five in the Reserve. However, over the course of his career he twice extended his period of service and ended up serving more than 25 years before his retirement in 1914. Although armourers were 'badged' and trained by the AOC most went on to serve with infantry battalions (one per battalion). Their job was to maintain and repair the unit's rifles, pistols and other mechanical equipment – including, oddly enough, bicycles. With his background as a gunsmith David was perfectly suited to the role.

On enlisting, David received the service number 655. His Army records showed that he was 5ft 7in tall, weighed 9st 4lbs and had brown eyes and dark brown hair. He was clearly a good soldier because by

MORRISON, David Thomson

the following March, after less than five months in the Army, he had been promoted to Armourer Sergeant, 2nd Class. David's Army records show that besides military training and instruction he also received a more general education at the Royal Military Asylum, Chelsea, and the Royal Hibernian Military School in Dublin.

On 8 September 1889, David married Catherine Elizabeth Worrall at St Saviour's Church, Birmingham. The couple had almost certainly met after David moved to the city to enlist. Catherine, known to friends and family as Lizzie, had been born in 1865 in the Aston area of Birmingham. Her father, Henry (1842-1894), was a pearl button maker and he and Catherine's mother, Lucy (née Paddon 1843-1901), had a total of ten children together.

Within weeks of marrying, David was posted to India and his new bride either accompanied him or followed shortly afterwards. Once in India David was sent to the Ordnance Corps base at Allahabad (modern Prayagraj in the state of Uttar Pradesh) in November 1889 and then, a month later, to the AOC arsenal at Rawalpindi (in Punjab province in modern Pakistan). In April 1990 he was assigned to the 2nd Battalion, The Highland Light Infantry based in Peshawar (in modern Pakistan)

On 5 September 1890 Catherine Morrison gave birth to a daughter, Jessie, in Peshawar. Two more daughters followed – Lucy on 1 March 1892 and Helen on 1 September 1895. Both girls were born in Fyzabad (modern Faizabad in Uttar Pradesh, India).

As David's family life prospered so, too, did his military career and on 1 March 1894 he was promoted to Armourer Sergeant 1st Class. However, life in India was starting to take its toll on his wife. During 1896 Catherine suffered frequent attacks of dyspepsia – a condition affecting the oesophagus, gullet and intestine – which led to vomiting and ultimately anaemia. She was sent to the hills to recuperate and prescribed iron tonics, but to little avail. In January 1897, an Army medical board recommended that Catherine, by this time pregnant with a fourth child, should return to England and that David should be allowed to go with her.

On 10 May 1897, two months after arriving back in England, David was posted to the 2nd Battalion, The Lincolnshire Regiment with whom he remained for a year before returning to the Ordnance Corps depot in Sheffield. Catherine, meanwhile, had given birth to another daughter, Lilian, on 18 June 1897. Lilian, however, died two years later and was one of two Morrison children to die in infancy. Another daughter, Elsie, was born in Sheffield on 3 January 1899, by which time it appears Catherine Morrison's health had improved significantly.

In January 1900 David Morrison was posted to South Africa where he saw action in the Second Boer War. It is not known to which regiment he was assigned, but his Army records show that he remained overseas until 1903 and was awarded the King's South Africa Medal with clasps for 'Cape Colony', 'Paardeburg' and 'Johannesburg'. The Battle of Paardeburg, fought at Paardeburg Drift in Orange Free State between 18 and 27 February 1900, was particularly significant. In it, a 4,000-strong Boer force under General Piet Cronje was besieged and eventually forced to surrender to a British and Canadian army commanded by Field Marshal Lord Frederick Roberts and General Horatio Kitchener.

In June 1903 David returned to England where he was to spend the next 11 years of his Army career. The following month he was transferred to the AOC base at Colchester, Essex, before being promoted to Staff Armourer Sergeant on 5 December. A posting to 1st Battalion, The Grenadier Guards followed

MORRISON, David Thomson

in March 1904 when his rank was redesignated as Armourer Quarter-Master-Sergeant. On 29 August, the same year Catherine gave birth to another daughter, Marjorie Primrose, in Windsor. The Morrisons were clearly moving around a great deal in this period because on 9 March 1906 a sixth surviving child, Grace, was born in Aldershot.

In 1909 David Morrison was presented with the Long Service and Good Conduct Medal together with a gratuity in recognition of his 21 years' military service. The same year he was promoted to Armourer Sergeant-Major and posted to the Rifle Brigade Depot in Winchester where he settled down to spend what he believed would be his final five years in the armed forces.

The family moved in to 10, Brassey Road, a comfortable five-room house which became No. 19 when the street was renumbered in 1913. In the 1911 Census all the Morrison daughters except Jessie were living at the house, with 19-year-old Lucy working as a dressmaker and Elsie, aged 12, a pupil at the County High School for Girls in Cheriton Road. Jessie, meanwhile, was living in London and working as a dressmaker.

19, Brassey Road, Winchester – David Morrison's home from 1913 until his death

David Morrison retired from the Army on 3 February 1914, but he had little opportunity to enjoy his new-found leisure time. When war broke out six months later, he immediately re-joined his old Corps as a volunteer and was assigned the rank of Warrant Officer 1st Class. He received the new service number A/1663 and served with the 12th Section of the Army Ordnance Corps. Few details of David's war record can be found but given that he was nearly 50 it is unlikely that he served overseas. It is believed that he probably served with the AOC at the Rifle Brigade Depot in Winchester.

David Morrison survived the war but just three months after the Armistice, he was suddenly taken ill – probably with Spanish flu – and died at his home on 24 February 1919. He was 53 years old. His obituary in the Hampshire Chronicle on 8 March 1919 stated:

> *MILITARY FUNERAL – The death took place on February 24th, at his residence Brassey Road, of Armourer Sergeant-Major David Thomas [sic] Morrison, Army Ordnance Corps. For five years prior to 1918 Armourer Sergeant-Major Morrison was at the Rifle Brigade Depot and he re-joined on the outbreak of war. In his earlier days he served in India and also in the South African War. He returned home from Stirling, where he had recently been employed, on February 14th, and was taken ill almost immediately, passing away as stated.*
>
> *The funeral with full military honours was last Saturday afternoon. The body – enclosed in a coffin covered with the Union Jack, and on which were placed beautiful floral emblems – was borne on a gun carriage from the R.G.A. (Royal Garrison Artillery) Camp, the escort, firing party, band and buglers being furnished from the Rifle Depot. The first part of the service was conducted at St Paul's Church, after which the cortege crossed the Rifle Depot Square to the cemetery at West Hill, where the interment took place.*

Following her husband's death Catherine Morrison continued to live at 19, Brassey Road before moving a few doors to No.7 in around 1930. Three of her daughters - Lucy, Marjorie and Grace – lived with her

MORRISON, David Thomson

throughout the 1930s. Lucy and Marjorie both worked as clerks while Grace was a teacher. The three daughters, who never married, remained at 7, Brassey Road, following their mother's death in 1948. Records show them living in the property in 1951 and Lucy was still there in 1954. She later moved to a new property in Bereweeke Avenue where she remained until her death in 1972, aged 80. Grace died in Winchester in 1988, aged 82, and Marjorie in 1991 at the age of 86.

Jessie Morrison also remained single. In 1939 she was working as a live-in domestic help for a family in Epsom and Ewell, Surrey. It is not known when she died. Helen Morrison, too, never married. In 1939 she was living in Bognor Regis and died in Winchester in 1981, aged 86. Elsie was the only Morrison daughter not to remain single. She married Wilfred Hurry in Gipping, near Stowmarket, Suffolk, in 1940 and died in Bury St Edmunds on 19 December 1992, aged 95. It is not known whether the couple had any children.

Medals and memorials for David Thomson Morrison

Armourer Sergeant-Major David Thomson Morrison was not entitled to any Great War medals because it is not believed that he served in a theatre of war between 1914-18. Together with his wife Catherine, he is buried at West Hill Cemetery (grave above), Winchester (Record Plan No. 63 and GR. 16609). David is listed in the records of the Commonwealth War Graves Commission, but his grave is not typical of those instituted by the CWGC. It is inscribed with the words:

**IN LOVING MEMORY
DAVID THOMPSON MORRISON
ARMOURER SERGEANT MAJOR R.O.A.C
Who fell asleep Feb 25th 1919
Aged 53 years
Peace Perfect Peace
Also his wife
Catherine Elizabeth Morrison**

David Morrison is also commemorated on the memorials at St Paul's and St Matthew's churches, Winchester, under the name A. Morrison

Researchers – DEREK WHITFIELD, JENNY WATSON and GERALDINE BUCHANAN

MULDOWNEY, John Henry

Private JOHN HENRY MULDOWNEY
7/15A, Greenhill Road, Winchester (No.13 today)
Service number 818241. 26th Battalion, Canadian Infantry
(New Brunswick Regiment)
Killed in action, France, 8 August 1918

John Henry Muldowney was born in Winchester on 15 April 1898. The son of Thomas William and Rosabella Muldowney, he was one of four children and known as Jack to family and friends. His father, who served as a soldier and then as a policeman in Winchester, became something of a local celebrity after being shot while tackling a gunman. Jack emigrated to the United States in his early teens and lived for several years in Boston. In 1916, aged 18, he travelled to Canada to enlist with the Canadian Expeditionary Force with whom he served on the Western Front until his death in August 1918.

Jack's father Thomas was born in Winchester in 1872. Thomas's own father, John (1818-1891), had been born in Dublin and went on to serve in the 22nd Regiment of Foot, reaching the rank of Sergeant. After being admitted as a Chelsea Pensioner in 1852 John went on to serve as a Sergeant in the Militia. In the 1861 Census he was living in Winchester with his wife Ellen (née Budd) – who was 17 years his junior - and three young children at 12, North View.

In 1881 John and Ellen were still living at 12, North View along with their three daughters and nine-year-old Thomas. On leaving school in 1887, Thomas joined the Royal Marines Artillery with the service number 3423. However, on 3 August 1893, he bought himself out of the Army and joined the police force. John Muldowney died in 1891 (possibly in Fareham lunatic asylum), but Thomas and his mother continued to live at 12, North View.

In 1896 Thomas married 23-year-old Rosabella Dowse in Winchester. Born in Southampton on 27 December 1872, Rosabella – known as Rose - was listed in the 1881 Census living at 64, Water Lane, Winchester, under her mother Priscilla's surname of Sandom. By the 1891 Census, however, she was known as Rosabella Dowse, having taken her stepfather James's name. Her occupation was domestic servant and she lived with a family called the Flights at their home at 91, High Street, Winchester.

Rose gave birth to three other children in addition to Jack: Ellen, known as Nellie, in 1897, Richard Ernest in 1901 and Edward Stanley in 1905. By the time that Jack was born, the Muldowneys had moved to 7, Greenhill Road, Winchester, which was the family's address in the 1901 Census. Also living at the house was Jack's 63-year-old grandmother, Ellen, who was recorded as being a retired monthly nurse. Women of this period were expected to rest in bed or at home for extensive periods after giving birth and care was provided either by female relatives (usually the mother or mother-in-law) or, for those who could afford it, by the monthly nurse. These weeks of confinement or 'lying-in' ended with the re-introduction of the mother to the community in the Christian ceremony of the churching of women.

On 24 October 1902 Thomas Muldowney and another police constable tackled an armed gunman called Howard Brunless during an incident in Winchester. Brunless shot PC Muldowney in the wrist during the violent confrontation but he was then overpowered by the other officer. The wound partially disabled Thomas and both officers were highly commended by the Winchester Watch Committee, the body which oversaw the city police force.

In 1905 seven-year-old Jack Muldowney, still living at 7, Greenhill Road, was enrolled at St Thomas Elementary Boys' School in Mews Lane. Like his younger brothers later, he had probably previously attended Western Infants School.

MULDOWNEY, John Henry

John Muldowney's parents, Thomas (left) and Rosabella, and his brother Edward, right

The years 1911-12 were a turbulent period for the Muldowney family. Although still only 12 years old, Jack left home in the early part of 1911 and was not recorded living at home in the census taken in April. In fact, it appears he was no longer even in the country as a note in the St Thomas School logbook states that he had 'left for America'. Although Jack's parents and younger brothers were still living in Greenhill Road, his sister, Ellen, had also left home and was living with her grandmother Ellen at 7, St John's Hospital (South), Winchester, and working as an apprentice dressmaker. Ellen Snr was recorded living at St John's as an inmate and she died there later the same year. The following year Thomas Muldowney, still aged only 39, resigned from the police force.

Today it seems inconceivable that Jack Muldowney should have left home so young and that his parents should have allowed him to do so. However, 100 years ago attitudes were very different and it was not uncommon for young children to leave home. They did so for a variety of reasons – to relieve the pressure on the family budget, to free up space in what were often overcrowded homes, or simply because they did not get on with one or both parents. That said, Jack was exceptionally young when he left home and his decision to seek a new life overseas was unusual and would not have been taken lightly.

Jack's enlistment papers from 1916 give some clues to his life after arriving in America. He gave his address as 35, Moreland Street, Roxbury, which was then a suburb of Boston in the state of Massachusetts. Pay records show that after enlisting Jack regularly sent money ($20) to his 'sister-in-law, Mrs E. Muldowney', who was living at 35, Moreland Street. Mystery surrounds the identity of Mrs E. Muldowney who would have had to have married one of Jack's brothers to have been his sister-in-law. However, no trace can be found of either brother moving to America, besides which they were surely too young? The possibility that the pay record was wrong and that the mystery woman was in fact Jack's sister Ellen can probably also be discounted as she married in Winchester in 1919.

The papers also provide a physical description of Jack – he was 5ft 8¾in tall with dark brown hair, grey eyes and a fair complexion. He had a 35in chest, three vaccination scars on his left arm and gave his religious denomination as Church of England. His next of kin was his mother, Rose, and her address was Tree Cottage, 15A, Greenhill Road, Winchester – the house had been renumbered shortly before the war and is the one listed in the Winchester War Service Register (WWSR). His stated occupation was labourer.

MULDOWNEY, John Henry

Above left: the modern 13, Greenhill Road, Winchester, which was No.7 and later 15A when the Muldowney family lived there. In 1911 Jack Muldowney emigrated to the United States where he lived at 35, Moreland Street, Roxbury, Boston (right)

On 14 June 1916, less than two months after his 18th birthday, Jack travelled to St John in the Canadian province of New Brunswick where he joined the 140th Battalion (St John's Tigers) the Canadian Expeditionary Force with the service number 818241.

Canadian Army records from the Great War are, unlike those for British servicemen, extensive and well preserved. This has allowed us to build an accurate picture of Jack Muldowney's military service. After enlisting he underwent a period of training in Canada before sailing to England aboard the SS Corsican on 25 September 1916. Interestingly, he was sentenced to 28 days detention earlier that month for being absent from duty which raises the question: was this because he returned to Boston to visit friends or relatives before heading off to war?

Jack arrived in England on 6 October 1916. On 4 November he was transferred to the Royal Canadian Regiment (RCR) and Princess Patricia's Canadian Light Infantry (PPCLI) Reserve for further training at Caesar's Camp at Shorncliffe, near Seaford, on the Sussex coast between Eastbourne and Brighton. Two mobilisation camps (North and South) were constructed at Seaford between 1914 and 1915 which initially served as accommodation and training bases for volunteers of Lord Kitchener's Third Army. The camps were later used for the same purpose by soldiers of the Canadian Expeditionary Force.

On 7 December 1916 Jack was admitted to Raven's Croft Military Hospital in Seaford suffering from bronchitis, probably brought on by conditions at his camp. He was discharged on New Year's Eve. January 1917 saw Jack transferred twice, first to the 7th Reserve Battalion and then to the 13th Reserve Battalion. On 20 April 1917 he transferred once more, this time to the 26th Battalion (known as The Fighting 26th, such was its reputation) which had been serving on the Western Front since 1915. Jack joined his unit in France towards the end of the following month.

Fresh from fighting at the Battle of Arras, which saw the Canadians capture Vimy Ridge, the 26th Battalion formed part of 5th Infantry Brigade, 2nd Canadian Division. Casualties during the Arras campaign had been heavy and Jack Muldowney was undoubtedly one of many men sent out to fill the depleted Canadian ranks.

Jack's first major experience of combat came at the Battle of Hill 70 (so-called because it rose 70 metres above sea level), near the coal mining town of Lens in northern France. The Canadian attack on the German stronghold opened on 15 August 1917 and was aimed at diverting enemy troops from the heavy

MULDOWNEY, John Henry

fighting further north at the Third Battle of Ypres. The Canadians succeeded in capturing most of their objectives on the slopes of Hill 70 but then had to face German counterattacks over the following days. The fighting, often hand-to-hand, was brutal, even by Great War standards and the Germans' use of poison gas left the Canadians gasping for air inside their restrictive respirators and struggling to see the advancing enemy through their fogged-up goggles.

On 17 August, as the Canadians fought to repel the repeated enemy onslaughts, Jack Muldowney was shot in the thigh by a German sniper and taken to a Casualty Clearing Station where a doctor removed the bullet. He was evacuated back to England and taken to Tooting Military Hospital in south London for treatment before being transferred to the Canadian Convalescent Hospital at Hillingdon House, Uxbridge, on 31 August.

On 25 September, his wound healed, Jack was discharged from hospital and transferred two days later to the 3rd Canadian Command Depot. Jack's wound meant that he did not take part in the Third Battle of Ypres in which the 26th Battalion distinguished itself during the capture of Passchendaele village in November 1917.

On 7 December Jack was declared fit for duty and sent to the 13th Reserve Battalion at Seaford shortly afterwards. He then spent more than three months in reserve before being transferred back to the 26th Battalion on 30 March 1918 after the Germans launched Operation Michael, the first of their spring offensives. On 20 April he joined up with his unit which was holding trenches near the village of Blaireville, south of Arras. The battalion spent the following three months in and out of the front line around Blaireville which was comparatively quiet as the Germans had switched the focus of their offensives to other parts of the Western Front.

From the end of July, the 26th Battalion was involved in extensive training for the Battle of Amiens, widely regarded as the start of the Allied drive to victory in the late summer and autumn of 1918. Surprise was a key element in the lead up to the battle, with troops only moved at night and fake movements made during the day to mask the Allies' actual intent. Significantly, the Canadian Corps – regarded by this stage of the war as the shock troops of the British Expeditionary Force – only moved south to the Amiens sector on 7 August, the day before the battle began.

The results of the battle, particularly on the first day, exceeded Allied commanders' wildest expectations. With more than 500 tanks and 800 aircraft spearheading the assault, British, Canadian, Australian and French troops punched a gap more than 15 miles long and up to eight miles deep (in the case of the Canadians) in the German lines on 8 August. Progress thereafter was slower, possibly because the rapid gains of the infantry had outrun the supporting artillery while many of the mechanically vulnerable tanks had broken down. Nevertheless, the Allied success on the opening day led General Erich Ludendorff to describe 8 August 1918 as 'the black day of the German army in the war'.

This success, however, came at a high price with casualties among the British, Canadian and Australian infantry on 8 August numbering some 8,000. Among them was Private Jack Muldowney who is believed to have been killed in the early stages of the battle as his battalion attacked the village of Marcelcave. Jack was just 20 years old when he died.

In February 1919, the sum of $23 and 78 cents was sent to his father Thomas in respect of his effects. Thomas himself had also fought in the war. He re-enlisted with the Royal Marines Artillery in August 1914 and served in France.

MULDOWNEY, John Henry

After the war Thomas and Rose Muldowney continued to live at 15A, Greenhill Road. Thomas's occupation is unknown, but he died in Winchester in 1934, aged 64. Rose remained in the house until her death in 1956 at the age of 86. Jack's sister Ellen married John Sampson in Winchester in 1919 and in 1927 the couple were recorded living in Sutton Scotney. She died in September 1956, aged 59.

Neither of Jack's brothers are mentioned in the WWSR so presumably they did not serve in the Great War. In June 1928 Edward Muldowney married Kathleen Tomlin in Andover. The couple had two sons: Kenneth born in November 1928 and Derek born in December 1929. In 1933 the family were living in Dummer, near Basingstoke, but in July of that year Edward died. He was just 28 years old. His wife died in Andover in March 1993 at the age of 91. Richard Muldowney married Gladys Winn in London in March 1940 but it is not known if they had any children. Richard died in September 1968, aged 67.

Medals and memorials for John Henry Muldowney

Private John Henry Muldowney was entitled to the British War Medal and the Victory Medal. He is buried at Wood Cemetery (above), Marcelcave, Somme, France (GR. A. 2). His name appears on the memorials at St Matthew's and St Paul's churches, Winchester, and on the St Thomas School memorial, which today is held at Kings School, Winchester.

Researchers – JENNY WATSON and DEREK WHITFIELD

Additional sources

- https://central.bac-lac.gc.ca/.item//?op=pdf&app=CEF&id=B6467-S008
- https://www.canada.ca/en/department-national-defence/services/military-history/history-heritage/casualty-identification-military/battle-hill-70-1917.html
- https://www.veterans.gc.ca/eng/remembrance/memorials/canadian-virtual-war-memorial/detail/278243
- http://saintjohnlibrary.com/research/overview.html
- http://www.blupete.com/DJ%20&%20Malcolm/War%20Diary%2026th.htm#Apr'18

NEWBY, William Ernest Herbert

Stoker 1st Class WILLIAM ERNEST HERBERT NEWBY
1, Ashley Terrace, Winchester (no longer stands)
Service number K/16532, HMS Queen Mary, Royal Navy
Killed in action, Battle of Jutland, 31 May 1916

William Ernest Herbert Newby – known to family and friends as Bert - was the youngest child of John and Annie Eliza Newby (née Bailey) and was born at Kilmeston, near Cheriton, Hampshire, on 12 July 1892. His father was born in London in about 1853 and by 1871 was working as a labourer and lodging in Shipton, near Andover. (John's mother was from Shipton which might explain why John was there in 1871.) Bert's mother was from Sherborne St John, near Basingstoke, Hampshire, and she was about 35 when she gave birth to him.

Bert had three older siblings: Edward John had been born in Andover in 1876, Elizabeth Annie, whose birth was registered in Winchester in 1878 and Maria Lucy who was born in Hursley, near Winchester, in 1882. These different birthplaces reflect the family's peripatetic existence, presumably driven by where John Newby could find work. In the 1881 Census, he was listed as an agricultural labourer in Hursley and the family's address was 'the Sheephouse'. However, ten years later, and by then living in the village of Kilmeston, John's occupation was given as an engine driver on a farm. The Newby's eldest child, 14-year-old Edward, was listed as a shepherd.

By 1895, the Newby family were living at 40, Wharf Street, Winchester. This property, which faced up the hill towards Chesil Street, was demolished in 1974 to make way for the residential development of Wharf Mill. By 1899, the Newbys had moved to 33, Eastgate Street, Winchester. This has also been demolished and was at the top of Eastgate Street which at that time came out at Durngate Place by The Willow Tree public house. No. 33 would have been opposite the pub in what is now Durngate Terrace.

In the 1901 Census, John Newby was an engine driver (stationary). Perhaps there was more opportunity in an expanding city for that skill rather than in the countryside. However, his wife Eliza was listed as a charwoman so there was perhaps still a need for extra money. Their son Edward, aged 24 and living at home, was working as a carman or carter for railway agents. Lucy Newby, aged 18, who was also at home, worked as a shop assistant at a stationers while eight-year-old Bert was at school.

In 1900 Bert's elder sister, Elizabeth, married Frederick Padwick, a brewer's cellar man. They lived at 101, Upper Brook Street where their only child Lillian was born on 2 November 1900. Sadly, Elizabeth died in 1903, aged only 25. At this stage George and Lillian probably went to live with his parents in nearby Middle Brook Street as a 'G. Padwick' only appears in Warren's Directory from 1901 to 1903. The 1911 Census supports this theory as it shows Frederick and Lillian living at his parents' home at 58, Lansdowne Terrace, Middle Brook Street.

Shortly after Elizabeth's death, Bert lost his father John who died in Winchester in 1904, aged only 52. His mother stayed on at 33, Eastgate Street, almost certainly with Bert as he was only about 13 at the time. Bert's older brother Edward and second sister Maria also probably remained at the house. In 1906 Maria (under the name Lucie Marie Newbie) married Alfred Stewart Meldrum in Winchester. By that time, Annie Newby was living at 10, Sussex Street, Winchester (No.19 today), presumably with Bert, who was then 13 and due to leave school, and possibly with Edward.

NEWBY, William Ernest Herbert

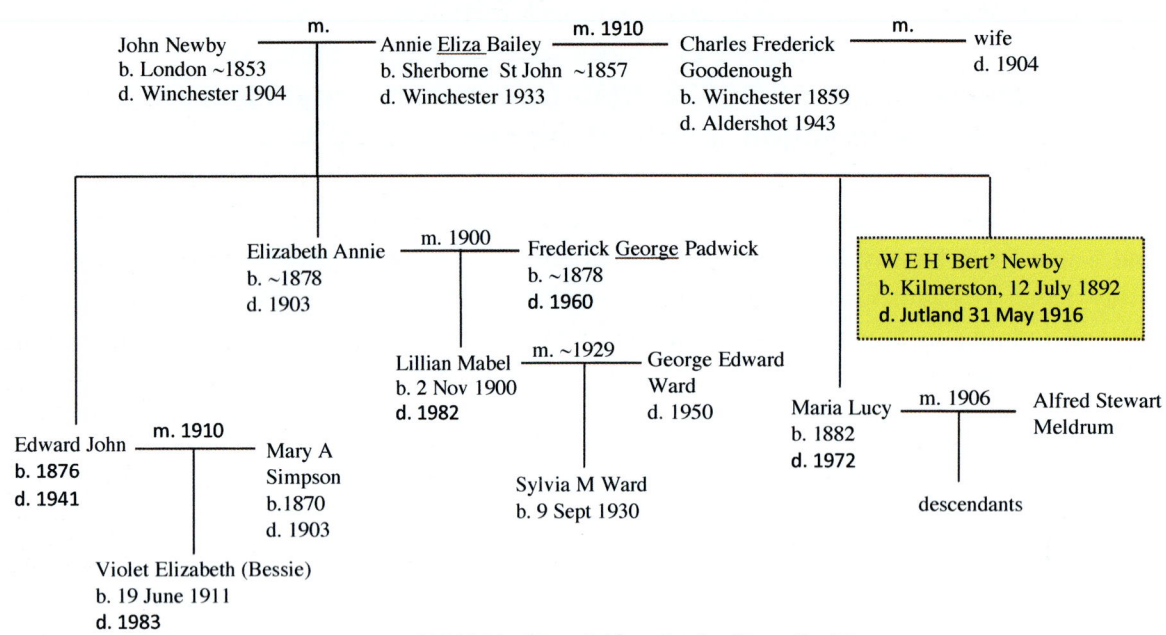

W.E.H. 'Bert' Newby's Family Tree

The year 1910 saw two weddings in the Newby family. First, Bert's widowed mother Annie married Charles Frederick Goodenough, a 51-year-old widower, whose first wife had died in 1904. Charles had been born in Winchester in 1859 and worked as a hire carman (carter). In the 1890s the two families had both lived in houses just a few doors apart at the top end of Eastgate Street, although their residencies only overlapped by one year – 1899. Bert's brother Edward also married in 1910. His wife was Mary A. Simpson and the couple married in Reading.

In the 1911 Census, the two pairs of newlyweds were both living at 22, Nuns Road, Hyde, Winchester, Charles Goodenough's address before he married Annie. Interestingly, on the census forms they were listed as two separate households, rather than Edward and Mary Newby being designated as visitors or relatives. Their census record allots them two rooms each, apart from the kitchen and any washing and toilet facilities which were presumably shared. Bert was with his new stepfather and mother, who was listed as 'deaf'. Both Charles and Bert were 'workers', i.e. employed by someone else, but worked 'at home'. Charles and Edward were still 'carmen' while Bert was working as an apprentice for a hot and cold water fitter. It seems he had inherited his father's practical skills.

Edward and Mary's daughter, Violet Elizabeth (known as Bessie), was born on 19 June 1911. As Edward Newby does not appear in Warren's Directories as a householder, it is probable that the two households remained at 22, Nuns Road with Charles continuing as the named householder. However, none of Charles's five children were living with him. They were all old enough to have left home.

Bert Newby enlisted with the Royal Navy as a stoker on 9 October 1912. He signed up for 12 years - five in active service and seven in the reserve. He gave his occupation as a whitesmith, a person who makes and repairs items made of tin. His motives for joining up will never be known. Perhaps it was the practical and mechanical side that appealed to him or a desire to get away from home and see the world?

Stokers were regarded within the Navy as the lowest of the low - uncouth, uneducated and ill-disciplined

NEWBY, William Ernest Herbert

men. They were, however, slightly better paid than ordinary seaman, a recognition by the Royal Navy that without stokers its ships would have been unable to move. Work conditions down in the 'stoke-hole' were appalling – hot, gloomy, filthy and dangerous. Stokers also had to contribute to their living costs if they wanted to eat adequately and be clothed 'safely' in items such as wooden clogs (leather soles melted) and fireproof woollen trousers.

19, Sussex Street, Winchester (above left), where young Bert Newby was living with his mother widowed Annie in 1906. The house was then No.10. Right: 22, Nuns Road, Hyde, Winchester, Bert's home in 1911 after his mother remarried

Bert Newby became K/16532, Stoker 2nd Class. His Navy records include a physical description: he was 5ft 6¾ins tall with a 34ins chest, brown hair, grey eyes and a fresh complexion. He also had tattoos on both forearms. Bert was around average height and build for the time which may have been a disadvantage when working in cramped spaces such as a ship's boiler when it needed cleaning, one of the most unpopular tasks amongst stokers.

One intriguing question is whether Bert Newby knew Charles Winter (see biography on page 371) before he signed up. Charles was also from the Winchester area and he enlisted in the Royal Navy as a stoker just one week after Bert. If they had not known each other before enlistment, they would certainly have soon met as both were sent on the same six-month initial training course. This was held at HMS Victory II, a shore-based training establishment near Crystal Palace, south London, for stokers and other sailors in mechanical roles.

Despite the increasing complexity of warships, a large part of the training still involved basic naval drill. For more relevant and practical experience, Bert Newby and Charles Winter then spent a month at HMS Renown, the stokers' training ship based at Portsmouth. There they were trained in getting coal from the bunker, loading a furnace and then removing the clinker and ash. Not only was this hard, physical work but dangerous, as methane could build up in coal storage areas. Only at the end of their time on HMS Renown would Bert and Charles have been allowed to practise lighting a furnace, which on all Royal Navy ships was the responsibility of a Stoker 1st Class.

After completing their naval and technical training at HMS Victory II, Bert and Charles were assigned to different ships. Bert was sent to HMS Vindictive, a cruiser of a type which was being used as a tender for HMS Vernon, a torpedo training ship based at Portsmouth. After only a fortnight, on 22 April 1913, he was transferred to HMS Minerva, also based at Portsmouth and which was part of the 6th Destroyer Flotilla. He left that ship on 29 August 1913, was promoted to Stoker 1st Class the next day, which meant a little more pay, and signed off until 9 October. Throughout his career, his end of year assessments always gave his character as 'very good' and his ability as 'satisfactory'.

NEWBY, William Ernest Herbert

Bert Newby's Royal Navy service record showing the ships on which he served
(Crown Copyright Image reproduced by courtesy of The National Archives)

Around this time, Bert's mother Annie and her second husband Charles Goodenough moved from Nuns Road to 1, Ashley Terrace, off Gladstone Street, Winchester. (Ashley Terrace was a row of houses between Gladstone Street and the railway station. It was demolished in the 1960s so that Station Approach could be made a through road to Newburgh Street and Upper High Street.) It is possible that Edward and Mary Newby and their daughter Bessie moved with them as again there is no mention of Edward in Warren's Directories. What supports this idea is that Edward appears in electoral records under that address in the 1920s.

Between October 1913 until March 1914 Stoker 1st Class Bert Newby moved between HMS Victory II and HMS Dido, a cruiser used as a depot (supply) ship. He also spent two weeks over Christmas 1913 at HMS Excellent, the gunnery training base on Whale Island near Portsmouth. A Stoker 1st Class was responsible for maintaining machinery throughout a ship, including guns, and was likely to be manning a gun during Battle Stations if not on stoking duty.

On 19 March 1914 Bert Newby was assigned to his final ship, HMS Queen Mary. Named after King George V's wife, Queen Mary was a battle-cruiser which had entered service the previous year. It was under the command of Captain Cecil Prowse and was attached to Rear-Admiral Sir David Beatty's First Battle-Cruiser Squadron, part of the Grand Fleet under Admiral Sir John Jellicoe. This fleet spent the entire Great War operating in the North Sea, keeping the German High Seas Fleet in port and defending the British coast and the Atlantic trade routes. On arriving on HMS Queen Mary, Bert would have been reunited with his fellow stoker from the Winchester area, Charles Winter, who had been on the ship since 6 November 1913 and was now also a Stoker 1st Class.

The Queen Mary had 42 furnaces to be kept going if top speed was required. Consequently, almost half of the ship's total crew complement were stokers – some 555 out of 1,266 men. A Stoker 1st Class would be spared the back-breaking task of bringing coal from the bunkers, but he would be the one to shovel the coal into the furnace. If top speed was required, this could be brutal work over the course of

NEWBY, William Ernest Herbert

a four-hour watch. Nevertheless, stokers took great pride in maintaining the requested speed, especially if an enemy ship was being pursued.

Bert and Charles would have been part of the visit of the First Battleship Squadron to Russia in June 1914. They first saw action in the Great War on 28 August 1914 at the Battle of Heligoland Bight when the First Battleship Squadron was sent to assist British destroyers and submarines which had been ordered to attack German ships patrolling the German coast, but which had then come under attack themselves by superior enemy forces. The British sank several German ships without loss and hailed the battle as a great victory. However, this triumphalism masked the poor communications between the Admiralty and the Grand Fleet and between British ships and submarines which came close to them firing on each other on several occasions.

Royal Navy stokers at work – they appear to be emptying ash from a furnace. This would have been a familiar task for Bert Newby

On 16 December 1914 HMS Queen Mary was part of a British force sent to intercept a German squadron on its way back from shelling the port towns of Scarborough, Hartlepool, and Whitby. The raid was an attempt to lure part of the British Grand Fleet out into the North Sea where the German High Seas Fleet was lying in wait. The British had been able to crack the German naval code and so knew about the raid in advance. However, they were unaware that the High Seas Fleet had left harbour and was planning an ambush. The British were only saved by the Kaiser's reluctance to endanger his fleet and Rear-Admiral Beatty's decision to turn his force back before attacking the superior German force.

HMS Queen Mary missed the next serious German attempt to engage part of the British Grand Fleet at the Battle of Dogger Bank on 24 Jan 1915 as she was in the middle of a refit. On 24-25 April 1916, the Germans raided the East Coast again, this time Yarmouth and Lowestoft, and Rear-Admiral Beatty was sent to intercept them. However, the German force managed to slip away in the bad weather.

The background to the Battle of Jutland has been described in the chapter on William J. Mitchell (see page 207). HMS Queen Mary was involved in the first phase of the battle as Beatty attempted to cut off the German scouting force under Rear-Admiral Franz Hipper from its base. At the same time, Hipper was trying to lure Beatty towards the German High Seas Fleet before Beatty had been joined by the rest of the British Grand Fleet under Admiral Jellicoe.

At 3.48pm on 31 May 1916 the German ships Seydlitz and Derfflinger opened fire on HMS Queen Mary which quickly responded. After five minutes of this exchange, a rolling German salvo crashed on to the deck of the British battle-cruiser. An eyewitness reported that a dazzling flashing red flame erupted from the ship where the shells had landed. Then there was a large explosion which rent the ship into two. Clouds of black debris shot hundreds of feet into the air. The ship sank quickly with the bow plunging downwards, the propellers still slowly turning. All that was left was a dark pillar of smoke like a vast palm tree.

NEWBY, William Ernest Herbert

A pillar of smoke belches from HMS Queen Mary after she was hit by German shells and exploded at the Battle of Jutland on 31 May 1916. Bert Newby and Charles Winter were among the 1,266 men who went down with the ship *(Public domain)*

Bert Newby and Charles Winter were among the 1,266 men who went down with HMS Queen Mary, one of three battle-cruisers among Beatty's force to be sunk in quick succession as a result of explosion. Only 20 men survived. The wreck of the Queen Mary was discovered in 1991, resting in pieces on the floor of the North Sea. Today it is designated as a protected place under the Protection of Military Remains Act 1986.

In June 1917, on the first anniversary of Bert's death, an In-Memoriam notice appeared in the Hampshire Chronicle immediately below those for William Mitchell. It is only from this entry that we know that that William Ernest Herbert Newby was known simply as Bert:

'Newby, Bert
Missed by Ethel and friends
At 11, Greenhill Road'

In 1917, the householder at 11, Greenhill Road, Fulflood, was a Charles Meacher. According to the 1911 Census, his youngest child was Ethel Rose. She would have been about 20 in 1917 and it is tempting to think that she may have been Bert Newby's sweetheart.

Bert's mother Annie and her second husband Charles remained at 1, Ashley Terrace after the war. In early 1915, Bert's brother Edward had lost his wife Mary when their daughter Bessie was only three years old. The electoral records show that Annie, Charles and Edward remained together at 1, Ashley Terrace throughout the 1920s.

Annie Goodenough died in 1933, aged 76. Her granddaughter Bessie was then 22 and had perhaps already become the family's housekeeper. Charles Goodenough remained listed in Warren's as the householder for 1, Ashley Terrace until 1940/1. However, the 1939 Register lists only Edward and Bessie Newby, not Charles Goodenough, as the residents at the property. Edward was a farm labourer, so had returned to his agricultural background, and Bessie a domestic servant. Charles Goodenough was found in the 1939 Register at the Public Assistance Institution (the former workhouse) on St Paul's Hill where he was described as an 'incapacitated patient'. Charles died in Aldershot in 1943 at the age of 84.

NEWBY, William Ernest Herbert

Edward Newby, Bert's brother, died in 1941, aged 65. The Warren's Directory of 1942 has Miss Newby (presumably his daughter Bessie) as the householder for 1, Ashley Terrace. Bessie never married and remained at the house until it was demolished in around 1964. She would then have been around retirement age and it may have been at that time that she moved to Southampton (there were several Newbys living in the city) where she died in 1983, aged 72.

The life of Bert's second sister Maria has been difficult to piece together. Her husband, Alfred Meldrum, whom she married in Winchester in 1906, is believed to have come from Portsmouth and worked as a linotype operator. The couple had several children over at least a 17-year span, many of whom their Uncle Bert would have known. Maria died in 1972 in Oxford, aged 89. She was the last of Bert Newby's three siblings to die.

Lillian Padwick, Bert's niece, lived with her widower father Frederick for many years after the war. In the 1939 Register they were living at 11, Stoney Lane, Weeke, Winchester. Lillian was listed as 'Mrs Ward'. A George Edward Ward had been the householder at the Red Bungalow, later 11, Stoney Lane, since 1929 so presumably he was Lillian's husband. The Register also showed that the couple had a daughter, Sylvia, who had been born on 9 September 1930.

George Ward remained the householder of 11, Stoney Lane in the 1940s but is believed to have died in Winchester in 1950, aged 57. Lillian was recorded as being the householder for the property in 1951 but she moved shortly afterwards. Her father Frederick died in Winchester in 1960. In the 1960s and 1970s, Lillian lived at 3, Chesil Terrace, Winchester. She died in Winchester in 1982 at the age of 81.

Medals and memorials for William Ernest Herbert Newby

William Ernest Herbert Newby was entitled to the 1914/15 Star, the British War Medal and the Victory Medal. His final resting place, HMS Queen Mary off the Danish North Sea coast, is a protected war grave. He is listed (above) on the Naval Memorial on Southsea Common in Portsmouth (PR. 19) and on the memorials at St Paul's and St Matthew's churches, Winchester.

Researchers – GERALDINE BUCHANAN,
JOSEPHINE COLEMAN and CHERYL DAVIS

Additional sources

- T. Chamberlain: *Life of a Stoker* – thesis, University of Exeter
  https://ore.exeter.ac.uk/repository/handle/10871/13844
- http://www.naval-history.net/xDKCas1916-05May-Jutland1.htm

NEWTON, Alan Herbert

2nd Lieutenant ALAN HERBERT NEWTON
Morn Dale, Bereweeke Road, Winchester (No. 24 today)
2nd Battalion, The Duke of Cambridge's Own (Middlesex Regiment)
Died of wounds, France, 7 April 1916

Alan Herbert Newton was born in Winchester on 10 March 1892, the son of Gertrude (née Eastment) and Thomas Edwin Newton. The second of four children, Alan came from a family of prosperous farmers on his father's side while his mother was the daughter of a Dorset magistrate. The Great War interrupted his blossoming career in land management when he joined the Army in 1915. Alan served on the Western Front where he died of wounds the following year.

The Newton family came from Twyford, near Winchester. Alan's grandparents lived in Shawford House, a large property between Twyford and the neighbouring village of Shawford. His grandfather, William Edwin Newton, was born in Britford, near Salisbury, in 1816 and married twice. His first wife, Sarah (née Cozens), was born in 1821 and in the 1841 Census the couple were recorded living in Twyford where William was a farmer. In 1842 Sarah gave birth to a son, William Jnr, and then a daughter, Mary, three years later. Both children were born in Twyford. However, Sarah Newton died in 1846, aged about 25.

William was still a widower in the 1851 Census which also revealed that he was still living at Shawford House and farming 530 acres. He employed 18 labourers and five boys. His sister Martha was also living at the house, presumably looking after young William and Mary.

In July 1856 William Newton, then aged 39, married for a second time. His new wife, Sarah (née Lywood), was ten years younger and had been born in Clatford, near Andover, Hampshire, in 1828. The couple had four children, all born in Twyford: Thomas in 1858, John in 1859, Florence in 1861 and Lywood in 1864. William Newton died in 1870 but the following year's census showed his widow and children still living at Shawford Farm along with a governess, two servants and the farm bailiff. It is not known where Thomas Newton went to school, although given that his family was wealthy, he may have attended Twyford Preparatory school.

By the time of the 1881 Census Sarah Newton had moved from Twyford to a house in Berrylands, near Kingston-upon-Thames, Surrey. Two of her children, John and Florence, were living with her along with two servants. Sarah was recorded as living on an annuity while John was working as a trainee architect. The youngest son, Lywood, was at boarding school in Buckinghamshire. Meanwhile, Thomas Newton had left home and was training as a land agent in Salisbury where he was lodging in Exeter Street.

On 8 May 1888, Thomas married 21-year-old Gertrude Eastment in Drayton, near Langport, Somerset. Gertrude had been born in Martock, Somerset, in October 1866 and was one of nine children. Her father, Francis, was a county magistrate, a salaried position, who had been born in Wincanton in 1831. He died in Sherborne, Dorset, in January 1882, leaving an estate of £10,674 5s 7d. (about £1.3 million today). Gertrude's mother was born Kate Grant (1841-1916) in Portsmouth and she also came from a prosperous family – her father was a banker and magistrate.

By 1891 Thomas Newton was working as a land agent in Winchester and living at 30c Hyde Street, which was to be more usually known as Exeter House, with Gertrude and their daughter Elsie who had been born in 1890. The young couple had one residential servant. Exeter House, built towards the end of the 1870s, was a large detached house in a ¼ acre of grounds and with its own carriage sweep.

NEWTON, Alan Herbert

Gertrude gave birth to three more children: Alan Herbert in 1892, Gertrude Joan in 1894 and Thomas Meade Bertram in 1896. All four children were born in Winchester, so Exeter House was probably Alan's birthplace. The 1901 census recorded the family as still living at Exeter House. Thomas was again listed as a land agent and auctioneer and he appears to have had his own business as the census recorded him as an employer. In September of the same year Thomas's mother, Alan's grandmother, Sarah died in Surrey at the age of 73.

Thomas Newton's business clearly continued to flourish in this period because in 1904 he and his family moved to the newly built Morn Dale in Bereweeke Road, Weeke, Winchester. (After the Newtons had left Exeter House, it became from 1906 the first home of Winchester High School for Girls, now The Westgate school. Rosewarne Court was built on its former site.) Morn Dale was a large 12-room house where, according to the 1911 Census, the Newtons employed two residential servants. The house is situated nearly opposite the later Bereweeke Avenue and was subsequently renamed 'Thornleys' and then 'Tregony'. Now it is 24, Bereweeke Road.

By 1911 Alan Newton, then 19 years old, was studying to be a land agent at Reading University College, no doubt with his father's approval. Alan was a member of the university's Officer Training Corps, but sport appears to have been his true love and he was secretary of the Reading Athletic Club hockey team and vice-captain of the tennis club in both 1911 and 1912. It is not clear whether the athletic club concerned was the Reading University College organisation or the prestigious Reading Athletic Club, one of the oldest in the United Kingdom. Formed in November 1881, Reading A.C. was one of the inaugural clubs that formed the sport's governing body, the Amateur Athletic Association.

Alan Newton's whereabouts in August 1914 when the Great War broke out are not known. However, in May 1915, aged 24, he was commissioned into the 2nd Battalion, The Duke of Cambridge's Own (Middlesex Regiment) with the rank of 2nd Lieutenant. His younger brother Thomas had enlisted as a Private with the Hampshire Regiment the previous year. On 2 June 1915 Alan joined his regiment on the Western Front in France. By this time, the 2nd Middlesex, a Regular Army unit, had been in France for seven months and had fought at the Battles of Neuve Chapelle and Aubers Ridge in the spring of 1915. The battalion, part of 23rd Brigade in 8th Division, saw action again in September 1915 at Bois Grenier, an unsuccessful diversionary attack that coincided with the Battle of Loos.

In January 1916, the 8th Division transferred to the Somme sector of the Western Front as part of the build-up for the major operation that was to be launched there on 1 July. The 8th Division attack on that fateful day was on the German-held village of Ovillers, just to the east of Albert. Alan Newton, however, never got a chance to fight in the Battle of the Somme because on April 7 1916, just a few weeks after his 24th birthday, he died of wounds, probably sustained during an artillery barrage or while raiding an enemy trench.

Probate records show that Alan left effects worth £170 1s 7d to his father. However, Thomas Newton himself died in Winchester in 1917 at the age of 58 and it was left to Alan's widowed mother Gertrude to apply for his medals after the war. Gertrude Newton remained at Morn Dale with her two daughters until 1918 when she moved to Arundel, 17, Christchurch Road, St Cross, Winchester. In 1921 the family moved again, to 1, Clifton Hill, Winchester, where they remained until Gertrude's death on 23 November 1939. In her will Gertrude left £10,285 to her daughters who took over the house on Clifton Hill and lived there until the early 1970s. Neither of the Newton sisters married: the 1939 National Register lists Elsie as a diocesan organiser for religious education and Gertrude as the chief clerk for motor taxation at Hampshire County Council. Elsie died in 1971 and Gertrude the following year.

NEWTON, Alan Herbert

Alan Newton's brother, Thomas, had an interesting military career. After enlisting with the 5th Battalion, The Hampshire Regiment he was commissioned into the 2nd Battalion, The Royal Berkshire Regiment with whom he served in France from 1916. However, in September 1915 he had gained his Royal Aero Club Aviators Certificate at the Military Flying School, Farnborough, which enabled him to subsequently transfer to the Royal Flying Corps with the rank of Captain. Thomas survived the war.

On 4 September 1918 Thomas married Edith Folkard, a 27-year-old bank manager's daughter, at St Andrew's Church, Farnham, Surrey. The couple, who are not believed to have had children, lived in Eashing, near Guildford, Surrey during the 1920s. When war broke out again in 1939 Thomas rejoined the RAF. He was killed, aged 44, in what is believed to have been an accident at Cranfield Aerodrome, Bletchley, Buckinghamshire, on 23 October 1940. His widow died in Buckinghamshire in 1975, aged 84.

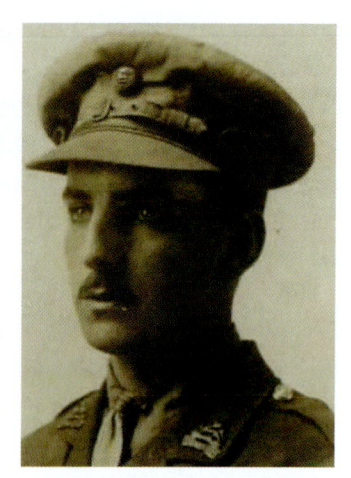

Alan Newton's brother, Thomas, who served in the Army and the Royal Flying Corps in the Great War

Medals and memorials for Alan Herbert Newton

Alan Herbert Newton was entitled to the British War Medal, the 1914-15 Star and the Victory Medal. He is buried at Millencourt Communal Cemetery Extension (below), Somme, Picardy, France (GR. C. 38). His headstone bears the inscription:
THE LORD IS MY SHEPHERD PSALM 23
He is commemorated on the memorials at St Matthew's and St Paul's Churches, Winchester, as well as that located at St Cross Chapel, Winchester. His name also appears on the memorial at Reading University College.

Researchers – JENNY WATSON, DEREK WHITFIELD and GERALDINE BUCHANAN

Additional sources

- Christine Grover: *Hyde from Dissolution to Victorian Suburb*. (Winchester, The Victorian Heritage Press, 2012)

NORGATE, Percy Douglas

Gunner PERCY DOUGLAS NORGATE
4, Brassey Road and 46, Andover Road, Winchester
Service number 153118. 233rd Siege Battery, Royal Garrison Artillery
Died in German captivity, France, 10 August 1918

Percy Douglas Norgate – he appears to have been known by his middle name - was born on 18 October 1879 in Bighton, near Alresford, Hampshire. His father, Michael, was a blacksmith who had been born in Bighton on 26 March 1837. His mother, Elizabeth (née Jacob), was a schoolteacher who was born in 1840 in Longwood, Hampshire, although her birthplace is also recorded as Tichbourne and Owslebury. The couple met when Elizabeth began lodging with Michael's parents (also called Michael and Elizabeth) in the family's home, The Knapp, after becoming a teacher at the Bighton village school in 1860.

Michael and Elizabeth married in Bighton on Christmas Eve 1862 and initially they lived with Michael's parents and his brother Alfred. They had 12 children in 18 years, all born at home except for one who arrived while the family were temporarily living elsewhere after a fire which had started in the smithy damaged their home.

Four children died in childhood. Owen, aged six, and six-month-old Ernest fell victim to scarlet fever within a week of each other in February 1869. Then in May 1880 Edward, aged eight, and Ethel, aged three, died within five days of each other, presumably following another outbreak of an infectious disease. One child was probably stillborn in 1871. The remaining children lived into adulthood. Douglas grew up with six sisters - Amy, who was born in 1865, Minnie (1867), Clara (1870 and the one Norgate sibling not born at The Knapp), Ellen (1874) and Mabel (1875). Only one sister, Mary (1881), was younger than Douglas.

Michael's father died in 1866 and his mother in 1873, long before their grandson Douglas was born. Michael's brother Alfred continued to live with the family until his death. In the 1871 Census he was described as an 'imbecile' and in the 1881 Census as 'an imbecile from childhood', but by then he was contributing to the household finances after inheriting an annuity.

On 10 August 1888, Bighton School Log recorded that eight-year-old Douglas won a school prize for attendance. One wonders whether he had any choice but to attend given that his mother had been the school's headmistress since 1864!

By 1891, Amy and Clara Norgate had left home as had 16-year-old Ellen who was working as a nurse maid in London. (Ellen kept a birthday book which has survived within the family and has proved invaluable for establishing actual dates of family events.) Minnie, then aged 24, was still at home and was an assistant school mistress working with her mother at Bighton School. Mabel, aged 15, was also still at home and was employed as a cook. Douglas, aged 11, and his younger sister Mary were still at school.

In about 1898, according to a family record, Douglas started to work in Winchester for Messrs Lipton Ltd, Grocers. However, he may also have worked in their Southampton branch as the 1901 Census records a Douglas Norgate boarding at 10, Magdalene Terrace in the St Mary's district of Southampton and working as a grocer's assistant. Douglas's uncle Alfred, the 'imbecile', died in 1904, aged 62, and his father, Michael, in 1909, at the age of 72. The two brothers had lived in the same house all their lives. In 1909 Douglas's mother retired from Bighton School after 49 years' service, 45 as headmistress.

NORGATE, Percy Douglas

By 1911 Douglas was back in Winchester, boarding in Sussex Street at 37 (now the site of Cowdray House) and working as the manager of a grocery business, presumably Lipton's. His mother Elizabeth was still living in Bighton along with his sister Minnie who had taken over as headmistress at the village school in 1909. Elizabeth also had two grandchildren with her on census night - Nelly Bartlett, aged 16, who was a pupil teacher, the third generation in the family to follow that profession, and Nelly's brother, 12-year-old Clement. These were the children of her eldest daughter Amy who had married in 1893 but whose husband, Samuel Bartlett, had been killed in a road accident in 1904.

Elizabeth Norgate died in May 1915 and so did not live to see her son Douglas marry Annie Barnett in Winchester later that year. Annie, then 28, was a dressmaker in her own account, as was her elder sister, Mabel. Both women had been recorded working at home in the 1911 Census. Home was 46, Andover Road, which lay between Victoria Road and Worthy Lane. (The terrace which included No.46 no longer exists and Albert Court now stands in its place.)

The 1911 Census recorded Annie's father, Thomas Barnett, aged 57, and her older brother, Charles, working as shoeing–smiths on their own account. Annie's mother, Mary, also 57, had been born in Northamptonshire. She married Thomas, who was from Leicestershire, in about 1884. Their three children were all born in Newmarket, Suffolk. According to Warren's Winchester Directory the family had moved to the city by 1893 and were living at 46, Andover Road.

The Winchester War Service Register gives Douglas's address as 4, Brassey Road (the address then and now). However, the only record of the couple living there is the 1919 Electoral Register (Douglas is marked as 'absent'); there is no trace of a Norgate living in Brassey Road in the relevant Warren's Directories. The assumption must be that Douglas and Annie lived there for only a short time. The couple had one child, John, born on 7 May 1916 when Douglas was still manager at Lipton's Groceries at 116/117, High Street. An article in the Hampshire Chronicle in March 1919 states that he had been a well-known figure in Winchester as manager of the Lipton's shop, having worked there for 20 years.

Unlike many of the men in this book, Douglas Norgate chose not to volunteer for military service at the start of the war. Nor was he called up in the early phases of conscription in 1916 which suggests that he may have successfully appealed against being conscripted at a Military Service Tribunal. These bodies, formed by local councils, heard applications for exemption from conscription and one common argument given by appellants was that they performed work crucial to the war effort. Further research would be required, but it is possible that Lipton's Grocers were involved in supplying food to the Army camps which sprang up around Winchester during the war and furthermore that Douglas argued that his role was crucial to the smooth-running of the business.

In April 1917, however, Douglas enlisted in the Army, almost certainly as a conscript. He joined the 233rd Siege Battery of the Royal Garrison Artillery as a gunner with the service number 153118. Siege Batteries were equipped with heavy howitzers which fired large calibre high explosive shells. As British artillery tactics developed during the Great War, heavy artillery was most often used to destroy or neutralise enemy guns and to bombard strongpoints, dumps, stores, roads and railways behind enemy lines. The 233rd Siege Battery formed part of 66th Heavy Artillery Group and took part in the Third Battle of Ypres (better known as Passchendaele) which was fought in Flanders between 31 July and 10 November 1917. It is likely that Douglas took part in some, or all, of the battery's engagements during the campaign.

NORGATE, Percy Douglas

Douglas was taken prisoner on 21 March 1918, the opening day of the German Spring Offensive on the Western Front. In just five hours the Germans fired one million artillery shells at positions held by the British Fifth Army – more than 3,000 every minute. The bombardment was followed by an attack by elite stormtroopers and by the end of the day 21,000 British soldiers, including Douglas, had been taken captured.

A British howitzer team in action on the Western Front in February 1918

Although the Hampshire Chronicle reported on 3 March 1919 that Douglas had been taken to Gustrow PoW Camp in north Germany, this does not seem possible as he died of intestinal catarrh (gastro-enteritis) on 10 August 1918 in a German war hospital at Valenciennes, close to the Western Front. He was 38 years old. Douglas was first buried in a German extension to the cemetery at Valenciennes. A nameplate was put on the coffin and the site was marked with a temporary wooden cross. Later, the coffin was exhumed and reburied in a British extension to what appears to be the same cemetery, now known as Valenciennes (St Roch) Communal Cemetery.

Douglas's personal effects amounted to £14 16s 3d, equivalent to about eight months' pay for a gunner (1s 2½d per day). On 3 September 1919, the money was authorised to be released, with his widow Annie receiving approximately one third and his son John two thirds. It is believed that in late 1919 or early 1920 Annie left 4, Brassey Road and moved back to her family home at 46, Andover Road as that is the address given on Army records for Douglas's next of kin.

Annie Norgate and her son remained in her parents' house until 1937. The 1938 Warren's Directory shows Annie as the named householder and in the 1939 Register, her occupation is listed as 'housekeeper', rather than 'unpaid domestic labour' which was the more usual description for married or widowed women in that record. The Register gives John Norgate's occupation as a clerk of works in local government. The third member of the household in 1939 was Mabel Newbury, Annie's sister, whose occupation is listed as dressmaker. It is not known why Mabel was living with her sister, but it is possible that her husband was serving in the forces.

Annie Norgate remained the named householder for 46, Andover Road until at least 1961, but by 1964 it had changed to her son John. Annie died in Winchester in 1968, aged about 81. She would have been the last person alive from the two families to have remembered Douglas. All his sisters were dead by then, along with Nelly and Augusta, the niece and nephew who had been staying with his mother at the time of the 1911 Census.

John Norgate continued to live at 46, Andover Road until 1972 when he would have been 56. By 1973, he had moved to 12, Lawn House, in Lawn Street, one of the new blocks of flats in the Friarsgate development. It is possible that the terrace that included 46, Andover Road was due for

NORGATE, Percy Douglas

demolition; the property was listed as empty in the 1973-4 Warren's Directory. John eventually retired to Brighton, Sussex, where he died, aged 75, in 1991.

Medals and memorials for Percy Douglas Norgate

Gunner Percy Douglas Norgate was entitled to the British War Medal and the Victory Medal. He is buried in Valenciennes (St Roch) Communal Cemetery (above), Nord, Pas-de-Calais, France (GR. V. R. 20). The family's personal inscription on his headstone is:

PEACE PERFECT PEACE WITH LOVED ONES FAR AWAY

He is remembered on the memorials at St Matthew's and St Paul's churches, Winchester, as P.D. Norgate. All Saint's in Bighton remembers him as D. Norgate. He is also commemorated as Percy D. Norgate on the war memorial at Holy Trinity Church, North Walls, Winchester, but it is not yet known what his or his family's connection was with that parish.

Researchers - GERALDINE BUCHANAN, JOSEPHINE COLEMAN and DEREK WHITFIELD

PAYNE, Henry John

Private HENRY JOHN PAYNE
68, Brassey Road, Winchester
Service number 85422. 123rd Company, Machine Gun Corps
Killed in action, Belgium, 5 August 1917

Henry John Payne was born in Compton, near Wantage, Berkshire, in April 1887. One of ten children, he was brought up in Berkshire but moved to Winchester shortly after marrying in 1915. He worked as a grocer and joined the Machine Gun Corps in late 1916. He was killed the following year during the Third Battle of Ypres, better known as Passchendaele.

Henry's parents, David and Martha Payne, were also born in Compton, as were his grandparents and siblings. David Payne (1850-1934) was the son of a journeyman blacksmith, also named David (born 1823), and his wife Caroline, (1822). David Payne Snr died some time before 1871, leaving his widow and young son living in Ilsley Road, Compton.

David Payne Jnr, who was already working as an iron moulder, married Martha in around 1873 and a daughter, Hannah, was born the following year. Martha went on to give birth to a further nine children: Charles (1875), Miriam (1877), Rose (1878), Lilian (1880), William (1882), Albert (1884), Lewis or Louis (1886), Henry (1887) and Ethel (1891)

In 1881 the family, who were Primitive Methodists, lived in Holey Road, Compton, where they remained for several years before moving within the village to 2, East Ilsley Road. The 1901 Census recorded William Payne working as an iron moulder like his father. Lewis, meanwhile, was a blacksmith and Albert a gardener. Daughter Rose was working as a barmaid (unusually, perhaps, for a Primitive Methodist) while Henry and Ethel were at school.

By 1911, Henry Payne had left Compton and was lodging with chimney cleaner Darius Husband and his wife at their home in Blossom End, Beale, near Reading. In that year's census Henry was listed as a grocer's assistant. In 1915 Henry married 32-year-old Edith Gutteridge in her hometown of Wallingford, Berkshire (now Oxfordshire), and by the following year the couple had moved to 68, Brassey Road, Winchester (the address then and now).

On 17 November 1915 Henry attested for military service under the Derby Scheme. This system had been introduced by the Minister for War, Lord Derby, as an attempt to solve the Army's manpower crisis. Under the scheme, men 'attested' their willingness to serve at a future date if called upon to do so. It was promoted as a half-way house between the old voluntary system of recruitment and conscription, which many opposed because, they argued, it infringed an individual's freedom to choose not to fight.

Henry's attestation form reveals that he was assigned to the 35th Battalion, Training Reserve with a service number that appears to be 8/81139 (it is barely legible). The form was later updated when Henry joined the Machine Gun Corps (MGC) on 4 December 1916.

68, Brassey Road, Winchester – Henry Payne moved here in 1916

PAYNE, Henry John

The gap of more than a year between his attestation and assignment to a fighting unit is unusual. However, married men who attested under the Derby Scheme had been promised that they would not be called up until the pool of able-bodied single men had been exhausted.

Henry Payne (service number 85422) was assigned to 123rd Company, MGC which served with the 41st Division from 1916. The MGC had been formed in October 1915 and quickly earned the nickname 'The Suicide Club', not simply because of its high casualty rates but also in recognition of the heroism shown by many machine-gun teams.

Shortly after the formation of the MGC, the Army replaced its obsolete Maxim machine guns with the Vickers, which became a standard gun for the next 50 years. The Vickers was fired from a tripod and cooled by water held in a jacket around the barrel. The gun weighed 28lbs, the tripod 20lbs and the water another 10lbs. Two men were needed to carry the equipment and two the ammunition. Each Vickers machine gun team also had two spare men. The gun fired a maximum of 500 rounds per minute.

After completing his training, Henry Payne transferred to the Western Front in 1917. The 41st Division, formed as part of Lord Kitchener's Fifth New Army, first saw action that year at the Battle of Messines (7-14 June) in Flanders. Today the battle is mostly remembered for the detonation of 19 huge mines beneath the German front line.

The 41st Division remained in Flanders for the Third Battle of Ypres (31 July-10 November), better known as Passchendaele. The 123rd Machine Gun Company fought in the Battle of Pilckem Ridge which opened the campaign on 31 July. For five days 41st Division attacked north of the Ypres-Commines Canal before being relieved on 4 August. Henry was killed in action the following day, aged 38, although the exact location of his death is unknown. His body was never found.

After the war, Henry's widow Edith continued to live at 68, Brassey Road until 1935. In 1942, at the age of 59, she married 23-year-old Douglas Smith who was from her hometown of Wallingford. It is not known when she died.

Medals and memorials for Henry John Payne

Private Henry John Payne was entitled to the British War Medal and the Victory Medal. He is remembered on the Ypres (Menin Gate) Memorial (Panel 35) and on the memorials at St Matthew's and St Paul's churches, Winchester. His name also appears on the memorial at the Primitive Methodist Chapel in Parchment Street, Winchester.

Researcher – JENNY WATSON

POWELL, Cyril Edward

Acting Bombardier CYRIL EDWARD POWELL
17, Prison Quarters, Winchester (no longer stands)
Service number 66865. 112th Battery, Royal Field Artillery
Died of wounds, France, 29 September 1916

Cyril Edward Powell was born on 23 April 1897, the third child of Edward Giles Powell and his wife Ada. His family were not from Winchester but moved to the city when his father was made principal warder at Winchester Prison. Cyril was underage when he enlisted in the Royal Field Artillery in 1914 and he died two years later of wounds received during the Battle of the Somme.

Cyril's father Edward was born on 1 September 1862 in Bullingham, Herefordshire. His first job, according to the 1881 Census, was working as a bootboy at the Mitre Hotel in Hereford. Cyril's mother was born Ada Baugh on 8 March 1867 in Ammely, Herefordshire.

Edward Powell's career in the prison service began in Cardiff where he was made assistant warder on 1 August 1890. The following year he and Ada married in Hereford. Two children were born in Cardiff - Gladys in 1893 and Eric a year later.

Edward became Assistant Warder at Shrewsbury Prison on 1 November 1894. On 23 April 1897 Ada gave birth to Cyril in Greenfields, Shrewsbury. He was christened at St Julian's Church, Shrewsbury, on 19 May 1897. The family were still living in the town when Cyril's sister Maud was born on 30 June 1898.

In 1900 the Powells moved to Cambridge where Edward was appointed warder at the city prison on 4 December. The 1901 Census shows the family living at 57, Richmond Rd, Chesterton, Cambridge. Later in 1901, however, the Powells were on the move once more because of Edward's work, this time back to Hereford. Here Cyril attended St Owen's School.

On 15 April 1909 Edward was promoted to principal warder at Winchester Prison. The following month, 12-year-old Cyril entered St Thomas Senior Church of England Boys' School but left in 1910 to go to work. The 1911 Census gives his occupation as 'clerk accountant' and shows that he was living with his family at 17, Prison Quarters, a house provided by the Prison Service which no longer stands. His 16-year-old brother Eric was serving as a boy soldier with the 3rd Battalion, The Coldstream Guards in Penge Barracks, south London.

When Britain declared war in August 1914, Cyril enlisted with the Royal Field Artillery (RFA) in Winchester despite being just 17 years old. Assigned the service number 66865, he was attached to the 112th Battery as a gunner and trumpeter. The 112th Battery, together with 110th and 111th Batteries, were with 24th Brigade RFA and served with the British 6th Division.

The 6th Division moved to the Western Front early in the war and saw action on the River Aisne in September 1914 and the following year at Hooge, near Ypres. However, Cyril did not go out to France until 1916 when 6th Division fought in the later stages of the Somme Offensive.

At the Battle of Morval (25-28 September 1916), the Division took part in attacks on the villages of Morval, Gueudecourt and Lesbœufs. These had been objectives during the earlier Battle of Flers–Courcelette (15–22 September) but remained in German hands. The opening day of the battle saw the British make their biggest advance on the Somme since mid-July. The three villages were captured, and heavy casualties inflicted on the Germans. Further south, in a coordinated attack, the French took

POWELL, Cyril Edward

Combles. However, fatigue and a lack of reserves prevented the British from exploiting the success further.

It is not known where and when Cyril was wounded, but presumably it was during the Battle of Morval. He died on 29 September 1916, aged 19. Although he served on the Western Front for a comparatively short time, Cyril did earn one promotion – to Acting Bombardier (the artillery equivalent of Acting Lance-Corporal).

On 11 September, shortly before Cyril's death, his father had moved from Winchester to Leicester to become principal warder at the city prison. Edward became chief warder II at Bedford Prison in December 1919 and finally chief warder II at Plymouth Prison in April 1920. The family's move away from Winchester in 1916 explains why Cyril's name does not appear in the Winchester War Register which was compiled in 1921. Edward and Ada later moved to 34, Ivy Street, Penarth, Glamorganshire. The 1939 National Register records them at this address together with daughter Maud who was single and a music teacher. Ada Powell received a Dependant's Pension on behalf of her son.

Cyril's brother Eric (service number 8657) fought in the war with the Coldstream Guards. He survived and in November 1919 married Clarissa Kerr in Leicester. He remained in the Army and was promoted to Lance-Corporal in 1920.

Medals and memorials for Cyril Edward Powell

Acting Bombardier Cyril Edward Powell was entitled to the British War Medal and the Victory Medal. He is buried at Guillemont Road Cemetery (above), Guillemont, Somme (GR. I. C. 10). His name appears on the memorials at St Matthew's and St Paul's churches, Winchester.

Researcher – JENNY WATSON

POWNEY, William Benjamin

Lance-Corporal WILLIAM BENJAMIN POWNEY
33, Lower Stockbridge Road, Winchester (76, Stockbridge Road today)
Service number 5779. 1st Battalion, The Royal Berkshire Regiment
Died of wounds, France, 16 May 1915

William Benjamin Powney was born in Salisbury in 1875, the second of the five children of Joseph and Mary Powney. Joseph, a boot retailer, was born in 1850 in Leicester. His wife had been born Mary Geary in London in 1846. The couple married at Lambeth, south London, in 1871.

In the 1881 Census the family were living at 36, Silver Street, Salisbury. The children included William, his elder brother Joseph, then aged eight, and two younger sisters, four-year-old Gertrude, and Florence, aged one. The family also employed a live-in domestic servant so were comparatively well-off.

William's mother died in Salisbury in 1884, aged just 38, possibly while giving birth to a third daughter, Violet, who was born that year. Two years later Joseph remarried. His new wife, Elizabeth (née Hunt), had been born in Overton, near Basingstoke, in 1854.

By 1891 the Powneys were living at Brown Street, Salisbury, with Joseph listed in that year's census as a shoe merchant. William, then 16, was an outfitter's assistant. Joseph Powney died in 1897, aged 47, at which point the family shoe business seems to have been taken over by the elder son, Joseph Jnr, who went on to marry Eliza Sewell in 1898. In the 1898 Kelly's Directory of Wiltshire, William was listed as a clothier, operating from 7, Minster Street, Salisbury. The previous entry in the directory is for his brother, Joseph Jnr, a boot and shoemaker at 36, Silver Street.

In 1899 William Powney enlisted in the Army in Reading, joining the 1st Battalion, The Royal Berkshire Regiment. It is likely that he knew Harold Forster, another of the Great War dead of Fulflood and Weeke, who joined the 1st Royal Berkshires the same year. (Harold's biography is on pp. 98).

William cannot be found on the 1901 Census, probably because his battalion was stationed in Ireland at the time. His stepmother, meanwhile, had moved with his three sisters to 7, Minster Street, Salisbury, and was recorded as 'living on own means'. On 5 September 1904, William's siter Gertrude married Loftus Harvey and the couple went on to have a daughter, Agnes, born around 1909. In 1911 they were living in Sutton, Surrey.

By the time of the 1911 Census, William Powney had left the Army and was living with his stepmother Elizabeth and sisters Florence and Violet at 33, Lower Stockbridge Road, Winchester. He was working as a nurseryman. His brother Joseph was still running his shoe shop in Salisbury and living at 5, Moberly Road with wife Eliza and their three children, Dorothy (born 1899), Margaret (1903), and Joseph (1907).

Minster Street, Salisbury, around the turn of the 20th Century. William Powney ran a clothing store here in 1898. His brother Joseph had a shoe shop in the town

POWNEY, William Benjamin

When the Great War broke out in August 1914, William Powney was 40 years old. He had probably joined the Army in 1899 for seven years with another five years in the Reserve. That period would have expired in 1911 so he was not compelled to re-enlist. However, William appears to have re-joined his old regiment as a volunteer, probably with his previous rank of Lance-Corporal.

Although the 1st Royal Berkshires arrived in France in August 1914, William did not join them until 9 February 1915. His first engagement was at the Battle of Festubert (15-25 May), part of a series of attacks by the British and French armies in the Second Battle of Artois (3 May-18 June 1915). William was wounded on 15 May when the 1st Royal Berkshires, as part of 6th Brigade in 2nd Division, attacked German positions along the Rue du Bois near the village of Richebourg. He died the following day, aged 40 or 41, one of more than 16,000 British casualties at Festubert.

Probate records confirm that William was living at 33, Lower Stockbridge Road (later renumbered as 76, Stockbridge Road) although they wrongly give his date of death as 10 May 1915. He left £226 16s 7d to his brother Joseph.

After the war, Joseph Powney continued to work in the shoe retail business. At some stage he, his wife Eliza and daughter Florence moved from Salisbury to Bournemouth where they were listed as living at 32, East Avenue in the 1939 National Register. Joseph died in Bournemouth in 1943, aged 76.

76, Stockbridge Road, Winchester (33, Lower Stockbridge Road in 1914) - William Powney's home in 1914

William's middle sister, Florence, married in 1913. Violet, his youngest sister, continued to live at 76, Stockbridge Road, Winchester, where she died in 1949, aged 66.

Medals and memorials for William Benjamin Powney

Lance-Corporal William Benjamin Powney was entitled to the 1914-15 Star, the British War Medal and the Victory Medal. He is buried (grave right) at Bethune Town Cemetery, Pas de Calais, France (GR. III. C. 82) and the inscription on his headstone reads:
HE DIED THAT WE MIGHT LIVE
William is remembered on the memorials at St Matthew's and St Paul's churches, Winchester.

Researchers – DEREK WHITFIELD, CHERYL DAVIS and STEVE JARVIS

PRIOR, George

Private GEORGE PRIOR
21, Cranworth Road, Winchester
Service number 907538. 5th Battalion, Canadian Infantry
Killed in action, France, 9 April 1917

George Prior was born in the village of Dean, Bedfordshire, on 7 February 1884, the son of George Thomas Prior and his wife Sarah. George Jnr spent his early years with his family in farming communities in eastern England before emigrating to Canada before the Great War. After his mother's death his father remarried and moved to Winchester, and this appears to be the reason his name appears on the Fulflood and Weeke memorials. George served with the Canadian Corps and was killed in the attack on Vimy Ridge in 1917.

George Prior Snr was born on 21 October 1847. His birthplace is given variously as Alconbury, Huntingdonshire, and Leighton, Bedfordshire. George Snr's father, Benjamin, was a farmer who had been born in Sawtry, Huntingdonshire, in about 1822. In 1851 he was farming 360 acres in Leighton, Bedfordshire, employing 12 labourers. George's mother was born Elizabeth Sanderson in Glatton, Huntingdonshire, in about 1825.

George Prior Snr married Sarah Braybrooks sometime in the late 1860s or early 1870s. Sarah had been born in Spaldwick, Huntingdonshire (now Cambridgeshire), in 1845 and was the daughter of Thomas and Sarah Braybrooks. Thomas, who was born in Hitchen, Hertfordshire, in about 1806 was a master fellmonger – a dealer in hides or skins, especially sheepskins.

By 1881 George Prior was running 546-acre Old Farm in Wigsthorpe, Northamptonshire, employing four men and four boys. At this stage he and Sarah had five children, all born in Wigsthorpe – Benjamin, aged nine, Florence, aged six, five-year-old Thomas, Elizabeth, aged three, and Mary, who was just ten months old. The family employed a domestic servant and a nursemaid.

Ten years later the Priors were living at The Grange in Wingland, near King's Lynn, Norfolk. George Snr was still a farmer. Benjamin, the elder son had left home, leaving Thomas, Elizabeth, Mary and seven-year-old George Jnr. He had been born in Dean, Bedfordshire, so it appears the family had been at another farm between leaving Wigsthorpe and arriving at Wingland.

Sarah Prior died in 1895, her death being registered in nearby Holbeach, Lincolnshire. Three years later, on 17 November 1898, George Snr remarried at St Peter's Church, Paddington, London. His new wife was Emily Etheridge, the daughter of the late Charles Etheridge, described as a farmer on the marriage certificate. The same document recorded George as being a widower, aged 51, and living at Wingland, Norfolk. Emily was living at 49, Chippenham Road, west London.

Emily, one of five siblings, had been born in Winchester in 1865 so she was some 18 years younger than her husband. Her father Charles worked as a cattle dealer and had been born in Winchester in about 1819. Her mother Jane was born in Stockbridge in about 1825. In 1871 the Etheridges were lodging at 16, High Street, Winchester.

George Prior Snr, who lived in Cranworth Road, Winchester. He would have ensured his son's name appeared on the Weeke and Fulflood war memorials

PRIOR, George

By 1881 Emily's parents appear to have both died and she was living at 18, Eastgate Street with her brother William, 34, a clerk in the Winchester births, marriages and deaths records office, and sister Elizabeth, 30. Emily, then 16, was working as a milliner. The three siblings were at the same address ten years later with Emily employed as a draper's assistant. She obviously moved to London sometime over the next few years as that is where she was living when she married George Snr in 1898.

It is unclear where George Jnr lived after his father remarried, but he probably remained in eastern England working on farms - he gave his occupation as farmer on his enlistment papers in 1916. In 1901 his sister Mary was living and working as a housekeeper in the home of her uncle James Wilkinson in Great Haddington, Northamptonshire. She was still there in 1911.

In the 1901 Census George Snr and Emily were living at the Farm House, Wingland, Norfolk, along with a domestic servant. However, there is no sign of George Jnr or any of the other children from his father's first marriage. In 1902 Emily gave birth to a daughter, Emily, followed by a son, Arthur, the following year.

21, Cranworth Road, Winchester - home to George Prior's father and stepmother by 1917 and his address in the WWSR

By 1911 the Priors had moved to Winchester and were living at Longmeade, a house in Fairfield Road with their two children and one servant. George Snr, by then 63, was recorded as being a retired farmer. By 1917 the family had moved to a larger house nearby at 21, Cranworth Road (the address then and now).

It is possible that George Jnr retained contact with his father, and he may even have come to live with him briefly in Winchester. However, there are also indications that father and son may have drifted apart, particularly in George Jnr's decision to name his sister Mary, rather than his father, as his next-of-kin on his enlistment papers. In 1916 Mary was living at Shawington, Newton Road, Rushden, Hertfordshire.

George Jnr emigrated to Canada sometime before the Great War, almost certainly to make a new life for himself. He settled as a farmer in Candahar in the rich farming belt of Saskatchewan province.

George enlisted with the Canadian Corps at Regina, Saskatchewan, on 28 March 1916. He served in the 5th Battalion, Canadian Infantry, also known as the Western Cavalry, which recruited in the provinces of Alberta, British Columbia, Manitoba and Saskatchewan. On George's attestation papers his date of birth is given as 7 February 1887, rather than 7 February 1884. This error was probably made when the original hand-written document was typed up – it is highly unlikely that another George Prior born on the same day of the same month in Bedfordshire also enlisted with the Canadian Corps.

The 5th Battalion Canadian Infantry had been raised on 10 August 1914 and departed for Britain on 29 September 1915. Training and reorganisation commenced upon arrival in Britain the following month. The battalion entered the theatre of operations in France on 14 February 1915, where it fought as part of the 2nd Infantry Brigade, 1st Canadian Division, in France and Flanders until the end of the war.

PRIOR, George

It is not known when George transferred to France or the extent of his service at the front before he died. All that is known for certain is that he died, aged 33, on 9 April 1917, the first day of the Battle of Arras. George's battalion had set off in driving sleet to attack German positions near Neuville-St-Vaast, a village which today stands about two miles south of the Canadian Memorial on Vimy Ridge. George was hit in the head by shrapnel from an exploding enemy shell and killed instantly. His body was never found.

After the war George Prior's father and stepmother continued to live in Winchester. George Snr died on 28 November 1934 at Sarum Road Nursing Home, aged 87. Probate records show that he was living at 37, Stuart Crescent, Stanmore, Winchester, when he died. George left £725 7s 1d to his widow Emily and their son Arthur who by then was working as a clerk. Emily Prior died in Southampton in 1944, aged 79.

George Prior's attestation paper dated 28 March 1916 – note the error with his date of birth

Probate for George Jnr's estate was not granted until 25 April 1935, more than 17 years after his death. He left £1,014 8s 3d to his sister Mary in England.

Mary Prior never married. In 1939 she and her sister Florence, also a spinster, were living together in Poole, Dorset. Mary was living in Southbourne, Bournemouth (in a house named Wingland), when she died in December 1975 at the age of 95. George Jnr's sister Elizabeth also remained unmarried. She lived in Boldre, near Lymington, Hampshire, towards the end of her life and died in Lymington Hospital in 1959, aged about 81. It is not known what became of Florence or George's brothers.

Medals and memorials for George Prior

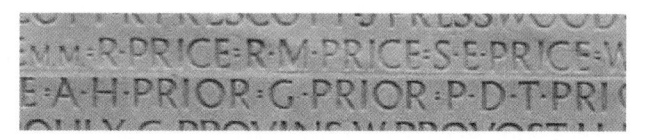

Private George Prior was entitled to the British War Medal and the Victory Medal. He is commemorated as G. Prior (above) on the Canadian National Vimy Memorial, Pas de Calais, France, and on the memorials at St Matthew's and St Paul's churches, Winchester.

Researchers – CHERYL DAVIS, STEVE JARVIS and DEREK WHITFIELD

RICHARDS, Frederick Charles

Private FREDERICK CHARLES RICHARDS
53, Lower Stockbridge Road, Winchester (116, Stockbridge Road today)
Service numbers 4/1793 and 200163. 1/4th Battalion, The Hampshire Regiment
Died in captivity, Turkey, between 29 April 1916 and 30 January 1917

Frederick Charles Richards was born in Winchester in the second quarter of 1894, the youngest child of Edward and Sarah Ann Richards. One of eight children, Fred, as he was known to family and friends, came from a solid working-class family. He worked as a hairdresser and joined the Territorials in 1912. He died a prisoner of the Turks after the fall of Kut-al-Amara, Mesopotamia (modern Iraq), in 1916.

Frederick's father Edward was born in Portsmouth in 1849. He spent his life working variously as a labourer, blacksmith, engine smith and ships smith. Frederick's mother was born Sarah Snook in Portsmouth on 25 January 1852. Her father, James (1827-1889), a shoemaker, had been born in Muny, Somerset. Her mother, Charlotte Barnden (1830-1912), was a Portsmouth girl.

Edward and Sarah married in Portsmouth on 5 November 1871 and went on to have eight children over the following 24 years. Of these, five were born in Portsmouth: Anne (1872-1916), Emma (1874-1948), Phoebe (1876-1935), Charlotte (1884-1967) and Alfred (1888-). Jane (1880-1947) was born in Pembroke, Wales, while Frederick and Winifred (1891-1983) were the only two siblings to be born in Winchester. Sarah gave birth to five other children who died.

In 1881 the Richards family were living at 13, Landport Street, Portsmouth, but ten years later they had moved to 21, King Alfred Place, Hyde, Winchester. Edward Richards was working as an engine smith and daughters Anne, Emma and Phoebe as laundresses. By 1901 the family had moved again, to 13, Egbert Road, Hyde. Edward was a general labourer and daughter Jane a packer in a steam laundry. In 1903 the Richards were at 19, Monks Road, Hyde.

It is not known which school Fred attended, but it was probably St Thomas Church of England Boys' School where his brother Alfred had been a pupil. Given that Alfred also went to the Wesleyan School in Parchment Street as an infant, it is possible that Fred had earlier followed him there too.

By 1911 the family were living at 53, Lower Stockbridge Road, a property which had eight rooms. The house was renumbered as 116, Stockbridge Road after the war and still stands today. Edward Smith was working as a ships smith while Fred, who by this time had left school, was an assistant in the railway refreshment bar at Winchester station. Among those also living in the house were Fred's sister Charlotte, her husband William Smith, a builder's labourer, and the couple's 11-month-old son, William Jnr. Alfred was also still living at home and working as an assurance collector.

The family continued to live at 53, Lower Stockbridge Road until 1914. However, they were not there during the war years and it is not until 1918 that Edward Richards reappears in the Warren's Winchester Directory, living at 29, Western Road, Fulflood. This is the house in which Fred's brother Alfred had lived between 1914 and 1917 before moving a few doors to No. 21 in 1918.

It is not clear where Fred's parents were living between 1915 and 1917. One complication is an entry in the Hampshire Regimental Journal of July 1917 announcing Fred's death. The entry not only gives the Richards's address as 15, North View, Fulflood, but states that before the war Fred had lived at the YMCA at 73, High Street, Winchester (today the Cote restaurant), and that Edward and Sarah had been

RICHARDS, Frederick Charles

73, High Street, Winchester – in 1914 this was the YMCA. Fred Richards may have lived here and certainly said farewell to friends in the building before going off to war

Right: 116, Stockbridge Road – this was 53, Lower Stockbridge Road in 1914 and home to Fred Richard's family

caretakers. The North View address may be an error as no record can be found of a Richards living there, or anywhere else in North View, between 1900 and 1918 although it is possible that the couple may have lodged at the house.

As for the YMCA connection, there is no Richards listed at 73, High Street before 1914. However, the Warren's Directory does show a 'Mrs Richards, caretaker' as the householder there between 1915 and 1917.

One explanation is that Edward and Sarah moved in with Alfred at 29, Western Road early in the war and then took over the house in 1918 when their son moved to No. 21. Another, more likely, explanation is that Edward and Sarah both lived at the YMCA between 1915 and 1917 before moving to Western Road. Evidence for this is contained in the Prisoner Comforts Fund ledger of Mrs Esme Bowker (see pp. 383) which gives the Richards' address in 1916 as the 'YMCA, Winton'. Fred's wartime battalion, the 1/4th Hampshires, also kept records of all the Winchester men who served with them. The list was probably compiled in 1914 or 1915 and the entry for Fred gives his address as 53, Lower Stockbridge Road. Scribbled in pencil next to that is the word 'YMCA'.

Although the precise whereabouts of Edward and Sarah during the war is something of a mystery they were certainly in Winchester. By 1918 they were back together at 29, Western Road and this is Fred

RICHARDS, Frederick Charles

Richards's address in the Winchester War Service Register, compiled in 1921. However, Fred never lived there. Instead he went to war in 1914 from either the family home in Stockbridge Road or from the YMCA.

The other interesting fact revealed in the Regimental Journal is that by 1914 Fred had found a new job, as an apprentice hairdresser working for J. & C. Yates at 4, Parchment Street, Winchester.

The list of Winchester men who served with the 1/4th Hampshires in the war. Fred Richards's address mentions 53, Lower Stockbridge Road and the YMCA. Note the entries for Eric Rule, Cecil Shefferd and George Soffe who all died in Turkish captivity and are also commemorated on the parish memorials

Fred Richards's first service number (4/1793) indicates that he joined the 4th Battalion, The Hampshire Regiment as a Territorial in 1912. Regimental records show that he sailed with the 1/4th Hampshires to India in October 1914, when the battalion split into two shortly after the outbreak of war.

At this point, however, something unexpected happened. Instead of transferring to Mesopotamia with the rest of his battalion in March 1915, Fred remained in India. Quite why this should have happened is unclear – possibly he was sick or perhaps he had been detached to serve with the 2/4th Battalion, which had arrived in India at the start of 1915. This second possibility is backed up by regimental records which reveal that in October 1915 the 2/4th Battalion sent 250 men as reinforcements to the 1/4th in Mesopotamia. This dovetails neatly with the date on Fred's Medal Index Card which shows that he entered the Asiatic theatre of war on 25 October 1915.

Once in Mesopotamia, Fred was assigned to 'A' Company of the 1/4th Hampshires. The company formed part of the British-Indian garrison at Kut-al-Amara which was besieged by the Turks for five months from 7 December 1915 until its surrender on 29 April 1916 (for details of the siege see pp. 378). Fred, who had been wounded on 11 December, in the early stages of the siege, was then marched off into captivity as a prisoner of war.

Uncertainty also surrounds the date of Fred Richards's death. The WWSR states it was on 17 June 1916, while Mrs Esme Bowker, widow of the 1/4th Battalion's Commanding Officer, states in her Prisoner Comforts Fund records that he died on 30 June 1916 during the march into captivity. However, the Commonwealth War Graves Commission gives the date of death as 30 January 1917.

One clue lies in the fact that Fred died at Nesibin (Nisibin) PoW camp in Turkey. We know this both from the WWSR and because Fred is commemorated on the Nisibin Memorial at Baghdad (North Gate) War Cemetery in Iraq. It seems reasonable, therefore, to conclude that he did not die on the march into captivity, but several months later after he reached his PoW camp. However, it is impossible to know with certainty the exact date of Fred's death - probably from disease - other than it was between 29 April 1916 and 30 January 1917. He was 21 years old.

Several months passed before news of Fred's death reached Winchester. The Hampshire Regimental Journal of July 1917 stated:

RICHARDS, Frederick Charles

RICHARDS. Pte. Fred Richards, Hampshire Regiment, died prisoner of war in Turkey, date, place, and cause unknown, youngest and much-loved son of Mr and Mrs E. Richards, late of Y.M.C.A., High Street, Winchester, aged 21.

Mr and Mrs E. Richards, of 15, North View, Winchester, late caretakers of the Y.M.C.A, High Street, have received official notice that their youngest son, Pte. F. Richards, 1793, who was shut up in Kut, wounded, and then taken prisoner of war, died as a prisoner of war between 29th April, 1916, and January 30th, 1917. He was an apprentice of Mr. Yates, hairdresser, Parchment Street, and said his last 'goodbye' at the Y.M.C.A. before sailing for India with the Hampshire Regiment on October 9th, 1914.

Fred's parents continued to live at 29, Western Road after the war. His father Edward died around 1924 and by 1926 the Warren's Directory shows the house listed in the names of his widow Sarah and her son-in-law William Smith. William and his wife Charlotte, Fred's sister, took over the house when Sarah died in 1934, aged 82. Charlotte, who had no further children, died in Winchester in 1967, aged 83.

Fred's brother Alfred also served with the Hampshire Regiment during the war, reaching the rank of Lance-Sergeant. However, he did not serve overseas. Alfred had married Birmingham-born Kate Webb in Winchester in 1913 and the couple had two children. They continued to live at 21, Western Road after the war (it is Alfred's address in the WWSR) but had moved to 3, Kingsgate Street by 1939, when Alfred was working as a greengrocer, fruiterer and market nurseryman. It is not known when Alfred died.

Several of Fred Richards's other siblings retained links with Winchester after the war. Phoebe married bricklayer Edward Mills in 1896 and the couple had two children. In 1901 they were living at 6, Saxon Road, Hyde and ten years later at 14, Owens Road. Phoebe died in Winchester in 1935 at the age of 59.

Jane Richards married Frederick Brealey, a baker, in Amesbury, Wiltshire, in June 1905. The couple, who had five children, lived in London and Devon but were back in Winchester by 1939. Jane was living at 63, Portal Road when she died, aged 66, in May 1947. Anne Richards married builder's labourer William Chivers in Alton in April 1904. Anne gave birth to two children in Alton, Hampshire, but the family were living at 41, Water Lane, Winchester, in 1911. However, Anne moved back to Alton where she died in 1916, aged 44.

Winifred Richards married Ernest Avery, a domestic gardener, in Winchester in November 1913. The couple, who had one daughter, were living in Dorking, Surrey, in 1939, but Winifred returned to Winchester where she passed away in March 1983 at the age of 91.

Emma was the only one of Fred's siblings to completely sever her ties with Winchester. After marrying Henry Lee in the city in January 1896, she moved to Kent and later Essex and had six children. Emma died in Chelmsford in December 1948, aged 74.

Medals and memorials for Frederick Charles Richards

Private Frederick Charles Richards was entitled to the 1914-15 Star, the British War Medal and the Victory Medal. He is commemorated on the Nisibin Memorial at Baghdad (North Gate) War Cemetery, Iraq (PR. Nisibin Mem. 250). His name also appears on the memorials at St Paul's, St Matthew's and St Thomas's churches, Winchester.

Researcher – DEREK WHITFIELD

RULE, Eric Granville Sutherland

Company Sergeant Major ERIC GRANVILLE SUTHERLAND RULE
10, St Paul's Terrace, Winchester (4, St Paul's Hill today)
Service numbers 4/25 and 200005. 1/4th Battalion, The Hampshire Regiment
Missing, presumed killed, Mesopotamia, 21 January 1916

Eric Granville Sutherland Rule's family roots lay in Scotland and the north of England, but he came to live and work in Winchester in the late 1890s. For more than a decade before 1914, Eric served as a part-time soldier with the Hampshire Regiment, initially with the 1st Volunteer Battalion and then as a Territorial with the 4th Battalion. During the Great War he served in India and Mesopotamia (modern Iraq). He was killed in January 1916 during an attempt to relieve the besieged British garrison at Kut-al-Amara. Eric Rule's name does not appear on the Winchester War Service Register, probably because his family had moved away from the city before it was compiled.

Eric was born in the village of Filford, near Farnham, Surrey, on 10 August 1878, the youngest son of Thomas Baillie Rule and his wife Elizabeth. Thomas had been born in 1825 in Dornoch, Sutherlandshire, in the Western Highlands. He worked variously as a carpet manufacturer, dealer and commission agent and was clearly a prosperous man - he is described as 'gentleman' under the heading 'Quality, Trade or Profession' on his son's baptism record (dated 1 December 1878). A further indication of Thomas's social standing is that in 1870 he was living with his family at 14, Hanley Road, Holloway, north London, next door to the very grand-sounding A.B. Dennistoun-Sword, solicitor.

Eric's mother was born Elizabeth Ord in the city of Durham in 1837. The daughter of hatter and wig maker John Ord and his wife Rebecca, Elizabeth came from a respectable background. However, the Ords were blighted by family tragedy. Of Elizabeth's 12 siblings, no fewer than seven died under the age of three and another aged just 11. However, Rebecca lived to be 88, surviving Elizabeth by 12 years.

Thomas and Elizabeth married in Bishopwearmouth, an area of Sunderland, County Durham, in 1867. Thomas's work took him around the country with the result that Eric and his six siblings were born in various locations in Scotland and England – Ellen Gertrude (1862-) in Glasgow; Arthur John Percy (1865-1876) in Leicester; Florence Annie (1868-) in Tottenham, north London; Edith Jessica Margaret (1870-1874) in Hornsey, north London, William Taylor (1872-1873) in Surrey, and Charles Campbell (1874-1941) in Dalston, north-east London. Again, it is interesting to note that despite Thomas Rule's apparent prosperity at least three of his six children died young. Diseases such as tuberculosis, scarlet fever and smallpox – not to mention cholera – were no respecters of class or status.

Thomas Rule died in the Guildford area in 1880, aged 55. The following year the family were living in Woking, Surrey, with his widow Elizabeth listed on that year's census as an 'annuitant' – in other words

RULE, Eric Granville Sutherland

she was receiving a pension, presumably provided by her late husband. It must have been a reasonable sum of money as Elizabeth was still able to afford to employ a servant. Elizabeth Rule died in Deal, Kent, in August 1890, aged 53. Intriguingly, probate for her estate was not granted until 1903 with Eric receiving £88 10s. Given his father's apparent wealth this seems a rather paltry sum.

The period immediately following his mother's death must have been a difficult time for Eric. The 1891 Census found him boarding at Kent County School in Burchington-on-Sea. It is possible that he spent school holidays with his surviving elder brother or sisters or with other family members.

After leaving school, Eric appears to have moved to Winchester for work and by 1901 was employed as an auctioneer's clerk, lodging at 6, Great Minster Street. Living at 2, Great Minster Street was Violet Mary Minter, who became Eric's wife just a few weeks after the census. Violet had been born Mary Ann Minter in the rural parish of Westleton, Suffolk. Her father, Clifton, was born in 1850 and worked as a master tailor. Her mother, Naomi, was born in 1852.

Eric Rule's home at 10, St Paul's Terrace, Winchester, a short distance from St Paul's Church. The house is now 4, St Paul's Hill

Eric and Violet married in Ipswich in the second quarter of 1901 but continued to live in Winchester. On 19 December 1902 Violet gave birth to a son, Gordon Granville, in Winchester. A daughter, Beryl Enid, followed on 19 April 1905. Nothing is known of the children's early education, but in 1914 Beryl entered the County High School for Girls in Cheriton Road.

The Rules lived at several addresses in Winchester. Between 1902 and 1903 they were at 36, Hyde Close and from 1904 to 1905 at Drysdale, a house in Owens Road. By 1911 the family were living at 10, St Paul's Terrace, Upper Stockbridge Road. (Houses in the road were renumbered after the war and it is now 4, St Paul's Hill). Living a few doors down the hill at No. 2 in 1914 was Andrew Bogie who fought in the same battalion as Eric during the war. Both men died in Mesopotamia.

Eric Rule had a deep interest in military matters. We know this because the Royal Hampshire Regiment Museum in Winchester holds in its archives several scrapbooks and collections of photographs that Eric compiled. These illustrate events such as the Boer War as well as the annual summer camps that he attended as a part-time soldier. The earliest, a series of photos of the Hampshire Regiment's 1st Volunteer Battalion on summer camp in Swanage, Dorset, dates from 1901. It shows that Eric joined the Regiment soon after he arrived in Winchester.

The 1908 Haldane Army reforms created the Territorial Force and saw the 1st Volunteer Battalion replaced by the 4th Battalion, The Hampshire Regiment. Eric merely swapped the old battalion for the new. He was clearly a respected soldier and won promotion regularly so that by 1914 he had reached the rank of Colour-Sergeant. Following Britain's declaration of war in August that year Eric volunteered for overseas service and sailed for India with the 1/4th Hampshires in October. After three months' training and acclimatising in India the battalion was sent to Mesopotamia as part of 6th Poona Division, arriving there on 18 March 1915.

RULE, Eric Granville Sutherland

Eric Rule's first summer camp with the Hampshire Regiment – at Swanage in 1901, shortly after he moved to live in Winchester. Eric is back row, centre

Lance-Corporal Eric Rule (rear) at summer camp with the Hampshire Regiment's 1st Volunteer Battalion in 1904

Butchers prepare meat at the Hampshire Regiment summer camp on Morn Hill, Winchester, in 1904

Men of the 4th Hampshires at their summer camp at Bulford, Wiltshire, in July 1912. Two years later, many of these part-time soldiers marched off to war

The Colours of the 4th Battalion, The Hampshire Regiment are consecrated at the summer camp of 1909. The battalion had been formed the previous year as part of the Haldane Army reforms

(All photos: Royal Hampshire Regiment Museum)

RULE, Eric Granville Sutherland

At some point, either in India or in Mesopotamia, Eric was promoted again, to Company Sergeant Major (CSM). This put him in charge of discipline, standards and administration within his company of around 250 men. (Although most records state that Eric was a CSM when he died, the Army Register of Soldiers' Effects, 1901-1929 states that he was Acting CSM.)

Eric Rule was killed on 21 January 1916 at the Battle of El-Hanna, an attack launched to try to break through to the 14,000 British and Indian troops under siege by Turkish forces at Kut-al-Amara. (For a full account of the siege of Kut and operations carried out by the 1/4th Battalion in Mesopotamia in 1915 see pp.377). It failed disastrously, with the 1/4th Hampshires losing 13 officers and 230 men killed, missing and wounded out of 16 and 339 in action. Eric Rule was among the dead, together with the battalion's Commanding Officer, Lieutenant Colonel Frederick Bowker, and Private Sidney Coles who lived at 44, Western Road, Winchester, a short distance from Eric.

Eric Rule was 37 years old when he died. Although his body was never found, and he was officially listed as missing, presumed killed, his wife Violet clung to the hope that he may have survived and been taken prisoner in the battle. An entry in the Hampshire Regimental Journal of July 1916 states:

> *MISSING - Mrs E.G. Rule, 10, St Paul's Terrace, Winchester, would be very grateful to anybody who could give her any definite news (first hand) of No. 25 Co-Sergt-Major E.G. Rule, 1/4th Hants Regt, reported missing in Mesopotamia since January 21st, 1916.*

The Army Registers of Soldiers' Effects, 1901-1929 shows that Violet Rule received £11 17s 9d on 25 July 1918 in respect of her late husband's effects. Violet and her children moved to Chelsea, west London, before the war ended – there is no entry for her in the Warren's Winchester Directory after 1916. Consequently, she would not have been in Winchester to provide the necessary information for Eric to be included in the WWSR. Violet died in Holborn, London, in 1931, her death being registered under her birth name Mary Ann.

Medals and memorials for Eric Granville Sutherland Rule

Company Sergeant Major Eric Granville Sutherland Rule was entitled to the 1914-15 Star, the British War Medal and the Victory Medal. He is commemorated on the Basra Memorial (above), Iraq (Panel No. 21 and 63) and on the memorials at St Paul's and St Matthew's churches, Winchester.

Researcher – DEREK WHITFIELD

SCADDEN, Alfred

Private ALFRED SCADDEN
10, Andover Road, Winchester (no longer stands)
Service number G/15680. 7th Battalion, The Buffs (East Kent Regiment)
Transferred from Kent Cyclists Battalion
Missing, believed killed in action, France, 5 October 1916

Alfred Scadden was born in Union Street, Winchester in 1889, the son of William and Annie Scadden (the name also appears as Scaddan, Scuddan and Scuddon). His parents were not from Winchester but moved to the city a few years before Alfred's birth. Alfred worked as an ironmonger before enlisting with the Kent Cyclists Battalion in 1915. He transferred to an infantry battalion and was killed in action, aged 27, during the later stages of the Battle of the Somme in 1916.

Alfred's father William was born on 10 April 1851 in Corfe Castle, Dorset. William's parents, Charles (born 1814) and Fanny (1814) and his five brothers were also from Corfe Castle. In 1851 Charles Scadden was working as a labourer in a clay pit with his family living in West Street, Corfe Castle. In the 1861 Census Charles was still working in clay pits while two of his sons were clay diggers and one a brickmaker's labourer. William, aged nine, was at school.

Alfred's mother Annie (1858-1924) was born in Leckford, near Stockbridge. It is not known when she and William married, but they must have lived in Southampton for a time because their three elder children, Bertie (1884), Charles (1884) and Fred (1886) were all born there.

By 1886 the Scaddens had moved to Winchester and were living on the east side of Union Street at No. 36 (subsequently demolished). After Alfred's birth in 1889 the couple went on to have two daughters – Elizabeth, born in Winchester in 1892, and Emily (1897). The 1901 Census records Alfred's father working as a saddler and harness maker and his older brother Charles as a bottle washer. Fred and Bertie, his other brothers, had left home. At some stage, the Scadden family moved to Middle Brook Street and then, in 1908, to 10, Andover Road (the house no longer stands). By the time of the 1911 Census only 21-year-old Alfred, his parents and sister Emily were living at home. Alfred was working as an ironmonger's assistant and Emily as a dressmaker.

Alfred did not join the rush to volunteer for military service when the Great War began in August 1914. Instead he waited until October 1915 before enlisting with the Kent Cyclists Battalion in Tonbridge (service number G15680). Given his choice of battalion it is likely that he was a keen cyclist.

Most of the British Army's cyclist battalions were Territorial units that formed part of Regular infantry regiments. However, four battalions - the Huntingdonshire, Highland, Northern and Kent Cyclists - were independent and without regimental affiliation. Although it had been touted as the new form of cavalry before the war, the bicycle proved to be of limited use in trench warfare.

In 1915 the first units of the Army Cyclist Corps were serving primarily in reconnaissance roles and as dispatch riders. They also engaged in traffic-directing duties and helping to locate stragglers and wounded troops on the battlefield. During the war years cyclists often found themselves confronted by difficult terrain, and on numerous occasions were forced to abandon their heavy Army issue machines.

The Army bicycle was designed to enable the rider to travel as a completely self-contained one-man fighting unit. Everything from his rifle to his cape and groundsheet could be stowed away on his bike. A small kitbag carried behind the seat held rations and personal items while an emergency tool kit hung from the crossbar. 'Cycle Artificers' were used to maintain the bikes and members of each battalion were trained as mechanics.

SCADDEN, Alfred

The Kent Cyclists on parade – Alfred Scadden joined the battalion in October 1915

The Army drew up regulations for the use of bikes. These included such gems as:

A cyclist standing with his cycle, with rifle attached to it, will salute with the right hand, as laid down in Section 19, returning the hand to the point of the saddle on the completion of the salute. When at ease, a cyclist, whether mounted or leading his bicycle, will salute by coming to attention, and turning his head to the officer he salutes. A party of cyclists on the march will salute on the command Eyes Right, which will be followed by Eyes Front, from the officer or NCO in charge.

The rate of marching, excluding halts, will generally vary from 8 to 10 miles per hour, according to the weather, the nature of the country, and the state of the roads. A column of battalion size should not be expected to cover more than 50 miles in a day under favourable conditions.

A Great War Army bicycle of the type that Arthur Scadden would have used

However, Alfred's time with the Kent Cyclists was brief. On 2 December 1915, the 1/1st Kent Cyclist Battalion moved to Chiseldon Camp, Swindon, Wiltshire, to be reorganised as an infantry battalion. It is believed that this was when Alfred transferred to the East Kent Regiment – known as The Buffs - and assigned to the 7th (Service) Battalion. The 7th Buffs had been raised at Canterbury, Kent, in September 1914 as part of Secretary of State for War Lord Kitchener's expansion of the British Army. The battalion came under the command of 55th Brigade in the 18th (Eastern) Division.

After a period of training, Alfred joined the 7th Buffs on the Western Front in time for the start of the Somme Offensive on 1 July 1916. Although the British suffered some 58,000 casualties on that disastrous first day of battle, the 18th Division, including the 7th Buffs, successfully achieved all its objectives. Attacking German positions near the village of Montauban at the southern end of a 13-mile front, 18th Division captured the formidable defensive systems known as The Loop, Pommiers Trench and Pommiers Redoubt.

One interesting footnote concerns the battalion attacking to the right of the 7th Buffs on 1 July, the 8th East Surreys. When the order came to go over the top at 7am Captain W.P. Nevill led his four platoons

SCADDEN, Alfred

into battle, each platoon kicking a football towards the German front line for the honour of scoring the first 'goal' Captain Nevill was killed but his platoons continued the advance. Two of the footballs were retrieved and one is now in the National Army Museum.

The 7th Buffs were in action again on 13-14 July when 18th Division was given the task of capturing Trones Wood, north of Montauban. Alfred's battalion led the attack, bombing their way up Maltzhorn Trench on the edge of the wood. After fierce German resistance and heavy British casualties, 18th Division eventually took Trones Wood in the early hours of 14 July.

Alfred and his battalion were out of the front-line during August but returned at the end of the following month for the Battle of Thiepval (26-28 September) and the Battle of the Ancre Heights (1-18 October). Among the objectives in the latter battle was Schwaben Redoubt which had been briefly captured on 1 July and then retaken by the Germans. The ferocious fighting around the Redoubt is vividly described by military historian Barry Cuttell:

> *This close-quarter work with bomb and bayonet was one of the most dangerous aspects of infantry work, during which all opposing sensations were experienced – fear-excitement, indecision-confidence, despondency-elation, despair-hope, what is today called a surge of adrenaline. Gains by both sides were made and lost, and at the end of the day the line had changed little. Losses were very heavy on both sides.*

Alfred Scadden is believed to have been killed, aged 27, in an attack on the Schwaben Redoubt on 5 October 1916. His body was never found. The British finally captured the Redoubt on 14 October.

Alfred's father William continued to live at 10, Andover Road immediately after the war. However, his name is not listed in Warren's Directory after 1920 which suggests that he may have died around that date. Annie Scadden, Alfred's mother, died in Winchester in 1924. Warren's lists a Miss Scadden at 10, Andover Road from 1920 to 1926 and she is almost certainly one of Alfred's sisters.

Medals and memorials for Arthur Scadden

Private Alfred Scadden was entitled to the British War Medal and the Victory Medal. His name appears (misspelt as Scuddan A – see above) on the Thiepval Memorial, Somme, France (Pier & Face 5D) and also on the memorials at St Matthew's and St Paul's churches, Winchester.

Researcher – JENNY WATSON

Additional sources
- Cuttell, Barry. *148 Days on the Somme* (Peterborough, GMS Enterprises, 2000).

SEWARD, John William

Sergeant JOHN WILLIAM SEWARD
16, Stockbridge Road, Winchester
Service numbers 355 and 26123. 101st Company, Machine Gun Corps
(Previously 2nd Battalion, Rifle Brigade)
Killed in action, France, 26 August 1917

John William Seward was born in Winchester on 26 November 1886, the eldest of eight children. A professional soldier with the Winchester-based Rifle Brigade, he served overseas in Malta and India before being sent to the Western Front in the early months of the Great War. John was brought up in east Winchester and it was not until mid-way through the war that his family moved to Stockbridge Road, a year before he was killed while serving with the Machine Gun Corps.

John's father, also named John, was born in Exeter in 1861, the son of labourer William Seward (born around 1824) and his wife Harriett (born 1825). Little is known of John Seward Snr's early years, but he married Esther Edwards at St Peter's Church, Winchester, in 1886, the same year that John Jnr was born.

Esther had been born in Winchester in 1863. Her father, George Edwards (1827-1907), worked variously as a bricklayer and labourer in the building trade, and later as a milkman. George married Jane Philpott in Winchester in 1854. Jane had been born in Longstock, near Stockbridge, Hampshire, in 1834. George and Jane went on to have nine children together. In the 1861 Census they were living in St John's Street, Winchester, with two young children and George's 80-year-old father, William, a butcher. By 1881 they had moved a short distance to 24, Cheesehill Street with Esther, then 18, working in domestic service. Ten years later, George was working as a milkman and living with Jane at 26, Wharf Hill, Winchester.

John Seward Snr spent much of his working life as a labourer, latterly to a sawyer in the timber business. Esther, meanwhile, looked after the couple's children, all of whom were born in Winchester apart from their eldest daughter, Louisa, who was born in Exeter in 1888. Besides John Jnr, the other children were Alice (born 1891), Harry (1893), Esther (1894), Charles (1896), George (1898) and Rosa (1900). With so many mouths to feed and only a small income, life for the Sewards would have been extremely hard, as it was for many working-class people in Winchester at the time.

The family regularly moved from one rental property to another. The 1891 Census showed them living at 72, Wales Street but two years later they had moved to 52, Canon Street. By 1895 they were at 13, Cheesehill Street and in 1897 at 20, Colebrook Street. The Sewards were at 68, Middle Brook Street between 1901 and 1905 and at 84, Middle Brook Street in 1907. From 1908 to 1910 they lived at 2, The Weirs and between 1911 and 1912 at 46, Canon Street. In the years when the family do not appear in any traceable official record it is likely that they were living with Esther's parents at 42, Wharf Hill.

John Seward Jnr entered St John's National School, Winchester, on 28 November 1893 when he was six years old. His sister Louisa enrolled at the school a few days later, on 4 December, aged five. Their address in the school logbook is 1, Wales Street. It is not known when John Jnr left school, but by the time of the 1901 Census, when he was 14, he was already working as an errand boy.

On 8 April 1904 John Jnr enlisted with the Rifle Brigade in Winchester. His attestation papers show that he lied about his age, giving it as 18 years and five months when in fact he was a year younger. He initially enlisted for three years' service (with nine years in the reserve) but later extended this to seven and then 12 years. John was described as 5ft 6½in tall with fair hair and blue eyes. He had a scar on the nape of his neck, tattooed dots on his left forearm and he gave his previous occupation as shoeing smith.

SEWARD, John William

He was assigned to the 2nd Battalion, Rifle Brigade (The Prince Consort's Own) with the service number 355 and sent to Chatham, Kent, for training.

John's Army career got off to an inauspicious start. In November 1904 he was confined to barracks for eight days for making an insolent reply to an NCO and he continued to have periodic run-ins with authority over the following years, but always for relatively minor offences of disobedience and insubordination. In 1905, his training completed, John embarked for Malta to join 4th Rifle Brigade and he remained there for more than a year. In December 1906 he was sent to India to serve with 2nd Rifle Brigade.

John's first posting was to Chaubattia, high in the Kumaon Hills in north-west India (in modern Uttarakhand state). Conditions here were tough: not only was the remote British base 50 miles from the nearest railway station, but disease – mainly malaria and enteric fever – exacted a constant and often deadly toll on soldiers of all ranks. Company training and musketry practice formed the backbone of the working day. John was also posted to Shahjahanpur on the River Ganges (in modern Uttar Pradesh, northern India) and Calcutta.

In 1908 John was awarded the Army Certificate of Education 3rd Class. The certificates had been introduced in 1861 to encourage soldiers to broaden what was all too often a rudimentary school education. The third-class certificate specified the standard for promotion to the rank of Corporal: the candidate was required to read aloud and to write from dictation passages from an easy narrative, and to work examples in the four compound rules of arithmetic and the reduction of money.

In the summer of 1911, while stationed at Fort William, Calcutta, John spent more than two weeks in hospital after contracting gonorrhoea. He was hospitalised with the same disease again, this time for two months, in early 1912 while stationed in Rawalpindi (in the Punjab province of modern Pakistan). John had either been re-infected or, more likely, the disease had flared up again, this time more severely. Treatment for venereal disease in the days before penicillin was notoriously unreliable and would later cause significant problems for the military authorities during the Great War.

The British Army base at Kuldana, India, where John Seward served from 1912 to 1914

SEWARD, John William

2nd Rifle Brigade form the guard of honour for King George V in Calcutta during the state visit of 1911-12

It is not known whether John was well enough to take part in the Calcutta Pageant in early January 1912 which marked the end of King George V's state visit to India. The 2nd Rifle Brigade formed the guard of honour for the royal party at the pageant, but Army records show that by 22 January John was in hospital being treated for VD. The same year brought more bad news with the death of John Seward Snr in Winchester, aged 53. John Jnr would probably have received the news by letter or telegram but would not have been able to attend the funeral given that India was many weeks away by ship.

By the start of 1914 John had been promoted to Lance-Corporal. The 2nd Rifle Brigade were stationed at Kuldana, some 7,000ft up in the Murree Hills in Rawalpindi district. Training here focused on mountain warfare and manoeuvres were frequently extremely hazardous! The battalion was due to return to England in October that year, but Britain's declaration of war hastened its departure.

As a Regular battalion of trained professional soldiers, 2nd Rifle Brigade was needed urgently on the Western Front to reinforce the British Expeditionary Force (BEF). Consequently, the War Office ordered the battalion to return from India early. Its place – and that of many other Regular Army units in India - was taken by Territorial battalions from England, including several dozen Winchester men of the 4th Battalion, The Hampshire Regiment.

On 26 August 1914 2nd Rifle Brigade received orders to return to England. By 8 September hundreds of men – and in many cases their families as well – plus tons of baggage and equipment had been transported to Bombay docks. The 1914 Rifle Brigade Chronicle recorded this impressive logistical feat:

Early on Tuesday morning, 8 September, both troop trains steamed into Princes' Dock, Bombay, only for us to find that we were not expected so soon and were not wanted for another week! Someone had blundered! However, we could not bed down for ten days on the quayside and so, at 10am, we started to embark on the S.S. Somali. By night the whole Battalion and all the baggage was on board and we had the first drink since Barakao, a free bottle of beer all round ... and a very welcome drink it was too, for the Battalion had man-handled quite 50 tons of baggage three times, marched 40 miles by road, entrained, travelled 1,700 miles by rail, dis-entrained and embarked – all in 132 hours!

SEWARD, John William

After a six-week voyage, 2nd Rifle Brigade arrived at Liverpool on 22 October 1914 and made their way by train down to Winchester. From here they marched the short distance to Hursley Park to join up with 25th Brigade, part of 8th Division, which was mobilising there.

On 25 October John Seward was appointed Acting-Corporal. It is likely that he took the opportunity to visit family and friends in Winchester before his battalion embarked for France, where it arrived on 7 November. Ten days later 2nd Rifle Brigade entered the front line for the first time, in trenches in front of the German-held village of Aubers, nine miles west of Lille in northern France. Almost immediately the weather, which had already been wet, took a turn for the worse. The Battalion Chronicle reported:

> *The trenches were full of mud and water on the 18th [November] and a heavy fall of snow made matters worse. On the night of the 18th a very hard frost set in, freezing the men's wet boots with the result that almost all ranks suffered badly from swollen feet. Tallow and Vaseline have since been provided, and sandbags with straw in them for the men's feet are now up in the trenches.*

Soldiers of 2nd Rifle Brigade training in mountain warfare in the Murree Hills in 1912

The severe weather led to more than 44 men being treated for frostbite of the feet on 22 November. For John Seward it must have seemed a far cry from the stifling heat and dust of India.

The 2nd Rifle Brigade did not take part in the First Battle of Ypres (19 October-22 November 1914) which saw the BEF suffer heavy casualties. However, the battalion did see action at the Battle of Neuve Chapelle between 10 and 13 March 1915. The battle, the BEF's first major planned offensive of the war, involved 40,000 troops and the heaviest British artillery bombardment to date. The assaulting battalions managed to capture Neuve Chapelle village, but communications difficulties meant reinforcements were not called up in time to capitalise on this success.

John Seward and his battalion had spent 2-9 March out of the front line, training for the battle. On the day of the attack they quickly took the German front line trenches but were then forced to dig in after losing a 'good many men' from the fire of two enemy field guns and a machine-gun. Over the following three days 2nd Rifle Brigade suffered grievously as the Germans counter-attacked in a bid to recapture lost ground. By 13 March five officers had been killed, five wounded and two had died of wounds. Among the other ranks, 83 had been killed and 269 wounded. Another 15 men were missing.

It is not known whether any letters written by John Seward from the front to his family have survived. However, correspondence from one of his comrades, Rifleman Frederick Peters, gives some idea of what the men of 2nd Rifle Brigade endured during the Battle of Neuve Chapelle. Writing to his mother on 21 March 1915, Frederick stated:

SEWARD, John William

I suppose you will have seen the letter I wrote to [sister] Edie by now so you will know that I came safely out of the big battle. No doubt you read all about it in the People [newspaper], but that was only the official reports. There will be a lot more details given when Sir John French [British Commander-in-Chief] issues his despatches. We were surprised to see what a big affair it was, according to the papers. We suddenly realised we had earnt a name in history, but we had a heavy price to pay for it. If you keep a look out in the People you will see the casualty lists published in three or four weeks' time and will find a lot of Rifle Brigade names in them, for we were right in the thick of it.

Frederick gave more details of the battle in a letter home on 13 April 1915:

I saw those pictures of Neuve Chapelle in that piece of paper and was around the two spots all day. The Germans were shelling it, and bricks, tiles, and rafters kept falling about us. The ground was like a nutmeg grater, one mass of big holes caused by the terrific explosions. A cemetery was torn up, and all the headstones were smashed to atoms and strewed the ground. Dead bodies were blown up; some were of our poor fellows who had been killed about there in August or September. Anyone who visited the place now and was ignorant that a war was on, would think an earthquake had taken place.

Less than a month later 2nd Rifle Brigade was in action again, at the Battle of Aubers Ridge. The battalion attacked near the village of Fromelles on 9 May with 24 officers and some 1,000 men. At 5am the following day when the battalion marched back to their billets 21 officers and 571 other ranks had been killed, wounded or were missing - the highest casualties of any unit involved that day. Among those who died were Rifleman Frederick Peters and Brigadier General Arthur Cole, the commander of 25th Brigade. The losses for the Aubers Ridge attack were just as catastrophic as any incurred more than a year later on 1 July 1916, the first day of the Battle of the Somme, but in 1915 it **was the loss of the experienced professionals from the pre-war regulars that was so keenly felt.**

John Seward was promoted to full Corporal on 10 May 1915, the day that 2nd Rifle Brigade came out of the line after Aubers Ridge. On 9 July John suffered gunshot wounds to the thigh and hand and was taken to 22nd General Hospital at Etaples. Four days later he was evacuated to the Horton (County of London) War Hospital in Epsom, Surrey, for treatment and rehabilitation. On 14 December 1915 he was posted to the 5th (Reserve) Battalion, Rifle Brigade, a depot/training unit based at Minster on the Isle of Sheppey where it formed part of the Thames and Medway Garrison.

In early 1916 John's military career took a new turn when he transferred to the Machine Gun Corps (MGC) and was sent to Grantham, Lincolnshire, for training. The MGC had been set up in October 1915 in response to the need for more effective use of heavy machine guns on the Western Front. One MGC Company, usually comprising ten Vickers heavy machine guns, was attached to each infantry brigade. Each weapon required a team of six to eight men - one fired, one fed the ammunition and the rest helped to carry the weapon, its ammunition, and spare parts.

The Vickers machine gun had a reputation for great solidity and reliability. This was demonstrated in an action in August 1916 during the Somme Offensive when the 100th Machine Gun Company fired their ten Vickers guns continuously for 12 hours. Using 100 barrels, they fired a million rounds without a failure. During the war, the MGC earned a reputation for heroism as a fighting force. Some 170,500 officers and men served in the MGC, with 62,049 becoming casualties, including 12,498 killed, earning it the nickname 'The Suicide Club'.

SEWARD, John William

John Seward remained in England until 24 April 1916 when he embarked for France with 102nd Machine Gun Company. There the unit was assigned to 102nd Brigade, part of 34th Division. At some point over the next six months John transferred to the 101st Machine Gun Company, part of 101st Brigade, also in 34th Division. Both companies saw action at the Battle of Albert (1-13 July 1916), the opening phase of the Somme Offensive, although the 102nd Company was transferred to 37th Division after 102nd Brigade suffered exceptionally heavy casualties on 1 July.

The surviving military records do not show which company John served with on the Somme. However, they do reveal that on 4 October 1916 he was promoted to Sergeant in 101st Machine Gun Company. One possible scenario is that John served with 102nd Company until early October, transferring to 101st Company when the bloodletting on the Somme left it short of experienced NCOs.

16, Stockbridge Road, Winchester – this was home to John Seward's family from 1916 to 1925

By the start of 1917 John Seward was a hardened war veteran. His 12-year period of service in the Army should have ended on 8 April 1916, but intriguingly – and for reasons unknown - it did not in fact do so until a year later. An entry in his Army records states: 'Continued in the service under the Military Service Act (Session 2) from 8-4-17'. The two Military Service Acts of 1916 (in January and May) introduced conscription in Britain for the first time, effectively putting the country on a 'total war' footing. One of the provisions stated that soldiers who had been discharged from the Army were eligible for service again. The implication here is that John *wanted* to leave the Army in April 1917 but was immediately conscripted back in.

John Seward's next taste of action came in the Arras Offensive of April and May 1917. On April 9 – the day after it is thought that he was conscripted – John went over the top in the First Battle of the Scarpe. The assault, fought in tandem with the Battle of Vimy, brought considerable early gains before bogging down. The Scarpe battle ended on 14 April, but after a fortnight out of the line John found himself in the fray once more at the Battle of Arleux (28-29 April).

In terms of BEF lives lost each day, the Arras Offensive, which ended on 16 May, was the bloodiest of the entire war, yet John Seward again emerged unscathed. In addition to his good fortune, one senses that he had developed into a fine soldier, no longer the headstrong, rebellious Rifleman of his India years but an effective and trusted NCO. Tragically, however, his luck was about to run out.

From March 1917 the German army in the Somme sector of the Western Front had begun to pull back to new, heavily fortified positions known as the Hindenburg Line. The BEF advanced in the wake of the German retirement and eventually encountered the outposts of the Hindenburg Line, including the village of Hargicourt, situated between the towns of Peronne and St Quentin. The British attacked Hargicourt in April 1917 but made only limited gains. On 26 August, in pouring rain, 34th Division attacked again and captured enemy positions east of the village on a front of more than a mile. As in

SEWARD, John William

April, casualties were heavy and among those killed was 30-year-old Sergeant John Seward. His body was never found, suggesting that he and his machine-gun team may have been hit by an artillery shell.

Two of John's brothers served in the war and survived. According to the Winchester War Service Register (WWSR), Charles Seward joined the Hampshire Regiment in October 1915 and fought in Mesopotamia before transferring to the Northumberland Fusiliers. He was wounded once. However, Army records indicate that instead of the Hampshires Charles served first with the Wiltshire Regiment.

George Seward, meanwhile, enlisted with the Hampshire Regiment in August 1915 and later transferred to the RAF. He served on the home front.

In 1916 John's widowed mother Esther moved to 8, Lower Stockbridge Road which was renumbered 16, Stockbridge Road in 1918. This is the address given for John Seward in the WWSR compiled in 1921. The 1918 Warren's Winchester Directory shows several of John's siblings living at the house, including his sister Louisa and her husband Joseph Thorpe, a labourer, who she had married in 1917.

Esther Seward remained at 16, Stockbridge Road – which still stands - until 1925 when she moved with her son Charles to Hutment 31, Alresford Road, Winchester. This was one of 57 huts which had served as married quarters at the military camp on Morn Hill during the Great War. The huts were taken over by the local council after the war and provided homes for between 30 to 40 families before being demolished in around 1927.

There is no trace of Esther in Warren's after 1927, but in 1939 she was living at Women Lodge, Beeding Hill, Sussex, with her daughter Esther Jnr and her son Charles and his wife Ellen who had married in 1937. She is thought to have died in Worthing, West Sussex, in 1940, aged 78. Charles Seward, who had been working as a pigman in 1939, died in Horsham, Sussex, in December 1973, aged 77. **Esther Seward Jnr never married and died in Worthing in 1951 at the age of 57.**

Louisa and Joseph Thorpe continued to live in Winchester and in 1939 were at 25, Fivefields Road (off Highcliffe Road). Louisa died in Winchester on 27 June 1952, aged 63. Sister Rosa married Percy Seymour in Winchester in 1919. Percy went on to serve in the RAF and the couple had at least one child, Ronald, who was born in 1924. Rosa died in Staffordshire in 1979, aged 78.

John's brother George married Edith Luce in Cirencester, Gloucestershire, in October 1918. He was serving as a labourer in the RAF at the time, stationed at Queensferry in North Wales. In 1935 Edith gave birth to a daughter, Sylvia, and in 1939 the family were living in Cirencester with George working as a builder's labourer. George died in Cirencester in 1958 at the age of 61. Alice Seward is believed to have married in Winchester in 1911 but no further trace of her can be found.

Medals and memorials for John William Seward

Sergeant John William Seward was entitled to the 1914 (Mons) Star, the British War Medal and the Victory Medal. He has no known grave, but his name appears on the Thiepval Memorial, Somme, France (Pier and Face 5 C and 12 C). He is also mentioned on the memorials at St Paul's and St Matthew's churches, Winchester.

Researchers – DEREK WHITFIELD, GERALDINE BUCHANAN and JENNY WATSON

SHEARS, Samuel

Private SAMUEL SHEARS
12, Ashley Terrace, Winchester (no longer stands)
Service numbers 1449, 144683 and 37762
4th Battalion, The Hampshire Regiment and Labour Corps
Died in Winchester, 5 February 1919

Samuel Shears was born in Wallop, near Andover, in the summer of 1866, the youngest child of George and Eliza Shears. Samuel joined the Hampshire Regiment as a professional soldier in his teens and later re-enlisted as a Territorial. He was 48 years old when the Great War broke out and never saw active service, almost certainly due to poor health. Instead, Samuel served on the home front, latterly with the Labour Corps, before being discharged on health grounds in August 1918. He died shortly afterwards.

Samuel's father George was also born in Wallop, in 1832, and worked as an agricultural labourer. In the 1851 Census George was recorded living with his parents and two sisters at Waterloo House in Broughton, near Stockbridge. His father Thomas, a woodman, had been born in Wallop in 1809 and his mother, Dinah, in 1808 in Houghton, near Stockbridge.

George married Eliza Wake in Winchester in 1851. Eliza had been born in Hursley, near Winchester, in 1829. As well as Samuel, the couple had six other children: Sarah, born in 1857, Thomas (1858), Josiah (1859), Eliza (1862), George (1863) and James (1864). In 1861 the family were living at Berry Court Cottage, Nether Wallop. Ten years later the Shears family had moved to Saxley Cottage, Upper Clatford, near Andover.

George Shears died in Andover in 1874. The years immediately following his death must have been difficult for his widow and their four children although, except for Samuel, all were old enough to work and bring in money to the household.

On 26 May 1884 Samuel enlisted with the 1st Battalion, The Hampshire Regiment in Winchester. At the time he signed up he was living at 10, George Yard, Andover, and his attestation papers reveal he was working as a chimney sweep. Still a few weeks short of his 18th birthday, Samuel was technically under-age when he enlisted, although on the attestation papers he stated that he was 19. He was issued with the service number 1449.

Samuel Shears spent ten years with the 1st Hampshires, serving in Malta, India and Burma. In 1887 he was serving overseas when his mother died in Andover, aged 59. Samuel was discharged from the Army on 30 January 1894 because he was suffering from epilepsy. His discharge papers reveal that he intended to live at 11, Terrace Row, Winchester.

In the summer of 1896 Samuel married Mary Laming in Winchester. His wife, a widow, had been born Mary Ward in Winchester in 1862. She married Henry Laming in Portsmouth in April 1882 and the couple had five children: Priscilla (1882-1968), Frances (1884-1925), Lily (1885-1980), Leonard (1888-1962) and Jessie (1893-1953). Henry Laming died in Portsmouth in October 1892, a few months before his daughter Jessie's birth.

Two years after they married, Samuel and Mary Shears had their first child, a daughter, Mabel, who was born in Winchester. A son, Samuel George (referred to here as Samuel Jnr), was born in 1900. By the time of the 1901 Census the family – which also included three of Samuel's stepchildren – were living at 12, Ashley Terrace (next to Gladstone Street but no longer standing today) in Winchester. Samuel was working as a railway carrier's carman. This involved driving a horsedrawn vehicle to transport

SHEARS, Samuel

goods; carmen were often employed by railway companies for local deliveries and collections. Samuel and his two children were still at Ashley Terrace in 1911, the year that Mary Shears died, aged 49.

Three years earlier, in July 1908, Samuel Shears had enlisted for four years with the 4th Battalion, The Hampshire Regiment, part of the new Territorial Force. His Army papers reveal that he was working as a carter for Chaplains & Co. Samuel gave his age as 33 when he was 42. It is unclear why he should do so. In 1912 he re-enlisted for a further four years.

When war broke out in August 1914 Samuel immediately became liable for military service but, unlike many of the younger men in his battalion, he chose not to volunteer to serve overseas. This may have been because of his age – he was 48 years old – or his fragile health.

While both 4th Hampshire battalions (the 1/4th and 2/4th) served abroad, Samuel – service number 144683 - remained at home in a non-combat role. Army records suggest that before transferring to the Labour Corps in 1917 he may have served with the 13th (Works) Battalion, The Devonshire Regiment (service number 58596). This unit was one of several labour companies set up by individual Army regiments to carry out the various non-combatant tasks involved in keeping the war effort running smoothly. These companies were transferred to the Labour Corps in February 1917.

The Labour Corps was made up of men who had been in the front line but who were unfit to return because of wounds or illness. They also included men who, on enlistment, were found to be too old or not fit enough to be sent to the front. Samuel Shears appears to have fallen into this second category. His duties on the home front would have included helping in stores, transporting equipment, repairing roads and possibly even manning theatres and cinemas. By November 1918, some 400,000 men served in the Labour Corps.

In April 1917 Samuel was transferred to the 3rd Battalion the Labour Corps. Less than two months later, on 7 June, he was assigned to 303 Reserve Labour Company and then on 18 July to 380 Home Service Labour Company with the service number 37762.

In August 1918 Samuel was discharged from the Army on health grounds for a second time, on this occasion for chronic bronchitis. On 2 September he was issued with the Silver War Badge, to distinguish him in civilian life as someone who had served in the military. He died in Winchester, aged 52, on 5 February 1919, possibly from Spanish flu exacerbated by his chest problems. It is not known whether Samuel was buried or cremated after his death. Interestingly, despite official records showing that Samuel died in Winchester, no trace can be found of him living in the city after 1916.

Samuel Shears Jnr also served in the Great War. In 1915 he enlisted twice in Winchester to serve with the Hampshire Carabiniers Yeomanry. His first attestation papers are dated 14 June 1915 when he was just 15 years old. His service number was 1764. Samuel Jnr enlisted again on 6 November and his second attestation papers state that he had previously served with the Carabiniers but been discharged. Samuel gave his age as 16 years and 9 days which, even if true, meant he was still underage for military service. However, he appears to have been accepted by the Army and was given the service number 45495 (later 210305). Despite his father's health problems, his physical condition was described as 'good' – he was 5ft 7ins tall, weighed 9st and had a 34in chest. His employment was given as vanman.

Samuel Jnr went on to serve in France with the Hampshire Carabiniers before being transferred to the 3rd Battalion, The Royal Worcestershire Regiment (service number 207339), possibly when the Carabiniers were disbanded in 1917. He also appears to have served with the Royal Warwickshire Regiment. Both Samuel Jnr and his father are listed in the Winchester War Service Register.

SHEARS, Samuel

Samuel Jnr survived the war and went on to marry Bessie Price in Winchester in 1925. In 1939 the couple were living at 59a Colebrook Street. Samuel Jnr died at the Royal Hampshire County Hospital Winchester in 1949, aged 48 or 49. He is buried at Magdalen Hill Cemetery (grave No.6 12/66 p.75 in register).

Of Samuel Shears Snr's other close family members, only two can be traced to Winchester after the Great War. His daughter Mabel died there in June 1975, aged 77. His sister Sarah had married Edward Spencer in 1874 and after his death in 1886 she lived at 52, Water Road, Winchester, with her five children. Sarah died of congestion of the lungs on 19 October 1934, aged 67.

Medals and memorials for Samuel Shears

Private Samuel Shears was not entitled to any military medals because he never served in a theatre of war. He is mentioned on the memorials at St Matthew's and St Paul's churches, Winchester.

Researcher – DEREK WHITFIELD

SHEFFERD, Cecil

Lance-Corporal CECIL SHEFFERD
Grangemont, 94, Fairfield Road, Winchester
Service numbers 4/1660 and 200107, 1/4th Battalion, The Hampshire Regiment
Died in Turkish captivity, Mesopotamia, 4 September 1916

Cecil Shefferd was born on 22 January 1893 in the splendid surroundings of Northington Grange, near Alresford, where his father worked at as a valet. Cecil's parents later moved to Winchester and here he excelled as a scholar before becoming a clerk with Hampshire County Council. A pre-war Territorial soldier with the 4th Battalion, The Hampshire Regiment, Cecil Shefferd served in Mesopotamia (modern Iraq) and was taken prisoner by the Turks following the fall of the British garrison at Kut-al-Amara. He died in captivity a few months later.

Cecil's father, Thomas Shefferd, was born in Itchen Stoke, near Alresford, on 21 June 1860. He was one of nine children. Thomas's parents had also been born in Itchen Stoke. His father, Charles Shefferd (1837-1905), worked as an agricultural labourer. His mother, Hannah (née Smith, 1837-1882) was the daughter of an agricultural labourer. Thomas, however, clearly decided that working on the land was not for him because in 1881 he was working as a footman for 94-year-old Anne Penelope Hoare (believed to be related to Sir Samuel Hoare, Home Secretary in Neville Chamberlain's government between 1939 and 1939) at her home in St James's Square, Pall Mall, London.

Cecil's mother was born Jane Marchant in the village of Handcross, near Crawley, Sussex, in 1861. Like Thomas, she came from a large family and had six siblings. Her father, Henry, was born in 1834 in Slaugham, Sussex, and worked as a brickmaker. Her mother was born in Brighton in 1837. In 1881 Jane was working as a schoolroom maid, one of six servants employed by GP John Lucas Worship and his wife Clara at their home, The Manor House in Sevenoaks, Kent.

Thomas and Jane married at St Matthew's Church, Redhill, Surrey, on 29 October 1891. Thomas's occupation on the marriage certificate is given as valet in Northington. A house had existed on the site of Northington Grange since the 17th Century, but in 1804 the four-storey red-brick property was transformed into a neoclassical Ancient Greek temple under the direction of architect William Wilkins. Further additions and alterations were made in the 1850s which proved to be a halcyon period. The owner, William Baring, 2nd Lord Ashburton, served in the government of Sir Robert Peel. His wife Harriet, a witty and sophisticated hostess, threw sumptuous parties at Northington Grange attended by Thomas Carlyle, Alfred Lord Tennyson and other society figures.

SHEFFERD, Cecil

By the time Thomas Shefferd arrived to work at the house – probably in the late 1880s – it had passed to Francis Barring, the 5th Lord Ashburton, who converted the orangery into a picture gallery to accommodate his paintings. Today the Grange is home to an internationally acclaimed opera company.

The Shefferds must have left the Grange shortly after Cecil's birth in 1893, because in 1895 Jane gave birth to a second son, Ronald, in Winchester. Two more sons, Charles and George, were also born in the city, in 1898 and 1900 respectively, and a daughter, Madeline Alfreda, in 1901.

Cecil Shefferd's father Thomas and mother Jane. Below: Northington Grange in around 1870. Cecil was born in the house on 22 January 1893 when his father was working there as a valet

By 1899, Thomas Shefferd was running The Old Red Deer public house at 92, Lower Stockbridge Road, Winchester (on the corner with Elm Road), which doubled as the family home. A few hundred yards away, on the corner of Lower Stockbridge Road and Andover Road, his brother William was publican of The Albion. The Old Red Deer closed in 1983 but the building survives with Winchester Travel Health on the corner and Fulflood Gallery & Framing next door. The Albion is still in business.

Cecil attended Western Infants School in Elm Road, Fulflood, before moving on to St Thomas Church of England Boys' School on 17 April 1899. He was clearly a good scholar because on 15 September 1905 he was admitted to Peter Symonds Boys School where he spent the next three years. His fees were paid by Hampshire County Council. Cecil also appears to have enjoyed amateur dramatics; a report in the Hampshire Chronicle of 19 October 1909 describes his portrayal of Mrs Homespun in a farce called 'Cherry Bounce', put on by boys of St Paul's Bible Class.

Cecil left Peter Symonds School on 7 April 1909 to help his father run The Old Red Deer. By 1911, however, Thomas had sold the business and the family had moved a short distance to Grangemont, 94, Fairfield Road, Winchester. The Census of that year shows Cecil working as a clerk for the County Council and his brother Ronald as a grocer's assistant. Oddly, Thomas is not mentioned on the census document, so his occupation is unknown. His name does, however, appear in the 1911 Warren's Directory and places him at 94, Fairfield Road.

SHEFFERD, Cecil

Right: 94, Fairfield Road, Winchester, which in 1914 was known as Grangemont. It was from here that Cecil Shefferd departed to go to war in October 1914

Cecil's Army service number 4/1660 indicates that he enlisted as a Territorial soldier with the 4th Battalion, The Hampshire Regiment before the Great War. Although a part-time soldier, Cecil would have received basic military training, particularly during the battalion's annual two-week summer camp.

When war broke out in August 1914 Cecil volunteered for service overseas. In October he sailed for India with the newly-formed 1/4th Hampshires. In March 1915, the battalion was sent to Mesopotamia and Cecil entered a theatre of war there on the 18th.

Cecil fought with the 1/4th Hampshires against the Ottoman Turks throughout 1915 and was wounded twice. In December he was among the contingent of Hampshire soldiers trapped by the Turks in the British garrison at Kut-al-Amara. (For details of the 1/4th Hampshires' actions in Mesopotamia in 1915 and the siege of Kut see pp. 377.) Cecil became a prisoner of war when the garrison surrendered on 29 April 1916 and he was marched off into captivity. He eventually reached the Yarbaschi PoW camp in the Amanus Mountains where prisoners were set to work on constructing the Baghdad railway. Cecil could only have been at the camp a short time because on 4 September he died, probably from disease. He was 23 years old.

Among the prisoners at Yarbaschi was Company Quarter Master Sergeant Andrew Bogie, also of the 1/4th Hampshires, who lived in St Paul's Terrace, Fulflood, a short distance from the Shefferd family. Andrew survived Cecil by less than three weeks, dying on 22 September 1916. It took several months for news of Cecil's death to reach his parents back in Winchester. The Hampshire Regimental Journal of April 1917 records:

> *SHEFFERD - Lance-Corporal C. Shefferd, Hampshire Regiment, taken prisoner at Kut, died in the hands of the Turks, date and place not known, aged 24, the eldest son of Mr and Mrs Shefferd, Grangemont, Fairfield Road, Winchester.*
>
> *Lce-Corpl. Cecil Shefferd, Hampshire Regt, who was taken prisoner at Kut, has died as a prisoner of war in the hands of the Turks, aged 24. Official notification of the sad fact was received last month. Lce.-Corpl. Cecil Shefferd was a son of Mr and Mrs T. Shefferd, of Grangemont, Fairfield Road, Winchester for whom much sympathy will be felt. Before joining the Forces, Lce.-Corpl. Shefferd was at the County Council Offices.*

The UK Army Registers of Soldiers Effects, 1901-29 shows that £21 7s 5d was paid to Cecil's father Thomas on 12 July 1917, presumably in respect of his effects and back pay. Thomas received a £9 10s war gratuity in September 1919.

Cecil's three brothers also fought in the Great War. Charles served in Mesopotamia as a sapper (he would have been too young to have gone off to war with Cecil) before transferring to the Royal

SHEFFERD, Cecil

Engineers where he was promoted to Sergeant. George and Ronald both served in France, with the Hampshire Regiment and the Royal Army Medical Corps respectively. All three survived the war. The four brothers are listed in the Winchester War Service Register.

Thomas and Jane Shefferd continued to live at Grangemont after the war. Thomas died in Winchester on 14 March 1927, aged 66. Probate records show he left £862 1s 9d to his wife. Jane passed away in Winchester on 10 February 1936 at the age of 75. She left £1878 16s 7d in her will.

George Shefferd married Edith Tilling (1902-1946) and the couple had a son, Maurice (1926-1976). George was living at 9, Walton Place, Winchester, when he died in 1946, aged 47. He is buried at Magdalen Hill Cemetery.

Cecil's sister Madeline married Edwin Tilbury (1900-1962) in Winchester in 1923. The couple had two children, Joan, (1924-2010), who was born in Easton, near Winchester, and George (1926-2006). Madeline died in Winchester in December 1973 at the age of 72, and Edwin in September 1962.

Charles Shefferd married Kate Kelsey in Winchester in 1924 and the couple had a son, Ronald (1925-1987). Kate passed away in Winchester in March 1974, aged 78. Charles, who worked for the Post Office, also died in Winchester, on 9 September 1981, aged 84.

Ronald Shefferd married Melinda Hollis (1880-1970) in Dartford, Kent, in 1920. Three years later, Melinda gave birth to a son, poignantly named Cecil. He was to be the couple's only child. Ronald died in 1961, aged 66.

Medals and memorials for Cecil Shefferd

Lance-Corporal Cecil Shefferd was entitled to the 1914-15 Star, the British War Medal and the Victory Medal. (A Great War Memorial Plaque to Cecil Shefferd, with supporting paper confirming his date of death, was sold for £80 by Dreweatt's of Bloomsbury on 28 September 2012.) After the war Cecil's body was disinterred and reburied in Baghdad (North Gate) War Cemetery, Iraq (GR. XXI. T. 23). He is mentioned on the memorials at St Matthew's and St Paul's churches, Winchester, as well as those at Peter Symonds School and the Hampshire County Council offices in Winchester. Cecil's name also appears on the St Thomas School memorial, which is today held by Kings School, Winchester.

Researcher - DEREK WHITFIELD

SIMMONS, John

2nd Lieutenant JOHN SIMMONS
36, Greenhill Road, Winchester
3rd Battalion, Rifle Brigade - attached to School of Bombing
(Previously service number 7198)
Killed accidentally, Aldershot, 21 August 1916

John Simmons was born on 24 March 1873 in Marylebone, London. At the age of just 15 he followed his father into the Army and served as a professional soldier for 28 years, latterly with the Winchester-based Rifle Brigade. He moved to the city in around 1914 when he helped to oversee the Rifle Brigade's preparations for war. Despite being in his forties, he was given a commission and served as a 2nd Lieutenant on the Western Front before being invalided home a few months later. He subsequently served as an instructor at the School of Bombing in Aldershot where he was killed in an accident in 1916. The Winchester War Service Register gives John's address as 4, Greenhill Road (his wife's address in 1921 when the Register was compiled), but this biography uses 36, Greenhill Road which was his home in 1914.

John was the only child of John George and Emily Simmons. John Snr had been born in Bloomsbury, London, in 1841. He joined the 2nd Battalion of the 60th Rifles (officially known as the King's Royal Rifle Corps) in March 1859. John spent much of his service overseas – in India and China and Ireland.

In 1865 John married Emily Reeve who had been born in Hayward's Heath, Sussex, in 1846. The 1871 Census recorded John Snr living at the Army barracks in Colchester, Essex; however, there is no mention of Emily. John rose through the ranks to become a Colour Sergeant before leaving the Army, in around 1875. By the time of the 1881 Census, John Simmons Snr was working as a clerk and living at 32, Southwark Bridge Road, London, with Emily and eight-year-old John Jnr who was at school. Two other families were also living at the same address. Two years later, John Snr died in Marylebone, aged just 42. No further trace can be found of Emily Simmons after 1881.

It appears that in 1884, the year after his father's death, 12-year-old John Simmons Jnr enrolled at King Edward School, Witley, Surrey. Situated in the village of Wormley, near Guildford, the boarding school was founded in 1553 by King Edward VI and Nicholas Ridley. John's conduct was recorded as good, but his attainment in the school band merely 'indifferent'. Despite this, when he left school in 1888, he joined the 2nd Battalion, The Queen's (Royal West Surrey) Regiment at Guildford as a band boy.

The 2nd Queen's Regiment had been formed in 1661 and was the senior English line infantry regiment of the British Army. John apparently signed up for six years because in August 1894 he transferred to the Army Reserve list, but in December of the same year he re-enlisted. It has not been possible to determine which regiment John joined on re-enlisting – his brief biography on the King Edward School website states that it was probably the 2nd Queen's, although a report in the Hampshire Chronicle after his death suggests that most of his career was spent with the Rifle Brigade. To further confuse matters, his marriage certificate states that he was serving with the Border Regiment.

Right: King Edward School, Witley, Surrey, which John Simmons attended before joining the Army in 1888

SIMMONS, John

The Royal Marine Barracks in Woolwich, London, in the mid-1800s. John Simmons was garrisoned here with the 5th Rifle Brigade in around 1910 by which time the building had become the Cambridge Barracks

On 9 June 1900 John Simmons married Helen Barrow in Marylebone. The youngest of seven children, Helen had been born in 1870 in the parish of St George's, Hanover Square, London. At the time of her marriage she was living at 4, Westmoreland Street, Marylebone. Thomas Barrow, Helen's father, was described on the marriage certificate as a caretaker but he had previously been the manager of a soup kitchen and a painter - presumably a decorator. (Interestingly, a missionary was recorded living with the Barrows in the 1881 Census. This, together with Thomas's role at the soup kitchen, suggests the family may have had Methodist connections. It would certainly help to explain why a memorial to John Simmons was placed in the Wesleyan Chapel in St Peter's Street, Winchester, after the war.)

As mentioned above, the couple's marriage certificate showed that in June 1900 John was serving with the Border Regiment in the Brigade Office at Shorncliffe Army Camp, near Folkestone, Kent, and had reached the rank of Sergeant. A few months later, in the 1901 Census, John was described as an Orderly Room Sergeant with '7 BRB', which was possibly a unit in the Border Regiment. An Orderly Room Sergeant is the chief clerk of an infantry battalion whose role is to assistant the adjutant. It suggests that John was probably more a military administrator by temperament than fighting soldier.

Helen Simmons was already pregnant when she married John and on Boxing Day 1900 she gave birth to a son, John George (after his paternal grandfather), in Hackney, London. The family were recorded living at 84, Shrubland Road, Hackney, in the 1901 Census and a second son, Harold, was born there on 18 July 1903.

Given that John was serving in England with the Border Regiment in 1900 and 1901, it is unlikely that he saw action in the Boer War. The details of his military career over the next ten years are unclear, but by the 1911 Census he had transferred to the 5th Battalion, The Rifle Brigade – a Special Reserve unit - based at Cambridge Barracks (the former Royal Marine Barracks) in Frances Street, Woolwich, London, and was working in the recruiting office with the service number 7198.

At some point over the next three years John transferred to the Rifle Brigade Depot at Winchester as a Colour Sergeant. His name first appears in the Warren's Winchester Directory in 1914 when he was listed living at 36, Greenhill Road (the address then and now), presumably with his family. He was at the same address in 1915. The house, which dated from 1912, was rented out by the Winchester Working Men's Housing Society.

On 8 September 1914, a month after the outbreak of war, John was appointed Warrant Officer 1st Class, the highest non-commissioned rank in the Army. As such, he would have helped to oversee the Rifle Brigade's preparations for war. It was a daunting task, the Winchester Depot becoming a scene of frantic activity as hundreds of Reservists arrived in response to the country's call to arms.

SIMMONS, John

Left to right: 36, Greenhill Road, Winchester - John Simmons's first Winchester home in 1914; 42, Nuns Road, Hyde, to where he and his family moved in 1916; 4, Greenhill Road, his widow's home from 1918-31

The strain of this enormous logistical exercise proved too much for John who was forced to take extended leave. However, he returned, apparently improved in health, and in December 1914 was given a commission with the rank of 2nd Lieutenant. The promotion of senior NCOs to commissioned officer rank was not uncommon in late 1914 and early 1915. As the Army expanded rapidly, it desperately needed suitable junior officers: many came from the public schools while others, like John Simmons, were promoted from the ranks.

John was soon sent to the Western Front. His Medal Index Card reveals that on 12 January 1915 he arrived in France where he joined up with 3rd Rifle Brigade, which had already distinguished itself in four months of fighting. The battalion occupied trenches near Armentieres in northern France where conditions during the winter of 1914-15 were appalling. Heavy rain and freezing temperatures led to hundreds of cases of trench foot, although the sodden battlefield did restrict the amount of fighting.

During the spring of 1915, 3rd Rifle Brigade relieved troops who had been involved in the Second Battle of Ypres (22 April-25 May). However, Rifle Brigade records show that on 25 May 1915 John Simmons was sent back to England because of sickness. No mention is made of the illness he was suffering from and he never returned to the front again.

In 1916 John moved from Fulflood with his family to 42, Nuns Road, Hyde, Winchester. He subsequently returned to Army life as an instructor at the School of Bombing at Aldershot and it was here that he was accidentally killed on 21 August 1916. On 26 August, the Hampshire Chronicle carried a report under the headline 'Tragic Death of Lieut. Simmonds' [sic] which stated:

> *Information of the death of Lieutenant J. Simmonds, Rifle Brigade, in a bombing accident was received at the Rifle Depot at Winchester on Monday evening, he having been killed in Aldershot that morning. Deceased was, it transpired, instructing a number of officers in what is known as 'demolitions' and when the accident happened he was demonstrating how to demolish barbed wire entanglements by the use of explosives. These were laid by the uprights supporting the wire with a time fuse attached. Deceased had set the fuse and was turning away when a sudden explosion took place and he was killed instantly.*

SIMMONS, John

An Army doctor who gave evidence to the inquest stated that John had suffered severe wounds in the blast, particularly down the left side of his body. Death, he said, would have been instantaneous. The Chronicle report also included the following details about John's Army career:

> *He joined the Rifle Depot at Winchester as a Colour Sergeant and at the time of the outbreak of war was the Sergeant Major at the Rifle Depot. The heavy work and the great strain entailed in this office during the autumn months of 1914 proved too much for him and he was granted leave. He returned much improved in health and was subsequently given a commission. Proceeding to France, he saw active service there, but was in the course of time invalided back and was more recently attached to the School of Bombing at Aldershot as instructor. A thorough soldier, and one who enjoyed the esteem of officers and rank and file alike, his death will be generally regretted by a wide circle of friends at Winchester, and the deepest sympathy will go out to Mrs Simmonds and her family (who still reside in Winchester) in their great sorrow. The late Lieut. Simmonds was a member of the 'William of Wykeham' Lodge of Freemasons who have sent a message of sympathy to the widow and family.*

John Simmons was buried at Aldershot Military Cemetery on 26 August 1916. Following her husband's death, his widow Mary remained at 42, Nuns Road until 1918 when she returned to Fulflood to live at 4, Greenhill Road. This is the address given for John in the Winchester War Service Register of 1921. Mary lived at 4, Greenhill Road until 1931 when she moved to 38, Andover Road, Winchester. From 1934 she shared the address with an Albert Hayter while the 1939 Register shows her widowed sister Henrietta also living there. (38, Andover Road is thought to be the house now named Whitecott, just north of the junction with Boscobel Road.) Mary Simmons died in Winchester in 1942, aged 71.

John Simmons' elder son, John George, enlisted in the Royal Flying Corps (from April 1918 the Royal Air Force) as a Boy in October 1917, just short of his 17th birthday nearly. He survived the war and served in Germany immediately after the Armistice. John Jnr married Edith Marks in Winchester in 1926 and the couple had a daughter, Jeanette, the following year. John later became a haulage driver and he and his family lived at 30, Clifton Road, Winchester, for more than 30 years. He died in Winchester in 1966 at the age of 65.

John Simmons' daughter Jeanette married Vincent Morgan in 1951 and they went on to have two children – Carol, born in Winchester in 1952, and Adrian, born in Portsmouth in 1967.

John Simmons' younger son Harold married Muriel Henning in Alresford, near Winchester, in 1930. A son, Geoffrey, was born in 1931 but he died the same year. In 1933, Muriel gave birth to a second son, Brian, in Winchester. No further details of him can be found. In 1939 Harold was working as a tailor's cutter and living with his family at 13, Western Road, Fulflood, where he remained until at least 1954. He died in Winchester in 1988, aged about 85.

SIMMONS, John

Medals and Memorials for John Simmons

2nd Lieutenant John Simmons was entitled to the 1914-15 Star, the British War Medal and the Victory Medal. In Winchester, he is listed on the memorials at St Matthew's Church, Weeke, St Paul's Church, Fulflood and St Bartholomew's Church, Hyde (where he is 'Simmonds'). His name also appears on the memorial from the Wesleyan Methodist Church, St. Peter's Street, Winchester, which is now kept at the United Church in Jewry Street. His connection with the Methodist church has not yet been positively established. John was buried in Aldershot Military Cemetery (PR. AH. 347) where his gravestone (pictured above) bears the following inscription:

IN LOVING MEMORY
OF MY DEAR HUSBAND
2nd LIEUT. JOHN SIMMONS
RIFLE BRIGADE
KILLED WHEN GIVING INSTRUCTION
IN BOMBING AT ALDERSHOT
21st AUGUST 1916. AGE 43.
WE CANNOT, LORD, THY PURPOSE SEE,
BUT ALL IS WELL THAT'S DONE BY THEE

Researchers – GERALDINE BUCHANAN, DEREK WHITFIELD, JOSEPHINE COLEMAN and CHERYL DAVIS

Additional sources

- King Edward School, Witley, website: John Simmons profile. http://fluencycontent2-schoolwebsite.netdna-ssl.com/FileCluster/KingEdwardsWitley/MainFolder/Old-Wits/In-Memoriam/WW1-1916/John_SIMMONS.pdf
- Kitchen, Leigh. *Drummer Boys – Boys Serving in the British Army.* https://gmic.co.uk/topic/23848-quotdrummer-boysquot-boys-serving-in-the-british-army/
- We would like to thank the Hyde900 group for their assistance in preparing this biography.

SMITH, Archibald Charles

Private ARCHIBALD CHARLES SMITH
13, Cheriton Road, Winchester
Service number 203512. 1/4th Battalion, The Hampshire Regiment
Died, Mesopotamia, 13 July 1917

Archibald Charles Smith was born in New Alresford, near Winchester, on 28 August 1881, the youngest of the five sons of Harry and Amelia Smith. Known to family and friends as Archie, he was married with four young children when he was conscripted into the Army in December 1916 after a series of appeals against military service. He died in Baghdad seven months later.

Archie's father Harry was born in New Alresford in 1855 and went on to work as a carpenter. Harry's father, Henry (1824-1874), was a blacksmith who had been born in Owslebury, near Winchester. In April 1846 Henry married Julia Holland (1825-1883) in Alresford. Julia had been born in Meonstoke, Hampshire, and she and Henry went on to have six children, including Harry. They lived in New Alresford all their married lives.

Archie's mother was born Amelia Ivey (some records have Ivery) in Ovington Down, near Alresford, in 1848. She was one of six children. Her father, Moses (1810-1850), had been born in nearby Ropley and worked as an agricultural labourer. Her mother, Ruth (née Gumbleton 1818-1898), was born in Upham, near Bishops Waltham. In 1841 the family were living in New Alresford and in 1871 in Ovington.

Harry and Amelia married in Alresford in April 1872. In January Amelia had given birth to the couple's first son, William. More sons followed: Alfred (1873-1909), Thomas (1877-1890), Bertram (1878-1961) and Archie himself in 1881. A daughter, Annie, was born in September 1880, but she died when only a few days old. Amelia herself died in Winchester in 1883, aged just 34.

The loss of his wife at such a young age must have been a shattering blow for Harry Smith who, for the next seven years, assumed sole responsibility for the family. In 1890, however, he remarried. His new wife was 30-year-old Ann Brown, the daughter of an agricultural labourer from Crawley, near Winchester. The marriage marked the end of the Smiths' ties with New Alresford because by 1891 Harry, Ann and the children were living at 27, Western Road, Winchester.

Archie attended St Michael's Infants School before moving on to St Thomas Senior Church of England Boys' School in February 1893. School records show the family living at 3, Avenue Terrace (3, Avenue Road today) where they remained until 1900 when Archie's father died. The following year Archie and his brother Bertram were boarding at 51, Western Road (now 9 Cheriton Road), the home of whitesmith Harry Legg and his family. Archie was working as a tailor and Bertram as a machinist.

SMITH, Archibald Charles

In January 1908 Archie married Annie Wiseman in Winchester and the following year moved to 53, Western Road which was renumbered 13, Cheriton Road in 1914. It is the same address today. (Still living at No. 51 – later 9, Cheriton Road - were Archie's brother Bertram, with his wife Elizabeth and their young daughter.) Annie, the daughter of labourer Francis Wiseman and his wife Ann, had been born in Ringwood in the New Forest in 1879. By 1901 she was working as a domestic housemaid at Sherriff & Ward department store (later absorbed into Debenhams) in Winchester High Street, one of 33 staff recorded as living on the shop premises.

Archie and Annie quickly started a family. Frederick (known as Jim) was born in July 1908, Robert Archibald Charles in May 1910, Ann Amelia (known as Mill) in August 1912 and Doris May (known as Jo) in October 1914.

When the Great War broke out in 1914 Archie was working for Messrs F.W. Flight & Sons, a firm of military tailors at 90, High Street, Winchester. With the demand for uniforms soaring, Archie would have been exceptionally busy and was clearly valued by his employer. So much so that the company successfully appealed for him before the local Military Service Tribunal on two or three occasions after Archie had received call-up papers following the introduction of conscription in 1916.

13, Cheriton Road, Winchester – previously 53, Western Road until the road was renamed and renumbered in 1914. This was Archie Smith's home. His brother Bertram lived at No.9 until 1939

However, the Tribunal eventually ruled that Archie was eligible for military service and in December 1916 he joined the 1/4th Battalion, The Hampshire Regiment. He would almost certainly have undergone some basic military training in England before being sent out to join the 1/4th Hampshires in Mesopotamia (modern Iraq). It is not known when he arrived there because his Medal Index Card does

The Sherriff & Ward store in Winchester High Street in the early 1900s. Archie Smith's wife Annie worked and lived here before she married. The store was later absorbed into Debenhams

SMITH, Archibald Charles

not state the date that he entered a theatre of war, although it is unlikely to have been in time to share in the Hampshires' triumphant entry into Baghdad on 13 March 1917.

A long spell of uneventful garrison duty in the occupied city then followed for the 1/4th Hampshires. In his book The Royal Hampshire Regiment 1914-1919, C.T. Atkinson paints a less than flattering picture of the city at the time:

> ... pleasant at a distance, with romantic traditions, it proved smelly and squalid, and its garrison had much unattractive work before they could make the famous city habitable, sanitary and healthy.

Within a short time, however, the Hampshires had licked the garrison into shape which enabled large numbers of troops to be sent on leave to India. Sickness rates were far lower than the previous two summers, but nevertheless it appears that 37-year-old Archie Smith succumbed to disease on 13 July 1917, although no cause of death is given in any of the official records. There is some confusion, too, over the date of his death with some records giving 3 July and 31 July, but the majority – including the Hampshire Regimental Journal - have 13 July. The Regimental Journal of August 1917 states:

> Pte. Archibald C. Smith, Hampshire Regiment, whose death on July 13th, while on active service in Mesopotamia, is officially reported, resided at 13, Cheriton Road. Winchester. In civilian life he was an expert hand in the employ of Messrs. F. Flight & Sons, military tailors, of Winchester, who appealed for him before the local Tribunal on two or three occasions. He was 37 years of age and leaves a widow and four children. A pathetic feature is that a letter, couched in cheery, homely terms, has reached the widow from her husband since she received the announcement of his death; he was at that time quite well.

Archie's widow Annie continued to live at 13, Cheriton Road after the war and was still there in 1929. She died in Winchester in 1963, aged 84.

It is possible that Archie's brother Bertram served in the war as a photograph exists of him in Army uniform. However, no record of military service can be found and, unlike Archie, he is not listed in the Winchester War Service Register. Bertram and his wife Elizabeth continued to live at 9, Cheriton Road until 1939 when they moved to No. 33. Elizabeth died in Winchester in April 1949, aged 71, while Bertram passed away in March 1961 at the age of 83.

Archie's brother Alfred, who had worked as a plumber, died in 1909, aged 36. No trace can be found of the other surviving brother, William.

All four of Archie and Annie's children married and moved away from Winchester, although Robert did live for a time in Vernham Road while working as a confectioner of cakes. He died in 1994. Frederick passed away in 1952, William in 1961 and Ann Amelia in 2006.

Archie's brother Bertram Smith in Army uniform.

Medals and memorials for Archibald Charles Smith

Private Archibald Charles Smith was entitled to the British War Medal and the Victory Medal. He is buried in Baghdad (North Gate) War Cemetery, Iraq (GR. XV. E. 11) and is mentioned on the memorials at St Matthew's and St Paul's churches, Winchester. His name also appears on the St Thomas Church of England Boys' School memorial, now held at Kings' School, Winchester.

Researcher – DEREK WHITFIELD

SMITH, Edwin Alfred

Private EDWIN ALFRED SMITH
11, Fairfield Road, Winchester
Service numbers 4/2844 and 200771. 1/4th Battalion, The Hampshire Regiment
Killed in action, Mesopotamia, 23-24 February 1917

Edwin Alfred Smith was born in Winchester in late 1887, the eldest child of Edwin Herbert and Charlotte Smith. The Smiths were a long-established Winchester family whose men traditionally worked in skilled professions, particularly carpentry. Teddy, as Edwin was known to family and friends, went on to earn his living as a wood carver. He was also an accomplished sportsman.

Teddy's father worked as a carpenter and joiner. He was born in Winchester in 1865, the son of Walter Smith (1825-1871), a Winchester-born carpenter, and his wife Emily (née Foyle), who had been born in Wilton, Wiltshire, around 1836. Emily's father, Henry, also worked as a carpenter. Interestingly, Edwin Snr's brother, Walter (Teddy's uncle), served in the Militia and in the 1881 Census was recorded as living at the Army Barracks in Winchester.

In 1871 Walter and Emily Smith were living at 6, Cheesehill Street, Winchester, with Emily working as a laundress. Ten years later, 16-year-old Edwin Snr was living with his mother and four brothers at the other end of the city at 5, Tower Street. Emily Smith died in Winchester in 1884, aged 48.

Teddy's mother was born Charlotte Whitear in Winchester in 1865. Her father, Jacob, born around 1839, was also a Wintonian and worked as a painter/decorator. Charlotte's mother was born Emma Abbott in Wimborne, Dorset, in around 1841. In 1871 the Whitears were living in Middle Brook Street, Winchester. Ten years later they had moved to 2, Colebrook Place, with Charlotte working as a dressmaker, a skill she would have learned from her seamstress mother. By 1901, Charlotte's parents had moved to Basingstoke. Emma Whitear died in Winchester in 1905, aged 64, and Jacob in Fareham the following year, aged 67.

Edwin Smith Snr and Charlotte Whitear married in Winchester in late 1887, around the time of Teddy's birth. Four years later the couple were living at 68, Sussex Street with Teddy and a second son, Walter, who had been born in 1889.

By 1901 the Smiths had moved to 11, Fairfield Road, Winchester (the house has the same address today). This was presumably a larger property given that the family had grown with the births of Winifred in 1892, Dorothy in 1894 and Clement in 1899. Two more daughters, Gladys and Nellie, were born in 1902 and 1904 respectively. The Smiths also took in a lodger whose rent would have supplemented the family income. The house at 11, Fairfield Road remained the Smith family home until at least 1939.

No record can be found of Teddy's education. On leaving school he served an apprenticeship with Messrs Thomas & Co., cabinet makers and upholsterers in Highcliffe, Winchester. The 1911 Census records his occupation as wood carver. Teddy also excelled at sport. He was a keen athlete and played for Winchester Football Club, winning several medals. Winchester FC's ground at the time was on land off the Stockbridge Road, opposite The Roebuck pub.

11, Fairfield Road, Winchester – Teddy Smith's home. His family lived here for more than 40 years

SMITH, Edwin Alfred

British troops in trenches in Mesopotamia. Teddy Smith served in the region for nearly two years before he was killed in February 1917 during the attempt to recapture Kut-al-Amara from the Turks

Teddy enlisted with the 4th Battalion, The Hampshire Regiment in September 1914, a month after war broke out. His original service number was 4/2844. Assigned to the 1/4th Battalion, he sailed to India in October and spent the next four months training and preparing for war. In March 1915 Teddy sailed with the 1/4th Hampshires for Mesopotamia (modern Iraq), arriving at Basra on the 18th.

Teddy served in one of the most inhospitable theatres of war for nearly two years during which time his physical fitness would have stood him in good stead. (For details of the 1/4th Hampshires' campaigns in Mesopotamia in 1915 and 1916 see pp. 377).

Teddy Smith was killed during operations to recapture the garrison town of Kut-al-Amara, which had fallen to the Turks after a five-month siege in April 1916. On 23-24 February 1917, the 1/4th Hampshires formed part of a British-Indian force which attacked across the River Tigris at Shumran

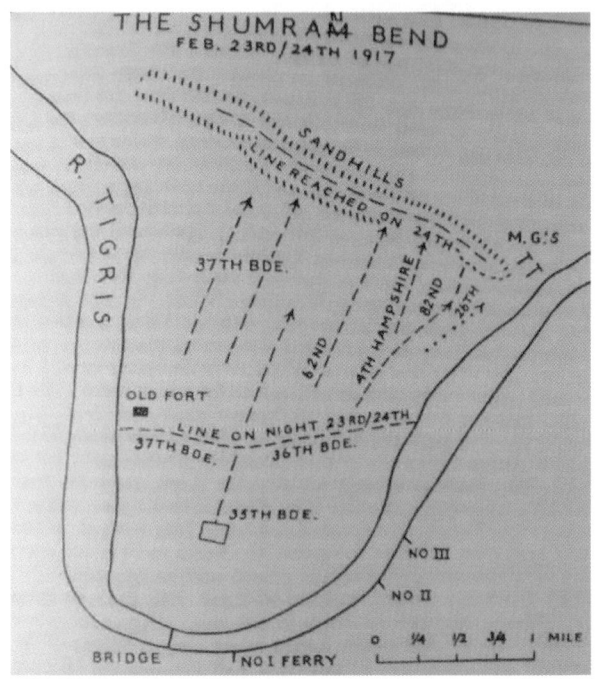

Map showing the 4th Hampshires' role at the Battle of Shumran Bend in which Teddy Smith was killed on 24 February 1917

Bend. Early on 23 February, more than 200 Hampshire soldiers joined hundreds of other troops in rowing pontoons full of men across the Tigris to attack Turkish positions. The operation was successful, but only after many of the pontoons had been hit by enemy fire which killed and wounded at least 100 Hampshires.

The battalion was in action again the following day, attacking Turkish positions on a ridge which ran across Shumran Bend. Of 450 men who went into battle 180 were killed or wounded, mainly by enemy machine-gun fire. It is unclear whether Teddy Smith was killed while rowing a pontoon across the Tigris on 23 February or in the attack the following day. Most of the official records give his date of death as

SMITH, Edwin Alfred

24 February, although the Regimental Journal gives the 23rd. He was 29 years old and his body was never found.

The Hampshire Regimental Journal of March 1917 stated:

SMITH - Killed in action, in Mesopotamia, on February 23rd-24th, 2844 Edwin Alfred (Teddy), eldest son of Mr. and Mrs. Smith, 11, Fairfield Road, Winchester.

Pte. Edwin Alfred (Teddy) Smith, Hampshire Regiment, who was killed in action on February 23rd, was the eldest son of Mr. and Mrs. E. H. Smith, of 11, Fairfield Road, Winchester. As a lad he served his apprenticeship with Messrs Thomas and Co, Highcliffe, but latterly took to carpentry. He was a keen athlete, and played for the Winchester Football Club, being the holder of several medals.

On 17 March 1917, the Hampshire Observer newspaper reported:

The Winchester Football Club has lost another of its players in the person of 'Teddy' Smith of Fairfield Road, who has ... been killed in action in Mesopotamia.

Teddy's youngest brother Clement also served in the Great War. He is believed to have been conscripted into the Training Reserve Regiment in February 1917, before transferring to the Royal Warwickshire Regiment as a private (service number 34905) and then the Manchester Regiment (service number 71097). He survived the war, receiving the British War Medal and the Victory Medal. No trace of Clement can be found in the records after 1920.

Teddy's other brother, Walter, served with the Hampshire Regiment in Egypt and Palestine. He was wounded in December 1917 but survived the war and went on to become a well-known grocer in Winchester. He died in 1955, aged 65. All three Smith brothers are listed in the Winchester War Service Register.

Teddy's parents both died in Winchester, his mother in 1924 and his father in 1936. His sister Winifred died in 1919, aged just 28, possibly from Spanish flu. Dorothy and Gladys Smith are both believed to have married and lived locally. The youngest sibling, Nellie, remained single and was still living at 11, Fairfield Road in 1939. She died in Southampton in 1990 at the age of 86.

Medals and memorials for Edwin Alfred Smith

Private Edwin Alfred Smith entitled to the 1914-15 Star, the British War Medal and the Victory Medal. He is commemorated on the Basra Memorial, Iraq, (Panel 21 and 63) and on the memorials at St Paul's and St Matthew's churches, Winchester, although on the latter his name is given as B.A. Smith.

Researchers – DEREK WHITFIELD AND CHERYL DAVIS

SMITH, Horace

Trooper HORACE SMITH
14, Gladstone Street, Winchester (no longer stands)
Service number D/3211. 5th (Princess Charlotte of Wales's) Dragoon Guards
(Previously with Duke of Cornwall's Light Infantry)
Died of wounds, France, 31 March 1918

Horace Smith was born in the village of Overton, near Basingstoke, in late 1891 and baptised there on 24 April 1892. Horace was the fifth of the six children of Francis and Emily Smith. Francis, who worked variously as a farmer, butcher and pub landlord, had been born in Wherwell, near Winchester, on 4 July 1855. His wife was born Emily Budd in Overton on 17 January 1858.

Francis Smith was the youngest of five children. His father, also called Francis, had been born in the remote hamlet of Hippenscombe, Wiltshire (about four miles northeast of Ludgershall), in 1809. In the 1861 Census Francis Snr was living with his wife Mary and their family at the White Lion Inn, Wherwell, where he worked as a victualler and butcher. Mary had been born in Chute, Wiltshire, about two miles from Hippenscombe. The Smiths were still living at the White Lion in 1871 when Francis Snr was a farmer of 188 acres, employing three men and one boy. He died in Winchester in 1880.

In 1881, the year after his father's death, Francis Jnr and his mother were recorded living in Compton, near Winchester, where Francis was working as a butcher.

Horace Smith's mother Emily was the youngest of the seven children of John Budd (1821-1897) and his wife Fanny (née Whitear, 1821-1891). The 1861 Census showed the Budds living in Winchester Street, Overton, where Emily's father was a master butcher.

Emily and Francis Jnr married in Whitchurch, Hampshire, in 1882. Two daughters, Annie and Fanny, were born in 1884 and 1885, followed by Henry (1888), Amelia (1889) and Horace (1891). In 1891 the family were living at the White Hart Hotel, Wherwell, where Francis was a licensed victualler and farmer. In 1894, Emily gave birth to a fourth daughter, Dorothy.

Despite the great depression in British agriculture at this time, Francis ventured into farming. In the 1901 Census, the Smiths were living in Winchester Street, Overton – possibly in the home of Emily's now deceased parents – with Francis working as a farmer. Four of the children, Henry, Amelia, Horace and Dorothy, were still at school. We know that Horace later attended St Thomas Church of England Boys' School in Winchester because his name appears on the school's war memorial.

In 1908 Horace Smith joined the Army. His military records, including his attestation form, have survived although several of the documents are damaged and others barely legible. Nevertheless, they enable a picture to be drawn of Horace's military career that is more rounded and detailed than some of the men in this book whose records were destroyed in the Blitz in 1940.

Horace enlisted in Winchester on 18 February 1908. Although only just 16, he stated that he was 18 so that he would be accepted into the Army. He was working as a butcher when he joined up and serving as a part-time soldier in the Militia with the 3rd Battalion, The Hampshire Regiment. Horace is shown enlisting for 12 years (including five in the Reserve) in the Somerset Light Infantry, but he actually joined the Duke of Cornwall's Light Infantry (DCLI) and was posted to the regimental depot in Bodmin on 20 February 1908. His service number is believed to have been 8944. On 19 June he was assigned to the 1st Battalion, DCLI.

SMITH, Horace

The records give a brief physical description of Horace: he was 5ft 7in tall with a 34in chest and he could read and write, although he had no formal educational qualifications. They also show that Horace was something of a rebel who was frequently in trouble with authority – the records contain details of no fewer than 29 breaches of Army discipline. These begin on 29 March 1908, just a month after joining the DCLI, when he was given 48 hours' detention for refusing to obey an order. Insolence to his superiors, being dirty on parade and asleep while on night guard duty are among Horace's other misdemeanours.

On 29 April 1909 Horace left the DCLI and transferred to the 5th (Princess Charlotte of Wales's) Dragoon Guards, a cavalry regiment, with the service number 3211. According to his records this was so that he could serve alongside his elder brother Henry who had joined the regiment in 1905. Another Dragoon, Trooper Charles Horsnell, enlisted in 1909 and a photograph of him in parade uniform has survived.

Horace was posted to Dublin where the 5th Dragoon Guards were based in 1909. In September 1910, the battalion moved to the British Army camp at the Curragh, in County Kildare, which is where Horace and Henry were both recorded living in the 1911 Irish Census.

Trooper Charles Horsnell of the 5th Dragoon Guards in parade uniform. Charles enlisted in 1909 and would have known Horace Smith

Although he continued to have frequent run-ins with authority, it appears that by the time the regiment returned to England in October 1912 Horace had started to mature as a soldier. His Employment Sheet dated 7 October 1913 stated that he had served as a Sergeant's batman for the previous three months and on it he is described as 'smart, respectful, hardworking and honest'.

Meanwhile, Horace's parents and sister Dorothy had moved to 14, Parchment Street, Winchester, where they were listed in the 1911 Census as boarding house keepers. Francis gave his name as Frank on the census document. The family later moved to 3, St John Street, Winchester, which was the address used for correspondence by the Army.

The 5th Dragoon Guards formed part of the British Expeditionary Force (BEF) – Britain's military response to the Britain's declaration of war on Germany on 5 August 1914. On 16 August, the regiment of 549 men – including Henry and Horace Smith – arrived at Le Havre aboard the troopship SS Cestrian and disembarked to form part of the 1st Cavalry Brigade.

Horace's first spell on the Western Front lasted just one month. His regiment was not involved in the battles of Mons (23 August) and Le Cateau (26 August) although it did come under German attack briefly on 24 August. On 1 September, as the BEF retreated southwards before the advancing German army, the 5th Dragoon Guards helped 1st Cavalry Brigade to repel a surprise attack by the German 4th Cavalry Division at the Battle of Nèry. The brigade captured 12 enemy guns in the action which saw three Victoria Crosses awarded to 'L' Battery, Royal Horse Artillery. The 5th Dragoon Guards lost its Commanding Officer, Lieutenant-Colonel G.K. Ansell, and about ten other men killed in the battle.

SMITH, Horace

British cavalry at Nery on 1 September 1914. The battle was Horace Smith's first taste of warfare

After Nèry, Horace's regiment continued to retreat south almost to Paris at which point the Allies counter-attacked at the Battle of the Marne (6-12 September). As the British advanced, the 5th Dragoon Guards attempted to capture the village of Sablonniere during which Horace was shot in the arm. He was taken to a field ambulance and eventually evacuated to England.

Horace was out of action until 30 October 1914 when he was posted to the 1st Cavalry Reserve Regiment based in England. He remained with the regiment for seven months until 17 June 1915 when he rejoined the 5th Dragoon Guards at Oudezeele in French Flanders.

Horace returned to a changed Western Front. The battles of 1914 had shown the lethal effect of modern firepower – particularly machine-guns and artillery – on massed cavalry charges. However, the British High Command still believed that cavalry was needed to exploit any planned breakthrough. This 'Big Push' would bring the return of mobile warfare and mounted units would exploit any breach using their superior speed to reach the enemy's rear positions and destroy supply and communications lines. Until that moment came, cavalrymen – who were trained to shoot like their infantry colleagues – could fight in a dismounted role where needed. This is what the 5th Dragoon Guards did at the Second Battle of Ypres in April and May 1915.

The next three years, however, were to prove immensely frustrating for cavalry units. The 5th Dragoon Guards saw no further action in 1915 and little of note during 1916, despite the British Army launching a major offensive on the Somme. With the 'volunteer armies' raised in the early months of the war now in the field, and soldiers from the British Dominions – Australia, Canada, New Zealand and South Africa – also on the Western Front in large numbers, there was less need for cavalry to operate as dismounted infantry.

Instead, Horace Smith's regiment spent most of 1916 away from the front line, training and providing working parties. Horace, however, still managed to get into trouble – on 21 September 1916 he was ordered to be confined to camp for seven days for ill-treating his horse. One month later, on 21 October, Horace's father Francis died in Winchester, aged 61. It is possible that Horace and his brother Henry were allowed compassionate leave to visit their family and to attend Francis's funeral.

For the 5th Dragoon Guards the early months of 1917 followed a similar pattern to 1916. The regiment was not involved in any front-line action but the regimental war diary does show that in February and

SMITH, Horace

March significant numbers of officers and men were sent on training courses – on the use of poison gas, musketry, veterinary practice and aeroplane signalling among others. It is not known if Horace attended any of these.

The early stages of the Arras Offensive (9 April-16 May 1917) offered hope that mounted cavalry might once more be used on the Western Front. On 9 April the 5th Dragoon Guards sent a detachment to Arras in the hope of exploiting British success there. However, while riding into the captured village of Fampoux the detachment came under German machine-gun and artillery fire which killed several men and 16 horses. The Dragoons were forced to seek cover and withdrew after dark. They tried again the following day but with no success.

The opening phase of the Battle of Cambrai (20 November-6 December 1917) also appeared to present an opportunity for a British breakthrough which the cavalry could exploit. On 20 November the 5th Dragoon Guards were deployed to the area of Grand Ravine, near Flesquieres. A squadron of mounted Dragoons then attempted to capture Flot Farm but had to withdraw after coming under machine-gun fire. On 24 November the 1st Cavalry Brigade was ordered to provide a battalion of dismounted troops to fight around Bourlon Wood, with the 5th Dragoon Guards contributing a company of men. These were relieved on 26 November. During the German counter-attack at Cambrai, which began on 30 November, dismounted Dragoons were in action again, this time at Gouzeaucourt.

Early 1918 saw Horace Smith's regiment in camp at Buire in the Somme valley where it provided working parties to repair trenches. By March, the 5th Dragoons were serving as dismounted troops and on the night of 9-10 March six officers and 160 men mounted a trench raid on German lines at Square Copse. However, the barbed wire they encountered was thicker than expected and the party had to retire under heavy machine-gun fire. It is not known if Horace took part in the raid.

By 19 March, the 5th Dragoon Guards had moved to Montecourt, about ten miles south-east of Peronne. The following day they received orders to disperse and man outposts in case of a German attack. Early on the morning of 21 March the Germans launched their Spring Offensive against British positions in the Somme valley and east of Arras with the aim of splitting the British from their French allies and winning the war at a stroke.

The British line in the south quickly gave way before the German artillery and infantry onslaught and troops retired westwards, conducting a fighting retreat as they went. On the afternoon of 21 March, the 5th Dragoon Guards received orders to dismount and reinforce troops of 17th Brigade in 24th Division around Small Foot Wood. The following day, after coming under heavy bombardment, the regiment retreated after one company was almost outflanked and cut off by the rapidly advancing enemy. The regiment then remounted and proceeded to the town of Athies before moving into position that night to cover the British retreat across the River Somme.

In the confusing and chaotic days that followed, the 5th Dragoon Guards withdrew westwards, sometimes on horseback, on other occasions fighting as dismounted infantry. On 24 March 190 men were formed into a dismounted brigade which moved to the town of Carnoy and then to Montauban where it engaged in heavy fighting. By 28 March, the regiment was holding trenches near the village of Hamel, about 18 miles south-east of Amiens, which the Germans attacked two days later. The 5th Dragoon Guards' regimental war diary recorded how events unfolded:

> *30th March – Intermittent shelling of front line and Hamel from 7.45am.*
> *11.30am – Very intense bombardment of front line, village and surroundings for two hours, when enemy launched a strong attack on brigade front with three battalions. Capt. H.O. Wiley with his squadron rallied parties of infantry who had retired from the front line and led them*

SMITH, Horace

back to the ... trenches, remaining there during the attack. Lieut. J. Jordan M.C. and 30 men from 'A' Squadron went to support 11th Hussars on right. The attack was completely repulsed on the whole brigade front with heavy loss to the enemy who left many dead on the wire.

Horace Smith was wounded by an exploding grenade during the German assault on Hamel. He was taken to 5th General Hospital at Rouen but died the following day. He was 26 or 27 years old. The Winchester War Service Register states that Horace was wounded three times in total. His Army records mention two of the occasions he was wounded (1914 and 1918) but not the third.

News of Horace's death did not immediately reach his mother back in Winchester. A telegram was sent to Emily, but to her old address at 3, St John's Street, not 14, Gladstone Street. The telegram was returned to the Cavalry administrative HQ in Kent which then had to track down Emily to inform her of her son's death.

On 4 October 1919 Emily wrote to the military authorities pleading for financial assistance. She stated that she had been widowed for three years and that her husband had been an invalid in his later years – implying that he had been unable to earn. Given that her other children were living in 'fair' circumstances, she was the only one of Horace's dependents who needed help. She continued:

It was my son's wish in case anything happened to him that I should have his effects, and he said it was not necessary to make a will as I was his next of kin. As I also am an invalid and a widow and nothing coming in, could I not be assisted from the funds that provide for widows of husbands and sons killed during the war?

On 29 April 1920 Emily applied for a dependent's pension. The application is thought to have been successful. Emily also received the three war medals to which Horace was entitled.

Although Francis Smith died in 1916, he continued to be listed as the householder at 14, Gladstone Street in Warren's Winchester Directory for another two years. By 1920, however, the address was listed under 'Mrs Smith' – presumably Emily. In 1939 Emily was living at St John's Hospital, Winchester. She died in Chandler's Ford, Hampshire, on 26 January 1947 at the age of 90.

Henry Smith, the brother with whom Horace served, was wounded in 1916 but survived the war. Both brothers are listed in the Winchester War Service Register.

Medals and memorials for Horace Smith

Trooper Horace Smith was entitled to the 1914 (Mons) Star, the British War Medal and the Victory Medal. He was buried in St Sever Cemetery Extension (right), Rouen, Seine-Maritime, France (GR. P. IX. 3. EB). Horace is mentioned on the memorials at St Matthew's and St Paul's churches, Winchester, and on the St Thomas School memorial, held today by Kings School, Winchester.

Researchers – CHERYL DAVIS, DEREK WHITFIELD and STEVE JARVIS

SOFFE, George

Private GEORGE SOFFE
8, Upper Stockbridge Road, Winchester
(later 17, St Paul's Hill - no longer stands)
Service number 4/2471. 1/4th Battalion, The Hampshire Regiment
Died in captivity, Mesopotamia, between 13 and 26 June 1916

George Soffe, the son of John and Charlotte Soffe, was born in Church Oakley, near Basingstoke, in March 1881. One of 13 siblings, George came to Winchester with his family in the late 1880s and although he later moved away his parents and several brothers and sisters remained in Fulflood. George's brother Henry was also killed in the Great War and his biography is on pp. 302. Three other brothers served in the war and survived.

The exact date of George's birth is unclear, but in the 1881 Census, taken on 2 April, his entry states he is less than one month old.

George's father, who was known as Tom, was born in Nursling, near Southampton, on 6 October 1836. His mother was born Charlotte Birch in Winchester in 1847, the daughter of James and Charlotte Birch. Tom and Charlotte married in Winchester in 1866 and quickly began a family. Besides George their children were: Rosa (1867-1940), Alfred (1868-1900), Frank (1869-1934), William (1870-1921), Henry (1872-1916), Constance (1874-1962), Frances (1875-1944), Charlotte (1876-1945), Caroline (1879-), Ernest (1880-1945), Frederick (1883-1939) and Arthur (1884-1954). Other than Alfred, William and Rosa, who were born in Winchester, and Frank who was born in Southampton, all the Soffe children were born in Church Oakley.

In 1871 the Soffes were living in Twyford, near Winchester, with George's father Tom employed as a gardener. Shortly afterwards the family moved to Church Oakley where Henry was born in 1872. The Soffes remained in the village at least until 1884, when Charlotte gave birth to Arthur. By 1891 they were living at No. 2 Worthy Road Cottages, near Headbourne Worthy rectory on the outskirts of Winchester. According to that year's census George and his brothers Frederick and Ernest were working as domestic gardeners like their father. Brother Henry, meanwhile, was employed as a groom and George's 17-year-old sister Constance as a kitchen maid.

We know little of George's education; the 1891 Census, compiled when he was 10 years old, fails to state whether he was at school or not. However, given that his other brothers went to school and that compulsory education from age five to ten had been introduced in 1870, it must be assumed that George also attended school, probably in Church Oakley.

In 1895 the Soffe family moved to 8, Upper Stockbridge Road, Winchester. The house was renumbered as 17, St Paul's Hill after the Great War but no longer stands. By 1901 Tom Soffe was a self-employed jobbing gardener and three of his sons - George, Frederick and Arthur - worked for him. Caroline, the only other of the Soffe children still at home, was employed as a domestic nurse. Sisters Rosa and Charlotte had moved to London where they were working as a nurse and a cook respectively in a large house in Hanover Square.

George's eldest brother Alfred, who had also moved away, died in Bromley, Kent, in 1900, aged 32. The following year Henry, another older brother, who by this time was working as an insurance agent, married and went to live with his new wife in Southampton.

By 1911 George Soffe, then 30 years old and still a bachelor, had left Winchester and was lodging and working as a gardener at Dairy House Farm in Woodington, East Wellow, near Romsey. His

SOFFE, George

younger brothers also remained in or around Winchester. Frederick, who by this time was married with two young children and working as a nurseryman, lived at 35, Western Road. Ernest, also married and with a son and a daughter, lived in Otterbourne while Arthur, who had enlisted as a gunner with the Royal Marines Artillery in 1902, was based in Portsmouth.

George Soffe was 33 when he enlisted with the 4th Battalion, The Hampshire Regiment in August 1914, shortly after the Great War began. Assigned to the 1/4th Hampshires, he volunteered for service overseas and sailed to India with his battalion in October. Four months later the 1/4th Hampshires deployed to Mesopotamia (modern Iraq), with George entering the Asiatic theatre of war on 18 March 1915.

Once in Mesopotamia, the 1/4th Hampshires were soon in action against the Turks. George would have been involved in helping to secure the British oil pipeline in Arabistan (present day Iran) and then in operations north of Basra on the Tigris and Euphrates rivers during the summer. Many men from the battalion succumbed to disease and heatstroke during this period but George appears to have come through unscathed.

George possibly served in 'A' Company of the 1/4th Hampshires. The company deployed to the British garrison town of Kut-al-Amara at the end of November 1915 after the Turks halted the advance towards Baghdad of a British-Indian force under General Sir Charles Townshend, forcing it to retreat to Kut. The Turks then surrounded the garrison and laid siege for five months before Townshend surrendered on 29 April 1916. (For details of the siege of Kut see pp. 378).

George Soffe was one of 188 officers and men of the 1/4th Hampshires taken prisoner when Kut fell. Along with 12,000 other British and Indian troops he was marched off as a prisoner of war, destined for PoW camps in Turkey. George, however, never made it. Some two months after setting off from Kut, he died at Mosul, probably from disease, aged 35. The exact date of his death is unclear - the Commonwealth War Graves Commission gives 26 June 1916 while the Winchester War Service Register (WWSR) gives the date as 20 June 1916 and other sources state that he died on 13 June 1916.

A short notice announcing George's death appeared in the Hampshire Regimental Journal of January 1917:

> *Soffe - On June 26th, at Mosul, Pte George Soffe, Hampshire Regiment (a prisoner of war from Kut), fifth son of Mr and Mrs J.T. Soffe, 8, Upper Stockbridge Road, Winchester, aged 34 [sic].*

Four of George's brothers served in the Great War. Henry (service number 17710) enlisted with the 2nd Battalion, The Hampshire Regiment in May 1915 when he was 43 years old. He was killed in action on 20 October 1916 at the Battle of Le Transloy during the latter stages of the Somme Offensive. Henry's biography is on pp. 302.

Three Soffe brothers survived the war. In December 1915 35-year-old Ernest, by then widowed, enlisted with the Hampshire Regiment in Southampton. He later transferred to the Machine Gun Corps (service number 63162) and served in Salonika, reaching the rank of Acting-Corporal. He finished the war in the Labour Corps (service number 486143) which suggests that he may have been deemed unfit to serve in the front line because of wounds or illness. Frederick Soffe joined the Royal Garrison Artillery (service number 3237) in July 1916 when he was 33 years old and living at 22, North View, Winchester. His enlistment papers show that he had previously been in the Army. Frederick also served in Salonika. Arthur Soffe, meanwhile, remained on the home front with the Royal Marine Artillery. All five Soffe brothers are listed in the WWSR.

SOFFE, George

This housing block was the site of 8, Upper Stockbridge Road, Winchester (later 17, St Paul's Hill), the home of George Soffe's parents at the start of the Great War. Judging by the cars in the background, the photograph was probably taken in the 1960s or 1970s. The block was later demolished

George's father Tom died in Winchester, aged 80, on 17 February 1917, just months after the deaths of George and Henry. Charlotte Soffe, George's mother, continued to live at 17, St Paul's Hill until around 1925 when she is believed to have moved in with her son Arthur. In 1939 Arthur was living at 39, Brassey Road, Winchester, together with his sister Rosa and his mother who by then was incapacitated. Rosa and Charlotte both died the following year, aged 73 and 93 respectively. Arthur, who had returned to working as a jobbing gardener after the Great War, passed away in Winchester in December 1954 at the age of 70.

Frederick Soffe also continued to live in Winchester after the war. In 1939 he was living with his wife and 29-year-old son at 177, Stanmore Lane, and was still working as a nurseryman. He died in December that year at the age of 57.

Ernest Soffe moved to Chandlers Ford after the war and he died there in 1945, aged 65. George's sisters Charlotte and Constance both married and went to live in Basingstoke where they died aged 67 and 87 respectively. Frances, who had married in 1900, passed away in Bromley, Kent, in 1944 at the age of 69.

Medals and memorials for George Soffe

Private George Soffe was entitled to the 1914 -15 Star, the British War Medal and the Victory Medal. His British War Medal and Great War Memorial Plaque, along with the original cardboard case and letter addressed to his father Tom, were put up for sale for £225 in around 2015 (see right). George is commemorated on the Basra Memorial, Iraq (PR. Panel 21 and 63.) and on the memorials at St Matthew's and St Paul's churches, Winchester.

Researcher – DEREK WHITFIELD

SOFFE, Henry James

Private HENRY JAMES SOFFE
8, Upper Stockbridge Road, Winchester
(later 17, St Paul's Hill – no longer stands)
Service number 17710. 2nd Battalion, The Hampshire Regiment
Killed in action, France, 20 October 1916

Henry James Soffe was born in Church Oakley, near Basingstoke, Hampshire, on 13 January 1872. Known as Harry to family and friends, he was one of 13 children born to John and Charlotte Soffe. The family moved to the Winchester area in the late 1880s and although Henry moved away after marrying, his parents and several brothers and sisters remained in Fulflood. Henry was one of two Soffe brothers killed in the Great War. Three others fought and survived.

The history of the Soffe family, both before and after the Great War, is covered in the biography of Henry's brother George on pp. 299. This biography will focus on Henry Soffe's life from the time of his marriage up until his death in 1916.

Henry married 26-year-old Maria Campbell in South Stoneham, near Southampton, early in 1901. Maria was the daughter of Henry and Elizabeth Campbell and had been born in Chipstead, near Banstead, Surrey. In 1891 she lived with her parents and three siblings in a large house in Chilworth, near Southampton, where her father worked as a gardener and domestic servant.

By the time of the 1901 Census, compiled a few months after their wedding, Henry and Maria Soffe were living at 46, Laundry Road, Shirley, Southampton. Henry was working as an assurance agent. On 18 August 1901 Marie gave birth to a daughter, Dorothy, in Shirley. A son, Henry, born in Rownhams, near Southampton, followed on 25 March 1904. By 1911, when his parents were living at 8, Upper Stockbridge Road, Winchester (later renamed and renumbered as 17, St Paul's Hill), Henry Soffe was working as a jobbing gardener and living with his wife and children at 4, Victoria Road, Freemantle, Southampton.

Henry was 43 years old when he volunteered for military service in Southampton in about May 1915. His brother George had enlisted with the 4th Battalion, The Hampshire Regiment on the outbreak of war in August 1914 and was fighting the Turks in Mesopotamia (modern Iraq) by the time Henry joined the Hampshires. Frederick and Ernest Soffe also enlisted within days of each other in December 1915 while the youngest brother, Arthur, a professional soldier since 1902, was already serving on the home front.

One can only guess at what motivated Henry to enlist at his age. Perhaps he was inspired by his brother George or wanted to show solidarity with him. It could be that he saw the war as an opportunity for adventure. Or he could have been guided by straightforward love for his country – clearly the Soffes were a patriotic family. Whatever his reasons, Henry would have been under no illusion about what he was letting himself in for. By May 1915 British newspapers were full of the names of men killed and wounded in action, particularly on the Western Front.

After completing his training at the end of 1915, Henry (service number 17710) joined up with the 2nd Battalion, The Hampshire Regiment. By this time, the 2nd Hampshires had spent eight months fighting at Gallipoli where they suffered heavy losses through combat and disease. Henry's military records show that he entered a theatre of war on 1 December 1915 which means that he may have served at Gallipoli for a short period before the 2nd Hampshires were evacuated to Egypt in January 1916.

In March 1916, the 2nd Hampshires moved to France where they were assigned to the Fourth Army as it prepared for the Somme Offensive. Between 1 and 10 July Henry fought at the Battle of Albert, the opening phase of the campaign. At the end of the month the Hampshires moved north to trenches near St Julien, near Ypres in Flanders, where a German gas attack on 8 August killed four officers and 125 men and wounded 120 more.

In early October 1916, the 2nd Hampshires returned south to reinforce 12th Division at the Battle of Le Transloy during the closing stages of the Somme campaign. After moving up to reserve trenches near the village of Gueudecourt, two companies of the Hampshires helped to capture a German position known as Hilt Trench. On 17 October, the whole battalion assembled in Hilt Trench for an assault on the next German position, Grease Trench. This began at 3.40am the following morning in pouring rain but, despite the weather, the Hampshires succeeded in overpowering the Germans in Grease Trench and took 200 prisoners. However, in the confusion, some troops were unaware they had reached their objective and continued almost as far as the German second line. They were then forced to retreat, and many troops were hit by rifle and machine-gun fire.

Over the next two days the Hampshires in Grease Trench were subjected to German counter-attacks and artillery fire. The battalion should have been relieved on the night of 19-20 October, but with the communication trenches deep in mud, the relieving battalion could not complete the manoeuvre in time. The Hampshires therefore had to remain in double-manned trenches until the evening of 20 October when they were finally relieved. This was the day that Henry Soffe was killed, along with 11 of his comrades. He was 44 years old.

The 2nd Hampshires received many congratulations from commanders for their gallantry and tenacity during the Battle of Le Transloy. In his book chronicling the Hampshire Regiment during the Great War, the military historian C.T. Atkinson writes:

> *18 October 1916 ranks among the 2nd Hampshire's most notable achievements. Success at that stage in the Somme was never easily obtained and needed dash and determination to no small degree.*

A short notice announcing Henry's death appeared in the Hampshire Regimental Journal in January 1917:

> *Soffe - Killed in action, in France, on October 20th, Pte. H. J. (Harry) Soffe, Hampshire Regiment, third son of Mr. and Mrs. J.T. Soffe, 8, Upper Stockbridge Road. Winchester, aged 44.*

Henry Soffe is listed in the Winchester War Service Register. His widow Maria died in Southampton in June 1939, aged 63. The couple's daughter Dorothy married in 1922 and lived in Southampton before moving to Guildford, Surrey, where she died in 1974, aged 73. Henry Soffe Jnr also married and lived in Southampton where he is believed to have died in 1969 at the age of 65.

Bancourt British Cemetery, on the Somme, where Henry Soffe is buried

SOFFE, Henry James

Medals and memorials for Henry James Soffe

Private Henry James Soffe was entitled to the 1914-15 Star, the British War Medal and the Victory Medal. He is buried in Bancourt British Cemetery, Pas de Calais, France (GR. X. B. 9) and is listed on the memorials at St Matthew's and St Paul's churches, Winchester.

Researcher – DEREK WHITFIELD

SOTHCOTT, Leopold George

Sapper LEOPOLD GEORGE SOTHCOTT
8, Greenhill Road, Winchester
Service number 177509. 288th Army Troops Company, Royal Engineers
Died of influenza, France, 29 October 1918

Leopold George Sothcott was born in Southampton on 8 July 1885, the eldest of James and Sarah Sothcott's five children. Although Leopold enlisted in Winchester and is mentioned on the memorials at St Matthew's and St Paul's churches, he spent most of his life in Southampton. His connection to Winchester is thought to come through his wife who lived in 8, Greenhill Road after the war. Leopold, who is not mentioned in the Winchester War Service Register, died of influenza while on active service less than a fortnight before the Armistice which brought the war to an end.

Leopold Sothcott's father James was born in Portsmouth in 1865. James's father, Thomas, was also from Portsmouth and had been born there in 1837. Thomas Sothcott worked as a brazier man and tinman - someone who made and repaired objects constructed of tin and other light metals. James's mother, Jane, was born in Odiham, near Basingstoke, in 1836. It appears that James's parents may have died when he was still quite young because in the 1871 Census, he and his brothers and sisters were recorded living with their aunt, Caroline Sothcott, a needlewoman.

Leopold's mother was born Sarah Hillier in Figheldean, near Amesbury, Wiltshire, in 1860. She and James married in Southampton in 1884 and Leopold was born the following year, followed by Ernest in 1885 and Winifred in 1889.

By 1891 the Sothcotts were living in Fir Grove Road, Millbrook, Southampton. James was a whitesmith – a craftsman who worked with white or light-coloured metals such as tin and pewter. Sarah went on to give birth to three more children: Hilda (1894), Leslie (1897) and Doris (1901).

On 25 April 1892, six-year-old Leopold enrolled at Freemantle National School, Southampton, having previously attended a dame school. This was an early form of private elementary school often found in areas of poverty and usually situated in the teacher's home. In 1898, at the age of 13, Leopold left school to start work and by 1901 he was a gas fitter's apprentice. That year's census showed his father working as an ironmonger and his brother Ernest as an errand boy. His other siblings were at school.

It was in this period that two of Leopold's uncles came to live and work in Winchester. In 1900 George Sothcott was living at 2, St Thomas Street while his brother William was at 25, Stockbridge Road. George worked as a gas fitter, so he may have helped Leopold with his job. By 1908 William Sothcott had left Winchester and George died around this time, but his widow continued to live in the city.

In 1908 Leopold Sothcott married 19-year-old Dora Tiller, the daughter of Southampton blacksmith William Tiller. On 7 November 1910 Dora gave birth to a daughter, Gwendoline. By 1911

Men of the Royal Engineers Signal Service, the unit that Leopold Sothcott served with during the Great War. Signals flags look primitive today but were vital to communications between 1914 and 1918

SOTHCOTT, Leopold George

Leopold had qualified as a gas fitter and was living with Dora, her father and baby Gwendoline at 19, Nelson Road, Freemantle, Southampton. Meanwhile, Leopold's father James was running a shop – probably a hardware store – in Southampton and employing two of his children, Hilda and Leslie.

It is not known precisely when Leopold enlisted to fight in the Great War. However, it is thought to have been in 1916 when he and his family moved to 32, Charlton Road, Shirley, as that is the address he gave when he joined up. Leopold enlisted with the Royal Engineers as Sapper 177509 and was assigned to 288th Army Troops Company, part of the Royal Engineers Signal Service.

At the outbreak of the Great War the Royal Engineers Signal Service comprised 12 Regular companies supported by a motorcyclist section of the Special Reserve and 29 signal companies of the Territorial Force. By 1918 the service had expanded to 589 companies, most of which operated on the Western Front.

The extensive use of artillery during the war produced a demand for dedicated signal sections, particularly for liaising with spotter aircraft. Other units aided in the movement of men and supplies to the front. Alongside this expansion in traditional forms of signalling, a whole new field of electronic warfare opened up thanks to the work of Signals Intelligence and the Wireless Observation Groups.

The revolution in signals technology between 1914 and 1918 enabled the British Army to make great strides in its military operations. By 1918 the old-style infantry attacks on trench systems were increasingly being replaced by more sophisticated 'combined arms' operations involving infantry, artillery, tanks, aircraft and cavalry. The Army's expanded signals branch also played a crucial role by ensuring that the separate weapons 'arms' were able to communicate with each other.

Nothing is known about where Leopold Sothcott served during the war. His Army pension records (under the name Southcott) show that he died on 29 October 1918 of influenza contracted while on active service. He was 33 years old. The same records give Dora Sothcott's address in early 1919 as 8, Greenhill Road, Winchester (the address then and now). Dora also appears in the Electoral Registers of 1920 and 1921 at the same address, although she, too, is incorrectly listed as Southcott. It is not known if Leopold ever lived in the house but given that his widow went to the trouble of ensuring his name appeared on the parish memorials he may well have done. For that reason, this biography uses 8, Greenhill Road as Leopold Sothcott's address.

After Leopold's death Dora received a grant of £6 from the military authorities on 12 December 1918. From 12 May 1919 she also received a pension of 23s 6d a week to help with the cost of bringing up her and Leopold's daughter Gwendoline. This ceased on 7 November 1926, Gwendoline's 16th birthday.

Leopold Sothcott's Army pension records showing his widow Dora living at 8, Greenhill Road

SOTHCOTT, Leopold George

Dora Sothcott is thought to have moved from Winchester back to Southampton where she remained for several years. By 1939 she was living in Boscombe, near Bournemouth. Dora never remarried and died in Bournemouth in 1985 at the age of 98. Gwendoline Sothcott married Herbert Griggs in 1932. The couple lived in Southampton and later in Somerset. Gwendoline died in Cambridgeshire in 2006, aged 95.

Medals and memorials for Leopold George Sothcott

Sapper Leopold George Sothcott was entitled to the British War Medal and the Victory Medal. He is buried at Busigny Communal Cemetery Extension (below), Nord, France (GR. II. A. 5) with the following inscription on his headstone:
ONLY THOSE THAT HAVE LOVED AND LOST KNOWETH THE MEANING OF GONE.
Leopold is mentioned on the memorials at St Matthew's and St Paul's churches, Winchester. His name also appears on the Southampton Main Memorial.

Researchers – JENNY WATSON and DEREK WHITFIELD

STEVENS, Ernest

2nd Lieutenant ERNEST STEVENS
21-22, Sussex Street, Winchester (no longer stand)
1st Battalion, Seaforth Highlanders
(Previously 8248, Regimental Quartermaster Sergeant)
Died of wounds, France, 2 February 1915

Ernest Stevens was born in Winchester on 9 May 1880, the first of the three children of Samuel and Emily Stevens. Samuel had been born in Winchester in 1858 and Emily (née Pottle) in Crawley, near Winchester, in the same year. The couple married in Portsmouth in 1879.

In the 1881 Census, Emily and baby Ernest were living with her brother John's family at 20, Sussex Street, Winchester. Ernest's father Samuel was away from home – his occupation was listed as a coachman. By 1891 the family, by then including a daughter, Ida, born in 1887, and a second son, Fred, born the following year, were living at Highland Terrace, Winchester. Samuel was working as a baker. Fred Stevens died in late 1891, aged three.

No trace of Ernest has yet been found on the 1901 Census when his family's address was 21, Sussex Street. His father gave his occupation as a baker, confectioner and a shopkeeper. In 1903 Ernest enlisted with the Seaforth Highlanders (Ross-shire Buffs, Duke of Albany's) and was assigned to the 1st Battalion which was posted to India shortly afterwards.

On 30 September 1907, Ernest married Ethel White in Peshawar, Bengal (part of modern Pakistan). Ethel had been born in Bengal in 1884 so it is possible that her father, Edwin, had a military background. Two of the couple's three daughters were born in India, Freda on 25 July 1908 and Doris in October 1912. By 1911 Ernest had reached the rank of Regimental Quartermaster Sergeant with the service number 8248. His address was 'Chanbattia', India.

Back in Winchester, Ernest's sister Ida married William Barker, a schoolmaster, in 1909. The couple went to live with Ida's father Samuel – by then a master baker – and mother Emily at 21-22, Sussex Street. (The houses, situated in Sussex Street between Newburgh Street and Gladstone Street, no longer stand.) The Stevens family remained there until 1920 when they moved to 11, Western Road, Winchester, which is the address given for Ernest in the Winchester War Service Register. This study, however, has opted for the Sussex Street address because, although almost all Ernest's military career was spent overseas, this was a house that he knew and where his family lived during the Great War.

When war broke out in August 1914, the 1st Seaforth Highlanders were stationed in Agra, India, as part of the Dehra Dun Brigade of the 7th (Meerut) Division. Over the following weeks the battalion mobilised for war before embarking for France. On October 12, the Dehra Dun Brigade arrived at Marseilles where it was renamed the 19th Indian Brigade.

The brigade immediately moved to northern France to form part of the Indian Corps at the Battles of La Bassée, Messines and Armentieres. These actions, between 10 October and 2 November 1914, were a series of attempts by the German and Allied armies to envelop each other's northern flank in what became known as the Race to the Sea. All proved inconclusive and both sides dug in from the Channel coast to the Swiss frontier, marking the start of trench warfare on the Western Front.

On 20 January 1915 Ernest Stevens was commissioned as a 2nd Lieutenant in the 1st Seaforth Highlanders. The battalion had suffered heavy losses among its officers in the autumn battles and urgently needed suitable replacements. Ernest may have impressed the Army authorities during the fighting, leading to him being recommended for promotion. However, he had little opportunity to make his mark as an officer. He died of wounds near Aubers Ridge, northern France, on 2 February 1915, less

STEVENS, Ernest

than a fortnight after being commissioned. It is believed he was shot in the head whilst part of a night-time trench-digging team.

Ernest's father Samuel served as a Lieutenant on the home front with the Hampshire Regiment and survived the war. In the 1939 National Register, Samuel was recorded still living at 11, Western Road, together with a housekeeper. He died there in 1943 at the age of 84. Ernest's mother Emily died in Winchester in 1926, aged 68.

At the time of Ernest's death his wife Ethel was listed living at The Bungalow, Holly Road, Orpington, Kent, so she may have returned to England from India after the outbreak of war. By the following month (March 1915) she had moved to Winchester - probably to be with her in-laws – where she gave birth to a third daughter, Marjorie. Although Ethel was in England there is some suggestion that at least one of the older daughters remained in India to continue her schooling. Ethel applied for her husband's 1914 (Mons) Star on 8 January 1918. She received £285 12s 1d in his will.

On 26 November 1920 Ethel Stevens and her three children left Liverpool aboard the ship City of Karachi bound for Bombay (Mumbai today). It is likely that she was returning to India to visit her parents, or even to live with them. No trace can be found of Ethel in any records after this date. Ernest and Ethel's eldest daughter, Freda, remained single and died in Camden, London, in the second quarter of 1981, aged 72. Middle daughter Doris is believed to have married and she died in Bognor Regis, Sussex, on 20 April 2009, aged 96. Marjorie, the youngest daughter, married Gordon Cummins in Paddington, London, in December 1939. However, Gordon died in Newgate Prison in 1942, aged just 27. Marjorie never remarried and she passed away in London in 2013 at the age of 98.

Medals and memorials for Ernest Stevens

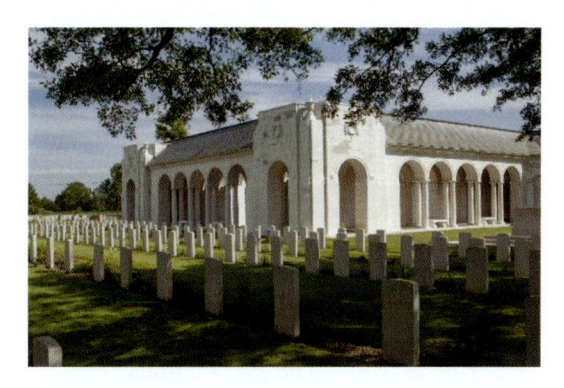

2nd Lieutenant Ernest Stevens was entitled to the 1914 (Mons) Star, the British War Medal and the Victory Medal. He is buried in Le Touret Military Cemetery (above), Richebourg-L'Avoue, Pas de Calais, France (GR. II. D. 4) and his name appears on the memorials at St Matthew's, St Paul's and St Thomas' churches, Winchester.

Researchers – CHERYL DAVIS and DEREK WHITFIELD

STROUD, Bertram Edward

Sergeant BERTRAM EDWARD STROUD
7, Western Road, Winchester, and 80, Stockbridge Road (No. 27 today)
Service number R/13747, 18th (Service) Battalion, King's Royal Rifle Corps
Killed in action, France, 10 October 1916

Bertram Edward Stroud was born in January 1886, in Newbridge, County Kildare, Ireland, the sixth of eight children. His father served in the Royal Artillery and the family moved around the country before settling in Winchester. Bertram served in the Merchant Navy but joined the King's Royal Rifle Corps (KRRC) in 1915. He reached the rank of Sergeant before being killed at the Battle of the Somme in October 1916 within a few days of his brother George (see biography on pp. 313).

Bertram's father, Richard, was born in Bramley, near Basingstoke, in 1847, the son of agricultural labourer Barzillai Stroud and his wife Sarah. Barzillai had been born in Silchester, near Basingstoke, in around 1818 and Sarah in the nearby village of Tadley in 1820.

In 1865 Richard Stroud enlisted with the Royal Artillery for 12 years. He met Margaret Jones (1852-1930), who had been born in Cornwall or Devon, and they married in Exeter in 1874. Margaret gave birth to four children in quick succession: Alice in Woolwich, south London, in 1874, and Florence (August 1876), Richard Jnr (September 1878) and Alfred (March 1880), all in Christchurch, Dorset.

By 1881, Richard was still serving with the Royal Artillery and living with Margaret and their four children at 37, New Street, St. John's Wood, north London. Another son, Arthur, was born in London the following year and then Bertram in Ireland in 1886.

Richard Stroud left the Army in February 1886, a month after Bertram's birth, and by 1891 he was working as a groom. He and Margaret had moved to Lower Lyeway, Ropley, near Alresford, and had two more children – George, born in Sherborne, near Basingstoke, in 1887 and Hetty, born in 1888 in Ropley. The two elder daughters, Florence and Alice were domestic servants and the other children at school.

By 1894 the Strouds had moved to Winchester and were living at 4, Greenhill Avenue. We know this because Bertram's cousin Albert had come to live with the family and was attending St Thomas Church of England Boys' School. Albert entered the school, aged eight, on 24 October 1894 after having previously been at Highcliffe School. The St Thomas School records reveal that his guardian was Richard Stroud of Greenhill Avenue. The reason behind this arrangement is unclear. Albert was the youngest son of Richard Stroud Snr's brother William who ran a grocer's store in Pamber, near Basingstoke. William remarried shortly afterwards and by 1901 had a baby son, named Barzillai after his grandfather.

Where Bertram went to school is not known, but by 1901 he was working as a plumber and living with his family at 4, Greenhill Road, Fulflood. His father was a jobbing gardener and younger brother George a house painter. Sister Hetty was still at school, but the other siblings had left home. In 1910 George emigrated to Canada.

Right: 7, Western Road, Winchester – Bertram Stroud's parents moved here shortly before the Great War

STROUD, Bertram Edward

There is no mention of Bertram Stroud in the 1911 Census in which his parents were recorded living at 7, Western Road, Winchester (the address then and now). However, Bertram's Army records from 1915 state that he was a merchant seaman when he enlisted so he was probably not living in Winchester at the time of the census. Intriguingly, on the same enlistment papers Bertram gave his address as 80, Upper Stockbridge Road (27, Stockbridge Road today), the home of Ernest and Laura Page. The papers also reveal that after Bertram's death the Army was requested to send his effects and medals to Ernest and Laura's daughter, Dorothy. Although Bertram was some 14 years older than Dorothy, there is just a hint here that the pair may have been romantically involved. (Dorothy's mother, Laura, was the stepsister of William Mitchell whose name also appears on the parish memorials. His biography is on pp. 207).

Richard Stroud, Bertram's father, died in Winchester in the first quarter of 1915. Bertram left the merchant navy shortly afterwards and on 31 May he enlisted (service number R/13747) with the KRRC in Poplar, east London. From there he was posted to the Rifles depot at Winchester. Many of his Army papers have survived and these enable us to paint a more rounded picture of Bertram, both as a man and a soldier. They reveal that he was 5ft 6ins tall, weighed 9st 4lbs and had a 37in chest. His rapid rise through the Army ranks is also charted. On 12 August 1915 he was promoted to Corporal, two days before being posted to the 18th (Service) Battalion (Arts and Crafts) KRRC which had been raised in early June at Gidea Park, Romford Essex. Just two months later, on 22 October, Bertram was promoted again, to Lance-Sergeant, and then to Acting Sergeant on 27 November.

Clearly Bertram possessed qualities that marked him out as a leader of men, qualities which probably had much to do with his age and previous experience of life at sea. At 28 he would have been older than many of his fellow volunteers in the battalion while his years in the merchant navy would have familiarised him with the importance of discipline and perhaps instilled a degree of self-assurance and confidence that caught the eye of his Army superiors.

The records contain other fascinating snippets of information. In August 1915 Bertram underwent dental treatment in Winchester to have no fewer than 12 'stumps' (presumably rotten teeth) removed, two teeth filled, and then upper and lower dentures fitted at a total cost of £3. It is possible that this was the first time that Bertram had ever visited a dentist - it would be another 33 years before the creation of the NHS introduced free health to all, not just those who could afford to pay for it.

The records also reveal one blip in Bertram's rise up the Army ladder. In February 1916, while the battalion was undergoing training at Aldershot, he was reprimanded for 'irregular conduct' and giving a false name to the Military Police in Guildford. It did not affect his career prospects, however, because on 3 May 1916, the day that the 18th KRRC transferred to France, he was made full Sergeant.

Bertram first saw action at the Battle of Flers-Courcelette (15-22 September 1916) during the Somme Offensive. The battle, which is best remembered for the first use of tanks in warfare, started badly for the 18th KRRC when a shell killed the battalion's Commanding Officer and three other officers a few minutes after Zero Hour. Only 15 tanks were used in the battle, but they caused panic among the German troops, many of whom threw down their weapons and fled. However, the tanks were slow and prone to mechanical failure and the German gunners, once over their initial shock, put several out of action.

A spotter plane flying over the battlefield sent the following message: 'Tank seen in main street Flers. Going on with large numbers of troops following it.' Such good news was rare during the Somme Offensive and these famous words were soon making headlines in newspapers across Britain. Although the Allies failed to achieve their initial objectives, they did capture the villages of Courcelette, Martinpuich and Flers as well as High Wood, which had been a thorn in the side for over two months.

STROUD, Bertram Edward

Bertram Stroud was in action again at the Battle of Le Transloy (1-18 October 1916) which aimed to build on the successes of the previous month. However, rain, fog and mud thwarted the best efforts of British troops. The 122nd Brigade went into the line on 3 October, about one and a half miles north of Flers. On 7 October the 18th KRRC took part in a failed attack on Bayonet Trench West, suffering heavy casualties in the process. The following day, 41st Division was withdrawn from the line, a process that took three days because of the appalling state of the battlefield. According to his Army papers, Bertram Stroud was killed between 3 and 10 October although most official records give the 10th. Bertram was 30 years old and his body was never found.

Bertram's brother George, who was serving with the 49th Battalion (Edmonton Regiment) Canadian Expeditionary Force, also fought on the Somme. He was killed two days before Bertram at the Battle of the Ancre Heights (1-18 October), just a few miles from the Le Transloy battlefield. Neither brother is listed in the Winchester War Service Register, presumably because they were not living in the city at the outbreak of war.

Bertram's mother Margaret continued to live at 7, Western Road until 1917 when she moved a short distance to 21, Elm Road, the home of her son Alfred. She died in Winchester in 1930. Alfred continued to live in Winchester until his death in March 1966, aged 86. Bertram's other surviving brother, Richard, is believed to have married in 1902 but no trace can be found of him after that date.

All three of Bertram's sisters married. The eldest, Alice (later Barnes) went to live in Shirley, Southampton, and had at least three children. She died in the New Forest in February 1953, aged 74. Florence (later Welch) lived at 14, Cheriton Road, Fulflood. She is known to have had one child and died in Winchester in March 1939 at the age of 62. Hetty (later Gale) moved to Southsea after marrying. She died in Basingstoke in September 1967, aged 77.

Finally, what of Dorothy Page, who may have been Bertram's girlfriend in Winchester? In 1919 she married 22-year-old Londoner George Pheby who had served with the London Regiment during the Great War. George died less than four years later in February 1923. Dorothy tried unsuccessfully to secure a widow's pension from the Army authorities, suggesting that George's death may have been related to an injury sustained while on active service. Dorothy never remarried. In 1939 she was recorded living with her mother at 27, Stockbridge Road and doing domestic work. She died in Southsea in July 1983, aged 83.

Medals and memorials for Bertram Edward Stroud

Sergeant Bertram Edward Stroud was entitled to the British War Medal and the Victory Medal. His body was never found and he is commemorated (above) on the Thiepval Memorial, Somme, France, (PR. 13A & 13B, Pier & Face). Bertram is also mentioned on the memorials at St Paul's and St Matthew's churches, Winchester.

Researchers –DEREK WHITFIELD and JENNY WATSON

Sergeant GEORGE STROUD
7, Western Road, Winchester
Service number 432686. 49th Battalion (Edmonton Regiment), Canadian Corps
Killed in action, France, 8 October 1916

George Stroud, the son of Richard and Margaret Stroud, was born in Sherborne St John, near Basingstoke, on 9 April 1887. George emigrated to Canada in 1910 but fought in the Great War after joining the Canadian Corps in 1915. He was killed at the Battle of the Somme in 1916, two days before his brother Bertram. The Stroud family's story up to the time that George emigrated can be found in Bertram's biography on pp. 310).

On 5 August 1910 George Stroud sailed from Liverpool for Quebec City. He arrived on 11 August and made his way to Edmonton in the province of Alberta. By 1911 George was lodging in a boarding house in the city and working as a house painter. In that year's census he gave his nationality as Canadian.

George met and then married Scottish-born Christina Furlough of Fort McMurray, Alberta, and the couple lived at 438, 18th Street, Edmonton. Their son Hugh was born there in 1915.

On 11 January 1915, five months after the start of the Great War, George Stroud joined the 49th Battalion (Edmonton Regiment) with the service number was 432686. The battalion, which formed part of the Canadian Expeditionary Force, recruited and mobilized in Edmonton. Most of its troops were British-born volunteers - conscription was not introduced in Canada until the end of the war.

On 3 June 1915 the 49th Battalion left Montreal on the SS Metagama bound for England. George was almost certainly on board. After arriving in England, the battalion celebrated Dominion Day in Folkestone on 1 July 1915 and then deployed to France on 9 October 1915. There it came under orders of 7th Infantry Brigade, part of the 3rd Canadian Division.

The 3rd Canadian Division first saw action in Flanders at the Battle of Mount Sorrel (2-13 June 1916). To divert British resources from the build-up for the Somme Offensive, German forces attacked an arc of high ground positions defended by the Canadian Corps, including the 3rd Division. The Germans captured the heights at Mount Sorrel and Hill 62 which the Allies immediately set about retaking. After an artillery bombardment lasting several days, three Divisions, including two Canadian, attacked on 13 June and recaptured most of their former positions. The battle cost the Canadians and British some 8,000 casualties, including the Canadian 3rd Division commander Major-General Malcolm Mercer.

George Stroud, who had probably been promoted to Sergeant by this time, fought next at the Battle of Flers-Courcelette (15-22 September 1916) during the Somme Offensive. George's brother Bertram fought in the same battle.

The Canadian 7th Brigade was involved in attacks aimed at capturing Regina Trench – one of the longest trench systems on the Somme battlefield - to the

The area around 18th Street, Edmonton – George Stroud lived near here from 1911 after emigrating to Canada

STROUD, George

west of the German-held village of Courcelette. Progress was slow in the face of stiff German resistance and George would have seen desperate close-quarter fighting.

As September turned to October the weather worsened, turning the Somme battlefield into a sea of mud. On 1 October, the British launched the Battle of the Ancre Heights. Regina Trench, still in German hands, was an objective on the opening day but that attack, too, failed. Seven days later the British tried again.

George Stroud is believed to have been killed during the attack on Regina Trench by Canadian 3rd Division on 8 October 1916. The Canadians fought bravely but could not crack the German defences. Small parties of troops did manage to break into sections of the trench but were never seen again. The 49th Battalion found their way into a trench blocked by newly laid barbed wire and suffered heavy losses from German machine-gun fire. It is possible that George Stroud was killed here. He was 29 years old.

The Canadian Expeditionary Force's Great War Book of Remembrance showing George Stroud's name

Two days later, on 10 October, George's brother Bertram, who was serving with the 18th King's Royal Rifle Corps, was killed in action at the Battle of Le Transloy. The battlefield on which he died was just a few miles from where George was killed. Neither brother's body was ever found.

After George's death, his widow Christina continued to live at 18th Street in Edmonton. According to the 1921 Canadian Census she was living there with their son Hugh and listed as a housekeeper.

George Stroud, like his brother Bertram, is not listed in the Winchester War Service Register.

Medals and memorials for George Stroud

Sergeant George Stroud was entitled to the British War Medal and the Victory Medal. He is commemorated (above) on the Canadian National Vimy Memorial at Vimy Ridge (right), Pas de Calais, France, and in the Canadian Expeditionary Force's Great War Book of Remembrance. He is also remembered on the memorials at St Matthew's and St Paul's churches, Winchester.

Researcher – JENNY WATSON

Additional sources

- http://www.albertagenealogy-research.ca/LER/Nominal_Roles/49thBnCEF.pdf
- http://www.albertagenealogy-research.ca/Admin/MilitaryEdmontonArticles.htm

THOMPSON, Richard James

Sergeant RICHARD JAMES THOMPSON, M.M.
41, Sussex Street, Winchester (no longer stands)
Service No. 54572. 117th Battery, Royal Field Artillery
Accidentally killed, France, 21 July 1916

Richard James Thompson, the eldest child, of William and Mary Thompson, was born in 1891 in Barracktown, County Cork. Richard's father had also been born in Cork, in 1831, and was some 27 years older than his wife and 60 years Richard's senior. He had already retired and was living as an Army pensioner when his son was born. Richard's mother was born Mary Mahoney in Glasson, County Westmeath, in 1858. She gave birth to a second son, Patrick, on 11 March 1892 in Cork and a daughter, Mary, in Barracktown, in 1894. It is likely that the family lived in the British Army barracks in Cork.

In the 1901 Census the Thompsons were recorded living at Rathbone Road, Cork, with the three children at school. Richard's father, then aged 70, was listed in the census as the caretaker of the Baptist Chapel in Bing Street, Cork. He was the only member of the family unable to read and write.

On 15 January 1909, 18-year-old Richard Thompson joined the Army at Fort Westmoreland, Cork. He was assigned to 116th Battery, Royal Field Artillery (RFA) as a gunner. His attestation form shows that he joined up for 12 years and was already serving as a Special Reservist (a part-time soldier similar to a Territorial) with the Royal Artillery in Cork.

On the attestation form Richard was described as 5ft 8in tall, with grey eyes, light brown hair and a fresh complexion. He weighed 8st 10lbs and his chest measured 33in. His physical development was said to be good. Richard had previously worked as a clerk and he gave his religion as Church of England. The records reveal that he later attended Army school, possibly the Royal Hibernian Military School in Dublin, and that he passed a class of instruction in cookery in May 1910 while based at Aldershot.

Richard's father died in Cork in 1911. That year's census showed that his mother Mary and brother Patrick – by then a railway engine cleaner – were the only members of the family still living at Rathbone Road. Richard's sister Mary had left home and was living in Bishop's Mill Lands, Bishopstown, Cork, with three sisters from the Bergin family. The sisters were running a private school where 17-year-old Mary was employed as a servant. In 1913 Richard's mother died in Cork, aged 54. His brother Patrick continued to work with the railway company.

By this time Richard had moved with the Army to England where he was living at 41, Sussex Street, Winchester. Interestingly, the Warren's Directories of 1912 and 1913 record the house being used by the Hampshire Carabiniers, a cavalry unit, possibly as a billet.

On 20 May 1914 Richard Thompson married Gwendoline Holt in Hartley Wintney, near Basingstoke. Gwendoline was the daughter of Alfred and Maria Holt and had been born on 23 January 1893 in Devonport where her father is believed to have been serving in the Army. By 1911 the family had moved to Farnborough where Alfred Holt worked as a steward at the local Conservative Club. After marrying, Richard and Gwendoline lived at 41, Sussex Street, Winchester. The house no longer stands.

When Britain went to war in August 1914, 23-year-old Richard Thompson had been a professional soldier for eight years. He was still serving with 117th Battery, RFA and had reached the rank of Bombardier, the artillery equivalent of Corporal.

During the war the RFA, the largest of the three branches of the Royal Artillery, provided close artillery support for the infantry and was responsible for the Army's medium calibre guns and howitzers which were deployed close to the front line.

THOMPSON, Richard James

A horse-drawn 18-pounder field gun is moved into position by a British artillery team during the Great War. This would have been a familiar sight to Sergeant Richard Thompson

The RFA's principal weapon in 1914 was the 15-pounder field gun although by 1916 most batteries were being issued with the improved 18-pounder. These guns fired shrapnel or high explosive shells on a low trajectory at a target that was usually visible. By 1916, an artillery brigade consisted of four batteries, each of six guns. The first three, A B and C batteries, were equipped with field guns while D battery used 4.5in howitzers. The howitzer fired its shell high into the air on a much steeper trajectory and was used to target concealed enemy positions, behind a wood or a hill, for example.

Together, the 116th, 117th and 118th Batteries, RFA, formed 26th Brigade which served with the British Army's 1st Division. The 1st Division, among the first to be deployed to France in August 1914, fought on the Western Front throughout the war and took part in most of the major actions. The early engagements included the Battle of Mons (23 August 1914) and the subsequent retreat (24 August-5 September), the First Battle of the Marne (6-10 September), the Battle of the Aisne (13-28 September), the First Battle of Ypres (19 October-22 November) and the winter operations of 1914-15.

On 23 October 1914 Richard was transferred to 117th Brigade, RFA. At the end of 1914, 1st Division moved south to the La Bassée front and took over the trenches at the Cuinchy Brickstacks where it came under German attack on 29 January 1915. The Division suffered heavy losses in the British attack on Aubers Ridge on 9 May 1915 and then again at the Battle of Loos (25 September-15 October 1915). At Loos, 1st Division was at the forefront of the fighting near the Lone Tree and Le Rutoire Farm and particularly in the unsuccessful, and costly, assault on the Hohenzollern Redoubt stronghold.

On 7 April 1915 Richard was promoted to Acting Sergeant and then full Sergeant two months later. This may have been in recognition of his performance in the field during the early phase of the war.

In early 1916 1st Division transferred to the Somme. During the Somme Offensive, Richard saw action around the village of Mametz and it was here, on 21 July 1916, that he was accidentally killed while on active duty. The circumstances of the accident are unknown, but it is possible that a shell exploded prematurely in a gun before being fired. Richard was 25 years old when he died.

Richard was posthumously awarded the Military Medal which was listed in the London Gazette on 12 September 1916. The Military Medal, which had only just been introduced, was awarded to soldiers below commissioned rank (i.e. non officers) for 'acts of gallantry and devotion to duty under fire'.

Richard Thompson's Army pension records show that his widow Gwendoline received a pension of 11shillings a week from 12 February 1917. The records also reveal that at that time she had moved from

THOMPSON, Richard James

Winchester and was living at The Peaceful Home inn in East Street, Alresford. (This is a private residential house today.)

Gwendoline Thompson remarried in Winchester on 9 October 1917. Her new husband, 30-year-old William Newman, had been born in Camberwell, south London, and worked as a printer's compositor. The couple went on to have two children. A daughter, named Gwendoline after her mother, was born in Winchester on 24 August 1918 and a son, Reginald, in Lambeth, south London, on 27 May 1921. (Reginald died in 1952 while fighting in the Korean War.) Gwendoline would almost certainly have lost her Army widow's pension when she remarried.

Gwendoline and William were living at 41, Sussex Street in 1920 but by 1939 they had moved to Dagenham, Essex, where William was still employed as a compositor. William died in Farnham, Surrey, in May 1973, aged 80, and Gwendoline in Aldershot on 18 March 1979 at the age of 86.

It is not known if Richard's brother Patrick fought in the Great War. On 18 June 1918 he married Sarah Holland at St Nicholas Church in Cork. On the marriage certificate he was listed as a fireman with the Great Southern and Western Railway, living at 9, Rockvale Street, Glanwire, Cork.

Richard Thompson is listed in the Winchester War Service Register.

Medals and memorials for Richard James Thompson

Sergeant Richard James Thompson was entitled to the 1914 (Mons) Star, the British War Medal and the Victory Medal. He is buried (grave right) at Dantzig Alley British Cemetery (GR. III. F. 6), Mametz, Somme, Pas de Calais, France. His name appears on the memorials at St Matthew's and St Paul's churches, Winchester.

Researchers DEREK WHITFIELD and JENNY WATSON

TONG, Herbert Lewis

Lance-Corporal HERBERT LEWIS TONG
88, Lower Stockbridge Road, Winchester (11, Stockbridge Road today)
Service Number 23003. 2nd Battalion, The Wiltshire Regiment
Died of wounds, France, 12 April 1917

Herbert Lewis Tong was born on 8 January 1896 in the parish of St Peter's Cheesehill, Winchester. He was the sixth surviving child of Edward and Louisa Tong. Edward Tong had been born in Rochester, Kent, in 1860. The next record found for Edward is his marriage on 26 March 1882 to Louisa Runyard at St Mark's Church, Regent's Park, London. Louisa had been born in 1862 and her family were from Wool, Dorset. In 1881, she was working as a servant to a wealthy London family.

Edward and Louisa's first child, Stephen George, was born in Rochester in 1883. By the birth of Augustine Henry (Harry) in 1885, the family were living in Wimborne, Dorset, where Edward worked as a journeyman cabinetmaker. A third son, Arthur Edward, was born there in 1888. However, by November 1892, Edward had become a lay clerk at Winchester Cathedral and the couple's subsequent known children were all born in the city - Edith May, their only daughter, in 1892, Herbert Lewis in 1896, Frank Percy in 1897 and Sidney James in 1899. There was another child, but it is not known when he or she was born or when they died. The Tongs come over as hard-working and aspirational.

By the 1901 Census, the family were living at 33, Bar End Road, Winchester (now No. 23), where Herbert, Edith, Frank and Sidney may have been born. Edward, still a lay clerk at Winchester Cathedral, further described his occupation as woodcarver. Their eldest son Stephen, by then 17, had followed in his father's footsteps and was an apprentice cabinet maker. Harry, 14, was an architect's clerk. Interestingly, Arthur, 13, was not at home on census night. He was recorded as boarding at 64/63 Kingsgate Street along with 15 other Winchester College quiristers (choristers). They would have been educated in a separate school within the College.

Edith, aged eight, and five-year-old Herbert were at school whilst Frank and Sydney were still at home. Herbert later went to All Saint's Elementary School, Highcliffe, Winchester, before progressing to Peter Symonds Grammar School in September 1908 when he was nearly 13. Herbert was obviously a bright boy as his fees were paid for by the school's governing body. However, he was not there for long as he left in April 1910 to be apprenticed to a pharmaceutical chemist.

By 1911, most of the Tong family were living at 88, Lower Stockbridge Road, Winchester. The house was renumbered 11, Stockbridge Road in 1918 and it remains that today. (Sadly, it is currently the derelict property in the row of shops between Elm Road and Western Road.) In 1909, Edward had been promoted to be a virger (verger) at the cathedral. He would have had to work against the background of the upheaval created by the replacing of the foundations spearheaded by the diver William Walker. His wife was assisting in a tobacconist's while Herbert had been a chemist's apprentice for a year.

23, Bar End Road, Winchester – Herbert Tong is believed to have been born here in 1896 when it was No. 33

TONG, Herbert Lewis

Of the other sons still at home, Harry, aged 25, was an architect's assistant and 23-year-old Arthur was working as a clerk in the music warehouse Teague & King in Lower Minster Street. Herbert's younger brother Frank had followed him to Peter Symonds in September 1910, also with the fees paid for by the governing body. He left on 19 July 1912, to become an apprentice at a piano warehouse. Sydney, 11, was still at school. There seems to have been a strong musical streak in the family as Herbert was the organist at St Lawrence's Church in The Square from 1915.

The currently derelict 11, Stockbridge Road, Winchester – this was 88, Lower Stockbridge until 1918. Herbert Tong had moved here with his family by 1911

Two of the Tong children had left home. The eldest, Stephen, had married and was living in Bournemouth with his wife Matilda and their three daughters. He had served his apprenticeship as a cabinet maker and was now earning a living making furniture. Meanwhile, Edith Tong, known as Edie, was boarding in a large hostel in Aldershot belonging to Thomas White & Co. Ltd, Military Outfitter. Edith's occupation was described as a draper's assistant.

In 1912 Arthur Tong, Herbert's brother, married Grace Comber at St Mathew's Church, Weeke. By the time that he enlisted in the Army in 1914 the couple already had one daughter and Grace was to give birth to a second in 1916, who lived to be 100.

In 1916 Herbert joined the 2nd Battalion, The Duke of Edinburgh's (Wiltshire Regiment) in Winchester. It is not yet known exactly when he joined up or whether he volunteered or was conscripted. The 2nd Wiltshires were a Regular Army battalion who had deployed to France in October 1914 with 21st Brigade, part of 7th Division, and fought in the major battles of that year and 1915.

In December 1915, 21st Brigade was transferred to 30th Division which saw action on 1 July 1916, the first day of the Somme Offensive. The 2nd Wiltshires were in the line near the village of Maricourt, at the junction of the British and French armies. The objective of 21st Brigade was the village of Montauban which was defended by a series of enemy strongpoints and trench systems. Much of the German wire had been cut by the British artillery bombardment and the assault initially made good progress. However, a single machine-gun caused almost 100 casualties among the Wiltshires who were bringing up supplies. Despite this and other pockets of German resistance, 30th Division was able to achieve all its objectives on 1 July, one of the few British successes that day.

The 21st Brigade was quickly back in action, attacking Trones Wood, on 8 July. The 2nd Wiltshires again took heavy casualties, losing their CO wounded and his replacement killed. Just two weeks later, on 23 July, the battalion took part in an attack towards Guillemont before being taken out of the line for rest and refitting. They did not return to the front until 18 October when they attacked the German Gird Line trench system, north east of the village of Flers, at the Battle of Le Transloy. The Wiltshires forced their way into the trenches but were then nearly wiped out by enfilade fire.

Herbert Tong's Medal Index Card does not state when he entered a theatre of war but, given that he had been promoted to Lance-Corporal by the time he died in April 1917, it is likely that he fought in at least one of the 2nd Wiltshires' engagements on the Somme.

TONG, Herbert Lewis

Herbert died on 12 April 1917 of wounds received during the First Battle of the Scarpe, the opening phase of the Arras Offensive (9 April-16 May 1917). On 9 April the 2nd Wiltshires had attacked the Hindenburg Line, a formidable German defensive position, and quickly came under heavy enemy artillery bombardment. The Wiltshire Regimental War Diary entry for that date stated:

At 11.38am the 21st Brigade attacked with the 2nd Wiltshire Regiment on their right ... The distance between the battalion and their objective (the Hindenburg Line) varied between 2000 and 2500 yards. Considerable hostile shelling was experienced throughout the advance which became more intense as it proceeded. To reach the objective, two sunken roads had to be crossed where heavy machine-gun fire was encountered. The advance continued right up to the enemy wire by which time the ranks were considerably depleted. It was found that though damaged the wire was not cut sufficiently for the troops to enter the enemy trenches. Shelter was sought in available shell holes but finally the troops had to fall back to the sunken road running from Neuville Vitasse to St Martin sur Coseul where they dug in.

When the 2nd Wiltshires came out of the line on 11 April they had lost 16 officers and 363 other ranks killed, wounded and missing. It is believed that Herbert, who died the following day aged 21, was among the casualties.

Four of Herbert's brothers also served in the Great War and survived. The elder two served on the Home Front. Stephen Tong joined up in 1914 and became a sapper in the Royal Engineers, reaching the rank of Corporal. His address in the Winchester War Service Register is 23, Greenhill Road (same number today). Harry Tong, meanwhile, became a Petty Officer in the Royal Naval Air Service (RNAS), which merged with the Royal Flying Corps in 1918 to become the Royal Air Force.

Arthur Tong must have been in the Army Cadet Force before enlisting in 1914 as he had been awarded an Army Proficiency Certificate. He had married Grace Comber at St Mathew's Church, Weeke, in 1912 and by the time he joined up he already had one daughter, aged about one (and was to have a second in 1916, who lived to be 100). He became a Private in the Oxfordshire & Buckingham Light Infantry and served in France. He was wounded on 28 October 1918. His address in 1921 was 12, Elm Road, Winchester.

Sydney, Herbert's youngest brother, served in Italy with the RNAS. Both Harry and Sydney must still have been based at home as in 1921 their address was given as 11, Stockbridge Road, Winchester.

After Herbert's death, his father Edward carved a wooden cross that was placed on his son's temporary grave in France in October 1917. Affixed to this was a brass memorial plaque from Edward and Louisa. It was later returned and today is held by Herbert's great nephew in Winchester.

In November 1925, Edward was promoted to Second Virger at Winchester Cathedral. The following year he retired, aged 65, on a pension of

Herbert Tong's father Edward on the day he retired as Second Virger at Winchester Cathedral in June 1926. He is pictured with a wooden maquette that he is believed to have carved.
(Photo: Winchester Cathedral)

TONG, Herbert Lewis

Above left: The memorial plaque to Herbert Tong which was attached to the wooden cross placed on his temporary grave in 1917. The plaque was later returned and is today held by Herbert's descendants. **Right:** the memorial to Herbert in St Lawrence's Church *(Photos: Merritt family)*

£60 a year. To mark his retirement, a photograph was taken of Edward with a maquette that he is believed to have carved and which would presumably have been used as a model by a stonemason in the cathedral.

After Edward's retirement, he and Louisa went to live in Bournemouth with their daughter Edith and her husband William Sapsed who had married in Winchester in 1920. Sadly, the marriage did not last and by 1932 Edward and Louisa were living in Southampton. Edward died in Romsey in 1942 and Louisa in Winchester in 1947. Edith passed away in 1962.

On his parents' move to Bournemouth, Arthur Tong moved from Elm Road with his wife Grace, two daughters and young son Donovan (Don) to take over the shop at 11, Stockbridge Road. By then it was a newsagent as well as a tobacconist and sweet shop. Don, who was born in 1923, had one wonderful memory of the shop. On the day that the refrigeration broke down, his parents allowed him to eat as much ice cream and ice lollies as he could manage!

Arthur Tong also had an interest in 7, Stockbridge Road as he is recorded in Warrens Directories as the householder there. (In Arthur's time, and for many decades after, it was a hairdresser's and is now the right-hand side of Pickards shop.) Arthur died in 1932, aged 44. Grace then took over running the shop on her own before she retired in 1953, at which point Norman Churchill took it over until the early 1990s. Grace went to live in a bungalow at 56, Stoney Lane, Weeke, next door to her son Don. Grace passed away in 1977 in Winchester.

In 1939 Herbert's eldest brother Stephen and his wife Matilda were living at Uplands, Bereweeke Road, Winchester. He was working as a builder/joiner/machinist. Stephen died in 1959 and Matilda in 1982.

Harry Tong resumed his career as an architect after the war and is thought to have designed several houses in the expanding suburb of Oliver's Battery. In fact, Harry designed 29, Compton Way for a family member and his brother Stephen built it. Herbert's great nephew now lives in the house.

Harry had married Amy Burton in Poole, Dorset, in October 1917. The 1921 Winchester War Register gives his address as 11, Stockbridge Road so perhaps initially they lived with his parents. They had two sons, both born in Winchester, Eric in 1919 and Raymond in 1922. By 1923, the family were living at 3, Battery Hill and by 1930 at 6, Eversley Place off Stanmore Lane. Harry died in Winchester in 1965 and Amy in 1982.

Frank Tong continued his musical career after the war. In 1939 he was working as a pianoforte tuner and regulator and living in London with his wife Marjorie. The couple had married in Winchester in 1922 and had one son, Peter. After Marjorie's death in 1942 Frank may have moved to Southampton to live with his mother as he died there in 1953.

Herbert's youngest brother, Sidney, is remembered by the family as being a very clever man who 'invented things'. He married Hilda Ballard (known as Margery) in January 1921. They did not have any children. At some stage, the couple moved to Dorset and both died within a few months of each other in 1980.

During the Second World War, Don Tong served with the RAF in Bomber Command. He married his wife Grace at St Paul's Church, Fulflood, in 1949 and later worked in the planning department at Winchester Rural District Council. Don died in 2009 and Hazel in 2018. They were the parents of Janice Merritt who has been very helpful in assisting with the compilation of this biography.

Herbert Tong is listed in the Winchester War Service Register.

Medals and memorials for Herbert Lewis Tong

Lance-Corporal Herbert Lewis Tong was entitled to the British War Medal and the Victory Medal. He is buried in Warlincourt Halte British Cemetery, Saulty, Pas de Calais, France (GR. VII. F. 7) – grave right. His name appears on the memorials at St Matthew's and St Paul's churches, Winchester, and on the Peter Symonds Grammar School Memorial. There is also a memorial plaque to Herbert at St Lawrence's Church, Winchester, where he was organist.

Researchers - GERALDINE BUCHANAN and JOSEPHINE COLEMAN

Additional sources

- Interview with Janice Merritt, great niece of Herbert Tong and who was brought up at 11, Stockbridge Road.
- The Wartime Memories Project. *2nd Battalion, The Wiltshire Regiment during the Great War.* https://wartimememoriesproject.com/greatwar/allied/alliedarmy-view.php?pid=847

TUNKS, Edward Joseph Austin

2nd Lieutenant EDWARD JOSEPH AUSTIN TUNKS
Rippledene, Sussex Street, Winchester (No. 98 today)
Service numbers 3806 and 5447. Argyll and Sutherland Highlanders and 4th Battalion, The Hampshire Regiment (attached to 2nd Battalion)
Killed in action, Belgium, 13 April 1918

Edward Joseph Austin Tunks, known as Jack to his family and friends, was born in Winchester in the first quarter of 1898. The elder son of Joseph and Alice Tunks, Jack came from a comfortable family background – his father was a master tailor. In the Great War he served as a Private with both the Argyll and Sutherland Highlanders and the Hampshire Regiment before being commissioned into the latter as a 2nd Lieutenant. He was killed in Belgium in 1918 during the German Spring Offensive.

Joseph Tunks, Jack's father, was born on 27 July 1872 in Willisborough, Kent, and was one of 13 children. His father, Joseph Snr, had been born in September 1851 in Ashford, Kent, and worked variously as a coal merchant's clerk, a tobacconist and a commercial traveller. Joseph Jnr's mother, Sarah, was born in Stepney, east London, in 1843. By 1891 the family had moved to 48, High Street, Lewes, Sussex, with 19-year-old Joseph Jnr already working as a tailor.

Jack's mother was born Alice Piper in Winchester in 1874. Alice's father, Edward (1842-1909), was a draper by trade (although, somewhat incongruously, he also appears as a butcher in the 1881 Census) who had been born in Lewes, Sussex. Alice's mother was born Eliza Corps (1846-1923) in Winchester. One of nine children, Eliza married Edward Piper in Winchester in 1868 and they also went on to have nine children. In 1891, the family were living at 12, Great Minster Street, Winchester, with Alice employed as an apprentice milliner.

Alice and Joseph Tunks married in 1897 and Jack was born the following year. In 1899 Alice gave birth to a second son, Arthur Cyril, who was known as Cyril. By 1901 the family were living at 25, Southgate Street, Winchester, with Joseph running his own tailoring business from the property. The 1911 Census records the family at 45, Southgate Street, with Joseph described as a master tailor. His business was prosperous enough for the family to employ a domestic servant. By 1914 Joseph and Alice had moved to a nine-room house in Sussex Street, Winchester, which they had named Rippledene by 1918. The property, which is 98, Sussex Street today, stands opposite the Hampshire Record Office.

No record of Jack Tunks's education can be found. He was 16 years old when the Great War began in August 1914 and therefore too young to enlist. However, his father did volunteer for the Hampshire Regiment and was posted to India. The Winchester War Service Register (WWSR) states that Joseph Tunks reached the rank of Sergeant and was wounded once.

According to the WWSR, Jack Tunks enlisted with the Argyll and Sutherland Highlanders in 1915. That would have meant he was under-age, but of course many young men did lie about their age in order to

TUNKS, Edward Joseph Austin

join the Army. It is possible that in late 1915, shortly before his 18th birthday, Jack enlisted under the Derby Scheme under which men 'attested' their willingness to serve in the forces and were then called up later. Jack may have attested at that stage, with the military authorities aware that he would be the correct age to serve in 1916. Surprisingly perhaps, Jack opted to join the Argyll and Sutherland Highlanders (service number 3806) rather than the Hampshire Regiment in which his father was serving.

However, Jack did subsequently transfer to the 4th Battalion, The Hampshire Regiment (service number 5447). It is not known whether he pressed the authorities for a switch, but it does seem more than coincidence that he was moved to what was effectively his 'home' battalion. Here, he impressed sufficiently to win a commission and become a 2nd Lieutenant. This promotion would have been followed by a period of officer training.

The official records state that Jack served only with the 4th Hampshires after he transferred from the Argyll and Sutherland Highlanders. However, this was clearly not the case because at the time that Jack was killed on the Western Front in 1918 both 4th Hampshire battalions – the 1/4th and 2/4th – were serving elsewhere in different theatres of war (the 1/4th in Persia, the 2/4th in Palestine). This confusion was created by the failure of the official records to indicate that Jack had was attached to the 2nd Battalion, The Hampshire Regiment after completing his officer training.

In the spring of 1917, the 2nd Hampshires were serving with 88th Brigade, part of 29th Division, on the Western Front. Jack's Medal Index Card shows him first entering a theatre of war (France) on 8 May 1917. On 6 June 1917 the 2nd Hampshires' war diary recorded that '2Lts DL Whitmarsh & EJA Tunks joined Battn' at Fieffes, about three miles south of the town of Candas, where the battalion was resting after fighting at the Battle of Arras two months earlier.

The Royal Hampshire Regiment's historian, C.T. Atkinson, described the period:

> *The 2nd had spent most of June near Candas, resting and reorganising. Nearly 200 reinforcements joined them soon after arriving there, but many of them were only 'C.2' [men were graded according to their physical fitness – C2 were deemed able to walk five miles and see and hear for ordinary purposes], mainly under-sized Londoners, and their musketry was little better than their physique; other drafts and returns from hospital brought the total reinforcements to 350 ... other ranks were up to 960 by July 1st.*

Initially, Jack was appointed battalion transport officer. During the Great War this appears to have been a means for some new officers to cut their teeth. By July 1917, Jack had joined the 2nd Hampshires' X Company where he would have been put in charge of a platoon (about 50 men). He did serve another spell as transport officer in October, but by December was back with X Company.

Jack first saw action on 16 August 1917 during the Battle of Langemarck, some two weeks after the start of the Third Ypres or Passchendaele campaign (31 July-15 November 1917) in Flanders. Attacking German positions to the north-west of the village of Langemarck, the 2nd Hampshires captured both of their objectives, despite having to cross waterlogged ground – several men fell into shell holes or got stuck in the bog and had to be hauled out with ropes. Soldiers of X Company armed with Mills bombs and hand grenades distinguished themselves by clearing several German blockhouses along a railway line, so it is likely that Jack was in the thick of the action. The battalion lost three officers and 43 men killed and missing in the engagement and a further 150 wounded, but received warm congratulations from 29th Division commander, Major-General Henry de Beauvoir de Lisle for their achievements.

On 9 October, in heavy rain, the 2nd Hampshires were in action again during another successful attack by 88th Brigade, this time along the Roulers railway line near the village of Les Cinq Chemins. C.T. Atkinson's account of the assault illustrates just how much British infantry tactics had improved by this stage of the war. One attack went in behind a 'creeping' artillery barrage:

TUNKS, Edward Joseph Austin

Advancing with two platoons in a front wave and one supporting, the company, well led and skilfully directed by Captain Cuddon, who was well backed up by Sergeants Trethewy and Parker, mastered its objective, despite stubborn opposition. Many Germans were accounted for, a Lewis gunner, Private Gosling, dispersing one party of 30 single-handed ...

The following month saw the 2nd Hampshires in action at the Battle of Cambrai, the battalion's stiffest fighting in the whole of 1917. The battle, which began on 20 November, saw the first massed use of tanks in the war (a total of 476 were thrown into the attack) as the British Third Army broke into the formidable German defensive system known as the Hindenburg Line. The attack achieved complete surprise and at first went well, with the Hampshires involved around the villages of Masnieres and Les Rues Vertes. However, the advance eventually stalled and on 30 November the Germans launched their biggest counter-attack against the British since 1914.

In the desperate fighting that followed, the Hampshires played a major part in blunting the Germans around Marcoing and enabling the British to conduct a comparatively orderly retreat where at one stage it appeared they would be routed. According to C.T. Atkinson, 'the fruits of General de Lisle's training were now reaped; platoons combined "fire and movement" as instructed and helped each other, carrying out the attack as if at practice ...' When the battle ended on 7 December the British had retreated almost to the positions they had started from on 15 November.

After Cambrai, the 2nd Hampshires spent a month out of the line. In January 1918 they returned to the trenches near Passchendaele. The ground here, according to Atkinson, was 'mainly morass, pitted with shell holes full of stinking liquid mud and water ... Of all the sectors any Hampshire battalion held this was perhaps the foulest'.

Unsurprisingly, given these conditions, Jack Tunks fell sick and on 5 February 1918 he was admitted to hospital. He did not return to duty until 28 March. A week earlier, the Germans had launched their Spring Offensive aimed at shattering Allied forces on the Western Front. When the first attack, on the centre and south of the British line, petered out on 5 April, they tried again further north. This second assault targeted British forces on the River Lys in Flanders and lasted from 7 to 29 April. It again proved unsuccessful, but it was to be Jack Tunks's final battle.

The 2nd Hampshires moved to the Lys sector along with the remainder of 88th Brigade on 10 April. They arrived by bus in the town of Bailleul to find it under artillery fire from the advancing Germans and crowded with refugees. Near the village of Steenwerck the battalion dug in along the railway to Armentieres, with Jack's company holding an outpost line. The following day the Hampshires beat off several German attacks, but at a cost of 40 killed and missing. On 13 April, the day of Jack's death, the British position on the Lys around Bailleul began to deteriorate. The 2nd Hampshires' war diary entry for that day states:

Today a warning was issued that a further withdrawal would be carried out owing to the capture of Neuve Eglise by the enemy. During the evening the enemy developed strong attacks against the Regiment on our left and ground was given to the enemy. The position held by the 88th Brigade was therefore becoming very precarious. Orders for withdrawal came through at 8pm by which time the enemy were making progress along the Nieppe-Bailleul road throwing up his white lights to guide the Infantry and nosing forward with light machine guns. At 10pm Companies withdrew in the order Y, Z, W & X, each Company covering its withdrawal by a Lewis Gun. The withdrawal of the Brigade was covered by the Royal Newfoundland and Monmouth Regiments. The Battalion was clear of the position slightly before 2am.

TUNKS, Edward Joseph Austin

Casualties:
Other Ranks
1 Killed
11 Wounded
5 Missing
1 Died of wounds
2Lt EJA Tunks Killed.

Jack Tunks was just 20 years old when he died. He had served on the Western Front for 11 months and been involved in some of the fiercest fighting of the war. On 11 December 1918 probate on his estate was granted to his mother Alice. Jack left effects valued at £132 11s 10d.

Alice Tunks died in Winchester in 1922, aged 48. Joseph Tunks, Jack's father, returned to civilian life in Winchester after the war and remarried in Kensington, west London in 1924. His new wife, Florence Hudson, had been born in 1888. She gave birth to a son, John, on 14 September 1924 by which time she and Joseph were living at 2, Jewry Street, Winchester. A daughter, named Florence after her mother, was born in 1926. The following year the Tunks family moved to 6, St Swithun's Villas, Canon Street, Winchester. Joseph Tunks died in Winchester in 1951, aged 78 and Florence Snr in Wiltshire in 1960 at the age of 60.

Jack Tunks's brother Cyril worked as a chemist's clerk before the war. He joined the Royal Navy in 1916 (service number F37258) and served on the home front until 5 September 1917 when he joined the Royal Flying Corps, which became the Royal Air Force in 1918. Cyril survived the war and in 1926 he married Lillian Hibberd in Winchester. The couple had two children – Michael, born in Winchester in 1928 and David, born in 1932 in Middlesex. Cyril died in Middlesex in 1955, aged 56.

Jack Tunks, his brother and father are all listed in the Winchester War Service Register.

Medals and memorials for Edward Joseph Tunks

2nd Lieutenant Edward Joseph Austin Tunks was entitled to the British War Medal and the Victory Medal. He is buried at Cabaret-Rouge British Cemetery (above), Souchez, Pas de Calais, France (GR. XX. D. 24). He is mentioned on the war memorials at four churches in Winchester - St Matthew's, St Paul's, St Thomas's and St Maurice's.

Researchers - DEREK WHITFIELD and CHERYL DAVIS

VANDELEUR, John Beauclerk

Lieutenant JOHN BEAUCLERK VANDELEUR
1, Romsey Road, Winchester
3rd Battalion, The Leicestershire Regiment
(Attached 3rd Battalion, The Worcestershire Regiment)
Killed in action, Belgium, 7 November 1914

John Beauclerk Vandeleur was born into a family with a strong military tradition on his father's side and aristocratic roots on his mother's. Originally from Holland, the Vandeleurs settled in Kilrush, County Clare, in the 17th Century and became the principal landowners there. One of John's ancestors, Major-General Sir John Ormsby Vandeleur (1763-1849), fought with Wellington at Waterloo and his father served with the Winchester-based Rifle Brigade and the Hampshire Regiment. John also joined the Army and was among the first Winchester men to see action – and die - in the Great War.

John Beauclerk Vandeleur was born in Winchester in 1887, the only son of Colonel John Ormsby Vandeleur and his wife Frederica. Despite his Irish roots, the Colonel had been born in Dorchester, Dorset, in 1840. His own father, also called John, was a Lieutenant-Colonel in the 10th Hussars.

No trace can be found of Lieutenant-Colonel Vandeleur, his wife Alice or baby John Ormsby in the 1841 Census and it may be that they had been posted overseas or were living in Ireland. The couple are also missing from the 1851 Census, but John Ormsby was recorded as a pupil at a school in Worksop, Staffordshire. Presumably, this was a prep school he attended prior to moving on to public school. John Ormsby eventually joined the Army and was commissioned into the Rifle Brigade as an Ensign (the Army rank that became 2nd Lieutenant from 1871) on 4 June 1858, the same year that Winchester became the regiment's HQ. The 1861 Census recorded John Ormsby Vandeleur living at the Rifle Brigade Barracks in Winchester and on 15 November the same year he was promoted to Lieutenant.

In 1870 John Ormsby married Frederica Jane Beauclerk in Christchurch (then in Hampshire). Frederica could trace her ancestry back to Charles II and Nell Gwyn - the couple had a child who later became the 1st Duke of St Albans. Frederica had been born in late 1850, probably at Winchfield House, Winchfield, Hampshire, as this was her address in the 1851 Census compiled just three months later. She was the daughter of Charles Beauclerk who, in 1850, had inherited Winchfield House and the surrounding estate from his father, the Reverend Lord Frederick Beauclerk, a younger son of the 5th Duke of St Albans. Frederica's mother was Penelope Hulke from nearby Yateley.

Charles Beauclerk died in 1867 and Frederica's older brother, Frederick, inherited Winchfield House. (He was to sell the property in 1908 and it still stands today.) Charles's widow, Penelope, then went to live in Christchurch with her other children which explains why Frederica's marriage to John Ormsby Vandeleur took place there.

VANDELEUR, John Beauclerk

Wellington College, Berkshire, where John Beauclerk Vandeleur was a pupil between 1901 and 1904

At the time of the 1871 Census, John Ormsby and Frederica Vandeleur were living at 6, Wellington Terrace, Cheriton, Hythe, in Kent. The following year the couple had their first child, a daughter called Alice Caroline, born in Gravesend. On 3 July 1872, John Ormsby was promoted to Captain, but just four months later, on 13 November, he retired from the Army. Why he did so is not known but it was not to be the end of his connection with the military.

By the second half of the 1870s, the Vandeleurs were living in South Stoneham, now part of Southampton. In 1876 or 1877 Frederica gave birth to a second daughter, Marie, and then a third, Evelyn, in 1878 or 1879. On 5 January 1878 John Ormsby returned to the Army when he was appointed to the 4th Administrative Battalion of the Hampshire Rifle Volunteers with the rank of Major.

The Hampshire Rifle Volunteers had been established in response to the fears of a French invasion in 1859-60 during the reign of Napoleon III. A total of 22 infantry corps and six artillery corps were formed in the county along with a further six infantry corps on the Isle of Wight. These were grouped into four Administrative Battalions with the 4th – John Ormsby's unit – based in Southampton. Some 20 years later, around the time John Ormsby was appointed, these loosely knit administrative battalions of independent local corps were reorganised as battalions of the Hampshire Rifle Volunteers, and in 1885 as Volunteer Battalions of The Hampshire Regiment. Thus, John Ormsby's unit became the 4th Volunteer Battalion, The Hampshire Regiment which in 1908 became part of the Army's Territorial Force.

Men of the Volunteer Battalions were part-time soldiers. As such, John Ormsby would not have received pay, other than for expenses, although given his and Frederica's background it is unlikely that they were hard up. John Ormsby's second Army career progressed steadily – in February 1880 he was promoted to Lieutenant-Colonel and then in April 1886 he was given the rank of Honorary Colonel.

John Ormsby and Frederica Vandeleur and their youngest two children, Marie and Evelyn, have not yet been found in the 1881 Census. However, their eldest daughter, Alice, was living with her grandmother, Penelope Beauclerk, in Hastings, East Sussex. Alice was to leave home permanently in 1896 when she married gentleman farmer Thomas Wodehouse in Knightsbridge, London, after which the couple went to live in Somerset.

By 1887 the Vandeleurs had moved to Winchester and were living at Hyde Abbey House, 23, Hyde Street. The move was almost certainly connected to John Ormsby's duties with the Hampshire Volunteers who by then had been absorbed into the Winchester-based Hampshire Regiment. John Beauclerk Vandeleur was born at Hyde Abbey House on 12 March 1887. Two years later, on 20 May 1889, Frederica gave birth to a fourth daughter, Janetta, in Winchester. In 1897, John Ormsby Vandeleur was made a Companion of the Bath (CB) in Queen Victoria's Diamond Jubilee Honours. He and Frederica also became grandparents the same year when Alice and Thomas Wodehouse had a daughter, Elinor, who was also known as Elison.

VANDELEUR, John Beauclerk

The Vandeleurs' Winchester homes: Hyde Abbey House (above), 7, Clifton Terrace (right) and 1, Romsey Road (below), where the family were living when Britain went to war in August 1914

On 9 June 1900 Colonel John Ormsby Vandeleur died at the Hampshire County Hospital, Winchester, aged 60. The cause of his death is unknown. Less than a year later, according to the 1901 Census, Frederica and her four younger children – including 14-year-old John Beauclerk – had moved from Hyde Abbey House to a new home at 7, Clifton Terrace, Winchester.

John Beauclerk Vandeleur was educated at Winton House Preparatory School, Andover Road, Winchester, under the direction of headmaster Dr E.F. Johns. There is also evidence that in 1901 he was tutored privately, along with two other boys, also possibly from military families, at Rosslyn, Hyde Park Road (now 8, Park Road, but still named Rosslyn House). In September 1901 John Beauclerk started at Wellington College where he joined Lynedoch House. He studied there for four years and was almost certainly a member of the College's Officer Training Corps.

From Wellington, John Beauclerk moved on to Sandhurst for officer training, but thereafter his early Army career becomes difficult to trace. In August 1905 he appears to have joined the 4th Battalion, The Oxford Light Infantry (OLI) which, in 1908, was transferred to the Army's Special Reserve and redesignated the 3rd Battalion. It seems therefore that John Beauclerk, like his father during his time with

VANDELEUR, John Beauclerk

the Hampshire Volunteers, was a part-time soldier which may have allowed him to continue living in Winchester, at least for some of the time.

It is known that John Beauclerk became involved in the fledgling Boy Scout movement there, working with Lieutenant Bramwell Withers of the Hampshire Regiment. In 1907 Lieutenant-General Robert Baden Powell had organised a Boy Scout Camp at Brownsea Island, Dorset, and shortly afterwards Withers formed Britain's first Boy Scout troop - known as 'Withers' Own' – in the city. Other than a suggestion that John Beauclerk may have been involved with the fraternal organisation the Royal Antediluvian Order of Buffaloes, nothing more is known of his social interests.

Winton House Preparatory School, Andover Road, Winchester, where John Beauclerk Vandeleur received his early education. The building has been demolished and Winton Close is on its site. *(Photo: Britain from Above)*

In April 1910 John Beauclerk joined the 2nd Battalion, The Durham Light Infantry as a 2nd Lieutenant, his first taste of life in the Regular Army. It appears to have been an experience he did not enjoy because in 1912, after two years with the battalion based in Colchester, he left.

Life was changing, too, for John Beauclerk's mother Frederica. The 1911 Census reveals that she and her daughters Marie, Evelyn and Janetta, had moved the short distance from Clifton Terrace to 1, Romsey Road (just down from the St James Tavern). With ten rooms, the Vandeleurs' new home was another large property, and the family employed a live-in servant. Alice, the eldest daughter, is believed to have moved to the United States some years earlier with her husband Thomas and daughter Elinor.

In October 1913, John Beauclerk Vandeleur was gazetted into the 3rd (Reserve) Battalion, The Leicestershire Regiment with the rank of Lieutenant. He was still with the battalion when Britain went to war in August 1914, but shortly afterwards he was attached to the 3rd Battalion, The Worcestershire Regiment and sent to the Western Front on active service.

The exact date that John joined the 3rd Worcesters is unknown – he was definitely not with the battalion when it landed in France on 16 August. Possibly it was after the Battle of Le Cateau (26 August) - during which the Worcesters, fighting as part of 7th Brigade in 3rd Division, suffered several officer casualties when a German shell hit the battalion HQ – or following the Battle of the Aisne (13-28 September). As the Allied and German armies then tried to outflank each other in a series of manoeuvres that became known as the 'Race to the Sea', the Worcesters were sent north to the Lys Valley where they fought at the Battle of La Bassée (10 October-2 November), losing a further 300 men killed or wounded, including 18 officers. Given that several sources state that John served in Flanders AND France, and

Right: Lieutenant Bramwell Withers, of the Hampshire Regiment, who set up Britain's first Boy Scout troop in Winchester. John Beauclerk Vandeleur helped him in his pioneering work

330

VANDELEUR, John Beauclerk

that the Worcesters' next fought in Flanders, it is likely that he had linked up with the battalion by La Bassée at the latest.

On 1 November 1914 the 3rd Worcesters were detached from 7th Brigade and reassigned to 4th Division. The 4th Division had earlier captured the town of Armentieres and Ploegsteert Wood (nicknamed Plugstreet by the British), just across the Belgian border, which it was having difficulty holding. At dusk on 2 November, the Worcesters moved forward to the front line just beyond the eastern edge of Ploegsteert Wood.

What followed for John Beauclerk and the men of the 3rd Worcesters is described, with typical military understatement, as four days of 'great discomfort' by Captain H. Sacke in his regimental history of the Great War. In fact, what the Worcesters endured was truly horrific. Cramped into shallow, waterlogged trenches, they were overlooked by the Messines Ridge from where German observers directed murderous artillery fire down on them. Matters eventually came to a head on 7 November, the events of which were vividly described by Captain Sacke:

> *In the darkness between 3 and 4am next morning (7 November) a very heavy shellfire was opened on the British line east of Ploegsteert Wood. For an hour shells crashed down on the Battalion's line. Then about 5am masses of German infantry came plunging through the fog. Such of the front-line defenders as had survived the bombardment manned their smashed parapets and fired swiftly into the advancing hordes; and on the left of the Battalion line the attack was stopped and held. But the centre and left of the Battalion's trenches had been practically obliterated by the bombardment, and there the German attack flooded over the defences of [the battalion's] 'C' Company. Most of the defenders were killed, but a few men managed to fight their way out in the fog and were able to get back to the wood behind in time to warn the reserve companies and Battalion Headquarters. A counter-attack was organised at once to retake the lost trenches. The counter-attack met the enemy inside the edge of the wood and a confused and desperate struggle ensued.*
>
> *Reinforcements were brought up ... but the lost trenches could not be regained. All through the night of November 7th/8th the remnants of the 3rd Worcestershire hung on to their position, and not until evening of the 8th was the Battalion finally relieved. The losses had been very heavy – over two hundred in all, including six officers [four killed and two wounded].*

Sacke records that Lieutenant John Beauclerk Vandeleur, aged 27, was one of the officers killed in Ploegsteert Wood. His body was never found. News of John Beauclerk's death quickly reached Winchester where the Hampshire Chronicle reported:

> *To the list of honoured dead more directly associated with Winchester has to be added the name of Lieut. John Beauclerk Vandeleur, of the 3rd Leicestershire Regiment, killed in action about November 10th [sic]. Mr J.B. Vandeleur, whose age was 27, was the only son of the late Col. J.O. Vandeleur CB of Ballinacourty, Castle Connell, Co. Limerick, and Mrs J.O. Vandeleur of 1, Romsey Road, Winchester. He was educated at Mr E.F. Johns', Winton House, and Wellington College, Berks. He interested himself in 1910 with Mr Withers at the Hampshire Depot in raising the Winchester Boy Scouts. Mr J.B. Vandeleur joined the 1st Leicestershire Regiment from the Special Reserve Battalion of the Regiment. He was gazetted to the Durham Light Infantry in 1910 and served with the 2nd Battalion at Colchester, leaving it two years ago for service in the old Leicestershire Militia.*

The mention in the Chronicle report of the 1st Leicestershire Regiment is interesting as no record has been found to date of John serving with that battalion. However, it is possible that the information is incorrect – the newspaper was dealing with dozens of similar reports for its editions at the time involving many different military units and mistakes were far from unknown.

In his will John left effects valued at £3,578 15s 5d (worth some £370,000 in 2020), with his sisters Marie and Evelyn acting as executors. In March 1916 Marie married Captain James Balfour in Colinton,

VANDELEUR, John Beauclerk

near Edinburgh. Captain Balfour, who also came from a military background, served in the 1st Battalion, The Highland Light Infantry and saw action on the Western Front and then in Mesopotamia (modern Iraq). He was killed in action there on 11 January 1917 and was buried at Kut-al-Amara, scene of the infamous siege. He and Marie had been married for just ten months and are unlikely to have had children. No further trace has been found of Marie until her death, aged about 76, on 15 August 1953. Her address then was 19A, Ashley Place, Westminster, London, and she is not thought to have remarried.

John Beauclerk's mother Frederica remained living at 1, Romsey Road until her death in 1926 at the age of 75. Her daughter Evelyn, who never married, was named as the householder for the property in the 1927 Kelly's Directory, but there is no further mention of any Vandeleur living in Winchester after that date. Nor has any trace been found of Evelyn in inter-war electoral records. At some point she moved to Ireland to live at West View, Greystones, County Wicklow. She died there in 1958, aged 79.

No further information about Alice Wodehouse has yet been found. In 1933 her daughter Elinor sailed from Southampton to South Africa to be a missionary. By 1939 she had returned to England and was working as a social worker in Devon. Elinor died in Oxford in October 1977, aged nearly 80. She appears to have never married.

Janetta Vandeleur, John's younger sister, married Winchester-born Algernon Drummond – of the Drummond Bank family - in Kensington, west London, in 1917. Algernon's father, also called Algernon, had been a Captain in the Rifle Brigade before leaving to work for the family bank. (Algernon Snr continued to maintain a Winchester connection and in the 1915 Warren's Directory was listed as the householder of Preston House, 26, Colebrook Street. After his death in 1932 his widow continued to live at the property with two of their daughters until at least 1939.)

Algernon Drummond Jnr also worked in banking, but during the Great War he served as a Chief Petty Officer in the Royal Navy Volunteer Reserve. The 1939 Register listed Janetta and Algernon Jnr living in Godstone, Surrey, with him working as a bank accountant and part-time volunteer ARP warden. The couple had four children and later moved to Milford on Sea, Hampshire. Janetta Drummond died at Birchy Hill Nursing Home, Sway, Hampshire, on 7 January 1958, aged 68.

Medals and memorials for John Beauclerk Vandeleur

Lieutenant John Beauclerk Vandeleur was entitled to the 1914 Star, the Victory Medal and the British War Medal. He has no known grave but is commemorated on the Ypres (Menin Gate) Memorial, Ypres (Ieper), West Flanders, Belgium - see above. (CMWG has two panel references - Panel 33/Y and Panel XXXIV). In Winchester, John's name is on the memorials at St Matthew's and St Paul's churches, Winchester. He also appears on two more Great War church memorials in the city – those at St Thomas's, Southgate Street, and Holy Trinity, North Walls. The fact that he appears on four memorials perhaps reflects which churches members of the Vandeleur family attended. John is also named on Wellington College's Roll of Honour.

Researchers: GERALDINE BUCHANAN, DEREK WHITFIELD, CHERYL DAVIS and JOSEPHINE COLEMAN

VANDELEUR, John Beauclerk

Additional sources

- Sacke, Captain FitzM. H. *The Worcestershire Regiment in the Great War, Vol I.* (G.T. Cheshire & Sons Ltd, Kidderminster, 1928. Reprinted 2002 by Naval & Military Press).
- Boyle, Colonel Gerald Edmund. *The Rifle Brigade Century: An Alphabetical List of the Officers of The Rifle Brigade, 1800-1905* (William Clowes & Sons Ltd, London, 1905). See pp.183-184. (On Forces War Records).
- British Army, Bond of Sacrifice: *Officers Died in the Great War 1914-1916*, pp. 415-6. (On findmypast.co.uk

VOKES, Basil

2nd Lieutenant BASIL VOKES
41, Western Road, Winchester (12, Cheriton Road today)
1/4th Battalion, Oxfordshire & Buckinghamshire Light Infantry
Previously Corporal 4861, 28th Battalion, The London Regiment (Artists Rifles)
Killed in action, France, 15 February 1917

Basil Vokes was the son of stonemason James Vokes whose business on the Stockbridge Road was once a familiar landmark in Fulflood. Basil attended the Winchester Diocesan Training College for Teachers and later worked in Surrey. During the Great War, he enlisted with the famous Artists Rifles before joining the Oxfordshire & Buckinghamshire Light Infantry. He was killed on the Western Front in an artillery bombardment in 1917.

Basil, the second son of James and Lavinia Vokes, was born in Winchester on 4 July 1883 and baptised on the 29th at St Matthew's Church, Weeke. His father had been born in Winchester in 1851. Basil's paternal grandfather was also called James but attempts to trace him have so far proved unsuccessful, mainly because Vokes is such a common name in Hampshire.

Basil's mother was born Lavinia Draper in Chale, on the Isle of Wight, in 1854. She was the fourth of six children born to labourer Mark Draper and his wife Jane (née White). At the age of 16, Lavinia became a live-in housemaid to a landowner and former Captain in the Hampshire Militia at 4, City Road, Winchester. This, presumably, was when she met James Vokes.

James and Lavinia married in Chale on 8 January 1879. They moved to the newly-built 1, Greenhill Road in Fulflood where their first son, Harold, was born the following year.

In the 1881 Census James was recorded as a 'Stonemason Journeyman' – meaning that he was learning his trade. Also living in the house was a visitor, Claude de Neville, an 'artist in fine arts' who is believed to have been in Winchester to visit his fiancée Hannah Taylor. The couple went on to marry in Winchester later that year.

By the 1891 Census the Vokes's house had been renumbered as 9, Greenhill Road (today it is No. 17). Basil's father was a fully qualified stonemason while Basil himself and brother Harold were both at school. Although it is not known which primary school they attended, the National Schools Admissions Register shows

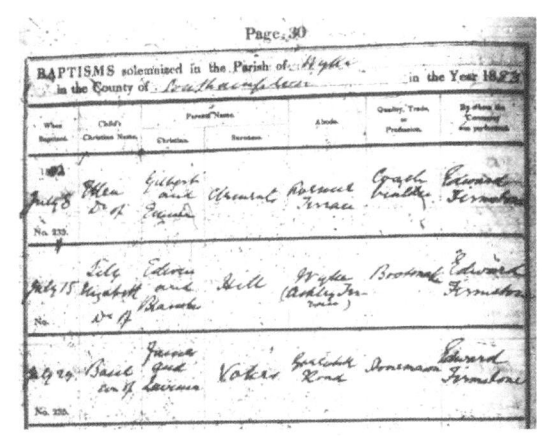

Basil Vokes's baptism record

VOKES, Basil

Basil was admitted to St Thomas National Church of England Boys' School in 1893. Years later, he would return there as a trainee teacher.

By 1901 the Vokes family were living at 3, Clifton Terrace, Winchester, a spacious home spread over five floors. Also living in the house were Lavinia's widowed mother and Emily Kervell, a 21-year-old Londoner who was employed as a general domestic servant. Harold, aged 25, had qualified as a Post Office clerk and Basil was a pupil-teacher at St Thomas School.

FULFLOOD MONUMENTAL WORKS.

HAVING taken over the above-named Premises,

MESSRS. VOKES & BECK

Beg to announce that they are prepared to execute all manner of STONE-WORK at moderate prices.

Estimates and Designs

Supplied for HEADSTONES, TOMBS, &c., in Granite, Marble, or Stone.

The advertisement in the Hampshire Chronicle of 6 September 1902 for stonemason James Vokes's new business

Basil's position as a pupil-teacher meant that he had shown promise in class and had been invited by his school to stay on beyond the normal leaving date. Pupil-teachers had to be at least 15 years old and be accepted by an Inspectorate. They also had to pass a medical and a written examination in reading and recitation, English, history, geography, arithmetic, algebra, Euclidean geometry and teaching.

Pupil-teachers were not permitted to work more than five hours a day and 20 hours in a week. They were examined annually by the Inspectorate and at the end of their period of service they usually sat a scholarship examination, with a 1st or 2nd class pass entitling the pupil to enter teacher training college. Basil duly passed the exam and in 1902, aged 19, he enrolled at Winchester Diocesan Training College, less than half a mile from his home in Clifton Terrace.

The year 1902 was also a landmark one for Basil's father. An advertisement in the Hampshire Chronicle of 6 September 1902 reveals that James Vokes had gone into business as a stonemason in Fulflood. The firm, Vokes & Beck, carried out all types of stonework, but the advertisement makes special mention of tombs and headstones. Over the following century, Vokes & Beck would go on to become part of the fabric of life in Fulflood. The firm still operates today, but from premises in Kings Worthy.

As his father ventured into business, Basil Vokes began his three years of teacher training. Part of this involved visiting local schools and the college magazine of the period features an article written by Basil about his experiences at Mount Pleasant School, an exceptionally large primary in Newtown, Southampton. Basil also seems to have been involved in college sporting events – especially football and cricket – although usually as referee or umpire.

Among Basil's contemporaries at teacher training college was Andrew Bogie who would later live in Winchester in St Paul's Terrace (St Paul's Hill today) and also become a master at St Thomas School. During the Great War he served with the 1/4th Battalion, The Hampshire Regiment and died after being captured by the Turks following the siege of Kut-al-Amara. Andrew is listed on the Fulflood and Weeke memorials and his biography is on pp. 37.

It is possible that Basil, like Andrew Bogie, joined the college's Volunteer Company, part of the Winchester-based Hampshire Regiment. In 1908, the Volunteer Company was transformed into 'B' Company of the 4th Territorial Battalion, The Hampshire Regiment.

In 1905 Basil took up his first teaching position at St James's School, Weybridge, Surrey. However, the excitement of beginning his career would have been tempered by the news of his brother Harold's death

VOKES, Basil

at the age of just 25. Three years later tragedy struck again when his mother Lavinia died at the age of 54 while visiting family in Chertsey, Surrey.

Besides his teaching duties, Basil enjoyed a busy social life in Weybridge. He sang with Weybridge Choral Society, joined the Freemasons, was elected secretary of the local bowling club and became Secretary of Weybridge Football Club and Honorary Secretary of the Emly Deanery Schools Football League. He also became an NCO in the local Volunteer Company (later reorganised into the Territorial Force).

Basil Vokes, back row, right (in cap), with the Winchester Diocesan Training College cricket team *(Photo: Winchester Training College: Roll Call of the Fallen)*

Basil lodged with a Mrs Sumner at Fieldview, Springfield Meadow, until her death in 1911. He then boarded at 11, Minorca Road with Ellen Huband, headmistress of St James's Girls' School.

Back in Winchester, James Vokes had moved to 41, Western Road where his niece, 31-year-old Bertha Macklin, was the live-in housekeeper. Bertha was the daughter of Arthur Macklin and his wife Ellen, the sister of Lavinia Vokes. In the census James described himself as a 'General Monumental and Stonemason'. Two years later, however, James died in Winchester, aged 61. His business partner, Mr Beck, continued to run the firm.

With his father's death, Basil Vokes no longer had any living immediate relatives, although he appears to have remained close to the Macklin family. Intriguingly, the 1914 Warren's Winchester Directory lists a 'Mrs Vokes' living at 41, Western Road. The identity of this person is a mystery as neither Basil nor Harold married and James Vokes did not remarry. It is possible, however, that Bertha Macklin titled herself Mrs Vokes to try to retain her lodgings.

Basil continued to teach at St James's School after the Great War had started. Indeed, he waited for more than a year before enlisting in St Pancras, London, with the 28th (County of London) Battalion, The London Regiment (Artists Rifles) on 1 November 1915.

The Artists Rifles had been founded in 1860 by a group of painters, sculptors, architects, poets and actors who feared a possible French invasion of Britain. Early members included the pre-Raphaelites as well as William Morris and the poet Algernon Swinburne. During the early part of the Great War, artists such as Paul and John Nash, the poets Wilfred Owen and Edward Thomas and the playwright Noel Coward joined the Artists Rifles which, because of the calibre of its recruits, produced more than 10,000 officers for service in other regiments between 1914 and 1918.

Basil's Army medical report reveals that he was 6ft tall, weighed 11 stone and had a 36in chest. He was promoted to Lance-Corporal on 24 November 1915 (probably because of his previous military experience) and then to Corporal on 24 March 1916. His movements over the next three months are uncertain, but he almost certainly did his officer training at Hare Hall Camp in Romford, Essex, where

VOKES, Basil

the Artists Rifles had their own Officer Training Corps (OTC). Here, he may have met Wilfred Owen who was completing his training around the same time.

In the 13 September 1916 edition of The London Gazette – the publication which recorded all commissioned officers' postings and changes of regiment – there is a notice stating that Basil has been transferred from the Artists' Rifles OTC to the Oxfordshire & Buckinghamshire Light Infantry (OBLI). Both were effective from 5 September.

Lance-Corpl. Basil Vokes, one of the teachers at St. James's School, who joined the Artists Rifles, was presented on leaving Weybridge with a wrist watch, case of brushes, razor, etc., from the members of the Weybridge Bowling Club, of which club he was secretary for a number of years.

The Surrey Advertiser of 8 January 1916 reports how St James's School marked Basil Vokes's departure for the war

Basil joined the 1/4th Battalion, OBLI (The Lightbobs as the regiment was known) on the Somme, near Courcelette, as the British offensive there was ending. He was assigned to 'C' Company and spent November and December 1916 in and out of the front line. Casualties were light by Great war standards, but the bitter winter of 1916-17 took a heavy toll on soldiers, with many suffering illness and frostbite.

Basil's battalion spent January 1917 training at different camps, with route marches between. By 7 February, the 1/4th OBLI were back on the Somme at Herbecourt, ten miles south-east of Courcelette, and two days later they moved into the front line there.

The battalion's war diary records how the men came under German artillery fire over the following days, with 'C' Company's positions bearing the brunt of the bombardments. The diary entry for 15 February 1917, the day Basil was killed, reads:

> *Brigade Support 1500 yards east of Flaucourt. 9.30am Several hostile aeroplanes over, which were 'strafed' by our Lewis gun. 10.15am Shelling in neighbourhood of Battalion HQ commenced. This continued, without cessation, till 1pm, being particularly fierce for about the first three-quarters of an hour. Several hundred shells were fired ... Several direct hits scored on dugouts occupied by Battalion HQ and C Company, also on a dump of French bombs on the road close by. Casualties: Killed 2Lt B. Vokes from a shell which burst just outside the entrance to C Company's HQ and 1 OR [Other Rank].*

In 1924, when Basil's body was exhumed for reburial, he was found to have suffered extensive shrapnel wounds to the upper part of his body.

Basil Vokes was 33 years old when he died. Although he was living in Weybridge when he enlisted, this study has chosen to give his address as 41, Western Road, Winchester, in recognition of the fact that his father was living there until 1913 and because of the Vokes family's close ties to Fulflood. His name is not listed in the Winchester War Service Register.

Right: 12, Cheriton Road, Winchester – this was 41, Western Road when Basil Vokes's father lived in the house. Although Basil lived and worked in Surrey, he would have visited his father here

VOKES, Basil

Medals and memorials for Basil Vokes

2nd Lieutenant Basil Vokes was entitled to the British War Medal and the Victory Medal. He was buried at Hem Farm Military Cemetery (above), Hem-Monacu, Somme, France. (GR. I. L. 6). Basil's name appears on the memorials at St Matthew's and St Paul's churches, the St Thomas School Memorial, now held at Kings School, Winchester, and the King Alfred's College Memorial, Winchester.

Researchers – DEREK WHITFIELD, CHERYL DAVIS and STEVE JARVIS

Additional sources

- We are grateful to the group that produced the website, Winchester Training College: Roll Call of the Fallen 1914-18 (https://wtcfallen.com/training-college/) for their assistance in producing this biography and for kindly allowing us to use their photographs.

WAKE, Frederick William

Acting Sergeant FREDERICK WILLIAM WAKE
64, Fairfield Road, Winchester
Service number 307105. 2/7th Battalion, The Hampshire Regiment
Died, Mesopotamia, 19 August 1919

Frederick William Wake was born in July 1885 in Medstead, near Alton, the youngest of four sons of Henry and Anne Wake. Frederick served in Mesopotamia (modern Iraq) and survived the Great War, only to die there in mysterious circumstances nine months later.

Frederick came from a prosperous background. His father, the son of Richard and Jane Wake, was born in Medstead in around 1818 and he went on to become a local farmer and landowner. William's mother Anne was Henry's second wife. His first, Harriett, had been ten years older while Anne was 23 years younger.

Henry appears not to have had any children with Harriett who died sometime between 1861 and 1871. In 1872 Henry married Anne (née Hewett), then a 31-year-old ladies' maid, in London. Anne had been born in Odiham, near Basingstoke and was the daughter of Thomas Hewett, a 'beer retailer' (possibly a publican), and his wife, Mary.

By 1881 Henry and Anne were living at Trinity House, Medstead, with their two elder sons, Henry Jnr, who was born in 1879, and George who arrived two years later. A third son, John, was born in 1883 and then Frederick in 1885. Nothing is known about where Frederick and his brothers were educated.

The family were still living at Trinity House in 1891, the year that Henry Wake died. Probate records show that Henry – who is described as a 'gentleman' in the records - left effects worth £2,3855 11s to his wife. This was a considerable sum for the time and may not have included any land or property that he owned.

By 1901 Anne Wake and her sons had moved to Towngate Farm, Medstead. Ten years later Henry Jnr had married, and he and his brother George were running Towngate Farm. George would go on to marry Marjorie Mallinson in 1916. Meanwhile, Frederick and brother John were working as clerks for Hampshire County Council, presumably in Winchester. When John married Florence Smith in 1914 the couple moved to the city, possibly with Frederick. By 1915 they were living at 64, Fairfield Road which is the address given for Frederick in the Winchester War Service Register.

In 1916 Frederick enlisted with the Hampshire Regiment. It is unclear whether he had volunteered for military service - perhaps under the Derby Scheme at the end of 1915 - or was one of the first men to be conscripted. He was assigned to the 2/7th Battalion which had been raised in Bournemouth in the opening weeks of the war before being sent to Secunderabad, in central southern India, early in 1915.

64, Fairfield Road, Winchester – Frederick Wake's address in the Winchester War Service Register

It is possible that Frederick completed some basic training in England before being sent out to Jabalpur in central India – to where the 2/7th Battalion had moved in March 1916 – but it is more likely that he

WAKE, Frederick William

was sent directly to the sub-continent on joining up. In that case he was in India for about a year before transferring to Mesopotamia with his battalion in the autumn of 1917. The 2/7th Hampshires had originally been expected to move to Egypt, but their destination was postponed and then changed. On 5 September 1917, a total of 23 officers and 859 other ranks, including Frederick Wake, boarded a troop ship at Bombay for the six-day voyage to Basra. From there the battalion was sent on by river and then train to the town of Azizieh.

Even for soldiers used to the heat and privations of India, Azizieh proved a miserable posting. The town stood amid flat countryside covered with liquorice scrub and disease was rife. Within weeks, the battalion's Commanding Officer had died of heart failure and 144 men were sick in hospital. Nevertheless, the battalion was kept busy training and providing work parties as well as troops for an Azizieh Mobile Column.

However, the 2/7th Hampshires saw little in the way of fighting. In January 1918 they moved to the town of Amara and remained there until the autumn. Few incidents occurred and the men busied themselves mainly with training and working on the town's defences. At the end of September, the battalion moved once more to the Jabal Hamrin mountain range (in the north-east of modern Iraq) where it was employed on road building until the end of the war a few weeks later.

Mystery surrounds both Frederick Wake's death and his rank when he died. The official records variously list him as Sergeant, Acting Sergeant and Acting Corporal. This biography has opted to follow the Winchester War Service Register's designation of Acting Sergeant. The fact that he reached the rank in such a comparatively short time indicates that Frederick excelled as a soldier.

As for the date and place of his death, this is generally agreed to have been at Basra on 19 August 1919. The 2/7th Hampshires, however, had been demobilised and returned to England in February, some six months earlier. One possible explanation is that Frederick was sick at the time of the battalion's demobilisation and remained in hospital in Basra until his death. Interestingly, Frederick is listed on the 1919 Electoral Register, which was obviously compiled before he died. His address is given as Towngate Farm, Medstead.

It is not known whether any of the other Wake brothers served in the Great War. As farmers, Henry and George may have been exempted from military service. John almost certainly would not, but no trace can be found of a military record. John remained in Winchester after the war and by 1930 was living at 27, Cranworth Road. Nine years later, and by then an education officer for Hampshire County Council, he and his wife Florence had moved to 2, Bereweeke Close. John died in Bournemouth in 1957, aged 74. Frederick's other brothers both died in Medstead, Henry in 1966, aged 87, and George in 1945 at the age of 64. Anne Wake, Frederick Wake's mother, died at Medstead in 1926, aged 75.

Medals and memorials for Frederick William Wake

Acting Sergeant Fredrick William Wake was entitled to the British War Medal and the Victory Medal. He is buried at Basra War Cemetery, Iraq, (GR. II. E. 11) and is mentioned on the memorials at St Matthew's and St Paul's churches, Winchester. His name also appears on the memorial at St Andrew's Church, Medstead (right), and on the commemorative plaque to Hampshire County Council employees who gave their lives in the Great War. This is situated on the wall just inside the main door to the authority's Castle Hill HQ in Winchester.

Researcher – DEREK WHITFIELD

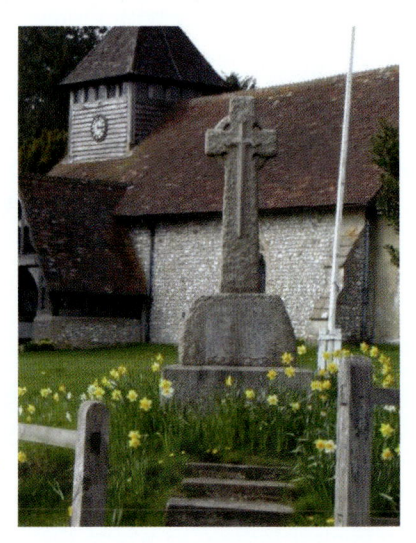

WAND-TETLEY, Clarence Ernest

Lieutenant Clarence Ernest Wand-Tetley
The Lodge, Bereweeke Road, Winchester (no longer stands)
9th (Service) Battalion, The Lancashire Fusiliers
Killed in action, Gallipoli, 21 August 1915

Clarence Ernest Wand was born on 22 July 1889, the eldest child of Ernest Wand, a commercial traveller and his wife Emily. He acquired the surname Wand-Tetley after his parents divorced and Emily married into the wealthy Tetley tea family. Clarence had only superficial links to Winchester – his mother and stepfather moved to Weeke only in 1915, the year of his death at Gallipoli. A talented sportsman, Clarence was an Oxford hockey Half Blue and played rugby for Harlequins.

Clarence Wand's father Ernest was born in Grantham, Lincolnshire, in October 1865. Ernest's father, Charles (1821-1887), worked as a butcher in Grantham. At the age of 15, Ernest Wand was an apprentice printer in the town, but by 1887 he had become a commercial traveller based in London. Clarence's mother had been born Emily Jane Lawes Harrison in Marlborough, Wiltshire, on 8 June 1864 but by the mid-1880s she and her family had moved to Paignton, Devon, where her father, Thomas, owned and ran the Esplanade Hotel.

Ernest Wand may have met Emily while travelling in the West Country on business. The couple married on 6 October 1888 at St John's Church in Paignton and Ernest's address on the marriage certificate was given as 11, Burton Crescent, St Pancras, London. The newlyweds settled down to married life in Paignton. After Clarence's birth there in 1889, Emily and Ernest had another son, Thomas, in 1890 followed by a daughter, Winifred, in 1894 and finally a third son, Joseph, in 1898.

By 1891 Thomas Harrison had handed over the running of the Esplanade Hotel to Ernest Wand. That year's census also revealed that Emily was helping with the book-keeping. The Esplanade, one of the two principal hotels in the town at the time, was also home for the Wand family. The building, minus its central tower, still stands and is trading as The Inn on the Green, with self-catering apartments.

The Wand family's circumstances had changed significantly by 1901. That year's census revealed that Emily was proprietor of the hotel; there was no mention of Ernest Wand in connection with the family – indeed, to date, no trace has been found of him in the census. Emily was living at the hotel with her two younger children while her two elder sons, Clarence, aged 11, and ten-year-old Thomas were boarders at Newton Abbot School, near Bovey Tracey, Devon, which was run by a clergyman/schoolmaster.

In 1903 Ernest and Emily Wand divorced - an unusual and expensive occurrence in those days – and the Esplanade Hotel was sold. Around the same time, Clarence and Thomas Wand left Newton Abbot School and were sent to Eastbourne College in Sussex. The rest of the family also moved to Eastbourne

WAND-TETLEY, Clarence Ernest

because from 1907-08 Clarence and Thomas were home boarders. Both brothers excelled at sport and Clarence won college colours for rugby.

At some stage, Emily met Joseph Tetley, the man who would become her second husband. Joseph had been born in Huddersfield, Yorkshire, in around 1850 and was the son of one of the founders of the Tetley tea company. He entered the family business in 1871 and, on the death of his father in 1889,

The Esplanade Hotel in Paignton, Devon, where Clarence Wand spent his childhood. It still as operates today as The Inn on the Green

took over the running of the company. The 1901 Census showed Joseph, then aged 51, living in Parrock Wood, Hartfield, Sussex. His nephew, William, who later inherited the tea business, was also living in the house, but Joseph's wife, Florence, whom he had married in 1878, was residing in a hotel in Brighton. This may have been for health reasons because on 9 January 1909 she died after a long illness.

Within three months Emily and Joseph were married in Eastbourne. This was remarkably quick: according to the social convention of the time, a spouse would normally wait at least a year before remarrying. The reason for the haste is not known; it does not appear to have been because Emily was pregnant as she was 46 at the time and there is no record of her having any more children.

The previous year, 1908, Clarence Wand had gone up to Oriel College, Oxford, where his sporting prowess again came to the fore. Clarence gained a hockey Half Blue and also played rugby at university as well as for Harlequins between 1909 and 1912.

By 1911 Joseph and Emily Tetley were living at Wildwood, Clay Hill, near Enfield, Middlesex, with the two youngest Wand-Tetley siblings. Clarence, although still at Oxford, was also at the house on the night of that year's census. Joseph and Emily's first recorded link with Winchester was in the 1915 Warren's Directory when they were listed living at The Lodge, Bereweeke Road.

This property, which no longer stands, was situated close to the southern corner of Bereweeke Road and Andover Road. It was later incorporated into Peter Symonds School and renamed Varley after the first headmaster. It appears that between 1918 and 1919 the Tetleys were not actually living at The Lodge, as that is the address in Warren's for George and Emily Dennistoun, the parents of James Dennistoun, whose name is also on the parish war memorials (his biography is on pp. 73). There may have been a connection between the Tetley and Dennistoun families as both gave The Lodge as the address in the Winchester War Service Register for their sons who fought between 1914-18.

It is not known what Clarence did between leaving Oxford in 1912 and the outbreak of the Great War but on 22 August 1914 he enlisted in the Army before being commissioned into the 9th (Service) Battalion, The Lancashire Fusiliers as a 2nd Lieutenant. He was made a temporary Lieutenant in December the same year. The 9th Lancashire Fusiliers, one of the first battalions raised for Kitchener's New Armies, were formed in Bury on 31 August 1914 and came under orders of 34th Brigade in 11th (Northern) Division. After initial training at the regimental depots, the infantry moved to Belton Park, near Grantham, and then, in April 1915, to Witley Camp, near Godalming, Surrey, for final training. At the end of July, the battalion sailed from Liverpool for Gallipoli, stopping at Alexandria in Egypt and the eastern Mediterranean island of Imbros on the way.

WAND-TETLEY, Clarence Ernest

Harlequins (in the plain tops) take on Richmond on 2 October 1909 in the first ever match at Twickenham Stadium. It is possible that Clarence Wand represented Harlequins in the game

Left: Clarence in his Eastbourne College rugby kit and, below left, his brother Thomas who was a POW in Germany for much of the war and who went on to enjoy a distinguished Army career

Right: A soldier's poem recalls the bloody events of 6 August 1915 when 11th Division landed at Suvla Bay on the Gallipoli Peninsula

"Suvla Bay" By One of the Boys.

You may talk of Balaclava,
And of Trafalgar Bay,
But what of the Eleventh Division
Who landed at Suvla Bay.
They were part of Kitchener's Army
Some of them left children and wives
But they fought for England's freedom.
Yes, fought for their very lives.
'Twas on the Sixth of August 1915,
When they made that terrible dash
And the Turks along the hill-side
Our boats were trying to smash.
The order came "fix bayonets,"
As out of the boats we got,
Every man there was a hero,
Who was facing the Turkish shot
Funnels of our ships got smashed
While the sea in some places was red
But we fought our way through the ocean;
To the beach that was covered with dead.
Creeping at last up the hill side
While shot and shell fell all around
We made a last desperate effort
And charged over the Turkish ground.
The Turks at last gave it up
When they saw the bayonets play
For they turned their backs on the British.
And retired from Suvla Bay

There were Lincolns, Dorsets and Staffs,
And Notts and Derbys too,
The Border regiment was there
The rough and ready crew.
Then we got the Manchesters,
With Lancashire Fusiliers by their side,
The boys of good old Lancashire
Who will fill your hearts with pride.
The Yorks, West Yorks and East Yorks.
The Yorks and Lanks as well.
Who fought for good old Yorkshire,
Were among the boys who fell.
The fighting Fifth were there,
Northumberland lads you know
While the Duke of Wellington's as well
Were keeping back the foe.
And far away on the hill side,
Lying beneath the clay,
Are some of the lads who died,
While trying to win the day.
So remember the Eleventh Division,
Who are all your brothers you know
How they fought and died heroes
While going to face the foe.

Price 2d. Each.
(Disabled Soldier.)

Members of the public watch the 9th Lancashire Fusiliers in training in December 1914 before the battalion's posting to Gallipoli the following year

WAND-TETLEY, Clarence Ernest

The Gallipoli campaign took place on Turkey's Gallipoli peninsula between 17 February 1915 and 9 January 1916. Among its principal architects was Britain's First Lord of the Admiralty Winston Churchill who argued that an operation against the Ottoman Turks would allow Britain to make full use of its powerful Navy and avoid the bloody stalemate of the Western Front. The Ottoman Empire was widely regarded to be crumbling and the initial plan was for the British and French fleets to take control of the Dardanelles Straits that provided a supply route to Russia. When this failed an alternative plan was hatched for an amphibious landing on the Gallipoli peninsula to capture the Ottoman capital of Constantinople and knock Turkey out of the war.

The amphibious attacks, launched by the Allied Mediterranean Expeditionary Force under General Sir Ian Hamilton, began on 25 April 1915 but quickly bogged down in the face of unexpectedly strong Turkish resistance. Further attacks in June also faltered before Hamilton made a final attempt to break the deadlock on the night of 6 August when British troops, including Lieutenant Clarence Wand-Tetley, landed at Suvla Bay at the start of a new offensive known as the Battle of Sari Bair.

The assault by 34th Brigade, including 9th Lancashire Fusiliers, went awry from the start. The destroyers conveying the brigade anchored 1,000 yards from their intended position and two lighters ran aground on reefs. Consequently, the 9th Lancashire Fusiliers had to wade ashore in the darkness up to their necks in water. Once on dry land they were pinned down by sniper fire and shelling. Their Commanding Officer was shot in the head around dawn and the battalion lost another six officers killed and seven wounded.

The Suvla Bay landings descended into chaos, due largely to the lethargic leadership of Lieutenant-General Sir Frederick Stopford, commander of IX Corps (of which 11th Division was a part). Stopford proved reluctant to order his troops to seize the high ground overlooking the bay and was eventually sacked. On 21 August his temporary replacement, Major-General Beauvoir De Lisle, ordered a fresh attack by 11th Division on the W Hills surrounding Suvla Bay. However, this also collapsed in confusion when the assaulting troops came under fire from Turkish artillery who, unlike their British counterparts, had a clear view of the entire Suvla battlefield.

Clarence Wand-Tetley was officially listed as missing on 22 August, although it is possible that he was killed in the previous day's fighting and his body never found. Aged just 26, he was one of 5,300 British casualties in the Suvla Bay attacks of 21 August. **Clarence was mentioned in one of Sir Ian Hamilton's final dispatches dated 28 January 1916** by which time the British and their allies had withdrawn from Gallipoli. The campaign, characterised by trench warfare and massed infantry attacks similar to the Western Front, cost the British some 250,000 men killed, wounded and missing.

Clarence's stepfather Joseph Tetley died on 16 May 1935. He had two listed addresses at the time of his death - 49, Mansell Street, London, and The Lodge, Winchester. He was buried at Magdalen Hill Cemetery, Winchester, on 20 May 1935 and left effects valued at £74,528 5s 9d (some £5 million today). Joseph's nephew William Tetley-Jones inherited the tea business but died the following year and his son, Tetley Ironside Tetley-Jones, took over the company until his death in 1990.

Emily Tetley, Clarence's mother, was listed as the householder for The Lodge in the Warren's Directories for 1936 and 1937, but by 1938 she had left Winchester. In the 1939 Register, she was living in Hastings, East Sussex, at the Albany Hotel, a large boarding house for the wealthy elderly or retired. Emily died on 22 June 1948 in Ealing, west London, leaving nearly £25,000 in her will, a considerable sum.

What became of Clarence's father, Ernest Wand? In the 1911 Census, an Ernest Wand, aged 45 and born in Grantham, Lincolnshire (as Clarence's father had been) was listed as a single man, boarding at 94, Clarence Gate Gardens, Marylebone, London. Intriguingly, given who his ex-wife had married, he was employed as a manager of a wholesale tea dealer. In July 1922, Ernest Wand appears to have been

WAND-TETLEY, Clarence Ernest

living in Watford, Hertfordshire. At the National Archives at Kew, there is an envelope (possibly dated 11 July 1922) addressed to an 'E. Wand, Esq., 10, Clifton Road, Watford, Herts.', which contains his son Charles [sic] Ernest Wand-Tetley's medal records. 'Charles' was a 'Lieut. in Lancs. Fus. dated 1915, KIA 22/8/15'.

From about 1929, Ernest Wand was a resident at Park End, Deacons Hill, Oxhey, Hertfordshire. He died from a heart attack on Oxhey golf course on 1 October 1938, aged 74. Ernest left £13,003 5s 2d in his will (more than £1 million today) so he did not die a poor man!

Clarence Wand-Tetley's two brothers also served in the Great War. Joseph Wand-Tetley was commissioned into the Northamptonshire Regiment in 1916 even though he was under-age. He served in France and was wounded in October 1918, the same year that he won the Military Cross. Joseph ended the war as a Lieutenant and later turned his hand to farming; in September 1921 he was living at Park Farm, Lurgashall, near Petworth, Sussex. He married Mabel Miles at East Ashford, Kent, in 1923 and the couple had a son. Joseph was still farming in 1939 while also serving as a volunteer Air Raid Warden. He died in Kent on 25 September 1988, aged about 90.

Clarence's other brother Thomas had a long and distinguished military career. In 1910 he was commissioned into the 1st Battalion, The Wiltshire Regiment and by 1912 had been promoted to Captain. In August 1914 he was sent to the Western Front where he was taken prisoner on 27 October. He suffered a severe neck wound before being captured and was subsequently mentioned in British Commander-in-Chief Sir John French's dispatches for gallant conduct on the field of battle. In 1917 Thomas was listed as a PoW at Holzminden, Germany, a prison camp for determined escapees.

Like Clarence, Thomas was a gifted sportsman and during his time as a PoW he came to realise the importance of physical fitness to morale. His work in this field resulted in a further mention in dispatches in September 1919 for valuable services rendered whilst a prisoner of war. In 1920, he received a third mention in dispatches for 'gallant conduct and determination displayed in escaping or attempting to escape from captivity'. He clearly succeeded in escaping as he was interned in Holland (a neutral country in the Great War) from 24 February 1918. On 29 August 1918 Thomas married Cecile Florence Tatham at St John's and St Philip's, the English Church in The Hague with the reception held at the British Legation. Cecile had been born in Natal, South Africa, on 20 September 1894.

On 19 November 1918, Thomas was repatriated to England. He devoted the rest of his Army career to improving fitness levels in the service and his expertise in this area was increasingly recognised. He also pursued his own sporting interests and in 1920 represented Great Britain in the modern pentathlon and fencing at the Olympic Games in Antwerp. Thomas also played hockey for the Army and Great Britain and was actively involved in amateur boxing.

On 2 February 1920 Cecile gave birth to a son, Peter, in Farnham, Surrey, followed by John, who was born near Fleet on 4 May 1922. In September 1923 Thomas moved to South Africa for nine months to train the physical instructors in the defence forces there. His family accompanied him and a third son, Nigel, was born there on 8 February 1924. After returning to England they lived mainly in London.

Thomas was awarded an OBE in June 1929. By 1938 he had been made a Colonel and was working at the War Office in the department of the Chief of the Imperial General Staff with responsibility for Army Physical Training. He retired in 1944 with the rank of Honorary Brigadier, but remained on the reserve list and was still in 'active service' as an Air Raid Warden

After the war, Thomas advised the Ministry of Health on the physical rehabilitation of servicemen. He died on Jersey on 4 February 1956, aged 65. His obituary in The Times stressed his pivotal role in raising standards of physical fitness in the Army and his sporting achievements, but also stated that 'he will long be remembered for his charm and modesty'. His wife Cecile died on Jersey on 9 January 1980.

WAND-TETLEY, Clarence Ernest

Thomas and Cecile's eldest son Peter was an early recruit into the SAS during the Second World War. He served behind enemy lines in Greece and received the Military Cross. Peter died in Wiltshire on 16 March 2003, aged 83. His biography, Special Forces Commander - The Life and Wars of Peter Wand-Tetley, OBE, MC, Commando, SAS, SOE and Paratrooper, by Col. Michael Scott, was published in 2011.

The middle son, John Wand-Tetley, worked as a hospital physician. He died suddenly at his home near Amersham, Buckinghamshire, on 28 December 1974, aged 52. He had a son, David, by his first marriage.

Nigel Wand-Tetley, Thomas and Cecile's youngest son, joined the Royal Navy in 1942 and retired as a Lieutenant-Commander in 1969, by which time he was known just as Nigel Tetley. The previous year he had competed in the Sunday Times Golden Globe single-handed, non-stop, round-the-world yacht race. Nigel was leading the event when his trimaran Victress broke up some 1,200 miles from the finish and he had to be rescued. It was said that he had pushed his boat too hard as he thought fellow competitor Donald Crowhurst was 'on his heels'. In the event it transpired that Crowhurst had falsified his radio record and logbook to make it appear that he had gone round the world. His abandoned boat was found in July 1969 in the Atlantic, an ocean it had never left. Crowhurst is believed to have committed suicide because he could not face the consequences of his deception if discovered. In 1970 Nigel Tetley wrote an account of his voyage, Trimaran Solo: The Story of Victress's Circumnavigation and Last Voyage. Tragically, Nigel was found dead in February 1972 near Dover. He was 47 and was survived by his wife, Eve, and three children.

Clarence sister Winifred married John Davidson in Winchester in 1919, probably at St Matthew's Church, Weeke. In 1939 she was living in Penarth, Glamorgan, with her husband, an agricultural officer with Glamorgan County Council. Winifred died in South Glamorgan in 1983, aged 89.

Clarence Wand-Tetley and his brothers Joseph and Thomas are both listed in the Winchester War Service Register where their surname is spelt Waud Tetley.

Medals and memorials for Clarence Ernest Wand-Tetley

Lieutenant Clarence Ernest Wand-Tetley was entitled to the 1914-15 Star, the British War Medal and the Victory Medal. His name appears on the memorials at St Matthew's and St Paul's Churches, Winchester, and on the Helles Memorial, near Sedd el Bahr, on the Gallipoli Peninsula (Panel 59-72 or 218-219). Clarence is also commemorated on both Eastbourne College War Memorials – one in the chapel (1924), the other in the hallway of the base of the tower of the Memorial Building (1930) – as well as on the Oriel College Memorial, Oxford and the Harlequins Rugby Club War Memorial.

Researchers – GERALDINE BUCHANAN, DEREK WHITFIELD and JENNY WATSON

Additional sources
- Eastbourne College Roll of Honour.
  https://www.eastbourne-college.co.uk/wp-content/uploads/2018/08/esorg-roll-of-honour-2018-08-15.pdf   November 2019, Clarence is listed as Charles on this website. This has been acknowledged as an error.
- Tatham Family Tree.
  https://www.saxonlodge.net/getperson.php?personID=I1373&tree=Tatham
- History of Tetley tea company and Tetley family tree.
  https://www.thegenealogist.co.uk/featuredarticles/2012/let-the-flavour-flood-out-42/

WARD, Donald Henry Charles

Lance-Corporal DONALD HENRY CHARLES WARD
51, Cheesehill Street, Winchester. (Family later moved to 63, Hatherley Road)
Service number 291033, 9th (Service) Battalion, The Devonshire Regiment
Killed in action, Belgium, 10 October 1917

Donald Henry Charles Ward was born in Winchester in 1898, the son of Charles and Caroline Ward. He was one of four children. Despite his humble background, Donald's father built a prosperous grocery business in Cheesehill (now Chesil) Street. This enabled the family to move to Hatherley Road at the end of the Great War. Donald enlisted in the Army in 1916 and served on the Western Front with the Devonshire Regiment. He was killed at the Battle of Passchendaele the following year.

Charles Ward, Donald's father, was born in Winchester on 24 March 1870. According to the 1871 Census, his own father, Jesse, was working as a servant but living at 12, Cheesehill Street (No.17 today), which is where Charles is thought to have been born. Jesse Ward had been born in Sparsholt, near Winchester, in around 1842. His wife, Emma, was from Chilcomb where she had been born in 1844. Emma is believed to have died in Winchester in 1874, aged 31.

By 1881, 11-year-old Charles Ward was living with his father – by then working as a general labourer - and older brother at 81, Cheesehill Street (No. 44 today). This was the home of Charles's 76-year-old widowed maternal grandmother, Elizabeth Burns. They shared the small house with three of Elizabeth's unmarried children so conditions must have been very cramped. Ten years later Charles Ward, with his father and brother, had moved again and were living at 21, St John's Road, Winchester, which was then a new development. Jesse Ward was still a labourer, as was his elder son, while Charles was working as a grocer's assistant.

In 1895 Charles married Caroline Kirby, the daughter of agricultural labourer Henry Kirby and his wife Elizabeth. The Kirby family lived in the rural hamlet of Up Somborne, near Winchester. Caroline had been born on 5 January 1871 and was the youngest of three children. Before marrying Charles, she had worked as a housemaid in the Vicarage, Ropley Dean, near Alresford, Hampshire.

Charles and Caroline are thought to have married at Up Somborne Church after which they went to live in Winchester in St John's Road, first at No. 28 and then at No. 43. On 4 May 1896 Caroline gave birth to a daughter, Lillian, followed two years later by Donald who was probably born at 43, St John's Road.

By 1900 the family had moved to 79, Cheesehill Street (50, Chesil Street today) and for the first time Charles Ward was listed as a grocer in Warren's Winchester Directory. The house stands next door but one to the property where Charles spent part of his childhood with his father and his grandmother, Elizabeth Burns. It is a double-fronted property and traces of a shop window can still be seen. Until recently it was home to the East Winchester Social Club.

The Wards were still at 79, Cheesehill Street when the 1901 Census was compiled. Donald, like his father, would probably have gone to St Peter's Cheesehill School. (The

43, St John's Road, Winchester - the house in which Donald Ward is thought to have been born in early 1898

WARD, Donald Henry Charles

school building, St Peter's Hall, is a private home today.) The 1901 Census also recorded Donald's grandfather Jesse, 59, working as a farm labourer. He was living in Martyr Worthy, near Winchester, with his father, 90-year-old Charles who, remarkably, was also still working – as a labourer in a park.

On 13 May 1902 Caroline Ward gave birth to a second son, Hector Cecil – probably at 79, Cheesehill Street. A second daughter, Millicent Kitty, was born on 17 February 1909, by which time the Ward grocery business and family home had moved further down Cheesehill Street to No. 51. The row of houses and businesses of which the property formed part, backed on to the Didcot and Newbury Railway loading bay for Winchester Chesil station, so the area would have been busy with commercial activity. The buildings were demolished by the 1950s and the area was later used as a car park for many years before becoming the site of the Chesil Lodge retirement complex.

The Wards were at 51, Cheesehill Street for the 1911 Census, by which time Charles was both a grocer and sub-postmaster, with Caroline assisting in the business. Donald, aged 13, was at school – probably All Saints Elementary which he would have attended from the age of seven.

Donald Ward was too young to volunteer for military service when war broke out in 1914. According to the Winchester War Service Register (WWSR) he joined up in September 1916, when he was 18, enlisting in Winchester with the 7th (Cyclist) Battalion, The Devonshire Regiment. Whether Donald volunteered or was conscripted is unclear. It is likely that he had helped his father with the family business by delivering groceries by bicycle so was a natural candidate for a cyclist battalion.

The 7th Devons were a Territorial unit and comprised two battalions – the 1/7th and the 2/7th. The latter had

St Peter's Hall, Winchester - a private home today. Earlier the building was St Peter's Cheesehill School which Donald Ward probably attended as a young boy.

Above: All Saints Primary School in St Catherine's Road - Donald is thought to have been a pupil there from 1905 to 1912 when it was known as All Saints Elementary School

Below: 50, Chesil Street, Winchester - this was 79, Cheesehill Street when the Wards moved here. Donald's father ran his grocery business from the property

348

WARD, Donald Henry Charles

been formed in 1914 when the original battalion filled up during the 'rush to the colours'. Neither battalion saw action overseas, but instead spent the war at various locations in England, including Kent, Suffolk, and Sussex. However, both supplied drafts for other fighting battalions in the regiment and at some stage Donald was transferred to the 9th (Service) Battalion, The Devonshire Regiment.

The precise date that Donald joined the 9th Devons is not known. However, given that he would have spent three months doing his basic training it was probably not until the late winter or early spring of 1917. Between then and his death in October 1917, Donald proved himself sufficiently on the battlefield to earn promotion to Lance-Corporal. Like his father, he appears to have been an enterprising young man.

The 9th Devons fought with 20th Brigade in 7th Division which has been described as 'one of the greatest fighting formations Britain ever put into the field'. Formed at Exeter in September 1914, the battalion was part of Lord Kitchener's Second New Army and carried out its initial training at Aldershot, Bisley and Haslemere before being sent to the Western Front in July 1915. The 9th Devons fought throughout the war with their sister service battalion the 8th Devons and saw action in 1915 at the Battle of Loos and in several operations during the Somme Offensive in 1916, the year that Donald Ward enlisted.

During January and February 1917, the 9th Devons were involved in continued fighting on the Somme. In that time the battalion received more than 200 reinforcements, including men from other Devon battalions. It is just possible that Donald was among them. Significantly, the 8th Devons also received large numbers of drafts in the same period, including men from the regiment's cyclist battalion.

In March and April, the 9th Devons took part in the pursuit of the German army as it withdrew to new fortified positions on the Hindenburg Line. This period culminated in the battalion helping to capture the village of Ecoust on 2 April, a considerable feat of arms involving fierce house-to-house fighting. It cost the 9th Devons 100 men killed and wounded, numbers that were partly made up by reinforcements later in the month. Again, Donald Ward may have been one of the drafts.

Donald was almost certainly serving with the 9th Devons by the time they returned to action between 7 and 10 May at the Second Battle of Bullecourt, during the latter stages of the Arras Offensive (9 April-16 May). The Arras campaign had begun promisingly with the Canadians capturing Vimy Ridge on the opening day while the British made significant gains astride the River Scarpe. However, as German resistance stiffened it swiftly descended into a bloody, attritional confrontation reminiscent of the Somme, although 7th Division, with the 8th and 9th Devons both prominent, did gain a foothold in the ruins of Bullecourt on 7 May and subsequently linked up with previously cut-off Australian troops.

Bullecourt cost the 9th Devons 130 more casualties and when the Arras campaign finally ended, they were withdrawn from the line to enjoy a spell of comparative quiet, resting, training and providing work parties.

As the British Army absorbed the lessons of the Somme and Arras so its infantry tactics began to develop, and this was apparent in the training carried out by the 9th Devons in the early summer of 1917. The battalion war diary records how troops practised attacking in platoons (typically around 50 men) organised into four sections of specialist fighters – riflemen, Lewis gunners, bombers (who threw hand grenades) and rifle grenadiers. Each section was led by a Corporal, aided by a Lance-Corporal (Donald Ward's rank).

From mid-June to mid-August 7th Division found itself back in the front line, holding Bullecourt and trenches to the north-west of the village. By then, however, Bullecourt was a relatively quiet zone and patrols sent out by the 9th Devons rarely met opposition. One feature of the period was the increasing use made by the Germans of concrete machine-gun posts, known as pill boxes. These would become all too familiar obstacles to the Devons, and the rest of the British Army, at the Third Battle of Ypres (or Passchendaele) later in the year.

In mid-August – with the Third Ypres campaign already underway - 7th Division was taken out of the line at Bullecourt and moved north for training near Bailleul, close to the Belgian border. On 29 August the 9th Devons moved to Proven, west of Ypres, and from there to Steenvorde. However, the battalion's entry into fighting east of Ypres did not take place just yet. Heavy rain was holding up the progress of the offensive and throughout September the troops continued to train behind the lines at St-Martin-au-Laert. On 29 September the 9th Devons moved by train to Abeele from where they marched to camp at Dickebusch, close to the fighting zone.

By the time the Devons entered the front line on the night of 30 September/1 October, the British Second Army, under General Sir Herbert Plumer, had achieved success at the battles of the Menin Road Ridge (20-25 September) and Polygon Wood (26 September). The latter, by capturing a significant section of the Germans' fourth defensive position, threatened their hold on Broodseinde Ridge. Over the following week the Germans launched at least 24 attacks and counter-attacks aimed at recovering the lost ground. Among the British units standing in their way were the 9th Devons who had taken over positions around Jetty Wood, on the eastern fringes of Polygon Wood. The battalion came under ferocious German artillery bombardment and was then attacked by enemy infantry, but it tenaciously clung on to its positions.

On 4 October, despite the resumption of heavy rain, Plumer sent his troops into action at the Battle of Broodseinde. The objective was to complete the British hold on the strategically important Gheluvelt Plateau by seizing Broodseinde Ridge and the Gravenstafel Spur. This would open a route to Passchendaele Ridge, the capture of which would put the British in control of much of the high ground in the Ypres Salient.

The 9th Devons were not directly involved in the Broodseinde fighting, but they were kept busy through the day, carrying supplies and bringing back the wounded. Once again, the British seized all their objectives, with 7th Division helping to secure a line between Noordenhoek and In Der Ster Cabaret (see map below).

Map showing the area of operations of the 8th and 9th Devons between 4 and 9 October 1917. Noordenhoek and In Der Ster Cabaret, both captured during the Battle of Broodseinde on 4 October, are on the right (Final Objective). Jolting Trench, where the 9th Devons were heavily bombarded on 10 October – the day Donald Ward was killed – is shown below Jay Barn, in the centre of the map

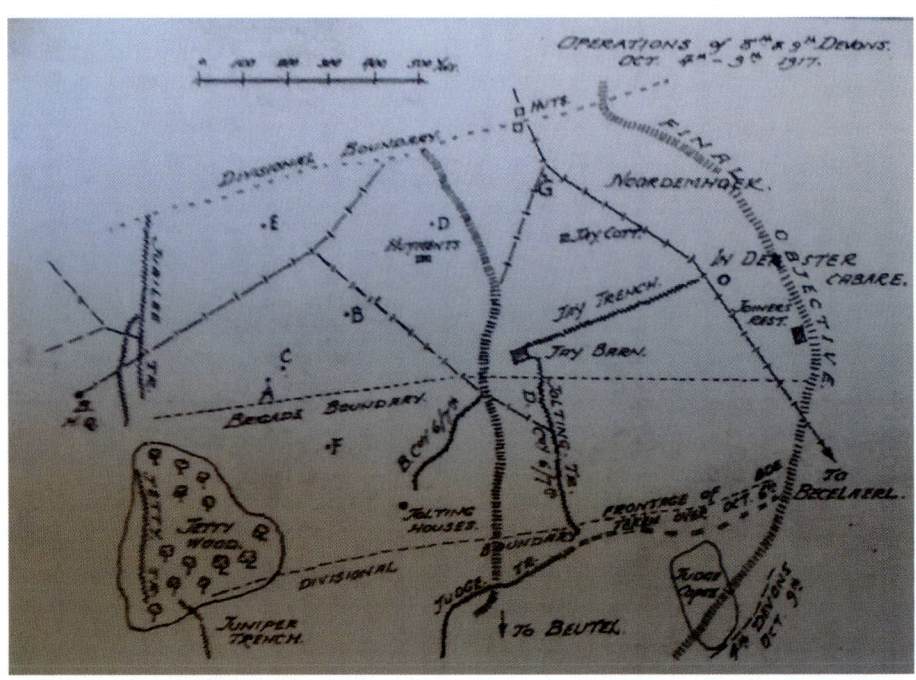

WARD, Donald Henry Charles

Broodseinde was the last successful 'bite and hold' attack of the Passchendaele campaign and caused senior German commanders to consider withdrawing from the salient. They were only saved by the weather which turned the battlefield into a quagmire once more and prevented the British from bringing up enough of their heavy guns quickly enough.

On 6 October, the Devons' HQ dug-out at Hooge Crater was severely shelled and the CO so badly shaken that he had to be relieved of command. That evening orders arrived for the battalion to move up to Polygon Wood where for the next two days it came under heavy bombardment. The casualty list rose steadily but, despite its sister battalion the 8th Devons being relieved on 8 October, the 9th Devons remained in the line in support of 22nd Brigade.

63, Hatherley Road, Winchester – Donald Ward's family had moved here by the spring of 1919, some 18 months after his death

The following day, with the rain still falling, Plumer – under pressure from his Commander-in-Chief Sir Douglas Haig - reluctantly ordered the start of the Battle of Poelcapelle which was intended to bring the British and Australians to within striking distance of Passchendaele. Just to the south, away from the main offensive, the 22nd Brigade also launched a series of attacks. That evening the 9th Devons took over Jolting Trench (see map on previous page) where, throughout the following day, they again came under heavy artillery bombardment. The waterlogged ground made digging to improve the trench impossible and the battalion, hopelessly pinned down, had to find what shelter they could amid the exploding shells. When they were finally relieved that evening, the 9th Devons had lost 270 officers and men killed, wounded and missing in six days of fighting. Among the dead was 19-year-old Lance-Corporal Donald Ward. His body was never found.

The WWSR gives Donald's date of death as 7 October. However, all the other available military records state that he was killed on the 10th which is the date used in this biography. The WWSR also states that Donald was killed at Hooge. Strictly speaking this is incorrect - Hooge lies some three miles to the south-west of the spot where Donald actually died – but the village had been the scene of bloody fighting earlier in the war and was therefore a familiar name to many in England.

After the war Charles Ward continued to run his grocery shop from 51, Cheesehill Street which, by 1921, had been renamed Chesil Street. The property was renumbered 48 in the same year before becoming No.41 by 1930. However, while Chesil Street was the base for the Wards' business interests, it was no longer the family home. Electoral records show that by the spring of 1919 Charles, Caroline and their surviving children were living at 63, Hatherley Road, Winchester, where they would remain until 1927 at least.

Charles was also registered at 51, Chesil Street but next to his entry are printed the words 'Abode – 63, Hatherley Road, Winchester'. The move to Hatherley Road is evidence that Charles Ward's business had thrived during the war years. The store may have furnished the mobilisation camps on nearby Morn Hill with supplies and it would certainly have been patronised by soldiers making their way down into Winchester along the Alresford Road.

WARD, Donald Henry Charles

The Ward family probably worshipped at either St Paul's or St Matthew's following their move to Hatherley Road and they would have been responsible for Donald's name appearing on St. Paul's war memorial. Why they gave Donald's address in the WWSR as 51, Cheesehill Street rather than their new home is unclear – perhaps it was because of their son's long-standing association with the eastern end of the city. This biography also uses 51, Cheesehill Street as Donald's address as it was from there that he went off to war in 1916.

Charles and Caroline Ward have not yet been found on the Electoral Register after 1927, although they do continue to figure in the local directories, with Charles listed in the 1928 Warren's Directory as the householder of 63, Hatherley Road. In 1930 he was still a grocer and sub-postmaster at 41, Chesil Street, but that year's Kelly's Directory also lists him for 3, Chesil Street (No. 2 today), a large house that still stands alongside Station Approach, the former access to Winchester Chesil Station. The same directory also contains the first mention of Hector Ward being a cycle director at No. 3. Hector, like his older brother, was clearly a keen cyclist. It also appears that around this time the Ward family moved from Hatherley Road to live at 3, Chesil Street, with Hector running his cycle business, the Chesil Cycle Depot, from the premises.

Charles Ward sold his grocery business as a going concern towards the end of the 1930s and by 1939 he and Caroline had moved to 3, Stoney Lane, Weeke. (The property stood at the Andover Road end on the south side.) Charles was still living there when he died on 4 May 1946, aged, 76. Caroline, who by this time had been incapacitated for several years, died in Winchester on 18 September 1947. She was also 76.

Lillian Ward, Donald's older sister, is not believed to have married. In the 1939 Register she was recorded living at 3, Stoney Lane where she was carrying out unpaid domestic duties – probably caring for her parents. Lillian is thought to have died in Bournemouth in 1992 at the age of 95.

Hector Ward was also living with his parents in 1939 and continued to run the Chesil Cycle Depot in Chesil Street. After his mother's death he became the named householder for 3, Stoney Lane and remained there until 1961 when he moved to 'Plaisance', a house on Petersfield Road in east Winchester. He sold the cycle business in 1966 and left Winchester in around 1972. Hector, who is also believed to have remained single, died on 23 July 1980, aged 78. He had been living in Falmouth, Cornwall.

Donald's younger sister Millicent married Horace Lucas in Winchester in 1933 and the couple had two children. The 1939 Register recorded Millicent living at 3, Stoney Lane where, presumably, she helped her sister Lillian look after her parents. Interestingly, there is no mention in the Register of Horace Lucas living at Stoney Lane. Millicent died in Weston Super Mare, Somerset, in 1987 at the age of 78. Horace passed away in Bristol in 2008, aged 101.

Medals and memorials for Donald Henry Charles Ward

Lance-Corporal Donald Henry Charles Ward was entitled to the British War Medal and the Victory Medal. He is commemorated on the Tyne Cot Memorial to the Missing, Zonnebeke, West Flanders, Belgium (Panel 38-40). Donald is mentioned on the memorials at St Matthew's and St Paul's, Winchester (where his initials appear incorrectly as DCH) and also on those at All Saints Church and St Peter Chesil, Winchester.

Researchers – GERALDINE BUCHANAN, DEREK WHITFIELD, CHERYL DAVIS and JOSEPHINE COLEMAN

Additional sources
- Atkinson, C.T. *The Devonshire Regiment 1914-1918, Vols I and II*. (Exeter, 1926. Reprinted by The Naval and Military Press).

WEDGE, Charles Edward

Private CHARLES EDWARD WEDGE
8, Andover Road, Winchester
Service number 7802. 2nd Battalion, The Wiltshire Regiment
Killed in action, France, 11 March 1915

Charles Edward Wedge was born in Winchester in 1891, the youngest of the nine children of James and Mary Wedge. Charles joined the Army in 1911 and was one five brothers who fought in the Great War. He was killed in action in 1915. An older brother, James, who served in the Royal Navy was killed in 1918 and his biography follows this on p. 359. Charles's father was a well-known figure in Winchester where he ran a plumbing and gas fitting business from the family home in Andover Road.

Thanks to a local newspaper article published in late 1914 or early 1915, a great deal is known about the Wedge family. James Wedge Snr, Charles's father, was born in Winchester in 1844. He served in the Navy from 1861-70, which included a posting to the west coast of Africa. In 1866 he took part in Dr David Livingstone's exploration of the Congo River, travelling some 200 miles upriver with the Christian missionary on HMS Archer. After Livingstone had preached a farewell sermon on board Archer, he was rowed to his own boat by a crew which included James Wedge. Livingstone never returned from his expedition and died in 1873. James later served on the ironclad battleship HMS Bellerophon.

James Wedge married three times. In 1868 he married 18-year-old Winchester-born Abigail Mary Smith in Ringwood, Hampshire. The couple had two daughters (stepsisters to Charles Wedge) – Emily, born in Ringwood in 1869, and Mary Ann (known as Marion), who was born in May 1871 in Shoeburyness, Essex. The 1871 Census lists Abigail living in Christchurch, near Bournemouth, with her baby daughter Emily. James, however, was lodging at a house in South Molton Street, London, and working as a gas manager (his father had also been a gas worker). Abigail died at some point over the next five years although the precise date is not known.

James Wedge remarried in Marylebone, London, in 1876. His second wife, Mary Ann London, had been born in Hound, Southampton, in 1850 and she gave birth to seven children in 14 years. These were: James Charles Thomas (referred to here as James Jnr), born in Bloomsbury, London, in December 1877; Maude (sometimes spelt Maud) Eugenie, born in Marylebone in August 1879 and John William, born in March 1880 in Broseley, Shropshire. Four more children were born in Winchester – Frederick Arthur in 1884; Thomas in 1886; Daisy in June 1888; and Thomas in June 1890.

The early years of their marriage saw James and Mary Ann Wedge move around the country as James looked for work. In 1881 they were living at Madeley, near Broseley, Shropshire. Today Madeley is part of Telford new town, but at the end of the 19th Century it was a busy mining and manufacturing community where James's skills as a gas fitter and plumber would have been in high demand.

By the time of the next census in 1891, James Wedge had moved back to Winchester and was living with his family at 1, Jubilee Villas, Kingsgate Street. He was still working as a plumber and gas fitter.

WEDGE, Charles Edward

The next ten years were a time of great change for James and Mary Wedge as, one by one, their children flew the nest. Marion, who had worked as a tailoress, was the first to go when she married Southampton-born gas worker George Avery in Winchester in 1891. The couple went on to have at least two children.

In 1893 James Wedge Jnr joined the Royal Navy and he remained in the service until his death in the Great War in 1918. However, he was based at Portsmouth so would no doubt have visited his family in Winchester when the opportunity arose.

In 1894, the eldest Wedge daughter, Emily, married plumber Arthur Cowling in Marylebone, London. They went on to live in London and had four children together. Maude Wedge married in Southampton in 1898. Her husband, Augustus Harris, was a coastguard with the Admiralty and they had a son, also called Augustus, in 1903.

In May 1900 John Wedge, Charles's brother, also married. His bride, Ida Lily Blaber, had been born in Walthamstow, Essex, in 1880. The couple had three children – Frederick, born in London in 1903 and Doris (1905) and Jack (1906), both born in Winchester.

These happy family events were punctuated by the death of Charles Wedge's mother Mary in 1895, aged 45. Five years later his father James took a third wife when he married Agnes Annie (née Morgan) in Winchester. In the 1901 Census the newly-weds were living at 11, Victoria Road, Winchester, together with James's youngest children, Daisy and Charles. Also living in the house was five-year-old Helen Parodi who had been adopted by James and Agnes.

In April 1905 Charles's brother James married Emily Forsdick in Portsmouth. Emily had been born in Nova Scotia, Canada, in 1882.

By 1911 James and Agnes Wedge had moved to 8, Andover Road, Winchester (the address then and now). The photograph above shows the family home and store with James Wedge posing rather nonchalantly at the front door. The advertising on the front of the building indicates that he had branched out from being just a plumber and gas fitter and was involved in other aspects of building work such as glazing and decorating. Interestingly, another of the services James offered was lock repairs – by coincidence, the shop at 8, Andover Road today is Croma Locksmiths.

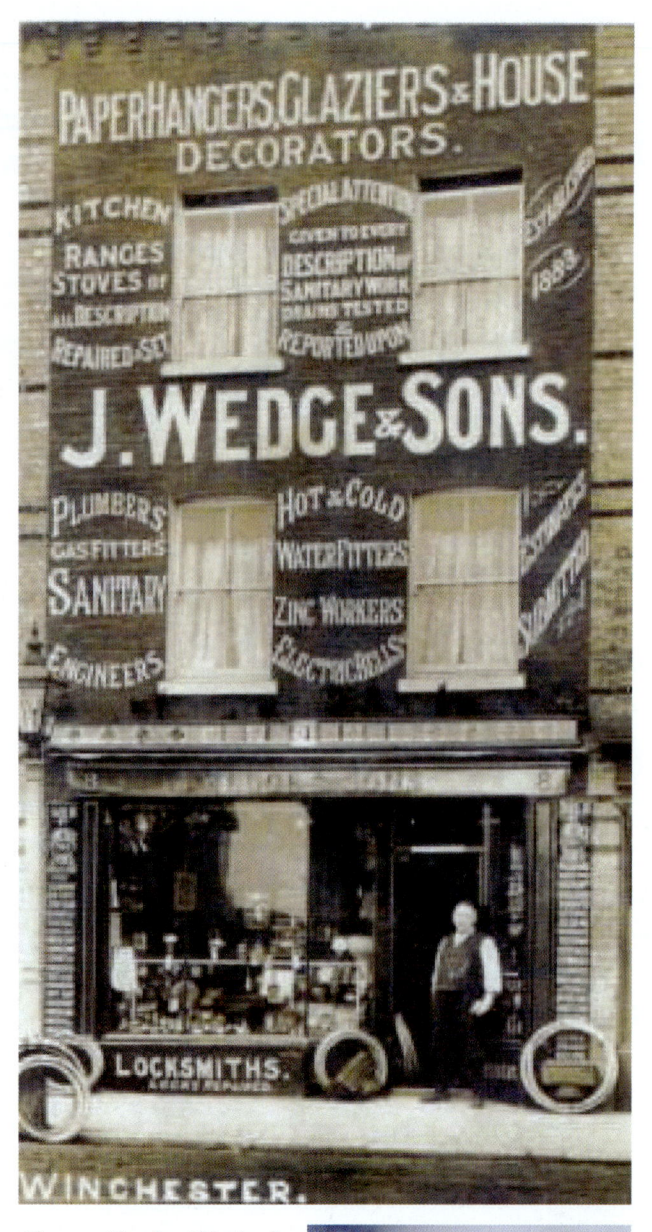

Above: Charles Wedge's father James pictured outside the family home and store at 8, Andover Road, Winchester, shortly before the Great War. Right: the house today

WEDGE, Charles Edward

A local newspaper article from late 1914 or early 1915 about James Wedge and his sons. The cutting was found in the personal effects of Jessie Ellen Wedge, daughter of James Wedge Jnr, and a niece of Charles Wedge. No trace has yet been found of Albert Wedge, bottom centre

Charles Wedge joined the Army in 1911, enlisting with the Wiltshire Regiment in Portsmouth. He was assigned to the 2nd Battalion and posted to Gibraltar as part of the British garrison. When war broke out in August 1914, the Army came under pressure to supply troops for the Western Front and the 2nd Wiltshires were recalled to England. The battalion arrived at Southampton on 3 September and from there moved to Lyndhurst in the New Forest where it came under the command of 21st Brigade, part of the newly-formed 7th Division.

On 7 October 1914, the 2nd Wiltshires were sent to the Western Front, landing at Zeebrugge in Belgium. As part of 7th Division, the battalion was ordered to assist in defending the port of Antwerp but by the time that the Division arrived the city had already fallen. The 7th Division was instead tasked with holding certain important bridges and other places that would help the westward evacuation of the Belgian army.

With the Belgians evacuated, 7th Division moved to Ypres in Flanders where its infantry battalions entrenched in front of the town, the first British troops to occupy an area that was to become synonymous with suffering in the Great War. The battalion suffered heavy losses at the First Battle of Ypres (19 October-22 November 1914) where Charles was wounded in the knee. He was evacuated home to England to recuperate and may have visited his father and other family members in Winchester.

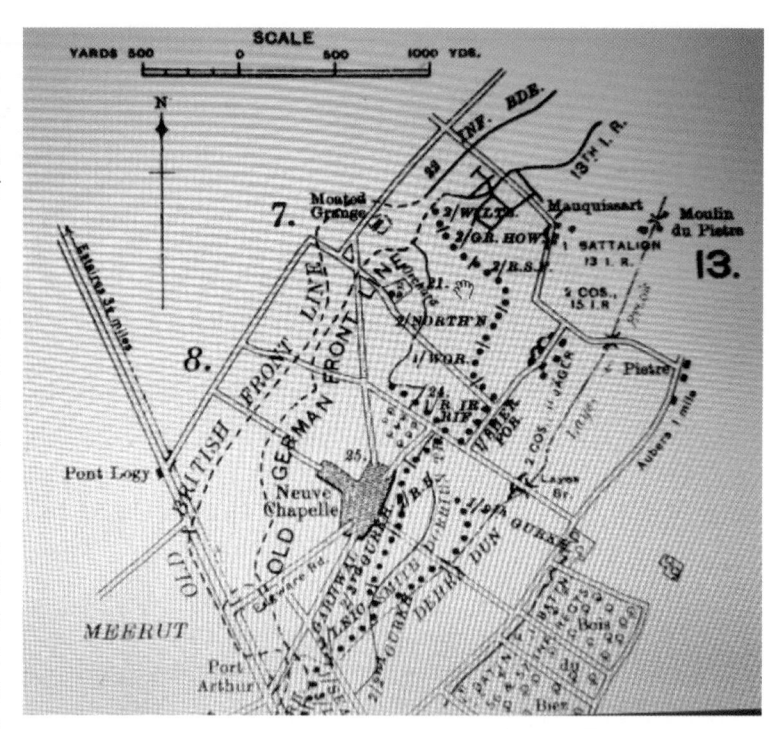

The Neuve Chapelle battlefield, 10-13 March 1915. Charles Wedge was killed between the Moated Grange and Mauquissart on 11 March while serving with the 2nd Wiltshires

In 1915 Charles returned to the Western Front in time to fight at the Battle of Neuve Chapelle (10-13 March). The battle was the first deliberately planned British offensive and its course set the pattern for attacks on the Western Front for much of the rest of the war. Tactical surprise and a break-in were achieved after careful initial planning, but the tempo of operations then slowed as communications problems led to a breakdown in command and control.

The attack, in the Artois region of northern France, was intended to rupture the German lines, enabling the British Army to rush to the Aubers Ridge and possibly as far as Lille. A French assault at Vimy Ridge was also planned to threaten the road, rail and canal junctions from the south as the British attacked from the north. However, the French part of the offensive was cancelled leaving the British to attack on their own, albeit with some French artillery support.

The battle opened on 10 March 1915 with attacks by British and Indian troops. By lunchtime, Neuve Chapelle village was in British hands although the further objective of Aubers Ridge had not been captured. In mid-afternoon, 21st Brigade, including the 2nd Wiltshires, was ordered to advance from positions between the Orchard and the Moated Grange towards the village of Mauquissart and then on to a mill called Moulin du Pietre (see map above). The advance began well but the troops soon came under enfilade fire and were forced to halt.

The attack resumed at 5.30pm and despite strong German resistance 21st Brigade continued to advance. As dusk fell, the 2nd Yorkshires and 2nd Royal Scots Fusiliers (the other battalions in 21st Brigade) battled their way through numerous ditches and hedgerows to assault the German lines. Lance-Corporal H. Wood of the 2nd Yorkshires later wrote:

> *We had to take the German trenches at the bayonet point and it ended in a glorious victory, and I will never forget it. We lost heavily, all our officers but one were killed and only a quarter of the battalion ... remains. It was slaughter for the enemy in some of the trenches. We saw dead bodies piled four feet high, and we sheltered from machine-gun fire behind them.*

WEDGE, Charles Edward

Meanwhile, the 2nd Wiltshires, supported by bombers, worked north from the Moated Grange to penetrate German defences. They captured one officer and 180 men before being halted. That night, as stretcher bearers tried to recover the dead and wounded from the battlefield, British troops, exhausted from battle, dug makeshift trenches to provide shelter from enemy machine-gun fire.

The Germans spent the night strengthening their defences and rushing reinforcements to the area. Early the following morning (11 March) they launched a strong assault against the 2nd Wiltshires to try to capture the Orchard and the Moated Grange as well as trenches they had lost the previous day. They succeeded in capturing a section of one trench before rifle fire from the Wiltshires halted the advance. (By coincidence, Charles Wedge's brother James was serving on the battleship HMS Venerable off the Belgian coast on 11 March when it bombarded German positions in support of the British attack at Neuve Chapelle.)

At daybreak, 21st Brigade received orders to attack from around the Moated Grange in the direction of Mauquissart with the objective of capturing Les Mottes Farm. However, the artillery bombardment which preceded the attack had little impact on German defences which had been fortified during the night. As a result, the leading waves of 21st Brigade troops were mown down as they advanced. Adding to the chaos, some British shells fell short of their targets, inflicting more casualties on the attackers. It is thought that Charles Wedge was among those killed in the assault. He was 23 or 24 years old.

In all, six Wedge brothers are believed to have served in the Great War. Charles and James Jnr were the only brothers known to have died and to be listed in the Winchester War Service Register (WWSR). James, who had joined the Navy in 1893, was killed in October 1918 when his ship struck a mine off the Belgian coast.

Frederick Wedge followed James into the Royal Navy in March 1900 (service number 209069) and the following year's census lists him as a 'Boy Sailor' at Devonport. He appears to have left the Navy in 1907 but re-joined at the start of the Great War and served as a Petty Officer 1st Class. In 1916 Frederick married Amy Rose Jackson in London. After the war, the couple moved to Canada from where they emigrated to the United States in 1924. Frederick and Amy, who were also known by the surname Bishop, lived in Los Angeles where Frederick was employed as a structural iron worker and rigger. They became American citizens in 1937. In 1942, during the Second World War, Frederick was registered on the US draft list but given that by then he was 59 years old it is unlikely that he was called up. Frederick died in Los Angeles on 3 January 1957, aged 72, and is buried at Valhalla Memorial Park, North Hollywood, under the name Frederick A. Bishop.

Thomas Wedge also joined the Navy before the war and in 1908 was part of a rescue team sent to Messina on the island of Sicily after it was hit by a devastating earthquake which killed 75,000 people. During the war he served as a stoker on the dreadnought battleship HMS Neptune and is believed to have fought at the Battle of Jutland in 1916. It is not known whether Thomas ever married. He is believed to have died in Newbury in 1934, aged 49.

John Wedge was the only brother besides Charles to serve in the Army. He joined the Royal Engineers as a Sapper and reached the rank of Corporal. John returned to Winchester after the war and continued to work as a plumber. He and wife Ida lived at 11, Victoria Road, his father's old home. John died in Winchester in 1956, aged 76. Of the couple's three children, Doris was the only one who remained in Winchester. She married Robert Wedge (no relation) and had three children of her own. She died in Winchester in 1980 at the age of 75.

A sixth brother, Albert, is listed in the newspaper article above as having served as a naval bandsman, but no trace has yet been found of him in any record.

WEDGE, Charles Edward

Charles's brother-in-law Augustus Harris, who had married Maude Wedge, served as a Petty Officer 1st Class on the destroyer HMS Mastiff which operated mainly in home waters. The last record of Maude is the 1911 Census which lists her as living with her husband and son at Stubbington Coastguard Station, near Fareham.

Daisy Wedge, Charles's sister, married Frederick Napier, a laboratory assistant, in Marylebone, London, in 1915. It is not known if they had any children. Daisy died in Winchester in 1966, aged 78. It is not known what became of Charles's stepsisters, Emily and Marion.

Charles Wedge's father James died in Winchester on 24 May 1917 and his stepmother Agnes in 1925. The address given for Charles and his brother James in the WWSR of 1921 is 6, Andover Road. The electoral registers of 1920 and 1921 show that this was the house that James's widow Emily moved to following his death, probably to be close to her mother-in-law at No. 8. Emily would almost certainly have been responsible for the names of her late husband and brother-in-law appearing in the WWSR with the address of 6, Andover Road. Likewise, she or Agnes would have ensured the brothers' names appeared on the parish war memorials. However, as neither Charles nor James Jnr ever lived at No. 6 this biography gives the family home at 8, Andover Road as their address.

Medals and memorials for Charles Edward Wedge

Private Charles Edward Wedge was entitled to the 1914 (Mons) Star, the British War Medal and the Victory Medal. His body was never found, and he is commemorated on the Le Touret Memorial (right), Pas de Calais, France, (Panel 33 and 34). He is also mentioned on the memorials at St Matthew's and St Paul's churches, Winchester.

Researchers – DEREK WHITFIELD, CHERYL DAVIS and STEVE JARVIS

WEDGE, James Charles Thomas

Chief Petty Officer (Gunnery Instructor) JAMES CHARLES THOMAS WEDGE
8, Andover Road, Winchester
Service number 171150. HMS M21, Royal Navy
Killed in action, English Channel, 21 October 1918

James Charles Thomas Wedge, the eldest of James and Mary Ann Wedge's seven children, was born in Bloomsbury, London, on 30 December 1877. A sailor with the Royal Navy from the age of 16, he served throughout the Great War before being killed just three weeks before the Armistice. This biography will focus primarily on James's life - full details of the Wedge family history can be found in the biography of James's younger brother, Charles, on pp. 353.

In January 1893, aged just 15, James Wedge Jnr joined the Royal Navy as a boy sailor. His service records give his occupation when he enlisted as plumber's mate, so he had probably previously worked for his father, a gas fitter and plumber. James's first posting was on the training ship HMS Boscawen based at Portland.

After completing his basic training, James served on several ships in quick succession, including the ironclad battleship HMS Inflexible, which operated as the Portsmouth Port Guard Ship, and the armoured cruiser HMS Undaunted. He won his first promotion, to Ordinary Seaman in December 1895, and was made Able Seaman in July the following year. James trained to be a gunner and spent much of the period between 1897 and 1910 based at the naval shore establishments HMS Victory I and the HMS Excellent, the Gunnery School at Whale Island, Portsmouth.

James was clearly a trusted and respected sailor. At the funeral of Queen Victoria in 1901, a year after being promoted to Petty Officer 2nd Class, he was chosen to be part of the brigade of servicemen who drew the gun carriage bearing the late monarch's coffin. He was selected to perform the same duty at the funeral of King Edward VII in 1910. For these services James received the Royal Victorian Medal.

On 23 April 1905 James married Emily Maud Forsdick in Milton, Portsmouth. Emily, who had been born in Nova Scotia, Canada, on 21 February 1882, was the daughter of George and Amelia Forsdick. In the 1901 Census George was listed working as a gun retailer and living in Portsmouth.

Emily gave birth to a daughter, Constance, in Portsmouth on 9 November 1907. In the 1911 Census, James, by then a Petty Officer 1st Class, was living with Emily and Constance at 16, Netley Street, Fratton, Portsmouth. A second daughter, Jessie Ellen, was born on 4 October 1913 when the family were living at 228, Twyford Avenue, Portsmouth. A son, Harold, was born in Portsmouth on 6 August 1918, just a few weeks before his father's death.

WEDGE, James Charles Thomas

At the start of the Great War in August 1914 James Wedge was serving on the London-class battleship HMS Venerable. Venerable formed part of the 5th Battle Squadron of the Channel Fleet and spent the opening weeks of the war helping to protect the British Expeditionary Force as it crossed to France. In late August she was used to transport part of the Portsmouth battalion of Marines to Ostend.

By late October Venerable was at Dover, serving as the flagship of Admiral Sir Horace Hood. On 27 October she anchored off the Belgian coast to help the Belgian army in the Battle of the Yser. Sluice gates had been opened to flood the area in front of the Belgian lines, but the water had not yet risen high enough to stop the Germans attacking. HMS Venerable took part in the bombardment of German army positions on both 27 and 28 October before withdrawing on the 30th. As a gunnery officer, James would have been at the forefront of operations on ship.

James Wedge with his wife Emily whom he married in 1905

By February 1915 only four battleships remained with the Channel Fleet. In March two of those four were sent to the Dardanelles, but HMS Venerable remained in the Channel to take part in further bombardments of the Belgian coast. On 11 March she bombarded the coast close to the Yser as part of moves to support the Battle of Neuve Chapelle. James brother Charles was killed in the battle the same day.

In May 1915 Venerable was also sent to the Dardanelles, replacing HMS Queen Elizabeth. Once there, she took part in the Suvla landings in August, bombarding Turkish positions to support the Allied troops on the beach. Again, James would have been in the thick of the action.

HMS Venerable – one of the two fighting ships that James Wedge served on in the Great War

WEDGE, James Charles Thomas

HMS M21 - James Wedge was killed when the ship hit a mine off Ostend on 21 October 1918

From the Dardanelles Venerable moved to the Adriatic to support the Italians and she remained there until early 1917. In December 1916, however, James Wedge, by now a Chief Gunnery Officer, returned to Portsmouth where he spent the next 12 months at HMS Excellent. In December 1917 he was transferred to HMS Attentive II, the shore establishment for the Dover Patrol.

Based at Dover and Dunkirk, the Dover Patrol's primary task was to prevent German shipping – chiefly submarines – from entering the English Channel en route to the Atlantic. The aim was to force the German Navy to travel via the much longer route around Scotland which was itself covered by the Northern Patrol.

The Dover Patrol was made up of cruisers, monitors, destroyers, armed trawlers, paddle minesweepers, armed yachts, motor launches, submarines, seaplanes, aeroplanes and even airships. It operated in the southern North Sea and the Dover Straits, carrying out anti-submarine patrols, escorting merchantmen, hospital and troopships, laying and sweeping mines and bombarding German positions on the Belgian coast.

James was posted to HMS M21, an M15-class monitor which had a crew of 69 officers and men. The ship's main armament was a 7.5in 50-caliber gun plus one 12-pounder and one 6-pounder anti-aircraft gun. She boasted a top speed of 11 knots.

On 23 April 1918, M21 took part in the Zeebrugge Raid, an attempt by the Royal Navy to block the Belgian port of Bruges-Zeebrugge by sinking obsolete ships at the mouth of the canal which led to the port. The port was used by the German Navy as a base for U-boats which were a threat to Allied control of the English Channel and southern North Sea.

The Zeebrugge Raid was carried out in conjunction with an attack on Ostend. Two of three blockships were scuttled in the narrowest part of the Bruges Canal and a submarine rammed the viaduct linking the shore and the mole (stone pier), to trap the German garrison. However, the blockships were sunk in the wrong place and after a few days the Germans had opened the canal to submarines at high tide. The British suffered 583 casualties in the action and the Germans just 24. The following month James was promoted to Acting Chief Petty Officer and was working as a Chief Gunnery Instructor. It is believed that he became a full Chief Petty Officer before his death.

James was killed on 21 October 1918, aged 40, when HMS M21 struck a mine off Ostend. The ship was taken in tow to Dover but sank off West Pier. James's body was never recovered.

Emily and the three children were living at 8, Highfield Street, Fratton, Portsmouth, when James died, but by 1920 she had moved to 6, Andover Road, Winchester, next door but one to her widowed mother-in-law Agnes Wedge. It is believed that Emily was responsible for the names of her late husband and her brother-in-law Charles – killed at Neuve Chapelle in 1915 - being listed in the Winchester War Service Register and on the memorials at St Matthew's and St Paul's.

From April 1919 Emily received a widow and dependent's pension of 33s 4d a week. This covered both her and the children although the children's pension ended when they reached 16.

James and Emily's daughter Constance went on to marry Alfred Long in Portsmouth in 1927. In the 1939 National Register the couple were recorded living at 9, Derlyn Road, Fareham, together with Emily and their eight-year-old son Richard. The family later returned to Winchester and by 1942 were living at 32, Hatherley Road where Emily died in 1955, aged 73. Constance died in 1957 at the age of 49.

James Wedge's son Harold in 1944 in his Royal Observer Corps uniform

Jessie Wedge, James and Emily's younger daughter, married Reginald Ashdown in Portsmouth in 1933. The couple had two children - Daphne, born in Portsmouth in 1936, and Melville, born in 1941 in Winchester. The family cannot be found on later records and may have moved abroad.

The 1939 National Register recorded Harold Wedge, James and Emily's son, living at 11, Victoria Road, Winchester, with his uncle John and aunt Ida. He was single and working as a heating engineer's clerk. During the Second World War Harold served with the Royal Observer Corps on the home front. He died in Winchester in 1961, aged 42.

Medals and memorials for James Charles Thomas Wedge

Chief Petty Officer James Charles Thomas Wedge was entitled to the 1914-15 Star, the British War Medal and the Victory Medal. He is commemorated on the Portsmouth Naval Memorial, Southsea. He is also mentioned on the memorials at St Matthew's and St Paul's churches, Winchester, and the Portsmouth City Memorial.

Researchers – DEREK WHITFIELD, CHERYL DAVIS, and STEVE JARVIS

WHITCHER, Edwin Walter

Private EDWIN WALTER WHITCHER
2, Avenue Road, Winchester
Service number 30267. 2/1st Derbyshire Yeomanry
Died, Canterbury, Kent, 24 September 1918

Edwin Whitcher was born in Winchester in 1880, one of eight children. For much of his life Edwin and his family lived outside the parish of Fulflood and Weeke and it was not until 1915 that he moved with his wife and children to 2, Avenue Road. Edwin joined the Army late in the war and died less than a month into his military service. His surname has various spellings in official records (including Whicher in the Winchester War Service Register) but this biography uses Whitcher.

Edwin's father, Frederick, was born in Up Somborne, near Winchester, in 1852. He spent most of his working life employed as a bricklayer. Edwin's mother was born Mary Elizabeth Goodchild (she was known in the records by either her first or middle name or both) in Winchester in 1852 and baptised on 23 May that year at St Peter's Church, Cheesehill.

Frederick's father, Charles (1823-1885), had also been born in Up Somborne. In the 1871 Census he was working as a labourer and living at 83, Cheesehill Street, Winchester (now 36, Chesil Street), with his wife Ann who had been born in Eldon, near King's Somborne, in 1824. In the 1881 Census, a Thomas Bignell was staying as a visitor at No.83. During the Great War, Thomas lost a son, Jesse, whose name also appears on the Fulflood and Weeke memorials. Jesse Bignell's biography is on pp. 32.

Charles and Ann Whitcher had three children, including Frederick who in 1871 was employed as an errand boy.

Edwin's other grandparents were John and Ann Goodchild. John (1812-1891) was born in Woodmancote, near Emsworth, near Portsmouth, and worked as an agricultural labourer and later as a gardener. Ann (1821-1888) was born in Otterbourne and worked as a laundress. In the censuses of 1851, 1861 and 1881 the Goodchilds were recorded living in Cheesehill Street, Winchester, a short distance from the Whitcher family.

Frederick Whitcher and Mary Goodchild married in Winchester in 1872 and by 1881 were living at 46, Cheesehill Street, a few doors away from Ann's parents. They already had at least four children – Elizabeth Annie (also known as Ann and Annie), who had been born in 1872, Alice Jane (1874-1956), Frederick (1877-1957) and Edwin, who was probably born at No. 46. Behind the house stood Winchester Chesil railway station and one can imagine the younger Whitcher children being enthralled by the activities in the animal loading bay that served it and by the frequent passing of steam trains.

In 1885 Mary Whitcher gave birth to another son, William Alfred (known as Alfred), and then Arthur Henry two years later. (Rather confusingly, two more children – Charles John and Nelly – are shown living with Frederick and Mary Whitcher in the 1911 Census despite not having figured in any earlier official records. Nelly's age was given as 28 which would mean she was born around 1883. Charles was 35 years old, making his date of birth around 1876. To add to the mystery the 1911 Census stated that although Mary Whitcher gave birth to eight children only six survived. To date it has not been possible to discover the identity of the two children who died before reaching adulthood, nor have any further records relating to Charles and Nelly Whitcher been uncovered.)

The Whitcher family moved to 6, Granville Place, Wharf Hill, Winchester, (same address today) in around 1884, remaining there until 1896. Edwin, aged four when they moved, probably went to St Peter's Cheesehill Elementary School from age five to 13. Meanwhile, his two older sisters went out to

WHITCHER, Edwin Walter

work as domestic servants. In the 1891 Census Elizabeth Annie is listed living at 16, The Square where she was a domestic servant to Mrs Adelaide Joyce. Mrs Joyce, a widow, had a son, 30-year-old Samuel, who worked as a dispenser of medicines, possibly from his mother's house.

In 1897 Frederick and Mary Whitcher moved a short distance to 10, Hillside Terrace, Winchester (later renumbered 71, Bar End Road). As the boys grew up, they followed their father into

Cheesehill Street in 1877. Edwin Whitcher was born here three years later

the building trade, as bricklayers and labourers. Edwin was working as a labourer when he married Annie Harriet Wild (1885-1964) in Winchester in 1908. Annie had been born in the city and grew up in St Clement's Street. Her father, George, was a chimney sweep. Her mother, Harriet, passed away in 1894 at the age of 52. In the 1901 Census 16-year-old Annie was listed as a domestic servant working for surveyor Robert Piper and his family at their home in Foundry Lane, off Colebrook Street.

After marrying, Edwin and Annie lived at 12, Staple Gardens, Winchester, until 1914. The 1911 Census shows Annie's father John Goodchild living with them at the property. The same census reveals that six of Edwin's siblings were still living at home at 10, Hillside Terrace (now 71, Bar End Road). Annie and Alice were out of work, Frederick and Arthur were employed as labourers and then there were the mysterious Charles John and Nelly, mentioned above. Edwin's other brother William was living at 8, Water Lane with his wife Daisy and their young son.

Edwin and Annie's first child, Doris, was born on 22 August 1913. Two years later the Whitchers moved to 2, Avenue Road, Fulflood (the address then and now), which was to be home to the Whitcher family until the 1960s. On 13 November 1916, Annie gave birth to a second daughter, Gladys May. The Whitchers' neighbours at 3, Avenue Road were Lot and Elizabeth Churcher whose sons Henry and Harry served in the Great War with the Hampshire Regiment. Henry was killed in action in September 1918, the same month that Edwin was to die. Henry's name is also on the Fulflood and Weeke memorials and his biography appears on page 55.

According to the Winchester War Service Register (WWSR), Edwin Whitcher did not enlist for military service until 1 September 1918, more than four years after the start of the Great War. It is not known why he joined up so late as all his other brothers enlisted much earlier. From June 1916 Edwin would have been liable for call-up under conscription, but for some reason he avoided the call to arms until just two months before the war ended. Although by then in his mid-30s, age was unlikely to have been a factor – across Britain thousands of married men of a similar age were swept into the forces by conscription. Nor would his work have marked him out for exemption. It is possible that Edwin was deemed physically unfit in the early years of the war before the military authorities changed their minds.

WHITCHER, Edwin Walter

Right: 2, Avenue Road, Winchester - where Edwin and Annie Whitcher moved in 1915.

In the end conscription probably did catch up with Edwin Whitcher. On 1 September 1918 he joined the 2/1st Derbyshire Yeomanry, a mounted Territorial unit who were serving on the home front at Ash, near Canterbury, Kent. The regiment had been formed in 1914 and for much of 1915 was based near King's Lynn in Norfolk. The following year the unit was converted to cyclists and consequently dismounted. By 1918 it was stationed at Ash as part of the 5th Cyclist Brigade in The Cyclist Division. On 24 September, after just over three weeks' service, Edwin died at Canterbury Military Hospital, aged 37. The cause of his death is not known, but possibly it was a result of Spanish flu which had reached southern England earlier that summer.

As stated above, all of Edwin's brothers served in the war and survived. Frederick volunteered with the Hampshire Regiment in November 1915 but later transferred to the Royal Army Service Corps, serving in the Mechanical Transport section. He was wounded in France in August 1917. William Whitcher, whose address in the WWSR, is 8, Westgate Lane, Winchester (a road which ran from the High Street to Sussex Street and disappeared during the building of the Hampshire County Council offices) volunteered with the 4th Battalion, The Hampshire Regiment in September 1914 and served in India and Mesopotamia. Arthur Whitcher is believed to have enlisted with the Royal Garrison Artillery in January 1916, possibly as an early conscript, and served as a gunner in Egypt. He is thought to have married Nina Street in the same year and his address in the WWSR is given as 12, St Catherine's Road, Winchester.

After the war Edwin's parents, Frederick and Mary, continued to live at 71, Bar End Road. Mary died in 1931, aged 79, and Frederick two years later at the age of 81. Annie Whitcher, Edwin's widow, remained the householder for 2, Avenue Road until her death, aged 79, in Winchester in 1964. However, she is not to be found there in the 1939 Register, just her two daughters, Doris and Gladys. Doris, who was listed as a domestic servant, died in Basingstoke in 1958, aged 45. Gladys married William G. Edwards in Winchester in 1945 and remained in the city until her death in 2003, aged 87.

The 1939 Register recorded Edwin's brother Frederick living with his wife Rose at 75, Milverton Road, Winchester (just around the corner from Annie Whitcher), and working as a general labourer/heavy worker. Frederick died in Winchester in 1957, aged 70.

William (Alfred) Whitcher was working as a bricklayer in 1939 and living with his wife Daisy at 69, Bar End Road, next door to where he had lived with his parents. The date and place of his death are unknown. Meanwhile, Edwin's other brother Arthur had moved with his wife Nina to Birmingham where he was employed as a gardener. He died in Birmingham in 1960, aged 73.

WHITCHER, Edwin Walter

Edwin's elder sister, Alice, continued to live in Winchester and is believed to have not married. She died in the city in 1956 at the age of 69. It is not known for certain what became of Edwin's eldest sister, Elizabeth Annie, but she possibly died in Manchester in 1943, aged 71.

Medals and memorials for Edwin Walter Whitcher

Private Edwin Walter Whitcher was not entitled to any military service medals because he never served in a theatre of war. After his death, his body was returned from Canterbury to Winchester and buried at St Giles Cemetery on the Alresford Road – headstone pictured right. Edwin's name appears on the memorials at St Matthew's Church, Weeke, St Paul's Church, Fulflood (where it is spelt Witcher), St Peter Chesil, Winchester (held at All Saints, Winchester) and the Methodist Church, Parchment Street, Winchester (held at the United Church, Jewry Street). As yet, the family's connection with that Methodist church is not known

Researchers – GERALDINE BUCHANAN, DEREK WHITFIELD and JENNY WATSON

WHITE, Frederick Alexander

Lance-Corporal FREDERICK ALEXANDER WHITE
36, Stockbridge Road, Winchester (no longer stands)
Service number 20024. 4th Battalion, The Grenadier Guards
Killed in action, France, 13 April 1918

Frederick Alexander White was born in Evercreech, Somerset, in 1888, the youngest of the seven surviving children of William and Emily White. William, a road contractor and former silk worker, had been born in Evercreech in 1849. His wife was born Emily Southway in 1852, also in Evercreech. The couple married in late 1869.

In the 1911 Census, Frederick was recorded living at Horrington, Wells, Somerset, and working as an assistant in the local asylum. His parents, meanwhile, had moved to 18, Lower Stockbridge, Road, Winchester. This large property appears to have been home to several businesses - including T. Barnett (blacksmith's shop), Hampshire County Council stores, A.S. Newman stores and G. Clements, coachbuilder – as well as being the White family home. It seems the house was later split into several smaller properties with the Whites taking over what became 36, Stockbridge Road when that was renumbered in 1918. It is unclear whether Frederick ever lived in the property, which no longer stands, but he would almost certainly have known it from visiting his parents.

It is not known when Frederick White enlisted, but given that he was not entitled to the 1914-15 Star it was obviously between 1916 and 1918. He was probably conscripted.

Frederick joined the 4th Battalion, The Grenadier Guards in Newport, but whether this was in South Wales or on the Isle of Wight is unclear. The 4th Grenadier Guards had been raised at Marlow in 1915 and the battalion moved to France in July the following year, coming under the orders of 3rd (Guards) Brigade, part of 31st Division.

In 1917 Frederick married Rosie Beaver of 6, Gatling Road, Plumstead, London. In 1911 Rosie had been working as an attendant at the Somerset and Bath Lunatic Asylum which is almost certainly where she and Frederick met.

Because Frederick's date of enlistment is unknown it has not been possible to trace where and when he fought. However, we do have a detailed account of the action in which he was killed: the Battle of Hazebrouck in 1918. The battle formed part of the Lys offensive (9-29 April 1918), the second major German assault that spring. Its aim was to win the war before large numbers of American troops arrived on the Western Front. The German plan was to break through the British First Army, then sweep aside the Second Army to the north before driving west to the English Channel. This would cut off British forces from one of their major supply lines which ran through the ports of Calais, Dunkirk and Boulogne.

After a two-day artillery bombardment, the Germans quickly broke through Allied defences between Festubert and Armentieres which was captured on 11 April. The following day the advance continued towards the important supply centre of Hazebrouck which lay some six miles to the west of Armentieres.

The Germans pressed forward again on 13 April, launching two separate attacks – one against British positions at Vieux Berquin and another between Bailleul and Neuve Eglise. The 4th Grenadier Guards, who had been transferred to 4th (Guards) Brigade in February 1918, were defending the sector around Vieux Berquin which covered the approach to Hazebrouck.

At the height of the fighting that day, the German hurled more than three divisions against the 4th (Guards) Brigade and other units who were defending the Nieppe Forest on a 4,000-yard front. The

WHITE, Frederick Alexander

assault, like that around Bailleul, met with only limited success and the Germans failed to make a decisive breakthrough.

The German Official History of the engagement dourly noted that 'the battle on 13th April was not fought under a lucky star'. By the end of the day the British had managed to move enough forces in front of Hazebrouck to establish a solid defensive barrier.

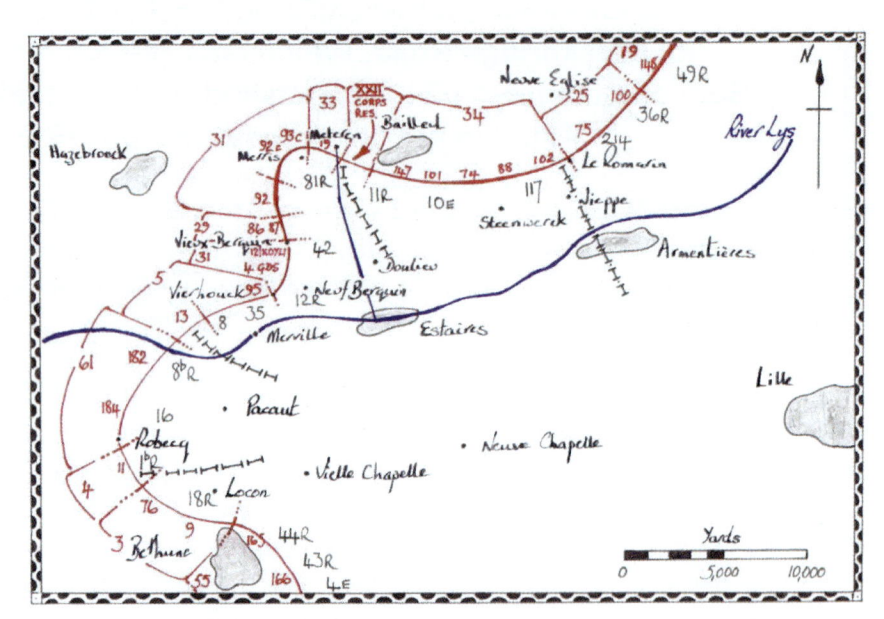

Map showing the position of the 4th Grenadier Guards near Vieux Berquin where Frederick White was killed on 13 April 1918

The British Official History recalls that after the war a German officer of the Alpine Corps wrote the following to a British officer:

> *To us, the 13th April 1918 was a disappointment. We were accustomed to definite success in obtaining our objectives everywhere, in Serbia, in front of Verdun, in Romania and Italy. For the first time, on this 13th April, we succeeded in gaining only a few hundred metres of ground. I think I must say that the defenders on the British front in April 1918 were the best troops of the many with whom we had crossed swords in the course of the four and a quarter years.*

Among those 'best troops' was Lance Corporal Frederick White who was killed in action that day, almost certainly in the Nieppe Forest. He was 30 years old. By a cruel twist of fate, the 4th (Guards) Brigade was transferred to GHQ Reserve on 20 May 1918 and took little further part in the war.

One of Frederick's brothers, Walter, who lived in Winchester, also served in the war and survived. He joined the Royal Engineers in 1917, probably as a conscript, and worked on road construction. Both Frederick and Walter are listed in the Winchester War Service Register.

Medals and memorials for Frederick Alexander White

**Lance-Corporal Frederick Alexander White was entitled to the British War Medal and the Victory Medal. He is buried at Aval Wood Military Cemetery (right), Vieux-Berquin, Nord, France (GR. III. C. 2) and the inscription on his headstone reads:
BUT AFTER TOIL COMES RESTING
AND CROWN WILL FOLLOW CROSS
Frederick is mentioned on the memorials at St Matthew's and St Paul's churches, Winchester, and on the United Church memorial, Winchester.**

Researchers – DEREK WHITFIELD, CHERYL DAVIS and STEVE JARVIS

WHITE, William Edward

Private WILLIAM EDWARD WHITE
32, Fairfield Road, Winchester
Service numbers 4/3002 and 200904. 1/4th Battalion, The Hampshire Regiment
Died in Turkish captivity, Mesopotamia, 22 July 1916

William Edward White was born in Winchester on 24 May 1895, the first child of William and Kate White. He worked alongside his father in a local ironmongery firm before enlisting with the Hampshire Regiment on the outbreak of war. William served in India and Mesopotamia (modern Iraq) and died, aged 21, after being taken prisoner by the Turks following the surrender of the British garrison at Kut-al-Amara.

William's father was born in Romsey in 1867 and spent most of his life working as a tinsmith. His father, Robert (born 1827), was also a Romsey man who worked as a carter. His mother, Emma, was born in Southampton in 1832.

William White Snr married Kate Elizabeth Scivier in Winchester in 1894. Kate had been born in Braishfield, near Romsey, in September 1868. She was the daughter of Charles Scivier (1838-1913), a labourer from Michelmersh, near Romsey, and Elizabeth Bevis (1847-1891) who was born in Hursley. In 1891, three years before she married William White, Kate was working as a maid at 15, Clifton Road, Winchester, the home of Lieutenant-Colonel Charles Wheatley, a retired officer in the Royal Artillery.

By 1897 William, Kate and their young son had moved to 32, Fairfield Road, Winchester (the address then and now), which had only been built two or three years earlier. The house was to remain the White family home through to the Great War and beyond. In March 1898 Kate gave birth to a second son, Herbert, and then in December 1900 a daughter, Dorothy.

William attended Western Infants School before moving on to St Thomas Church of England Boys' School on 2 February 1903. He left St Thomas's on 23 July 1909, shortly after his 14th birthday, to start working. By 1911 he was a whitesmith's apprentice with Messrs Kingdon & Co. ironmongers in Winchester High Street, where his father also worked.

William enlisted with the 4th Battalion, The Hampshire Regiment on Salisbury Plain, immediately after the outbreak of war in August 1914. When the battalion split into two – the 1/4th and 2/4th - he was assigned to the former with the service number 4/3002. After volunteering for overseas service, he sailed to India in October, arriving the following month. Four months later he was with the 1/4th Hampshires when they deployed to Mesopotamia and entered a theatre of war on 18 March 1915.

William would have taken part in the 1/4th Battalion's campaigning in Arabistan and southern Mesopotamia in the spring and summer of 1915. This included a gruelling month spent countering a Turkish-Arab threat to the British oil pipeline at Ahwaz in Arabistan

32, Fairfield Road, Winchester – the Whites moved here in the late 1890s

369

(part of modern Iran). The Hampshires then took part in the capture of Amara, on the River Tigris, on 4 June and the key town of Nasiriyah, on the Euphrates, on 25 July.

In early December, William found himself among a 200-strong force of Hampshire soldiers that formed part of the British-Indian garrison at Kut-al-Amara, between Basra and Baghdad. For five months the Turks besieged Kut which eventually surrendered on 29 April 1916 and William and 12,000 other British and Indian were marched off into captivity. He died – possibly from sickness or wounds – on 22 July 1916. He was 21 years old. (For more details of the siege of Kut and the 1/4th Hampshires' actions in Mesopotamia in 1915 see pp. 377)

It is not known whether William ever reached a prisoner-of-war camp in Turkey. If he did, then he died very shortly after arriving. Alternatively, he may have fallen ill and died on the march from Kut. News of William's death took a long time to reach England. An entry in the Hampshire Regimental Journal of July 1917 states:

An advertisement in the Hampshire Chronicle for T.M. Kingdon & Co. ironmongers which was based in Winchester High Street. William White worked there before the Great War

WHITE - On July 22nd, 1916, whilst a prisoner of war, Pte. W. E. White, 1/4th Battalion, Hampshire Regiment (son of Mr and Mrs W. White, of 32, Fairfield Road, Winchester), formerly in the employ of Messrs Kingdon & Co., High Street, Winchester, aged 21 years.

Pte. W. E. White, 1/4th Hants Regiment. son of Mr and Mrs W. White, 32, Fairfield Road, Winchester, has died while a prisoner of war presumably in Turkey. The official notification received by his parents this week states that his death took place on July 22nd of last year. Pte. White, who was 21 years of age, was formerly with Messrs. Kingdon & Co., ironmongers, of Winchester, where his father is also employed. Much sympathy has been felt with Mr and Mrs White in their long period of anxiety, and especially at the still sadder information which reached them this week.

William White's father died in Winchester in 1936, aged 69. His mother Kate was still at 32, Fairfield Road in 1939 along with his sister Dorothy and her husband Frank Hutchings. Kate White died in 1948, aged 79. Dorothy was still living at the house when she passed away in 1986, at the age of 86. No record can be found of William's brother Herbert, though it is possible that he married and moved to London.

William White is listed in the Winchester War Service Register.

Medals and memorials for William Edward White

Private William Edward White was entitled to the 1914-15 Star, the British War Medal and the Victory Medal. He is buried in Baghdad (North Gate) War Cemetery, Iraq (GR. XXI. X. 40) and is mentioned on the memorials at St Matthew's and St Paul's churches, Winchester. William's name also appears on the St Thomas Church of England Boys' School memorial, which is now held at Kings School, Winchester.

Researchers – DEREK WHITFIELD and CHERYL DAVIS

WINTER, Charles John

Stoker 1st Class CHARLES JOHN WINTER
Sparsholt, Hampshire
Service number SS 1129943, Royal Navy, HMS Queen Mary
Killed in action, Battle of Jutland, 31 May 1916

Charles John Winter never lived in the parish of St Matthew with St Paul but his widowed mother, Sarah, had moved into the area by 1917 and she would have been responsible for getting his name on the parish memorials. Charles is one of three Royal Navy sailors listed on the memorials who died at the Battle of Jutland. He and fellow stoker Bert Newby were serving on HMS Queen Mary when it exploded after being hit by a salvo of German shells in the opening phase of the battle on 31 May 1916.

Charles was born in Sparsholt, near Winchester, on 30 June 1890, the eldest surviving child of Henry William Winter, an agricultural labourer, and Sarah Uityciah (née Funnell). Charles's father had been born about 1854 in Colemore, East Hampshire, where his mother, (Charles Winter's grandmother) Ann, had also been born. Henry's father George had been born in Cheriton.

By 1861, Henry and his parents were living in the hamlet of Dean, in the parish of Sparsholt, near Winchester. Henry was then aged seven and had two younger siblings, William and Jane. By 1871, he had left home and was lodging in Crawley at the Jolly Sportsman Inn (which used to stand just up the hill from The Fox) and working, like his father, as an agricultural labourer.

Henry married Sarah Funnell in 1885 and the marriage was registered in Winchester. Sarah came from a quite different background to Henry. She was born in 1856 in the parish of St George, Hanover Square, London, the daughter of George and Uityciah Funnell. By the 1871 Census, the Funnells were living in Grosvenor Mews and George was a domestic coachman.

By 1891, Henry and Sarah were lodging with a widow in Church Street, Sparsholt. Henry was by then a groom (an occupation that might explain the meeting of the two families) and gardener. Sarah gave birth to Charles on 30 June 1890. By 1901 Henry was a dairyman working on a farm and he and Sarah were living in Lower Deane. Charles, by then 10 years old, was presumably attending St Stephens Church of England School in Sparsholt. He had two siblings – Helen, born on 19 July 1894 and Mary Alice, born about 1898, but who died in 1904, aged six. All the children were born in the parish of Sparsholt. There was another child, but when he or she was born or died is not known.

In 1911, Charles and his parents were lodging in a four-room house in Littleton. Henry, then aged 57, was a cowman on a farm and 20-year-old Charles a domestic gardener. Charles's sister Helen, 16, had left home and was in domestic service with a Mrs Trask and her daughter in Watley/The Cottage in Sparsholt.

Charles joined the Royal Navy at Portsmouth on 16 October 1912. His reasons for enlisting are, of course, unknown but it may have been out of economic necessity - the Winter family seem to have always hovered around the breadline. Stokers were paid a little more than the equivalent rank of seaman: a Stoker 2nd Class earned 1s 8d a day plus free kit, board and lodgings. Charles may also have wanted to get away from home to see the world, enticed by the glamorous images of the recruiting poster. In fact, he visited few countries during his brief naval career. It has been suggested that those recruits with an agricultural background would have had little idea of what they were letting themselves in for as stokers.

Charles signed up to serve for five years and then to transfer to the Royal Naval Reserve for seven. This was only a week after Bert Newby, who at the time lived in Hyde, Winchester, enlisted as a stoker. If they did not know each other before they enlisted, they would certainly have met in training. Charles had to pass a basic literary test and his physical characteristics were listed: 'Height 5ft 5ins., Chest 37 ins., Hair Brown, Eyes Hazel, Complexion Fresh'.

As Stoker 2nd Class 1129943, Charles was sent to HMS Victory II, a shore-based training establishment near Crystal Palace, south London. Here he would have joined Stoker 2nd Class Bert Newby for their six months training. A stoker's life has been described more graphically in an anonymous poem entitled An Anonymous Stoker, an extract from which is printed below.

After training, Charles Winter and Bert Newby were assigned to different ships. On 9 April 1913, Charles was posted to HMS Maidstone, a submarine depot ship. The role of such a ship was to service submarines and to store their supplies. The ship had only been commissioned at Portsmouth the day before Charles enlisted in 1912. For his time on HMS Maidstone, his captain was Captain Frank Brandt who was also in charge of the Eighth Submarine Flotilla. On 3 September 1913, Charles left HMS Maidstone and joined HMS Queen Mary.

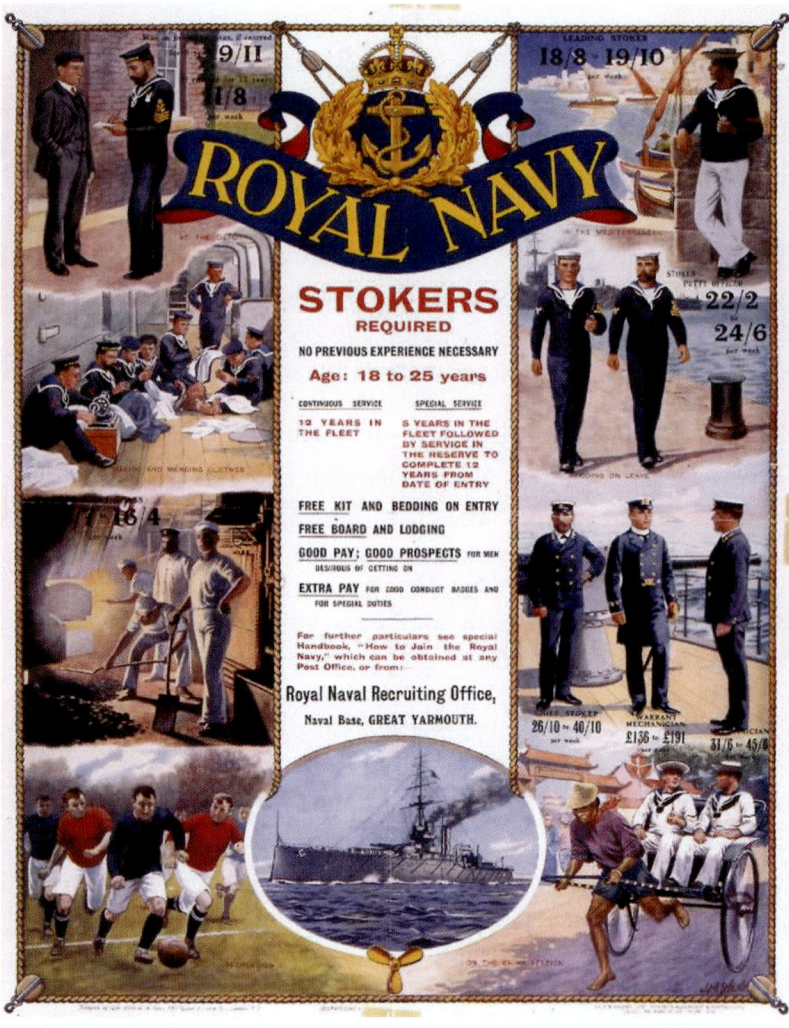

A recruitment poster for Royal Navy stokers from around 1910. Despite the enticing images, the reality of a stoker's life aboard ship was anything but glamorous as the poem below shows

An Unknown Stoker

For every hour of every day, they keep the watch in hell,
For if the fires ever fail, their ship's a useless shell.
When ships converge to have a war, upon the angry sea,
The men below just grimly smile at what their fate might be.

They're locked below like men fore-doomed. Who hear no battle cry,
It's well assured that if they're hit, the men below will die.
For every day's a war down there, when the gauges all read red,
Twelve hundred pounds of superheated steam, can kill you mighty dead.

A few weeks later, on 6 November, Charles was promoted to Stoker 1st Class. In all his end-of-year assessments his character was rated as 'very good' and his ability 'satisfactory'. He did see a little more of the world than he had done previously on HMS Maidstone, where he had been confined to the North Sea. As part of Rear-Admiral Sir David Beatty's First Battle Cruiser Squadron, he was part of a visit to the French naval base of Brest in February 1914. Charles would also have been with the Squadron when

WINTER, Charles John

it visited Russia in June 1914. By then, he had been joined on board by his fellow trainee from the Winchester area, Bert Newby, also now a Stoker (1st Class). A description of HMS Queen Mary's role in the naval war from 1914 until 1916 when it was sunk at the Battle of Jutland on 31 May is found in the biography of Bert Newby on page 235.

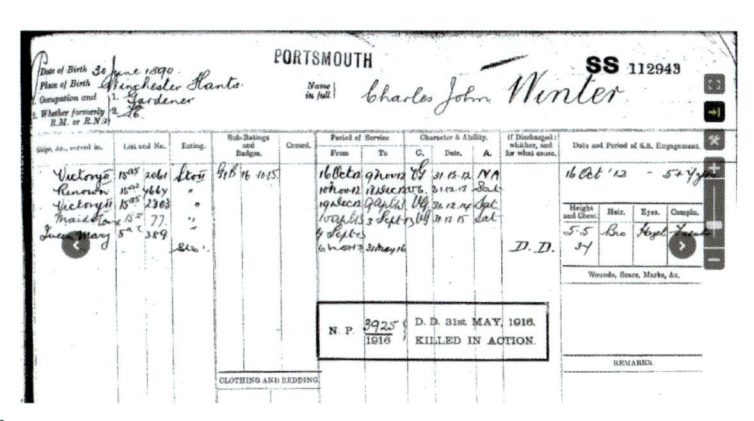

Above: Stoker Charles Winter's Royal Navy service record and, below, HMS Queen Mary, the ship on which he died at the Battle of Jutland on 31 May 1916

On Charles's service papers was starkly written 'DD [Discharged Dead] Killed in Action on 31 May 1916'. His father had died in the late spring/early summer of 1915, aged about 61, so his mother Sarah had to endure the loss of a husband and son in the space of just 12 months.

As the next of kin, Sarah received Charles's war gratuity in 1917. Her address was given as Pond Cottage, Weeke Without, a house that still stands on the Stockbridge Road. According to Warren's Directories, that remained her address until 1921-22. It is not known if she lived there in 1915 and 1916 or if Charles ever visited the house. Charles Winter is listed at the address in the Winchester War Service Register (WWSR) of 1921.

In the summer of 1917, Helen Winter, Charles's sister and the only surviving child, married Gilbert Paintin, the marriage being registered in Winchester. Gilbert was born on 29 September 1894 and is probably the Gilbert Paintin whose birth was registered at Headington, Oxfordshire. The next possible mention of him is in the 1911 Census when he was 17. This states that he was an inmate at a reformatory in Bengeo, Hertfordshire, and that he worked as a farm labourer. He is not in the WWSR although it is believed that he may have served in the Army Service Corps during the Great War as a driver.

Helen and Gilbert must have lived with Sarah Winter at Pond Cottage for a while as Gilbert Paintin is registered there in the Electoral Rolls in 1919. Their first child, Charles, seems to have been born on 9 March 1916, more than a year before they married. After 1921, there is no further mention in Winchester in either the street directories or electoral registers of Sarah Winter, her daughter and her son-in-law. However, Charles Winter's Navy pension records lists 12, Poulsome Place (which no longer exists), Middle Brook Street, as a contact address for his mother after she had left Pond Cottage. Presumably, she was a lodger there.

Pond Cottage, Weeke - the home of Charles Winter's mother Sarah until 1921. It is not known if he ever visited his family there.

373

The wreck of HMS Queen Mary showing clearly that it was blown in two at Jutland. The site, now a war grave, is the last resting place of Charles Winter and Bert Newby
(Photo: Royal Navy)

In 1925 and 1926, Sarah, Helen and Gilbert appear in the electoral registers at Lancen Farm, Lane End, Longwood, in the parish of Cheriton. (The same address appears in Charles's pension records.) It is possible that they moved there as Sarah Winter's father-in-law George had come from the area and there might still have been family around.

By 1927, Gilbert and Helen Paintin were living at No.18 Hutment on the Alresford Road, Winchester, but Sarah was no longer with them. The huts, which provided basic accommodation, were left over from the Army camps on Morn Hill during the Great War.

The final mention of Sarah Winter is her death in 1934 which was registered in Droxford. She was 77 years old. By the 1939 Register, Gilbert and Sarah Paintin were living at 4, The Grange, Westbourne, near Chichester, Sussex, with Gilbert employed as a general builders' labourer. The couple had had ten children in total. Charles, who was born in 1916 and who may be their eldest child, was still living with them, aged 22 and was an agricultural labourer. Gilbert died in 1958 and Helen in 1961, aged 66. Both deaths were registered in Chichester.

Medals and memorials for Charles John Winter

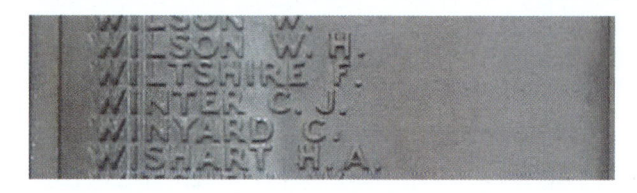

Stoker 1st Class Charles John Winter was entitled to the 1914-15 Star, the British War Medal and the Victory Medal. He is not in the Winchester War Service Register of 1921 as he never lived in Winchester, but he is commemorated on the Portsmouth Naval Memorial (Panel 20) on Southsea Common for those with no known grave. His name appears on the memorials at St Paul's and St Mathew's churches, Winchester, but not on the Sparsholt War Memorial.

Researchers: GERALDINE BUCHANAN,
JOSEPHINE COLEMAN and CHERYL DAVIS

Additional sources

- Chamberlain, Terry. *Stokers – The Lowest of the Low? A Social History of Royal Navy Stokers 1850-1950.* PhD thesis, University of Exeter, 2013. https://ore.exeter.ac.uk/repository/handle/10871/13844
- Corbett, Sir Julian. *Official History Naval Operations Great War, Vol. III* (Longmans, 1923).
- http://www.naval-history.net/xDKCas1916-05May-Jutland1.ht

Appendix i – The 4th Hampshires in Mesopotamia

The 4th Battalion, The Hampshire Regiment in the Great War

Of the 91 men listed on the memorials at St Matthew's and St Paul's churches, no fewer than 17 (nearly 1 in 5) served with the 4th Battalion, The Hampshire Regiment. This disproportionately high number reflected both the role that the battalion played in Winchester life and the social dynamics of enlistment in the early months of the war.

The 4th Hampshires were a Territorial Force (TF) battalion created under the Army reforms of 1908. In 1914 they were one of six TF infantry and cyclist battalions serving with the Hampshire Regiment, whose barracks and depot were situated just off Southgate Street in Winchester.

The TF battalions recruited locally – the 5th Hampshires, for example, drew many of their men from around Southampton and the 7th Battalion from Bournemouth. The 4th Battalion recruited in Winchester and north Hampshire. This close connection to an area meant that TF battalions became more recognised and supported by the local community than Regular Army units.

Territorial soldiers trained at weekends or in the evenings and went away to a summer camp. They were not obliged to serve overseas, but the terms of their enlistment meant that in the event of war they could be called upon for full-time service. The physical criteria for joining the TF were the same as for the Regular Army but the lower age limit was 17.

The 4th Hampshires were on Salisbury Plain for their annual summer camp when the Great War began on 4 August 1914. Men from Winchester and elsewhere immediately flocked to enlist and the battalion was soon 'oversubscribed'. The Army's solution was to authorise the formation of 2nd-Line units which were distinguished by a '2/' prefix from the original unit (prefixed '1/'.) Thus the 4th Hampshires were split into the 1/4th Battalion and 2/4th Battalion.

The backbone of the 1/4th Battalion was the pre-war Territorial soldiers. The War Office decided that units such as these were experienced enough for them to replace Regular Army units overseas, particularly in India.

On 9 October 1914, the 1/4th Hampshires sailed for Bombay, arriving a month later. From there they travelled to the British Army base at Poona (Pune in the modern state of Maharashtra in western India), where they were assigned to

The 2/4th Hampshires on their way to their base at Quetta, India, in 1915

Appendix i – The 4th Hampshires in Mesopotamia

the 2nd Indian Division of the Indian Army. In January 1915, the battalion moved again, to Rawalpindi (in the state of Punjab in modern Pakistan).

The 2/4th Hampshires, by contrast, had little military experience despite a smattering of pre-war soldiers in their ranks. They were also desperately short of equipment and supplies. However, in December 1914 they, too, were ordered to India, arriving in January 1915. They were posted to Quetta (in Baluchistan in modern Pakistan), on the North West Frontier.

Both battalions had to acclimatise and get to grips with the very unfamiliar conditions of Indian service. They also had to begin training - the 2/4th did theirs in the mountains around Quetta. Several NCOs were appointed from the ranks around this time, among them Henry Churcher of the 2/4th Battalion, who lived in Avenue Road, Fulflood.

The 2/4th Hampshires remained in India until April 1917. In that time, they supplied hundreds of men as drafts for other battalions fighting in different theatres of war, but primarily Mesopotamia (modern Iraq). And it was there that the 1/4th Hampshires found themselves next in March 1915.

The Mesopotamia Campaign 1915-16

Map of lower Mesopotamia where the 1/4th Hampshires fought in 1915-16

Most people have heard of the Battles of the Somme and Passchendaele and perhaps even the Gallipoli campaign. Few, however, are aware that thousands of British troops fought in Mesopotamia (modern Iraq) during the Great War and that the Army suffered one of its most humiliating defeats there. Moreover, for many of those Fulflood and Weeke men who joined the 4th Hampshires in 1914 in a spirit of excitement and adventure, Mesopotamia would be their graveyard.

Appendix i – The 4th Hampshires in Mesopotamia

The British were in Mesopotamia for one primary reason: oil. With the Royal Navy increasingly reliant on oil-powered ships it was vital that the oilfields and pipeline be protected from the Ottoman Turks who were fighting alongside Germany and Austria-Hungary in the Great War. Mesopotamia was also of major geo-strategic importance – as Iraq is today. Back in 1914 the British Empire had to protect the Persian Gulf because of its proximity to India. There were worrying signs, too, of increasing German military and economic influence in the area with many Turkish regiments advised or even commanded by German officers.

In 1915 the focus of the War Office in London was on the Western Front and Gallipoli and responsibility for the Mesopotamia campaign was initially left largely to the British Indian Army. The subsequent 'mission creep' – pushing on beyond the original military goal - and confusion between the authorities in London and India when the campaign began to unravel lay at the heart of the disaster that overtook the Army at Kut-al-Amara in 1916.

Mission Creep: March-December 1915

The Allied Army – initially 6th (Poona) Division under Major-General Charles Townshend - arrived in Mesopotamia soon after war broke out. By the end of November, the port of Basra had been secured and the town of Qurna was captured the following month. On 18 March 1915, the 1/4th Hampshires arrived at Basra from India as part of build-up of British and Indian forces in Mesopotamia. However, other elements necessary for a deeper advance up the Tigris and Euphrates rivers, particularly medical and logistical support, were not increased.

The Hampshires were initially employed north of Basra on steamers on the River Euphrates, operating against Turkish communications. They took no part in a hard-fought engagement at Shaiba (12-15 April 1915) in which the British successfully defeated a Turkish attempt to retake Basra. With the port city secure once more, the battalion was ordered to Ahwaz in Arabistan (in modern Iran) to confront Turkish forces threatening the pipeline there. The Hampshires spent a month operating in difficult terrain – often swampy – and increasing heat, but the Turks refused to give battle and the battalion returned to Basra.

The Allies, by this time strengthened by the arrival of the 12th Division under Major General George Gorringe and the 6th Cavalry Brigade commanded by Major-General Sir Charles Melliss VC, returned to the offensive and on 4 June captured the town of Amara. Conditions were far from ideal: the flooding of the Tigris resulted in waterlogged ground while the extremes of heat and swarms of flies must have seemed utterly alien to the Winchester men. Private Charles Douglas of 22, Cheriton Road (then 36, Western Road) died around this time, probably from heatstroke. The operations around Amara saw the British use a variety of vessels – particularly flat-bottomed bellums - to cross the flooded ground and attack Turkish positions. This became known as 'Townshend's Regatta'.

The advance northwards continued, with the commanders justifying each new objective as necessary to protect the one previously captured. In truth, Basra could have been defended comparatively easily once Qurna and Amara had been taken.

The next attack, on the town of Nasiriyah, 28 miles up the Euphrates from Amara, followed a month later. The first assault on 14 July using boats failed. A second attempt was made on 24 July, with the 1/4th Hampshires in the thick of the fighting in temperatures that reached 110 Fahrenheit. In one 24-hour period alone, 15 men collapsed with heatstroke, one dying. The Turks eventually withdrew and Nasiriyah was occupied on 25 July. The Hampshires, having suffered 30 per cent casualties, were then taken out of the line and returned to Amara. Just eight officers and 167 men remained fit for duty.

Appendix i – The 4th Hampshires in Mesopotamia

General Sir John Nixon, senior commander of the British Indian Army, ordered a further advance, despite misgivings from Townshend. Kut-al-Amara was taken on 27 September 1915, but crucially the Turkish forces there escaped and regrouped. More troops were sent to reinforce 6th Division which advanced again to Ctesiphon, just 18 miles from Baghdad. Here the Allies and Turks fought an inconclusive battle on 22 November. After the battle, with his supply lines stretched beyond their limits, Townshend decided to withdraw to Kut pursued by the Turks.

The exhausted troops of 6th Division reached Kut on 3 December 1915, having marched 44 miles in just 36 hours. The garrison had stockpiles of supplies and, with reinforcements expected to arrive within a month, Townshend took the fateful decision to stand at Kut and defend the town.

The Siege of Kut: 7 December 1915-29 April 1916

Kut stands on a peninsula two miles long by one mile wide within a horseshoe bend of the River Tigris. The population in 1915 was around 6,200, mainly Arabs, most of whom chose to stay during the siege. The arrival of Townshend's 6th Division pushed that figure up to nearly 21,000. Of these, 197 were men of the 1/4th Hampshires, comprised mainly of the battalion's Headquarters and A Company, plus drafts from other battalions such as the 2/4th.

The Hampshires within Kut were led by Major Foster Footner, from Romsey, who commanded nine officers and 187 other ranks. The battalion came under orders of Major-General Melliss's 30th Brigade.

The siege began on 7 December 1915. Relief was expected to arrive quickly, and this was the major factor in the decision to allow the native population to stay in Kut. However, it had a huge impact on the availability of food for the troops.

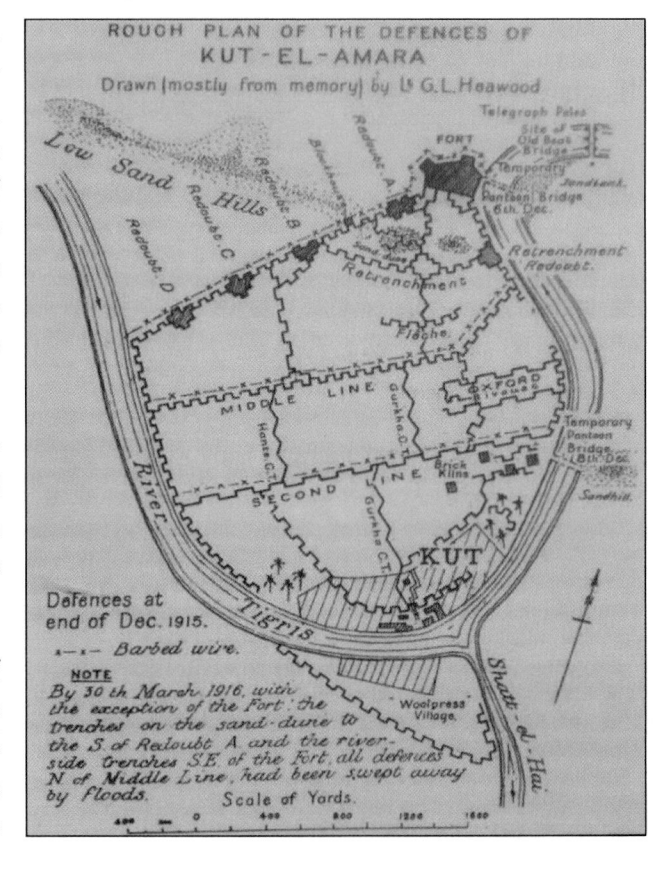

The town was subjected to shelling, sniper fire and attacks by aircraft as well as frontal assaults by Turkish infantry, particularly in the early stages when British losses numbered between 150 and 200 each day. Private Fred Richards, of Stockbridge Road, Winchester, was among those wounded. However, Turkish casualties were also very heavy and so they settled in for a long siege aimed at starving the defenders into submission.

The food situation within Kut quickly became serious. Fresh meat ran out at the end of December and three-quarter rations were introduced in mid-January. Mules and horses were slaughtered to supplement supplies, but many Indian troops refused to eat horseflesh because it was against their religion. Rations were cut again in February by which time the hospital was filled with men suffering from dysentery, scurvy, malaria, gastroenteritis and pneumonia. By the end of the siege, up to 80 soldiers a day were dying in Kut, many from starvation.

Appendix i – The 4th Hampshires in Mesopotamia

The winter weather added to the misery of the Kut garrison. Heavy rain left men soaked to the skin, filled trenches with water, and leaked through the hospital roof. The nights were also bitterly cold.

On 29 April 1916, with food supplies exhausted and all hope of relief gone, Major-General Townshend surrendered the Kut garrison and its 13,309 personnel to the Turks. Of these, 2,689 were British, including 277 officers, and 10,440 were Indian (204 officers), including 3,248 camp followers. During the five-month siege 1,025 men had died from enemy action, 721 from disease and 72 were missing. A further 2,500 men had been wounded and 1,450 were in hospital.

Indian prisoners after the fall of Kut on 29 April 1916. Given their weakened condition, many British and Indian troops succumbed to disease during the brutal march into captivity

Efforts to relieve Kut: January-April 1916

The British did not stand idly by and abandon Kut to its fate and made several attempts to break through to the besieged garrison.

On 4 January 1916, a relief force under Lieutenant-General Sir Fenton Aylmer advanced up the Tigris to Sheik Saad (see map right) which was captured five days later after fierce fighting. The next objective, known as The Wadi, was taken on 14 January at which point the Turks withdrew to strong defensive positions at the Hanna Defile (Um-El-Hanna).

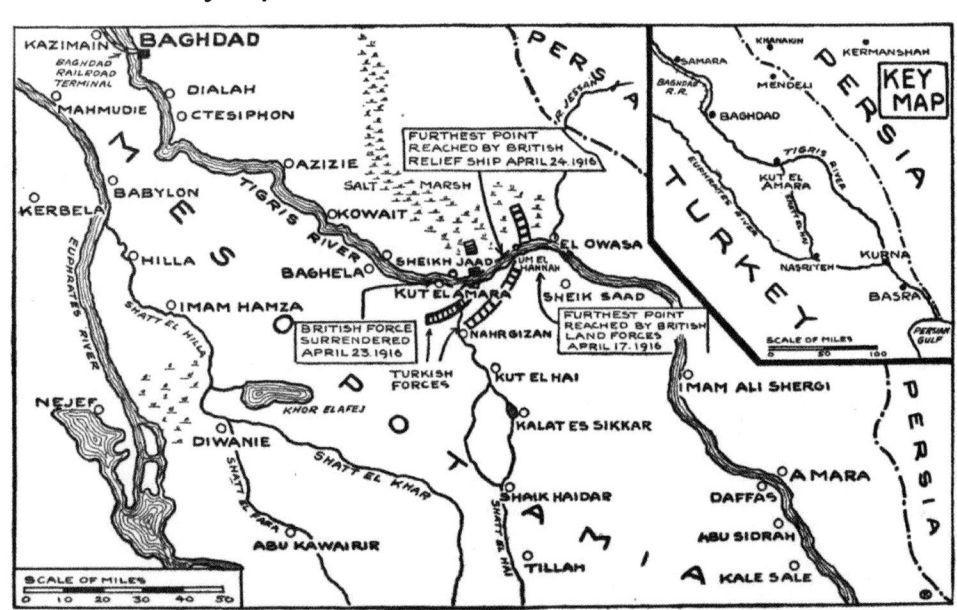

Appendix i – The 4th Hampshires in Mesopotamia

On 21 January, the Relief Force attacked at El-Hanna in atrocious conditions. Thick mud made the movement of troops and equipment difficult and the Turks had had time to improve their defences which were a mile in depth.

Among the attacking British force were 345 men of the 1/4th Hampshires who were particularly eager for success given that many of their comrades were trapped inside Kut.

The attack was a disaster. After shelling the Turkish positions, the British and Indian troops advanced in heavy rain over flat ground which afforded neither cover nor surprise. The 9th Brigade, which four 1/4th Hampshires had managed to infiltrate, attempted to reinforce a group of around 60 men who had got within 50 yards of the Turkish trenches. However, they were quickly driven back.

THE BATTLE OF UMM-EL-HANNAH
January 21st 1916.
Shewing the position of the Regiments which launched the attack. The nearest troops behind our second line were 1000 yards from the Turks

On a day of heavy casualties, the Hampshires suffered particularly badly. They went into battle with 16 officers and 339 other ranks and came out with three and 64 respectively. Among those killed was the Battalion's Commanding Officer, Lieutenant-Colonel Francis Bowker, a pre-war soldier who lived in the village of Longparish, near Andover. Two men listed on the Fulflood and Weeke memorials also lost their lives - Company Sergeant Major Eric Rule, of St Paul's Terrace, and Private Sidney Coles, of Western Road.

One account describes how a group of Hampshires were cut down:

> *A small batch of the Hants were seen to advance at walking pace some 1,800 yards without taking cover. At 400 yards from the enemy one officer and two men were left. They walked coolly on and were within 300 yards of the Turkish trenches when the officer, the last of that forlornest of forlorn hopes, fell.*

The attack was abandoned and the British soldiers, cold and wet, withdrew. Those unfortunate enough to be wounded on the battlefield had to crawl back as best they could through the mud and slime. Many, like Eric Rule and Sidney Coles were never seen again. For several months, the shattered remnants of the 1/4th Hampshires were fit for nothing more than camp and guard duties.

The British refused to give up on Kut. Another major relief effort was launched on 8 March 1916 with an attack on Duijaila Redoubt. This, too, failed and casualties were again high. Several more attempts to break the siege were made throughout April, including a bid to buy the garrison's freedom (Captain T.E. Lawrence was part of the negotiating team) and a daring attempt to run the Tigris blockade by steamer. All ended in failure.

The Relief Force suffered 23,000 casualties in the fighting, including 10,000 in just three weeks in April during the final desperate attempts to relieve Kut.

Left: Lieutenant-Colonel Francis Bowker – the 1/4th Hampshires' Commanding Officer who was killed at the Battle of El-Hanna

Appendix i – The 4th Hampshires in Mesopotamia

The March into Captivity: Summer 1916

Nine men of the 1/4th Hampshires died in Kut during the siege which left ten officers and 178 other ranks to march out of the garrison when it surrendered on 29 April 1916. The captured men marched together as far as Shumran where the officers and rank and file were separated.

British officers fared far better in Turkish captivity than their men. From Shumran most officers continued their journeys up the Tigris by barge. They were then split into four groups and marched nearly 400 miles to various PoW camps. Many had shared donkeys to ride or at least to carry their belongings. They also received better food.

Most officers ended up at the Turkish prisoner-of-war camps at Afion Kara Hissar, Kastamuni, Changri, Kedos and Yozgad. Their treatment there depended largely on the character of the camp commandant, but each received a small amount of regular pay which invariably went back to the Turks to pay for food and accommodation.

Major-General Townshend fared best of all. He was imprisoned on an island overlooking Constantinople where he spent the remainder of the war in relative luxury.

For the British and Indian NCOs and men, life as a prisoner of the Turks was to be brutal and often short. Most of the men were already weakened by the privations they had endured during the siege, but worse was to come. At Shumran they were issued with coarse black biscuits which they ate dry without soaking them in water first. The unfamiliar food, weeks old, wreaked havoc with the men's digestive systems and the following morning 91 had died. In total, nearly 300 men died at Shumran in the first week of captivity, including Private Charles Hammond of Clifton Road, Winchester, who is remembered on the Fulflood and Weeke memorials.

In a letter, Regimental Sergeant Major William Leach of the 1/4th Hampshires described the men's physical condition:

> *After five months of siege these men were as weak as rats from starvation, none of them fit to march five miles; they were full of dysentery, beriberi, malaria and enteritis; they had no*

Appendix i – The 4th Hampshires in Mesopotamia

doctors; no medical stores, and no transport; the hot weather, just beginning, would have meant in those deserts much sickness and many deaths, even among troops who were fit, well cared for and well supplied.

The prisoners were marched 100 miles to Baghdad in just eight days, herded and beaten along the way by the Arab conscripts who formed part of the escort. By time they reached Baghdad many men had bartered all their possessions, including their shoes. Others had had them stolen while they slept. Some of the sickest prisoners were returned to the British, but deaths continued at the rate of around 19 each day. Private Francis Forder, of North View, Fulflood, was left at Baghdad after becoming sick and died there in mid-July. He, too, is commemorated on the parish memorials.

From Baghdad the march northwards continued, to Tikrit, Samarra and then Mosul which the first group of other ranks reached on 3 June. Around 100 soldiers remained at Mosul to receive treatment, but most died there, including Private George Soffe of Stockbridge Road, Winchester.

From Mosul the trek continued to the railhead at Ras-Al-Hain, some 200 miles to the north-west, travelling via Dolabia, Rumailan, Kabir, Nisibin and Kochhisar. Many men remained in these places to work on the Baghdad Railway, among them Fred Richards, who bravely endured the long march to Nisibin despite the wounds he had received in the fighting at Kut. He died at Nisibin (now Nusaybin on the modern Turkey-Syrian border) sometime before the end of January 1917.

Some soldiers owed their lives to the Germans they encountered on the march. Appalled at the treatment being meted out to fellow Europeans, these Germans remonstrated forcefully with the Turks and arranged for medical help and better work conditions in the camps.

Conditions on the journey to Ras-Al-Hain were perhaps the worst of the entire march. Almost certain death at the hands of the Arab guards awaited those unable to keep up, as one British officer recounted:

> *The tail of the column was an awful place ... For the most part British soldiers stayed with their friends until they were dead ... I shall never forget one soldier who could go no farther. He fell resignedly on the floor, the stump of a cigarette in his mouth, and with a tiredness born of long suffering, buried his head in his arms to shut out the disappearing column and smoked on ... I saw another man crawling on all fours over the desert in the dark quite alone.*

Those prisoners taken to hospital en route did not always fare better. An Army chaplain wrote about his visit to one 'hospital' in Nisibin on 29 June:

> *I thought I had witnessed horror enough in these frightful hospital conditions, but another more terrible sight had got to be seen. There was a small, dark, dank room, with no windows to it, only a few feet square. Something told me to go inside this room, and there to my horror I saw two British soldiers, absolutely naked, lying in the own faeces, which had not been cleaned up for several days. They were both dying and, thank God, one was unconscious. The other said to me 'Oh, sir, please kneel down and ask God may let me die quickly. I can no longer stand these horrors'.*

They were horrors repeated a thousand times over on the road to Ras-Al-Hain.

After reaching the railhead, most of the British prisoners continued over the Taurus Mountains on foot to Asia Minor where they were dispersed among the smaller work camps. The soldiers worked mainly on railway construction projects at Ras-Al-Hain, Afion Kara Hissar (where Company Sergeant Major Frank Coles of Andover Road, Winchester, died), Mamourie, Bagtsche and Yarbaschi (Colour Sergeant Andrew Bogie of St Paul's Hill, Winchester, and Private Cecil Shefferd of Fairfield Road, Winchester, both died here). Other prisoners ended up at Entilli (where Private Leslie Jacob of Western Road,

Appendix i – The 4th Hampshires in Mesopotamia

Winchester, died), Kedos, Adana, Airan (Private Frank Chapman of Andover Road, Winchester, died here), Angora, Tarsus, Changri, Daridja, Mosul and Baghdad.

Conditions in the camps were poor. Bagtsche was known as 'The Cemetery' and was eventually closed down in 1917 when details of conditions there were leaked to the outside world. Yarbaschi closed the same year for the same reason.

Survival rates among the Kut prisoners differed markedly. Of the ten 1/4th Battalion officers captured all survived while only 50 of the original 178 rank and file made it home again. Of the 13,309 soldiers who surrendered at Kut, 13,078 went into captivity. Of these at least 4,718 died, more than 3,000 on the march into captivity. This figure, however, does not include the men who died from other causes such as Spanish Flu. After the war survivors erected a plaque in the crypt at St Paul's Cathedral dedicated to those who died in the siege and afterwards in captivity. The total given is 5,746.

Mrs Bowker's Comforts Fund

Mrs Esme Bowker was the widow of Lieutenant-Colonel Francis Bowker, Commanding Officer of the 1/4th Hampshires, who was killed at the Battle of El Hanna on 21 January 1916. After his death Mrs Bowker resolved to do all she could to help those men of the battalion who had become prisoners of the Turks.

Her Comforts Fund, started in July 1916, raised money for parcels to send out to the prisoners. Mrs Bowker did this by having each prisoner 'adopted' by someone in Britain.

The Comforts Fund ledger, held by the Royal Hampshire Regiment Museum in Winchester, is a treasure trove of information and includes the prisoners' names, addresses and next of kin, which camp they were being held in, the name of their adopters, details of the parcels sent to them and what became of the men. It even lists their height and boot and cap sizes.

Right: Extracts from Mrs Bowker's ledger showing (from top) a list of the names of prisoners, including Fred Richards, Charles Hammond and George Soffe; a record of which camp each soldier was interned in, including Frank Coles and Frank Chapman; and details of the parcels sent out to the prisoners

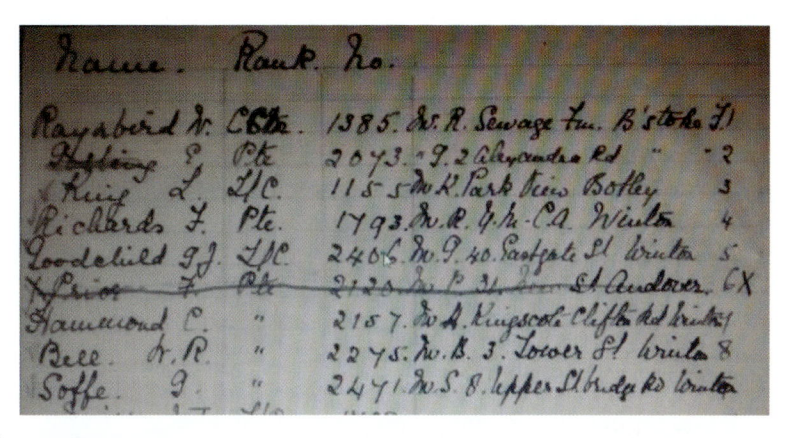

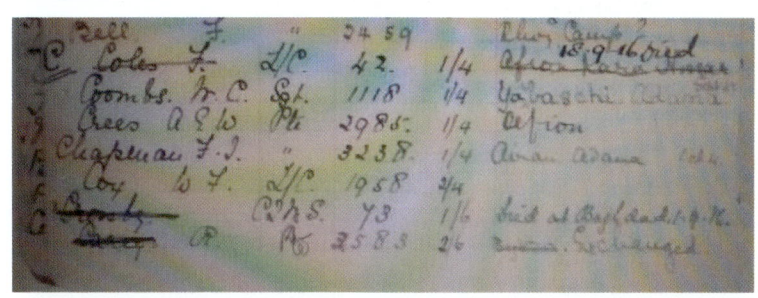

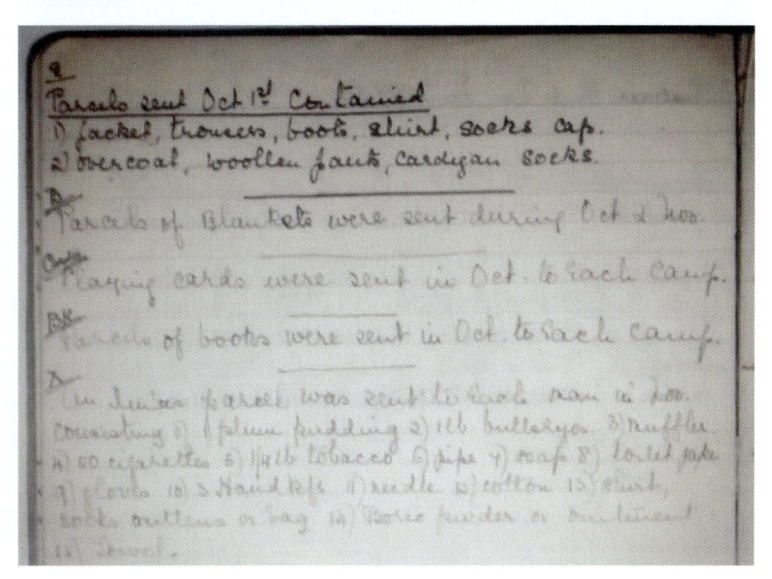

383

Appendix i – The 4th Hampshires in Mesopotamia

Regimental Sergeant Major William Leach

Senior NCOs played a critical role in helping the soldiers to endure the long months of captivity. Regimental Sergeant Major William 'Billy' Leach of the 1/4th Hampshires became revered among his men for the selfless work he did on their behalf.

William had been born in Salisbury and before the war he trained to be a teacher at the Diocesan Training College in Winchester. In 1914 he was a teacher at St Thomas Church of England Elementary Boys' School in the city and lived at 2, Alswitha Terrace, Hyde.

During the long march into captivity, William would have been among the most senior ranked officers because the Turks had separated the commissioned officers from the rank and file. His notebooks, held by the Royal Hampshire Regiment Museum, record details of the march such as distances travelled, rations issued to individual soldiers and his battalion's dwindling numbers. William spent time at Nisibin, but in Mrs Bowker's Comforts Fund Ledger he is also recorded at Afion Kara Hissar, Yarbaschi and Adano. He was 'adopted' by Mrs Bowker herself and she records him as being 5ft 10ins tall with size 8 boots.

RSM William 'Billy' Leach

William's notebooks describe in detail something of the prisoners' daily routine as well as hospital admissions and deaths. He was also responsible for the distribution of parcels, letters and clothing. William was not only popular among his own men, but also with Turks and Germans who allowed him to travel around the country and visit the PoW camps.

On 2 May 1918 William Leach died of typhus, contracted while looking after the sick. One NCO who assisted with his funeral at Nisibin wrote:

> *The funeral was the best conducted one that I have witnessed as a prisoner of war, and several Germans attended. Sergeant Major Leach won respect and popularity by his unfailing courtesy, willingness to help others, and hard work on behalf of the prisoners at Nisibin, from captives and captors alike. His going was a sad loss to the British community at Nisibin and to all the little groups of Englishmen in isolated camps for miles around.*

Captain Floyd of the 4th Hampshires expressed his admiration for William in a letter to Mrs Bowker:

> *I tried to get Leach along as a servant, but he would not leave the men. He is the best man I have ever struck. Some new orderlies who joined us at Kastamouni told me that the work he did with the men on the trek (from Kut) was wonderful. All those poor men who had to trek as prisoners owe Leach a heavy debt of gratitude.*

William Leach was buried at Nisibin but after the war his body was removed and reinterred at Baghdad North Gate Cemetery. Today it lies in an unmarked grave because it proved impossible to identify the remains of the soldiers when they were moved from Nisibin.

William is commemorated on the memorials at King Alfred College, Winchester, and St Thomas Church of England Boys' School, the latter held today by Kings School, Winchester.

Appendix i – The 4th Hampshires in Mesopotamia

A Winchester Welcome Home: February 1919

Ten officers and 178 other ranks marched out of Kut and into captivity on 29 April 1916. Whilst all the officers survived the war only about 40 of the rank and file saw England again.

An official welcome home took place in Winchester on 20 February 1919 and was organised by Mrs Bowker, widow of the deceased Commanding Officer, together with Reginald Harris (whose son Captain James Harris, of Wyke Croft, Weeke, escaped from captivity and is believed to be the only Kut survivor from the parish) and the Mayor and Mayoress. The 40 or so officers and men formed up on Castle Hill where photographs were taken and then marched to the Guildhall, preceded by the Hampshire Depot Band.

Kut survivors of the 1/4th Hampshires in Winchester on 20 February 1919 for the official welcome home reception. Captain James Harris, believed to be the only survivor from Fulflood and Weeke, is sitting in the front row, second from the left

The men sat down to a meal in the Banqueting Hall with a menu (below) that was supposed to be amusing. Given what they had endured, one wonders how funny the soldiers found it. A programme of musical entertainment followed, and Mr Harris then gave a speech in which he spoke of the roller-coaster of emotions that the soldiers' families and friends at home had experienced during their long confinement. He continued:

> *I will not dwell on what you suffered during your two and a half years of captivity. I am sure we do not know, and probably it will never be known, what sufferings you went through ... But we cannot forget the gallant fellows who have not come home. They have died like British heroes, their memory will never be forgotten, and we tender to those whom they have left behind to mourn, our sympathy.*

In his response, Major Footner went out of his way to praise Regimental Sergeant Major Leach for all his efforts for the men on the march and in the prison camps.

For many of the soldiers present it was the first reunion they had enjoyed with their comrades since the march into captivity. It would not be the last – an annual Kut Garrison Dinner for the 1/4th Hampshire survivors was held for many years to come.

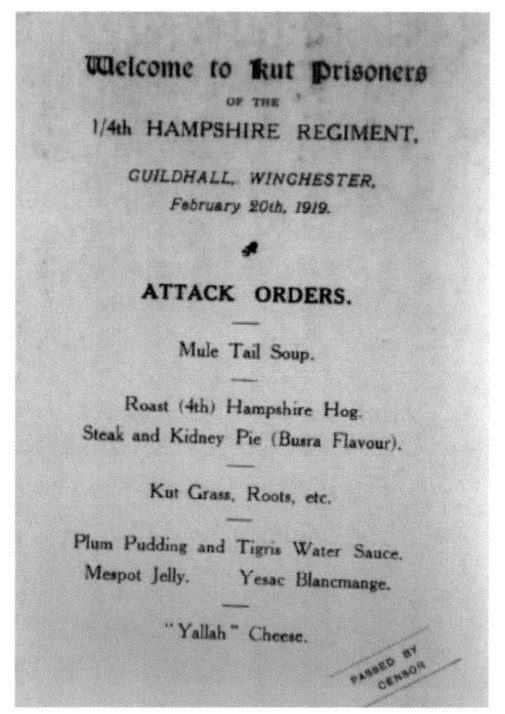

```
Welcome to Kut Prisoners
        OF THE
1/4th HAMPSHIRE REGIMENT,

   GUILDHALL, WINCHESTER,
      February 20th, 1919.

        ATTACK ORDERS.

         Mule Tail Soup.

       Roast (4th) Hampshire Hog.
  Steak and Kidney Pie (Busra Flavour).

        Kut Grass, Roots, etc.

  Plum Pudding and Tigris Water Sauce.
  Mespot Jelly.    Yesac Blancmange.

          "Yallah" Cheese.
```

Appendix i – The 4th Hampshires in Mesopotamia

The Fulflood and Weeke Survivors

Mrs Bowker's ledgers provide a list of the Winchester men who served with the 1/4th Hampshires during the Great War. From this, it has been possible to extract the names of the following men from Fulflood and Weeke who saw action in Mesopotamia or Persia and survived. (The addresses are from the Great War period and may have changed since due to renumbering):

2572 Frederick Corps – 23, Fairfield Road.

2794 Ernest Dumper – 2, Elm Road.

1685 Frederick Green – 17, Greenhill Road.

2251 Edgar Glover - 7, Cranworth Road.

1706 Percival Charles Meacher – 6, Greenhill Road.

3028 Edward F. Mills – 28, Greenhill Road.

2265 Ernest Pearce – 39, Brassey Road.

11 Henry Ross – 35, Clifton Road. (Invalided home).

1492 Ralph Snow – 41, Fairfield Road.

2405 Arthur Saunders – 60, Western Road.

2806 Frederick Savage – 4, Elm Road.

2401 Joseph John Tunks – 41, Sussex Street (father of 2nd Lt. Edward Tunks, see pp. 323)

2528 Charles H. Winkworth – 32, Clifton Road.

2855 Albert Harry Wilson – 78a, Western Road.

2859 John Robert Watts – The Lodge, Highfield, Andover Road.

2714 Charles Young – 6, Stockbridge Road.

The 1/4th Hampshires gradually rebuilt their strength after the Battle of El-Hanna and continued to serve in Mesopotamia before moving to Persia in late 1917. Some men served with Major-General Lionel Dunsterville in 1918, reaching the key oil field and port of Baku on the Caspian Sea. The 2/4th Hampshires spent much of the war in India and supplied hundreds of drafts to their parent battalion in Mesopotamia. They moved to Egypt in the spring of 1917 and fought in the Palestine campaign under General Edmund Allenby before transferring to the Western Front in 1918. There they distinguished themselves in the battles of the 'Hundred Days' leading up to the Armistice. The battalion served as part of the Army of Occupation in Germany after the war and was disbanded on 31 October 1919.

DEREK WHITFIELD

Additional sources

- Brook, Lieutenant-Colonel F. *2/4th Battalion Hampshire Regiment 1914-1919.* (Uckfield, The Naval and Military Press).
- Crowley, Patrick. *Kut 1916: The Forgotten British Disaster in Iraq.* (Stroud, The History Press, 2009).
- Leach, Regimental Sergeant Major W. *Diaries and Notebooks.* (Unpublished. Held by the Royal Hampshire Regiment Museum, Winchester.)
- The Comforts Fund Ledgers of Mrs Esme Bowker (M1830) and Lists of PoWs *(M1830)*, The Royal Hampshire Regiment Museum, Winchester.
- Winchester Training College Roll Call of the Fallen 1914-1918.
  https://wtcfallen.com/mesopotamia/

Appendix ii   The Battles of 1916 - 18

The British Offensives of 1916-18

The British Army took part in several major offensive campaigns on the Western Front between 1916 and 1918, but this section focuses on four – the battles of the Somme, Arras, Passchendaele (known more accurately as the Third Battle of Ypres) and the Hundred Days. The British did, of course, mount other offensives during the war – such as the battles of Neuve Chapelle and Loos in 1915 and Cambrai in 1917 - but these were smaller in scale and duration and involved fewer of the men who are the subject of this book. Details of these engagements, plus the Gallipoli campaign, the First and Second Battles of Ypres and the early actions of the war (Mons, Le Cateau, the Marne and the Aisne, for example) are given in the biographies of those men who died in them. Similarly, the Battle of Jutland, the major naval engagement of the war, is discussed in the relevant profiles.

The offensives listed below were not single engagements but rather a series of battles fought over several weeks or months. Each offensive involved several phases, some more successful than others. The purpose here is to help the reader understand more about these campaigns and battles by providing an historical context and a chronological framework.

Many of the men featured in the book fought in one or more of the offensives. Readers wishing to learn more about the Mesopotamia campaign, in which almost 1 in 5 of the Weeke and Fulflood soldiers died, should turn to Appendix i.

The Somme: 1 July-18 November 1916

The Somme offensive was a joint Anglo-French operation. It took place in Picardy either side of the River Somme which, in 1916, marked the boundary between the British Expeditionary Force (BEF) and the French army. The original plan envisaged the French taking the leading role. However, this changed after the Germans attacked at Verdun in early 1916, forcing the French to transfer thousands of troops there from the Somme.

The tragedy of the first day of the offensive (57,470 British casualties, including 19,240 dead) has cast a long shadow over the rest of the campaign. However, there were successes. On 1 July, the French made their biggest advance of the war to date. Even the British achieved some gains, notably at Montauban and Mametz. The first phase of the offensive also saw tactical innovation by the British with a bold dawn attack on the Bazentin Ridge.

The period between mid-July and the end of August developed into a desperate attritional slog as the British tried to secure better positions from which to launch the next phase of the offensive. The summer fighting for Pozieres, High Wood and Delville Wood was among the bloodiest of the entire campaign.

September saw the Allies inflict a series of defeats on the Germans who, together with their losses at Verdun, suffered 130,000 casualties during the month. However, Allied momentum slowed in October and November when bad weather turned the battlefield into a sea of mud. Much of the criticism subsequently levelled at the British Commander-in-Chief, Sir Douglas Haig, stemmed from his refusal to call a halt to the campaign when it became clear that it was pointless to throw exhausted troops into battle in such appalling conditions.

The British suffered 450,000 casualties on the Somme. German losses were almost as high, and manpower would be an increasing problem for the German army in 1917 as it struggled to find an answer to the problem of fighting a war on two fronts with dwindling resources.

Appendix ii   The Battles of 1916 - 18

The Somme Offensive comprised the following battles and phases:

Phase 1: 1-17 July 1916

Battle of Albert (1-13 July) – capture of Montauban, Mametz, Fricourt, Contalmaison and La Boisselle.

Battle of Bazentin Ridge (14-17 July) – capture of Longueval, Trones Wood and Ovillers. Featured successful surprise dawn attack on 14 July.

Phase 2: July-September 1916

Battle of Delville Wood (15 July-3 September).

Battle of Pozieres (23 July-3 September) – Australians involved in fierce fighting for German stronghold of Mouquet Farm.

Battle of Guillemont (3-6 September) – capture of the German stronghold of Guillemont.

Battle of Ginchy (9 September) – capture of Ginchy.

Phase 3: September-November 1916

Battle of Flers-Courcelette (15-22 September) – capture of Martinpuich. Featured first use of tanks in warfare.

Battle of Morval (25-28 September) – capture of Combles, Lesboeufs and Gueudecourt.

Battle of Thiepval Ridge (26-28 September) – fought in conjunction with the Battle of Morval.

Battle of Le Transloy (1-18 October) – capture of Eaucourt l'Abbaye, Le Sars and attacks on the Butte de Warlencourt. Bad weather hampered British.

Battle of the Ancre Heights (1 October-11 November) – capture of the Schwaben Redoubt, Stuff Redoubt and Regina Trench.

Battle of the Ancre (13-16 November) – capture of Beaumont Hamel, an objective on 1 July.

Arras: 9 April-16 May 1917

The BEF launched the Arras Offensive to draw German troops away from the area of the River Aisne where the French planned to launch a major attack in May 1917. The opening Battle of Vimy Ridge and the First Battle of the Scarpe were highly encouraging. The Canadians captured the strategic high point of Vimy Ridge on the opening day, and to the east of Arras British troops advanced more than three miles, the biggest Allied success of the war up to that point. Enemy resistance then stiffened, and the offensive bogged down. Final attempts to outflank the Germans at Bullecourt proved hugely costly.

On the plus side, the offensive did succeed in diverting German troops away from the French sectors. It also showed that British commanders had learned lessons from the Somme and were now capable of mounting successful set-piece attacks against strongly fortified German positions. However, the gains in territory were offset by the 158,000 British and Canadian casualties and by the subsequent failure of the French offensives to the south. Ultimately, Arras had little impact on the strategic or tactical situation on the Western Front.

Phase 1: 9-14 April 1917

Battle of Vimy Ridge (9-12 April) – Canadians capture Vimy Ridge.

First Battle of the Scarpe (9-14 April) – British attack east of Arras and advance more than three miles in places.

First Battle of Bullecourt (10-11 April) – a flanking operation south of Arras. British and Australians suffer heavy losses.

Appendix ii   The Battles of 1916 - 18

German attack on Lagnicourt (15 April) – a German flanking operation.

Phase 2: 23-24 April 1917

Second Battle of the Scarpe (23-24 April) – British attack on a nine-mile front on both sides of the River Scarpe. Gavrelle and Guemappe captured but Rouex remains in German hands.

Attack on La Coulotte (23 April) – subsidiary Canadian assault.

Phase 3: 28-29 April 1917

Battle of Arleux (28-29 April) – aims to tie down German forces which could be sent to French sector. Canadians capture Arleux.

Phase 4: 3-16 May 1917

Third Battle of the Scarpe (3-4 May 1917) – assault on German fortification of Boiry Riegel. Called off after British suffer heavy losses.

Second Battle of Bullecourt (3-16 May 1917) – British and Australians attack Bullecourt which is eventually taken. However, further attacks on the Hindenburg Line fail.

Capture of Rouex (13-14 May)

Third Battle of Ypres (Passchendaele): 31 July-10 November 1917

Along with the Somme, the Third Battle of Ypres (commonly known as Passchendaele) is the best-known of the British offensives of the Great War. The aim of commanders was to win control of the ridges to the south and east of the Belgian town of Ypres and then advance to capture the German railhead at Roulers. Ultimately, the British wanted to clear the German army from the Belgian coast as far as Holland.

To this day the battle remains mired in controversy – over the choice of Flanders for the offensive, for example, and whether the British objectives were simply unrealistic given the nature of warfare in 1917. More than anything, however, it is the images of a landscape destroyed by war and of soldiers floundering in mud that have shaped popular perceptions of the campaign.

The first phase of the offensive was planned by General Sir Hubert Gough, commander of the British Fifth Army. An aggressive soldier (a 'thruster' in Army parlance), Gough - in conjunction with Sir Douglas Haig – set ambitious objectives for his divisions. The battle started well, but heavy rain then slowed progress as the waterlogged battlefield hindered the movement of men and guns.

Gough's troops also found themselves pitted against an enemy who had perfected defence in depth, employing lightly-held front lines behind which they placed scattered strong points – such as pill boxes - to disrupt any Allied advance. Once the British were disorganised, the Germans would launch counter-attacks with specially trained divisions kept out of range of Allied artillery. Allied attacks often succeeded in penetrating the German front line but failed to get past the second.

In early September, Gough was relieved of responsibility for the battle which passed to General Sir Herbert Plumer, commander of Second Army. A meticulous planner, Plumer aimed to use the Germans' own tactics against themselves. Rather than try to break through the German lines, as Gough had, he selected a small part of the front, pounded it with heavy artillery and then attacked in strength behind a 'creeping barrage'. Having over-run the German position to a depth of about 1,500 yards, the attacking troops then dug in and waited for the Germans to counter-attack. When they did, instead of exhausted, disorganised troops they were confronted by a well organised defensive line. Moreover, the British defenders were covered by their own artillery which was able to break up the German counter-attacks.

Appendix ii The Battles of 1916 - 18

Plumer's so-called 'bite and hold' tactics were successful at the battles of the Menin Ridge Road, Polygon Wood and Broodseinde when the ground was dry. However, when the rain returned in early October, the problems of manoeuvre on the battlefield manifested themselves once more. The final stage of the campaign, like that on the Somme, resulted in appalling casualties in unspeakable conditions before the BEF finally took the village of Passchendaele.

The Third Ypres campaign demonstrated the British ability to break into fortified defences and then hold them against enemy counter-attacks. It also led the German high command to seriously consider withdrawing from the Ypres Salient.

Preliminary Phase: 7-14 June 1917

Battle of Messines (7-14 June) – British detonate 19 mines under Messines Ridge, south of Ypres, then attack and capture much of the high ground as a strategic prelude to the Third Battle of Ypres.

Phase 1: 31 July-25 August

Battle of Pilckem Ridge (31 July-2 August) – British Fifth Army attacks across Gheluvelt Plateau in bad weather. Gains made in the north of the sector but attack quickly bogs down.

Capture of Westhoek (10 August)

Battle of Langemarck (16-18 August) – Despite less ambitious objectives, British attacks fail because of bad weather and German resistance. General Sir Hubert Gough relieved of responsibility for planning battle.

Phase 2: 20 September-9 October 1917

Battle of the Menin Ridge Road (20-25 September) – after weeks of preparation, General Sir Herbert Plumer's Second Army attacks on an eight-mile front. Greater emphasis on heavy artillery destroying German fortified positions. Most objectives seized and German counter-attacks broken up.

Battle of Polygon Wood (26 September-3 October) – British and Australian 'bite and hold' tactics succeed again. All objectives taken and held.

Battle of Broodseinde (4 October) – British and Australians complete capture of Gheluvelt Plateau and Broodseinde Ridge.

Battle of Poelcapelle (9 October) – return of heavy rain blunts British and French assault and gains in front of Passchendaele are lost to German counter-attacks.

Phase 3: 12 October-10 November 1917

First Battle of Passchendaele (12 October) – British and New Zealand troops attempt to gain ground around Passchendaele. Rain hinders movement of artillery support. German counter-attacks retake most of lost ground.

Second Battle of Passchendaele (26 October-10 November) – after British capture Poelcapelle on 22 October, Canadian Corps launches a three-phase attack on Passchendaele which is finally taken on 6 November. Last remaining high ground in the area is captured on 10 November.

The Hundred Days: 8 August-11 November 1918

The Hundred Days Campaign ended the Great War. Starting with the Battle of Amiens on 8 August 1918, the Allies launched a series of large-scale attacks against an enemy much weakened after the failure of its own offensives in the spring and early summer. The attacks, orchestrated by Field Marshal Ferdinand Foch, who had been appointed Supreme Allied Commander in March 1918, shattered the Hindenburg Line defences, pushed the Germans out of France and culminated in the Armistice of 11 November.

Appendix ii   The Battles of 1916 - 18

There were no phases as such during the Hundred Days, just a rapid series of victories against which the German armies had no reply. The offensives involved attacks by British and Dominion forces as well as the French, American and Belgian armies.

Some military historians regard the Hundred Days Campaign as a triumph of British 'combined arms' warfare in which innovative coordinated attacks involving infantry, artillery, aircraft and particularly tanks finally broke the Western Front stalemate. Others argue that Allied success between August and November 1918 was due more to German weakness in manpower and morale than any new way of fighting. They point out that while tanks were effective at the Battle of Amiens (8 August), success thereafter was due to the tried and tested combination of infantry and artillery.

The following battles saw the greatest British involvement.

Picardy: 8-11 September 1918

Battle of Amiens (8-11 August) – Australian, Canadian, British and French forces smash a 15-mile wide gap in German lines and advance up to eight miles. British use 500 tanks to spearhead attack which achieves complete surprise. Momentum slows in following days as advance outruns supporting artillery.

The Somme: 21-29 August 1918

Battle of Albert (21-22 August) – Albert recaptured and Germans pushed back on a 34-mile front.

Battle of the Scarpe 1918 (26-30 August) – Canadians advance three miles and capture Monchy-le-Preux and Wancourt.

Second Battle of Bapaume (29 August) – Bapaume retaken.

Advance to the Hindenburg Line: 26 August-18 September 1918

Battle of the Scarpe 1918 (26 August) – British First Army joins the offensive north of the Somme.

Battle of Mont St Quentin (31 August) – Fourth Army resumes attack. Australians cross the Somme and break the German lines at Mont St Quentin and Peronne.

Battle of the Drocourt-Queant Line (2 September) – British and Canadians push Germans out of last major defence system before the Hindenburg Line.

Battle of Havrincourt (12 September) – Havrincourt captured. Evidence that German fighting spirit is weakening.

Battle of Epehy – British, Australian and French forces clear German outposts in front of Hindenburg Line.

Flanders: 28 September-2 October 1918

Fifth Battle of Ypres (28 September-2 October 1918) – in Flanders, the British Second Army and the Belgian Army join Foch's Grand Offensive, a series of sequential attacks along the Western Front.

Battle for the Hindenburg Line: 29 September-10 October 1918

Battle of St Quentin Canal (29 September-10 October) – British, Australian, American and French forces break through one of the most heavily defended sections of the Hindenburg Line after massive British artillery bombardment.

Second Battle of Cambrai – British First and Third Armies also breach Hindenburg Line.

The final weeks: 17 October-11 November 1918

Battle of Courtrai (14-19 October) – British, French and Belgian forces attack in Flanders. Ostend, Lille and Douai recaptured on 17 October. Bruges and Zeebrugge fall two days later.

Appendix ii   The Battles of 1916 - 18

Battle of the Selle (17-25 October) – Germans forced out of new defensive positions behind the River Selle by British armies. Unprecedented number of Germans surrender.

Battle of Valenciennes (1-2 November 1918) – British and Canadians capture Valenciennes.

Battle of the Sambre (4 November 1918) – British and French Armies cross the Sambre Canal (poet Wilfrid Owen killed here) to threaten Maubeuge and Namur. To the south American forces advance north out of the Argonne forest. The Sambre is the last major battle fought by the British in the Great War.

DEREK WHITFIELD

Appendix iii The "Missing Men"

Fulflood and Weeke dead not listed on the parish memorials

The following men from the parish died in the Great War - or afterwards from its effects - but their names do not appear on the memorials at St Matthew's and St Paul's churches. They are listed in the Winchester War Service Register of 1921 but addresses may differ today because of renumbering. The list is not exhaustive.

1. 2nd Lieutenant DOUGLAS COWAN. Little Meade, Cheriton Road, Weeke, Winchester. Commissioned into The Hampshire Regiment in 1912, he was deployed with the 1st Battalion to France on the outbreak of war in August 1914. He was killed in action at Cambrai on 26 August 1914. Entitled to the 1914 (Mons Star), British War Medal and Victory Medal.

2. Acting Sergeant Instructor ARTHUR CHARLES STUART CAINEY. 14, (previously 83) Brassey Road, Winchester. Born in Chelsea, London in 1893, the son of Charles and Louisa Cainey, who were living in Hammersmith in 1901. The family moved to Winchester where Arthur attended Peter Symonds Grammar School and later Winchester Diocesan Training College before becoming a teacher. He enlisted as an instructor with the Army Gymnastic Staff (service number 342 Army Gymnastic Staff) on 12 January 1915 when he was living at 14, Brassey Road. Later transferred to The Northamptonshire Regiment (service number 50869), reaching the rank of Acting Sergeant Instructor. Married Nella Guyatt in Lymington, Hampshire, in 1916. The couple were living in New Milton when Arthur was demobilised from the Army on 26 February 1919. He died on 17 March 1924 and is mentioned on the Peter Symonds School War Memorial.

3. Private HARRY EADE. 18, North View, Winchester. Enlisted as a Band Boy with the Hampshire Regiment in May 1914, before becoming a Private. Killed in action on 18 May 1918 while serving with the 2nd Hampshires in France.

4. Captain ARTHUR W. GALE DSO. 2, Clifton Road, Winchester. Joined the Dragoon Guards in August 1914 before transferring to the Life Guards. Later commissioned and promoted to Captain. Won the DSO and mentioned in dispatches in 1916. Killed in action in Belgium on 10 April 1916.

5. Lieutenant HARRY E. GERMAIN. 76, Stockbridge Road, Winchester. Enlisted with the Canadian Corps as a Staff Sergeant in August 1914, suggesting he had previous military experience. Commissioned and promoted to Lieutenant. Wounded on 8 June 1917, possibly at the Battle of Messines (7-14 June 1917). Died of his wounds at Calais the following month.

6. Private HARRY MATON. 10, North View, Winchester. Enlisted with the Army Service Corps in 1910. Served in Salonika and died from disease on 10 November 1918, the day before the Armistice. Two brothers also fought in the war and survived. Tom, who had joined the Gloucestershire Regiment in 1903, served in France, winning the Military Medal and Bar. Edward Maton enlisted in August 1915, also with The Glosters, but later transferred to The Northamptonshire Regiment and served in France. He was promoted to Corporal and awarded the Military Medal in 1918.

7. Private WILLIAM WADE. 1A, Newburgh Street, Winchester. Joined the Hampshire Carabiniers Yeomanry in May 1916. Wounded on 1 February 1917 and then killed in action at Ypres on 3 February 1917. Entitled to the British War Medal and the Victory Medal.

Appendix iv   A Guide to the British Army 1914 - 18

Structure of the British Army in the Great War

Not all readers will be familiar with the British Army's structure and its often-bewildering nomenclature. This section provides a simplified structure of the Army hierarchy which can be used as an accompanying reference tool to the biographies. There is also a more detailed explanation of the role and development of the infantry Battalion which was the unit that most British soldiers in the Great War regarded as their home.

Building blocks – the basic organisational structure

Infantry soldier - he was part of a Battalion (around 1,000 men) This was subdivided into four Companies, which were each subdivided into four Platoons, which were each subdivided into four Sections.

Several Battalions - were under command of a Brigade (around 5,000 men).

Several Brigades - were under command of a Division (around 20,000 men).

Several Divisions - were under command of a Corps.

Several Corps - were under command of an Army.

Several Armies (the British eventually had five on the Western Front) – were under command of a General Headquarters (GHQ)

GHQ – was under command of the War Office.

The *Artillery* was organised slightly differently:

Soldier - he was part of a Battery or Ammunition Column (which was subdivided into Sections).

Several Batteries and an Ammunition Column - were under command of a Brigade.

Several Brigades - were under command of a Division.

The *Cavalry* also had a different structure. The term 'cavalry' only applied to Regular Army units. Mounted Territorial Force units were known as yeomanry:

Soldier – he was part of a Troop (around 40 men).

Several Troops - were under command of a Squadron (around 160 men).

Several Squadrons – were under command of a Cavalry Regiment (around 550 men)

Several Cavalry Regiments – were under command of a Cavalry Brigade (around 1,750 men).

Several Cavalry Brigades – were under command of a Cavalry Division (around 7,000 men).

Structure and role of the Battalion

Each infantry Battalion belonged to a Regiment. The British infantry Regiments of 1914-18 were based on counties and been created under the Childers Reforms of 1881. Each Regiment was commanded by a full Colonel and was usually divided into two Regular Battalions, plus a Reserve Battalion and several Territorial Force (part-time) Battalions.

Regiments never fought as Regiments, but as individual numbered Battalions. These in turn were attached to Brigades, Divisions, Corps and Armies (see above). In 1914 a full-strength Battalion comprised 1,107 officers and men. Commanded by a Lieutenant-Colonel, it had a Headquarters, Machine-Gun Section and four Companies.

Appendix iv   A Guide to the British Army 1914 - 18

The *Headquarters* was made up of the Commanding Officer, his Second in Command, an Adjutant (Battalion staff officer), the Quartermaster, plus the Orderly Room staff, Pioneers, Signallers, and Stretcher Bearers. There would also be a Medical Officer and a Padre plus an Armourer from the Army Ordnance Corps. In total there were four officers, one Warrant Officer (the Regimental Sergeant Major), eight Sergeants and 61 Other Ranks plus the Medical Officer and the Padre.

The *Machine-Gun Section* had two Maxim Guns and was commanded by a Second Lieutenant or a Lieutenant. He had one Sergeant and 16 men under his command. In February 1915, the Machine-Gun Section had its strength increased from two to four machine-guns, and the old Maxims were gradually replaced by the Vickers Machine-Gun. In October 1915, the Machine-Gun Section in every battalion was disbanded, and the personnel transferred with their equipment to the newly-formed Machine-Gun Corps. The Vickers were replaced at Battalion level by the Lewis light machine gun. Initially there were four in every Battalion, formed into a Lewis Gun Section, but this had increased to 36 by 1918.

An infantry *Company* was lettered from A to D (or W-Z in some regiments) and was commanded by a Major or Captain. He had a Second in Command, normally a Captain. There was also a Company Sergeant Major, and a Company Quarter Master Sergeant. In total there were 227 officers and men in a Company.

A Company was split into four *Platoon*s, each one numbered. Numbers 1-4 always served in A Company, numbers 5-8 in B, numbers 9-12 in C, and numbers 13-16 in D. In total the four platoons comprised eight Sergeants, nine Corporals, four Drummers, four Batmen and 188 Privates. Each Platoon was commanded by a Second Lieutenant or a Lieutenant, with a Platoon Sergeant as his right-hand man.

Each Platoon was made up of four *Section*s, of 12 men, each commanded by a Non-Commission Officer (NCO) - usually a Corporal.

Shortly after the outbreak of war in 1914, Territorial Force Battalions were authorised to form Reserve or 2nd Line units. They were distinguished by a '2/' prefix from their parent unit (prefixed '1/'). Initially these were formed from men who had not volunteered for overseas service, and the recruits who were pouring in. Later they, too, were mobilised for overseas service and new 3rd Line units were created to supply drafts to the two service Battalions. In this way the six pre-war Territorial Force infantry Battalions of the Hampshire Regiment grew to 17 after 1914.

As the Great War progressed the strength of a Battalion varied greatly because of casualties, sickness and transfers. Heavy losses meant that by the time of the Third Battle of Ypres (Passchendaele) in 1917, the average infantry Battalion was around 450 officers and men - less than half its pre-war strength.

Street Index

Index to street addresses

The list below contains the more significant addresses mentioned in the biographies. The page number refers either to the page on which a photograph of the property appears (* in photo column), otherwise to the first page of the relevant biography. House numbers are the current numbers. A table relating current addresses to previous addresses is on page 400.

NLS = No Longer Stands.

Street Name	House no / name	Photo?	NLS	Surname	Initials	Page
Andover Road	2	*		COLES	F	65
Andover Road	4	*		CHAPMAN	F J	54
Andover Road	5	*		DOWSE	C	83
Andover Road	8	*		WEDGE	C E	354
Andover Road	8			WEDGE	J C T	359
Andover Road	10		NLS	SCADDEN	A	266
Andover Road	15			FRANCIS	A E	103
Andover Road	17	*		BUCK	J H	47
Andover Road	46		NLS	NORGATE	P D	245
Ashley Terrace	1		NLS	NEWBY	W H E	235
Ashley Terrace	12		NLS	SHEARS	S	276
Avenue Road	2	*		WHITCHER	E W	365
Avenue Road	3	*		CHURCHER	H T	56
Avenue Road	14	*		FORSTER	H T	99
Bar End Road	23	*		TONG	H	318
Bereweeke Road	14 (Bereweeke House)	*		GOULD	H C H	123
Bereweeke Road	Morn Dale			NEWTON	A H	242
Bereweeke Road	The Lodge		NLS	DENNISTOUN	J R	73
Bereweeke Road	The Lodge		NLS	WAND-TETLEY	C	341
Brassey Road	4			NORGATE	P D	245
Brassey Road	19	*		MORRISON	D Th	228
Brassey Road	30			HOUNSLOW	G H	150
Brassey Road	68	*		PAYNE	H Y	249
Brassey Road	72			KETLEY	C W	168
Brassey Road	86	*		ILLINGWORTH	T W	153
Cheshil Street	2			BIGNELL	J	32
Cheesehill Street	50			WARD	D H C	348

Street Index

Street Name	House no / name	Photo?	NLS	Surname	Initials	Page
Cheriton Road	7			MIDDLETON	B C	202
Cheriton Road	12	*		VOKES	B	337
Cheriton Road	13	*		SMITH	A C	289
Cheriton Road	22	*		DOUGLAS	C E G	78
Cheriton Road	Lincolnville	*		HAWKER	C W S	135
Cheriton Road	Westgate School			DOBSON	F W	76
Chilbolton Avenue	Langhouse		NLS	MACLACHLAN	R C	182
Chilbolton Avenue	Piper's Farm		NLS	HAWKINS	S M	136
Chilbolton Avenue	Piper's Field		NLS	GYE	D A	124
Clifton Road	26	*		BURGESS	F E	48
Clifton Road	37	*		HAMMOND	C W	129
Clifton Road	32	*		FORSTER	H T	129
Clifton Terrace	7	*		VANDELEUR	J B	329
Cranworth Road	6	*		HILL	A S	144
Cranworth Road	21	*		PRIOR	G	256
Cranworth Road	25	*		MORRAH	J	221
Cromwell Terrace	1		NLS	BISHOP	L N	35
Eastgate Street	17	*		CLARK	R	60
Elm Road	1	*		FIFIELD	B J	90
Elm Road	9	*		JACOB	L J	156
Elm Road	14	*		MITCHELL	W J	211
Elm Road	24	*		MITCHELL	W J	211
Fairfield Road	11	*		SMITH	E A	291
Fairfield Road	32	*		WHITE	W E	369
Fairfield Road	40	*		CLARK	R J	60
Fairfield Road	64	*		WAKE	F W	339
Fairfield Road	69			HILL	A S	141
Fairfield Road	90 (Venclyst)	*		INGE	S G	154
Fairfield Road	94 (Grangemont)	*		SHEFFERD	C	281
Gladstone Street	2		NLS	MAIDMENT	H G	193
Gladstone Street	14		NLS	SMITH	H	294

Street Index

Street Name	House no / name	Photo?	NLS	Surname	Initials	Page
Greenhill Road	1			EDWARDS	F	88
Greenhill Road	4	*		SIMMONS	J	285
Greenhill Road	8			SOTHCOTT	L G	305
Greenhill Road	10	*		LOVELOCK	G	179
Greenhill Road	13	*		MULDOWNEY	J	232
Greenhill Road	25	*		LAWRENCE	A E	171
Greenhill Road	36	*		SIMMONS	J	285
Greenhill Road	69	*		GOODRIDGE	G	113
Greenhill Road	95			HALLS	H C	126
Greenhill Terrace	8	*		DAWKINS	F	71
Hatherlehiy Road	63	*		WARD	D H C	351
High Street	73	*		RICHARDS	F C	259
Hyde Close	Drill Hall	*		MALE	R	198
Hyde Street	23 (Hyde Abbey House)	*		VANDELEUR	J B	329
Links Road	Culduthel	*		FRASER	F A	107
Milverton Road	11			LEVER	G T	175
Milverton Road	17	*		GOODYEAR	G F	119
Newburgh Street	11	*		JOHNSON	A L	162
North View	30	*		FORDER	F J	95
Nuns Road	22	*		NEWBY	W E H	237
Nuns Road	42	*		SIMMONS	J	285
Parchment Street	Old Post Office	*		MALE	R H	198
Prison Quarters	11		NLS	POWELL	C E	251
Romsey Road	1	*		VANDELEUR	J B	329
Romsey Road	14	*		HEAD	F J	140
St. Cross Road	55	*		CHAPMAN	F J	54
St. John's Road	43	*		WARD	D H C	347

Street Index

Street Name	House no / name	Photo?	NLS	Surname	Initials	Page
St. Paul's Hill	4	*		RULE	E G S	263
St. Paul's Hill	17		NLS	SOFFE	G	299
St. Paul's Hill	17		NLS	SOFFE	H	302
St. Paul's Hill	20	*		BOGIE	A W	38
Stockbridge Road	11	*		TONG	H L	319
Stockbridge Road	15	*		LAWRENCE	A E	171
Stockbridge Road	16	*		SEWARD	J W	274
Stockbridge Road	27			MITCHELL	W J	207
Stockbridge Road	27			STROUD	B E	310
Stockbridge Road	34		NLS	BIGNELL	J	32
Stockbridge Road	36		NLS	WHITE	F A	367
Stockbridge Road	76	*		POWNEY	W B	254
Stockbridge Road	116	*		RICHARDS	F	259
Stockbridge Road	176			MALE	R H	197
Stockbridge Road	188	*		BREADMORE	P G	42
Sussex Street	19	*		NEWBY	W E H	237
Sussex Street	21-22		NLS	STEVENS	E	308
Sussex Street	25		NLS	FORBES	J	93
Sussex Street	41		NLS	THOMPSON	R J	315
Sussex Street	98			TUNKS	E J A	323
Union Street	9	*	NLS	HILL	A S	142
Weeke	Arnwood		NLS	HAWKER	C W S	132
Weeke	Butts Close Cottage			HILL	N W	146
Weeke	Piper's Farm		NLS	HAWKINS	S M	136
Weeke	Pond Cottage	*		WINTER	C J	379
Weeke	Wyke Hill House	*		DRAKE	T H	86
Western Road	7			STROUD	B E	310
Western Road	7	*		STROUD	G	313
Western Road	16	*		GAMBLING	A W	110
Western Road	44	*		COLES	S J	68
Western Road	57	*		JACOB	L E	157

Street Index

Street re-naming/re-numbering

Many of Winchester's streets were re-named and/or re-numbered during or after the War. At that time there was some inconsistency in usage between "new" and "old" addresses and this is reflected in the data used in our researches. We have attempted in the biographies to distinguish consistently between addresses current in the period and their modern equivalents. The table below lists the more significant addresses noted in the biographies to have been changed and their modern variants.

Previous Address Street	No/name	Present Address Street	No/name
Avenue Terrace	3	Avenue Road	3
Bar End Road	33	Bar End Road	23
Brassey Road	7	Brassey Road	13
Brassey Road	10	Brassey Road	19
Cheriton Road	County High School (girls)	Cheriton Road	Westgate School
Clifton Road	36a (Kingscote)	Clifton Road	37
Greenhill Road	7/15a	Greenhill Road	13
Greenhill Road	1/9	Greenhill Road	17
Hillside Terrace	10	Bar End Road	71
Lower Stockbridge Road	18	Stockbridge Road	36
Lower Stockbridge Road	19	Stockbridge Road	38
Lower Stockbridge Road	33	Stockbridge Road	76
Lower Stockbridge Road	53	Stockbridge Road	116
Lower Stockbridge Road	56 / 86	Stockbridge Road	15
Lower Stockbridge Road	88	Stockbridge Road	11
North View	18	North View	5
North View	19	North View	4
North View	20	North View	3
St. Pauls Terrace	10	St. Paul's Hill	4
St. Paul's Terrace	20	St. Paul's Hill	2
Stockbridge Road	5	Stockbridge Road	10
Stockbridge Road	8	Stockbridge Road	16
Stockbridge Road	9	Stockbridge Road	18
Stockbridge Road	19	Stockbridge Road	38
Stockbridge Road	80	Stockbridge Road	27
Stockbridge Road	Trevenna	Stockbridge Road	176
Sussex Street	10	Sussex Street	19
Sussex Street	Rippledene	Sussex Street	98
Upper Stockbridge Road	8	St. Paul's Hill	17
Western Road	12	Cheriton Road	41
Western Road	36	Cheriton Road	22
Western Road	41	Cheriton Road	12
Western Road	50	Cheriton Road	7
Western Road	51	Cheriton Road	9
Western Road	53	Cheriton Road	13
Western Road	68	Western Road	44
Western Road	79	Western Road	57

Bibliography

Winchester primary sources

The Winchester War Service Register (Winchester: 1921).

The Hampshire Chronicle and Hampshire Observer newspapers. Available to view on micro-film at the Hampshire Record Office, Winchester.

Warren's and Kelly's Winchester & District Directories – at Hampshire Record Office.

Kelly's Directories of Southampton & Neighbourhood – at Hampshire Record Office.

Other Winchester sources

Best, Jen and Beaumont James, Tom (ed.). *Debt of Honour: Winchester City's First World War Dead.* (Gloucester: 2018). See also https://debtofhonourwinchester.weebly.com/

Brinkman, Barrie. Weeke Local History. http://www.weekehistory.co.uk.

Jarvis, Steve and Jenny. War Memorials/Rolls of Honour for Hampshire - http://hampshirewarmemorials.com/

Page, William (ed.). Parishes: Weeke (Wyke), in *A History of the County of Hampshire: Volume 3*, (London, 1908), pp. 451-453. *British History Online* http://www.british-history.ac.uk/vch/hants/vol3/pp451-453.

Whitfield, Derek. *To What Extent and Why did the Voluntary Ethic Characterise Winchester's Response to War in 1914-15?* MA dissertation, University of Birmingham, 2015. Available to view at the Hampshire Record Office, Winchester.

Winchester Training College Roll Call of the Fallen 1914-1918 - https://wtcfallen.com/

Winchester College at War - https://www.winchestercollegeatwar.com/

The Hampshire Regiment

Atkinson, C.T. *The Royal Hampshire Regiment 1914-1918, Volume II* (Glasgow: 1952).

Brook, Lt. Col. *2/4th Battalion Hampshire Regiment 1914-1919* (Uckfield: n.d.).

The Hampshire Regimental Journals for 1914 to 1919.

The Hampshire Regimental War Diaries for 1914 to 1919, especially those for the 1st, 2nd, 1/4th, 2/4th, 12th and 15th Battalions. Available to view at The Royal Hampshire Regiment Museum, Southgate Street, Winchester, and the Hampshire Record Office, Winchester.

Leach, Regimental Sergeant Major W. *Diaries and Notebooks.* (Unpublished). Also, the Comforts Fund Ledgers of Mrs Esme Bowker (M1830) and Lists of PoWs (M1830). Held by The Royal Hampshire Regiment Museum, Winchester.

The Rifle Brigade and the King's Royal Rifle Corps

Regimental Journals for the war period can be viewed at The Royal Green Jackets (Rifles) Museum, Winchester, and the Hampshire Record Office, Winchester.

Official Histories

Edmonds, Brig. Gen. Sir James E. *Military Operations: France and Belgium.* Vols for 1914 to 1918 (London: 1932-1938).

Moberly, Brig. Gen. F.J. *The Campaign in Mesopotamia, 1914-18.* Vols I-IV (London: 1923-27).

Secondary sources

Beckett, I.F.W. *Territorials: A Century of Service.* (London: 2008).

Bourne, J.M. *Who's Who in World War One* (London: 2001).

Crowley, P. *Kut 1916: The Forgotten British Disaster in Iraq* (Stroud: 2009).

Cuttell, B. *One Day on the Somme – 1ˢᵗ July 1916* (Peterborough: 1998).

Cuttell, B. *148 Days on the Somme – 2ⁿᵈ July to 26ᵗʰ November 1916* (Peterborough: 2000).

Duckers, P. *British Campaign Medals of the First World War* (Oxford 2011).

Gregory, A. *The Last Great War: British Society and the First World War* (Cambridge: 2008).

Griffith, P. *Battle Tactics of the Western Front: The British Army's Art of Attack 1916-18* (London: 1994).

Holmes, R. *Soldiers: Army Lives and Loyalties from Redcoats to Dusty Warriors* (London: 2011).

McCrery, N. *Final Wicket: Test and First-Class Cricketers Killed in the Great War* (Barnsley: 2015).

Messenger, C. *Call to Arms: The British Army 1914-18* (London: 2005).

Middlebrook, M. *The First Day on the Somme* (London: 1971).

McCarthy, C. *The Somme: The Day-by-day Account* (London: 1993).

Nichols, J. *Cheerful Sacrifice: The Battle of Arras 1917* (Barnsley: 1990).

Philpott, W. *Bloody Victory: The Sacrifice on the Somme* (London: 2009).

Renshaw, A. *Wisden on the Great War, The Lives of Fallen Cricketers 1914-1918* (London: 2014).

Sheffield, G. *Forgotten Victory: The First World War – Myths and Realities* (London: 2001).

Todman, D. *The Great War – Myth and Memory* (London: 2005).

Travers, T. *The Killing Ground: The British Army, the Western Front and the Emergence of Modern Warfare, 1900-1918* (London: 1987).

Simkins, P. *Kitchener's Army* (Manchester: 1988).

Stevenson, D. *1914-1918: The History of the First World War* (London: 2004).

Strachan, Hew. *The First World War* (London: 2003).

Websites

Ancestry - https://www.ancestry.com/

British Newspaper Archive - https://www.britishnewspaperarchive.co.uk/

Commonwealth War Graves Commission (GB) - https://www.cwgc.org

Find My Past - https://www.findmypast.co.uk/

Forces War Records - https://www.forces-war-records.co.uk/

Great War Forum – https://www.greatwarforum.org/

Hampshire Record Office - https://www.hants.gov.uk/librariesandarchives/archives

Imperial War Museum: 'Lives of the First World War' - https://livesofthefirstworldwar.iwm.org.uk

National Archives, Kew - https://www.nationalarchives.gov.uk/

Royal British Legion: 'Everyone Remembered' - https://www.everyoneremembered.org.

The Long, Long Trail: Researching Soldiers of the British Army in the Great War of 1914-1919 - https://www.longlongtrail.co.uk.

The Western Front Association – http://www.westernfrontassociation.com/